THE CHALLENGE OF DEMOCRACY

American Government in a Global World

BRIEF EDITION   SEVENTH EDITION

Kenneth Janda
Northwestern University

Jeffrey M. Berry
Tufts University

Jerry Goldman
Northwestern University

Updated and Abridged by
Kevin W. Hula
Loyola College in Maryland

WADSWORTH
CENGAGE Learning

Australia • Brazil • Japan • Korea • Mexico • Singapore • Spain • United Kingdom • United States

WADSWORTH
CENGAGE Learning

The Challenge of Democracy: American Government in a Global World, Brief Edition, Seventh Edition
Kenneth Janda
Jeffrey M. Berry
Jerry Goldman
Kevin W. Hula

Acquisitions Editor: Edwin Hill

Senior Development Editor: Lisa Kalner Williams

Assistant Editor: Katherine Hayes

Marketing Manager: Amy Whitaker

Marketing Assistant: Samantha Abrams

Marketing Communications Manager: Heather Baxley

Project Manager, Editorial Production: Susan Miscio

Manufacturing Buyer: Miranda Klapper

Permissions Editor: Katie Huha

Text Researcher: Maria Maimone

Production Service: Books By Design, Inc.

Text Designer: Cia Boynton

Photo Manager: Jennifer Meyer Dare

Photo Researcher: Stacey Dong

Cover Image and Designer: Harold Burch

Compositor: NK Graphics

For product information and technology assistance, contact us at
Cengage Learning Academic Resource Center, 1-800-423-0563
For permission to use material from this text or product, submit all requests online at **www.cengage.com/permissions.** Further permissions questions can be e-mailed to **permissionrequest@cengage.com.**

Library of Congress Control Number: 2008934719

ISBN-13: 978-0-547-21631-7

ISBN-10: 0-547-21631-9

Wadsworth, Cengage Learning
25 Thomson Place
Boston, MA 02210-1202
USA

Cengage Learning products are represented in Canada by Nelson Education, Ltd.

For your course and learning solutions, visit
academic.cengage.com.
Purchase any of our products at your local college store
or at our preferred online store **www.ichapters.com.**

Printed in Canada
3 4 5 6 7 12 11 10 09

Brief Contents

Contents

Preface

The Seventh Edition of *The Challenge of Democracy,* Brief Edition, is an abridged and updated version of the Tenth Edition of *The Challenge of Democracy.* As always, our goal was to streamline the larger text without diminishing any of the qualities that have made it so successful. In addition, we sought to make the text as current as possible by incorporating events occurring throughout 2008.

Key Content Updates

The text includes coverage of the latest political events that have emerged since the publication of the last edition. Key updates include discussion of the following:

- The 2008 congressional elections and the balance of the 111th Congress, in addition to an expanded discussion of the significance of a party's control of Congress.

- The 2008 presidential campaign and election, including analysis of the nomination process, the impact of the primary calendar, and the Democratic Party's delegate controversies in Michigan and Florida.

- The decline of public funding in presidential elections.

- Developments from the White House during George W. Bush's final term in office, including updated analysis of President Bush's domestic and foreign public approval rating, his handling of the war in Iraq, the federal response to Hurricane Katrina, and the president's authority to detain unlawful enemy combatants, among other topics.

- The politics of global climate change.

- Critical court cases covering the Second Amendment, same-sex marriage, and enemy combatant detainees.

- Nine entirely new chapter opening vignettes.

- A key partnership with the Associated Press that brings you the most up-to-date news to engage students in your classroom.

- AmericansGoverning.com, an online collection of videos, short-form documentaries, primary sources, and other documents designed to spark student interest.

Thematic Framework

Because we wanted to write a book that students would actually read, we sought to discuss politics—a complex subject—in a captivating and understandable way. American politics is not dull, and its textbooks need not be either. But equally important, we wanted to produce a book that students would credit for stimulating their thinking about politics. While offering all the essential information about American government and politics, we believed that it was most important to give students a framework for analyzing politics that they could use long after their studies ended.

To accomplish these goals, we built *The Challenge of Democracy* around three dynamic themes that are relevant to today's world: the clash among the values of *freedom, order, and equality;* the tensions between *pluralist and majoritarian visions of democracy;* and the fundamental ways that *globalization* is changing American politics.

Freedom, Order, and Equality

The first theme is introduced in Chapter 1 ("Dilemmas of Democracy"), where we suggest that American politics often reflects conflicts between the values of freedom and order and between the values of freedom and equality. These value conflicts are prominent in contemporary American society and they help to explain political controversy and consensus in earlier eras.

For instance, in Chapter 2 ("The Constitution") we argue that the Constitution was designed to promote order and it virtually ignored issues of political and social equality. Equality was later served, however, by several amendments to the Constitution. In Chapter 12 ("Order and Civil Liberties") and Chapter 13 ("Equality and Civil Rights") we demonstrate that many of this nation's most controversial issues represent conflicts among individuals or groups who hold differing views on the values of freedom, order, and equality. Views on issues such as abortion are not just isolated opinions; they also reflect choices about the philosophy citizens want government to follow. Yet choosing among these values is difficult, sometimes excruciatingly so.

Pluralist and Majoritarian Visions of Democracy

The second theme, also introduced in Chapter 1, asks students to consider two competing models of democratic government. One way that government can make decisions is by means of *majoritarian* principles—that is, by taking the actions desired by a majority of citizens. A contrasting model of government, *pluralism,* is built around the interaction of decision makers in government with groups concerned about issues that affect them.

These models are not mere abstractions; we use them to illustrate the dynamics of the American political system. In Chapter 9 ("The Presidency") we discuss the problem of divided government. More often than not over the past forty years, the party that controlled the White House did not control both houses of Congress. When these two branches of government are divided between the two parties, majoritarian government is difficult. Even when the same party controls both branches, the majoritarian model is not always realized. In Chapter 7 ("Interest Groups") we see the forces of pluralism at work. Interest groups of all types populate Washington, and these organizations represent the diverse array of interests that define our society. At the same

time, the chapter explores ways in which pluralism favors wealthier, better-organized interests.

Globalization's Impact on American Politics

The third theme, the impact of globalization on American politics, is introduced in Chapter 1 and then discussed throughout the text. The traditional notion of national sovereignty holds that each government is free to govern in the manner it feels best. As the world becomes a smaller place, however, national sovereignty is tested in many ways. When a country is committing human rights violations—putting people in jail for merely disagreeing with the government in power—should other countries try to pressure it to comply with common norms of justice? Do the democracies of the world have a responsibility to use their influences to try to limit the abuses of the powerless in societies where they are abused? These are just a few of the questions we explore.

Throughout the book we stress that students must make their own choices among the competing values and models of government. Although the four of us hold diverse and strong opinions about which choices are best, we do not believe it is our role to tell students our own answers to the broad questions we pose. Instead, we want our readers to learn firsthand that a democracy requires thoughtful choices. That is why we titled our book *The Challenge of Democracy.*

Features of This Edition

The Seventh Edition of *The Challenge of Democracy,* Brief Edition, includes a number of useful pedagogical features for students.

Chapter-Opening Vignettes

As in previous editions, each chapter begins with a vignette designed to draw students into the substance of that chapter while simultaneously examining one or more of the themes of the book, and relating chapter content to current world events.

For example, Chapter 1 ("Dilemmas of Democracy") looks at the meltdown of the home mortgage industry in the United States and introduces the concept of globalization by showing the ties between a home foreclosure in the United States, a bank in Scotland, and a small village in Norway. In Chapter 5 ("Participation and Voting") we examine recent pro-democracy protests in Myanmar to begin our examination of how politically active the residents of the United States are and how they most frequently participate in the political system. Other topics include the repeated failure of the European Union to ratify a constitution for Europe (Chapter 2, "The Constitution"), the challenges competing lobbyists pose to increasing fuel efficiency of vehicles and reducing the carbon footprint of the United States (Chapter 7, "Interest Groups"), the alternative intelligence analysis from the Pentagon in the lead-up to the war in Iraq (Chapter 10, "The Bureaucracy"), and the challenges policymakers in Congress and on the Federal Reserve Board face when global markets slide (Chapter 14, "Policymaking and the Budget"). More than three-quarters of the vignettes in this edition are either entirely new or significantly revised.

"Politics of Global Change" and "Compared with What?"

Two boxed features appear in *The Challenge of Democracy,* Brief Edition. The first, "Politics of Global Change" (found in Chapters 2, 3, 5, 8, 9, 11, and 13), examines various elements of political change, some troubling, some hopeful, particularly in light of the spread of globalization. Topics include the growth of electoral democracy around the world (Chapter 5, "Participation and Voting"); the politics of parliamentary fragmentation and coalition government in India (Chapter 8, "The Congress"); and changes in international support for the global war on terrorism (Chapter 9, "The Presidency").

We firmly believe that students can better evaluate how our political system works when they compare it with politics in other countries, so a second boxed feature, "Compared with What?" (found in Chapters 1, 4, 6, 7, 10, 12, and 14), in-

troduces a comparative perspective to the book, challenging students to compare the American political system with that of other countries around the world. In Chapter 1 ("Dilemmas of Democracy"), for example, we present international polling data showing significant differences in the importance people place on the competing values or order and freedom. In Chapter 6 ("Political Parties, Campaigns, and Elections"), we compare the choices voters in the United States face at the polls to the choices Canadians have on their ballots. In Chapter 14 ("Policymaking and the Budget"), we look at the differences in tax burdens across thirty countries to contextualize the rates taxpayers in the United States pay.

"Do It!"

In the margins of each chapter, we offer a suggested activity for students to undertake. These activities are intended to help students learn more about their communities, develop a more personal understanding of the topic at hand, and become politically active on topics of their own choosing.

In-Text Reference Materials

Key terms in each chapter are defined in the margins. At the end of the book, we have included a copy of the Declaration of Independence and the Constitution for student reference.

For the Instructor: Innovative Teaching Tools

Our job as authors did not end with writing this text. From the beginning, we have been centrally involved with producing a tightly integrated set of instructional materials to accompany the text. With help from other political scientists and educational specialists at Cengage Learning, these ancillary materials have grown and improved over time.

Teaching Support

■ *Online Instructor's Resource Manual.* This resource provides instructors with material that relates directly to the thematic framework and organization of the book. Revised and updated for this edition by Mary Beth Melchior, it includes learning objectives; chapter synopses; detailed full-length lectures (including a lecture format that encourages class participation); ideas for class, small group, and individual projects and activities; and Internet resources. Media lectures are also available. These lecture activities help students connect the material in the text with music and television programming they are exposed to every day. To access this manual, visit the password-protected instructor website at **www.cengage .com/politicalscience/janda.**

■ *Diploma Testing Instructor CD.* Thoroughly updated by P. S. Ruckman of Rock Valley College, this CD-ROM provides over 1,500 test questions in identification, multiple-choice, and essay formats. Diploma Testing provides instructors with all the tools they need to create, author, edit, customize, and deliver multiple types of tests. Instructors can import questions directly from the test bank, create their own questions, or edit existing algorithmic questions.

■ *PowerPoint Slides.* PowerPoint slides, which include figures from the text and brief outlines of chapter content, are available on the password-protected instructor website at **www.cengage.com/politicalscience/ janda.**

■ *In-Class "Clicker" Quizzes.* Multiple-choice quizzes, delivered in PowerPoint format and compatible with "clicker" technology, are available for download on the password-protected instructor website. Each clicker quiz consists of ten questions, and there is one quiz for every chapter in the text. As a motivator for students, half of the questions are available on the student website as pre-class quizzes; students who make an effort to answer these ques-

tions ahead of time are rewarded by being better prepared for in-class quizzes.

■ *CL NewsNow (powered by The Associated Press).* Bring the news right into your classroom! CL NewsNow PowerPoint slides allow instructors to engage students in events that are shaping the world right now. Use the slides to take a class poll or engage in a lively debate related to these stories, which may be downloaded from our password-protected instructor website at **www.cengage.com/ politicalscience/janda.** No in-class Internet connection required! The Associated Press also provides a live newsfeed that can be accessed on the student and instructor websites.

■ *CL Interactives (powered by The Associated Press).* These multimedia-learning tools walk students through the history of a present-day conflict or debate, and include visuals, animations, and questions for further discussion or research. Interactives and accompanying questions are also embedded in PowerPoint and available on the instructor's website to help spark in-class discussion. Marginal icons throughout the text point students to relevant CL Interactives, which are accessible at **www.cengage.com/ politicalscience/janda.** Both CL NewsNow and CL Interactives are ideal tools to use with "clickers."

■ *USpolitics.org.* The Seventh Edition continues to be supported by USpolitics.org, Kenneth Janda's personal website for *The Challenge of Democracy.* His site offers a variety of teaching aids to instructors who adopt any version of *The Challenge of Democracy* for courses in American politics. It is divided into two sides: the student side is open to all users, but the instructor side is limited to teachers who register online at uspolitics.org as *Challenge* adopters. The site offers some material not contained in Cengage Learning's own website, yet it also provides convenient links to the publisher's site.

Online Learning

Cengage Learning now offers the following exciting option for online learning.

- The Premium Website for *The Challenge of Democracy* offers a variety of rich online learning resources designed to enhance the student experience. These resources include podcasts, critical thinking activities, simulations, animated learning modules, timelines, flashcards and videos. Chapter resources are correlated with key chapter learning concepts, and users can browse or search for content in a variety of ways.

For information on the teaching tools that accompany *The Challenge of Democracy,* please contact your Cengage Learning sales representative.

For the Student: Effective Learning Aids

- *Student Website.* The student website, accessible at **www.cengage.com/politicalscience/janda,** offers a wide array of resources for students. Included are ACE Practice Tests, material from the *Study Guide* written by Kevin Davis of North Central Texas College–Corinth, chapter outlines, Internet exercises, and selected readings. Online appendices, such as *Federalist* Nos. 10 and 51, the Articles of Confederation, Presidents of the United States, Justices of the Supreme Court Since 1900, and Party Control of the Presidency and Congress, are available as general resources for students. The student website also hosts "In Our Own Words," a new audio feature. Spoken in the voice of the textbook authors, "In Our Own Words" provides insight into each chapter that will help students prepare for class.

- *IDEAlog10.0,* an earlier version of which won the 1992 Instructional Software Award from the American Political Science Association, is also available on the student website and is closely tied to the text's "value conflicts" theme. IDEAlog 10.0 first asks students to rate themselves on the two-dimensional tradeoff of freedom versus order and freedom versus equality. It then presents them with twenty questions, ten dealing with the conflict of freedom versus order and ten pertaining to freedom versus equality. Students' responses to these questions are classified according to libertarian, conservative, liberal, or communitarian ideological tendencies.

Acknowledgments

We acknowledge the contributions of those whose advice and assistance have been of great value, including David Bishop, Stu Baker, Claire Stewart, Eric Eberthardt, Zachary Cook, Tali Parensky, Matthew Wolfe, Tom Wyler, Patricia Conley, and Paul Manna.

We would also like to thank reviewers who gave us advice on preparing the Seventh Edition of *The Challenge of Democracy,* Brief Edition. They are Gary Aguiar, South Dakota State University; Alice Bartee, Missouri State University; Jonathan Buckstead, Austin Community College; William Hall, Bradley University; and John Sitton, Indiana University of Pennsylvania.

We invite your questions, comments, and suggestions about *The Challenge of Democracy,* Brief Edition at cod@northwestern.edu.

K.J.
J.G.
J.M.B.
K.W.H

Dilemmas of Democracy

CHAPTER 1

- The Globalization of American Government
- The Purposes of Government
- A Conceptual Framework for Analyzing Government
- The American Governmental Process: Majoritarian or Pluralist?
- Democracy and Globalization

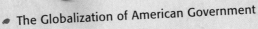

This icon will direct you to resources and activities on the website: www.cengage.com/polisci/janda/chall_dem_brief/7e

ENTERING 2009, MILLIONS OF homeowners in the United States feared meeting rising mortgage rates while their houses lost value in a declining market. Many had already lost their homes, as had Colorado truck driver Roger Rodriguez. His story illustrates how the aggressive sale of subprime mortgage loans hurt American homeowners, led to massive losses in financial institutions worldwide, and harmed ordinary people abroad. Taken together, these accounts demonstrate the effects of globalization on American life and raise the question of government's role in protecting its citizens.

In 2004, Mr. Rodriguez took out an $88,000 mortgage loan at a 6.3 percent interest rate from the CIT Group finance company to consolidate his debts.[1] An adjustable-rate mortgage (ARM), its rate would double after two years. Known as a *subprime* loan, it cost more than a prime, fixed-rate mortgage, for which his credit rating and monthly income were too low to qualify. When accepting the ARM, Mr. Rodriguez could just afford his low introductory monthly payment. In 2006, he lost his job after an accident; his income was cut in half; and his mortgage payment jumped by more than a third. In early 2007, a Denver law firm began foreclosure proceedings, and he filed for bankruptcy, owing $85,976.48 on his original loan.

However, Mr. Rodriguez did not owe the money to the CIT Group, for it had sold his loan to a unit of the Royal Bank of Scotland (RBS) in a package of mortgage-backed securities. In turn, RBS repackaged the securities with others into a trust called Soundview 2005-1, which it sold in pieces for $778 million to investors worldwide, who were attracted by high returns from subprime rates. Beginning in 2006, U.S. houses began to decline in value. Many loans in Soundview defaulted when their rates were reset, and the trust's value plummeted.

This scenario played out for countless mortgage-backed securities held across the globe. In 2007, RBS, Swiss UBS, the Bank of

Our main interest in this text is the purpose, value, and operation of government as practiced in the United States. We probe the relationship between individual freedoms and personal security, and how government ensures security by establishing order through making and enforcing its laws. We also examine the relationship between individual freedom and social equality as reflected in government policies, which often confront underlying dilemmas such as these. As the subprime mortgage collapse indicates, however, we live in an era of **globalization**—a term for the increasing interdependence of citizens and nations across the world. So we must consider how politics at home and abroad interrelate—which is increasingly important to understanding our government.[5]

We hope to improve your understanding of the world by analyzing the norms, or values, that people use to judge political events. Our purpose is

globalization The increasing interdependence of citizens and nations across the world.

China, and Norway's Terra Gruppen—among other foreign financial institutions—lost billions of dollars because of U.S. mortgage failures. Foreign citizens were hurt too. Four Norwegian villages near the Arctic Circle lost some $64 million from public investments in devalued mortgage-backed securities bought from Terra Securities.[2]

From 2000 to 2007, finance companies had aggressively sold subprime ARMs at low introductory rates to people patently unable to repay the loans when the rates were reset. An international organization estimated that about 15 percent of all U.S. mortgages were subprime and that about 20 percent risked default.[3] Because financial institutions had invested heavily in complex packages of mortgage securities with dubious value, they concealed from one another how much they held in subprime loans, generating mutual distrust and reluctance to lend to one another.

Trillions of dollars were linked to the U.S. mortgage market, and investors all over the world lost money. Major investment banks at home and abroad were forced to write down the value of their holdings. In mid-December 2007 the U.S. Federal Reserve System coordinated efforts with the European Central Bank and national banks in England, Switzerland, and Canada to extend credit to their cash-starved banks.[4]

Faced with even greater losses in 2008 and later as more loans would be reset to higher rates, pressure built for government to do something—but what? Free market principles frown on government bailing out greedy lenders or borrowers hoping for quick profits in a rising housing market. The government's limited mortgage relief plan in late 2007 was attacked by lenders (who feared losing money from existing loans) and by borrowers who failed to meet the plan's strict criteria for relief. With homeowners losing value as house prices decline and with millions of mortgage rates to be reset through 2011, pressure for government action increased. But what can government do to help? What *should* it do?

not to preach what people ought to favor in making policy decisions; it is to teach what values are at stake.

Teaching without preaching is not easy; no one can completely exclude personal values from political analysis. But our approach minimizes the problem by concentrating on the dilemmas that confront governments when they are forced to choose between important policies that threaten equally cherished values, such as freedom of speech and personal security.

A prominent scholar defined **politics** as "the authoritative allocation of values for a society."[6] Every government policy reflects a choice between conflicting values. All government policies reinforce certain values (norms) at the expense of others. We want you to interpret policy issues (for example, should assisted suicide go unpunished?) with an understanding of the fundamental values in question (freedom of action versus order and protection of life) and the broader political context (liberal or conservative politics).

By looking beyond the specifics to the underlying normative principles, you should be able to make more sense out of politics. Our framework for analysis does not encompass all the complexities of American government, but it should help your knowledge grow by improving your comprehension of political information. We begin by considering the basic purposes of government. In short, why do we need it?

 ## The Globalization of American Government

Most people do not like being told what to do. Fewer still like being coerced into acting a certain way. Yet billions of people in countries across the world willingly submit to the coercive power of government. They accept laws that state on which side of the road to drive, what constitutes a contract, how to dispose of human waste—and how much they must pay to support the government that makes these coercive laws.

In the first half of the twentieth century, people thought of government mainly in territorial terms. Indeed, a standard definition of **government** was the legitimate use of force—including firearms, imprisonment, and execution—within specified geographical boundaries to control human behavior. The term is also used to refer to the body authorized to exercise that power. Since the Peace of Westphalia in 1648 ended the Thirty Years' War in Europe, international relations and diplomacy have been based on the principle of **national sovereignty,** defined as "a political entity's externally recognized right to exercise final authority over its affairs."[7] Simply put, national sovereignty means that each national government has the right to govern its people as it wishes, without interference from other nations.

Although the League of Nations and later the United Nations were supposed to introduce supranational order into the world, even these international organizations explicitly respected national sovereignty as the guiding principle of international relations. The UN Charter, Article 2.1, states, "The Organization is based on the principle of the sovereign equality of all its Members."

National sovereignty, however, is threatened under globalization. Consider the international community's concern with starving refugees in the Darfur region of Sudan. The UN Security Council resolved to send troops to end the ethnic conflict that cost some 400,000 lives. The Sudanese government, suspected of causing the conflict, opposed the UN action as violating its sovereignty. Nevertheless, the humanitarian crisis in Sudan became closely monitored by the UN, which took action against a member state.

Global forces also generate pressures for international law. Consider the 1982 Law of the Sea Treaty, which governs maritime law from mineral

government The legitimate use of force to control human behavior; also, the organization or agency authorized to exercise that force.

national sovereignty "A political entity's externally recognized right to exercise final authority over its affairs."

rights to shipping lanes under an International Seabed Authority. Although President Reagan did not sign it, the treaty came into force in 1994 when it was ratified by sixty nations. President Clinton then signed the treaty, but conservative senators kept it from being ratified, fearing loss of U.S. sovereignty. After global warming began to melt the Arctic ice, the U.S. Navy backed the treaty for guaranteeing free passage through international straits, and oil and mining companies favored its 350-mile grant of mineral rights around Alaska. It was reported out of committee for Senate consideration in 2007 with President Bush's support.[8]

Our government, you might be surprised to learn, is worried about this trend of holding nations accountable to international law. In fact, in 2002, the United States "annulled" its signature to the 1998 treaty to create an International Criminal Court that would define and try crimes against humanity.[9] Why would the United States oppose such an international court? One reason is its concern that U.S. soldiers stationed abroad might be arrested and tried in that court.[10] Another reason is the death penalty, which has been abolished by more than half the countries in the world and all countries in the European Union. Indeed, in 1996, the International Commission of Jurists condemned our death penalty as "arbitrarily and racially discriminatory," and there is a concerted campaign across Europe to force the sovereign United States of America to terminate capital punishment.[11]

As the world's sole superpower, should the United States be above international law if its sovereignty is threatened by nations that don't share *our* values? What action should we follow if this situation occurs?

Although this text is about American national government, it recognizes the growing impact of international politics and world opinion on

U.S. politics. We are closely tied through trade to former enemies (we now import more goods from communist China than from France and Britain combined) and thoroughly embedded in a worldwide economic, social, and political network. More than ever before, we must discuss American politics while casting an eye to other countries to see how foreign affairs affect our government and how American politics affects government in other nations.

The Purposes of Government

All governments require their citizens to surrender some freedom as part of being governed. Why do people surrender their freedom to this control? To obtain the benefits of government. Throughout history, government seems to have served two major purposes: maintaining order (preserving life and protecting property) and providing public goods. More recently, some governments have pursued a third and more controversial purpose: promoting equality.

Maintaining Order

Maintaining order is the oldest objective of government. **Order** in this context is rich with meaning. Let's start with "law and order." Maintaining order in this sense means establishing the rule of law to preserve life and to protect property. To the seventeenth-century English philosopher Thomas Hobbes (1588–1679), preserving life was the most important function of government. In his classic philosophical treatise, *Leviathan* (1651), Hobbes described life without government as life in a "state of nature." Without rules, people would live as predators do, stealing and killing for their personal benefit. In Hobbes's classic phrase, life in a state of nature would be "solitary, poor, nasty, brutish, and short." He believed that a single ruler, or sovereign, must possess unquestioned authority to guarantee the safety of the weak to protect them from the attacks of the strong. He believed that complete obedience to the sovereign's strict laws was a small price to pay for the security of living in a civil society. Hobbes's philosophy explains why some Iraqi citizens may have preferred Saddam Hussein's tyranny to the disorder that came with unbridled freedom after his fall.

Most of us can only imagine what a state of nature would be like. But in some parts of the world, people live in a state of lawlessness. It occurred in Bosnia in 1995 after the former Yugoslavia collapsed, and again in Liberia in 2003 when both rebel and government forces, consisting largely of teenage and preteen children, plunged the country into chaos. It also occurred in the Darfur region of Sudan, where, as mentioned above, many thousands have fled from armed militias or been killed since 2003. Throughout history, authoritarian rulers have used people's fears of civil disorder to justify taking power and becoming the new established order.

INTERACTIVE 1.1

 Darfur's Plight

order Established ways of social behavior. Maintaining order is the oldest purpose of government.

Hobbes's conception of life in the cruel state of nature led him to view government primarily as a means of guaranteeing people's survival. Other theorists, taking survival for granted, believed that government protected order by preserving private property (goods and land owned by individuals). Foremost among them was John Locke (1632–1704), another English philosopher. In *Two Treatises on Government* (1690), he wrote that the protection of life, liberty, and property was the basic objective of government. His thinking strongly influenced the Declaration of Independence, which identifies "Life, Liberty, and the pursuit of Happiness" as "unalienable Rights" of citizens under government.

Not everyone believes that the protection of private property is a valid objective of government. The German philosopher Karl Marx (1818–1883) rejected the private ownership of property used in the production of goods or services. Marx's ideas form the basis of **communism,** a complex theory that gives ownership of all land and productive facilities to the people—in effect, to the government. In line with communist theory, the 1977 constitution of the former Soviet Union declared that the nation's land, minerals, waters, and forests "are the exclusive property of the state." In addition, "The state owns the basic means of production in industry, construction, and agriculture; means of transport and communication; the banks, the property of state-run trade organizations and public utilities, and other state-run undertakings."[12] Even today's market-oriented China still clings to the principle that all land belongs to the state, and not until 2007 did it pass a law that protected private homes and businesses.[13]

Providing Public Goods

After governments have established basic order, they can pursue other ends. Using their coercive powers, they can tax citizens to raise funds to spend on **public goods,** which are benefits and services that are available to everyone, such as education, sanitation, and parks. Public goods benefit all citizens but are not likely to be produced by the voluntary acts of individuals. The government of ancient Rome, for example, built aqueducts to carry fresh water from the mountains to the city. Road building is another public good provided by the government since ancient times.

Some government enterprises that have been common in other countries—running railroads, operating coal mines, generating electric power—are politically controversial or even unacceptable in the United States. Many Americans believe public goods and services should be provided by private business operating for profit.

Promoting Equality

The promotion of equality has not always been a major objective of government. It gained prominence in the twentieth century, in the aftermath of industrialization and urbanization. Confronted by the contrast of poverty

communism A political system in which, in theory, ownership of all land and productive facilities is in the hands of the people and all goods are equally shared. The production and distribution of goods are controlled by an authoritarian government.

public goods Benefits and services, such as parks and sanitation, that benefit all citizens but are not likely to be produced voluntarily by individuals.

amid plenty, some political leaders in European nations pioneered extensive government programs to improve life for the poor. Under the emerging concept of the welfare state, government's role expanded to provide individuals with medical care, education, and a guaranteed income "from cradle to grave." Sweden, Britain, and other nations adopted welfare programs aimed at reducing social inequalities. This relatively new purpose of government has been by far the most controversial. People often oppose taxation for public goods (such as building roads and schools) because of its cost alone. They oppose more strongly taxation for government programs to promote economic and social equality on principle.

The key issue here is the government's role in redistributing income, that is, taking from the wealthy to give to the poor. Charity (voluntary giving to the poor) has a strong basis in Western religious traditions; using the power of the state to support the poor does not. Using the state to redistribute income was originally a radical idea, set forth by Marx as the ultimate principle of developed communism: "from each according to his ability, to each according to his needs."[14] This extreme has never been realized in any government, not even in communist states. But over time, taking from the rich to help the needy has become a legitimate function of most governments.

That function is not without controversy, however. Especially since the Great Depression of the 1930s, the government's role in redistributing income to promote economic equality has been a major source of policy debate in the United States. In 2006, for example, Democrats in the Senate blocked a bill passed in the House that would have raised the minimum wage from $5.15 to $7.25. They objected to the bill because it would have also cut the estate tax for the wealthy. The minimum wage increase was ultimately passed in 2007, but only by attaching it to a bill funding the war effort in Iraq.

Government can also promote social equality through policies that do not redistribute income. For example, in 2000 Vermont passed a law allowing persons of the same sex to enter a "civil union" granting access to similar benefits enjoyed by persons of different sexes through marriage. In 2003, Canada granted full marriage rights to same-sex partners—the same year that Massachusetts courts allowed same-sex marriages. In this instance, laws advancing social equality may clash with different social values held by other citizens. Most states prohibit such marriages.

IDEAlog.org

How do you feel about government programs that reduce income differences between rich and poor? Take IDEAlog's self-test.

A Conceptual Framework for Analyzing Government

Citizens have very different views on how vigorously they want government to maintain order, provide public goods, and promote equality. Of the three objectives, providing public goods usually is less controversial than maintaining order or promoting equality. After all, government spending for highways, schools, and parks carries benefits for nearly every citizen. Moreover, these services merely cost money. The cost of maintaining order and promoting equality is greater than money; it usually means a tradeoff of basic values.

To understand government and the political process, you must be able to recognize these tradeoffs and identify the basic values they entail. You need to take a much broader view than that offered by examining specific political events. You need to use political concepts. A *concept* is a generalized idea of a class of items or thoughts. It groups various events, objects, or qualities under a common classification or label.

The framework that supports this text consists of five concepts that figure prominently in political analysis. We regard these five concepts as especially important to a broad understanding of American politics, and we use them repeatedly. This framework will help you evaluate political events long after you have read this book.

The five concepts that we emphasize relate to (1) what government tries to do and (2) how it decides to do it. The concepts that relate to what government tries to do are *order, freedom,* and *equality.* All governments by definition value order; maintaining order is part of the meaning of government. Most governments at least claim to preserve individual freedom while they maintain order, although they vary widely in the extent to which they succeed. Few governments even profess to guarantee equality, and governments differ greatly in policies that pit equality against freedom. Our conceptual framework should help you evaluate the extent to which the United States pursues all three values through its government.

How government chooses the proper mix of order, freedom, and equality in its policymaking has to do with the process of choice. We evaluate the American governmental process using two models of democratic government: *majoritarian* and *pluralist.* Many governments profess to be democracies. Whether they are or not depends on their (and our) meaning of the term. Even countries that Americans agree are democracies, such as the United States and Britain, differ substantially in the type of democracy they practice. We can use our conceptual models of democratic government both to classify the type of democracy practiced in the United States and evaluate the government's success in fulfilling that model.

The five concepts can be organized into two groups:

1. Concepts that identify the values pursued by government:

   ■ Freedom

   ■ Order

   ■ Equality

2. Concepts that describe models of democratic government:

   ■ Majoritarian democracy

   ■ Pluralist democracy

First we examine freedom, order, and equality as conflicting values pursued by government. Later in this chapter, we discuss majoritarian democracy and pluralist democracy as alternative institutional models for implementing democratic government.

The Concepts of Freedom, Order, and Equality

These three terms—*freedom, order,* and *equality*—have a range of connotations in American politics. Both *freedom* and *equality* are positive terms that politicians have learned to use to their own advantage. Consequently, *freedom* and *equality* mean different things to different people at different times, depending on the political context in which they are used. *Order,* however, has negative connotations for many people because it brings to mind government intrusion in private lives. Except during periods of social strife or external threat (e.g., after September 11, 2001), few politicians in Western democracies call openly for more order. Because all governments infringe on freedom, we examine that concept first.

Freedom. *Freedom* can be used in two major senses: freedom *of* and freedom *from.* Franklin Delano Roosevelt used the word in each sense in a speech he made shortly before the United States entered World War II. He described four freedoms: freedom *of* religion, freedom *of* speech, freedom *from* fear, and freedom *from* want. **Freedom of** is the absence of constraints on behavior. It is freedom to do something. In this sense, *freedom* is synonymous with *liberty.* **Freedom from** suggests immunity from something undesirable or negative, such as fear and want. In the modern political context, *freedom from* often connotes the fight against exploitation and oppression. The cry of the civil rights movement in the 1960s, "Freedom Now!" conveyed this meaning. If you recognize that *freedom* in the latter sense means immunity from discrimination, you can see that it comes close to the concept of equality.[15] In this book, we avoid using *freedom* to mean "freedom from"; for this sense of the word, we simply use *equality.* When we use *freedom,* we mean "freedom of."

Order. When *order* is viewed in the narrow sense of preserving life and protecting property, most citizens would concede the importance of maintaining order and thereby grant the need for government. But when *order* is viewed in the broader sense of preserving the social order, people are more likely to argue that maintaining order is not a legitimate function of government. *Social order* refers to established patterns of authority in society and to traditional modes of behavior. However, it is important to remember that social order can change. Today, perfectly respectable men and women wear bathing suits that would have caused a scandal a hundred years ago.

A government can protect the established order by using its **police power**—its authority to safeguard residents' safety, health, welfare, and morals.

---

freedom of An absence of constraints on behavior, as in *freedom of speech* or *freedom of religion.*

freedom from Immunity, as in *freedom from want.*

police power The authority of government to maintain order and safeguard citizens' safety, health, welfare, and morals.

The extent to which government should use this authority is a topic of ongoing debate in the United States and is constantly being redefined by the courts. After September 11, 2001, new laws were passed increasing government's power to investigate suspicious activities by foreign nationals in order to deter terrorism. Despite their desire to be safe from further attacks, some citizens feared the erosion of their civil liberties.

Most governments are inherently conservative; they tend to resist social change. But some governments aim to radically restructure the social order. Social change is most dramatic when a government is overthrown through force and replaced. This can occur through an internal revolution or a "regime change" effected externally. Societies can also work to change social patterns more gradually through the legal process. Our use of the term *order* in this book encompasses all three aspects: preserving life, protecting property, and maintaining traditional patterns of social relationships.

Equality. Like *freedom* and *order, equality* is used in different senses to support different causes. **Political equality** in elections is easy to define: each citizen has one and only one vote. This basic concept is central to democratic theory, a subject we explore at length later in this chapter. But when some people advocate political equality, they mean more than "one person, one vote." These people contend that an urban ghetto dweller and the chairman of the board of Microsoft are not politically equal despite the fact that each has one vote. Through occupation or wealth, some citizens are more able than others to influence political decisions. For example, wealthy citizens can exert influence by advertising in the mass media or contacting friends in high places. Lacking great wealth and political connections, most citizens do not have such influence. Thus, some analysts argue that equality in wealth, education, and status—that is, **social equality**—is necessary for true political equality.

There are two routes to promoting social equality: providing equal opportunities and ensuring equal outcomes. **Equality of opportunity** means that each person has the same chance to succeed in life. This idea is deeply ingrained in American culture. The U.S. Constitution prohibits titles of nobility, and owning property is not a requirement for holding public office. Public schools and libraries are free to all. For many people, the concept of social equality is satisfied by offering equal opportunities for advancement—it is not essential that people actually end up being equal. For others, true social equality means nothing less than **equality of outcome**.[16] They believe that society must see to it that people are equal. According to this view, it is not enough that governments provide people with equal opportunities; they must also design policies to redistribute wealth and status so that economic and social equality are achieved.

Some link equality of outcome with the concept of government-supported **rights**—the idea that every citizen is entitled to certain benefits of government, that government should guarantee its citizens adequate (if not equal) housing, employment, medical care, and income. If citizens are entitled to

political equality Equality in political decision making: one vote per person, with all votes counted equally.

social equality Equality in wealth, education, and status.

equality of opportunity The idea that each person is guaranteed the same chance to succeed in life.

equality of outcome The concept that society must ensure that people are equal, and governments must design policies to redistribute wealth and status to achieve economic and social equality.

rights The benefits of government to which every citizen is entitled.

government benefits as a matter of right, government efforts to promote equality of outcome become legitimized.

Clearly, the concept of equality of outcome is very different from that of equality of opportunity, and it requires a much greater degree of government activity. It also clashes more directly with the concept of freedom. By taking from one person to give to another, which is necessary for the redistribution of income and status, the government creates winners and losers. The winners may believe that justice has been served by the redistribution. The losers often feel strongly that their freedom to enjoy their income and status has suffered.

Two Dilemmas of Government

The two major dilemmas facing American government in the early years of the twenty-first century stem from the oldest and the newest objectives of government: maintaining order and promoting equality. Both order and equality are important social values, but government cannot pursue either without sacrificing a third important value: individual freedom. The clash between freedom and order forms the *original* dilemma of government; the clash between freedom and equality forms the *modern* dilemma of government. Although the dilemmas are very different, each involves trading off some amount of freedom for another value.

The Original Dilemma: Freedom Versus Order.   The conflict between freedom and order originates in the very meaning of *government* as the legitimate use of force to control human behavior. How much freedom a citizen must surrender to government is a dilemma that has occupied philosophers for hundreds of years. The original purpose of government was to protect life and property, to make citizens safe from violence. How well is the American government doing today in providing law and order to its citizens? More than 35 percent of the respondents in a 2002 national survey said that there were areas within a mile of their home where they were "afraid to walk alone at night."[17]

Contrast the fear of crime in urban America with the sense of personal safety while walking in Moscow, Warsaw, or Prague when the old communist governments still ruled in Eastern Europe. It was common to see old and young strolling late at night along the streets and in the parks of those cities. The communist regimes gave their police great powers to control guns, monitor citizens' movements, and arrest and imprison suspicious people, which enabled them to do a better job of maintaining order. Communist governments deliberately chose order over freedom.

In the abstract, people value both freedom and order; in real life, the two values inherently conflict. By definition, any policy that strengthens one value takes away from the other. In a democracy, policy choices hinge on how much citizens value freedom and how much they value order.

Compared with What?

The Importance of Order and Freedom in Other Nations

Compared with citizens in twenty-nine other nations, Americans do not value order very much. The World Values Survey asked respondents to select which of four national goals was "very important":

- Maintaining order in the nation
- Giving people more say in important government decisions
- Fighting rising prices
- Protecting freedom of speech

The United States ranked twenty-eighth in the list of those selecting "maintaining order" as very important. Although American citizens do not value government control of social behavior as much as others, Americans do value freedom of speech more highly. Citizens in only three countries favor protecting freedom of speech more than citizens in the United States.

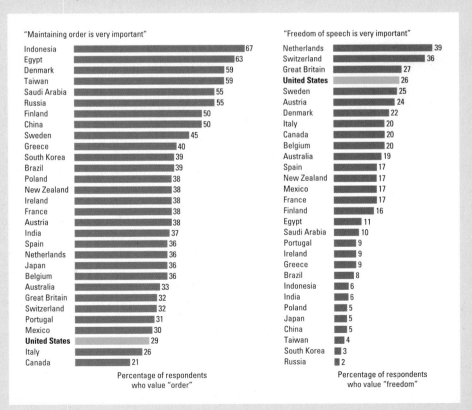

"Maintaining order is very important"

Country	Percentage
Indonesia	67
Egypt	63
Denmark	59
Taiwan	59
Saudi Arabia	55
Russia	55
Finland	50
China	50
Sweden	45
Greece	40
South Korea	39
Brazil	39
Poland	38
New Zealand	38
Ireland	38
France	38
Austria	38
India	37
Spain	36
Netherlands	36
Japan	36
Belgium	36
Australia	33
Great Britain	32
Switzerland	32
Portugal	31
Mexico	30
United States	29
Italy	26
Canada	21

Percentage of respondents who value "order"

"Freedom of speech is very important"

Country	Percentage
Netherlands	39
Switzerland	36
Great Britain	27
United States	26
Sweden	25
Austria	24
Denmark	22
Italy	20
Canada	20
Belgium	20
Australia	19
Spain	17
New Zealand	17
Mexico	17
France	17
Finland	16
Egypt	11
Saudi Arabia	10
Portugal	9
Ireland	9
Greece	9
Brazil	8
Indonesia	6
India	6
Poland	5
Japan	5
China	5
Taiwan	4
South Korea	3
Russia	2

Percentage of respondents who value "freedom"

Source: These are combined data from the 1999–2001 and 2005–2007 Waves of the World Values Survey. See Ronald Inglehart, "Materialist/Postmaterialist Priorities Among Publics Around the World," discussion paper presented at ISR, University of Michigan, February 14, 2008.

The Modern Dilemma: Freedom Versus Equality.   Popular opinion has it that freedom and equality go hand in hand. In reality, these two values usually clash when governments enact policies to promote social equality. Because social equality is a relatively recent government objective, deciding between policies that promote equality at the expense of freedom, and vice versa, is the modern dilemma of politics. Consider these examples:

- During the 1970s, the courts ordered the busing of schoolchildren to achieve equal proportions of blacks and whites in public schools. This action was motivated by concern for educational equality, but it also impaired freedom of choice.

- During the 1980s, some states passed legislation that went beyond giving men and women equal pay for equal work to the more radical notion of pay equity—equal pay for comparable work. Women were to be paid at a rate equal to men's even if they had different jobs, providing the women's jobs were of "comparable worth" (meaning the skills and responsibilities were comparable).

- During the 1990s, Congress prohibited discrimination in employment, public services, and public accommodations on the basis of physical or mental disabilities. Under the 1990 Americans with Disabilities Act, businesses with twenty-five or more employees could not pass over an otherwise qualified disabled person in employment or promotion, and new buses and trains had to be made accessible to them.

The clash between freedom and order is obvious, but the clash between freedom and equality is more subtle. Americans, who think of freedom and equality as complementary rather than conflicting values, often do not notice the clash between those two values. When forced to choose between them, however, Americans are far more likely than people in other countries to choose freedom over equality.

The conflicts among freedom, order, and equality explain a great deal of the political conflict in the United States. The conflicts also underlie the ideologies that people use to structure their understanding of politics.

Ideology and the Scope of Government

Some people hold an assortment of values and beliefs that produce contradictory opinions on government policies. Others organize their opinions into a **political ideology**: a consistent set of values and beliefs about the proper purpose and scope of government.

How far should government go to maintain order, provide public goods, and promote equality? We can analyze answers to this question by referring to philosophies about the proper scope of government—the range of permissible activities. Imagine a continuum. At one end is the belief that

political ideology A consistent set of values and beliefs about the proper purpose and scope of government.

FIGURE 1.1   Ideology and the Scope of Government

MOST
GOVERNMENT

LEAST
GOVERNMENT

POLITICAL THEORIES		
Totalitarianism	Libertarianism	Anarchism

ECONOMIC THEORIES		
Socialism	Capitalism	Laissez Faire

POPULAR POLITICAL LABELS IN AMERICA	
Liberal	Conservative

We can classify political ideologies according to the scope of action that people are willing to allow government in dealing with social and economic problems. In this chart, the three lines map out various philosophical positions along an underlying continuum ranging from "most" to "least" government. Notice that conventional politics in the United States spans only a narrow portion of the theoretical possibilities for government action. In popular usage, liberals favor a greater scope of government, and conservatives want a narrower scope. But over time, the traditional distinction has eroded and now oversimplifies the differences between liberals and conservatives. See Figure 1.2 on page 19 for a more discriminating classification of liberals and conservatives.

government should do everything; at the other is the belief that government should not exist. These extreme ideologies—from "most government" to "least government"—and those that fall in between are shown in Figure 1.1.

Totalitarianism. **Totalitarianism** is the belief that government should have unlimited power. A totalitarian government controls all sectors of society: business, labor, education, religion, sports, the arts, and others. A true totalitarian favors a network of laws, rules, and regulations that guides every aspect of individual behavior.

Socialism. Whereas totalitarianism refers to government in general, socialism pertains to government's role in the economy. Like communism, **socialism** is an economic system based on Marxist theory. Under socialism (and communism), the scope of government extends to ownership or control of the basic industries that produce goods and services (communications, heavy industry, transportation). Although socialism favors a strong role for government in regulating private industry and directing the economy,

INTERACTIVE 1.2

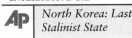 *North Korea: Last Stalinist State*

totalitarianism A political philosophy that advocates unlimited power for the government to enable it to control all sectors of society.

socialism A form of rule in which the central government plays a strong role in regulating existing private industry and directing the economy, although it does allow some private ownership of productive capacity.

it allows more room than communism does for private ownership of productive capacity.

Communism in theory was supposed to result in a withering away of the state, but communist governments in practice tended toward totalitarianism, controlling economic, political, and social life through a dominant party organization. Some socialist governments, however, practice **democratic socialism**. They guarantee civil liberties (such as freedom of speech and freedom of religion) and allow their citizens to determine the extent of the government's activity through free elections and competitive political parties. The governments of Britain, Sweden, Germany, and France, among other democracies, have at times been avowedly socialist.

Capitalism. Capitalism also relates to the government's role in the economy. In contrast to both socialism and communism, **capitalism** supports free enterprise—private businesses operating without government regulations. Some theorists, most notably the late economist Milton Friedman, argue that free enterprise is necessary for free politics.[18] Whether this argument is valid depends in part on our understanding of democracy, a subject we discuss later in this chapter.

The United States is decidedly a capitalist country, more so than most other Western nations. But our government does extend its authority into the economic sphere, regulating private businesses and directing the overall economy. Both American liberals and conservatives embrace capitalism, but they differ on the nature and amount of government intervention in the economy that is necessary or desirable.

Libertarianism. **Libertarianism** opposes all government action except that which is necessary to protect life and property. For example, libertarians believe that social programs that provide food, clothing, and shelter are outside the proper scope of government. They also oppose any government intervention in the economy. This kind of economic policy is called **laissez faire**, a French phrase that means "let (people) do (as they please)." Such an extreme policy extends beyond the free enterprise advocated by most capitalists.

Anarchism. Anarchism stands opposite totalitarianism on the political continuum. Anarchists oppose all government in any form. As a political philosophy, **anarchism** values absolute freedom above all else. Like totalitarianism, it is not a popular philosophy, but it does have adherents on the political fringes. Discussing old and new forms of anarchy, Joseph Kahn said, "Nothing has revived anarchism like globalization."[19]

Liberals and Conservatives. As shown in Figure 1.1, practical politics in the United States ranges over only the central portion of the continuum. The extreme positions, totalitarianism and anarchism, are rarely argued in public debate. And in this era of distrust of "big government," few Ameri-

democratic socialism
A socialist form of government that guarantees civil liberties such as freedom of speech and religion. Citizens determine the extent of government activity through free elections and competitive political parties.

capitalism The system of government that favors free enterprise (privately owned businesses operating without government regulation).

libertarianism A political ideology that is opposed to all government action except as necessary to protect life and property.

laissez faire An economic doctrine that opposes any form of government intervention in business.

anarchism A political philosophy that opposes government in any form.

Anarchists in Action
Anarchism as a philosophy views government as an unnecessary evil used by the wealthy to exploit the poor. In June 2007, scores of young anarchists were among hundreds in the streets of the German city of Rostock, protesting the G8 summit meeting of leaders of wealthy nations in nearby Heiligendamm. *(AP Photo/ Markus Schreiber)*

can politicians would openly advocate socialism. Most debate is limited to a narrow range of political thought. On one side are people commonly called *liberals;* on the other are *conservatives.* In popular usage, liberals favor more government, conservatives less. This distinction is clear when the issue is government spending to provide public goods. **Liberals** are willing to use government to promote equality but not order. Thus, they generally favor generous government support for education, wildlife protection, public transportation, and a whole range of social programs. **Conservatives** want smaller government budgets and fewer government programs. They support free enterprise and argue against government job programs, regulation of business, and legislation of working conditions and wage rates. In short, they prefer to use government to promote order rather than equality.

In other areas, liberal and conservative ideologies are less consistent. The differences no longer hinge on the narrow question of the government's role in providing public goods. Liberals still favor more government and conservatives less, but this is no longer the critical difference between them. Today, that difference stems from their attitudes toward the purpose of government. Conservatives support the original purpose of government: to maintain social order. They are willing to use the coercive power of the state to force citizens to be orderly. But they would not stop with defining, preventing, and punishing crime. They tend to want to preserve traditional patterns of social relations—the domestic role of women and the importance of religion in school and family life, for example.

liberals Those who are willing to use government to promote equality but not order.

conservatives Those who are willing to use government to promote order but not equality.

Liberals are less likely than conservatives to want to use government power to maintain order. Liberals do not shy away from using government coercion, but they use it for a different purpose: to promote equality. They support laws that ensure equal treatment of homosexuals in employment, housing, and education; laws that force private businesses to hire and promote women and members of minority groups; and laws that require public transportation to provide equal access to the disabled. Conservatives do not oppose equality, but they do not value it to the extent of using the government's power to enforce it. For liberals, the use of that power to promote equality is both valid and necessary.

A Two-Dimensional Classification of Ideologies

DO IT!

Take the IDEAlog.org quiz and see where you fit in Figure 1.2.

To classify liberal and conservative ideologies more accurately, we have to incorporate the values of freedom, order, and equality into the classification. We can do this using the model in Figure 1.2. It depicts the conflicting values along two separate dimensions, each anchored in maximum freedom at the lower left. One dimension extends horizontally from maximum freedom on the left to maximum order on the right. The other extends vertically from maximum freedom at the bottom to maximum equality at the top. Each box represents a different ideological type: libertarians, liberals, conservatives, and communitarians.[20]

Libertarians value freedom more than they value order or equality (we will use *libertarian* for people who have libertarian tendencies but may not accept the whole philosophy). In practical terms, libertarians want minimal government intervention in both the economic and the social spheres. For example, they oppose affirmative action laws and laws that restrict transmission of sexually explicit material. Liberals value freedom more than order but not more than equality. They oppose laws that ban sexually explicit publications but support affirmative action. Conservatives value freedom more than equality but would restrict freedom to preserve social order. Conservatives oppose affirmative action but favor laws that restrict pornography.

Finally, at the upper right in Figure 1.2, we have a group that values both equality and order more than freedom. Its members support both affirmative action laws and laws that restrict pornography. We will call this new group **communitarians**. The term is used narrowly in contemporary politics to reflect the philosophy of the Communitarian Network, a political movement founded by sociologist Amitai Etzioni.[21] This movement rejects both the liberal-conservative classification and the libertarian argument that "individuals should be left on their own to pursue their choices, rights, and self-interests."[22] Like liberals, Etzioni's communitarians believe that there is a role for government in helping the disadvantaged. Like conservatives, they believe that government should be used to promote moral values—preserving the family through more stringent divorce laws and limiting the dissemination of pornography, for example.[23] However, the Communitar-

libertarians Those who are opposed to using government to promote either order or equality.

communitarians Those who are willing to use government to promote both order and equality.

FIGURE 1.2   Ideologies: A Two-Dimensional Framework

The four ideological types are defined by the values they favor in resolving the two major dilemmas of government: how much freedom should be sacrificed in pursuit of order and equality, respectively. Test yourself by thinking about the values that are most important to you. Which box in the figure best represents your combination of values?

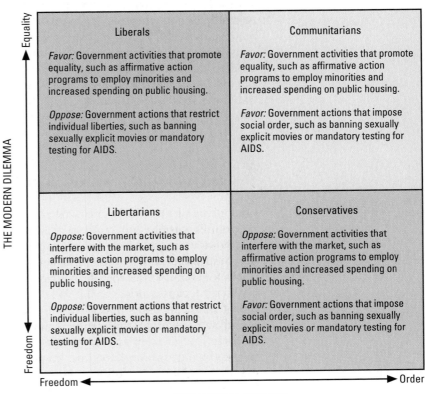

Liberals

Favor: Government activities that promote equality, such as affirmative action programs to employ minorities and increased spending on public housing.

Oppose: Government actions that restrict individual liberties, such as banning sexually explicit movies or mandatory testing for AIDS.

Communitarians

Favor: Government activities that promote equality, such as affirmative action programs to employ minorities and increased spending on public housing.

Favor: Government actions that impose social order, such as banning sexually explicit movies or mandatory testing for AIDS.

Libertarians

Oppose: Government activities that interfere with the market, such as affirmative action programs to employ minorities and increased spending on public housing.

Oppose: Government actions that restrict individual liberties, such as banning sexually explicit movies or mandatory testing for AIDS.

Conservatives

Oppose: Government activities that interfere with the market, such as affirmative action programs to employ minorities and increased spending on public housing.

Favor: Government actions that impose social order, such as banning sexually explicit movies or mandatory testing for AIDS.

THE MODERN DILEMMA — Equality / Freedom

Freedom ◄——————► Order

THE ORIGINAL DILEMMA

---

ian Network is not dedicated to big government. According to its platform, "The government should step in only to the extent that other social subsystems fail, rather than seek to replace them."[24] Our definition of communitarian (small "c") clearly embraces the Communitarian Network's philosophy, but it is broader: communitarians favor government programs that promote both order and equality, somewhat in keeping with socialist theory.

By analyzing political ideologies on two dimensions rather than one, we can explain why people can seem to be liberal on one issue (favoring a broader scope of government action) and conservative on another (favoring less government action). The reason hinges on the purpose of a given government action: Which value does it promote: order or equality? According to our typology, only libertarians and communitarians are consistent in their attitudes toward the scope of government activity, whatever its purpose. Libertarians value freedom so highly that they oppose most government efforts to enforce either order or equality. Communitarians (in our use) are inclined to trade off freedom for both order and equality. Liberals and conservatives, in contrast, favor or oppose government activity depending on its purpose. As you will learn in Chapter 4, large groups of Americans fall into each of the four ideological categories. Because Americans increasingly choose four different resolutions to the original and modern dilemmas of government, the simple labels *liberal* and *conservative* no longer describe contemporary political ideologies as well as they did in the 1930s, 1940s, and 1950s.

The American Governmental Process: Majoritarian or Pluralist?

Opponents of the widely criticized farm subsidy program argue that the program is wasteful and tends to channel taxpayer money to the wealthy. The program grew out of legislation passed by Congress in 1920 to stabilize food prices and reduce farm bankruptcies in the long term. When prices for commodities rose, farmers planted more and the increase in supply, in turn, caused prices to fall. When prices fell, farmers could be driven out of business. And if lots of farmers went out of business, then the reduced acreage under cultivation would result in less supply and cause prices to rise. The new law created price supports that would go to farmers to provide an income floor and keep food supplies stable, even during years when the market prices paid to farmers fell.

Over time, as many small family farms became uneconomical and were replaced by much larger farms owned by huge agribusiness concerns, these subsidy payments were increasingly sent to wealthy corporations and landowners. Some subsidy recipients were people who owned farmland but weren't themselves farmers, such as late night talk show host David Letterman. Despite the criticism over the billions of taxpayer dollars sent each year to wealthy landowners, no wholesale reform has occurred and subsidies have continued.[25]

Why does a program so widely denigrated survive? The dynamic is a familiar one: apathy versus intensity. The average citizen cares little about farm subsidies, as few of us know enough about the program to figure out how subsidies work or how much they cost us as taxpayers. But farmers care passionately about farm subsidies because price supports directly affect how much money they make each year. As a result, the interest groups that represent farmers energetically promote farm subsidies in Congress. In the United States, majority opinion often falls victim to a much smaller minority—a minority that takes advantage of the apathy of the majority.

To this point, our discussion of political ideologies has centered on conflicting views about the values government should pursue. We now examine how government should decide what to do. In particular, we set forth two criteria for judging whether a government's decision-making process is democratic, one emphasizing majority rule and the other emphasizing the role of interest groups.

The Theory of Democratic Government

Americans have a simple answer to the question, "Who should govern?" It is, "The people." Unfortunately, this answer is too simple. It fails to say who *the people* are. Should we include young children? Recent immigrants? Illegal aliens? This answer also fails to indicate how "the people" should do the governing. Should they be assembled in a stadium? Vote by mail? Choose representatives to govern for them? We need to take a close look at what "government by the people" really means.

The word *democracy* originated in Greek writings around the fifth century B.C. *Demos* referred to the common people, the masses; *kratos* meant "power." The ancient Greeks were afraid of **democracy**, which they viewed as rule by rank-and-file citizens. That fear is evident in the term *demagogue*. We use that term today to refer to a politician who appeals to and often deceives the masses by manipulating their emotions and prejudices.

Many centuries after the Greeks defined *democracy*, the idea still carried the connotation of mob rule. When George Washington was president, opponents of a new political party disparagingly called it a *democratic* party. No one would do that in politics today. In fact, the names of more than 20 percent of the world's political parties contain some variation of the word *democracy*.[26]

There are two major schools of thought about what constitutes democracy. The first believes democracy is a form of government, and it emphasizes the procedures that enable the people to govern: meeting to discuss issues, voting in elections, and running for public office, for example. The second sees democracy in the substance of government policies, in freedom of religion and providing for human needs. The *procedural* approach focuses on how decisions are made; the *substantive* approach is concerned with what government does.

The Procedural View of Democracy. **Procedural democratic theory** sets forth principles that describe how government should make decisions. These principles address three distinct questions:

1. *Who* should participate in decision making?

2. *How much* should each participant's vote count?

3. *How many* votes are needed to reach a decision?

According to procedural democratic theory, all adults within the boundaries of the political community should participate in government decision making. We refer to this principle as **universal participation**. How much should each participant's vote count? According to procedural theory, all votes

democracy A system of government in which, in theory, the people rule, either directly or indirectly.

procedural democratic theory A view of democracy as being embodied in a decision-making process that involves universal participation, political equality, majority rule, and responsiveness.

universal participation The concept that everyone in a democracy should participate in governmental decision making.

should count equally. This is the principle of political equality. Note that universal participation and political equality are two distinct principles. It is not enough for everyone to participate in a decision; all votes must carry equal weight.

Finally, procedural theory prescribes that a group should decide to do what the majority of its participants wants to do. This principle is called **majority rule.** (If participants divide over more than two alternatives and none receives a majority, the principle usually defaults to *plurality* rule, in which the group should do what the largest group of participants wants, even if fewer than half of those involved hold that view.)

A Complication: Direct Versus Indirect Democracy.   Universal participation, political equality, and majority rule are widely recognized as necessary for democratic decision making. Small, simple societies can achieve all three with direct or **participatory democracy,** in which all members of the group meet to make decisions, observing political equality and majority rule. However, in the United States and nearly all other democracies, participatory democracy is rare. Clearly, all Americans cannot gather at the Capitol in Washington, D.C., to decide defense policy.

Believing that participatory democracy on the national level was both impossible and undesirable, the framers of the Constitution instituted indirect democracy, that is, **representative democracy.** In such a system, citizens participate in government by electing public officials to make government decisions on their behalf. Within the context of representative democracy, we adhere to the principles of universal participation, political equality, and majority rule to guarantee that elections are democratic. But what happens after the election?

Suppose the elected representatives do not make the decisions the people would have made if they had gathered for the same purpose. To account for this possibility in representative government, procedural theory provides a fourth decision-making principle: **responsiveness.** Elected representatives should follow the general contours of public opinion as they formulate complex pieces of legislation.[27]

By adding responsiveness to deal with the case of indirect democracy, we now have four principles of procedural democracy:

- Universal participation
- Political equality
- Majority rule
- Government responsiveness to public opinion

The Substantive View of Democracy.   According to procedural theory, the principle of responsiveness is absolute: the government should do what the majority wants, regardless of what that is. At first this seems a reasonable way to protect the rights of citizens in a representative democ-

majority rule The principle—basic to procedural democratic theory—that the decision of a group must reflect the preference of more than half of those participating; a simple majority.

participatory democracy A system of government where rank-and-file citizens rule themselves rather than electing representatives to govern on their behalf.

representative democracy A system of government where citizens elect public officials to govern on their behalf.

responsiveness A decision-making principle, necessitated by representative government, that implies that elected representatives should do what the majority of people wants.

racy. But what about the rights of minorities? To limit the government's responsiveness to public opinion, we must look outside procedural democratic theory to substantive democratic theory. **Substantive democratic theory** focuses on the substance of government policies, not on the procedures followed in making those policies. It argues that in a democratic government, certain principles must be embodied in government policies. Substantive theorists would reject a law that requires Bible reading in schools because it would violate a substantive principle, the freedom of religion. The core of the substantive principles of American democracy is embedded in the Bill of Rights and other amendments to the U.S. Constitution.

In defining the principles that underlie democratic government—and the policies of that government—most substantive theorists agree on a basic criterion: government policies should guarantee *civil liberties* (freedom of behavior such as freedom of religion and freedom of expression) and *civil rights* (powers or privileges that government may not arbitrarily deny to individuals, such as protection against discrimination in employment and housing). But agreement among substantive theorists breaks down when discussion moves from civil rights to *social rights* (adequate health care, quality education, decent housing) and *economic rights* (private property, steady employment). For example, some insist that policies that promote social equality are essential to democratic government.[28] Others restrict the requirements of substantive democracy to policies that safeguard civil liberties and civil rights.

A theorist's political ideology tends to explain his or her position on what democracy really requires in substantive policies. Conservative theorists have a narrow view of the scope of democratic government and a narrow view of the social and economic rights guaranteed by that government. Liberal theorists believe that a democratic government should guarantee its citizens a much broader spectrum of social and economic rights.

Procedural Democracy Versus Substantive Democracy. The problem with the substantive view of democracy is that it does not provide clear, precise criteria that allow us to determine whether a government is democratic. Substantive theorists are free to promote their pet values— separation of church and state, guaranteed employment, equal rights for women, or whatever else—under the guise of substantive democracy.

The procedural viewpoint also has a problem. Although it presents specific criteria for democratic government, those criteria can produce undesirable social policies that prey on minorities. This clashes with **minority rights**—the idea that all citizens are entitled to certain rights that cannot be denied by the majority. One way to protect minority rights is to limit the principle of majority rule by requiring a two-thirds majority or some other extraordinary majority when decisions must be made on certain subjects. Another way is to put the issue in the Constitution, beyond the reach of majority rule.

Clearly, procedural democracy and substantive democracy are not always compatible. In choosing one over the other, we are also choosing to

---

IDEAlog.org

Should the government try to improve the standard of living for all poor Americans? Take IDEAlog's self-test.

substantive democratic theory The view that democracy is embodied in the substance of government policies rather than in the policymaking procedure.

minority rights The benefits of government that cannot be denied to any citizens by majority decisions.

focus on either procedures or policies. As authors of this text, we favor a compromise between the two. On the whole, we favor the procedural conception of democracy because it more closely approaches the classical definition of *democracy:* "government by the people." And procedural democracy is founded on clear, well-established rules for decision making. But the theory has a serious drawback: it allows a democratic government to enact policies that can violate the substantive principles of democracy. Thus, pure procedural democracy should be diluted so that minority rights and civil liberties are guaranteed as part of the structure of government.

Institutional Models of Democracy

Some democratic theorists favor institutions that tie government decisions closely to the desires of the majority of citizens. If most citizens want laws against the sale of pornography, then the government should outlaw pornography. If citizens want more money spent on defense and less on social welfare (or vice versa), the government should act accordingly. For these theorists, the essence of democratic government is majority rule and responsiveness. Other theorists place less importance on these principles. They do not believe in relying heavily on mass opinion; instead, they favor institutions that allow groups of citizens to defend their interests in the public policymaking process.

Both schools hold a procedural view of democracy but differ in how they interpret "government by the people." We can summarize these theoretical positions using two alternative models of democracy. As a model, each is a hypothetical plan, a blueprint, for achieving democratic government through institutional mechanisms. The *majoritarian* model values participation by the people in general; the *pluralist* model values participation by the people in groups.

The Majoritarian Model of Democracy.

The **majoritarian model of democracy** relies on our intuitive notion of what is fair. It interprets "government by the people" as government by the *majority* of the people. To force the government to respond to public opinion, the majoritarian model depends on several mechanisms that allow the people to participate directly.

The popular election of government officials is the primary mechanism for democratic government in the majoritarian model. Citizens are expected to control their representatives' behavior by choosing wisely in the first place and by reelecting or voting out public officials according to their performance.

Majoritarian theorists also see elections as a means for deciding government policies. An election on a policy issue is called a *referendum.* When a policy question is put on the ballot by the action of citizens circulating petitions and gathering a required minimum number of signatures, it is called an *initiative.* Twenty-one states allow their legislatures to put referenda before the voters and give their citizens the right to place initia-

majoritarian model of democracy The classical theory of democracy in which government by the people is interpreted as government by the majority of the people.

Now *That's* a Town Meeting
For almost 600 years, citizens of Appenzell Inner-Rhodes, the smallest canton (like a township) in Switzerland, have gathered in the town square on the last Sunday in April to make political decisions by raised hands. At a recent meeting, Appenzellers adopted a leash law for dogs, approved updating property files on a computer, chose a new building commissioner, and acted on other public business before adjourning until the next year. *(Marc Hutter/Appenzell)*

tives on the ballot. Five other states make provision for one mechanism or the other.[29] Sixteen states also allow for the *recall* of state officials, a means of forcing a special election for an up or down vote on a sitting governor or state judge.

In the United States, no provisions exist for referenda at the federal level. However, Americans strongly favor instituting a system of national referenda.[30] The most fervent advocates of majoritarian democracy would like to see modern technology used to maximize the government's responsiveness to the majority. Some have proposed incorporating public opinion polls or using computers for referenda.[31]

The majoritarian model contends that citizens can control their government if they have adequate mechanisms for popular participation. It also assumes that citizens are knowledgeable about government and politics, want to participate in the political process, and make rational decisions in voting for their elected representatives.

Critics contend that Americans are not knowledgeable enough for majoritarian democracy to work. They point to research that shows that only 26 percent of a national sample of voters said that they "followed what's going on" in government "most of the time." More (32 percent) said that they followed politics "only now and then" or "hardly at all."[32] Some believe that instead of quick and easy mass voting on public policy, what we need is more deliberation by citizens and their elected representatives. Defenders of majoritarian democracy respond that the American public has coherent and stable opinions on the major policy questions.[33]

An Alternative Model: Pluralist Democracy.   For years, political scientists struggled valiantly to reconcile the majoritarian model of democracy with polls that showed a widespread ignorance of politics among the American people. When only a little more than half of the adult population bothers to vote in presidential elections, our form of democracy seems to be government by *some* of the people.

The 1950s saw the evolution of an alternative interpretation of democracy, one tailored to the limited knowledge and participation of the real electorate, not the ideal one. It was based on the concept of *pluralism:* that modern society consists of innumerable groups that share economic, religious, ethnic, or cultural interests. Often people with similar interests organize formal groups. When an organized group seeks to influence government policy, it is called an **interest group**. Many interest groups regularly spend a great deal of time and money trying to influence government policy (see Chapter 7). Among them are the American Hospital Association, the National Association of Manufacturers, the National Education Association, the Associated Milk Producers, and the National Organization for Women.

The **pluralist model of democracy** interprets "government by the people" to mean government by people operating through competing interest groups. According to this model, democracy exists when many (plural) organizations operate separately from the government, press their interests on the government, and even challenge the government.[34] Compared with majoritarian thinking, pluralist theory shifts the focus of democratic government from the mass electorate to organized groups. It changes the criterion for democratic government from responsiveness to mass public opinion to responsiveness to organized groups of citizens.

A decentralized, complex government structure offers the access and openness necessary for pluralist democracy. For pluralists, the ideal system is one that divides government authority among numerous institutions with overlapping authority. Under such a system, competing interest groups have alternative points of access to present and argue their claims. When the National Association for the Advancement of Colored People could not get Congress to outlaw segregated schools in the South, it turned to the federal court system, which did what Congress would not do. According to the ideal of pluralist democracy, if all opposing interests are allowed to organize and if the system can be kept open so that all substantial claims have an opportunity to be heard, the decision will serve the diverse needs of a pluralist society. Countries going through the process of democratization can find the emergence of pluralism a challenge as new groups mean new demands upon government.

interest group An organized group of individuals that seeks to influence public policy. Also called a *lobby.*

pluralist model of democracy An interpretation of democracy in which government by the people is taken to mean government by people operating through competing interest groups.

On one level, pluralism is alive and well. Interest groups in Washington are thriving, and the rise of many citizen groups has broadened representation beyond traditional business, labor, and professional groups.[35] But on another level, political scientist Robert Putnam has documented declining participation in a wide variety of organizations. Americans are less inclined to be active members of civic groups like parent-teacher associations, the League of Woman Voters, and the Lions Club. Civic participation is a fundamental part of American democracy because it generates the social glue that helps to generate trust and cooperation in the political system.[36]

The Majoritarian Model Versus the Pluralist Model.
In majoritarian democracy, the mass public, not interest groups, controls government actions. The citizenry must be knowledgeable about government and willing to participate in the electoral process. Majoritarian democracy relies on electoral mechanisms that harness the power of the majority to make decisions. Conclusive elections and a centralized structure of government are mechanisms that aid majority rule. Cohesive political parties with well-defined programs also contribute to majoritarian democracy, because they offer voters a clear way to distinguish alternative sets of policies.

Pluralism does not demand much knowledge from citizens in general. It requires specialized knowledge only from groups of citizens, in particular their leaders. In contrast to majoritarian democracy, pluralist democracy seeks to limit majority action so that interest groups can be heard. It relies on strong interest groups and a decentralized government structure—mechanisms that interfere with majority rule, thereby protecting minority interests. We could even say that pluralism allows minorities to rule.

An Undemocratic Model: Elite Theory.
If pluralist democracy allows minorities to rule, how does it differ from **elite theory**—the view that a small group of people (a minority) makes most important government decisions? According to elite theory, important government decisions are made by an identifiable and stable minority that shares certain characteristics, usually vast wealth and business connections.[37] Elite theory appeals to many people, especially those who believe that wealth dominates politics.

According to elite theory, the United States is not a democracy but an **oligarchy,** a system in which government power is in the hands of an elite. Although the voters appear to control the government through elections, elite theorists argue that the powerful few in society manage to define the issues and constrain the outcomes of government decisions to suit their own interests. Clearly, elite theory describes a government that operates in an undemocratic fashion.

Political scientists have conducted numerous studies designed to test the validity of elite theory. Not all of those studies have come to the same conclusion, but the preponderance of evidence documenting government decisions on many different issues does not generally support elite theory—at least in the sense that an identifiable ruling elite usually gets its way.[38] Not

elite theory The view that a small group of people actually makes most of the important government decisions.

oligarchy A system of government in which power is concentrated in the hands of a few people.

surprisingly, elite theorists reject this view. They argue that studies of decisions made on individual issues do not adequately test the influence of the power elite. Rather, they contend that much of the elite's power comes from its ability to keep things off the political agenda—that is, its power derives from its ability to keep people from questioning fundamental assumptions about American capitalism.[39]

Elite theory remains part of the debate about the nature of American government and is forcefully argued by radical critics of the American political system.[40] Although we do not believe that the scholarly evidence supports elite theory, we do recognize that contemporary American pluralism favors some segments of society over others. The poor are chronically unorganized and are not well represented by interest groups. In contrast, business is better represented than any other sector of the public.[41] Thus, one can endorse pluralist democracy as a more accurate description than elitism in American politics without believing that all groups are equally well represented.

Elite Theory Versus Pluralist Theory.   The key difference between elite theory and pluralist theory lies in the durability of the ruling minority. In contrast to elite theory, pluralist theory does not define government conflict in terms of a minority versus the majority; instead, it sees many minorities vying with one another in each policy area. Pluralist democracy makes a virtue of the struggle between competing interests. It argues for government that accommodates this struggle and channels the result into government action. According to pluralist democracy, the public is best served if the government structure provides access for different groups to press their claims in competition with one another.

Note that pluralist democracy does not insist that all groups have equal influence on government decisions. In the political struggle, wealthy, well-organized groups have an inherent advantage over poorer, inadequately organized groups. In fact, unorganized segments of the population may not even get their concerns placed on the agenda for government consideration. This is a critical weakness of pluralism. However, pluralists contend that so long as all groups are able to participate vigorously in the decision-making process, the process is democratic.

 Democracy and Globalization

Most countries are neither majoritarian nor pluralist; rather, most are governed in an authoritarian manner or are struggling to move out of an authoritarian tradition but are not yet true democracies. By a "true democracy," we mean countries that meet the criteria for a procedural democracy (universal participation, political equality, majority rule, and government responsiveness to public opinion) and have established substantive policies supporting such civil liberties as freedom of speech and freedom of association, which create the necessary conditions for the practice of democracy. Until recently, fewer than twenty countries fully met all the criteria necessary to be judged a true democracy.[42] What is encouraging, however, is that today the world is awash in countries that are trying to make a transition to democracy. In Africa alone, perhaps twenty countries are moving in some fashion toward a democratic form of government.[43] But **democratization** is a difficult process, and many countries fail completely or succeed only in the short run and then lapse into a form of authoritarianism.

One reason that democratization can be so difficult is that ethnic and religious conflict is epidemic. Such conflict complicates efforts to democratize because antagonisms can run so deep that opposing groups do not want to grant political legitimacy to each other. As a result, ethnic and religious rivals are often more interested in achieving a form of government that oppresses their opponents (or, in their minds, maintains order) than in establishing a real democracy. These internal challenges can raise significant challenges for the global community. After toppling the Taliban government in Afghanistan and Saddam Hussein's regime in Iraq, the U.S. government faced the much more daunting task of creating enduring democratic institutions in two countries rife with ethnic, tribal, and religious conflicts.

The political and economic instability that typically accompanies transitions to democracy also makes new democratic governments vulnerable to attack by their opponents. The military will often revolt and take over the government on the grounds that progress cannot occur until order is restored. In other countries, opposition comes from segments of the people themselves. In Iraq, for instance, many rejected democracy because of opposition to the American occupation of their country. Many Islamic fundamentalists are hostile to the United States because they associate our form of government with modernity. And they regard modernity as a threat to the moral principles of their religion and their way of life.[44]

Despite such difficulties, strong forces are pushing authoritarian governments toward democratization. Nations find it difficult to succeed economically in today's world without establishing a market economy, and market economies (that is, capitalism) give people substantial freedoms. Thus, authoritarian rulers may see economic reforms as a threat to their regime.

American Democracy: More Pluralist Than Majoritarian

It is not idle speculation to ask what kind of democracy is practiced in the United States. The answer to this question can help us understand why our government can be called democratic despite a low level of citizen participation in politics and despite government actions that run contrary to public opinion.

Throughout this book, we probe to determine how well the United States fits the two alternative models of democracy: majoritarian and pluralist. If

democratization A process of transition as a country attempts to move from an authoritarian form of government to a democratic one.

our answer is not already apparent, it soon will be. We argue that the political system in the United States rates relatively low according to the majoritarian model of democracy but fulfills the pluralist model very well. Yet the pluralist model is far from a perfect representation of democracy. Its principal drawback is that it favors the well organized, and the poor are the least likely to be members of interest groups. As one advocate of majoritarian democracy once wrote, "The flaw in the pluralist heaven is that the heavenly chorus sings with a strong upper-class accent."[45]

This evaluation of the pluralist nature of American democracy may not mean much to you now. But you will learn that the pluralist model makes the United States look far more democratic than the majoritarian model would. Eventually you will have to decide the answers to three questions: Is the pluralist model truly an adequate expression of democracy, or is it a perversion of classical ideals designed to portray America as democratic when it is not? Does the majoritarian model result in a "better" type of democracy? If so, could new mechanisms of government be devised to produce a desirable mix of majority rule and minority rights? These questions should play in the back of your mind as you read about the workings of American government in meeting the challenge of democracy.

Summary

The challenge of democracy lies in making difficult choices—choices that inevitably bring important values into conflict. This chapter has outlined a normative framework for analyzing the policy choices that arise in the pursuit of the purposes of government.

The three major purposes of government are to maintain order, provide public goods, and promote equality. In pursuing these objectives, every government infringes on individual freedom. But the degree of that infringement depends on the government's (and, by extension, its citizens') commitment to order and equality. What we have, then, are two dilemmas. The first—the original dilemma—centers on the conflict between freedom and order.

The second—the modern dilemma—focuses on the conflict between freedom and equality.

Some people use political ideologies to help them resolve the conflicts that arise in political decision making. These ideologies define the scope and purpose of government. At opposite extremes of the continuum are totalitarianism, which supports government intervention in every aspect of society, and anarchism, which rejects government entirely. An important step back from totalitarianism is socialism. Democratic socialism, an economic system, favors government ownership of basic industries but preserves civil liberties. Capitalism, another economic system, promotes free enterprise. A significant step short of anarchism is libertarianism, which allows government to protect life and property but little else.

In the United States, the terms *liberal* and *conservative* are used to describe a narrow range toward the center of the political continuum. The usage is probably accurate when the scope of government action is being discussed—that is, liberals support a broader role for government than do conservatives. But it is easier to understand the differences among libertarians, liberals, conservatives, and communitarians and their views on the scope of government if the values of freedom, order, and equality are incorporated into the description of their political ideologies. Libertarians choose freedom over both order and equality. Communitarians are willing to sacrifice freedom for both order and equality. Liberals value freedom more than order and equality more than freedom. Conservatives value order more than freedom and freedom more than equality.

Most scholars believe the United States is a democracy. But what kind of democracy is it? The answer depends on the definition of *democracy*. Some believe democracy is procedural; they define *democracy* as a form of government in which the people govern through certain institutional mechanisms. Others hold to the substantive theory, claiming a government is democratic if its policies promote civil liberties and rights.

In this book, we emphasize the procedural conception of democracy, distinguishing between direct (participatory) and indirect (representative) democracy. In participatory democracy, all citizens gather to govern themselves according to the principles of universal participation, political equality, and majority rule. In an indirect democracy, the citizens elect representatives to govern for them. If a representative government is elected mostly in accordance with the three principles just listed and is also usually responsive to public opinion, then it qualifies as a democracy.

Procedural democratic theory has produced rival institutional models of democratic government. The classical majoritarian model, which depends on majority votes in elections, assumes that people are knowledgeable about government, want to participate in the political process, and carefully and rationally choose among candidates. The pluralist model of democracy, which depends on interest group interaction with government, argues that democracy in a complex society requires only that government allow private interests to organize and press their competing claims openly in the political arena. Unlike elite theory, the belief that the United States is run by a powerful minority, the pluralist model argues that different minorities win on different issues. These concepts underlie three questions for you to consider:

- Which is better: to live under a government that allows individuals complete freedom to do whatever they please or to live under one that enforces strict law and order?

- Which is better: to let all citizens keep the same share of their income or to tax wealthier people at a higher rate to fund programs for poorer people?

- Which is better: a government that is highly responsive to public opinion on all matters or one that responds deliberately to organized groups that argue their cases effectively?

These are enduring questions. The framers of the Constitution dealt with them, and their struggle is the appropriate place to begin our analysis of how these competing models of democracy have animated the debate about the nature of the American political process.

CL **Resources:** Videos, Simulations, News, Timelines, Primary Sources

The Constitution

CL

This icon will direct you to resources and activities on the website: www.cengage.com/polisci/janda/chall_dem_brief/7e

"YOU ARE THE 'CONVENTIONISTS' of Europe. You therefore have the power vested in any political body: to succeed or to fail," claimed Chairman Valéry Giscard d'Estaing in his introductory speech on February 26, 2002, to the members of the Convention on the Future of Europe. The purpose of the convention, according to Chairman Giscard d'Estaing, was for the members to "agree to propose a concept of the European Union which matches our continental dimension and the requirements of the 21st century, a concept which can bring unity to our continent and respect for its diversity." If the members succeeded, he reassured them, no doubt they would in essence write "a new chapter in the history of Europe."[1] Integrating and governing twenty-five nation-states—many of them at one time or another bitter enemies— with a population of 500 million is, to say the least, a daunting task.

Over two centuries earlier, from his home at Mount Vernon, George Washington penned a letter to James Madison on March 31, 1787. "I am glad to find," Washington wrote, "that Congress have recommended to the States to appear in the Convention proposed to be holden in Philadelphia in May. I think the reasons in favor, have the preponderancy of those against the measure."[2] Roughly two months later, in May, Washington would be selected by a unanimous vote to preside over the Constitutional Convention, known then as the Federal Convention, which was charged with revising the Articles of Confederation. Acting beyond its mandate, the body produced instead a new document altogether, which remains the oldest operating national constitution in the world.

The heads of state or government from twenty-eight countries signed the treaty establishing a constitution for Europe on October 29, 2004, and submitted the text to their respective governments for ratification. Unlike the U.S. Constitution, which required ratification by only nine of the thirteen states, the European constitution required ratification by *all* the signatories. As Americans discovered under the Articles of Confederation, unanimity is difficult to achieve. After ratification by nine European countries, voters in France and the Netherlands rejected the constitution in May and June 2005, dooming the document.

Although the processes on both sides of the Atlantic may have differed in 1787 and today, the political passions that these efforts spawned have been equally intense and highlight the fragility inherent in designing a constitution. And no wonder. The questions that challenged America's founders and confronted the women and men charged with setting a future course for Europe do not have easy or obvious answers. Guenter Burghardt, head of the European Commission delegation to the United States, noted several parallels in a speech in Berlin on June 6, 2002. Today, he remarked, Europeans are asking the same kinds of questions that confronted the delegates at Philadelphia: "How can a balance be achieved in the representation of large and small states? How much power should be conferred upon the federal level, and what should be the jurisdiction of the EU [European Union] today? What fundamental set of values underpins political unity? Is there a European equivalent to 'life, liberty and the pursuit of happiness'?"[3]

The next attempt at a solution took the form of a new treaty, called the Treaty of Lisbon or the Reform Treaty, which was signed on December 13, 2007, during a European summit. The Reform Treaty presented a still-longer version of the previous constitutional text, but dropped nearly all the statelike symbols and terminology (the European flag and anthem, among others). To further the process of European integration, member states were to ratify the treaty before the next European elections in 2009. The treaty's prospects were good, because only Ireland was constitutionally required to ratify by referendum; all other nations could ratify the Reform Treaty in their respective legislatures. However, ratification was blocked when Irish voters rejected the treaty in their June 2008 referendum. Declan Ganley, a leader in the anti-treaty movement declared, "this is democracy in action . . . and Europe needs to listen to the voice of the people."[4]

The American experience is sure to shed light on the issues emerging in Europe's quest for unity. This chapter poses some questions about the U.S. Constitution. How did it evolve? What form did it take? What values

Better Luck Next Time?
With each stroke of the pen projected onto a giant screen, the twenty-seven member states of the European Union signed the Treaty of Lisbon on December 13, 2007. Declaring that the new treaty marked a "watershed in European Integration," the president of the European Commission, José Manuel Barroso, exhorted the signatory states to "honor their commitments" by ratifying the document quickly. Irish voters refused, shooting down the treaty (53.4 percent to 46.6 percent) in a national referendum. *(Eric Feferberg/AFP/Getty Images)*

does it reflect? How can it be altered? And which model of democracy, majoritarian or pluralist, does it better fit? In these answers may lie hints of the formidable tasks facing the European Union.

The Revolutionary Roots of the Constitution

Compared to the European Constitution, which runs hundred of pages, the Constitution of the United States is startlingly short—just 4,300 words. But those 4,300 words define the basic structure of our national government. (In contrast, the failed European constitution was more than 60,000 words long. The proposed Reform Treaty was over 68,500 words.) A comprehensive document, the Constitution divides the government into three branches and describes the powers of those branches, their relationship to each other, the interaction between the government and the governed, and the relationship between the national government and the states. The Constitution makes itself the supreme law of the land and binds every government official to support it.

Most Americans revere the Constitution as political scripture. To charge that a political action is unconstitutional is akin to claiming that it is unholy. So the Constitution has taken on symbolic value that has strengthened its authority as the basis of American government. Strong belief in the Constitution has led many politicians to abandon party for principle when constitutional issues are at stake.

The U.S. Constitution, written in 1787 for an agricultural society huddled along the coast of a wild new land, now guides the political life of a massive urban society in the nuclear age. To fully understand the reasons for the stability of the Constitution—and of the political system it created—we must first look at its historical roots, which lie in colonial America.

Freedom in Colonial America

Although they were British subjects, the American colonists in the eighteenth century enjoyed a degree of freedom denied most other people in the world at that time. In Europe, ancient custom and the relics of feudalism restricted private property, compelled support for established religion, and restricted access to trades and professions; Americans were relatively free of such controls. Also, in America, colonists enjoyed almost complete freedom of speech, press, and assembly.[5]

By 1763, Britain and the colonies had reached a compromise between imperial control and colonial self-government. America's foreign affairs and overseas trade were to be controlled by the king and Parliament (the British legislature); the rest was left to home rule. But the cost of administering the colonies was substantial. Because Americans benefited the most, their English countrymen contended that Americans should bear that cost.

The Road to Revolution

The British believed that taxing the colonies was the obvious way to meet the costs of administering the colonies. The colonists did not agree. They especially did not want to be taxed by a distant government in which they had no representation. During the decade preceding the outbreak of hostilities in 1775, this issue was to convert increasing numbers of colonists from loyal British subjects seeking the rights of Englishmen to revolutionaries seeking the end of British rule over the American colonies.

On the night of December 16, 1773, a group of colonists reacted to a British duty on tea by organizing the Boston Tea Party. A mob boarded three ships and emptied 342 chests of that valuable substance into Boston Harbor. In an attempt to reassert British control over its recalcitrant colonists, Parliament passed the Coercive (or "Intolerable") Acts (1774). One act imposed a blockade on Boston until the tea was paid for; another gave royal governors the power to quarter British soldiers in private homes. Now the taxation issue was secondary; more important was the conflict between British demands for order and American demands for liberty. The Virginia and Massachusetts assemblies summoned a continental congress, an assembly that would speak and act for the people of all the colonies.

The First Continental Congress met in Philadelphia in September 1774. The objective of the assembly was to restore harmony between Great Britain and the American colonies. A leader of the Continental Congress, called the president, was elected. (The terms *president* and *congress* in American government trace their origins to the First Continental Congress.) In October 1774, the delegates adopted a statement of rights and principles; many of these later found their way into the Declaration of Independence and the Constitution. For example, the congress claimed a right "to life, liberty, and property" and a right "peaceably to assemble, consider of their grievances, and petition the king." Then the congress adjourned, planning to reconvene in May 1775.

Revolutionary Action

By early 1775, however, a movement that the colonists themselves were calling a revolution had already begun. Colonists in Massachusetts were fighting the British at Concord and Lexington. Delegates to the Second Continental Congress, meeting in May, faced a dilemma: Should they prepare for war, or should they try to reconcile with Britain? As conditions deteriorated, the Second Continental Congress remained in session to serve as the government of the colony-states.

On June 7, 1776, the Virginia delegation called on the Continental Congress to resolve "that these United Colonies are, and of right ought to be, free and Independent States, that they are absolved from all allegiance to the British Crown, and that all political connection between them and the State of Great Britain is, and ought to be, totally dissolved." A committee

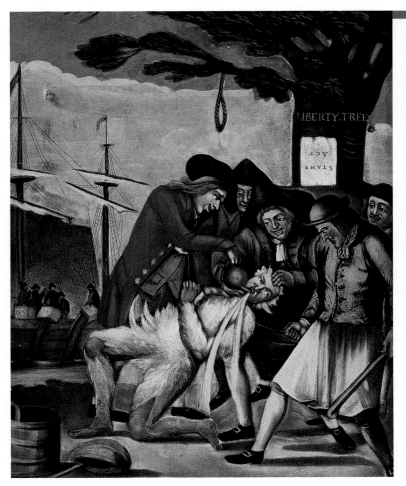

Uniquely American Protest
Americans protested the Tea Act (1773) by holding the Boston Tea Party (*background, left*) and by using a unique form of painful punishment, tarring and feathering, on the tax collector (see "Stamp Act" upside-down on the Liberty Tree). An early treatise on the subject offered the following instructions: "First, strip a person naked, then heat the tar until it is thin, and pour upon the naked flesh, or rub it over with a tar brush. After which, sprinkle decently upon the tar, whilst it is yet warm, as many feathers as will stick to it." (*Courtesy of the John Brown Library at Brown University*)

of five men was appointed to prepare a proclamation expressing the colonies' reasons for declaring independence.

The Declaration of Independence

Thomas Jefferson, a young farmer and lawyer from Virginia, drafted the proclamation. Jefferson's document, the **Declaration of Independence**, expressed simply, clearly, and rationally the arguments in support of separation from Great Britain.

The principles underlying the declaration were rooted in the writings of the English philosopher John Locke and had been expressed many times before by speakers in congress and in the colonial assemblies. Locke argued that people have God-given, or natural, rights that are inalienable—that is, they cannot be taken away by any government. According to Locke, all legitimate political authority exists to preserve these natural rights and

Declaration of Independence
Drafted by Thomas Jefferson, the document that proclaimed the right of the colonies to separate from Great Britain.

is based on the consent of those who are governed. The idea of consent is derived from **social contract theory,** which states that the people agree to establish rulers for certain purposes and have the right to resist or remove rulers who violate those purposes.[6]

Jefferson used similar arguments in the Declaration of Independence:

> We hold these truths to be self-evident, that all men are created equal, that they are endowed by their Creator with certain unalienable rights, that among these are life, liberty, and the pursuit of happiness. That to secure these rights, governments are instituted among men, deriving their just powers from the consent of the governed. That whenever any form of government becomes destructive of these ends, it is the right of the people to alter or to abolish it, and to institute new government, laying its foundation on such principles, and organizing its power in such form, as to them shall seem most likely to effect their safety and happiness.

Jefferson's simple yet impassioned statement of faith in democracy reverberates to this day. He went on to list the many deliberate acts of the king that had exceeded the legitimate role of government. Finally, Jefferson declared that the colonies were "Free and Independent States," with no political connection to Great Britain.

The major premise of the Declaration of Independence is that the people have a right to revolt if they determine that their government is denying them their legitimate rights. The long list of the king's actions was evidence of such denial, so the people had the right to rebel and form a new government. On July 2, 1776, the Second Continental Congress finally voted for independence. The vote was by state, and the motion carried 11 to 0. (Rhode Island was not present, and the New York delegation, lacking instructions, did not cast its yea vote until July 15.) Two days later, on July 4, the Declaration of Independence was approved with few changes.

The War of Independence lasted far longer than anyone had expected. It began in a moment of confusion, when a shot rang out as British soldiers approached the town of Lexington on the way to Concord, Massachusetts, on April 19, 1775. The end came six and a half years later, on October 19, 1781, with Lord Cornwallis's surrender of his six-thousand-man army at Yorktown, Virginia. It was a costly war: more died and were wounded in relation to the population than in any other conflict except the Civil War.[7]

From Revolution to Confederation

By declaring their independence from England, the colonies left themselves without any real central government, so the revolutionaries proclaimed the creation of a republic. Strictly speaking, a **republic** is government without a monarch, but the term had come to mean a government based on the consent of the governed, whose power is exercised by representatives who are

social contract theory The belief that the people agree to set up rulers for certain purposes and thus have the right to resist or remove rulers who act against those purposes.

republic A government without a monarch; a government rooted in the consent of the governed, whose power is exercised by elected representatives responsible to the governed.

responsible to them. A republic need not be a democracy, and this was fine with the founders; at that time, democracy was associated with mob rule and instability (see Chapter 1). The revolutionaries were less concerned with determining who would control their new government than with limiting the powers of that government. They had revolted in the name of liberty, and now they wanted a government with sharply defined powers. To make sure they got one, they meant to define its structure and powers in writing.

The Articles of Confederation

Barely a week after the Declaration of Independence was signed, the Second Continental Congress received a committee report entitled "Articles of Confederation and Perpetual Union." A **confederation** is a loose association of independent states that agree to cooperate on specified matters. In a confederation, the states retain their sovereignty, which means that each has supreme power within its borders. The central government is weak; it can only coordinate, not control, the actions of its sovereign states.

The **Articles of Confederation**, the compact among the thirteen original colonies that established the United States, was finally adopted on November 15, 1777. The Articles jealously guarded state sovereignty; their provisions clearly reflected the delegates' fears of a strong central government. Under the Articles, each state, regardless of its size, had one vote in the congress. Votes on financing the war and other important issues required the consent of at least nine of the thirteen states.

The common danger—Britain—forced the young republic to function under the Articles, but this first try at a government was inadequate to the task. The delegates had succeeded in crafting a national government that was largely powerless. The Articles failed for at least four reasons. First, they did not give the national government the power to tax. As a result, the congress had to plead for money from the states to pay for the war and carry on the affairs of the new nation. Second, the Articles made no provision for an independent leadership position to direct the government (the president was merely the presiding officer of the congress). The omission was deliberate—the colonists feared the reestablishment of a monarchy— but it left the nation without a leader. Third, the Articles did not allow the national government to regulate interstate and foreign commerce. (When John Adams proposed that the confederation enter into a commercial treaty with Britain after the war, he was asked, "Would you like one treaty or thirteen, Mr. Adams?").[8] Finally, the Articles could not be amended without the unanimous agreement of the congress and the assent of all the state legislatures; thus, each state had the power to veto any changes to the confederation.

The goal of the delegates who drew up the Articles of Confederation was to retain power in the states. This was consistent with republicanism, which viewed the remote power of a national government as a danger to

confederation A loose association of independent states that agree to cooperate on specified matters.

Articles of Confederation The compact among the thirteen original states that established the first government of the United States.

liberty. In this sense alone, the Articles were a grand success: they completely hobbled the infant government.

Disorder Under the Confederation

Once the Revolution ended and independence was a reality, it became clear that the national government had neither the economic nor the military power to function. Freed from wartime austerity, Americans rushed to purchase goods from abroad. Debt mounted, and bankruptcy followed for many.

The problem was particularly severe in Massachusetts, where high interest rates and high state taxes were forcing farmers into bankruptcy. In 1786 and 1787, farmers under the leadership of Daniel Shays, a Revolutionary War veteran, carried out a series of insurrections to prevent the foreclosure of their farms by creditors. With the congress unable to secure funds from the states to help out, the governor of Massachusetts eventually called out the militia and restored order.[9] Shays's Rebellion demonstrated the impotence of the confederation and the urgent need to suppress insurrection and maintain domestic order.

From Confederation to Constitution

Order, the original purpose of government, was breaking down under the Articles of Confederation. The "league of friendship" envisioned in the Articles was not enough to hold the nation together in peacetime. So in 1786, Virginia invited the states to attend a convention at Annapolis to explore revisions to the Articles of Confederation. Although only five states sent delegates, they seized the opportunity to call for another meeting in Philadelphia the next year. The congress agreed to the convention but limited its mission to "the sole and express purpose of revising the Articles of Confederation."

Shays's Rebellion lent a sense of urgency to the task before the Philadelphia convention. The congress's inability to confront the rebellion was evidence that a stronger national government was necessary to preserve order and property—to protect the states from internal as well as external dangers. "While the Declaration was directed against an excess of authority," remarked Supreme Court Justice Robert H. Jackson some 150 years later, "the Constitution [that followed the Articles of Confederation] was directed against anarchy."[10]

The Constitutional Convention officially opened on May 25, 1787. Although its delegates were authorized only to revise the Articles of Confederation, within the first week of debate, Edmund Randolph of Virginia presented a long list of changes, suggested by fellow Virginian James Madison, that would replace the weak confederation of states with a powerful national government. The delegates unanimously agreed to debate Randolph's proposal, which was called the **Virginia Plan**. Almost immediately, then, they rejected the idea of amending the Articles of Confederation, working instead to create an entirely new constitution.

The Virginia Plan

The Virginia Plan dominated the convention's deliberations for the rest of the summer, making several important proposals for a strong central government:

- That the powers of the government be divided among three separate branches: a **legislative branch** for making laws, an **executive branch** for enforcing laws, and a **judicial branch** for interpreting laws.

- That the legislature consist of two houses. The first would be chosen by the people and the second by the members of the first house from among persons nominated by the state legislatures.

- That each state's representation in the legislature be in proportion to taxes paid to the national government or in proportion to its free population.

- That an executive of unspecified size be selected by the legislature and serve for a single term.

- That the national judiciary include one or more supreme courts and other lower courts, with judges appointed for life by the legislature.

- That the executive and a number of national judges serve as a council of revision, to approve or veto (disapprove) legislative acts. Their veto could be overridden, however, by a vote of both houses of the legislature.

- That the scope of powers of all three branches be far greater than that assigned the national government by the Articles of Confederation and include the power of the legislature to override state laws.

By proposing a powerful national legislature that could override state laws, the Virginia Plan clearly advocated a new form of government. It was a mixed structure, with more authority over the states and new authority over the people.

Madison was a monumental force in the ensuing debate on the proposals. However, the constitution that emerged from the convention bore only partial resemblance to the document Madison wanted to create. He endorsed seventy-one specific proposals, but he ended up on the losing side on forty of them.[11] And the parts of the Virginia Plan that were ultimately adopted in the U.S. Constitution were not adopted without challenge. Conflict revolved primarily around the basis of representation in the legislature, the method of choosing legislators, and the structure of the executive branch.

Virginia Plan A set of proposals for a new government, submitted to the Constitutional Convention of 1787; included separation of the government into three branches, division of the legislature into two houses, and proportional representation in the legislature.

legislative branch The lawmaking branch of government.

executive branch The law-enforcing branch of government.

judicial branch The law-interpreting branch of government.

The New Jersey Plan

When in 1787 it appeared that much of the Virginia Plan would be approved by the big states, the small states united in opposition. William Paterson of New Jersey introduced an alternative set of resolutions, written to preserve the spirit of the Articles of Confederation by amending rather than replacing them. The **New Jersey Plan** included the following proposals:

- That a single-chamber legislature have the power to raise revenue and regulate commerce.

- That the states have equal representation in the legislature and choose the members of that body.

- That a multiperson executive be elected by the legislature, with powers similar to those listed in the Virginia Plan but without the right to veto legislation.

- That a supreme judiciary tribunal be created with a very limited jurisdiction. (There was no provision for a system of national courts.)

- That the acts of the legislature be binding on the states—that is, be regarded as the "supreme law of the respective states," with force used to compel obedience.

The New Jersey Plan was defeated in the first major convention vote, 7 to 3. However, the small states had enough support to force a compromise on the issue of representation in the legislature.

The Great Compromise

The Virginia Plan's provision for a two-chamber legislature was never seriously challenged, but the idea of representation according to population generated heated debate. The small states demanded equal representation for all states. A committee was created to resolve the deadlock. It consisted of one delegate from each state, chosen by secret ballot. After working through the Independence Day recess, the committee reported reaching the **Great Compromise** (sometimes called the *Connecticut Compromise* because it was proposed by Roger Sherman of the Connecticut delegation). Representation in the House of Representatives would be apportioned according to the population of each state. Initially, there would be fifty-six members. Revenue-raising acts would originate in the House. Most important, the states would be represented equally in the Senate, by two senators each. Senators would be selected by their state legislatures, not directly by the people.

The delegates accepted the Great Compromise. The smaller states got their equal representation and the larger states their proportional representation. The small states might dominate the Senate and the big states might control the House, but because all legislation had to be approved by both chambers, neither group would be able to dominate the other.

New Jersey Plan Submitted by the head of the New Jersey delegation to the Constitutional Convention of 1787, a set of nine resolutions that would have, in effect, preserved the Articles of Confederation by amending rather than replacing them.

Great Compromise Submitted by the Connecticut delegation to the Constitutional Convention of 1787, and thus also known as the *Connecticut Compromise,* a plan calling for a bicameral legislature in which the House of Representatives would be apportioned according to population and the states would be represented equally in the Senate.

Compromise on the Presidency

Conflict replaced compromise when the delegates turned to the executive branch. They agreed on a one-person executive—a president—but they disagreed on how the executive would be selected and the term of office. The delegates distrusted the people's judgment; some feared that popular election would arouse public passions. Consequently, the delegates rejected the idea. At the same time, representatives of the small states feared that election by the legislature would allow the larger states to control the executive.

Once again they compromised, creating the *electoral college,* a cumbersome system consisting of a group of electors chosen for the sole purpose of selecting the president and vice president. Each state legislature would choose a number of electors equal to the number of its representatives in Congress. Each elector would then vote for two people. The candidate with the most votes would become president, provided that the number of votes constituted a majority; the person with the next greatest number of votes would become vice president. (This procedure was changed in 1804 by the Twelfth Amendment, which mandates separate votes for each office.) If no candidate won a majority, the House of Representatives would choose a president, with each state casting one vote.

The electoral college compromise eliminated the fear of a popular vote for president. At the same time, it satisfied the small states. If the electoral college failed to produce a president—which the delegates expected would happen—an election by the House would give every state the same voice in the selection process.

The delegates agreed that the president's term of office should be four years and that the president should be eligible for reelection with no limit on the number of terms.

The delegates realized that removing a president from office would be a very serious political matter. For that reason, they involved the other two branches of government in the process. The House alone was empowered to charge a president with "Treason, Bribery, or other high Crimes and Misdemeanors" by a majority vote. The Senate was given sole power to try such impeachments. It could convict and thus remove a president only by a two-thirds vote. The chief justice of the United States was required to preside over the Senate trial.

 ## The Final Product

Once the delegates resolved their major disagreements, they dispatched the remaining issues relatively quickly. A committee was appointed to draft a constitution. The Preamble, which was the last section to be drafted, begins with a phrase that would have been impossible to write when the convention opened. This single sentence sets forth the four elements that form the foundation of the American political tradition:[12]

■ *It creates a people:* "We the People of the United States" was a dramatic departure from a loose confederation of states.

■ *It explains the reason for the Constitution:* "in Order to form a more perfect Union" was an indirect way of saying that the first effort, under the Articles of Confederation, had been inadequate.

■ *It articulates goals:* "[to] establish Justice, insure domestic Tranquility, provide for the common defense, promote the general Welfare, and secure the Blessings of Liberty to ourselves and our posterity"—in other words, the government exists to promote order and freedom.

■ *It fashions a government:* "do ordain and establish this Constitution for the United States of America."

The Basic Principles

In creating the Constitution, the founders relied on four political principles that together established a revolutionary new political order: republicanism, federalism, separation of powers, and checks and balances.

Republicanism is a form of government in which power resides in the people and is exercised by their elected representatives. The framers were determined to avoid aristocracy (rule by a hereditary class), monarchy (rule by one), and direct democracy (rule by the people). A republic was both new and daring; no people had ever been governed by a republic on so vast a scale. Indeed, the framers themselves were far from sure that their government could be sustained. After the convention ended, Benjamin Franklin was asked what sort of government the new nation would have. "A republic," he replied, "if you can keep it."

Federalism is the division of power between a central government and regional units. It makes citizens subject to two different bodies of law. A federal system stands between two competing government structures. On one side is unitary government, in which all power is vested in a central government. On the other side stands confederation, a loose union with powerful states. The Constitution embodied a division of power, but it conferred substantial powers on the national government at the expense of the states.

According to the Constitution, the powers vested in the national and state governments are derived from the people, who remain the ultimate sovereign. National and state governments can exercise their powers over persons and property within their own spheres of authority. But by participating in the electoral process or amending their governing charters, the people can restrain both the national and the state governments if necessary to preserve liberty.

The Constitution lists the powers of the national government and the powers denied to the states. All other powers remain with the states. However, the Constitution does not clearly describe the spheres of authority

republicanism A form of government in which power resides in the people and is exercised by their elected representatives.

federalism The division of power between a central government and regional governments.

FIGURE 2.1   The Constitution and the Electoral Process

The framers were afraid of majority rule, and that fear is reflected in the electoral process for national office described in the Constitution. The people, speaking through the voters, participated directly only in the choice of their representatives in the House. The president and senators were elected indirectly, through the electoral college and state legislatures. (Direct election of senators did not become law until 1913, when the Seventeenth Amendment was ratified.) Judicial appointments are, and always have been, far removed from representative links to the people. Judges are nominated by the president and approved by the Senate.

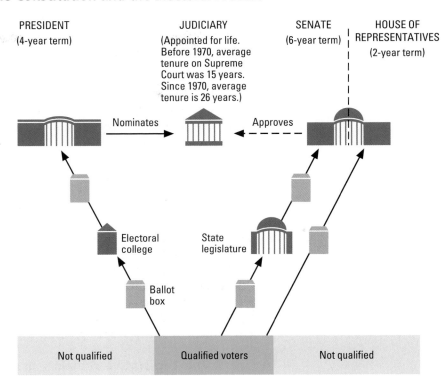

within which these powers can be exercised. As we will discuss in Chapter 3, limits on the exercise of power by the national government and the states have evolved as a result of political and military conflict; moreover, the limits have proved changeable.

Separation of powers and checks and balances are two distinct principles, but both are necessary to ensure that one branch does not dominate the government. **Separation of powers** is the assignment of the lawmaking, law-enforcing, and law-interpreting functions of government to independent legislative, executive, and judicial branches, respectively. Separation of powers safeguards liberty by ensuring that all government power does not fall into the hands of a single person or group of people. However, the Constitution constrained majority rule by limiting the people's direct influence on the electoral process (see Figure 2.1). In theory, separation of powers means that one branch cannot exercise the powers of the other branches. In practice, however, the separation is far from complete. One scholar has

separation of powers The assignment of lawmaking, law-enforcing, and law-interpreting functions to separate branches of government.

suggested that what we have instead is "separate institutions sharing powers."[13]

Checks and balances is a means of giving each branch of government some scrutiny of and control over the other branches. The aim is to prevent the exclusive exercise of certain powers by any one of the three branches. For example, only Congress can enact laws. But the president (through the veto power) can cancel them, and the courts (by finding that a law violates the Constitution) can strike them down. The process goes on as Congress and the president sometimes begin the legislative process anew, attempting to reformulate laws to address the flaws identified by the Supreme Court in its decisions. In a "check on a check," Congress can override a president's veto by an **extraordinary majority**, two-thirds of each chamber. Congress is also empowered to propose amendments to the Constitution, counteracting the courts' power to invalidate. Figure 2.2 depicts the relationship between separation of powers and checks and balances.

The Articles of the Constitution

In addition to the Preamble, the Constitution contains seven articles. The first three establish the separate branches of government and specify their internal operations and powers. The remaining four define the relationships among the states, explain the process of amendment, declare the supremacy of national law, and explain the procedure for ratifying the Constitution.

Article I: The Legislative Article.   In structuring their new government, the framers began with the legislative branch because they thought lawmaking was the most important function of a republican government. Article I is the most detailed and therefore the longest of all the articles. It defines the bicameral (two-chamber) character of the Congress and describes the internal operating procedures of the House of Representatives and the Senate. Section 8 of Article I expresses the principle of **enumerated powers**, which means that Congress can exercise only the powers that the Constitution assigns to it. Eighteen powers are enumerated; the first seventeen are specific powers (for example, the power to regulate interstate commerce).

The last clause in Section 8, known as the **necessary and proper clause** (or the *elastic clause*), gives Congress the means to execute the enumerated powers (see the Appendix). This clause is the basis of Congress's **implied powers**—those powers that Congress must have in order to execute its enumerated powers. For example, the power to levy and collect taxes (clause 1) and the power to coin money and regulate its value (clause 5), when joined with the necessary and proper clause (clause 18), imply that Congress has the power to charter a bank. Otherwise, the national government would have no means of managing the money it collects through its power to tax. Implied powers clearly expand the enumerated powers conferred on Congress by the Constitution.

checks and balances A government structure that gives each branch some scrutiny of and control over the other branches.

extraordinary majority Majority greater than that required by majority rule, that is, greater than 50 percent plus one.

enumerated powers The powers explicitly granted to Congress by the Constitution.

necessary and proper clause The last clause in Section 8 of Article I of the Constitution, which gives Congress the means to execute its enumerated powers. This clause is the basis for Congress's implied powers. Also called the *elastic clause*.

implied powers Those powers that Congress requires in order to execute its enumerated powers.

FIGURE 2.2   Separation of Powers and Checks and Balances

Separation of powers is the assignment of lawmaking, law-enforcing, and law-interpreting functions to the legislative, executive, and judicial branches, respectively. The phenomenon is illustrated by the diagonal from upper left to lower right in the figure.

Checks and balances give each branch some power over the other branches. For example, the executive branch possesses some legislative power, and the legislative branch possesses some executive power. These checks and balances are listed outside the diagonal.

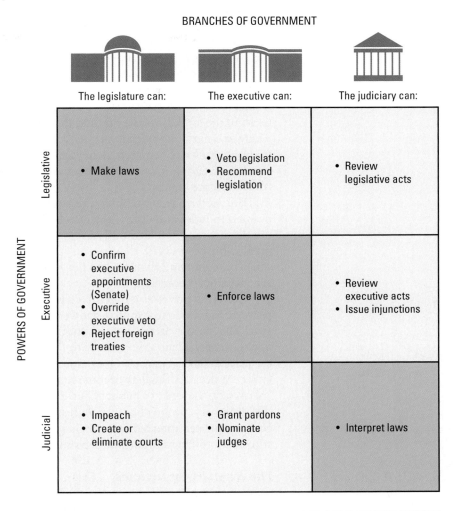

BRANCHES OF GOVERNMENT

	The legislature can:	The executive can:	The judiciary can:
Legislative	• Make laws	• Veto legislation • Recommend legislation	• Review legislative acts
Executive	• Confirm executive appointments (Senate) • Override executive veto • Reject foreign treaties	• Enforce laws	• Review executive acts • Issue injunctions
Judicial	• Impeach • Create or eliminate courts	• Grant pardons • Nominate judges	• Interpret laws

POWERS OF GOVERNMENT

Article II: The Executive Article.   Article II sets the president's term of office, the procedure for electing a president through the electoral college, the qualifications for becoming president, and the president's duties and powers. The last include acting as commander in chief of the military; making treaties (which must be ratified by a two-thirds vote in the Senate); and appointing government officers, diplomats, and judges (again, with the advice and consent of the Senate).

The president also has legislative powers—part of the constitutional system of checks and balances. For example, the Constitution requires that the president periodically inform the Congress of the "State of the Union" and of the policies and programs that the executive branch intends to advocate in the coming year. Today this is done annually, in the president's State of the Union address. Under special circumstances, the president can also convene or adjourn Congress. Additionally, the duty to "take Care that the Laws be faithfully executed" in Section 3 has provided presidents with a reservoir of power.

Article III: The Judicial Article.   The third article was left purposely vague. The Constitution established the Supreme Court as the highest court in the land. But beyond that, the framers were unable to agree on the need for a national judiciary, or its size, its composition, or the procedures it should follow. They left these issues to the Congress, which resolved them by creating a system of federal—that is, national—courts separate from the state courts.

Unless they are impeached, federal judges serve for life. They are appointed to indefinite terms "during good Behavior," and their salaries cannot be lowered while they hold office. These stipulations reinforce the separation of powers; they see to it that judges are independent of the other branches and that they do not have to fear retribution for their exercise of judicial power.

Congress exercises a potential check on the judicial branch through its power to create (and eliminate) lower federal courts. Congress can also restrict the power of the federal courts to decide cases. And, as we have noted, the president appoints—with the advice and consent of the Senate—the justices of the Supreme Court and the judges of the lower federal courts. In recent decades this has become highly politicized.

Article III does not explicitly give the courts the power of **judicial review,** the authority to invalidate congressional or presidential actions. That power has been inferred from the logic, structure, and theory of the Constitution and from important decisions by the Supreme Court itself.

The Remaining Articles.   The remaining four articles of the Constitution cover a lot of ground. Article IV requires that the judicial acts and criminal warrants of each state be honored in all other states, and it forbids discrimination against citizens of one state by another state. This provision promotes equality; it keeps the states from treating outsiders differently from their own citizens. The origin of this clause can be traced to the Articles of Confederation. Article IV also allows the addition of new states and stipulates that the national government will protect the states against foreign invasion and domestic violence.

Article V specifies the methods for amending (changing) the Constitution. We will have more to say about this shortly.

An important component of Article VI is the **supremacy clause,** which asserts that when they conflict with state or local laws, the Constitution, national laws, and treaties take precedence. The stipulation is vital to the operation of federalism. In keeping with the supremacy clause, Article VI

judicial review The power to declare government acts invalid because they violate the Constitution.

supremacy clause The clause of Article VI of the Constitution that asserts that national laws take precedence over state and local laws when they conflict.

requires that all national and state officials, elected or appointed, take an oath to support the Constitution. The article also mandates that religion cannot be a prerequisite for holding government office.

Article VII describes the ratification process, stipulating that approval by conventions in nine states would be necessary for the Constitution to take effect.

The Framers' Motives

What forces motivated the framers? Surely economic issues were important, but they were not the major issues. The single most important factor leading to the Constitutional Convention was the inability of the national or state governments to maintain order under the loose structure of the Articles of Confederation. Certainly order required the protection of property, but the framers had a view of property that extended beyond their portfolios of government securities. They wanted to protect their homes, their families, and their means of livelihood from impending anarchy.

Although they disagreed bitterly on the structure and mechanics of the national government, the framers agreed on the most vital issues. For example, three crucial features of the Constitution—the power to tax, the necessary and proper clause, and the supremacy clause—were approved unanimously and without debate. Indeed, the motivation to create order was so strong that the framers were willing to draft clauses that protected the most undemocratic of all institutions: slavery.

The Slavery Issue

The institution of slavery was well ingrained in American life at the time of the Constitutional Convention, and slavery helped shape the Constitution, although it is mentioned nowhere by name. It is doubtful, in fact, that there would have been a Constitution if the delegates had had to resolve the slavery issue.

The question of representation in the House of Representatives brought the issue close to the surface of the debate at the Constitutional Convention and led to the Great Compromise. Representation in the House was to be based on population. But who would be counted in the "population"? Eventually the delegates agreed unanimously that in apportioning representation in the House and in assessing direct taxes, the population of each state was to be determined by adding "the whole Number of free Persons" and "three fifths of all other Persons" (Article I, Section 2). The phrase "all other Persons" is, of course, a substitute for "slaves."

The three-fifths clause gave states with large slave populations (in the South) greater representation in Congress than states with small slave populations (in the North). The compromise left the South with 47 percent of the House seats, a sizable minority, but in all likelihood a losing one on slavery issues.[14] The overrepresentation resulting from the South's large slave populations translated into greater southern influence in selecting the president as well, because the electoral college was based on the size of the states' congressional delegations. The three-fifths clause also undertaxed states with large slave populations.

Another issue centered on the slave trade. Several southern delegates were uncompromising in their defense of it, while other delegates favored prohibition. The delegates compromised, agreeing that the slave trade could not be ended until twenty years had elapsed (Article I, Section 9). Also, the delegates agreed, without serious challenge, that fugitive slaves be returned to their masters (Article IV, Section 2).

In addressing these points, the framers in essence condoned slavery. Clearly, slavery existed in stark opposition to the idea that "all men are created equal," and though many slaveholders, including Jefferson and Madison, agonized over it, few made serious efforts to free their own slaves. Most Americans seemed indifferent to slavery. Nonetheless, the eradication of slavery proceeded gradually in certain states. By 1787, Connecticut, Massachusetts, New Jersey, New York, Pennsylvania, Rhode Island, and Vermont had abolished slavery or provided for gradual emancipation. This slow but perceptible shift on the slavery issue in many states masked a volcanic force capable of destroying the Constitutional Convention and the Union.

 ## Selling the Constitution

On September 17, 1787, nearly four months after the Constitutional Convention opened, the delegates convened for the last time to sign the final version of their handiwork. Because several delegates were unwilling to sign the document, the last paragraph was craftily worded to give the impression of unanimity: "Done in Convention by the Unanimous Consent of the States present." However, before it could take effect, the Constitution had to be ratified by a minimum of nine state conventions. In each, support was far from unanimous.

The proponents of the new charter, who wanted a strong national government, called themselves *Federalists*. The opponents of the Constitution were quickly dubbed *Antifederalists*. They claimed, however, that they were true Federalists because they wanted to protect the states from the tyranny of a strong national government. The viewpoints of the two groups formed the bases of the first American political parties.

The *Federalist* Papers

Beginning in October 1787, an exceptional series of eighty-five newspaper articles defending the Constitution appeared under the title *The Federalist: A Commentary on the Constitution of the United States*. The essays bore the pen name "Publius" and were written primarily by James Madison and

Alexander Hamilton, with some assistance from John Jay. Logically and calmly, Publius argued in favor of ratification. Reprinted extensively during the ratification battle, the *Federalist* papers remain the best single commentary we have on the meaning of the Constitution and the political theory it embodies.

Not to be outdone, the Antifederalists offered their own intellectual basis for rejecting the Constitution. In several essays, the most influential authored under the pseudonyms "Brutus" and "Federal Farmer," they attacked the centralization of power in a strong national government, claiming it would obliterate the states, violate the social contract of the Declaration of Independence, and destroy liberty in the process. They defended the status quo, maintaining that the Articles of Confederation established true federal principles.[15]

Of all the *Federalist* papers, the most magnificent and most frequently cited is *Federalist* No. 10, written by James Madison. He argued that the proposed constitution was designed "to break and control the violence of faction." "By a faction," Madison wrote, "I understand a number of citizens, whether amounting to a majority or minority of the whole, who are united and actuated by some common impulse of passion, or of interest, adverse to the rights of other citizens, or to the permanent and aggregate interests of the community."

Madison was discussing what we described in Chapter 1 as *pluralism*. What Madison called factions are today called interest groups or even political parties. According to Madison, "The most common and durable source of factions has been the various and unequal distribution of property." Madison was concerned not with reducing inequalities of wealth (which he took for granted) but with controlling the seemingly inevitable conflict that stems from them. The Constitution, he argued, was well constructed for this purpose.

Through the mechanism of representation, wrote Madison, the Constitution would prevent a "tyranny of the majority" (mob rule). The government would not be controlled directly by the people; rather, it would be controlled indirectly by their elected representatives. And those representatives would have the intelligence and understanding to serve the larger interests of the nation. Moreover, the federal system would require that majorities form first within each state, then organize for effective action at the national level. This and the vastness of the country would make it unlikely that a majority would form that would "invade the rights of other citizens."

The purpose of *Federalist* No. 10 was to demonstrate that the proposed government was not likely to be ruled by any faction. Contrary to conventional wisdom, Madison argued, the key to controlling the evils of faction is to have a large republic—the larger, the better. The more diverse the society is, the less likely it is that an unjust majority can form. Madison certainly had no intention of creating a majoritarian democracy; his view of popular government was much more consistent with the model of pluralist democracy discussed in Chapter 1.

Madison pressed his argument from a different angle in *Federalist* No. 51. Asserting that "ambition must be made to counteract ambition," he argued that the separation of powers and checks and balances would control tyranny from any source. If power is distributed equally across the three branches, then each branch has the capacity to counteract the other. In Madison's words, "usurpations are guarded against by a division of the government into distinct and separate departments." Because legislative power tends to predominate in republican governments, legislative authority is divided between the Senate and the House of Representatives, which have different methods of selection and terms of office. Additional protection comes through federalism, which divides power "between two distinct governments"—national and state—and subdivides "the portion allotted to each . . . among distinct and separate departments."

The Antifederalists wanted additional separation of powers and additional checks and balances, which, they maintained, would eliminate the threat of tyranny entirely. The Federalists believed that this would make decisive national action virtually impossible. But to ensure ratification, they agreed to a compromise.

A Concession: The Bill of Rights

IDEAlog.org

Do you think the government should or should not restrict violence and sex on cable television? Take IDEAlog's self-test.

Despite the eloquence of the *Federalist* papers, many prominent citizens, including Thomas Jefferson, were unhappy that the Constitution did not list basic civil liberties—the individual freedoms guaranteed to citizens. The omission of a bill of rights was the chief obstacle to the adoption of the Constitution by the states. The colonists had just rebelled against the British government to preserve their basic freedoms. Why didn't the proposed Constitution spell out those freedoms?

The answer was rooted in logic, not politics. Because the national government was limited to those powers that were granted to it and because no power was granted to abridge the people's liberties, a list of guaranteed freedoms was not necessary. In *Federalist* No. 84, Hamilton went even further, arguing that the addition of a bill of rights would be dangerous. Because it is not possible to list all prohibited powers, wrote Hamilton, any attempt to provide a partial list would make the remaining areas vulnerable to government abuse.

But logic was no match for fear. Many states agreed to ratify the Constitution only after George Washington suggested that a list of guarantees be added through the amendment process. More than one hundred amendments were proposed by the states. These were eventually narrowed down to twelve, which Congress approved and sent to the states. Ten of them became part of the Constitution in 1791, after securing the approval of the required three-fourths of the states. Collectively, these ten amendments are known as the **Bill of Rights**. They restrain the national government from tampering with fundamental rights and civil liberties and emphasize the limited character of the national government's power (see Table 2.1).

Bill of Rights The first ten amendments to the Constitution. They prevent the national government from tampering with fundamental rights and civil liberties and emphasize the limited character of national power.

TABLE 2.1   The Bill of Rights

The first ten amendments to the Constitution are known as the Bill of Rights. The following is a list of those amendments, grouped conceptually. For the actual order and wording of the Bill of Rights, see the Appendix.

Guarantees	Amendment
Guarantees for Participation in the Political Process	
No government abridgment of speech or press; no government abridgment of peaceable assembly; no government abridgment of petitioning government for redress.	1
Guarantees Respecting Personal Beliefs	
No government establishment of religion; no government prohibition of free religious exercise.	1
Guarantees of Personal Privacy	
Owners' consent necessary to quarter troops in private homes in peacetime; quartering during war must be lawful.	3
Government cannot engage in unreasonable searches and seizures; warrants to search and seize require probable cause.	4
No compulsion to testify against oneself in criminal cases.	5
Guarantees Against Government's Overreaching	
Serious crimes require a grand jury indictment; no repeated prosecution for the same offense; no loss of life, liberty, or property without due process; no taking of property for public use without just compensation.	5
Criminal defendants will have a speedy public trial by impartial local jury; defendants are informed of accusation; defendants may confront witnesses against them; defendants may use judicial process to obtain favorable witnesses; defendants may have legal assistance for their defense.	6
Civil lawsuits can be tried by juries if controversy exceeds $20; in jury trials, fact-finding is a jury function.	7
No excessive bail; no excessive fines; no cruel and unusual punishment.	8
Other Guarantees	
The people have the right to bear arms.	2
No government trespass on unspecified fundamental rights.	9
The states or the people retain all powers not delegated to the national government or denied to the states.	10

Ratification

The Constitution officially took effect on its ratification by the ninth state, New Hampshire, on June 21, 1788. However, the success of the new government was not ensured until July 1788, by which time the Constitution was ratified by the key states of Virginia and New York after lengthy debate.

The reflection and deliberation that attended the creation and ratification of the Constitution signaled to the world that a new government could be launched peacefully. The French observer Alexis de Tocqueville (1805–1859) later wrote:

> That which is new in the history of societies is to see a great people, warned by its lawgivers that the wheels of government are stopping, turn its attention on itself without haste or fear, sound the depth of the ill, and then wait for two years to find the remedy at leisure, and then finally, when the remedy has been indicated, submit to it voluntarily without its costing humanity a single tear or drop of blood.[16]

 ## Constitutional Change

The founders realized that the Constitution would have to be changed from time to time. To this end, they specified a formal amendment process—a process that was used almost immediately to add the Bill of Rights. With the passage of time, the Constitution also has been altered through judicial interpretation and changes in political practice.

The Formal Amendment Process

The amendment process has two stages: proposal and ratification. Both are necessary for an amendment to become part of the Constitution. The Constitution provides two alternative methods for completing each stage (see Figure 2.3). Amendments can be proposed by a two-thirds vote in both the House of Representatives and the Senate or by a national convention, summoned by Congress at the request of two-thirds of the state legislatures. All constitutional amendments to date have been proposed by the first method.

A proposed amendment can be ratified by a vote of the legislatures of three-fourths of the states or by a vote of constitutional conventions held in three-fourths of the states. Congress chooses the method of ratification. It has used the state convention method only once, for the Twenty-first Amendment, which repealed the Eighteenth Amendment (on Prohibition). Note that the amendment process requires the exercise of extraordinary majorities (two-thirds and three-fourths). The framers purposely made it difficult to propose and ratify amendments. They wanted only the most significant issues to lead to constitutional change. Calling a national con-

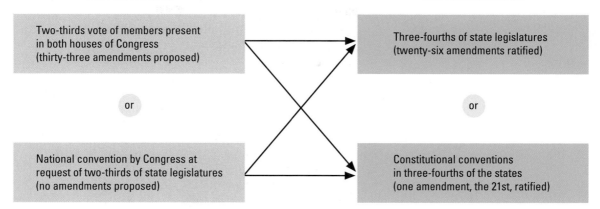

FIGURE 2.3   Amending the Constitution

PROPOSAL STAGE

RATIFICATION STAGE

Two-thirds vote of members present in both houses of Congress (thirty-three amendments proposed)

Three-fourths of state legislatures (twenty-six amendments ratified)

or

or

National convention by Congress at request of two-thirds of state legislatures (no amendments proposed)

Constitutional conventions in three-fourths of the states (one amendment, the 21st, ratified)

Amending the Constitution requires two stages: proposal and ratification. Both Congress and the states can play a role in the proposal stage, but ratification is a process that must be fought in the states themselves. Once a state has ratified an amendment, it cannot retract its action. However, a state may reject an amendment and then reconsider its decision.

vention to propose an amendment has never been tried. Certainly the method raises several thorny questions, the most significant of which concerns what limits, if any, there are on the business of the convention. Would a national convention called to consider a particular amendment be within its bounds to rewrite the Constitution? No one really knows.

Most of the Constitution's twenty-seven amendments were adopted to help keep it abreast of changes in political thinking. The first ten amendments (the Bill of Rights) were the price of ratification, but they have been fundamental to our system of government. The last seventeen amendments fall into three main categories: they make public policy, correct deficiencies in the government's structure, or promote equality (see Table 2.2).

Since 1787, about ten thousand constitutional amendments have been introduced, but only a fraction have passed the proposal stage. However, once an amendment has been voted by the Congress, chances of ratification are high. Only six amendments submitted to the states have failed to be ratified.

Interpretation by the Courts

In *Marbury* v. *Madison* (1803), the Supreme Court declared that the courts have the power to nullify government acts when they conflict with the

TABLE 2.2 Constitutional Amendments: 11 Through 27

No.	Proposed	Ratified	Intent*	Subject
11	1794	1795	G	Prohibits an individual from suing a state in federal court without the state's consent.
12	1803	1804	G	Requires the electoral college to vote separately for president and vice president.
13	1865	1865	E	Prohibits slavery.
14	1866	1868	E	Gives citizenship to all persons born or naturalized in the United States (including former slaves); prevents states from depriving any person of "life, liberty, or property, without due process of law"; and declares that no state shall deprive any person of "the equal protection of the laws."
15	1869	1870	E	Guarantees that citizens' right to vote cannot be denied "on account of race, color, or previous condition of servitude."
16	1909	1913	E	Gives Congress the power to collect an income tax.
17	1912	1913	E	Provides for popular election of senators, who were formerly elected by state legislatures.
18	1917	1919	P	Prohibits the making and selling of intoxicating liquors.
19	1919	1920	E	Guarantees that citizens' right to vote cannot be denied "on account of sex."
20	1932	1933	G	Changes the presidential inauguration from March 4 to January 20 and sets January 3 for the opening date of Congress.
21	1933	1933	P	Repeals the Eighteenth Amendment.
22	1947	1951	G	Limits a president to two terms.
23	1960	1961	E	Gives citizens of Washington, D.C., the right to vote for president.
24	1962	1964	E	Prohibits charging citizens a poll tax to vote in presidential or congressional elections.
25	1965	1967	G	Provides for succession in event of death, removal from office, incapacity, or resignation of the president or vice president.
26	1971	1971	E	Lowers the voting age to eighteen.
27	1789	1992	G	Bars immediate pay increases to members of Congress.

*P: amendments legislating public policy; G: amendments correcting perceived deficiencies in government structure; E: amendments advancing equality.

Constitution. (We will elaborate on this power, known as judicial review, in Chapter 11.) The exercise of judicial review forces the courts to interpret the Constitution. In a way, this makes a lot of sense. The judiciary is the law-interpreting branch of the government; as the supreme law of the land, the Constitution is fair game for judicial interpretation. Judicial review is the courts' main check on the other branches of government. But in interpreting the Constitution, the courts cannot help but give new meaning to its provisions. This is why judicial interpretation is a principal form of constitutional change.

Political Practice

The Constitution is silent on many issues. It says nothing about political parties or the president's cabinet, for example, yet both have exercised considerable influence in American politics. Some constitutional provisions have fallen out of use. The electors in the electoral college, for example, were supposed to exercise their own judgment in voting for president and vice president. Today the electors function simply as a rubber stamp, validating the outcome of election contests in their states.

Meanwhile, political practice has altered the distribution of power without changes in the Constitution. The framers intended Congress to be the strongest branch of government. But the president has come to overshadow Congress. Presidents such as Abraham Lincoln and Franklin Roosevelt used their powers imaginatively to respond to national crises, and their actions paved the way for future presidents to enlarge the powers of the office.

DO IT!

Volunteer to check original source documents for the Constitutional Sources Project at www.consource.org.

An Evaluation of the Constitution

The U.S. Constitution is one of the world's most praised political documents. It is the oldest written national constitution and one of the most widely copied, sometimes word for word. It is also one of the shortest. The brevity of the Constitution may be one of its greatest strengths. The framers simply laid out a structural framework for government; they did not describe relationships and powers in detail. For example, the Constitution gives Congress the power to regulate "Commerce . . . among the several States," but it does not define *interstate commerce*. Such general wording allows interpretation in keeping with contemporary political, social, and technological developments.

The generality of the U.S. Constitution stands in stark contrast to the specificity of most state constitutions. The constitution of California, for example, provides that "fruit and nut-bearing trees under the age of four years from the time of planting in orchard form and grapevines under the age of three years from the time of planting in vineyard form . . . shall be exempt from taxation" (Article XIII, Section 12). Because they are so specific, most state constitutions are much longer than the U.S. Constitution.

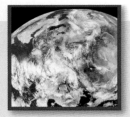

Politics of Global Change

A New Birth of Freedom: Exporting American Constitutionalism

When the founders drafted the U.S. Constitution in 1787, they hardly started from scratch. Leaders such as James Madison and John Adams drew on the failed experiences of the Articles of Confederation to chart a new course for our national government. They also leaned heavily on the ideas of great democratic thinkers of the past. Today, given the two-hundred-twenty-year track record of the United States, it is no wonder that many other nations have looked to the American experience as they embark on their own democratic experiments.

In the past fifteen years especially, democratizing countries on nearly every continent have developed new governing institutions by drawing at least in part on important principles from the U.S. Constitution and Bill of Rights. This is certainly the case in the former communist countries of Eastern Europe, which are in their second decade of newly established democratic rule. Enshrining democratic ideals in a written constitution corresponds to the ascendancy of freedom worldwide (see the accompanying figure).

Echoing the U.S. Declaration of Independence and the Constitution's preamble, for example, Article 1 of the Estonian constitution declares unequivocally, ". . . the supreme power of the state is vested in the people." Specific guarantees protecting individual rights and liberties are also written in great detail in the constitutions of these new democracies. The Latvian constitution, for example, takes a strong stand on the defense of privacy, stating that "everyone has the right to inviolability of his or her private life, home and correspondence."

Some of these newly democratic nations, however, have opted for a constitutional design with a separation of powers less rigid than one established by the American model. A parliamentary system poses fewer constraints on executive authority as long as it is sustained by a legislative majority. As long as prime ministers are backed by the popular vote ex-

Freedom, Order, and Equality in the Constitution

The revolutionaries constructed a new form of government—a *federal* government—that was strong enough to maintain order but not so strong that it could dominate the states or infringe on individual freedoms. In

pressed via a parliamentary majority, they can remain in office indefinitely. However, they can be removed from office as soon as they lose their popular support by means of a parliamentary non-confidence vote. For instance, if an election changes the composition of the parliament, the new majority can select a new prime minister. Under the same scenario, the U.S. president—who can be removed from office only by impeachment—is forced to govern facing a hostile majority and possible gridlock.

Because there is no ready-made formula for building a successful democracy, only time will tell whether these young constitutions will perform well in practice.

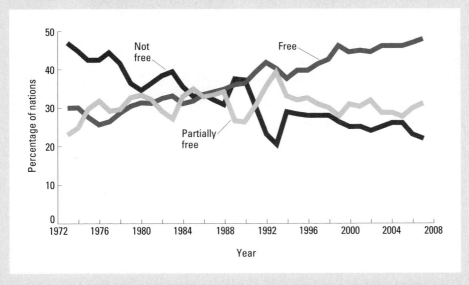

Sources: International Institute for Democracy, *The Rebirth of Democracy: 12 Constitutions of Central and Eastern Europe*, 2nd ed. (Amsterdam: Council of Europe, 1996); A. E. Dick Howard, "Liberty's Text: 10 Amendments That Changed the World," *Washington Post*, 15 December 1991, p. C3; Freedom House, "Freedom in the World 2008," available at www.freedomhouse.org/uploads/fiw08launch/FIW08Tables.pdf (accessed 16 March 2008).

short, the Constitution provided a judicious balance between order and freedom. It paid virtually no attention to equality.

Consider social equality. The Constitution never mentioned *slavery*, a controversial issue even when it was written. As we have seen, the Constitution implicitly condones slavery in several articles. Not until ratification

Designated Pourer
The Eighteenth Amendment, which was ratified by the states in 1919, banned the manufacture, sale, or transportation of alcoholic beverages. Banned beverages were destroyed, as pictured here. The amendment was spurred by moral and social reform groups, such as the Woman's Christian Temperance Union, founded by Evanston, Illinois, resident Frances Willard in 1874. The amendment proved to be an utter failure. People continued to drink, but their alcohol came from illegal sources. *(© Bettmann/Corbis)*

of the Thirteenth Amendment in 1865 was slavery prohibited. The Constitution was designed long before social equality was ever conceived as an objective of government. In fact, in *Federalist* No. 10, Madison held that protection of the "diversities in the faculties of men from which the rights of property originate" is "the first object of government."

More than a century later, the Constitution was changed to incorporate a key device for the promotion of social equality: the income tax. The Sixteenth Amendment (1913) gave Congress the power to collect an income tax; it was proposed and ratified to replace a law that had been declared unconstitutional in an 1895 court case. The income tax had long been seen as a means of putting into effect the concept of *progressive taxation*, in which the tax rate increases with income. The Sixteenth Amendment gave progressive taxation a constitutional basis.[17] Progressive taxation promotes social equality through the redistribution of income—that is, high-income people are taxed at higher rates to help fund social programs that benefit lower-income people taxed at lower rates.

Social equality itself has never been, and is not now, a prime *constitutional* value. The Constitution has been much more effective in securing order and freedom. Nor did the Constitution take a stand on political equality. It left voting qualifications to the states, specifying only that people who could vote for "the most numerous Branch of the State Legislature" could also vote for representatives to Congress (Article I, Section 2). Most states at that time allowed only taxpaying or property-owning white males to vote. Such inequalities have been rectified by several amendments. The United States is not unique in revisiting the balance among freedom, order, and equality within its constitution. Many other nations have pursued equally dramatic changes to their constitutions over the last decade. (See "Politics of Global Change: A New Birth of Freedom.")

The Constitution and Models of Democracy

Think back to our discussion of the models of democracy in Chapter 1. Which model does the Constitution fit: the pluralist or majoritarian? Actually, it is hard to imagine a government framework better suited to the pluralist model of democracy than the Constitution of the United States. It is also hard to imagine a document more at odds with the majoritarian model. Consider Madison's claim, in *Federalist* No. 10, that government inevitably involves conflicting factions. This concept coincides perfectly with pluralist theory (see Chapter 1). Then recall his description in *Federalist* No. 51 of the Constitution's ability to guard against the concentration of power in the majority through separation of powers and checks and balances. This concept—avoiding a single center of government power that might fall under majority control—also fits perfectly with pluralist democracy.

The delegates to the Constitutional Convention intended to create a republic, a government based on majority consent; they did not intend to create a democracy, which rests on majority rule. They succeeded admirably in creating that republic. In doing so, they also produced a government that developed into a democracy—but a particular type of democracy. The framers neither wanted nor got a democracy that fit the majoritarian model. They may have wanted and they certainly did create a government that conforms to the pluralist model.

Summary

The U.S. Constitution is more than a historic document, an antique curiosity. Although over two hundred years old, it still governs the politics of a mighty modern nation. It still has the power to force from office a president who won reelection by a landslide. It still has the power to see the country through government crises.

The Constitution was the end product of a revolutionary movement aimed at preserving existing liberties. That movement began with the Declaration of Independence, which proclaimed that everyone is entitled to certain rights (among them, life, liberty, and the pursuit of happiness) and that government exists for the good of its citizens. When government denies those rights, the people have the right to rebel.

War with Britain was only part of the process of independence. Some form of government was needed to replace the British monarchy. The Americans chose a republic and defined the structure of that republic in the Articles of Confederation. The Articles were a failure, however. Although they guaranteed the states the independence they coveted, they left the central government too weak to deal with disorder and insurrection.

The Constitution was the second attempt at limited government. It replaced a loose union of powerful states with a strong but still limited national government, incorporating four political principles: republicanism, federalism, separation of powers, and checks and balances. Republicanism is a form of government in which power resides in the people and is exercised by their elected representatives. Federalism is a division of power between the national government and the states. The federalism of the Constitution conferred substantial powers on the national government at the expense of the states. Separation of powers is a further division of the power of the national government into legislative (lawmaking), executive (law-enforcing), and judiciary (law-interpreting) branches. Finally, the Constitution established a system of checks and balances, giving each branch some scrutiny of and control over the others.

When work began on ratification, a major stumbling block proved to be the failure of the Constitution to list the individual liberties the Americans had fought to protect. With the promise to add a bill of rights, the Constitution was ratified. The subsequent ten amendments guaranteed participation in the political process, respect for personal beliefs, and personal privacy. They also contained guarantees against government's overreaching in criminal prosecutions. Over the years the Constitution has evolved through the formal amendment process, the exercise of judicial review, and political practice.

The Constitution was designed to strike a balance between order and freedom. It was not designed to promote equality; in fact, it had to be amended to redress inequality. The framers had compromised on many issues, including slavery, to ensure the creation of a new and workable government. The framers had not set out to create a democracy. Faith in government by the people was virtually nonexistent two centuries ago. Nevertheless, they produced a democratic form of government. That government, with its separation of powers and checks and balances, is remarkably well suited to the pluralist model of democracy. Simple majority rule, which lies at the heart of the majoritarian model, was precisely what the framers wanted to avoid.

The framers also wanted balance between the powers of the national government and the states. The exact balance was a touchy issue, skirted by the delegates at the Constitutional Convention. Some seventy years later, a civil war was fought over that balance of power. That war and countless political battles before and after it have demonstrated that the national government dominates the state governments in our political system. In the next chapter, we look at how a loose confederation of states has evolved into a "more perfect Union."

CL **Resources:** Videos, Simulations, News, Timelines, Primary Sources

Federalism

This icon will direct you to resources and activities on the website: www.cengage.com/polisci/janda/chall_dem_brief/7e

CL

ON AUGUST 29, 2005, A CATEGORY 4 hurricane named Katrina—the worst in a century—slammed ashore, unleashing 125-mile-per-hour winds, torrential rains, and sea surges that overwhelmed dikes, berms, floodwalls, and levees across the Gulf Coast. Damage estimates of $150 billion exceeded those of any other natural disaster in the United States. New Orleans, a low-lying city at the mouth of the Mississippi River, suffered the worst loss of life and property. More than thirteen hundred city residents died in the hurricane and its aftermath. The vast majority evacuated ahead of the storm. Yet despite repeated warnings, more than 100,000 residents, mostly poor and black, remained trapped within the city limits because they lacked the transportation to leave. City services crumbled. Disorder reigned. Communication and power were nonexistent. Many police officers abandoned their duties to protect their families and themselves. Thousands of sick, elderly, and poor people assembled at New Orleans's Superdome to ride out the storm and its aftermath, without air-conditioning, running water, or working toilets. They were finally evacuated after six days.[1]

In addition to the natural catastrophe, Hurricane Katrina will be remembered as a national tragedy that uncovered the coordination failures of our governmental structure. Many deaths in New Orleans might have been avoided had government acted swiftly. But which government was supposed to act? The city government was knocked out of commission. The Louisiana state government was overwhelmed by the magnitude of the damage. The national government awaited instructions from the governors of the affected states. Under our federal system of government, it is sometimes difficult to determine who is in charge of such a complex disaster and who has the resources to address it.

A chain of unfortunate events left New Orleans in a dismal state. Local and state authorities failed at planning the defense of the city. First responders were simply overwhelmed by the magnitude of the disaster. The Federal Emergency Management Agency (FEMA), the agency with the mandate to handle emergency situations, was unable to cope, partly because its director was a political appointee of the Bush administration with no relevant experience in disaster management. Louisiana governor Kathleen Babineaux Blanco contacted President

INTERACTIVE 3.1

 Katrina's Aftermath

In this chapter, we examine American federalism in theory and in practice. Is the division of power between the nation and states a matter of constitutional principle or practical politics? How does the balance of power between the nation and states relate to the conflicts between freedom and order and between freedom and equality? Does the growth of federalism abroad affect us here at home? Does federalism reflect the pluralist or the majoritarian model of democracy?

George W. Bush and said, "Give me everything you've got." (Bush was on vacation at his Texas ranch. Several days after the hurricane struck, his aide showed him a DVD of news coverage to demonstrate the seriousness of the problem.) But her request was imprecise, and she did not request military assistance. The president was reluctant at first to send in troops trained for combat when the city needed troops trained in police procedures. The National Guard, normally under the governor's control, fit the need, but the governor resisted federalizing the force because that would mean turning command and control over to the national government. In the end, the military was the only institution ready to cope with the disaster, but it could act only with a presidential declaration overriding all other authorities. Lurking in the background was the principle of federalism and the desirable extent of national intervention in local and state affairs.[2]

One key element of federalism is the respective sovereignty, or quality of being supreme in power or authority, of national and state governments. In the case of Hurricane Katrina, this distinction between different sovereignties becomes murkier because many decisions were supposed to be shared by different levels of government. Evacuation, for instance, was a responsibility shared by both the state and federal authorities. Ideology—in this case, the belief in maintaining strict controls on the powers of the national government—cast a shadow on the catastrophe. Generally conservatives tend to be more reluctant to exercise national power in matters such as public health, safety, and welfare.

Sovereignty also affects political leadership. A governor may not be a president's political equal, but governors have their own sovereignty apart from the national government. Regarding the political response to the damage caused by Hurricane Katrina, the national government blamed the state government for failing to request the specific help needed or to give up command and control. The state government underlined the inability of FEMA to deal with the necessities of the displaced population.[3] And local officials stressed the fact that national and state authorities seemed preoccupied with the press. Unfortunately for the people of New Orleans who were left behind in this tragedy, the same questions will keep on resonating in their heads: "Is anybody out there listening? Does anybody out there care?"[4]

 ## Theories and Metaphors

The delegates who met in Philadelphia in 1787 tackled the problem of making one nation out of thirteen independent states by inventing a new political form—federal government—that combined features of a confederacy with features of unitary government (see Chapter 2). Under the principle of **federalism,** two or more governments exercise power and authority over the same people and the same territory. For example, the governments

federalism The division of power between a central government and regional governments.

of the United States and Pennsylvania share certain powers (the power to tax, for instance), but other powers belong exclusively to one or the other. As James Madison wrote in *Federalist* No. 10, "The federal Constitution forms a happy combination . . . [of] the great and aggregate interests being referred to the national, and the local and particular to state governments." So the power to coin money belongs to the national government, but the power to grant divorces remains a state prerogative. By contrast, authority over state militia may sometimes belong to the national government and sometimes to the states. The history of American federalism reveals that it has not always been easy to draw a line between what is "great and aggregate" and what is "local and particular."*

Nevertheless, federalism offered a solution to citizens' fears that they would be ruled by majorities from different regions and different interests and values. Federalism also provided a new political model. The history of American federalism is full of attempts to capture its true meaning in an adjective or metaphor. By one reckoning, scholars have generated nearly five hundred ways to describe federalism.[5] We will concentrate on two such representations: dual federalism and cooperative federalism.

Dual Federalism

The term **dual federalism** sums up a theory about the proper relationship between the national government and the states. This theory has four essential parts. First, the national government rules by enumerated powers only. Second, the national government has a limited set of constitutional purposes. Third, each government unit—nation and state—is sovereign within its sphere. And fourth, the relationship between nation and states is best characterized by tension rather than cooperation.[6]

Dual federalism portrays the states as powerful components of the federal system—in some ways, the equals of the national government. Under dual federalism, the functions and responsibilities of the national and state governments are theoretically different and practically separate from each other. Dual federalism sees the Constitution as a compact among sovereign states. Of primary importance in dual federalism are **states' rights,** a concept that reserves to the states all rights not specifically conferred on the national government by the Constitution. Claims of states' rights often come from opponents of a national government policy. Their argument is that the people have not delegated the power to make such policy, and thus the power remains in the states or the people. Proponents of states' rights believe that the powers of the national government should be interpreted

dual federalism A view that holds the Constitution is a compact among sovereign states, so that the powers of the national government are fixed and limited.

states' rights The idea that all rights not specifically conferred on the national government by the Constitution are reserved to the states.

---

*The phrase Americans use to refer to their central government—*federal government*—muddies the waters even more. Technically, we have a federal system of government that includes both national and state governments. To avoid confusion from here on, we use the term *national government* rather than *federal government* when we are talking about the central government.

Made in the U.S.A.
Young boys working in a Macon, Georgia, cotton mill (1909). The U.S. Supreme Court decided in 1918 that Congress had no power to limit the excesses of child labor. According to the Court, that power belonged to the states, which resisted imposing limits for fear such legislation would drive businesses to other (less restrictive) states. *(Library of Congress)*

narrowly. They insist that the activities of Congress should be confined to the enumerated powers. They support their view by quoting the Tenth Amendment: "The powers not delegated to the United States by the Constitution, nor prohibited by it to the States, are reserved to the states respectively, or to the people." Conversely, those people favoring national action frequently point to the Constitution's elastic clause, which gives Congress the **implied powers** needed to execute its enumerated powers (see Chapter 2).

Political scientists use a metaphor to describe dual federalism. They call it *layer-cake federalism;* the powers and functions of national and state governments are as separate as the layers of a cake (see Figure 3.1). Each government is supreme in its own "layer," its own sphere of action; the two layers are distinct; and the dimensions of each layer are fixed by the Constitution.

Dual federalism has been challenged on historical and other grounds. Some critics argue that if the national government is really a creation of the states, it is a creation of only thirteen states—those that ratified the Constitution. The other thirty-seven states were admitted after the national government came into being and were created by that government out of land it had acquired. Another challenge has to do with the ratification process. Remember that special conventions in the original thirteen states, not the states' legislatures, ratified the Constitution. Ratification, then, was an act of the people, not the states. Moreover, the Preamble to the Constitution begins, "We the people of the United States," not, "We the States."

DO IT!
See how your state compares with the nation at www.fedstats.gov/qf.

implied powers Those powers that Congress requires in order to execute its enumerated powers.

FIGURE 3.1   Metaphors for Federalism

The two views of federalism
can be represented
graphically.

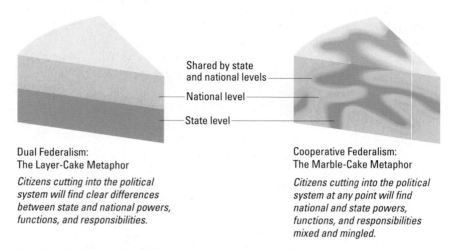

Shared by state
and national levels

National level

State level

Dual Federalism:
The Layer-Cake Metaphor

Citizens cutting into the political
system will find clear differences
between state and national powers,
functions, and responsibilities.

Cooperative Federalism:
The Marble-Cake Metaphor

Citizens cutting into the political
system at any point will find
national and state powers,
functions, and responsibilities
mixed and mingled.

The question of where the people fit into the federal system is not handled well by dual federalism.

Cooperative Federalism

Cooperative federalism, a phrase coined in the 1930s, is a different theory of the relationship between national and state governments. It acknowledges the increasing overlap in state and national functions and rejects the idea of separate spheres, or layers, for the states and the national government. Cooperative federalism has three elements. First, national and state agencies typically undertake governmental functions jointly rather than exclusively. Second, nation and states routinely share power. Third, power is not concentrated at any government level or in any agency; this fragmentation of responsibilities gives people and groups access to many centers of influence.

The bakery metaphor used to describe this kind of federalism is a *marble cake.* The national and state governments do not act in separate spheres; they are intermingled. Their functions are mixed in the American federal system. Critical to cooperative federalism is an expansive view of the Constitution's supremacy clause (Article VI), which specifically subordinates state law to national law and charges every judge to disregard state laws that are inconsistent with the Constitution, national laws, and treaties.

In contrast to dual federalism, cooperative federalism blurs the distinction between national and state powers. Some scholars argue that the layer-cake metaphor has never accurately described the American political structure.[7] The national and state governments have many common objectives and have often cooperated to achieve them. In the nineteenth century,

cooperative federalism A view that holds that the Constitution is an agreement among people who are citizens of both state and nation, so there is little distinction between state powers and national powers.

for example, cooperation, not separation, made it possible to develop transportation systems such as canals and to establish state land-grant colleges.

A critical difference between the theories of dual and cooperative federalism is the way they interpret two sections of the Constitution that set out the terms of the relationship between the national and state governments. Article I, Section 8, lists the enumerated powers of Congress and then concludes with the **elastic clause**, which gives Congress the power to "make all Laws which shall be necessary and proper for carrying into Execution the foregoing Powers." The Tenth Amendment reserves for the states or the people "powers" not given to the national government or denied to the states by the Constitution. Dual federalism postulates an inflexible elastic clause and a capacious Tenth Amendment. Cooperative federalism postulates suppleness in the elastic clause and confines the Tenth Amendment to a self-evident, obvious truth.

The Dynamics of Federalism

Although the Constitution defines a kind of federalism, the actual balance of power between nation and states has always been more a matter of politics than of formal theory. Three broad principles help to underscore why. First, rather than operating in a mechanical fashion, American federalism is a flexible and dynamic system. The Constitution's inherent ambiguities about federalism generate not only constraints but also opportunities for politicians, citizens, and interest groups to push ideas that they care about. Second, due to this flexibility, public officials across levels of government often make policy decisions based on pragmatic considerations without regard to theories of what American federalism should look like. Politics and policy goals rather than pure theoretical or ideological commitments about federalism tend to dominate decision making. Third, there is a growing recognition among public officials and citizens that public problems (those involving tradeoffs between freedom, order, and equality) cut across governmental boundaries. This section develops the first claim; we explore the other two later in this chapter.

The overall point these three claims illustrate is that understanding American federalism requires knowing more than simply the powers that the Constitution assigns the different levels of government. Real understanding requires recognizing the forces that can prompt changes in relationships between the national government and the states. In this section, we focus on four specific forces: national crises and demands, judicial interpretation, the expansion of grants-in-aid, and the professionalization of state governments.

National Crises and Demands

The elastic clause of the Constitution gives Congress the power to make all laws that are "necessary and proper" to carry out its responsibilities. By

elastic clause The last clause in Section 8 of Article I of the Constitution, which gives Congress the means to execute its enumerated powers. This clause is the basis for Congress's implied powers. Also called the *necessary and proper clause*.

using this power in combination with its enumerated powers, Congress has been able to increase the scope of the national government tremendously. The greatest change has come in times of crisis and national emergency, such as the Civil War, the world wars, the Great Depression, and the aftermath of 9/11. Consider the last two of these examples.

The problems of the Great Depression proved too extensive for either state governments or private businesses to handle, so the national government assumed a heavy share of responsibility for providing relief and pursuing economic recovery. Under the New Deal, President Franklin D. Roosevelt's response to the depression, Congress enacted various emergency relief programs to stimulate economic activity and help the unemployed. Many measures required the cooperation of national and state governments. Through the regulations it attached to funds, the national government extended its power and control over the states.[8]

Some call the New Deal era revolutionary. There is no doubt that the period was critical in reshaping federalism in the United States, and the interaction between the national and state governments clearly resembled the marble-cake metaphor more than the alternative. But perhaps the most significant change was in the way Americans thought about their problems and the role of the national government in solving them. Difficulties that at one time had been seen as personal or local problems were now national problems, requiring national solutions. The general welfare, broadly defined, became a legitimate concern of the national government.

In other respects, however, the New Deal was not very revolutionary. For example, Congress did not claim any new powers to address the nation's economic problems. It simply used its constitutional powers to suit the circumstances.

More recently, concerns over terrorist attacks on U.S. soil have expanded national power. The month after the events of September 11, 2001, the Congress swiftly passed and the president signed into law the USA-PATRIOT Act (P.L. 107-56). Among other provisions, the law expanded significantly the surveillance and investigative powers of the Department of Justice. After some disagreement about its structure and organization, federal policymakers also created the Department of Homeland Security in 2002, a new department that united over twenty separate federal agencies under a common administrative structure.[9] These efforts sparked much debate regarding the appropriate limits of the national government's power over the lives of American citizens and the prerogatives of other levels of government.

Legislation is one prod the national government has used to achieve goals at the state level. The Voting Rights Act of 1965 is a good example. Section 2 of Article I of the Constitution gives the states the power to specify qualifications for voting. But the Fifteenth Amendment (1870) provides that no person should be denied the right to vote "on account of race, color, or previous condition of servitude." Before the Voting Rights Act, states could not specifically deny blacks the right to vote, but they could require that voters pass literacy tests or pay poll taxes, requirements that virtually disenfranchised blacks in many states. The Voting Rights Act was designed to correct this political inequality (see Chapter 13). The act gives officials of the national government the power to decide whether individuals are qualified to vote in all elections, including primaries and national, state, and local elections. The constitutional authority for the act rests on the second section of the Fifteenth Amendment, which gives Congress the power to enforce the amendment through "appropriate legislation."

Judicial Interpretation

The Voting Rights Act was not a unanimous hit. Its critics adopted the language of dual federalism and insisted that the Constitution gives the states the power to determine voter qualifications. Its supporters claimed that the Fifteenth Amendment guarantee of voting rights takes precedence over states' rights and gives the national government new responsibilities.

The conflict was ultimately resolved by the Supreme Court, the umpire of the federal system. The Court settles disputes over the powers of the national and state governments by deciding whether the actions of either are unconstitutional (see Chapter 11). In the nineteenth and early twentieth centuries, the Supreme Court often decided in favor of the states. Then for nearly sixty years, from 1937 to 1995, the Court almost always supported the national government in contests involving the balance of power between nation and states. Since 1995, the Supreme Court has tended to favor states' rights, but not without some important exceptions.

Ends and Means.   Early in the nineteenth century, the nationalist interpretation of federalism triumphed over states' rights. In 1819, under Chief Justice John Marshall, the Supreme Court expanded the role of the national government in *McCulloch* v. *Maryland*. The Court was asked to rule whether Congress had the power to establish a national bank and, if so, whether states had the power to tax that bank. In a unanimous opinion that Marshall wrote, the Court conceded that Congress had only the powers conferred on it by the Constitution, which nowhere mentioned banks. However, Article I granted to Congress the authority to enact all laws "necessary and proper" to the execution of Congress's enumerated powers. Marshall gave a broad interpretation to this elastic clause: "Let the end be legitimate, let it be within the scope of the constitution, and all means which are appropriate, which are plainly adapted to that end, which are not prohibited, but consistent with the letter and spirit of the constitution, are constitutional."

The Court clearly agreed that Congress had the power to charter a bank. But did the states (in this case, Maryland) have the power to tax the bank? Arguing that "the power to tax involves the power to destroy," Marshall insisted that states could not tax the national government because the bank represents the interests of the whole nation; a state may not tax those it does not represent. Therefore, a state tax that interferes with the power of Congress to make law is void.[10]

Commerce for a New Nation. Especially from the late 1930s to the mid-1990s, the Supreme Court's interpretation of the Constitution's **commerce clause** was a major factor that increased the national government's power. The third clause of Article I, Section 8, states that "Congress shall have Power . . . To regulate Commerce . . . among the several States." In early Court decisions, beginning with *Gibbons* v. *Ogden* in 1824, Chief Justice Marshall interpreted the word *commerce* broadly to include virtually every form of commercial activity. But later courts would take a narrower view of that power.[11]

States' Rights and Dual Federalism. Roger B. Taney became chief justice in 1836, and during his tenure (1836–1864), the Court's federalism decisions began to favor the states. The Taney Court took a more restrictive view of commerce and imposed firm limits on the powers of the national government. As Taney saw it, the Constitution spoke "not only in the same words, but with the same meaning and intent with which it spoke when it came from the hands of its framers and was voted on and adopted by the people of the United States." In the infamous *Dred Scott* decision (1857), for example, the Court decided that Congress had no power to prohibit slavery in the territories.[12]

Federalism and the New Deal. The judicial winds shifted again during the Great Depression. After originally disagreeing with FDR's and the Congress's position that the economic crisis was a national problem demanding national action, in 1937, with no change in personnel, the Court began to alter its course and upheld several major New Deal measures. Perhaps the Court was responding to the 1936 election returns (Roosevelt had been reelected in a landslide, and the Democrats commanded a substantial majority in Congress). Or perhaps the Court sought to defuse the president's threat to enlarge the Court with justices sympathetic to his views. In any event, the Court abandoned its effort to maintain a rigid boundary between national and state power.

The Umpire Strikes Back. In the 1990s, a series of important U.S. Supreme Court rulings involving the commerce clause suggested that the states' rights position was gaining ground. The Court's 5 to 4 ruling in *United States* v. *Lopez* held that Congress exceeded its authority under the commerce clause when it enacted a law in 1990 banning the possession of a gun in or near a school.[13] A conservative majority, headed by Chief Justice William H. Rehnquist, concluded that having a gun in a school zone "has nothing to do with 'commerce' or any sort of economic enterprise, however broadly one might define those terms." Justices Sandra Day O'Connor, Antonin Scalia, Anthony Kennedy, and Clarence Thomas, all

commerce clause The third clause of Article I, Section 8, of the Constitution, which gives Congress the power to regulate commerce among the states.

appointed by Republicans, joined in Rehnquist's opinion, putting the brakes on congressional power.

Another Slice of the Layer Cake.   Another piece of gun control legislation, known as the Brady Bill, produced similar results. The 1993 bill mandated the creation by November 1998 of a national system to check the background of prospective gun buyers in order to weed out, among others, convicted felons and the mentally ill. In the meantime, it created a temporary system that called for local law enforcement officials to perform background checks and report their findings to gun dealers in their community. Several sheriffs challenged the law.

The Supreme Court agreed with the sheriffs, delivering a double-barreled blow to the local-enforcement provision in June 1997. In *Printz* v. *United States,* the Court concluded that Congress could not require local officials to implement a regulatory scheme imposed by the national government. In language that seemingly invoked layer-cake federalism, Justice Antonin Scalia, writing for the five-member conservative majority, argued that locally enforced background checks violated the principle of dual sovereignty by allowing the national government "to impress into its service— and at no cost to itself—the police officers of the 50 States." In addition, the scheme violated the principle of separation of powers, by congressional transfer of the president's responsibility to faithfully execute national laws to local law enforcement officials.[14]

Federalism's Shifting Scales.   In 2000, the Court struck down congressional legislation that had allowed federal court lawsuits pursuing money damages for victims of crimes "motivated by gender." The Violence Against Women Act violated both the commerce clause and Section 5 of the Fourteenth Amendment. The majority declared that "the Constitution requires a distinction between what is truly national and what is truly local."[15]

The recent pattern promoting states' rights in federalism cases is not without significant exceptions. Perhaps the best-known decision bucking the trend is *Bush* v. *Gore.* In that decision the Court overruled the Florida Supreme Court's interpretation of Florida election law and ordered a halt to Florida ballot recounts, effectively ending the 2000 presidential election contest. In *Lawrence and Garner* v. *Texas,* an unrelated case from 2003, the Court also ruled against the states when it declared unconstitutional, by a 6 to 3 vote, a Texas law that had outlawed homosexual conduct between consenting adults. In the process, the decision also overturned a prior Court decision from the 1980s that had upheld Georgia's authority to maintain a similar law.[16]

Grants-in-Aid

Since the 1960s, the national government's use of financial incentives has rivaled its use of legislation and judicial interpretation as a means of shaping

IDEAlog.org

One of the questions in the IDEAlog self-test deals with stricter gun-control laws. How did you answer that question?

relationships between national and state governments. The principal method the national government uses to make money available to the states is grants-in-aid.

A **grant-in-aid** is money paid by one level of government to another level of government, to be spent for a specific purpose. Most grants-in-aid come with standards or requirements prescribed by Congress. Many are awarded on a matching basis: a recipient must make some contribution of its own, which is then matched by the national government. Grants-in-aid take two general forms: categorical grants and block grants.

Categorical grants target specific purposes, and restrictions on their use typically leave the recipient relatively little discretion. Recipients today include state governments, local governments, and public and private non-profit organizations. There are two kinds of categorical grants: formula grants and project grants. As their name implies, **formula grants** are distributed according to a particular formula, which specifies who is eligible for the grant and how much each eligible applicant will receive. The formulas may weigh such factors as state per capita income, number of school-age children, urban population, and number of families below the poverty line. Most grants, however, are **project grants**, awarded on the basis of competitive applications. Recent grants have focused on health (substance abuse and HIV-AIDS programs); natural resources and the environment (asbestos and toxic pollution); and education, training, and employment (for the disabled, the homeless, and the aged).

In contrast to categorical grants, Congress awards **block grants** for broad, general purposes. They allow recipient governments considerable freedom in deciding how to allocate money to individual programs. Whereas a categorical grant might be given to promote a very specific activity—say, developing an ethnic heritage curriculum—a block grant might be earmarked for elementary, secondary, and vocational education. The state or local government receiving the block grant would then choose the specific educational programs to fund with it.

Grants-in-aid are a method of redistributing income. Money is collected by the national government from citizens of all fifty states and then allocated to other citizens, supposedly for worthwhile social purposes. Many grants have worked to remove gross inequalities among states and their citizens. But the formulas used to redistribute this income are not impartial; they are highly political, established through a process of congressional horse trading. Whatever its form or purpose, grant money comes with strings attached. Some strings are there to ensure that the money is used for the purpose for which it was given. Other regulations are designed to evaluate how well the grant is working. Still others are designed to achieve some broad national goal, a goal that is not always closely related to the specific purpose of the grant. For example, in October 2000, President Bill Clinton signed legislation establishing a tough national standard of .08 percent blood-alcohol level for drunk driving. States that refused to impose this lower standard by 2004 stood to lose millions in government

grant-in-aid Money provided by one level of government to another, to be spent for a given purpose.

categorical grant A grant-in-aid targeted for a specific purpose by formula or by project.

formula grant A categorical grant distributed according to a particular formula that specifies who is eligible for the grant and how much each eligible applicant will receive.

project grant A categorical grant awarded on the basis of competitive applications submitted by prospective recipients.

block grant A grant-in-aid awarded for general purposes, allowing the recipient great discretion in spending the grant money.

highway construction money.[17] Not surprisingly, every state with a higher blood alcohol standard responded to the legislation by passing its own law lowering the standard to .08 percent.

Professionalization of State Governments

A final important factor that has produced dynamic changes in the American federal system has been the emergence of state governments as more capable policy actors. Not long ago, states were described as the weak links in the American policy system. In an oft-quoted book, former North Carolina governor Terry Sanford leveled heavy criticisms at the states, calling them ineffective, indecisive, and inattentive organizations that may have lost their relevance in an increasingly complicated nation and world.[18] Writing nearly twenty years earlier, journalist Robert Allen was even less kind; he called the states "the tawdriest, most incompetent, most stultifying unit in the nation's political structure."[19]

How times have changed. Since the 1960s especially, states have become much more capable and forceful policy actors. These changes have contributed to dynamic changes in the American federal system. If the situation was so bleak less than four decades ago, what happened since then?[20]

First, the states have made many internal changes that have fostered their capabilities. Both governors and state legislators now employ more capably trained and experienced policy staff rather than part-time assistants. Second, legislatures now meet more days during the year, and elected officials in states receive higher salaries than in the past. Third, the appeal of higher salaries has helped to attract more highly qualified people to run for state office. Fourth, the increasing ability of states to raise revenue, through state tax and budgetary reforms that have transpired since the 1960s, has given states greater leverage in designing and directing policy. And, fifth, the unelected officials who administer state programs in areas such as transportation, social services, and law enforcement have become better educated. For instance, professional and service occupations account for more than the half of all jobs at the state and local levels. In 2006, professional workers represented one-fifth of all state and local government employees. Most of these professional jobs require a college degree.[21]

Changes in national policy have also helped the states to develop. Many federal grants-in-aid include components designed explicitly to foster capacity-building measures in state governments. One example is the Elementary and Secondary Education Act (ESEA), which became law in 1965. This act, passed as part of President Lyndon Johnson's Great Society effort, was designed to provide federal assistance to the nation's disadvantaged students. Although it is often overlooked, Title V of the law contained several provisions designed to strengthen state departments of education, the agencies that would be responsible for administering the bulk of other programs contained in the ESEA. Those new capabilities, which subsequent federal laws and internal state efforts have fostered, continue to influence the shape of both federal and state education policy, especially during the most recent revision of the ESEA as the No Child Left Behind Act of 2001.[22]

All of this is not to say that the states are without problems of their own. In some ways, they have been victims of their own success. Now that state capitals have become more viable venues where citizens and interest groups can agitate for their causes, the states have begun to face ever-increasing demands. Those requests can strain state administrators and legislative or gubernatorial staffs who, although better educated and equipped than their predecessors, still struggle to set priorities and please their constituents.

Ideology, Policymaking, and American Federalism

American federalism appears to be in constant motion. This is due in large part to what some political scientists call policy entrepreneurs—citizens, interest groups, and officials inside government—who attempt to persuade others to accept a particular view of the proper balance of freedom, order, and equality. The American federal system provides myriad opportunities for interested parties to push for their ideas.

In essence, the existence of national and state governments—specifically, their executive, legislative, and judicial branches and their bureaucratic agencies—offers these entrepreneurs several different venues where they can attempt to influence policy and politics. The most creative of these entrepreneurs can work at multiple levels of government simultaneously.

In this section, we explore how views about American federalism can influence the shape of the nation's politics and policy. We also relate these issues to our ongoing discussion of political ideology, which we introduced in Chapter 1 (see Figure 1.2 on page 19).

Ideology, Policymaking, and Federalism in Theory

To begin our discussion in this section, it will be helpful to return to the cake metaphors that describe dual and cooperative federalism. Looking at those models of the nation's federal system helps to capture some of what could be considered conventional wisdom about political ideology and federalism—in particular, the views of conservatives and liberals. In their efforts to limit the scope of the national government, conservatives are often associated with the layer-cake metaphor. In contrast, liberals, believing that one of the functions of the national government is to bring about equality, are more likely to find the marble-cake metaphor more desirable.

Conservatives are often portrayed as believing that different states have different problems and resources and that returning control to state governments would promote diversity. States would be free to experiment with alternative ways to confront their problems. Another view often attributed to conservatives is that the national government is too remote, too tied to special interests, and not responsive to the public at large. The national government overregulates and tries to promote too much uniformity. States, on the other hand, are closer to the people and better able to respond to specific local needs.

In contrast, pundits and scholars often argue that what conservatives hope for, liberals fear. Liberals remember, so the argument goes, that the states' rights model allowed political and social inequalities and supported racism. Blacks and city dwellers were often left virtually unrepresented by white state legislators, who disproportionately served rural interests. Liberals believe the states remain unwilling to protect the rights or provide for the needs of their citizens, whether those citizens are consumers seeking protection from business interests, defendants requiring guarantees of due process of law, or poor people seeking a minimum standard of living.

These ideological conceptions of federalism reveal a simple truth: federalism is not something written or implied in the Constitution; the Constitution is only the starting point in the debate.

In 1969, Richard Nixon advocated giving more power to state and local governments. Nixon wanted to decentralize national policies through an effort called *New Federalism.* Nixon's New Federalism called for combining and reformulating categorical grants into block grants. The shift had dramatic implications for federalism. Block grants were seen as a way to redress the imbalance of power between Washington and the states and localities. New Federalism was nothing more than dual federalism in modern dress.

After the administration of President Jimmy Carter, who made some headway in reorganizing federal efforts in domestic policy but by no means supported the extensive block-grant approach of Nixon, Ronald Reagan took office in 1981. Reagan promised a "new New Federalism" to restore a proper constitutional relationship between the federal, state, and local governments. The national government, he said, treated "elected state and local officials as if they were nothing more than administrative agents for federal authority."[23]

Reagan's commitment to reducing federal taxes and spending meant that the states would have to foot an increasing share of the bill for government services (see Figure 3.2). In the late 1970s, the national government funded between 25 and 30 percent of all state and local government spending. By the late 1980s, its contribution had declined to roughly 17 percent. That figure inched up steadily throughout the Clinton presidency and has hovered between 23 and 26 percent of state and local spending since then.

Ideology, Policymaking, and Federalism in Practice

Despite the apparent consistencies between presidential preferences regarding federalism and refrains such as "liberals love the national government"

FIGURE 3.2   The National Government's Contribution to State and Local Governments

In 1960, the national government contributed
roughly 11 percent of total
state and local spending.
After rising in the 1960s and
1970s, the total stood at
almost 30 percent by 1978.
The national share declined
during the 1980s and by
1990 was approximately
17 percent. It has inched
back up to the point at
which such spending represents more than 23 percent
of the total.

Source: Calculations from Historical Tables, Budget of the United
States Government, FY2009
Table 15.2 (adjusted to
2005 dollars).

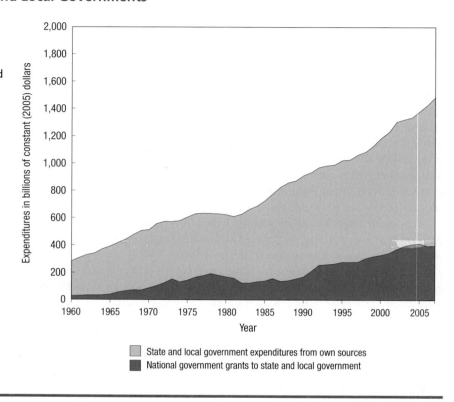

State and local government expenditures from own sources
National government grants to state and local government

---

and "conservatives favor states' rights," these simplifications are often misleading. To grasp the differences between conservatives and liberals, one has to understand not only these general labels but also the purposes of government under discussion. Consider an example from the debates over the federal preemption of state power.

National Intervention in State Functions.   The power of Congress to enact laws that have the national government assume total or partial responsibility for a state government function is called **preemption.**[24] When the national government shoulders a new government function, it restricts the discretionary power of the states. Congressional prohibition of state or local taxation of the Internet is an example of complete preemption.[25] It represents a loss billions of dollars to state and local governments. Partial preemption occurs with the enactment of minimum national standards that states must meet if they wish to regulate the field. The Do Not Call Implementation Act of 2003 is an example of partial preemption. States

preemption The power of
Congress to enact laws by which
the national government assumes
total or partial responsibility for a
state government function.

retained authority to regulate telemarketing provided they met the minimum standards spelled out by the act.[26]

Congressional preemption statutes infringe on state powers in two ways: through mandates and restraints. A **mandate** is a requirement that a state undertake an activity or provide a service in keeping with minimum national standards. A mandate might require that states remove specified pollutants from public drinking water supplies. In contrast, a **restraint** forbids state government from exercising a certain power. A restraint might prohibit states from dumping sewage into the ocean.

Preemption is a modern power. Congress passed only twenty-nine preemptive acts before 1900. In the ensuing sixty years, Congress had preempted the power of states to legislate in certain areas an additional 153 times. The pace of preemption has accelerated. By 2000, or in just forty years, Congress enacted an additional 329 preemption statutes.[27] From 2001 to 2005, 64 new laws have preempted state authority.[28] The vast majority of these recent preemption efforts were partial preemptions dealing with terrorism or environmental protection.

The increased use of preemption has given birth to a new theory of federalism. The pressure to expand national power inherent in cooperative federalism has reduced the national government's reliance on fiscal tools such as grants-in-aid. Instead, the national government has come to rely on regulatory tools such as mandates and restraints to assure the supremacy of federal policy. According to this view, cooperative federalism has morphed into **coercive federalism**.[29]

Constraining Unfunded Mandates.
State and local government officials have long voiced strong objections to the national government's practice of imposing requirements on the states without providing the financial

Label Me
Food labeling follows a single national standard today as a result of the Nutrition Labeling and Education Act of 1990. The act preempted the states from imposing different labeling requirements. *(© Sara-Maria Vischer/The Image Works)*

Nutrition Facts
Serving Size ¾ cup (31g)
Servings Per Container about 11

Amount Per Serving	Cinnamon Toast Crunch	with ½ cup skim milk
Calories	130	170
Calories from Fat	30	30

	% Daily Value**	
Total Fat 3g*	5%	5%
Saturated Fat 0.5g	2%	2%
Trans Fat 0g		
Polyunsaturated Fat 0.5g		
Monounsaturated Fat 2g		
Cholesterol 0mg	0%	1%
Sodium 220mg	9%	12%
Potassium 45mg	1%	7%
Total Carbohydrate 25g	8%	10%
Dietary Fiber 1g	4%	4%
Sugars 10g		
Other Carbohydrate 14g		
Protein 1g		

Vitamin A	10%	15%
Vitamin C	10%	10%
Calcium	10%	25%
Iron	25%	25%
Vitamin D	10%	25%
Thiamin	25%	30%
Riboflavin	25%	35%
Niacin	25%	25%
Vitamin B$_6$	25%	25%
Folic Acid	25%	25%
Vitamin B$_{12}$	25%	35%
Phosphorus	4%	15%
Magnesium	2%	6%
Zinc	25%	30%
Copper	2%	2%

* Amount in cereal. A serving of cereal plus skim milk provides 3g total fat, less than 5mg cholesterol, 280mg sodium, 250mg potassium, 30g total carbohydrate (16g sugars) and 5g protein.
** Percent Daily Values are based on a 2,000 calorie diet. Your daily values may be higher or lower depending on your calorie needs:

	Calories	2,000	2,500
Total Fat	Less than	65g	80g
Sat Fat	Less than	20g	25g
Cholesterol	Less than	300mg	300mg
Sodium	Less than	2,400mg	2,400mg
Potassium		3,500mg	3,500mg
Total Carbohydrate		300g	375g
Dietary Fiber		25g	30g

mandate A requirement that a state undertake an activity or provide a service in keeping with minimum national standards.

restraint A requirement laid down by act of Congress prohibiting a state or local government from exercising a certain power.

coercive federalism A view that the national government may impose its policy preferences on the states through regulations in the form of mandates and restraints.

support needed to satisfy them. By 1992, more than 170 congressional acts had established partially or wholly unfunded mandates.[30] One of the early results of the Republican-led 104th Congress (1995–1997) was the Unfunded Mandates Relief Act of 1995. The legislation requires the Congressional Budget Office to prepare cost estimates of any proposed national legislation that would impose more than $50 million a year in costs on state and local governments or more than $100 million a year in costs on private business. It also requires a cost analysis of the impact of agency regulations.

Many mandates have fallen outside the precise contours of the Relief Act. Although it is likely that the cost estimates have served to temper or withdraw some mandates, the Relief Act has acted merely as a "speed bump," slowing down others rather than deterring new efforts at regulation.[31] (It is important to note that the law does not apply to legislation protecting constitutional rights and civil rights or to antidiscrimination laws.)

The act's critics argue that large proportions of state appropriation budgets still must cover the costs of programs imposed by the national government. The National Conference of State Legislatures estimated, for example, that Real ID—a federally mandated program that requires states to issue driver's licenses and identification cards—will cost $11 billion through 2012.[32] Since 2001, the national government has passed along more than $100 billion worth of unfunded mandates to the states.[33]

If Republicans were expecting a return of powers to the states during the presidency of George W. Bush, then they were likely disappointed. On his watch, the national government increased its power over the states. Through coercive federalism, the national government now calls the tune for still more activities that were once the sole province of individual states.

 ## Federalism and Electoral Politics

While federalism affects the shape of American public policy, it also plays a significant role in electoral politics. We will have much more to say about elections in Chapter 6. For now, we focus on the ways that federalism is related to the outcome of state and national elections.

National Capital–State Capital Links

State capitals often serve as proving grounds for politicians who aspire to national office. After gaining experience in a state legislature or serving in a statewide elected position (governor or attorney general, for example), elected officials frequently draw on that experience in making a pitch for service in the U.S. House, Senate, or even the White House. The role that state political experience can play in making a run for the presidency seems to have become increasingly important in recent decades. Consider that four of the last six candidates who were elected to the highest office in the land, a period dating back to 1976, had formerly served as governors: Jimmy Carter (Georgia), Ronald Reagan (California), Bill Clinton (Arkansas), and George W. Bush (Texas). George H. W. Bush and Barack Obama are the exceptions to this otherwise long streak.

It is hard to underestimate the value of previous political experience in attempting to mount a campaign for national office. In addition to simply learning the craft of being a politician, experience in state politics can be critically important for helping a candidate to build up a network of contacts, staunch constituents, and potential fundraisers. Past governors also have the benefit of being plugged into organizations such as the National Governors Association and the Republican and Democratic governors' groups, which can help to cultivate national-level name recognition, friendships, and a reputation in Washington. Finally, considering that presidential elections are really a series of fifty different state-level contests, given the structure of the electoral college, a candidate for the White House can benefit tremendously from a friendly governor who can call into action his or her own political network on the candidate's behalf.

Congressional Redistricting

Perhaps even more important than activities on the campaign trail is the decennial process of congressional redistricting, which reveals crucial connections between federalism and the nation's electoral politics. Most generally, redistricting refers to the process of redrawing boundaries for electoral jurisdictions. This process occurs at all levels of government, and becomes an extremely high-stakes game in the two years after each decennial national census in the United States. During that window of time, the U.S. Census Bureau produces and releases updated population counts for the nation. Those figures are used to determine the number of seats that each state will have in the U.S. House, which are apportioned based on population.

While it is relatively straightforward to determine how many seats each state will have, where the new district lines will be drawn is a complicated and highly political affair. Even in states that may not have lost or gained seats due to population shifts within a state—some areas grow at a rapid rate, while others lose population, for example—the task of redistricting carries huge stakes. In large part, this is because state legislatures typically have the task of drawing the lines that define the congressional districts in their states. Given that this process happens only once every ten years and because the careers of U.S. House members and their party's relatively long-term fortunes in Congress can turn on decisions made in these state-level political debates, it is no wonder that the redistricting process commands significant national attention.

Evidence that federalism has become increasingly intertwined with the politics of congressional redistricting was revealed in Texas in 2003. Frustrated by the lack of Republican representation in his state's congressional delegation and hoping to increase the GOP majority in Congress, U.S. House majority whip Tom DeLay worked with legislators in Texas's Republican-controlled state legislature to reopen the redistricting question that had been settled prior to the 2002 midterm elections. Democratic state legislators took drastic measures to deny the state house a quorum. They fled to an undisclosed location in Oklahoma—some on state representative James E. "Pete" Laney's private plane. The plot thickened when shortly after this turn of events, it was learned that DeLay had called to service the Federal Aviation Administration and the Department of Homeland Security, the latter being the new office designed to protect the nation against terrorist attacks, to track down Laney's plane and pinpoint the location of the Texas Democrats. The controversy eventually produced a report by the inspector general of the U.S. Transportation Department and congressional hearings to probe the matter. Republicans tended to defend DeLay as simply performing constituent service by intervening as he did, while Democrats chastised DeLay's effort as an inappropriate use of the nation's resources, especially during a time of war and heightened concerns over terrorism.[34] DeLay was indicted in 2005 for money laundering. He resigned from Congress in 2006.

Federalism and the American Intergovernmental System

We have concentrated in this chapter on the roles the national and state governments play in shaping the federal system. Although the Constitution explicitly recognizes only national and state governments, the American federal system has spawned a multitude of local governments as well. A 2002 census counted over eighty-seven thousand.[35] It is worth considering these units because they help to illustrate the third main principle we outlined near the beginning of this chapter: a growing recognition among public figures and citizens that public problems cut across governmental boundaries.

Americans are citizens of both nation and state, but they also come under the jurisdiction of various local government units. These units include **municipal governments,** the governments of cities and towns. Municipalities, in turn, are located in (or may contain or share boundaries with) counties, which are administered by **county governments.** (Sixteen states further divide counties into townships.) Most Americans also live in a **school district,** which is responsible for administering local elementary and secondary educational programs. They also may be served by one or more **special districts,** government units created to perform particular functions, typically when those functions—such as fire protection and water purification and distribution—are best performed across jurisdictional bounda-

municipal government The government unit that administers a city or town.

county government The government unit that administers a county.

school district An area for which a local government unit administers elementary and secondary school programs.

special district A government unit created to perform particular functions, especially when those functions are best performed across jurisdictional boundaries.

Whose Rules?
Grand Staircase–Escalante National Monument in southern Utah was established by presidential decree in 1996. It sits on 1.7 million acres of austere and rugged land. The decree irked local residents, who had hoped for greater industrial development, which is now barred. They have fought back by claiming ownership of hundreds of miles of dirt roads, dry washes, and riverbeds in the monument. The conflicting signs illustrate the controversy. On the left, the local government, Kane County, approves use of all-terrain vehicles. On the right, the national government signals just the opposite. *(Kevin Maloney for the* New York Times*)*

ries. All of these local governments are created by state governments, either in their constitutions or through legislation.

In theory, at least, one benefit of localizing government is that it brings government close to the people; it gives them an opportunity to participate in the political process, to have a direct impact on policy. From this perspective, overlapping governments appear compatible with a majoritarian view of democracy.

The reality is somewhat different, however. In fact, voter turnout in local contests tends to be very low, even though the impact of individual votes is much greater. Furthermore, the fragmentation of powers, functions, and responsibilities among national, state, and local governments makes government as a whole seem complicated and hence incomprehensible and inaccessible to ordinary people. In addition, most people have little time to devote to public affairs. These factors tend to discourage individual citizens from pursuing politics and, in turn, enhance the influence of organized groups, which have the resources—time, money, and know-how—to sway policymaking (see Chapter 7). Instead of bringing government closer to the people and reinforcing majoritarian democracy, then, the system's complexity tends to encourage pluralism.

The large number of governments also makes it possible for government at some level to respond to the diversity of conditions that prevail in different parts of the country. States and cities differ enormously in population, size, economic resources, climate, and other characteristics. Smaller political units are better able to respond to particular local conditions and can generally do so more quickly than larger units. Smaller units, however,

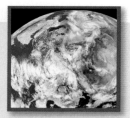

Politics of Global Change

Federalism, Iraqi Style

The United States and its coalition of willing partners deposed the Baathist regime of Saddam Hussein in Iraq in 2003. What form of government will ultimately replace unitary dictatorial rule? In October 2005 the Iraqi people approved a new constitution that established a federal system with separate legislative, executive, and judicial functions. Whereas the United States made its transition from a highly dispersed system under the Articles of Confederation to a more centralized federal arrangement, Iraq has now moved from a highly centralized and unitary system under dictator Saddam Hussein to a more distributed federal system under its new constitution.

The situation in Iraq is very complicated. Ethnic, tribal, and religious groups demand resources, territory, and autonomy. Arabs, Kurds, and Turkomen are the main ethnic groups. Although the population is almost entirely Muslim, the people divide into majority Shiite and minority Sunni sects. The Sunnis held sway under Saddam Hussein. Now the Shiites dominate. Too little acknowledgment of group demands risks violent disruption. But giving too much authority to the various groups and the regions where they concentrate will fuel the very nationalisms that will divide Iraq.

Former U.S. ambassador to Croatia Peter Galbraith, a critic of the Bush administration's Iraq policy but a strong defender of the new Iraqi constitution, argues that "there is no meaningful Iraqi identity. In the north, you've got a pro-Western Kurdish population. In the south, you've got a Shiite majority that wants a 'pale version of an Iranian state.' And in the center you've got a Sunni population that is nervous about being trapped in a system in which it would be overrun."

These divisions over ethnic and religious lines were expressed in parliamentary elections and constitutional

may not be able to muster the economic resources to meet some challenges. Consequently, in a growing number of areas, citizens have come to see the advantages of coordinating efforts and sharing burdens across levels of government.

Supreme Court Justice Anthony Kennedy once observed that "federalism was our Nation's own discovery. The Framers split the atom of sovereignty. It was the genius of their idea that our citizens would have two political capacities, one state and one federal, each protected from incursion by the other."[36] The promises and challenges of federalism in the

craftsmanship. The Kurds chose pro-autonomy leaders and opted for a constitution with strong regional control. The Shiites voted for religious parties and supported a decentralized republic along the lines of the early U.S. confederation. Many Sunnis who initially opted out of elections supported a strong central government, fearing that the Kurds and Shiites might marginalize them. In such a context, federalism is the best political tool to accommodate conflicting interests. Indeed, the Iraqi constitution provides the foundations for a loose federal system in which only fiscal and foreign affairs will be handled by the national government.

Three years after the approval of the Iraqi Constitution, the country is at a stalemate. The three-way divide among Shiites, Sunni Arabs, and Kurds turns a pluralistic democracy into an unsuitable device for reaching consensus. According to the Iraqi national security adviser, Mowaffak al-Rubaie, "[r]esolution can be achieved only through a system that incorporates regional federalism, with clear, mutually acceptable distributions of power be-tween the regions and the central government. Such a system is in the interest of all Iraqis and is necessary if Iraq is to avoid partition or further civil strife."

The challenge of democracy is to find that delicate balance ensuring enough regional autonomy to satisfy ethnic or religious solidarity but not so much autonomy as to splinter the entire enterprise. American views of democracy may complicate the situation. An Iraq that emulates America's free-style democracy may promote the seeds of its own destruction by giving every zealot a forum. But constraining Iraqi democracy by ruling some extreme viewpoints out of bounds may call into question one of the reasons America intervened in Iraq in the first place: to plant a viable democracy in the Middle East.

Sources: Edward Wong, "The World: New Wars in Iraq; Making Compromises to Keep a Country Whole," *New York Times,* 4 January 2004, sec. 4, p. 4; David Brooks, "Divided They Stand," *New York Times,* 25 August 2005; "Iraq's Constitution," *Wall Street Journal,* 15 October 2005, p. A5; Mowaffak al-Rubaie, "Federalism, Not Partition: A System Devolving Power to the Regions Is the Route to a Viable Iraq," *Washington Post,* 18 January 2008, p. A19.

twenty-first century face nations around the globe (see "Politics of Global Change: Federalism, Iraqi Style").

Federalism and Pluralism

Our federal system of government was designed to allay citizens' fears that they might be ruled by a majority in a distant region with whom they did not necessarily agree or share interests. By recognizing the legitimacy of the states as political divisions, the federal system also recognized the importance of diversity. The existence and cultivation of diverse interests are hallmarks of pluralism.

Both of the main competing theories of federalism support pluralism, but in somewhat different ways. The layer-cake approach of dual federalism aims to decentralize government, shifting power to the states. It recognizes the importance of local rather than national standards and applauds the diversity of those standards. The variety allows the people at least a choice of policies under which to live, if not a direct voice in policymaking.

In contrast, the marble cake of cooperative federalism is perfectly willing to override local standards for national ones depending on the issue at stake. Yet this view of federalism, while more amenable to national prerogatives, is highly responsive to all manner of pressures from groups and policy entrepreneurs, including pressure at one level of government from those unsuccessful at other levels. By blurring the lines of national and state responsibility, this kind of federalism encourages petitioners to try their luck at whichever level of government offers them the best chance of success.

Summary

The government framework outlined in the Constitution was the product of political compromise, an acknowledgment of the original thirteen states' fear of a powerful central government. The division of powers sketched in the Constitution was supposed to turn over "great and aggregate" matters to the national government, leaving "local and particular" concerns to the states. The Constitution does not explain, however, what is great and aggregate and what is local and particular.

Federalism comes in many varieties. Two stand out because they capture valuable differences between the original and modern visions of a federal government. Dual, or layer-cake, federalism wants to retain power in the states and keep the levels of government separate. Cooperative, or marble-cake, federalism em-phasizes the power of the national government and sees national and state governments working together to solve national problems. In its own way, each view supports the pluralist model of democracy.

One of the enduring features of American federalism has been the system's great ability to adapt to new circumstances. Several factors have produced changes in the nature of the system. National crises and demands from citizens frustrated with the responsiveness of state governments, judicial interpretations of the proper balance between states and the national government, changes in the system of grants in aid, and the professionalism of state governments have all contributed to changes in the American federalism.

Because the Constitution treats federalism in an ambiguous and sometimes seemingly contradictory way, it is difficult to pin clear ideo-

logical labels on particular theories of federalism. Although it is common to hear political pundits and politicians associate conservatism with dual federalism and liberalism with cooperative federalism, in practice these labels do not tend to correlate as well as casual glances would suggest. Rather, it is the combination of ideology and the specific policy context—how one prioritizes freedom, order, and equality—rather than ideology alone that drives conceptions of the proper national-state balance across several policy areas.

Although it is accurate to say that the national government's influence has grown significantly since the New Deal of the 1930s and the Great Society of the 1960s, it is also the case that citizens and elected officials alike have come to appreciate the intergovernmental nature of problems confronting the nation. Today

the answer to the question, "Which level of government is responsible?" is frequently, "All of them." Certainly there exists some separation between the national government and states; the flavors of the marble cake have not swirled together so much that they are indistinguishable. Still, given the mixed messages present in the Constitution and debates that date back to the country's founding over the proper role for the national government and the states, for better or for worse, it is likely that American federalism will remain in constant flux well into the future.

CL **Resources:** Videos, Simulations, News, Timelines, Primary Sources

Public Opinion, Political Socialization, and the Media

This icon will direct you to resources and activities on the website: www.cengage.com/polisci/janda/ chall_dem_brief/7e

FORMER IRAQI PRESIDENT
Saddam Hussein was hanged in Baghdad on December 29, 2006. His supporters in the Middle East took to the streets to protest his death. The United Nations special representative for Iraq, Ashraf Qazi, said that the United Nations could not support the execution. "Based on the principle of respect for the right to life, the United Nations remains opposed to capital punishment, even in the case of war crimes, crimes against humanity, and genocide."[1]

Mr. Qazi's reaction was shared by many government officials and citizens around the world. Almost all European and South American countries have abolished the death penalty. In many countries, including South Korea, the death penalty is legal but not practiced because of public concerns about the fairness of its use. More than two-thirds of the countries in the world have either totally abolished the death penalty or have not carried out any executions in the past ten years.[2]

However, there was also plenty of global support for the death penalty: capital punishment is still practiced in countries such as China, Pakistan, and Japan. It is legal in many countries in Africa and the Middle East, where hanging and firing squads are the most common methods of execution.[3] The use of capital punishment is relatively uncontroversial in the United States, where public opinion differs from that in Europe. Americans show consistently high support for the death penalty. In 2007, 69 percent of all respondents were in favor of the death penalty for murder, while only 27 percent were opposed.[4]

We can learn much about the role of public opinion in America by reviewing how our government has punished violent criminals. During most of American history, government execution

of people who threatened the social order was legal. In colonial times, capital punishment was imposed not just for murder but also for anti-social behavior—denying the "true" God, cursing one's parents, committing adultery, practicing witchcraft, even being a rebellious child.[5] Over the years, writers, editors, and clergy argued for abolishing the death sentence, and a few states responded by eliminating capital punishment. But the outbreak of World War I fed the public's fear of foreigners and radicals, leading to renewed support for the death penalty. The security needs of World War II and the postwar fears of Soviet communism fueled continued support for capital punishment.

After anticommunist hysteria subsided in the late 1950s, public opposition to the death penalty increased. But public opinion was neither strong enough nor stable enough to force state legislatures to outlaw it. In keeping with the pluralist model of democracy, efforts to abolish the death penalty shifted from the legislative arena to the courts. The opponents argued that the death penalty is cruel and unusual punishment and is therefore unconstitutional. Their argument apparently had some effect on public opinion: in 1966, a plurality of respondents opposed the death penalty for the first (and only) time since the Gallup Organization began polling the public on the question of capital punishment.

The states responded to this shift in public opinion by reducing the number of executions, until they stopped completely in 1968 in anticipation of a Supreme Court decision. By then, however, public opinion had again reversed in favor of capital punishment. Nevertheless, in 1972, the Court ruled in a 5–4 decision that the death penalty as imposed by existing state laws was unconstitutional.[6] The decision was not well received in many states, and thirty-five state legislatures passed new laws to get around the ruling. Meanwhile, as the nation's homicide rate increased, public approval of the death penalty jumped almost ten points and continued climbing.

In 1976, the Supreme Court changed its position and upheld three new state laws that let judges consider the defendant's record and the nature of the crime in deciding whether to impose a sentence of death.[7] The Court also rejected the argument that punishment by death violates the Constitution, and noted that public opinion favors the death penalty. Through the end of the 1970s, however, only three criminals were executed. Eventually the states began to heed public concern about the crime rate. Over one thousand executions have taken place since the 1976 Supreme Court ruling.[8]

Although public support for the death penalty remains high, Americans are divided on the issue. A majority of white Americans favor the death penalty for a person convicted of murder, while a majority of African Americans oppose the death penalty.[9] Conservatives are more likely to support the death penalty than liberals. Eighty-one percent of all Republicans favor the death penalty, whereas only 60 percent of all Democrats do. Many Americans are concerned that innocent persons have been executed.[10] Indeed, since 1973, over 125 death row inmates have been exonerated of their crimes by new evidence such as DNA testing.[11]

The use of the death penalty also varies by state. Fourteen states plus the District of Columbia do not have the death penalty. Of the thirty-six states that do, the vast majority of executions have taken place in Texas.[12] With more than three thousand inmates already on death row across the United States, the number of death sentences has been decreasing as the courts give more defendants life sentences without parole. Because nearly all executions in the United States are carried out by lethal injection, the Supreme Court put the death penalty on hold for seven months in 2007–2008 while it considered the constitutionality of that method. In April 2008 it ruled that lethal injection did not constitute cruel and unusual punishment. Two months later the Court established an important limitation: among crimes against individuals, only homicide could be punished by death. In ruling the death penalty unconstitutional for crimes against individuals in which no life was taken, the Supreme Court cited "evolving standards of decency" and a public consensus about the death penalty.[13]

The history of public thinking on the death penalty reveals several characteristics of public opinion:

1. *The public's attitudes toward a given government policy can vary over time, often dramatically.* Opinions about capital punishment tend to fluctuate with threats to the social order. The public is more likely to favor capital punishment in times of war and when fear of foreign subversion and crime rates are high.

2. *Public opinion places boundaries on allowable types of public policy.* Stoning or beheading criminals is not acceptable to the American public (and surely not to courts interpreting the Constitution). Until recently, administering a lethal injection to a murderer was not controversial.[14]

3. *If asked by pollsters, citizens are willing to register opinions on matters outside their expertise.* People clearly believe execution by lethal injection is more humane than electrocution, asphyxiation in the gas chamber, or hanging. But how can the public know enough about execution to make these judgments?

4. *Governments tend to respond to public opinion.* State laws for and against capital punishment have reflected swings in the public mood. The Supreme Court's 1972 decision against capital punishment came when public opinion on the death penalty was sharply divided; the Court's approval of capital punishment in 1976 coincided with a rise in public approval of the death penalty.

5. *The government sometimes does not do what the people want.* Although public opinion overwhelmingly favors the death penalty for murder, there were only forty-two executions in 2007 (but over sixteen thousand murders that year).[15]

INTERACTIVE 4.1

 1,000th Execution

The last two conclusions bear on our discussion of the majoritarian and pluralist models of democracy discussed in Chapter 1. Here we probe more deeply into the nature, shape, depth, and formation of public opinion in a democratic government. What is the place of public opinion in a democracy? How do people acquire their opinions? What are the major lines of division in public opinion? How do individuals' ideology and knowledge affect their opinions?

Public Opinion and the Models of Democracy

Public opinion is simply the collective attitudes of the citizens on a given issue or question. Opinion polling, which involves interviewing a sample of citizens to estimate public opinion as a whole, is such a common feature of contemporary life that we often forget it is a modern invention, dating only from the 1930s (see Figure 4.1). In fact, survey methodology did not develop into a powerful research tool until the advent of computers in the 1950s.

Before polling became an accepted part of the American scene, politicians, journalists, and everyone else could argue about what the people wanted, but no one really knew. Today, sampling methods and opinion

public opinion The collected attitudes of citizens concerning a given issue or question.

FIGURE 4.1   Gallup Poll Accuracy

One of the nation's oldest polls was started by George Gallup in the 1930s. The accuracy of the Gallup Poll in predicting presidential elections over nearly fifty years is charted here. Although it is not always on the mark, its predictions have been fairly close to election results. The poll was most notably wrong in 1948, when it predicted that Thomas Dewey, the Republican candidate, would defeat the Democratic incumbent, Harry Truman, underestimating Truman's vote by 5.4 percentage points. In 1992, the Gallup Poll was off by an even larger margin, but this time it did identify the winner, Bill Clinton.

Source: The Gallup Organization, www.gallup.com/poll/9442/Election-Polls-Accuracy-Record-Presidential-Elections.aspx.

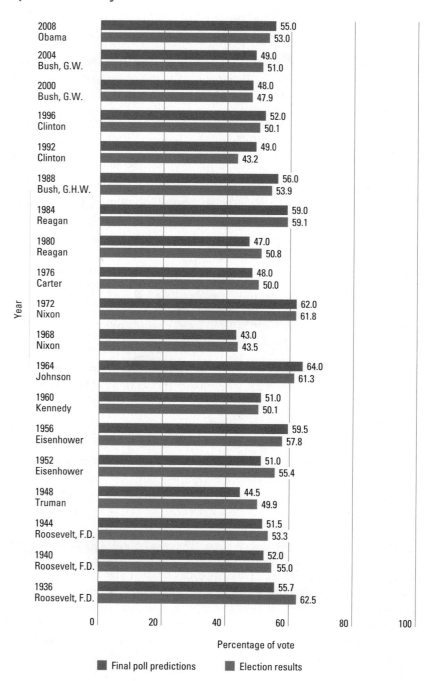

polling have altered the debate about the majoritarian and pluralist models of democracy. Now that we know how often government policy runs against majority opinion, it becomes harder to defend the U.S. government as democratic under the majoritarian model. Even at a time when Americans overwhelmingly favored the death penalty for murderers, the Supreme Court decided that existing state laws applying capital punishment were unconstitutional. Even after the Court approved new state laws as constitutional, relatively few murderers were actually executed.

The two models of democracy make different assumptions about public opinion. The majoritarian model assumes that a majority of the people hold clear, consistent opinions on government policy. The pluralist model assumes that the public is often uninformed and ambivalent about specific issues, and opinion polls frequently support that claim. What are the bases of public opinion? What principles, if any, do people use to organize their beliefs and attitudes about politics? Exactly how do individuals form their political opinions? We look for answers to these questions in this chapter. In later chapters, we assess the effect of public opinion on government policies. The results should help you make up your own mind about the viability of the majoritarian and pluralist models in a functioning democracy.

 ## Political Socialization

Public opinion is grounded in political values. People acquire their values through **political socialization**, a complex process through which individuals become aware of politics, learn political facts, and form political values. Think for a moment about your political socialization. What is your earliest memory of a president? When did you first learn about political parties? If you identify with a party, how did you decide to do so? If you do not, why don't you? Who was the first liberal you ever met? The first conservative? Obviously, the paths to political awareness, knowledge, and values differ among individuals, but most people are exposed to the same influences, or agents of socialization, especially in childhood through young adulthood. These influences are family, school, community, peers, and, of course, television.

Political socialization continues throughout life. As parental and school influences wane in adulthood, peer groups (neighbors, coworkers, club members) assume a greater importance in promoting political awareness and developing political opinions.[16] Because adults usually learn about political events from the mass media—newspapers, magazines, television, and radio—the media emerge as socialization agents. Older Americans are more likely to rely on newspaper and television news for political information, while younger Americans are more likely to turn to radio, magazines, or the Internet.[17]

Regardless of how people learn about politics, they gain perspective on government as they grow older. They are likely to measure new candidates

political socialization The complex process by which people acquire their political values.

(and new ideas) against the old ones they remember. Their values also may change. Finally, political learning comes simply through exposure and familiarity. One example is the act of voting, which people do with increasing regularity as they grow older.

 ## Social Groups and Political Values

No two people are influenced by precisely the same socialization agents in precisely the same way. Still, people with similar backgrounds do share learning experiences; this means they tend to develop similar political opinions. In this section, we examine the ties between people's social backgrounds and their political values. We do this by looking at responses to two questions posed by the 2004 National Election Study administered by the University of Michigan's Center for Political Studies.

The first question deals with abortion. The interviewer said, "There has been some discussion about abortion during recent years. Which opinion on this page best agrees with your view? You can just tell me the number of the opinion you choose":

1. "By law, abortion should never be permitted" [13 percent agreed].

2. "The law should permit abortion only in case of rape, incest, or when the woman's life is in danger" [32 percent].

3. "The law should permit abortion for reasons other than rape, incest, or danger to the woman's life, but only after the need for the abortion has been clearly established" [18 percent].

4. "By law, a woman should be able to obtain an abortion as a matter of personal choice" [37 percent].[18]

Those who chose the last category most clearly valued individual freedom over order imposed by government. Moreover, evidence shows that the pro-choice respondents also have concerns about broader issues of social order, such as the role of women and the legitimacy of alternative lifestyles.[19]

The second question pertained to the role of government in guaranteeing employment:

> Some people feel the government in Washington should see to it that every person has a job and a good standard of living. Suppose that these people are at one end of the scale. . . . Others think the government should just let each person get ahead on his own. Suppose these people are at the other end. . . . Where would you put yourself on this scale, or haven't you thought much about this?

Excluding those people who "haven't thought much" about this question, 34 percent of the respondents wanted government to provide every person with a living, and 19 percent were undecided. That left 47 percent who wanted the government to leave people alone to "get ahead" on their own. These respondents, who opposed government efforts to promote equality, apparently valued freedom over equality.

Overall, the responses to each of these questions were divided approximately equally. Over a third of the respondents (37 percent) felt that government should not set restrictions on abortion, and just short of a majority (47 percent) thought the government should not guarantee everyone a job and a good standard of living. However, sharp differences in attitudes emerged for both issues when the respondents were grouped by socioeconomic factors: education, income, region, race, religion, and sex. The differences are shown in Figure 4.2 as positive and negative deviations from the national averages for each question. Bars that extend to the right identify groups that are more likely than most Americans to sacrifice freedom for a given value of government, either equality or order. Next, we examine the opinion patterns more closely for each socioeconomic group.

Education

Education increases people's awareness and understanding of political issues. Higher education also promotes tolerance of unpopular opinions and behavior and invites citizens to see issues in terms of civil rights and liberties.[20] This result is clear in the left-hand column of Figure 4.2, which shows that people with more education are more likely to view abortion as a matter of a woman's choice.[21] College-educated individuals confronted with a choice between personal freedom and social order tend to choose freedom.

With regard to the role of government in reducing income inequality, the right-hand column in Figure 4.2 shows that people with more education also tend to favor freedom over equality. The higher their level of education is, the less likely respondents were to support government-guaranteed jobs and living standards.

Income

In many countries, differences in social class, based on social background and occupation, divide people in their politics.[22] In the United States, the vast majority of citizens regard themselves as "middle class." Yet as Figure 4.2 shows, wealth is consistently linked to opinions favoring a limited government role in promoting order and equality. Wealth and education have a similar impact on opinion: the groups with more education and higher income favor freedom.

Region

Early in our country's history, regional differences were politically important—important enough to spark a civil war between North and

FIGURE 4.2   Group Deviations from National Opinion on Two Questions

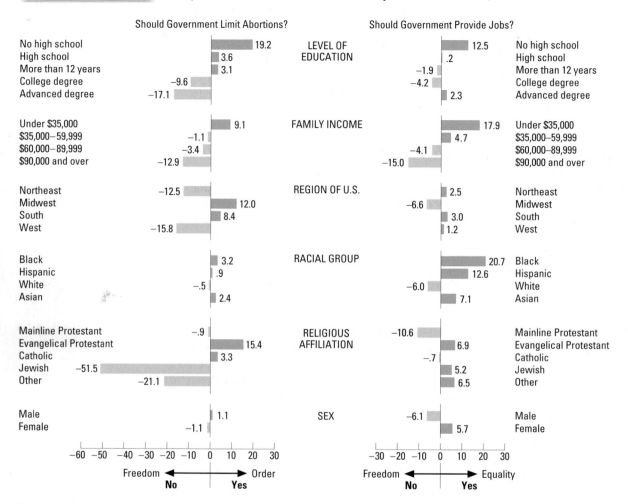

Two questions—one on abortion (representing the dilemma of freedom versus order) and the other on the government's role in guaranteeing employment (freedom versus equality)—were asked of a national sample in 2004. Public opinion for the nation as a whole was sharply divided on each question. These two graphs show how respondents in several social groups deviated from overall public opinion. The longer the bars are next to each group, the more its respondents deviated from the expression of opinion for the entire sample. Bars that extend to the left show group opinions that deviate toward freedom. Bars that extend to the right show deviations away from freedom, toward order or equality.

Source: Data from *2004 National Election Study,* Center for Political Studies, University of Michigan.

South. For nearly a hundred years after the Civil War, regional differences continued to affect American politics. The moneyed Northeast was thought to control the purse strings of capitalism. The Midwest was long regarded as the stronghold of isolationism in foreign affairs. The South was practically a one-party region, almost completely Democratic. And the individualistic West pioneered its own mixture of progressive politics.

In the past, differences in wealth fed cultural differences between regions. In recent decades, however, the movement of people and wealth away from the Northeast and Midwest to the Sunbelt states in the South and Southwest has equalized the per capita income of the regions. One product of this equalization is that the "solid South" is no longer solidly Democratic. In fact, the South has tended to vote for Republican candidates for president since 1968, and the majority of southern members of Congress are now Republicans.

Figure 4.2 shows greater differences among the four major regions of the United States on social issues than on economic issues. Respondents in the Northeast and West were more likely to support abortion rights than residents of the South and Midwest. People in the Midwest were somewhat less supportive of government efforts to equalize income than were people elsewhere.

Race and Ethnicity

In the early twentieth century, the major ethnic minority groups in America were immigrants from Ireland, Italy, Germany, Poland, and other European countries. They came to the United States in waves during the late 1800s and early 1900s and found themselves in a strange land, usually without money and unable to speak English. Moreover, their religious backgrounds, mainly Catholic and Jewish, differed from that of the predominantly Protestant earlier settlers. These urban ethnics and their descendants became part of the great coalition of Democratic voters that President Franklin Roosevelt forged in the 1930s. And for years after, the European ethnics supported liberal candidates and causes more strongly than the original Anglo-Saxon immigrants did.[23]

From the Civil War through the civil rights movement of the 1950s and 1960s, African Americans fought to secure basic political rights such as the right to vote. Initially mobilized by the Republican Party, the party of Lincoln, following the Civil War, African Americans later forged strong ties with the Democratic Party during the New Deal era. Today, African Americans are still more likely to support liberal candidates and identify with the Democratic Party. African Americans make up almost 13 percent of the population, with sizable voting blocs in southern states and northern cities.

Hispanics are the most rapidly growing racial or ethnic group in American society, slightly surpassing African Americans as the largest U.S. minority group according to the 2000 Census.[24] Hispanics are commonly but inaccurately regarded as a racial group, though they consist of both whites and non-whites. People of Latin American origin are often called Latinos. If they speak Spanish, they are also known as Hispanics. Hispanics (consisting of groups as different as Cubans, Mexicans, Peruvians, and Puerto Ricans) have lagged behind blacks in mobilizing and gaining political office. However, they make up approximately 15 percent of the nation's population and constitute over 35 percent of the population in California and Texas and 43 percent in New Mexico.[25]

Asians account for approximately 5 percent of the population, and Native Americans constitute just over 1 percent. Like other minority groups, their political impact is greatest in the cities or regions where they are concentrated and greater in number. Scholars are conducting more surveys of minority groups in order to have large enough numbers of respondents to make generalizations about racial and ethnic differences in public opinion and political values.[26]

We do know that blacks and members of other minorities display similar political attitudes on questions pertaining to equality. The reasons are twofold.[27] First, racial minorities (excepting second-generation Asians) tend to have low **socioeconomic status**, a combination of education, occupation, status, and income. Second, all racial minorities have been targets of racial prejudice and discrimination and have benefited from government actions in support of equality. The right-hand column in Figure 4.2 clearly shows the effects of race on the freedom-equality issue. All minority groups, particularly African Americans, are more likely than whites to favor government action to improve economic opportunity. The abortion issue produces less difference, although minority groups favor government restrictions on abortion slightly more than whites do.

Religion

Since the last major wave of European immigration in the 1930s and 1940s, the religious makeup of the United States has remained fairly stable. A recent study indicated that approximately 51 percent of the population is Protestant, about 24 percent is Catholic, 1.7 percent is Jewish, 6.5 reports some other faith, and about 16 percent denies any religious affiliation.[28] For many years, analysts found strong and consistent differences in the opinions of Protestants, Catholics, and Jews. Protestants were more conservative than Catholics, and Catholics tended to be more conservative than Jews.

As Figure 4.2 indicates, religiosity has little effect on attitudes about economic equality but has a powerful influence on attitudes about social order. Evangelicals (such as Baptists and Pentecostals) strongly favor government action to limit abortion. Jews overwhelmingly favor abortion rights. Differences among religious groups have emerged across many contemporary social and political issues. Evangelical Protestants are also more likely than members of other religious groups to oppose gay marriage and support the death penalty. Evangelicals and Jews are more likely to express

socioeconomic status Position in society, based on a combination of education, occupational status, and income.

support for Israel in Middle Eastern politics. Religious beliefs have been at the center of national and local debates over issues such as stem cell research, human cloning, and the teaching of evolution or intelligent design as the appropriate explanation for the development of life on Earth.[29]

Gender

Men and women differ with respect to their political opinions on a broad array of social and political issues. As shown in the right-hand column of Figure 4.2, women are more likely to favor government actions to promote equality. Women are also consistently more supportive than men of both affirmative action and government spending for social programs. They are consistently less supportive of the death penalty and going to war.[30] Men and women differ less on the abortion issue (see the left-hand column of Figure 4.2). Contemporary party politics is marked by a gender gap: women tend to identify with the Democratic Party more than men do (see Figure 6.2 on page 160). In the 2004 presidential election, 48 percent of the female voters supported Bush's reelection compared to 55 percent of the male voters.[31] A similar gender gap occurred in the 2008 presidential race. While 56 percent of all female voters cast ballots for Barack Obama, only 49 percent of the male voters did so. John McCain received support from 43 percent of the female voters and 48 percent of the male voters.

INTERACTIVE 4.2

 Stem Cell Research

From Values to Ideology

We have just seen that differences in groups' responses on two survey questions reflect those groups' value choices between freedom and order and between freedom and equality. But to what degree do people's opinions on specific issues reflect explicit political ideology (the set of values and beliefs that they hold about the purpose and scope of government)? Political scientists generally agree that ideology influences public opinion on specific issues; they have much less consensus on the extent to which people explicitly think in ideological terms.[32] They also agree that the public's ideological thinking cannot be categorized adequately in conventional liberal-conservative terms.[33]

The Degree of Ideological Thinking in Public Opinion

Although today's media frequently use the terms *liberal* and *conservative*, some people think these terms are no longer relevant to American politics. Political candidates often talk about bringing voters together rather than dividing them along partisan or ideological lines. Most voters don't tend to use ideological labels when discussing politics.[34]

In one poll, voters were asked what they thought when someone was described as "liberal" or "conservative."[35] Few responded in explicitly political terms. Rather, most people gave dictionary definitions: "'liberals' are generous (a *liberal* portion). And 'conservatives' are moderate or cautious (a *conservative* estimate)."[36] The two most frequent responses for *conservative* were "fiscally responsible or tight" (17 percent) and "closed-minded" (10 percent). For *liberal,* the top two were "open-minded" (14 percent) and "free-spending" (8 percent). Only about 6 percent of the sample mentioned "degree of government involvement" in describing liberals and conservatives. The tendency to respond to questions by using ideological terms grows with increasing education, which helps people understand political issues and relate them to one another. People's personal political socialization can also lead them to think ideologically.

The Quality of Ideological Thinking in Public Opinion

What people's ideological self-placement means in the early twenty-first century is not clear. At one time, the liberal-conservative continuum represented a single dimension: attitudes toward the scope of government activity. Liberals were in favor of more government action to provide public goods, and conservatives were in favor of less. The simple distinction is not as useful today. Many people who call themselves liberals no longer favor government activism in general, and many self-styled conservatives no longer oppose it in principle. As a result, many people have difficulty deciding whether they are liberal or conservative.

Studies of the public's ideological thinking find that two themes run through people's minds when they are asked to describe liberals and conservatives. First, people associate liberals with change and conservatives with tradition. This theme corresponds to the distinction between liberals and conservatives on the exercise of freedom and the maintenance of order.[37]

The other theme has to do with equality. The conflict between freedom and equality was at the heart of President Roosevelt's New Deal economic policies (social security, minimum wage legislation, farm price supports) in the 1930s. The policies expanded the interventionist role of the national government in order to promote greater economic equality, and attitudes toward government intervention in the economy served to distinguish liberals from conservatives for decades afterward.[38] Attitudes toward government interventionism still underlie opinions about domestic economic policies.[39] Liberals support intervention to promote their ideas of economic equality; conservatives favor less government intervention and more individual freedom in economic activities.

In Chapter 1, we proposed an alternative ideological classification based on people's relative evaluations of freedom, order, and equality. We described liberals as people who believe that government should promote equality, even if some freedom is lost in the process, but who oppose surrendering freedom to government-imposed order. Conservatives do not oppose equality in and of itself but put a higher value on freedom than on equality when the two conflict. Yet conservatives are not above restricting freedom when threatened with the loss of order. So both groups value freedom, but one is more willing to trade freedom for equality, and the other is more inclined to trade freedom for order. If you have trouble thinking about these tradeoffs on a single dimension, you are in good company. The liberal-conservative continuum presented to survey respondents takes a two-dimensional concept and squeezes it into a one-dimensional format.[40]

IDEAlog.com

How did you answer the questions about abortion and government-guaranteed employment on the self-test?

Ideological Types in the United States

Our ideological typology in Chapter 1 (see Figure 1.2 on page 19) classifies people as liberals if they favor freedom over order and equality over freedom. Conversely, conservatives favor freedom over equality and order over freedom. Libertarians favor freedom over both equality and order—the opposite of communitarians. By cross-tabulating people's answers to the two questions from the 2004 National Election Study about freedom versus order (abortion) and freedom versus equality (government job guarantees), we can classify respondents according to their ideological tendencies. As shown in Figure 4.3, a substantial portion of respondents falls within each of the quadrants. This finding indicates that people do not decide about government activity according to a one-dimensional ideological standard. Figure 4.3 also classifies the sample according to the two dimensions in our ideological typology. (Remember, however, that these categories—like the

FIGURE 4.3   **Respondents Classified by Ideological Tendencies**

In the 2004 election survey, respondents were asked whether abortion should be a matter of personal choice or regulated by the government, and whether government should guarantee people a job and a good standard of living or people should get ahead on their own. (The questions are given verbatim at the beginning of the "Social Groups and Political Values" section of this chapter.) These two questions presented choices between freedom and order and between freedom and equality. People's responses to the two questions showed no correlation, demonstrating that these value choices cannot be explained by a simple liberal-conservative continuum. Instead, their responses can be more usefully analyzed according to four different ideological types.

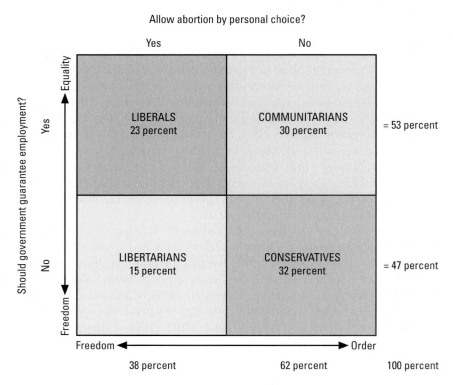

Source: 2004 National Election Study, Center for Political Studies, University of Michigan.

letter grades A, B, C, and D for courses—are rigid. The respondents' answers to both questions varied in intensity but were reduced to a simple yes or no to simplify this analysis. Many respondents would cluster toward the center of Figure 4.3 if their attitudes were represented more sensitively.) The conservative response pattern was the most common, followed by the communitarian pattern. The sample suggests that more than three-quarters of the electorate favor government action to promote order or increase equality, or both.

The ideological tendencies illustrate important differences among different social groups. Communitarians are prominent among minorities and among people with little education and low income, groups that tend to look favorably on the benefits of government in general. Libertarians are concentrated among people with more education and with higher income, who tend to be suspicious of government interference in their lives. People in the southern states tend to be communitarians, those in the Midwest tend to be conservatives, and those in the Northeast are inclined to be liberals. Men are more likely to be conservative or libertarian than women, who tend to be liberal or communitarian.[41]

This more refined analysis of political ideology explains why even Americans who pay close attention to politics find it difficult to locate themselves on the liberal-conservative continuum. Their problem is that they are liberal on some issues and conservative on others. Forced to choose along just one dimension, they opt for the middle category: moderate. However, our analysis also indicates that many people who classify themselves as liberals or conservatives do fit these two categories in our typology. There is value, then, in the liberal-conservative distinction, as long as we understand its limitations.

 # Forming Political Opinions

We have seen that people acquire political values through socialization and that different social groups develop different sets of political values. We also have learned that some people, but only a minority, think about politics ideologically, holding a consistent set of political attitudes and beliefs. But how do those who are not ideologues—in other words, most citizens—form political opinions? How informed are people about politics? What can we say about the quality of public opinion?

Political Knowledge

In the United States today, the level of education is high and media coverage of national and international events is extensive, yet the average American displays an astonishing lack of political knowledge.[42]

In a study of political knowledge, political scientists Delli Carpini and Keeter analyzed approximately thirty-seven hundred individual survey items that measured some type of factual knowledge about public affairs.[43] They found that "many of the basic institutions and procedures of government are known to half or more of the public, as are the relative positions of the parties on many major issues."[44] Yet, political knowledge is not randomly distributed within our society. "In particular, women, African Americans, the poor, and the young tend to be substantially less knowledgeable about politics than are men, whites, the affluent, and older citizens."[45] Changing news formats in the past twenty years—the emergence of around the clock cable news and the Internet—do not seem to have increased the level of political knowledge for most Americans.[46] Education is the strongest single predictor of political knowledge.

Researchers have not found any meaningful relationship between political sophistication and self-placement on the liberal-conservative scale—that is, people with equal knowledge about public affairs and levels of conceptualization are as likely to call themselves liberals as conservatives.[47]

Equal levels of political understanding, then, may produce quite different political views as a result of individuals' unique patterns of political socialization. However, individuals who strongly believe in certain causes may be impervious to information that questions their beliefs; they may even create false memories that support their beliefs.[48]

Costs, Benefits, and Cues

Perhaps people do not think in ideological terms or know a wide variety of political facts, but they can tell whether a policy is likely to directly help or hurt them. The **self-interest principle** states that people choose what benefits them personally.[49] The principle plays an obvious role in how people form opinions on policies with clear costs and benefits. Taxpayers tend to prefer low taxes to high taxes. Smokers tend to oppose bans on smoking in public places. Some people evaluate incumbent presidents according to whether they are better or worse off than they were four years ago. Group leaders often cue group members, telling them what they should support or oppose.[50]

In some cases, individuals are unable to determine personal costs or benefits. This tends to be true of foreign policy. Here, many people have no opinion, or their opinions are not firmly held and are likely to change quite easily given almost any new information. For example, public approval of the war in Iraq and of former president George W. Bush's handling of the war varied with positive news such as Iraqi elections and negative news such as the number of military casualties.

Public opinion that is not based on a complicated ideology may also emerge from the skillful use of cues. Individuals may use heuristics—mental shortcuts that require hardly any information—to make fairly reliable political judgments.[51] For instance, citizens can use political party labels to compensate for low levels of information about the policy positions of candidates.[52] Similarly, citizens take cues from trusted government officials and interest groups regarding the wisdom of bills pending in Congress or the ideology of Supreme Court nominees.

Political Leadership

Public opinion on specific issues is molded by political leaders, journalists, and policy experts. Politicians serve as cue givers to members of the public. Citizens with favorable views of a politician may be more likely to support his or her values and policy agenda. In one study, 49 percent of respondents were uncomfortable with the statement, "I have never believed the Constitution required our schools to be religion free zones," when it was presented anonymously; only 34 percent claimed to be uncomfortable when the statement was attributed to former president Bill Clinton.[53] In a different study, African Americans were presented with a statement about the need for blacks to rely more on themselves to get ahead in society; respondents agreed with the statement when it was attributed to black political figures (Jesse

self-interest principle The implication that people choose what benefits them personally.

Compared with What?

Exploring Our Image Around the World

Compared with citizens from other countries around the world, Americans have a very favorable view of the United States. In 2007, the Pew Research Center asked citizens around the world if they had a favorable or unfavorable view of the United States. The results for twenty-five countries are listed below. The image of the United States is most favorable in Sub-Saharan Africa, Israel, Japan, and India. Negative views of the United States prevail in the Muslim world as well as European countries such as France and Germany. Although many respondents voiced negative views of the United States when asked this general question, majorities in nearly all countries expressed admiration for U.S. science and technology. In most parts of the world, respondents also said that they liked U.S. music, movies, and television.

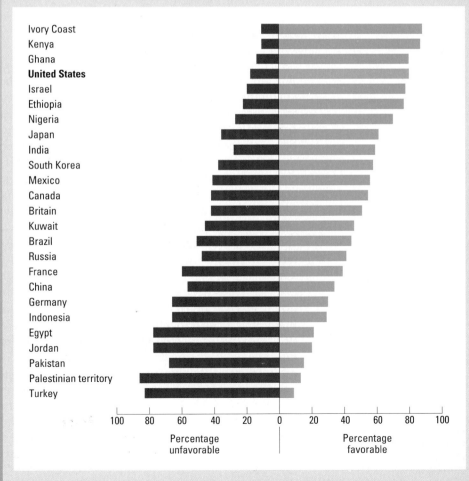

Source: Pew Global Attitudes Project, "Global Unease with Major World Powers," 27 June 2007, http://pewglobal.org/reports/display.php?ReportID=256.

Jackson and Clarence Thomas) and disagreed when the statement was attributed to white political figures (George Bush and Ted Kennedy).[54]

Politicians routinely make appeals to the public on the basis of shared political ideology and self-interest. Competition and controversy among political elites provide the public with a great deal of information. But politicians are well aware that citizen understanding of and support for an issue depend on how issues are framed. They compete to provide a story line or idea that suggests the essence of political events and policy issues.[55]

The ability of political leaders to affect public opinion has been enhanced enormously by the growth of the broadcast media, especially television.[56] The majoritarian model of democracy assumes that government officials respond to public opinion. But the evidence is substantial that this causal sequence is reversed—that public opinion responds instead to the actions of government officials.[57] If this is true, how much potential is there for public opinion to be manipulated by political leaders through the mass media?

The Media in America

"We never talk anymore" is a common lament of couples who are not getting along very well. In politics, too, citizens and their government need to communicate in order to get along well. *Communication* is the process of transmitting information from one individual or group to another. *Mass communication* is the process by which information is transmitted to large, heterogeneous, widely dispersed audiences. The term **mass media** refers to the means for communicating to these audiences. The mass media are commonly divided into two types. *Print media* (newspapers, magazines) communicate information through the publication of written words and pictures. *Broadcast media* (radio, television) communicate information electronically through sounds and images. The worldwide network of personal computers, commonly called the Internet, can also be classified as broadcast technology, and the Internet has grown in size so that it also qualifies as a mass media.

Our focus here is on the role of the media in promoting communication from government to its citizens and from citizens to their government. In totalitarian governments, information flows more freely in one direction (from government to people) than in the other. In democratic governments, information must flow freely in both directions; a democratic government can respond to public opinion only if its citizens can make their opinions known. Moreover, the electorate can hold government officials accountable for their actions only if voters know what their government has done, is doing, and plans to do. Because the mass media (and increasingly the group media) provide the major channels for this two-way flow of information, they have the dual capability of reflecting and shaping our political views.

mass media The means employed in mass communication, often divided into print media and broadcast media.

The media are not the only means of communication between citizens and government. Agents of socialization (especially schools) function as "linkage mechanisms" that promote such communication. In the next three chapters, we discuss other major mechanisms for communication: voting, political parties and election campaigns, and interest groups.

The Internet

Alongside the four most traditional forms of mass media—newspapers, magazines, radio, and television—the Internet has rapidly grown into an important conduit for political information. What we today call the Internet began in 1969 when, with support from the U.S. Defense Department's Advanced Research Projects Agency, computers at four universities were linked to form ARPANET. In its early years, the Internet was used mainly to transmit e-mail among researchers. In 1991, a group of European physicists devised a standardized system for encoding and transmitting a wide range of materials, including graphics and photographs, over the Internet, and the World Wide Web (WWW) was born. In January 1993 there were only fifty websites.[58] Today there are over 100 million sites and over a billion Web users.[59] The Internet was soon incorporated into politics, and today virtually every government agency and political organization has a website.

The Internet has also created a new venue for traditional print media outlets to offer their wares. On the Web, local publications such as the *Topeka Capital Journal* are no more difficult to access than national newspapers such as the *New York Times*. What television networks such as ABC and CNN offer in national and international news exists alongside the local coverage of individual stations such as Baltimore's WJZ, and Americans are logging in for news from all these outlets.

More than 70 percent of Americans use the Internet, and most of them are under the age of sixty-five.[60] Internet users tend to be well educated and concentrated in large cities and suburbs. Those individuals who rely on the Internet as their main source of news tend to be very critical of traditional news media; they are much more likely to say that news organizations are politically biased.[61]

Private citizens operate their own websites on politics and public affairs, daily posting their political thoughts and critical comments. These blogs (short for weblogs) have had dramatic effects on news reporting. In 2004, conservative "bloggers" exposed flaws in a *CBS Evening News* broadcast that questioned whether George W. Bush had served as claimed in the Texas Air National Guard. The blogs criticizing the network's reporting were publicized in the established media. Subsequently, Dan Rather, the anchorman at CBS with the longest tenure in network news, was forced to depart, short of completing twenty-five years in the chair. In early 2005, Eason Jordan, the chief news executive at CNN, resigned after bloggers assailed him for suggesting in a speech in Switzerland that the U.S. military deliberately targeted and killed journalists.[62]

Private Ownership of the Media

In the United States, people take private ownership of the media for granted. In other Western democratic countries, the print media (both newspapers and magazines) are privately owned, but the broadcast media often are not. Private ownership of both print and broadcast media gives the news industry in America more political freedom than any other in the world, but it also makes the media more dependent on advertising revenues. To make a profit, the news operations of the mass media in America must appeal to the audiences they serve. The primary criterion of a story's **newsworthiness** is usually its audience appeal, which is judged according to its potential impact on readers or listeners, its degree of sensationalism (exemplified by violence, conflict, disaster, or scandal), its treatment of familiar people or life situations, its close-to-home character, and its timeliness.[63]

Media owners can make more money by either increasing their audiences or acquiring additional publications or stations. A decided trend toward concentrated ownership of the media increases the risk that a few major owners could control the news flow to promote their own political interests. In fact, the number of *independent newspapers* has declined as newspaper chains (owners of two or more newspapers in different cities) have acquired more newspapers. Only about four hundred dailies are still independent, and many of these papers are too small and unprofitable to invite acquisition.

As with newspapers, chains sometimes own television stations in different cities, and ownership sometimes extends across different media. None of the three original television networks remains an independent corporation: the Walt Disney Company owns ABC, General Electric owns NBC, and, until 2006, Viacom owned CBS (along with Paramount Pictures, MTV, Comedy Central, and other entertainment companies). To improve its market value for stockholders, Viacom split off CBS into a new corporation including cable networks (Showtime), publishing (Simon & Schuster), radio (Infinity Broadcasting), outdoor advertising, and television (CBS, the CW, and TV stations).[64] The Fox Network is owned by Rupert Murdoch's News Corporation, which also controls 20th Century Fox movie studios, Fox News, the FX cable channel, MySpace, publisher HarperCollins, and the well-known *Wall Street Journal* newspaper.[65]

Government Regulation of the Media

Although most of the mass media in the United States are privately owned, they do not operate free of government regulation. The broadcast media, however, are subject to more regulations than the print media.

The Federal Communications Act of 1934 created the **Federal Communications Commission (FCC)** to regulate the broadcast and telephone industries. The FCC has five members (no more than three from the same political party) nominated by the president for terms of five years. The commissioners can be removed from office only through impeachment and conviction.

newsworthiness The degree to which a news story is important enough to be covered in the mass media.

Federal Communications Commission (FCC) An independent federal agency that regulates interstate and international communication by radio, television, telephone, telegraph, cable, and satellite.

CHANGE
WE CAN BELIEVE IN
Iowa.BarackObama.com

The Oprah Factor
Oprah Winfrey is the host of the highest-rated talk show in television history. *The Oprah Winfrey Show* boasts an audience of 46 million viewers a week in the United States, and it airs in 134 countries around the world. A magazine editor, film producer, actress, and philanthropist, Oprah Winfrey is one of the most widely known and admired women around the world. During the 2008 election cycle, Oprah endorsed Democrat Barack Obama in his bid for the presidency. The Federal Communication Commission does not require that talk show hosts provide equal airtime for all candidates. And any promotion of political candidates on Winfrey's show does not count as a campaign contribution. *(Scott Olson/Getty Images)*

Consequently, the FCC is considered an independent regulatory commission: it is insulated from political control by the president or Congress. (We discuss independent regulatory commissions in Chapter 10.) Today, the FCC's charge includes regulating interstate and international communications by radio, television, telephone, telegraph, cable, and satellite.

For six decades—as technological change made television commonplace and brought the invention of computers, fax machines, and satellite transmissions—the communications industry was regulated under the basic framework of the 1934 law that created the FCC. Then, pressured by businesses that wanted to exploit new electronic technologies, Congress, in a bipartisan effort, swept away most existing regulations in the Telecommunications Act of 1996.

The 1996 law relaxed or scrapped limitations on media ownership. For example, broadcasters were previously limited to owning only twelve TV stations and forty radio stations. Now there are no limits on the number of TV stations one company may own, as long as its coverage does not extend beyond 35 percent of the market nationwide. The 1996 law set no national limits for radio ownership and relaxed local limits. In addition, it lifted rate regulations for cable systems, allowed cross-ownership of cable and telephone companies, and allowed local and long-distance telephone companies to compete with one another and to sell television services. Although even those who wrote the law could not predict its long-range effect, the law quickly spurred a series of media group megamergers and expanded ownership of local stations by the networks.

The First Amendment to the Constitution prohibits Congress from abridging the freedom of the press. Over time, *the press* has come to mean all the mass media, and the courts have decided many cases that define how far freedom of the press extends under the law. The most important of these cases are often quite complex. Usually the courts strike down government attempts to restrain the press from publishing or broadcasting the information, reports, or opinions it finds newsworthy. One notable exception concerns strategic information during wartime; the courts have supported censorship of information such as the sailing schedules of troop ships or the planned movements of troops in battle. Otherwise, they have recognized a strong constitutional case against press censorship.

Because the broadcast media are licensed to use the public airwaves, they are subject to additional regulation, beyond that applied to the print media, of the content of their news coverage. The basis for the FCC's regulation of content lies in its charge to ensure that radio and television stations "serve the public interest, convenience, and necessity." With its **equal opportunities rule,** the FCC requires any broadcast station that gives or sells time to a candidate for public office to make an equal amount of time available under the same conditions to all other candidates for that office. The **reasonable access rule** requires that commercial stations make their facilities available for the expression of conflicting views or issues from all responsible elements in the community. Two related rules were struck down by a U.S. court of appeals in 2000. The *political editorial rule* required stations that endorsed a candidate to provide free reply time to political opponents. The *personal attack rule* required stations to provide free response time to candidates and others whose integrity was attacked on the air. Opponents of these rules had long charged that they stifled debate by discouraging broadcasters from adopting editorial positions.[66]

 ## Reporting and Following the News

In this section we discuss how the media cover political affairs, and we examine where citizens acquire their political knowledge. We also look at what people learn from the media, and we probe the media's effects on public opinion, the political agenda, and political socialization.

Covering National Politics

Washington, D.C., has by far the biggest press corps of any city in the world—nearly 7,000 congressionally accredited reporters: 2,000 from newspapers, 1,800 from periodicals, 2,500 from radio and television, and over 300 photographers.[67] Only a small portion of these reporters is admitted to fill the fifty seats in the White House press briefing room. As recently as the Truman administration, reporters enjoyed informal personal relationships with the president. Today, the media's relationship with the president is mediated primarily through the Office of the Press Secretary.

White House correspondents rely heavily on information they receive from the president's staff, each piece carefully crafted in an attempt to

equal opportunities rule Under the Federal Communications Act of 1934, the requirement that if a broadcast station gives or sells time to a candidate for any public office, it must make available an equal amount of time under the same conditions to all other candidates for that office.

reasonable access rule An FCC rule that requires broadcast stations to make their facilities available for the expression of conflicting views or issues by all responsible elements in the community.

control the news report. The most frequent form is the news release, a prepared text distributed to reporters in the hope that they will use it verbatim. A daily news briefing enables reporters to question the press secretary about news releases. A news conference provides an opportunity to question high-level officials in the executive branch—including the president on occasion. News conferences appear to be freewheeling, but officials tend to rehearse precise answers to anticipated questions.

Occasionally, information is given "on background," which means that reporters can use the information but cannot identify the source except in a vague reference such as "a senior official says." Information that is disclosed "off the record" cannot be printed. Journalists who violate these well-known conditions risk losing their welcome at the White House.

Reporters occasionally benefit from leaks of information released by officials who are guaranteed anonymity. The best-known example was a source known as "Deep Throat" during the Watergate scandal. Deep Throat provided *Washington Post* reporter Bob Woodward critical information linking the Nixon White House to crimes committed during the 1972 campaign and the subsequent cover-up. Facing impeachment, President Nixon ultimately chose to resign. Despite rampant speculation, Deep Throat's identity was kept secret for over thirty years, until he and his family revealed that he was W. Mark Felt, the number two man at the FBI during Watergate. Officials may leak news to interfere with others' political plans or to float ideas ("trial balloons") past the public and other political leaders to gauge their reactions. Sometimes a carefully placed leak turns into a gusher of media coverage through the practice of "pack journalism"—the tendency of journalists to adopt similar viewpoints toward the news simply because they hang around together, exchanging information and defining the day's news with one another.

Most news about Congress comes from innumerable press releases issued by its 535 members and from an unending supply of congressional reports, but reporters also learn about Congress from other media sources such as C-SPAN (the Cable Satellite Public Affairs Network).

Presenting the News

Media executives, news editors, and prominent reporters function as **gatekeepers** in directing the news flow: they decide which events to report and how to handle the elements in those stories. Only a few individuals—no more than twenty-five at the average newspaper or news magazine and fifty at each of the major television networks—qualify as gatekeepers, defining the news for public consumption.[68] They not only select what topics go through the gate but also are expected to uphold standards of careful reporting and principled journalism. In contrast to the print and broadcast media, the Internet has no gatekeepers and thus no constraints on its content. While it is a powerful research tool with the ability to deliver information quickly, it can spread factual errors and rumors as well.

INTERACTIVE 4.3

CIA Leak Investigation

INTERACTIVE 4.4

Who's Who in the Watergate Scandal

gatekeepers Media executives, news editors, and prominent reporters who decide which events to report and which elements in those stories to emphasize.

The established media cannot communicate everything about public affairs. There is neither space in newspapers or magazines nor time on television or radio to do so. Time limitations impose especially severe constraints on television news broadcasting. Each half-hour network news program devotes only about twenty minutes to the news (the rest of the time is taken up by commercials), and there is even less news on local television.

During elections, personification encourages **horse race journalism,** in which media coverage becomes a matter of "who's ahead in the polls, who's raising the most money, who's got TV ads and who's getting endorsed." U.S. television presents elections as contests between individuals rather than as confrontations between representatives of opposing parties and platforms. Studies of network news coverage of recent presidential campaigns have shown that more stories are shown covering the horse race than policy issues.[69] The public's reaction to this coverage is mixed. Over three quarters of Americans say that they want more coverage of candidates' positions on the issues; almost half would also like less coverage of who is leading in the polls.[70]

Where the Public Gets Its News

Until the early 1960s, most people reported getting more political news from newspapers than from any other source. Television nudged out newspapers as the public's major source of news in the early 1960s. Today, 70 percent of Americans name television or cable news networks as their primary source for news.[71] Eleven percent cite newspapers as their primary news source. A little over 9 percent of Americans claim that the Internet is their primary source of news. Over half of the public consults multiple sources of news during the day—perhaps reading the paper at breakfast, checking the Internet at work, and ending the day watching television news.[72] On average, Americans spend a little over an hour a day getting the news from one or multiple sources. Older Americans spend more time watching, reading, or listening to news; people under the age of thirty spend less.[73]

More and more Americans are getting news online. The top online news sites include Yahoo! News, MSNBC, and CNN. Each of these websites is viewed by roughly 25 million people per month.[74] Internet users are also visiting the online versions of print newspapers such as the *New York Times* and *USA Today.* Fewer Americans mention blogs or online news and opinion magazines such as Slate.com and Salon.com, although these are more popular with young people. Internet users of all age groups report receiving news stories in e-mails from friends.

horse race journalism Election coverage by the mass media that focuses on which candidate is ahead rather than on national issues.

What People Remember and Know

If, as surveys indicate, 80 percent of the public reads or hears the news each day, how much political information do these people absorb? By all accounts, not much. In a 2007 survey of new media usage, only 69 percent of the respondents could name the vice president (Richard Cheney), only 49 percent could identify Nancy Pelosi as the Speaker of the House, and only 29 knew that Robert Gates was the secretary of defense—at a time when the debate over the ongoing war in Iraq dominated daily political news.[75]

Numerous studies have found that those who rely on television for their news score lower on tests of knowledge about public affairs than those who rely on print media.[76] Among media researchers, this finding has led to the **television hypothesis**—the belief that television is to blame for the low level of citizens' knowledge about public affairs.[77] We know that television tends to squeeze public policy issues into one-minute or, at most, two-minute fragments, which makes it difficult to explain candidates' positions.

Television also tends to cast abstract issues in personal terms to generate the visual content that the medium needs.[78] However, other research has questioned the hypothesis and found that "television was more successful in communicating information about topics that were of low salience [significance] to the audience, while print media were superior in conveying information about topics that had high salience."[79] Regardless of how well newspapers convey information, readership is declining.

Influencing Public Opinion

Americans overwhelmingly believe that the media exert a strong influence on their political institutions, and almost nine out of ten Americans believe that the media strongly influence public opinion.[80] However, measuring the extent of media influence on public opinion is difficult.[81] Because few of us learn about political events except through the media, it could be argued that the media create public opinion simply by reporting events. Consider the dismantling of the Berlin Wall in 1989. Surely the photographs of joyous Berliners demolishing that symbol of oppression affected American public opinion about the reunification of Germany.

The media can have dramatic effects on particular events. Soon after the scandal involving President Clinton's relationship with Monica Lewinsky broke in January 1998, he gave the State of the Union address before Congress and a television audience of 50 million. Clinton focused on his accomplishments (a robust economy, record low unemployment and inflation, and a virtually balanced budget) and on his proposals for child care, education, and health care. To counter his image as a philandering male, he positioned himself as an able president. And his strategy paid off, according to a poll of viewers: only 33 percent had been "very confident" in his ability to carry out his duties prior to watching the address, but 48 percent were very confident afterward.[82] The February Gallup Poll found that 70 percent of the public approved of Clinton's job performance, the highest rating of his presidency.

Documenting general effects of media on opinions about general issues in the news is difficult. Doris Graber, a leading scholar on the media, reported several studies that carefully documented media influence. For

television hypothesis The belief that television is to blame for the low level of citizens' knowledge about public affairs.

example, more pretrial publicity for serious criminal cases leads to full trials rather than settlement through plea-bargaining; media attention to more obscure foreign policy issues tends to force them on the policy agenda.[83] Also, television network coverage of the returns on the night of the 2000 presidential election may have profoundly affected public opinion toward both major candidates. In a report commissioned by cable news network CNN, three journalism experts concluded that the networks' unanimous declarations of George W. Bush's victory that night "created a premature impression" that he had defeated Al Gore before the Florida outcome had been decided. The impression carried through the postelection challenge: "Gore was perceived as the challenger and labeled a 'sore loser' for trying to steal the election."[84]

Setting the Political Agenda

Despite the media's potential for influencing public opinion, most scholars believe that the media's greatest impact on politics is found in their power to set the **political agenda**—a list of issues that people identify as needing government attention. Those who set the political agenda define which issues government decision makers should discuss and debate.

The mass media in the United States have traditionally played an important role in defining the political agenda. Television, which brings pictures and sound into almost every home, has enormous potential for setting the political agenda. A careful study designed to isolate and examine television's effects on public opinion concluded, "By attending to some problems and ignoring others, television news shapes the American public's political priorities."[85] Indeed, the further removed a viewer is from public affairs, "the stronger the agenda-setting power of television news."[86]

One study found varying correlations between media coverage and what the public sees as "the most important problem facing this country today," depending on the type of event. Public opinion was especially responsive to media coverage of recurring problems such as inflation and unemployment.[87] The media's ability to influence public opinion by defining "the news" makes politicians eager to influence media coverage. Politicians attempt to affect not only public opinion but also the opinions of other political leaders.[88]

The president receives a daily digest of news and opinion from many sources. In a curious sense, the mass media have become a network for communicating among attentive elites, all trying to influence one another or to assess others' weaknesses and strengths. If the White House is under pressure on some policy matter, it might supply a representative to appear for fifteen minutes of intense questioning on *Meet the Press* or the *NewsHour with Jim Lehrer*. The White House's goal would be to influence the thinking of other insiders (who faithfully watch these programs) as much as to influence opinions among the relatively few news sophisticates in the public who watch these particular programs.

political agenda A list of issues that need government attention.

Socializing the Citizenry

The mass media act as important agents of political socialization.[89] Young people who rarely follow the news by choice nevertheless acquire political values through the entertainment function of the broadcast media. Years ago, children learned from radio programs; now they learn from television. What children learned from radio was quite different from what they are learning now, however. In the golden days of radio, youngsters listening to popular radio dramas heard repeatedly that "crime does not pay." The message never varied: criminals are bad; the police are good; criminals get caught and are severely punished for their crimes.

Television today does not portray the criminal justice system in the same way, even in police dramas. Consider programs such as *24* and *In Justice,* which have portrayed police and FBI agents as lawbreakers. Other series, such as *Law and Order, Prison Break,* and *The Shield,* sometimes portray a tainted criminal justice system and institutionalized corruption.[90] Certainly one cannot easily argue that television's entertainment programs help prepare law-abiding citizens.

So the media play contradictory roles in the process of political socialization. On the one hand, they promote popular support for government by joining in the celebration of national holidays, heroes' birthdays, political anniversaries, and civic accomplishments. On the other hand, the media erode public confidence by publicizing citizens' grievances, airing investigative reports of agency malfeasance, and even showing dramas about crooked cops.[91]

 Evaluating the Media in Government

Are the media fair or biased in reporting the news? What contributions do they make to democratic government? What effects do they have on freedom, order, and equality?

Is Reporting Biased?

News reports are presented as objective reality, yet critics of modern journalism contend that news is filtered through the ideological biases of the owners and editors (the gatekeepers) and of the reporters themselves. Even citizens tend to be skeptical of the news. Democrats and Republicans show distinct differences in which media organizations they find most credible (see Figure 4.4). The argument that news is politically biased has two sides. On the one hand, news reporters are criticized in best-selling books for tilting their stories in a liberal direction, promoting social equality and undercutting social order.[92] On the other hand, wealthy and conservative media owners are suspected—in other best-selling books—of preserving inequalities and reinforcing the existing order by serving a relentless round of entertainment that numbs the public's capacity for critical analysis.[93]

FIGURE 4.4 Partisanship and the Credibility of the News

Respondents were asked to rate broadcast and print media according to whether the respondent believes "all or most" or "nothing" of what the organization says. The table lists the results broken down by partisan identification. In general, Republicans are more skeptical of the media than Democrats. Republicans rate the Fox News channel and the *Wall Street Journal* most highly, while Democrats favor the *NewsHour with Jim Lehrer,* CNN, and National Public Radio.

Source: "Section 5: Media Credibility," In *Online Papers Modestly Boost Newspaper Readership,* Pew Center for the People and the Press, 30 July 2006, http://people-press.org.

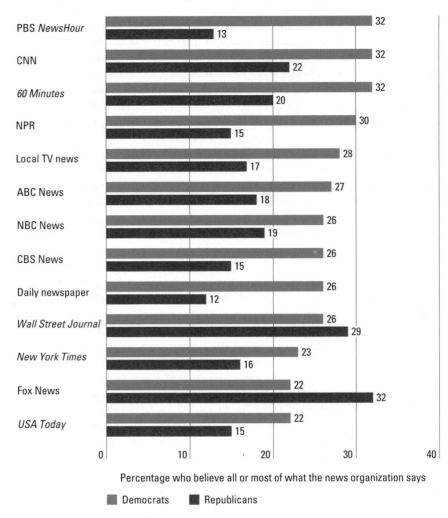

Percentage who believe all or most of what the news organization says

■ Democrats ■ Republicans

Although the picture is far from clear, available evidence seems to confirm the charge of liberal leanings among reporters in the major news media. In a 2004 survey of 547 journalists, 34 percent considered themselves "liberal," compared with only 7 percent who said they were "conservative."[94] Content analysis of the tone of ABC, CBS, and NBC network coverage of presidential campaigns from 1988 to 2004 concluded that Democratic candidates received much more "good press" than Republicans in every election but 1988, when the Republican candidate benefited from better press.[95] However, one medium—talk radio—is dominated by conservative views.

To some extent, working journalists in the national and local media are at odds with their own editors, who tend to be more conservative.[96] The editors, in their function as gatekeepers, tend to tone down reporters' liberal leanings by editing their stories or not placing them well in the medium. Newspaper publishers are also free to endorse candidates, and almost all daily newspapers once openly endorsed one of the two major party candidates for president (usually the Republican candidate). A survey of newspaper endorsements in the 2000 presidential election showed that newspapers with large circulations were much more likely to endorse a candidate than smaller newspapers. Newspapers that did endorse a candidate favored Republican George W. Bush more than two to one, although Democrat Al Gore was backed almost as often as Bush in newspapers with the largest circulations.[97]

In the 2004 presidential election, the trade journal *Editor and Publisher* counted 213 newspaper endorsements for John Kerry compared with 205 for George W. Bush.[98] There was significant variation in support for candidates among newspaper chains. One survey of papers found Knight-Ridder to be the most pro-Kerry chain, with 18 of its papers endorsing him and only 2 endorsing Bush. On the other end of the spectrum, the same study found 16 MediaNews Group papers endorsing Bush, with only 2 in the Kerry corner. Gannett, sometimes thought of as a Republican-leaning chain, gave the nod to Kerry in 26 of its papers and to Bush in 19.[99]

Without question, incumbents—as opposed to challengers—enjoy much more news coverage simply from holding office and issuing official statements. The less prominent that the office is, the greater is the advantage from such free news coverage. Noncampaign news coverage leads to greater incumbent name recognition at election time, particularly for members of Congress (see Chapter 8). This coverage effect is independent of any bias in reporting on campaigns. For more prominent offices such as the presidency, however, a different news dynamic may come into play. When a powerful incumbent runs for reelection, journalists may feel a special responsibility to counteract his or her advantage by putting the opposite partisan spin on the news.[100] Thus, whether the media coverage of campaigns is seen as pro-Democratic (and therefore liberal) or pro-Republican (and therefore conservative) depends on which party is in office at the time.

A study of newspaper stories written in the last weeks of the 2000 presidential campaign showed that both major party candidates received negative coverage. Fifty-six percent of the stories written about the Democratic heir apparent, Al Gore, were negative. George W. Bush received negative coverage in 51 percent of the stories.[101]

Contributions to Democracy

In a democracy, communication must move in two directions: from government to citizens and from citizens to government. In fact, political communication in the United States seldom goes directly from government to citizens without passing through the media. The point is important because news reporters tend to be highly critical of politicians; they consider it their job to search for inaccuracies in fact and weaknesses in argument—practicing **watchdog journalism**.[102] Some observers have characterized the news media and the government as adversaries—each mistrusting the other, locked in competition for popular favor while trying to get the record straight. To the extent that this is true, the media serve both the majoritarian and the pluralist models of democracy well by improving the quality of information transmitted to the people about their government.[103]

The mass media transmit information in the opposite direction by reporting citizens' reactions to political events and government actions. The press has traditionally reflected public opinion (and often created it) while defining the news and suggesting courses of government action. But the media's role in reflecting public opinion has become much more refined in the information age. After commercial polls (such as the Gallup and Roper polls) were established in the 1930s, newspapers began to report reliable readings of public opinion. By the 1970s, some news organizations acquired their own survey research divisions. Occasionally print and electronic media have joined forces to conduct major national surveys. For example, the well-respected New York Times/CBS News Poll conducts surveys that are first aired on the *CBS Evening News* and then analyzed at length in the *Times*.

Although polls sometimes create opinions just by asking questions, their net effect has been to generate more accurate knowledge of public opinion and to report that knowledge back to the public. Although widespread knowledge of public opinion does not guarantee government responsiveness to popular demands, such knowledge is necessary if government is to function according to the majoritarian model of democracy.

Effects on Freedom, Order, and Equality

The media in the United States have played an important role in advancing equality, especially racial equality. Throughout the civil rights movement of the 1950s and 1960s, the media gave national coverage to conflict in the South, as black children tried to attend white schools and civil rights workers were beaten and even killed in the effort to register black voters. Partly because of this media coverage, civil rights moved up on the political agenda, and coalitions were formed in Congress to pass new laws promoting racial equality. Women's rights have also been advanced by the media, which have reported instances of blatant sexual discrimination exposed by groups working for sexual equality. In general, the mass media offer spokespersons for any disadvantaged group an opportunity to state their case before a national audience and to work for a place on the political agenda.

Although the media are willing to encourage government action to promote equality at the cost of some personal freedom, they resist government attempts to infringe on freedom of the press to promote order.[104]

watchdog journalism
Journalism that scrutinizes public and business institutions and publicizes perceived misconduct.

While the public tends to support a free press in theory, public support is not universal and wavers in practice. Asked whether it is more important "that the government be able to censor news stories it feels threaten national security OR that the news media be able to report stories they feel are in the national interest," about one-third of the respondents in a 2006 national survey favored government censorship.[105]

The media's ability to report whatever they wish, whenever they wish, certainly erodes efforts to maintain order. For example, sensational media coverage of terrorist acts gives terrorists the publicity they seek; portrayal of brutal killings and rapes on television encourages copycat crimes, committed "as seen on TV." Freedom of the press is a noble value and has been important to democratic government. But we should not ignore the fact that democracies sometimes pay a price for pursuing it without qualification.

Summary

Public opinion does not rule in America. On most issues, it merely sets general boundaries for government policy. People form their values through the process of political socialization. The most important socialization agents in childhood and young adulthood are family, school, community, and peers. Members of the same social group tend to experience similar socialization processes and thus to adopt similar values. People in different social groups that hold different values often express vastly different opinions. Differences in education, race, and religion tend to produce sharp divisions of opinion today on questions of order and equality.

Most people do not think about politics in ideological terms. When asked to do so by pollsters, however, they readily classify themselves along a liberal-conservative continuum. Many respondents choose the middle category, moderate, because the choice is safe. Others choose it because they have liberal views on some issues and conservative views on others. Their political orientation is better captured by a two-dimensional framework that analyzes ideology according to the values of order and equality. Responses to the survey questions we used to establish our ideological typology divide the American electorate as liberals, conservatives, libertarians, and communitarians. The one-fifth of the public that gave liberal responses—favoring government action to promote equality but not to impose order—was exceeded by the one-third of the public that gave conservative responses to promote order. At about 30 percent of the public, the communitarians, who wanted government to impose both order and equality, clearly exceeded the libertarians, who wanted government to do neither.

In addition to ideological orientation, many other factors influence the forming of political opinions. When individuals stand to benefit or suffer from proposed government policies, they usually base their opinions of these policies on self-interest. When citizens lack information on which to base their opinions, they usually respond anyway, which leads to substantial fluctuations in poll results, depending on how questions are worded and on intervening events.

Sometimes the public shows clear and settled opinions on government policy, conforming to the majoritarian model. However, public opinion is often not firmly grounded in knowledge and may be unstable on given issues. Moreover, powerful groups often divide on what they want government to do. This lack of consensus leaves politicians with a great deal of latitude in enacting specific policies, a finding that conforms to the pluralist model. Of course, politicians' actions are under close scrutiny by journalists reporting in the mass media.

The mass media transmit information to large, heterogeneous, and widely dispersed audiences through print and broadcasts. The main function of the mass media is entertainment, but the media also perform the political functions of reporting news, interpreting news, influencing citizens' opinions, setting the political agenda, and socializing citizens about politics. The broadcast media operate under technical, ownership, and content regulations imposed by the government, which tend to promote the equal treatment of political contests on radio and television more than in newspapers and news magazines.

Washington, D.C., hosts the biggest press corps in the world, but only a portion of those correspondents concentrate on the presidency. Because Congress is a more decentralized institution, it is covered in a more decentralized manner. All professional journalists recognize rules for citing sources that guide their reporting. What actually gets reported in the media depends on the media's gatekeepers, the publishers and editors.

Although Americans today get more news from television than from newspapers, newspapers usually do a more thorough job of informing the public about politics. Despite heavy exposure to news in the print and electronic media, the ability of most people to retain much political information is shockingly low. The media's most important effect on public opinion is in setting the country's political agenda. The role of the news media may be more important for affecting interactions among attentive policy elites than in influencing public opinion. The media play more subtle, contradictory roles in political socialization, both promoting and undermining certain political and cultural values. Reporters from the national media tend to be more liberal than the public, as judged by their tendency to vote for Democratic candidates and by their own self-descriptions. However, if the media systematically demonstrate pronounced bias in their news reporting, it tends to work against incumbents and front-runners, regardless of their party, rather than a bias in favor of liberal Democrats.

From the standpoint of majoritarian democracy, one of the most important effects of the media is to facilitate communication from the people to the government through the reporting of public opinion polls. The media zealously defend the freedom of the press, even to the point of encouraging disorder by granting extensive publicity to violent protests, terrorist acts, and other threats to order.

CL **Resources:** Videos, Simulations, News, Timelines, Primary Sources

Participation and Voting

CHAPTER 5

- Democracy and Political Participation
- Unconventional Participation
- Conventional Participation
- Participating Through Voting
- Explaining Political Participation
- Participation and Freedom, Equality, and Order
- Participation and the Models of Democracy

This icon will direct you to resources and activities on the website: www.cengage.com/polisci/janda/chall_dem_brief/7e

MR. PAR PAR LAY, A COMEDIAN IN
Myanmar (formerly known as Burma), had a favorite joke: A Burmese man goes to India to have his toothache treated. The Indian dentist wonders why he came all the way to India. "Don't you have a dentist in Myanmar?" he asks. "Oh, yes we do," says his patient. "But in Myanmar, we are not allowed to open our mouths."[1] Unfortunately for Mr. Par Par Lay, the military government of Myanmar did not think it was funny. He and other comedians began to disappear.

In the autumn of 2007, the military regime also suppressed a pro-democracy movement led by Buddhist monks. There are almost 500,000 Buddhist monks in Myanmar, and they are the most highly respected members of Burmese society.[2] They usually have little contact with the secular world, except for emerging in the morning with begging bowls, to ask for food. Families are proud to donate rice, food, and clothing to the monks.

But as the military government continued to repress political dissenters and the economy worsened, the monks took to the streets.[3] For several days, thousands of monks paraded through the capital city of Yangon to protest against the government. They were joined and protected by supporters, who walked alongside them

Though foreign journalists were forbidden in the country, information flowed out through photos, videos, and audio files on the Internet. Other nations issued statements of support for the monks and harsh condemnations of the military regime's continued suppression of human rights. The United States imposed an economic boycott and financial sanctions against prominent members of the military government.[4]

In the end, at least thirty people were killed and hundreds detained by the government. The monks returned to their monasteries. But the political actions of the monks and ordinary citizens in Myanmar sent a message to the Burmese government and the international community about their desire for a better life. Around the world, ordinary citizens take action—marching, voting, writing letters, boycotting products—in an effort to make their governments responsive to their needs and ideals.

Although most people in the United States think of political participation primarily in terms of voting, many other forms of political activity lie within the bounds of democracy. How politically active are Americans in general? How do they compare with citizens of other countries? How much and what kind of participation is necessary to sustain the pluralist and majoritarian models of democracy?

In this chapter, we seek to answer these and other important questions about popular participation in government. We begin by studying participation in democratic government, distinguishing between conventional and unconventional participation. Then we evaluate the nature and extent of both types of participation in American politics. Next, we study the expansion of voting rights and voting as the major mechanism for mass participation in politics. Finally, we examine the extent to which the various forms of political participation serve the values of freedom, equality, and order and the majoritarian and pluralist models of democracy.

Democracy and Political Participation

Government ought to be run by the people. That is the democratic ideal in a nutshell. But how much and what kind of citizen participation are necessary for democratic government? Champions of direct democracy believe that if citizens do not participate directly in government affairs, making government decisions among themselves, they should give up all pretense of living in a democracy. More practical observers contend that people can govern indirectly through their elected representatives. And they maintain that choosing leaders through elections—formal procedures for voting—is the only workable approach to democracy in a large, complex nation.

Elections are a necessary condition of democracy, but they do not guarantee democratic government. Before the collapse of communism, the former Soviet Union regularly held elections in which more than 90 percent of the electorate turned out to vote, but it certainly did not function as a democracy, because there was only one party. Both the majoritarian and the pluralist models of democracy rely on voting to varying degrees, but both models expect citizens to participate in politics in other ways. For example, they expect citizens to discuss politics, form interest groups, contact public officials, campaign for political parties, run for office, and even protest government decisions.

We define **political participation** as "those actions of citizens that attempt to influence the structure of government, the selection of government officials, or the policies of government or to support government and politics."[5] This definition embraces both conventional and unconventional forms of political participation. **Conventional participation** is relatively routine behavior that uses the established institutions of representative government, especially campaigning for candidates and voting in elections. **Unconventional participation** is relatively uncommon behavior that challenges or defies established institutions or the dominant culture (and thus is personally stressful to participants and their opponents).

Voting, displaying a campaign poster in the front yard, and writing letters to public officials are examples of conventional political participation; staging sit-down strikes in public buildings, spray-painting political slogans on walls, and chanting slogans outside officials' windows are examples of unconventional participation. Political demonstrations can be conventional (carrying signs outside an abortion clinic) or unconventional (linking arms to prevent entrance to the clinic). Terrorism is an extreme case of unconventional political behavior. Indeed, the U.S. legal code defines **terrorism** as "premeditated, politically motivated violence perpetrated

political participation Actions of private citizens by which they seek to influence or support government and politics.

conventional participation Relatively routine political behavior that uses institutional channels and is acceptable to the dominant culture.

unconventional participation Relatively uncommon political behavior that challenges or defies established institutions and dominant norms.

terrorism Premeditated, politically motivated violence perpetrated against noncombatant targets by subnational groups or clandestine agents.

against noncombatant targets by subnational groups or clandestine agents, usually intended to influence an audience."[6] Timothy McVeigh, a decorated veteran of the 1991 Gulf War, chose to bomb the federal building in Oklahoma City in 1995 because it would provide good camera coverage. Executed in 2001 for taking 168 lives, McVeigh said he bombed the building because the national government had become a police state hostile to gun owners, religious sects, and patriotic militia groups.[7]

Unconventional methods of participation figure in popular politics as disadvantaged groups resort to them in lieu of more conventional forms of participation used by most citizens. Let us look at both kinds of political participation in the United States.

INTERACTIVE 5.1

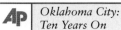 *Oklahoma City: Ten Years On*

 ## Unconventional Participation

On Sunday, March 7, 1965, a group of about six hundred people set out to march fifty miles from Selma, Alabama, to the state capital at Montgomery. The marchers were demonstrating in favor of voting rights for blacks. At the time, Selma had fewer than five hundred registered black voters, out of fifteen thousand who were eligible.[8] Alabama governor George Wallace declared the march illegal and sent state troopers to stop it. The two groups met at the Edmund Pettus Bridge over the Alabama River at the edge of Selma. The peaceful marchers were disrupted and beaten by state troopers and deputy sheriffs—some on horseback—using clubs, bullwhips, and tear gas. The day became known as Bloody Sunday.

The march from Selma was a form of unconventional political participation. Marching fifty miles in a political protest is certainly not common; moreover, the march challenged the existing institutions that prevented blacks from participating conventionally—voting in elections—for many decades. In contrast to some later demonstrations against the Vietnam War, this 1965 civil rights march posed no threat of violence. The brutal response to the marchers helped the rest of the nation understand the seriousness of the civil rights problem in the South. Unconventional participation is stressful and occasionally violent, but sometimes it is worth the risk.

Support for Unconventional Participation

Unconventional political participation has a long history in the United States. The Boston Tea Party of 1773 was the first in a long line of violent protests against British rule that eventually led to revolution. Yet we know less about unconventional political participation than about conventional participation. The reasons are twofold. First, it is easier to collect data on conventional practices, so they are studied more frequently. Second, political scientists are biased toward institutionalized, or conventional, politics. In fact, some basic works on political participation explicitly exclude any behavior that is "outside the system."[9]

INTERACTIVE 5.2

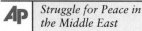 *Struggle for Peace in the Middle East*

What Motivates a Suicide Bomber?

In her farewell video, a twenty-two-year-old Palestinian woman and mother of two pledged to use her body as shrapnel to kill Israelis. In mid-January 2004, Reem al-Riyashi carried out a suicide bombing, killing three Israeli soldiers and a security guard and wounding nine others. Her husband and other family members said they were unaware of her plans. In her video, she professed her love for her daughter, age one, and son, age three, and said, "I am convinced that God will help and take care of my children." Reem al-Riyashi is only one of many worldwide who have sacrificed themselves for political causes in recent years. *(Handout/Reuters New Media Inc./Corbis)*

One major study of unconventional political action asked people whether they had engaged in or approved of ten types of political participation outside of voting.[10] Of these activities, signing petitions was clearly regarded as conventional, in the sense that the behavior was widely practiced. Most people claimed that they would never join a strike or occupy a building in protest. In fact, when political activities interfere with people's daily lives (occupying buildings, for example), disapproval is nearly universal. Most Americans would allow public meetings for religious extremists but not for people who want to "overthrow the government."[11] Many do not think it is important for a democracy to allow acts of civil disobedience (see Figure 5.1). When protesters demonstrating against the Vietnam War disrupted the 1968 Democratic National Convention in Chicago, they were clubbed by the city's police. Although the national television audience saw graphic footage of the confrontations, most viewers condemned the demonstrators, not the police.

The Effectiveness of Unconventional Participation

Vociferous antiabortion protests discourage many doctors from performing abortions but have not led to the outlawing of abortion. Does unconventional participation ever work (even when it provokes violence)? Yes. Antiwar protesters helped convince President Lyndon Johnson not to seek reelection in 1968, and they heightened public concern over U.S. participation in the Vietnam War. The unconventional activities of civil rights workers also

FIGURE 5.1 How Americans Rate the Importance of Participation in a Democracy

A survey asked Americans about the importance of people's rights in a democracy. Respondents thought that it is very important that a democratic government respect the rights of minorities and treat everybody equally. Large majorities also claimed a democratic government should take the views of citizens into account and give the people opportunities to participate in public decision making. However, most Americans do not believe that civil disobedience is the route to ensure that the government achieves these goals: over 40 percent did not think it was important for a democracy to allow acts of civil disobedience when citizens oppose the government's actions.

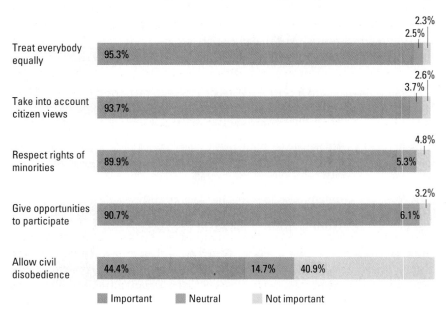

Source: International Social Survey Programme (ISSP) 2004: Citizenship Survey, available at www.zacat.gesis.org.

produced notable successes. Dr. Martin Luther King Jr. led the 1955 Montgomery bus boycott that sparked the civil rights movement. He used **direct action** to challenge specific cases of discrimination, assembling crowds to confront businesses and local governments and demanding equal treatment in public accommodations and government.

Denied the usual opportunities for conventional political participation, members of minorities used unconventional politics to pressure Congress to pass a series of civil rights laws in 1957, 1960, 1964, and 1968—each one in some way extending federal protection against discrimination by reason of race, color, religion, or national origin. The 1964 act also prohibited discrimination in employment on the basis of sex. In addition, the Voting Rights Act of 1965 put state electoral procedures under federal supervision, increasing the registration of black voters and the rate of black voter turnout (especially in the South). The civil rights movement shows that social change can occur, even when it is violently opposed at first.

Although direct political action and the politics of confrontation can work, using them takes a special kind of commitment. Studies show that

direct action Unconventional participation that involves assembling crowds to confront businesses and local governments to demand a hearing.

direct action appeals most to those who both (1) distrust the political system and (2) have a strong sense of political efficacy—the feeling that they can do something to affect political decisions.[12] Whether this combination of attitudes produces behavior that challenges the system depends on the extent of organized group activity.[13] The decision to use unconventional behavior also depends on the extent to which individuals develop group consciousness—identification with their group and awareness of its position in society, its objectives, and its intended course of action.[14] These characteristics were present among blacks and young people in the mid-1960s and are strongly present today among blacks and, to a lesser degree, women.

Unconventional Participation in America and the World

Although most Americans may disapprove of using certain forms of participation to protest government policies, U.S. citizens are just as likely as citizens of other countries to express interest in politics and donate money or raise funds for political causes. Two-thirds of Americans report having signed a petition. Almost 40 percent have boycotted certain products, and U.S. citizens are almost as likely to take direct action in politics as citizens in European democracies. Compared with citizens in other nations, Americans are not markedly apathetic.[15]

Is something wrong with a political system if citizens resort to unconventional—and widely disapproved of—methods of political participation? To answer this question, we must first learn how much citizens use conventional methods of participation.

DO IT!

Look for grassroots action in your area at http://grassroots.wikia.com/wiki/Main_Page.

 ## Conventional Participation

A practical test of the democratic nature of any government is whether citizens can affect its policies by acting through its institutions: meeting with public officials, supporting candidates, voting in elections. Citizens should not have to risk their life and property to participate in politics, and they should not have to take direct action to force the government to hear their views. The objective of democratic institutions is to make political participation conventional—to allow ordinary citizens to engage in relatively routine, nonthreatening behavior to get the government to heed their opinions, interests, and needs.

In a democracy, a group gathering at a statehouse or city hall to dramatize its position on an issue—say, a tax increase—is not unusual. Such a demonstration is a form of conventional participation. The group is not powerless, and its members are not risking their personal safety. But violence can erupt between opposing groups. Circumstances, then, often determine whether organized protest is or is not conventional. Conventional political behaviors fall into two major categories: actions that show support for government policies and those that try to change or influence policies.

Supportive Behavior

Supportive behaviors are actions that express allegiance to country and government. When we recite the Pledge of Allegiance or fly the American flag on holidays, we are showing support for the country and, by implication, its political system. Such ceremonial activities usually demand little initiative by citizens. The simple act of turning out to vote is in itself a show of support for the political system. Other supportive behaviors, such as serving as an election judge in a nonpartisan election or organizing a holiday parade, demand greater initiative.

At times, perceptions of patriotism move people across the line from conventional to unconventional behavior. In their eagerness to support the American system, they break up a meeting or disrupt a rally of a group they believe is radical or somehow "un-American." Radical groups may threaten the political system with wrenching change, but superpatriots pose their own threat. Their misguided excess of allegiance denies nonviolent means of dissent to others.[16]

Influencing Behavior

Citizens use **influencing behaviors** to modify or even reverse government policy to serve political interests. Some forms of influencing behavior seek particular benefits from government; other forms have broad policy objectives.

Particular Benefits.   Some citizens try to influence government to obtain benefits for themselves, their immediate families, or their close friends. Serving one's self-interest through the voting process is certainly acceptable in democratic theory. Each individual has only one vote, and no single voter can wangle particular benefits from government through voting unless a majority of the voters agree.

Political actions that require considerable knowledge and initiative are another story. Individuals or small groups that influence government officials to advance their self-interest may secretly benefit without others knowing. Those who quietly obtain particular benefits from government pose a serious challenge to a democracy. Pluralist theory holds that groups ought to be able to make government respond to their special problems and needs. Majoritarian theory holds that government should not do what a majority does not want it to do. A majority of citizens might very well not want the government to do what any particular person or group seeks if it is costly to other citizens.

Citizens often ask for special services from their local government. Such requests may range from contacting the city forestry department to remove a dead tree in front of a house to calling the county animal control

supportive behavior Actions that express allegiance to government and country.

influencing behavior Behavior that seeks to modify or reverse government policy to serve political interests.

center to deal with a vicious dog in the neighborhood. Studies of such "contacting" behavior find that it tends not to be empirically related to other forms of political activity. Contacting behavior is related to socioeconomic status: people of higher socioeconomic status are more likely to contact public officials.[17]

Americans demand much more of their local government than of the national government. Although many people value self-reliance and individualism in national politics, most people expect local government to solve a wide range of social problems. A study of residents of Kansas City, Missouri, found that more than 90 percent thought it was the city's responsibility to provide services in thirteen areas, including maintaining parks, setting standards for new home construction, demolishing vacant and unsafe buildings, ensuring that property owners clean up trash and weeds, and providing bus service. The researcher noted that "it is difficult to imagine a set of federal government activities about which there would [be] more consensus."[18]

Citizens can also mobilize against a project. Dubbed the "not-in-my-back-yard," or NIMBY, phenomenon, some citizens pressure local officials to stop undesired projects from being located near their homes. Contributing money to a candidate's campaign is another form of influencing behavior. Here too the objective can be particular or broad benefits.

Several points emerge from this review of "particularized" forms of political participation. First, approaching government to serve one's particular interests is consistent with democratic theory, because it encourages input from an active citizenry. Second, particularized contact may be a form of participation unto itself, not necessarily related to other forms of participation. Third, such participation tends to be used more by citizens who are advantaged in knowledge and resources. Fourth, particularized participation may serve private interests to the detriment of the majority.

Broad Policy Objectives.   We come now to what many scholars have in mind when they talk about political participation: activities that influence the selection of government personnel and policies. Here too we find behaviors that require little initiative (such as voting) and behaviors that require high initiative (attending political meetings, persuading others how to vote). Later in this chapter, we focus on elections as a mechanism for participation. For now, we simply note that voting to influence policy is usually a low-initiative activity. It actually requires more initiative to register to vote in the United States than to cast a vote on election day.

Other types of participation to affect broad policies require high initiative. Running for office requires the most (see Chapter 6). Some high-initiative activities, such as attending party meetings and working in campaigns, are associated with the electoral process; others, such as attending legislative hearings and writing letters to Congress, are not. Studies of citizen contacts in the United States show that about two-thirds deal with broad social issues and only one-third are for private gain.[19]

Few people realize that using the court system is a form of political participation, a way for citizens to press for their rights in a democratic society. Although most people use the courts to serve their particular interests, some also use them, as we discuss shortly, to meet broad objectives. Going to court demands high personal initiative.[20] It also requires knowledge of the law or the financial resources to afford a lawyer.

People use the courts for both personal benefit and broad policy objectives. A person or group can bring **class-action suits** on behalf of other people in similar circumstances. Lawyers for the National Association for the Advancement of Colored People pioneered this form of litigation in the famous school desegregation case, *Brown* v. *Board of Education* (1954).[21] They succeeded in getting the Supreme Court to outlaw segregation in public schools, not just for Linda Brown, one of the children on whose behalf the lawsuit was brought in Topeka, Kansas, but for all others "similarly situated"—that is, for all other black students who wanted to attend desegregated schools. This form of participation has proved to be effective for organized groups, especially those who have been unable to gain their objectives through Congress or the executive branch.

Individual citizens can also try to influence policies at the national level by direct participation in the legislative process. One way is to attend congressional hearings, which are open to the public and occasionally held outside Washington. To facilitate citizen involvement, national government agencies are required to publish all proposed and approved regulations in the daily *Federal Register* and to make government documents available to citizens on request.

Conventional Participation in America and the World

How often do Americans contact government officials and engage in other forms of conventional political participation compared with citizens in other countries? The most common political behavior in most industrial democracies is voting for candidates. In the United States, however, voting for candidates is less common than it is in other countries. When voting turnout in the United States over more than half a century was compared with historical patterns of voting in twenty-three other democratic countries, the United States ranked at the *bottom* of the pack. This is a political paradox: Americans are as likely as citizens in other countries to engage in many forms of political participation, but when it comes to voting, Americans rank dead last.[22]

Other researchers have noted this paradox and written: "If, for example, we concentrate our attention on national elections we will find that the United States is the least participatory of [all] five nations." But looking at the other indicators, they found that "political apathy, by a wide margin, is lowest in the United States. Interestingly, the high levels of overall involvement reflect a rather balanced contribution of both . . . conventional

class-action suit A legal action brought by a person or group on behalf of a number of people in similar circumstances.

and unconventional politics."[23] Clearly, low voter turnout in the United States constitutes a puzzle, to which we will return.

 ## Participating Through Voting

The heart of democratic government lies in the electoral process. Whether a country holds elections—and if so, what kind—constitutes the critical difference between democratic and nondemocratic government. Elections institutionalize mass participation in democratic government according to the three normative principles of procedural democracy discussed in Chapter 1: electoral rules specify *who* is allowed to vote, *how much* each person's vote counts, and *how many* votes are needed to win.

Again, elections are formal procedures for making group decisions. *Voting* is the act individuals engage in when they choose among alternatives in an election. **Suffrage** and the **franchise** both mean the right to vote. By formalizing political participation through rules for suffrage and for counting ballots, electoral systems allow large numbers of people, who individually have little political power, to wield great power. Electoral systems decide collectively who governs and, in some instances, what government should do. The simple fact of holding elections is less important than the specific rules and circumstances that govern voting. According to democratic theory, everyone should be able to vote. In practice, however, no nation grants universal suffrage. All countries have age requirements for voting, and all disqualify some inhabitants on various grounds: lack of citizenship, criminal record, mental incompetence, and so forth. What is the record of enfranchisement in the United States?

Expansion of Suffrage

The United States was the first country to provide for general elections of representatives through mass suffrage, but the franchise was far from universal. When the Constitution was framed, the idea of full adult suffrage was too radical to consider seriously. Instead, the framers left the issue of enfranchisement to the states, stipulating only that individuals who could vote for "the most numerous Branch of the State Legislature" could also vote for their representatives to the U.S. Congress (Article I, Section 2).

Initially, most states established taxpaying or property-holding requirements for voting. Virginia, for example, required ownership of twenty-five acres of settled land or five hundred acres of unsettled land. The original thirteen states began to lift such requirements after 1800. Expansion of the franchise accelerated after 1815 with the admission of new "western" states (Indiana, Illinois, Alabama), where land was more plentiful and widely owned. By the 1850s, the states had eliminated nearly all taxpaying and property-holding requirements, thus allowing the working class—at least

suffrage The right to vote. Also called the *franchise*.

franchise The right to vote. Also called *suffrage*.

its white male members—to vote. Extending the vote to blacks and women took more time.

The Enfranchisement of Blacks.

The Fifteenth Amendment, adopted shortly after the Civil War, prohibited the states from denying the right to vote "on account of race, color, or previous condition of servitude." But the states of the old Confederacy worked around the amendment, reestablishing old voting requirements (poll taxes, literacy tests) that worked primarily against blacks. Because the amendment said nothing about voting rights in private organizations, some southern states denied blacks the right to vote in the "private" Democratic primary elections held to choose the party's candidates for the general election. Because the Democratic Party came to dominate politics in the South, the "white primary" effectively disenfranchised blacks despite the Fifteenth Amendment. Also, in many areas of the South, the threat of violence kept blacks from the polls.

The extension of full voting rights to blacks came in two phases, separated by twenty years. In 1944, the Supreme Court decided in *Smith* v. *Allwright* that laws preventing blacks from voting in primary elections were unconstitutional, holding that party primaries are part of the continuous process of electing public officials.[24] The Voting Rights Act of 1965, which followed Selma's Bloody Sunday by less than five months, suspended discriminatory voting tests. It also authorized federal registrars to register voters in seven southern states, where less than half of the voting-age population had registered to vote in the 1964 election. For good measure, in 1966 the Supreme Court ruled in *Harper* v. *Virginia State Board of Elections* that state poll taxes are unconstitutional.[25] Although long in coming, these actions by the national government to enforce political equality within the states dramatically increased the registration of southern blacks (see Figure 5.2).

The Enfranchisement of Women.

Women also had to fight long and hard to win the right to vote. Until 1869, women could not vote anywhere in the world.[26] Women began to organize to obtain suffrage in the mid-1800s. Known then as *suffragettes,* the early feminists initially had a limited effect on politics. Their first major victory did not come until 1869, when Wyoming, while still a territory, granted women the right to vote. No state followed suit until 1893, when Colorado enfranchised women.

Between 1896 and 1918, twelve other states gave women the vote. Most of these states were in the West, where pioneer women often departed from traditional women's roles. Nationally, the women's suffrage movement intensified, often resorting to unconventional political behaviors (marches, demonstrations), which occasionally invited violent attacks from men and even other women. In 1919, Congress finally passed the Nineteenth Amendment, which prohibits states from denying the right to vote "on account of sex." The amendment was ratified in 1920, in time for the November election.

FIGURE 5.2 Voter Registration in the South, 1960, 1980, and 2000

As a result of the Voting Rights Act of 1965 and other national actions, black voter registration in the eleven states of the old Confederacy nearly doubled between 1960 and 1980. In 2000, there was very little difference between the voting registration rates of white and black voters in the Deep South.

Sources: Data for 1960 and 1980 are from U.S. Bureau of the Census, *Statistical Abstract of the United States, 1982–1983* (Washington, D.C.: U.S. Government Printing Office, 1983), p. 488; data for 2000 come from the U.S. Census Bureau, Current Population Report, P20-542, Table 3, Internet release, 27 February 2002.

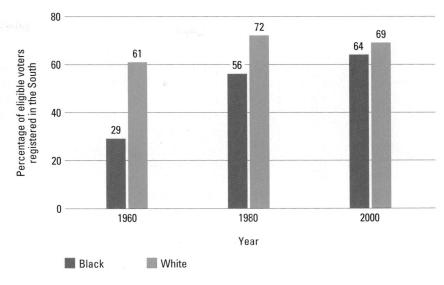

Evaluating the Expansion of Suffrage in America. The last major expansion of suffrage in the United States took place in 1971, when the Twenty-sixth Amendment lowered the voting age to eighteen. For most of its history, the United States has been far from the democratic ideal of universal suffrage. However, compared with other countries, it looks pretty democratic.[27] Women did not gain the vote on equal terms with men until 1921 in Norway; 1922 in the Netherlands; 1944 in France; 1946 in Italy, Japan, and Venezuela; 1948 in Belgium; and 1971 in Switzerland. Women are still not universally enfranchised. While women in Kuwait voted for the first time in 2006, women in Saudi Arabia, for example, still lack the right to vote.[28] Of course, no one at all can vote in the United Arab Emirates. In South Africa, blacks, who outnumber whites by more than four to one, were not allowed to vote freely in elections until 1994. With regard to voting age, nineteen of twenty-seven countries that allow free elections also have a minimum voting age of eighteen. None has a lower age.

Voting on Policies

Disenfranchised groups have struggled to gain voting rights because of the political power that comes with suffrage. Belief in the ability of ordinary citizens to make political decisions and to control government through the power of the ballot box was strongest in the United States during the Progressive era, which began around 1900 and lasted until about 1925.

The Fight for Women's Suffrage . . . and Against It

Militant suffragettes demonstrated outside the White House prior to ratification of the Nineteenth Amendment to the Constitution, which gave women the right to vote. Congress passed the proposed amendment in 1919, and it was ratified by the required number of states in time for the 1920 presidential election. Suffragettes' demonstrations were occasionally disrupted by men—and other women—who opposed extending the right to vote to women. *(Library of Congress)*

Progressivism was a philosophy of political reform that trusted the goodness and wisdom of individual citizens and distrusted "special interests" (railroads, corporations) and political institutions (traditional political parties, legislatures). Such attitudes resurfaced among followers of H. Ross Perot and others who share this populist outlook. Perot, a wealthy businessman, ran for president in 1992 and 1996 on a platform critical of the major parties for supporting the North American Free Trade Agreement (NAFTA) and for avoiding difficult issues such as the national deficit.

The leaders of the Progressive movement were prominent politicians (former president Theodore Roosevelt, Senator Robert La Follette of Wisconsin) and eminent scholars (historian Frederick Jackson Turner, philosopher John Dewey). Not content to vote for candidates chosen by party leaders, the Progressives championed the **direct primary**—an election, run by the state governments, in which the voters chose the party's candidates for the general election. Wanting a mechanism to remove elected candidates from office, the Progressives backed the **recall,** a special election initiated by a petition signed by a specified number of voters. Although eighteen states provide for the recall of state officials, only one state governor had ever been unseated until 2003, when California voters threw out Governor Gray Davis in a bizarre recall election that placed movie actor Arnold Schwarzenegger in the governor's mansion.

The Progressives also championed the power of the masses to propose and pass laws, approximating the citizen participation in policymaking that is the hallmark of direct democracy. They developed two voting mechanisms for policymaking that are still in use:

progressivism A philosophy of political reform based on the goodness and wisdom of the individual citizen as opposed to special interests and political institutions.

direct primary A preliminary election, run by the state government, in which the voters choose each party's candidates for the general election.

recall The process for removing an elected official from office.

■ A **referendum** is a direct vote by the people on a proposed law or on an amendment to a state constitution. The measures subject to popular vote are known as *propositions*. Twenty-four states permit popular referenda on laws, and all but Delaware require a referendum for a constitutional amendment. Most referenda are placed on the ballot by legislatures, not voters.

■ The **initiative** is a procedure by which voters can propose an issue to be decided by the legislature or by the people in a referendum. The procedure involves gathering a specified number of signatures from registered voters (usually 5 to 10 percent of the total in the state), then submitting the petition to a designated state agency. Twenty-four states currently provide for some form of voter initiative.

Over 300 propositions have appeared on state ballots in general elections since 2000. In 2008, voters in 36 states cast ballots on 153 propositions, passing almost two-thirds of them. Some of these propositions dealt with the most controversial topics in contemporary politics. Voters in California, Florida, and Arizona voted to enact Constitutional amendments banning same-sex marriage. In Colorado and South Dakota voters rejected propositions intended to ban abortions.[29]

What conclusion can we draw about the Progressives' legacy of mechanisms for direct participation in government? One seasoned journalist paints an unimpressive picture. He notes that an expensive "industry" developed in the 1980s that makes money by circulating petitions, then managing the large sums of money needed to run a campaign to approve (or defeat) a referendum.[30] In 1998, opponents of a measure to allow casino gambling on Native American lands in California spent $25.8 million. This huge sum, however, pales in comparison to the $66.2 million spent during the campaign by the tribes that supported the measure. The initiative passed.[31]

Clearly, citizens can exercise great power over government policy through the mechanisms of the initiative and referendum. What is not clear is whether these forms of direct democracy improve the policies made by representatives elected for that purpose.

Voting for Candidates

We saved for last the most visible form of political participation: voting to choose candidates for public office. Voting for candidates serves democratic government in two ways. First, citizens can choose the candidates they think will best serve their interests. Second, voting allows the people to reelect the officials they guessed right about and to kick out those they guessed wrong about. In Chapter 6, we look at the factors that underlie voting choice. Here, we examine Americans' reliance on the electoral process.

In national politics, voters seem content to elect just two executive officers—the president and vice president—and to trust the president to

referendum An election on a policy issue.

initiative A procedure by which voters can propose an issue to be decided by the legislature or by the people in a referendum. It requires gathering a specified number of signatures and submitting a petition to a designated agency.

appoint a cabinet to round out his administration. But at the state and local levels, voters insist on selecting all kinds of officials. Every state elects a governor (and forty-five elect a lieutenant governor). Forty-two states elect an attorney general; thirty-nine, a treasurer; and thirty-seven, a secretary of state. The list goes on, down through the superintendent of education, secretary of agriculture, controller, board of education, and public utilities commissioners. Elected county officials commonly include commissioners, a sheriff, a treasurer, a clerk, a superintendent of schools, and a judge (often several). At the local level, voters elect all but about 600 of 15,300 school boards across the nation.[32] Instead of trusting state and local chief executives to appoint lesser administrators (as we do for more important offices at the national level), we expect voters to choose intelligently among scores of candidates they meet for the first time on a complex ballot in the polling booth.

In the American version of democracy, the laws recognize no limit to voters' ability to make informed choices among candidates and thus to control government through voting. The reasoning seems to be that elections are good; therefore, more elections are better, and the most elections are best. By this thinking, the United States clearly has the best and most democratic government in the world because it is the undisputed champion at holding elections. The author of a study that compared elections in the United States with elections in twenty-six other democracies concluded:

> No country can approach the United States in the frequency and variety of elections, and thus in the amount of electoral participation to which its citizens have a right. No other country elects its lower house as often as every two years, or its president as frequently as every four years. No other country popularly elects its state governors and town mayors; no other has as wide a variety of nonrepresentative offices (judges, sheriffs, attorneys general, city treasurers, and so on) subject to election. . . . The average American is entitled to do far more electing—probably by a factor of three or four—than the citizen of any other democracy.[33]

However, the United States ranks near the bottom of industrialized democracies in voter turnout. How do we square low voter turnout with Americans' devotion to elections as an instrument of democratic government? To complicate matters further, how do we square low voter turnout with the fact that Americans seem to participate in politics in various other ways?

Explaining Political Participation

As you have seen, political participation can be unconventional or conventional, can require little or much initiative, and can serve to support the government or influence its decisions. This section begins our examination of some factors that affect the most obvious forms of political participation,

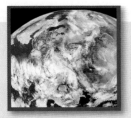

Politics of Global Change

The Growth of Electoral Democracy

Social scientist Larry Diamond says an electoral democracy exists if its citizens "can choose and replace their leaders in regular, free, and fair elections." Using data from Freedom House, a non-profit organization supporting electoral democracy around the world, he tallied the growth of electoral democracies from 1973 to 2007. The lines in this figure can be analyzed in three stages: (1) the period from 1974 to 1989 represents a "third wave" of democratization (the others were in 1828–1926 and 1943–1962) caused by social modernization and international influences; (2) the boom from 1989 to 1994 was sparked by the collapse of communism; and (3) a plateau was reached after 1995.

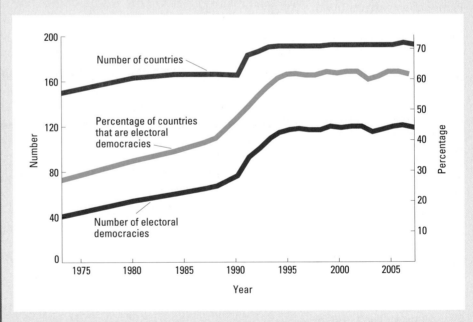

Source: Larry Diamond, *The Spirit of Democracy* (New York: Times Books, 2008), p. 22 and Appendix, Table 2. He kindly supplied data for 2007.

with particular emphasis on voting. Our first task is to determine how much variation there is in patterns of participation within the United States over time.

Patterns of Participation Over Time

Were Americans more politically apathetic in the 1990s than they were in the 1960s? The answer lies in Figure 5.3, which plots several measures of participation from 1952 through 2004. The graph shows a steady pattern of participation over the years (with upward spurts in 1992 because Ross Perot's candidacy added a new dimension to the presidential race and in 2004 following the close 2000 election and because of interest surrounding the war in Iraq). Otherwise, participation varied little across time in the percentage of citizens who worked for candidates, attended party meet-

FIGURE 5.3   Electoral Participation in the United States Over Time

Participation patterns from five decades show that in the 1980s, Americans participated in election campaigns about as much as or more than they did in the 1950s on every indicator except voting. The graph shows little variation over time in the percentage of citizens who worked for candidates, attended party meetings, and tried to persuade people how to vote. In fact, interest in election campaigns and efforts at persuasion tended to increase. Voting turnout during this period tended to decline, but it did show spurts in 1992 (when Ross Perot won 19 percent of the vote as a third candidate) and in 2004 (following the razor-close 2000 presidential election). This long-term decline in turnout runs counter to the rise in educational level, a puzzle that is discussed in the text.

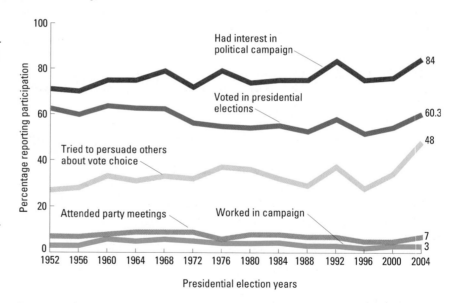

Source: American National Election Surveys, University of Michigan, available at www.umich .edu/~nes/nesguide/gd-index.htm; Harold W. Stanley and Richard G. Niemi, *Vital Statistics on American Politics, 2005–2006* (Washington, D.C.: Congressional Quarterly Press, 2006), Table 1.1. The percentage voting in elections is based on the eligible voter population, not the voting-age population.

ings, and tried to persuade people how to vote. *The only line that shows a downward trend is voting in elections.* Not only is voter turnout low in the United States compared with that in other countries, but turnout has basically declined over time. Moreover, while voting has decreased, other forms of participation have remained stable or even increased. What is going on? Who votes? Who does not? Why? And does it really matter?

The Standard Socioeconomic Explanation

Researchers have found that socioeconomic status is a good indicator of most types of conventional political participation. People with more education, higher incomes, and white-collar or professional occupations tend to be more aware of the impact of politics on their lives, to know what can be done to influence government actions, and to have the necessary resources (time and money) to take action. So they are more likely to participate in politics than are people of lower socioeconomic status. This relationship between socioeconomic status and conventional political involvement is called the **standard socioeconomic model** of participation.[34]

Unconventional political behavior is also related to socioeconomic status. Those who protest against U.S. government policies tend to be better educated. Moreover, this relationship holds in other countries too. One scholar notes: "Protest in advanced industrial democracies is not simply an outlet for the alienated and deprived; just the opposite often occurs."[35] In one major way, however, those who engage in unconventional political behavior differ from those who participate more conventionally: protesters tend to be younger.

Younger people are more likely to take part in demonstrations or boycotts, and less likely to participate in conventional politics.[36] Younger people engage in more voluntary and charitable activities, but older Americans are more likely to vote, identify with the major political parties, and contact public officials.[37] Voting rates tend to increase as people grow older, until about age sixty-five, when physical infirmities begin to lower rates again.[38]

Two other variables, race and gender, have been related to participation in the past, but as times have changed, so have those relationships. Blacks, who had very low participation rates in the 1950s, now participate at rates comparable to that of whites, when differences in socioeconomic status are taken into account.[39] Women also exhibited low participation rates in the past, but gender differences in political participation have almost disappeared.[40] (The one exception is in attempting to persuade others how to vote, which women are less likely to do than men.)[41] Research on the social context of voting behavior has shown that married men and women are more likely to vote than those of either sex living without a spouse.[42]

Of all the social and economic variables, education is the strongest single factor in explaining most types of conventional political participation (see Figure 5.4).[43] The strong link between education and electoral

standard socioeconomic model A relationship between socioeconomic status and conventional political involvement: people with higher status and more education are more likely to participate than those with lower status.

FIGURE 5.4   Effects of Education on Political Participation

Education has a powerful effect on political participation in the United States. These data from a 2004 sample show that level of education is directly related to five forms of conventional political participation. (Respondents tend to overstate whether they voted.)

Source: This analysis was based on the 2004 National Election Study done by the Center for Political Studies, University of Michigan, and distributed by the Inter-University Consortium for Political and Social Research, Ann Arbor, Michigan.

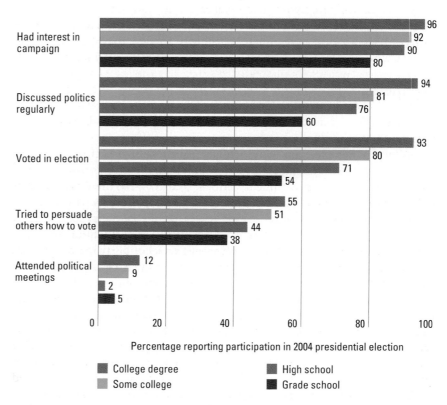

Percentage reporting participation in 2004 presidential election

- College degree
- Some college
- High school
- Grade school

participation raises questions about low voter turnout in the United States both over time and relative to other democracies. The fact is that the proportion of individuals with college degrees is greater in the United States than in other countries. Moreover, that proportion has been increasing steadily. Why, then, is voter turnout in elections so low? And why has it dropped over time?

Low Voter Turnout in America

Voting is a low-initiative form of participation that can satisfy all three motives for political participation: showing allegiance to the nation, obtaining particularized benefits, and influencing broad policy. How then do we explain the decline in voter turnout in the United States?

The Decline in Voting Over Time.   The graph of voter turnout in Figure 5.3 shows that one of the sharpest drops in turnout took place between the 1968 and 1972 elections. It was during this period (in 1971, actually) that Congress proposed and the states ratified the Twenty-sixth Amendment, which expanded the electorate by lowering the voting age from twenty-one to eighteen. Because people younger than twenty-one are much less likely to vote, their eligibility reduced the overall national turnout rate (the percentage of those eligible to vote who actually vote). Although young nonvoters inevitably vote more often as they grow older, some observers estimate that the enfranchisement of eighteen-year-olds accounts for about one or two percentage points in the total decline in turnout since 1952, but that still leaves more than ten percentage points to be explained.[44]

Why has voter turnout declined since 1968, while the level of education has increased? Many researchers have tried to solve this puzzle.[45] Some attribute most of the decline to changes in voters' attitudes toward politics. One major factor is the growing belief that government is not responsive to citizens and that voting does no good. Another is a change in attitude toward political parties, along with a decline in the extent and strength of party identification.[46] This puzzle is compounded by the fact that the decline in turnout is not occurring evenly across the United States. Participation in the South seems to be gradually increasing.

According to the age explanation, turnout in the United States is destined to remain a percentage point or two below its highs of the 1960s because of the lower voting rate of citizens younger than twenty-one. Turnout rates do increase as young people age, which suggests that voting is habit forming.[47] Despite these trends, the Obama campaign stimulated a wave of young voters to turn out at the polls in 2008. Voters under thirty accounted for 17 percent of the votes cast in 2000 and 2004, but they cast 18 percent of the vote in 2008 when over two million more eighteen-to-twenty-nine-year-olds turned out. More significantly, the percentage of eligible voters under age thirty who cast ballots is estimated to have increased from 35 percent in 1996 to roughly 50 percent in 2008.

U.S. Turnout Versus Turnout in Other Countries. Scholars cite two factors to explain the low voter turnout in the United States compared with that in other countries. First are the differences in voting laws and administrative machinery.[48] In a few countries, voting is compulsory, and turnout obviously is extremely high. But other methods can encourage voting: declaring election days to be public holidays or providing a two-day voting period. The United States does none of these things.

Furthermore, nearly every other democratic country places the burden of registration on the government rather than on the individual voter. This is important. Voting in the United States is a two-stage process, and the first stage (going to the proper officials to register) requires more initiative than the second stage (going to the polling booth to cast a ballot). In most American states, the registration process is separated from the voting process in both time (usually voters have to register weeks in advance of the

Go Vote

Rap mogul Sean "Diddy" Combs visited a polling station in New York City on Super Tuesday in 2008 in an effort to motivate New Yorkers to vote in the state's primary. Combs had tackled low voter turnout in the 2004 election cycle with the motto "vote or die." For Super Tuesday in 2008 he shortened the already pithy slogan to "go vote." *(Jemal Countess/Getty Images)*

election) and geography (often voters have to register somewhere other than their polling place). The seven states that do allow citizens to register and vote on the same day have consistently higher voter participation rates.[49] Turnout is higher in Oregon, where everyone votes by mail.[50] Moreover, registration procedures often have been obscure, requiring potential voters to call around to find out what to do. People who move (and younger people move more frequently) have to reregister. If we compute voter turnout on the basis of those who are registered to vote, about 80 percent of Americans vote, a figure that moves the United States to the middle (but not the top) of all democratic nations.[51] Since 1995, the so-called motor-voter law has required states to allow citizens to register by mail (similar to renewing drivers' licenses) and at certain agencies that provide public assistance.[52] In the 2001–2002 election cycle, over 42 percent of all voter registration applications were submitted through state motor vehicle offices.[53] Although registration rose to its highest level for a congressional election since 1970, the voting rate in 1998 declined by almost 2.4 percent below the comparable 1994 election.[54]

The second factor usually cited to explain low turnout in American elections is the lack of political parties that mobilize the vote of particular social groups, especially lower-income and less-educated people. American parties do make an effort to get out the vote, but neither party is as closely linked to specific groups as are parties in many other countries, where certain parties work hand in hand with ethnic, occupational, or religious groups. Research shows that strong party-group links can significantly increase turnout.[55] Similarly, citizens are more likely to turn out to vote when the elections are competitive or close.[56]

To these explanations for low voter turnout in the United States—the traditional burden of registration and the lack of strong party-group links—we add another. Although the act of voting requires low initiative, the process of learning about dozens of candidates on the ballot in American elections requires a great deal of initiative. Some people undoubtedly fail to vote because they feel inadequate to the task of deciding among candidates for the many offices on the ballot in U.S. elections.

Teachers, newspaper columnists, and public affairs groups tend to worry a great deal about low voter turnout in the United States, suggesting that it signifies some sort of political sickness—or at least that it gives us a bad mark for democracy. Others are less concerned.[57] One scholar argues:

> Turnout rates do not indicate the amount of electing—the frequency of occasion, the range of offices and decisions, the "value" of the vote—to which a country's citizens are entitled. . . . Thus, although the turnout rate in the United States is below that of most other democracies, American citizens do not necessarily do less voting than other citizens; most probably, they do more.[58]

Participation and Freedom, Equality, and Order

As we have seen, Americans participate in government in a variety of ways, and to a reasonable extent, compared with citizens of other countries. What is the relationship of political participation to the values of freedom, equality, and order?

Participation and Freedom

From the standpoint of normative theory, the relationship between participation and freedom is clear: individuals should be free to participate in government and politics in the way they want and as much as they want. And they should be free not to participate as well. Ideally, all barriers to participation, such as restrictive voting registration and limitations on campaign expenditures, should be abolished, as should any schemes for compulsory voting. In theory, freedom to participate also means that individuals should be able to use their wealth, connections, knowledge, organizational power (including sheer numbers in organized protests), or any other resource to influence government decisions, provided they do so legally. Of all these resources, the individual vote may be the weakest—and the least important—means of exerting political influence. Obviously, then, freedom as a value in political participation favors those with the resources to advance their own political self-interest.

Participation and Equality

The relationship between participation and equality is also clear. Each citizen's ability to influence government should be equal to that of every other citizen, so that differences in personal resources do not work against the poor or otherwise disadvantaged. Elections, then, serve the ideal of equality better than any other means of political participation. Formal rules for counting ballots—in particular, one person, one vote—cancel differences in resources among individuals.

At the same time, groups of people who have few resources individually can combine their votes to wield political power. Various European ethnic groups exercised this type of power in the late nineteenth and early twentieth centuries, when their votes won them entry to the sociopolitical system and allowed them to share in its benefits (see Chapter 4). More recently, blacks, Hispanics, homosexuals, and the disabled have used their voting power to gain political recognition. However, minorities often have had to use unconventional forms of participation to win the right to vote. As two major scholars of political participation put it, "Protest is the great equalizer, the political action that weights intensity as well as sheer numbers."[59]

Participation and Order

The relationship between participation and order is complicated. Some types of participation (pledging allegiance, voting) promote order, and so are encouraged by those who value order; other types promote disorder, and so are discouraged. Many citizens—men and women alike—even resisted giving women the right to vote for fear of upsetting the social order by altering the traditional roles of men and women.

Both conventional and unconventional participation can lead to the ouster of government officials, but the regime—the political system itself—is threatened more by unconventional participation. To maintain order, the government has a stake in converting unconventional participation to conventional participation whenever possible. Think about the student unrest on college campuses during the Vietnam War when thousands of protesting students stopped traffic, occupied buildings, destroyed property, and behaved in other unconventional ways. Confronted by such civil strife and disorder, Congress took action. On March 23, 1971, it enacted and sent to the states the proposed Twenty-sixth Amendment, lowering the voting age to eighteen. Three-quarters of the state legislatures had to ratify the amendment before it became part of the Constitution. Astonishingly, thirty-eight states (the required number) complied by July 1, establishing a new speed record for ratification.[60] As one observer argued, the right to vote was extended to eighteen-year-olds not because young people demanded it but because "public officials believed suffrage expansion to be a means of institutionalizing youths' participation in politics, which would, in turn, curb disorder."[61]

Participation and the Models of Democracy

Ostensibly, elections are institutional mechanisms that implement democracy by allowing citizens to choose among candidates or issues. But elections also serve several other important purposes:[62]

- *Elections socialize political activity.* The opportunity to vote for change encourages citizens to refrain from demonstrating in the streets. Elections transform what might otherwise be sporadic citizen-initiated acts into a routine public function. This helps preserve government stability by containing and channeling away potentially disruptive or dangerous forms of mass political activity.

- *Elections institutionalize access to political power.* They allow ordinary citizens to run for political office or to play an important role in selecting political leaders. Working to elect a candidate encourages the campaign worker to identify problems or propose solutions to the newly elected official.

- *Elections bolster the state's power and authority.* The opportunity to participate in elections helps convince citizens that the government is responsive to their needs and wants, which reinforces its legitimacy.

Participation and Majoritarianism

Although the majoritarian model assumes that government responsiveness to popular demands comes through mass participation in politics, majoritarianism views participation rather narrowly. It favors conventional, institutionalized behavior, primarily voting in elections. Because majoritarianism relies on counting votes to determine what the majority wants, its bias toward equality in political participation is strong. Clearly, better-educated, wealthier citizens are more likely to participate in elections, and get-out-the vote campaigns cannot counter this distinct bias.[63] Because it favors collective decisions formalized through elections, majoritarianism has little place for motivated, resourceful individuals to exercise private influence over government actions.

Majoritarianism also limits individual freedom in another way: its focus on voting as the major means of mass participation narrows the scope of conventional political behavior by defining which political actions are "orderly" and acceptable. By favoring equality and order in political participation, majoritarianism goes hand in hand with the ideological orientation of communitarianism (see Chapter 1).

Participation and Pluralism

Resourceful citizens who want the government's help with problems find a haven in the pluralist model of democracy. A decentralized and organizationally complex form of government allows many points of access and accommodates various forms of conventional participation in addition to voting. For example, wealthy people and well-funded groups can afford to hire lobbyists to press their interests in Congress. In one view of pluralist democracy, citizens are free to ply and wheedle public officials to further their own selfish visions of the public good. From another viewpoint, pluralism offers citizens the opportunity to be treated as individuals when dealing with the government, to influence policymaking in special circumstances, and to fulfill (insofar as possible in representative government) their social potential through participation in community affairs.

Summary

To have "government by the people," the people must participate in politics. Conventional forms of participation—contacting officials and voting in elections—come most quickly to mind. However, citizens can also participate in politics in unconventional ways: staging sit-down strikes in public buildings, blocking traffic, and so on. Most citizens disapprove of most forms of unconventional political behavior. Yet blacks and women used unconventional tactics to win important political and legal rights, including the right to vote.

People are motivated to participate in politics for various reasons: to show support for their country, obtain particularized benefits for themselves or their friends, or influence broad public policy. Their political actions may demand little political knowledge or personal initiative, or a great deal of both.

The press often paints an unflattering picture of political participation in America. Clearly, the proportion of the electorate that votes in general elections in the United States has dropped and is far below that in other nations. When compared with other nations on a broad range of conventional and unconventional political behavior, however, the United States tends to show as much or more citizen participation in politics. Voter turnout in the United States suffers by comparison with that of other nations because of differences in voter registration requirements. We also lack institutions (especially strong political parties) that increase voter registration and help bring those of lower socioeconomic status to the polls.

People's tendency to participate in politics is strongly related to their socioeconomic status. Education, one component of socioeconomic status, is the single strongest predictor of conventional political participation in the United States. Because of the strong effect of socioeconomic status, the political system is potentially biased toward the interests of higher-status people. Pluralist democracy, which provides many avenues for resourceful citizens to influence government decisions, tends to increase this bias. Majoritarian democracy, which relies heavily on

elections and the concept of one person, one vote, offers citizens without great personal resources the opportunity to influence government decisions through elections.

Elections serve to legitimize government simply by involving the masses in government through voting. Whether voting means anything depends on the nature of voters' choices in elections. The range of choices available is a function of the nation's political parties, the topic of the next chapter.

CL   **Resources:** Videos, Simulations, News,
▶ Timelines, Primary Sources

Political Parties, Campaigns, and Elections

This icon will direct you to resources and activities on the website: www.cengage.com/polisci/janda/ chall_dem_brief/7e

WHAT IS "THE FASTEST-GROWING political party" in the United States? The Libertarian Party, Green Party, and American Independent Party—among others—claim to be "the fastest growing" in scores of postings on the Internet. The Democratic and Republican parties—already fully grown—stand above the controversy. The two major parties took 99 percent of the more than 125 million votes for president in 2008.[1] Minor parties can tout scattered electoral gains from small beginnings, but their victories pale before the massive electoral success of the Democratic Party and the Republican Party. Unlike elections in most other democracies, elections in the United States are ruled by a party duopoly.

The extent of the Democrats' and Republicans' supremacy in the electoral process can be seen in comparison with the Libertarian Party. Although its claim to be the "fastest growing" may be disputed, the Libertarian Party is certainly the third largest in the United States. Founded in 1971, the party embraces the libertarian philosophy set forth in Chapter 1 (see page 16). The preamble to its party platform begins, "As Libertarians, we seek a world of liberty; a world in which all individuals are sovereign over their own lives, and no one is forced to sacrifice his or her values for the benefit of others."[2] Unlike many active members in the Democratic and Republican parties, most Libertarians seem aware of and committed to their party's platform. The national party maintains a headquarters in Washington, D.C., and its website links to party organizations in all fifty states, where the party claims some

elected officials at the state and local levels. The party is also more active than any other minor party in nominating candidates to run in national elections.

Libertarian candidates for president and vice president have run in all ten presidential elections since 1972. In the 2006 national election, the party nominated far more candidates for the U.S. House (114 out of 435 up for election) and the U.S. Senate (18 out of 33) than any other minor party.[3] But despite its clear and consistent philosophy, its national and state organizations, and its record of nominating candidates, the Libertarian Party has not fared well at the polls.

No Libertarian presidential candidate ever won more than 1 million votes. The party's best showing was 921,300 presidential votes in 1980—the only time that a Libertarian candidate won more than 1 percent of the vote.[4] In the congressional races of 2006, all its 114 House candidates together won less than 1 percent of the total vote cast in House elections, and its 18 Senate candidates won less than 1 percent of the vote in Senate elections.[5]

No Libertarian Party candidate was ever elected to Congress. It is true that Ron Paul, the Libertarian Party presidential candidate in 1988, and Bob Barr, the Libertarian Party presidential candidate in 2008, both served in Congress. However, both individuals ran and were elected to Congress as Republicans. Ron Paul ultimately sought the Republican nomination for president in 2008. Indeed, no member in Congress belongs to any third party, although two senators are independents.

U.S. politics is dominated by a two-party system. The Democratic and Republican parties have dominated national and state politics for more than 125 years. Their domination is closer to complete than that of any pair of parties in any other democratic government. Although all democracies have some form of multiparty politics, very few have a stable two-party system, Britain being the most notable exception. Most people take our two-party system for granted, not realizing that it is arguably the most distinctive feature of the American government.

Why do we have any political parties? What functions do they perform? How did we become a nation of Democrats and Republicans? Are parties really necessary for democratic government, or do they get in the way of citizens and their government? In this chapter, we answer these questions by examining political parties, perhaps the most misunderstood element of American politics.

And what of the election campaigns conducted by the two major parties? In this chapter, we also consider how those campaigns have changed over time, how candidates are nominated in the United States, what factors are important in election campaigns, and why voters choose one candidate over another. In addition, we address these other important questions: Do election campaigns function more to inform or to confuse voters? How important is money in conducting a winning election campaign? What are the roles of party identification, issues, and candidate attributes in influencing voters' choices and thus election outcomes? How do campaigns, elections, and parties fit into the majoritarian and pluralist models of democracy?

 ## Political Parties and Their Functions

According to democratic theory, the primary means by which citizens control their government is by voting in free elections. Most Americans agree that voting is important. Of those surveyed after the 2004 presidential campaign, 92 percent felt that elections made the government "pay attention to what the people think."[6] Americans are not nearly as supportive of the role that political parties play in elections, however. When asked whether Ross Perot should run for president in 1996 as "head of a third party which would also run candidates in state and local races" or "by himself as an independent candidate," 60 percent of a national sample favored his running without a party.[7]

Nevertheless, Americans are quick to condemn as "undemocratic" countries that do not hold elections contested by political parties. In truth, Americans have a love-hate relationship with political parties. They believe that parties are necessary for democratic government; at the same time, they think parties are somehow "obstructionist" and not to be trusted. This distrust is particularly strong among younger voters. To better appreciate the role of political parties in democratic government, we must understand exactly what parties are and what they do.

What Is a Political Party?

A **political party** is an organization that sponsors candidates for political office *under the organization's name.* The italicized part of this definition is important. True political parties select individuals to run for public office through a formal process of **nomination,** which designates them as the parties' official candidates. This activity distinguishes the Democratic and Republican parties from interest groups. The AFL-CIO and the National Association of Manufacturers are interest groups. They often support candidates in various ways, but they do not nominate them to run as their avowed representatives. If they did, they would be transformed into political parties. In short, the sponsoring of candidates designated as representatives of the organization is what defines an organization as a party.

Most democratic theorists agree that a modern nation-state cannot practice democracy without at least two political parties that regularly contest elections. In fact, the link between democracy and political parties is so close that many people define *democratic government* in terms of competitive party politics.

Party Functions

Parties contribute to democratic government through the functions they perform for the **political system**—the interrelated institutions that link people with government. Four of the most important party functions are nominating candidates for election to public office, structuring the voting choice in elections, proposing alternative government programs, and coordinating the actions of government officials.

Nominating Candidates. Without political parties, voters would confront a bewildering array of self-nominated candidates, each seeking votes on the basis of personal friendships, celebrity status, or name. Parties can provide a form of quality control for their nominees through the process of peer review. Party insiders, the nominees' peers, usually know the strengths and faults of potential candidates much better than average voters do and thus can judge their suitability for representing the party.

In nominating candidates, parties often do more than pass judgment on potential office seekers. Sometimes they go so far as to recruit talented individuals to become party candidates. In this way, parties help not only to ensure a minimum level of quality among candidates who run for office but also to raise the quality of those candidates.

political party An organization that sponsors candidates for political office under the organization's name.

nomination Designation as an official candidate of a political party.

political system A set of interrelated institutions that links people with government.

Structuring the Voting Choice.   Political parties also help democratic government by structuring the voting choice—reducing the number of candidates on the ballot to those who have a realistic chance of winning. Established parties—those with experience in contesting elections—acquire a following of loyal voters who guarantee the party's candidates a predictable base of votes. The ability of established parties to mobilize their supporters has the effect of discouraging nonparty candidates from running for office and discouraging new parties from forming. Consequently, the realistic choice is between candidates offered by the major parties, reducing the amount of new information that voters need to make a rational decision.

Proposing Alternative Government Programs.   Parties also help voters choose candidates by proposing alternative programs of government action—the general policies their candidates will pursue if they gain office. Even if voters know nothing about the qualities of the parties' candidates, they can vote rationally for candidates of the party that has policies they favor. The specific policies advocated vary from candidate to candidate and from election to election. However, candidates of the same party tend to favor policies that fit their party's underlying political philosophy, or ideology.

In many countries, parties' names, such as *Conservative* and *Socialist,* reflect their political stance. The Democrats and Republicans have issue-neutral names, but many minor parties in the United States have used their names to advertise their policies: the Prohibition Party, the Socialist Party, and even the Reform Party. The neutrality of the two major parties' names suggests that their policies are similar. This is not true. As we shall see, they regularly adopt very different policies in their platforms.

Coordinating the Actions of Government Officials.   Finally, party organizations help coordinate the actions of public officials. A government based on the separation of powers, such as that of the United States, divides responsibilities for making public policy. The president and the leaders of the House and Senate are not required to cooperate with one another. Political party organizations are the major means for bridging the separate powers to produce coordinated policies that can govern the country effectively.

A History of U.S. Party Politics

The two major U.S. parties are among the oldest in the world. In fact, the Democratic Party, founded in 1828 but with roots reaching back into the late 1700s, has a strong claim to being the oldest party in existence. Its closest rival is the British Conservative Party, formed in 1832, two decades before the Republican Party was organized in 1854. Several generations of

Americans have supported the Democratic and Republican parties, which have become institutionalized in our political process.

The Emergence of the Party System

Today we think of party activities as normal, even essential, to American politics. It was not always so. The Constitution makes no mention of political parties, and none existed when the Constitution was written in 1787. It was common then to refer to groups pursuing some common political interest as *factions.* Although factions were seen as inevitable in politics, they were also considered dangerous. One argument for adopting the Constitution— proposed in *Federalist* No. 10 (see Chapter 2)—was that its federal system would prevent factional influences from controlling the government.

The debate over ratification of the Constitution produced two factions. Those who backed the Constitution were loosely known as *Federalists,* their opponents as *Antifederalists.* At this stage, the groups could not be called parties because they did not sponsor candidates for election. We can classify George Washington as a Federalist because he supported the Constitution, but he was not a factional leader and actually opposed factional politics. During Washington's administration, however, the political cleavage sharpened between those who favored a stronger national government and those who wanted a less powerful, more decentralized national government.

Members of the first group, led by Alexander Hamilton, proclaimed themselves Federalists. Members of the second group, led by Thomas Jefferson, called themselves Republicans. (Although they used the same name, they were *not* the Republicans as we know them today. Indeed, Jefferson's followers were later known as the Democratic Republicans.) Disheartened by the political split in his administration, Washington spoke out against "the baneful effects" of parties in his farewell address in 1796. Nevertheless, parties already existed in the political system. For the most part, from that time to the present, two major political parties have competed for political power.

The Current Party System: Democrats and Republicans

By 1820, the Federalists were no more. In 1828, the Democratic Republican Party split in two. One wing, led by Andrew Jackson, became the Democratic Party. The other later joined forces with several minor parties and formed the Whig Party, which lasted for two decades.

In the early 1850s, antislavery forces (including Whigs and antislavery Democrats) began to organize. They formed a new party, the Republican Party, to oppose the extension of slavery into the Kansas and Nebraska territories. It is this party, founded in 1854, that continues as today's Republican Party. In 1860, the Republicans nominated Abraham Lincoln and successfully confronted a Democratic Party deeply divided over slavery.

The election of 1860 is considered the first of three critical elections under the current party system.[8] A **critical election** is marked by a sharp change in existing patterns of party loyalties among groups of voters. This change, which is called an **electoral realignment,** lasts through several subsequent elections.[9] When one party in a two-party system regularly enjoys support from most of the voters, it is called the *majority party;* the other is called the *minority party.*

The 1860 election divided the country between the northern states, which mainly voted Republican, and the southern states, which were overwhelmingly Democratic. The victory of North over South in the Civil War cemented Democratic loyalties in the South, particularly following the withdrawal of federal troops after the 1876 election. For forty years, from 1880 to 1920, no Republican presidential candidate won even one of the eleven states of the former Confederacy.

A second critical election, in 1896, transformed the Republican Party into a true majority party when, in opposition to the Democrats' inflationary free silver platform, a link was forged between the Republican Party and business. Voters in the heavily populated Northeast and Midwest surged toward the Republican Party, many of them permanently.

A third critical election occurred in 1932, when Franklin Delano Roosevelt led the Democratic Party to majority party status by uniting southern Democrats, northern urban workers, middle-class liberals, Catholics, Jews, and white ethnic minorities in the "Roosevelt coalition." (The relatively few blacks who voted at that time tended to remain loyal to the Republicans, the "party of Lincoln.") Democrats held control of both houses of Congress in most sessions from 1933 through 1994. In 1994, Republicans gained control of Congress for the first time in forty years. They retained control after the 1996 elections—the first time that Republicans took both houses in successive elections since Herbert Hoover's presidency. In 2006, Democrats regained control of both the House and the Senate after a decade of Republican dominance.

The North-South coalition of Democratic voters forged by Roosevelt in the 1930s has completely crumbled. Since 1952, in fact, the South has voted more consistently for Republican presidential candidates than for Democrats, and rural voters have become decidedly more Republican.[10] The majority of southern senators and representatives are now Republicans. However, the Democratic coalition of urban workers and ethnic minorities still seems intact, if weakened. Some scholars say that in the 1970s and 1980s we were in a period of **electoral dealignment,** in which party loyalties have become less important to voters as they cast their ballots. Others counter that partisanship increased in the 1990s in a gradual process of realignment not marked by a single critical election.[11] We examine the influence of party loyalty on voting later in this chapter.

critical election An election that produces a sharp change in the existing pattern of party loyalties among groups of voters.

electoral realignment The change in voting patterns that occurs after a critical election.

electoral dealignment A lessening of the importance of party loyalties in voting decisions.

The American Two-Party System

The critical election of 1860 established the Democratic and Republican parties as the major parties in our **two-party system**. In a two-party system, most voters are so loyal to one or the other of the major parties that independent candidates or candidates from a third party (which means any minor party) have little chance of winning office. Third-party candidates tend to be most successful at the local or state level. Since the current two-party system was established, relatively few minor-party candidates have won election to the U.S. House; very few have won election to the Senate, and none has won the presidency. However, we should not ignore the special contributions of certain minor parties, among them the Anti-Masonic Party, the Populists, and the Progressives of 1912. In this section, we study the fortunes of minor or third parties in American politics. We also look at why we have only two major parties, explain how federalism helps the parties survive, and describe voters' loyalty to the two major parties today.

Minor Parties in America

Minor parties have always figured in party politics in America. Most true minor parties in our political history have been of four types:[12]

- *Bolter parties* are formed from factions that split off from one of the major parties. Seven times in thirty-six presidential elections since the Civil War, disgruntled leaders "bolted the ticket" and challenged their former parties. Bolter parties have occasionally won significant proportions of the vote. However, with the exception of Teddy Roosevelt's Progressive Party in 1912 and possibly George Wallace's American Independent Party in 1968, bolter parties have not affected the outcome of presidential elections.

- *Farmer-labor parties* represent farmers and urban workers who believe that they, the working class, are not getting their share of society's wealth. The People's Party, founded in 1892 and nicknamed the "Populist Party," was a prime example of a farmer-labor party. The Populists won 8.5 percent of the vote in 1892 and became the first third party since 1860 to win any electoral votes. Flushed by success, they endorsed William Jennings Bryan, the Democratic candidate, in 1896. When he lost, the party quickly faded. Farm and labor groups revived many Populist ideas in the Progressive Party in 1924. The party died in 1925.

- *Parties of ideological protest* go further than farmer-labor parties in criticizing the established system. These parties reject prevailing doctrines and propose radically different principles, often favoring more government activism. The Socialist Party has been the most successful party of ideological protest. Even at its high point in 1912,

two-party system A political system in which two major political parties compete for control of the government. Candidates from a third party have little chance of winning office.

however, it garnered only 6 percent of the vote, and Socialist candidates for president have never won a single state. In recent years, the sound of ideological protest has been heard more from rightist parties, arguing for the radical disengagement of government from society. Such is the program of the Libertarian Party, which stresses freedom over order and equality. In contrast, the Green Party protests from the left, favoring government action to preserve the environment.

■ *Single-issue parties* are formed to promote one principle, not a general philosophy of government. The Free Soil Party of the 1840s and 1850s worked to abolish slavery. The Prohibition Party, the most durable example of a single-issue party, opposed the consumption of alcoholic beverages. The party has run candidates in every presidential election since 1884. Recently, however, its platform has grown to include other conservative positions, including right-to-life, limiting immigration, and withdrawal from the World Bank.

Minor parties, then, form primarily to express discontent with the choices offered by the major parties and to work for their own objectives within the electoral system.[13]

How have minor parties fared historically? As vote getters, they have not performed well. However, bolter parties have twice won more than 10 percent of the vote. More significant, the Republican Party originated in 1854 as a single-issue third party opposed to slavery in the nation's new territories; in its first election, in 1856, the party came in second, displacing the Whigs.

As policy advocates, minor parties have a slightly better record. At times, they have had a real effect on the policies adopted by the major parties. Women's suffrage, the graduated income tax, and the direct election of senators all originated in third parties.[14]

Most important, minor parties function as safety valves. They allow those who are unhappy with the status quo to express their discontent within the system and contribute to the political dialogue. Surely this was the function of Ralph Nader's candidacy and of the Green Party in 2000. If minor parties and independent candidates indicate discontent, what should we make of the numerous minor parties that took part in the 2008 election? Not much. The number of third parties that contest elections is much less important than the total number of votes they receive. Despite the presence of numerous minor parties in every presidential election, the two major parties usually collect over 95 percent of the vote, as they did in 2008.

Why a Two-Party System?

The history of party politics in the United States is essentially the story of two parties that have alternating control of the government. With relatively few exceptions, Americans conduct elections at all levels within the two-party system. This pattern is unusual in democratic countries, where multiparty systems are more common. Why does the United States have only two major parties? The two most convincing answers to this question stem from the electoral system in the United States and the process of political socialization here.

In the typical U.S. election, two or more candidates contest each office, and the winner is the single candidate who collects the most votes, whether those votes constitute a majority or not. When the two principles of *single winners* chosen by a *simple plurality* of votes govern the election of members of a legislature, the system (despite its reliance on pluralities rather than majorities) is known as **majority representation.** Think about how American states choose representatives to Congress. A state entitled to ten representatives is divided into ten congressional districts; each district elects one representative. Majority representation of voters through single-member districts is also a feature of most state legislatures.

Alternatively, a legislature might be chosen through a system of **proportional representation,** which would award legislative seats to a party in proportion to the total number of votes it wins in an election. Under this system, the state might have a single statewide election for all ten seats, with each party presenting a list of ten candidates. Voters could vote for the entire party list they preferred, and the party's candidates would be elected from the top of each list, according to the proportion of votes won by the party. Thus, if a party got 30 percent of the vote in this example, its first three candidates would be elected.

Although this form of election may seem strange, more democratic countries use it than use our system of majority representation. Proportional representation tends to produce (or perpetuate) several parties, because each can win enough seats nationwide to wield some influence in the legislature. In contrast, our system of elections forces interest groups of all sorts to work within the two major parties, for only one candidate in each race stands a chance to be elected under plurality voting. Therefore, the system tends to produce only two parties.

The rules of our electoral system may explain why only two parties tend to form in specific election districts, but why do the same two parties (Democratic and Republican) operate within every state? The contest for the presidency is the key to this question. A candidate can win a presidential election only by amassing a majority of electoral votes from across the entire nation. Presidential candidates try to win votes under the same party label in each state in order to pool their electoral votes in the electoral college. The presidency is a big enough political prize to induce parties to harbor uncomfortable coalitions of voters (southern white Protestants allied with northern Jews and blacks in the Democratic Party, for example) just to win the electoral vote and the presidential election.

The American electoral system may force U.S. politics into a two-party mold, but why do the same two parties reappear from election to election? After more than one hundred years of political socialization, the Republicans and Democrats today have such a head start in structuring the vote

majority representation
The system by which one office, contested by two or more candidates, is won by the single candidate who collects the most votes.

proportional representation
The system by which legislative seats are awarded to a party in proportion to the vote that party wins in an election.

that they discourage challenges from new parties. In addition to political socialization within the public, the two parties in power write laws that make it hard for minor parties to get on the ballot, such as requiring petitions with thousands of signatures.[15]

The Federal Basis of the Party System

Focusing on contests for the presidency is a convenient and informative way to study the history of American parties, but it also oversimplifies party politics to the point of distortion. Even during its darkest defeats for the presidency, a party can still claim many victories for state offices. Victories outside the arena of presidential politics give each party a base of support that keeps its machinery oiled and running for the next contest.[16]

Party Identification in America

The concept of **party identification** is one of the most important in political science. It signifies a voter's sense of psychological attachment to a party, which is not the same as voting for the party in any given election. Scholars measure party identification simply by asking, "Do you usually think of yourself as a Republican, a Democrat, an independent, or what?"[17] Voting is a behavior; identification is a state of mind. For example, millions of southerners voted for Dwight Eisenhower for president in 1952 and 1956 but continued to consider themselves Democrats. The proportions of self-identified Republicans, Democrats, and independents (no party attachment) in the electorate since 1952 are shown in Figure 6.1. Three significant points stand out:

- The number of Republicans and Democrats combined far exceeds the proportion of independents in every year.

- The number of Democrats consistently exceeds that of Republicans.

- The number of Democrats has shrunk over time, to the benefit of both Republicans and independents, and the three groups are now almost equal in size.

Although party identification predisposes citizens to vote for their favorite party, other factors may cause voters to choose the opposition candidate. If they vote against their party often enough, they may rethink their party identification and eventually switch. Apparently this rethinking has gone on in the minds of many southern Democrats over time. In 1952, about 70 percent of white southerners thought of themselves as Democrats, and fewer than 20 percent thought of themselves as Republicans. By 2002, white southerners were only 25 percent Democratic, 35 percent Republican, and 40 percent independent. Much of the nationwide growth in the proportion of Republicans and independents (and the parallel drop in the number of Democrats) stems from changes in party preferences among

party identification A voter's sense of psychological attachment to a party.

FIGURE 6.1 Distribution of Party Identification, 1952–2008

In every presidential election since 1952, voters across the nation have been asked, "Generally speaking, do you usually think of yourself as a Republican, a Democrat, an independent, or what?" Most voters think of themselves as either Republicans or Democrats, but the proportion of those who think of themselves as independents has increased over time. The size of the Democratic Party's majority has also shrunk. Nevertheless, most Americans today still identify with one of the two major parties, and Democrats still outnumber Republicans.

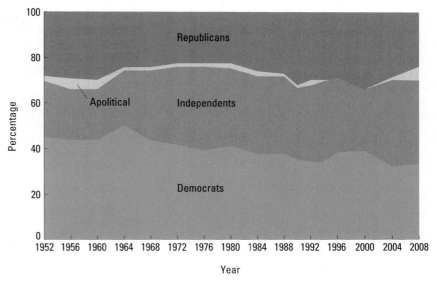

Source: National Election Studies Guide to Public Opinion and Electoral Behavior, www .electionstudies.org/nesguide/nesguide.htm. The 2008 figure is from a PEW Report, "An Even More Partisan Agenda for 2008," 24 January 2008.

white southerners and from the migration of northerners, which translated into substantial gains in the number of registered Republicans by 2002.[18]

Who are the self-identified Democrats and Republicans in the electorate? Figure 6.2 shows party identification by various social groups in 2008. The effects of socioeconomic factors are clear. People who have lower incomes and less education are more likely to think of themselves as Democrats than as Republicans. However, citizens with advanced degrees (such as college faculty) are slightly more Democratic. The cultural factors of religion and race produce even sharper differences between the parties. Jews are strongly Democratic compared with other religious groups, and African Americans are also overwhelmingly Democratic. In addition, American politics has a gender gap: women tend to be more Democratic than men.

The influence of region on party identification has changed over time. Because of the high proportion of blacks in the South, Democrats still outnumber Republicans by a wide margin (in party identity, but not in voting because of lower turnout among low-income blacks). Republicans are most numerous in the South and the Midwest. The East and the West have proportionately more independents than the central portion of the United States. Despite the erosion of Democratic strength in the South, we still see elements of Roosevelt's old Democratic coalition of socioeconomic groups.

FIGURE 6.2   Party Identification by Social Groups

Respondents to a 2008 election survey were grouped by seven socioeconomic criteria—income, education, religion, sex, race, region, and age—and analyzed according to their self-descriptions as Democrats, independents, or Republicans. As income increases, people become more likely to vote Republican. The same is true in the case of education, except for those holding advanced degrees. Protestants are far more likely to be Republican than those without religious affiliation, while women, Hispanics, and all non-white groups are more likely to be Democrats. Easterners are least likely to be Republican. The main effect of age was to reduce the proportion of independents as respondents grew older. Younger citizens who tend to think of themselves as independents are likely to develop an identification with one party or another as they mature.

Source: PEW Research Center Survey, January 9–13, 2008.

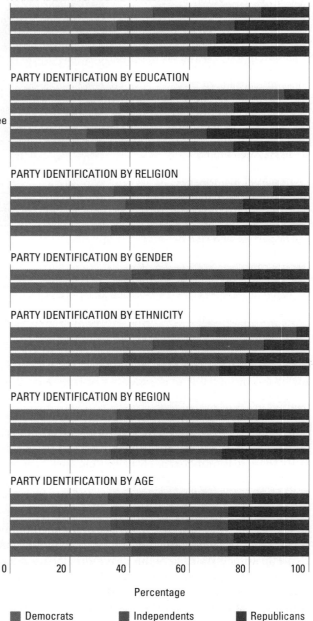

PARTY IDENTIFICATION BY INCOME

Under $30,000
$30,000–$74,999
$75,000–$99,999
Over $100,000

PARTY IDENTIFICATION BY EDUCATION

No high school
High school
Post high school, no degree
College degree
Advanced degree

PARTY IDENTIFICATION BY RELIGION

Unaffiliated
Catholic
Other
Protestant

PARTY IDENTIFICATION BY GENDER

Female
Male

PARTY IDENTIFICATION BY ETHNICITY

Black
Other
Hispanic
White

PARTY IDENTIFICATION BY REGION

East
West
South
Midwest

PARTY IDENTIFICATION BY AGE

18–29
30–41
42–53
54–64
65+

0   20   40   60   80   100

Percentage

■ Democrats   ■ Independents   ■ Republicans

Perhaps the major change in that coalition has been the replacement of white European ethnic groups by blacks, attracted by the Democrats' backing of civil rights legislation in the 1960s.

Studies show that about half the citizens in the United States adopt their parents' party. But it often takes time for party identification to develop. The youngest group of voters is most likely to be independent, but people now in their mid-twenties to mid-forties, who were socialized during the Reagan and first Bush presidencies, are heavily Republican. The oldest group is not only strongly Democratic but also shows the greatest partisan commitment (fewest independents), reflecting the fact that citizens become more interested in politics as they mature.

Americans tend to find their political niche and stay there.[19] The enduring party loyalty of American voters tends to structure the vote even before an election is held, even before the candidates are chosen. Later we will examine the extent to which party identification determines voting choice. But first we will look to see whether the Democratic and Republican parties have any significant differences between them.

Party Ideology and Organization

George Wallace, a disgruntled Democrat who ran for president in 1968 on the American Independent Party ticket, complained that "there isn't a dime's worth of difference" between the Democrats and Republicans. Humorist Will Rogers said, "I am not a member of any organized political party—I am a Democrat." Wallace's comment was made in disgust, Rogers's in jest. Wallace was wrong; Rogers was close to being right. Here we will dispel the myth that the parties do not differ significantly on issues and explain how they are organized to coordinate the activities of party candidates and officials in government.

Differences in Party Ideology

George Wallace notwithstanding, there is more than a dime's worth of difference between the two parties. In fact, the difference amounts to many billions of dollars—the cost of the different government programs supported by each party. Democrats are more disposed to government spending to advance social welfare (and hence to promote equality) than are Republicans. And social welfare programs cost money, a lot of money. Republicans, however, are not averse to spending billions of dollars for the projects they consider important. Although President George W. Bush introduced a massive tax cut, he also revived spending on missile defense, backed a $400 billion increase in Medicare, and proposed building a space platform on the moon for travel to Mars. One result was a huge increase in the budget deficit and a rare *Wall Street Journal* editorial against the GOP "spending spree."[20]

FIGURE 6.3 Ideologies of Party Voters and Party Delegates in 2008

Contrary to what many people think, the Democratic and Republican parties differ substantially in their ideological centers of gravity. When citizens were asked to classify themselves on an ideological scale, more Republicans than Democrats described themselves as conservative. When delegates to the parties' national conventions were asked to classify themselves, the differences between the parties grew even sharper.

Source: New York Times/CBS News Poll, 2008 Democratic National Delegate Survey and 2008 Republican National Survey, cited in *The New York Times*, 1 September 2008, p. A14.

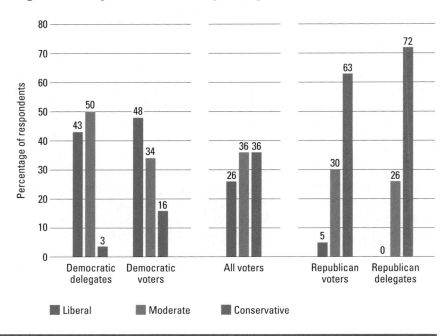

Voters and Activists. One way to examine the differences is to compare party voters with party activists. When such a comparison was done in 2008, it was found that 16 percent of those who identified themselves as Democratic voters described themselves as conservatives, compared with 63 percent of those who identified themselves as Republican voters. The ideological gap between the parties is even larger among party activists (see Figure 6.3). Only 3 percent of the delegates to the 2008 Democratic convention considered themselves conservatives compared with 72 percent of the delegates to the Republican convention.

Platforms: Freedom, Order, and Equality. For another test of party philosophy, we can look at the **party platforms**—the statements of policies— adopted in party conventions. Although many people feel that party platforms do not matter very much, several scholars have demonstrated that winning parties tend to carry out much of their platforms when in office.[21] Party platforms also matter a great deal to the parties' convention delegates. The wording of a platform plank often means the difference between victory and defeat for factions within a party.

The platforms adopted by the Democratic and Republican conventions in 2004 were strikingly different in style and substance and these differences reflected different preferences for freedom, order, and equality. For

party platform The statement of policies of a national political party.

Clashing Visions
Debates provide candidates with opportunities to highlight their own strengths and their opponents' weaknesses, although style sometimes trumps substance. During the presidential debates in 2008, John McCain and Barack Obama attempted to differentiate themselves and their visions of America while appealing to undecided voters in the middle of the political spectrum. *(AP Photo/Ron Edmonds)*

example, the 2004 Republican platform warned of "abortion" twelve times, while the Democrats said merely, "Abortion should be safe, legal, and rare." Republicans spoke glowingly about "free trade" twenty-two times, while the Democrats promised only "to include strong and enforceable labor and environmental standards in the core of new free trade agreements." Republicans repeatedly (twenty-three times) praised their position on "taxes," a problematic subject mentioned only eleven times by Democrats, who were more likely to talk about "jobs" (forty-seven times to thirty-six for Republicans).

In 2008, the Republican convention called for several amendments to the Constitution that reflected their values and priorities. Their platform called for a balanced budget amendment, an amendment to guarantee rights for crime victims, an amendment to end abortion and guarantee rights for the unborn, and an amendment to prevent same-sex marriage. In the Democratic Party's platform, the only amendment proposed was the equal rights amendment to prohibit gender discrimination. While both platforms recognized many of the same threats facing the United States, the Republicans identified the "gravest threat" as nuclear terrorism. For Democrats, the "greatest threat" was global climate change.[22]

Different But Similar. Democrats and Republicans have very different ideological orientations. Yet many observers claim that the parties are really quite similar in ideology compared with the different parties of other countries. Although both Republicans and Democrats favor a market economy over a planned economy more than parties elsewhere, Republicans do so more strongly than Democrats. A major cross-national study of party positions in Western countries since 1945 concludes that the United States experiences "a form of party competition that is as ideologically (or non-ideologically) driven as the other countries we have studied."[23]

National Party Organization

American parties parallel our federal system: they have separate national and state organizations (and functionally separate local organizations). At the national level, each major party has four main organizational components:

- *National convention.* Every four years, each party assembles thousands of delegates from the states and U.S. territories (such as Puerto Rico and Guam) in a **national convention** for the purpose of nominating a candidate for president. This presidential nominating convention is the supreme governing body of the party. It determines party policy through the platform, formulates rules to govern party operations, and designates a national committee, which is empowered to govern the party until the next convention.

- *National committee.* The **national committee**, which governs each party between conventions, is composed of party officials representing the states and territories, including the chairpersons of their party organizations. The Republican National Committee (RNC) has about 150 members, and the Democratic National Committee (DNC) has approximately 450 elected and appointed members. The chairperson of each national committee is chosen by the party's presidential nominee, then duly elected by the committee. If the nominee loses the presidential election, the national committee usually replaces the nominee's chairperson.

- *Congressional party conferences.* At the beginning of each session of Congress, Republicans and Democrats in each chamber hold separate **party conferences** (the House Democrats call theirs a *caucus*) to select their party leaders and decide committee assignments. The party conferences deal only with congressional matters and have no structural relationship to each other and no relationship to the national committee.

- *Congressional campaign committees.* Democrats and Republicans in the House and Senate also maintain separate **congressional campaign committees,** each of which raises its own funds to support its candidates in congressional elections. The separation of these organizations from the national committee tells us that the national party structure is loose; the national committee seldom gets involved with the election of any individual member of Congress. Moreover, even the congressional campaign organizations merely supplement the

national convention A gathering of delegates of a single political party from across the country to choose candidates for president and vice president and to adopt a party platform.

national committee A committee of a political party composed of party chairpersons and party officials from every state.

party conference A meeting to select party leaders and decide committee assignments, held at the beginning of a session of Congress by Republicans or Democrats in each chamber.

congressional campaign committee An organization maintained by a political party to raise funds to support its own candidates in congressional elections.

funds that senators and representatives raise on their own to win reelection.

It is tempting to think of the national party chairperson sitting at the top of a hierarchical party organization that not only controls its members in Congress but also issues orders to the state committees and on down to the local level. Few notions could be more wrong.[24] In fact, the RNC and DNC do not even really direct or control presidential campaigns. Prospective nominees hire their own campaign staffs during the party primaries to win delegates who will support them for nomination at the party conventions. The main role of a national committee is to support the eventual nominee's personal campaign staff in the effort to win the general election.

For many years, the role of the national committees was essentially limited to planning for the next party convention. The committee would select the site, issue the call to state parties to attend, plan the program, and so on.[25] In the 1970s, the roles of the DNC and RNC began to expand— but in different ways.

In 1968, during the Vietnam War, an unpopular President Lyndon Johnson was challenged for renomination by prominent Democrats, including senators Robert Kennedy and Eugene McCarthy. On March 31, after primary elections had begun, Johnson announced he would not run for reelection. Vice President Hubert Humphrey then announced his candidacy. A month later Senator Kennedy was assassinated. Although Humphrey did not enter a single primary, he won the nomination over McCarthy at a riotous convention angry at the war and the role of party bosses in picking Humphrey. In an attempt to open the party to broader participation, a party commission formulated new guidelines for selecting delegates to the next convention in 1972. These guidelines promised party members a "full, meaningful and timely opportunity" to participate in the process and required that state delegations starting in 1972 include women, blacks, and young people "in reasonable relationship to the group's presence in the population of the state."[26]

The DNC threatened to deny seating at the 1972 convention to any state delegation that did not comply with the guidelines. Never before had a national party committee imposed these kinds of rules on a state party organization, but it worked. To comply with the new guidelines, many more states began to use primaries to select convention delegates.

While the Democrats were busy in the 1970s with *procedural* reforms, the Republicans were making *organizational* reforms.[27] Republicans were not inclined to impose quotas on state parties through their national committee. Instead, the RNC strengthened its fundraising, research, and service roles. Republicans acquired their own building and their own computer, and in 1976 they hired the first full-time chairperson of either national party. The new RNC chairman, William Brock, expanded the party's staff, launched new publications, held seminars, conducted election analyses, and advised candidates—things that national party committees in other countries had been doing for years.

The vast difference between the Democratic and Republican approaches to reforming the national committees shows in the funds raised by the DNC and RNC during election campaigns. During Brock's tenure as chairman of the RNC, the Republicans raised three to four times as much money as the Democrats, and they raised more of their funds in small contributions (less than $100) than the Democrats.

Slow to respond to the Republicans' organizational initiatives, the Democrats acquired their own building in the 1990s and enhanced their computer system for fundraising. After former Vermont governor Howard Dean became the new chair of the DNC in 2005, he pushed a program to build the party's strength in all fifty states. His plan clashed with that of Rahm Emanuel (D-Ill.), the new head of the Democratic Congressional Campaign Committee, who favored focusing resources on "winnable" races in selected states. The clash itself showed the dispersion of power in the national party organization, but the party benefited from both efforts. Thanks largely to Emanuel's fervent work with congressional candidates, the Democrats won control of the Congress in the 2006 election, and state party leaders across the nation praised Dean for improving their organizations.[28]

State and Local Party Organizations

At one time, both major parties were firmly anchored by strong state and local party organizations. Big-city party organizations, such as the Democrats' Tammany Hall in New York City and the Cook County Central Committee in Chicago, were called *party machines*. A **party machine** was a centralized organization that dominated local politics by controlling elections—sometimes by illegal means, often by providing jobs and social services to urban workers in return for their votes. These patronage and social service functions of party machines were undercut when the government expanded its social services. As a result, most local party organizations lost their ability to deliver votes and thus to determine the outcome of elections.

The individual state and local organizations of both parties vary widely in strength, but research has found that "neither the Republican nor Democratic party has a distinct advantage with regard to direct campaign activities."[29] Whereas once both the RNC and the DNC were dependent for their funding on "quotas" paid by state parties, now the funds flow the other way. In addition to money, state parties also receive candidate training, poll data and research, and campaigning instruction.[30]

party machine A centralized party organization that dominates local politics by controlling elections.

Decentralized But Growing Stronger

The absence of centralized power has always been the most distinguishing characteristic of American political parties. Moreover, the rise in the proportion of citizens who call themselves "independents" suggests that our already weak parties are in further decline.[31] However, there is evidence that our political parties *as organizations* are enjoying a period of resurgence. Indeed, both national parties have globalized their organizations, maintaining branches in over a dozen nations.[32] And more votes in Congress are being decided along party lines. In fact, a specialist in congressional politics has concluded, "When compared to its predecessors of the last half-century, the current majority party leadership is more involved and more decisive in organizing the party and the chamber, setting the policy agenda, shaping legislation, and determining legislative outcomes."[33]

The Model of Responsible Party Government

According to the majoritarian model of democracy, parties are essential to making the government responsive to public opinion. In fact, the ideal role of parties in majoritarian democracy has been formalized in the four principles of **responsible party government**:[34]

1. Parties should present clear and coherent programs to voters.

2. Voters should choose candidates according to the party programs.

3. The winning party should carry out its program once in office.

4. Voters should hold the governing party responsible at the next election for executing its program.

How well do these principles describe American politics? You've learned that the Democratic and Republican platforms are different and that they are much more ideologically consistent than many people believe. So the first principle is being met fairly well. To a lesser extent, so is the third principle: once parties gain power, they usually do what they said they would do. From the standpoint of democratic theory, the real question lies in principles 2 and 4: Do voters really pay attention to party platforms and policies when they cast their ballots? And if so, do voters hold the governing party responsible at the next election for delivering, or failing to deliver, on its pledges? To answer these questions, we must consider in greater detail the parties' role in nominating candidates and structuring the voters' choice in elections. At the conclusion of this chapter, we return to evaluating the role of political parties in democratic government.

Parties and Candidates

An **election campaign** is an organized effort to persuade voters to choose one candidate over others competing for the same office. An effective campaign requires sufficient resources to acquire and analyze information about voters' interests, develop a strategy and matching tactics for appealing to these

responsible party government A set of principles formalizing the ideal role of parties in a majoritarian democracy.

election campaign An organized effort to persuade voters to choose one candidate over others competing for the same office.

Compared with What?

The Voter's Burden in the United States and Canada

No other country requires its voters to make as many decisions in a general election as the United States does. Compare these two facsimiles of official specimen ballots for the 2008 general election in the United States and the 2006 general election in Canada. The long U.S. ballot is just a *portion* of the one that confronted voters in the city of Evanston, Illinois. In addition to the multiple offices listed here, the full ballot also asked voters to check yes or no on the retention of scores of incumbent judges. By contrast, the straightforward Canadian ballot (for the Notre-Dame-de-Grâce–Lachine district in Montreal) simply asked citizens to choose one from seven party candidates running for the House of Commons for that district. (Incidentally, the Liberal Party candidate won.) It is no wonder that voting is so complicated in the United States and so simple in Canada.

Vote for Only One

FOR THE CANADIAN HOUSE OF COMMONS

◯　Alexandre Lambert	*Bloc Québécois*
◯　Allen F. Mackenzie	*Conservative*
◯　Pierre-Albert Sévigny	*Green*
◯　Marlene Jennings	*Liberal*
◯　Earl Wertheimer	*Libertarian*
◯　Rachel Hoffman	*Marxist-Leninist*
◯　Peter Deslauriers	*New Democratic*

interests, deliver the candidate's message to the voters, and get voters to cast their ballots.[35]

In the past, political parties conducted all phases of the election campaign. Today, however, candidates seldom rely much on political parties to conduct their campaigns. How do candidates plan their campaign strategy and tactics now? By hiring political consultants to devise clever "sound

---

Voter Ballot for the 2008 United States General Election
Cook County, Illinois, Tuesday, November 4

President and Vice President (Vote for 1)

❐ Barack Obama & Joe Biden	*Democrat*
❐ John McCain & Sarah Palin	*Republican*

U.S. Senator (Vote for 1)

❐ Richard J. Durbin	*Democrat*
❐ Steve Sauerberg	*Republican*

Representative in Congress, 9th District (Vote for 1)

❐ Janice D. Schakowsky	*Democrat*
❐ Michael Benjamin Younan	*Republican*

Illinois State Senator, 9th District (Vote for 1)

❐ Jeffrey M. Schoenberg	*Democrat*
❐ Brendan Appel	*Republican*

Illinois Assembly Representative, 18th District

❐ Julie Hamos	*Democrat*

Water Reclamation Commissioner (Vote for 3)

❐ Frank Avila	*Democrat*
❐ Kathleen Therese Meany	*Democrat*
❐ Cynthia M. Santos	*Democrat*
❐ David Clearwater	*Republican*
❐ Paul Chialdikas	*Republican*
❐ Daniel Flores	*Republican*

State's Attorney (Vote for 1)

❐ Anita Alvarez	*Democrat*
❐ Tony Peraica	*Republican*

Circuit Clerk (Vote for 1)

❐ Dorothy A. Brown	*Democrat*
❐ Diane Shapiro	*Republican*

Recorder of Deeds (Vote for 1)

❐ Eugene "Gene" Moore	*Democrat*
❐ Gregory Goldstein	*Republican*
❐ Terrence A. Gilhooly	*Green*

Board of Review, 2nd District (Vote for 1)

❐ Joseph Berrios	*Democrat*
❐ Lauren Elizabeth McCracken-Quirk	*Republican*
❐ Howard Kaplan	*Green*

Supreme Court Judge, 1st District (Vacancy of McMorrow)

❐ Anne M. Burke	*Democrat*

Appellate Court Judge, 1st District (Vacancy of Burke)

❐ Sharon Johnson Coleman	*Democrat*

Appellate Court Judge, 1st District (Vacancy of Cambell)

❐ John O. Steele	*Democrat*

Circuit Court Judge Full Circuit (Vacancy of Disko)

❐ Dennis J. Burke	*Democrat*

Circuit Court Judge Full Circuit (Vacancy of Glowacki)

❐ Jesse G. Reyes	*Democrat*

Circuit Court Judge Full Circuit (Vacancy of Healy)

❐ Maureen Ward Kirby	*Democrat*

Circuit Court Judge Full Circuit (Vacancy of Keehan)

❐ Marilyn F. Johnson	*Democrat*

Circuit Court Judge Full Circuit (Vacancy of Lott)

❐ Thomas J. Byrne	*Democrat*

Circuit Court Judge Full Circuit (Vacancy of Montelione)

❐ Debra B. Walker	*Democrat*

Circuit Court Judge Full Circuit (Vacancy of Murphy)

❐ Kristyna Colleen Ryan	*Democrat*

Circuit Court Judge Full Circuit (Vacancy of Nowicki)

❐ Michael B. Hyman	*Democrat*

Circuit Court Judge Full Circuit (Vacancy of Thomas)

❐ Joan Powell	*Democrat*

---

bites" (brief, catchy phrases) that capture voters' attention on television, not by consulting party headquarters. How do candidates deliver their messages to voters? By conducting media campaigns, not by counting on party regulars to canvass the neighborhoods. Beginning with the 2004 election, presidential and congressional candidates have also relied heavily on the Internet to raise campaign funds and mobilize supporters.[36]

Increasingly, election campaigns have evolved from being party centered to being candidate centered.[37] Whereas the parties virtually ran election campaigns in the past, now they exist mainly to support candidate-centered campaigns by providing services or funds to their candidates. Nevertheless, we will see that the party label is usually a candidate's prime attribute at election time.

Perhaps the most important change in American elections is that candidates do not campaign just to get elected anymore. It is now necessary to campaign for *nomination* as well. Party organizations once controlled that function. For most important offices today, however, candidates are no longer nominated *by* the party organization but are nominated *within* the party. Party leaders seldom choose candidates themselves; they organize and supervise the election process by which party *voters* choose the candidates. Because almost all aspiring candidates must first win a primary election to gain their party's nomination, those who would campaign for election must first campaign for nomination.

The distinguishing feature of the nomination process in American party politics is that it usually involves an election by party voters. Virtually no other political parties in the world nominate candidates to the national legislature through party elections.[38] In more than half the world's parties, local party leaders choose legislative candidates, and their national party organization must usually approve those choices.

Democrats and Republicans nominate their candidates for national and state offices in varying ways across the country because each state is entitled to make its own laws governing the nomination process. (This is significant in itself, for political parties in most other countries are largely free of laws stating how they must select their candidates.) We can classify their nomination practices by the types of party elections held and the level of office sought.

Nomination for Congress and State Offices

In the United States, almost all aspiring candidates for major offices are nominated through a **primary election**, a preliminary election conducted within the party to select its candidates. Forty states use primary elections alone to nominate candidates for all state and national offices, and primaries figure in the nomination process in all the other states. The rules governing primary elections vary greatly by state and can change between elections. Hence, it is difficult to summarize the types of primaries and their incidence. Every state uses primary elections to nominate candidates for statewide office, but about ten states also use party conventions to place names on the primary ballots.[39] The nomination process, then, is highly decentralized, resting on the decisions of thousands, perhaps millions, of the party rank and file who participate in primary elections.

There are four major types of primary elections, and variants of each type are used about equally across all states to nominate candidates for

primary election A preliminary election conducted within a political party to select candidates who will run for public office in a subsequent election.

state and congressional offices.[40] At one end of the spectrum stand **closed primaries,** in which voters must register their party affiliation to vote on that party's potential nominees. At the other end stand **open primaries,** in which any voter, regardless of party registration or affiliation, can choose either party's ballot. In between are **modified closed primaries,** in which individual state parties decide whether to allow those not registered with either party to vote with their party registrants; and **modified open primaries,** in which all those not already registered with a party can choose any party ballot and vote with party registrants.

Nomination for President

The decentralized nature of American parties is readily apparent in how presidential hopefuls must campaign for their party's nomination for president. Each party formally chooses its presidential and vice-presidential candidates at a national convention held every four years in the summer prior to the November election. Until the 1960s, party delegates chose their party's nominee at the convention, sometimes after repeated balloting over several candidates who divided the vote and kept anyone from getting the majority needed to win the nomination. The last time that either party needed more than one ballot to nominate its presidential candidate was in 1952, when the Democrats took three ballots to nominate Adlai E. Stevenson. Since 1972, both parties' nominating conventions have simply ratified the results of the complex process for selecting the convention delegates. Most minor parties, like the Green Party in 2008, still tend to use conventions to nominate their presidential candidates.

Selecting Convention Delegates.   No national legislation specifies how state parties must select delegates to their national conventions. Instead, state legislatures have enacted a bewildering variety of procedures, which often differ for Democrats and Republicans in the same state. The most important distinction in delegate selection is between the presidential primary and the local caucus.

A **presidential primary** is a special primary held to select delegates to attend the party's national nominating convention. Party supporters typically vote for the candidate they favor as their party's nominee for president, and candidates win delegates according to a variety of formulas. Most Democratic presidential primaries are *proportional,* so candidates who win at least 15 percent of the vote divide the delegates from that state in proportion to the percentage they won. Most Republican primaries are *winner-take-all,* so the candidate receiving the most votes in a state takes all of that state's convention delegates.

Delegate selection by **caucus/convention** has several stages. It begins with local meetings, or caucuses, of party supporters to choose delegates to attend a larger subsequent meeting, usually at the county level. Most delegates selected in the local caucuses openly back one of the presidential

closed primary A primary election in which voters must declare their party affiliation before they are given the primary ballot containing that party's potential nominees.

open primary A primary election in which voters need not declare their party affiliation and can choose one party's primary ballot to take into the voting booth.

modified closed primary A primary election that allows individual state parties to decide whether they permit independents to vote in their primaries and for which offices.

modified open primary A primary election that entitles independent voters to vote in a party's primary.

presidential primary A special primary election used to select delegates to attend the party's national convention, which in turn nominates the presidential candidate.

caucus/convention A method used to select delegates to attend a party's national convention. Generally a local meeting selects delegates for a county-level meeting, which in turn selects delegates for a higher-level meeting; the process culminates in a state convention that selects the national convention delegates.

candidates. The county meetings, in turn, select delegates to a higher level. The process culminates in a state convention, which selects the delegates to the national convention.

Primary elections were first used to select delegates to nominating conventions in 1912. Now parties in about forty states rely on presidential primaries in some form, which generate approximately 80 percent of the delegates.[41] Because nearly all delegates selected in primaries are publicly committed to specific candidates, one can easily tell before a party's summer nominating convention who is going to be its nominee. Indeed, we have been learning the nominee's identity earlier and earlier, thanks to the **front-loading** of primaries. This term describes the tendency during the past two decades for states to move their primaries earlier in the calendar year to gain more attention from the media and the candidates.[42] In 2008 so many states pushed their delegate selection process so far toward the beginning of the year that more than half of the delegates to both conventions were selected by February 5—when twenty-four states held simultaneous primary elections or caucuses to select convention delegates. Prior to 2000, New Hampshire's primary (the first in the nation) had never occurred that early.

Campaigning for the Nomination.   The process of nominating party candidates for president is a complex, drawn-out affair that has no parallel in any other nation.[43] Would-be presidents announce their candidacy and begin campaigning many months before the first convention delegates are selected. Soon after one election ends, prospective candidates quietly begin lining up political and financial support for their likely race nearly four years later. By historical accident, two small states, Iowa and New Hampshire, have become the testing ground of candidates' early popularity with party voters. Accordingly, each basks in the media spotlight once every four years.

The Iowa caucuses and the New Hampshire primary have served different functions in the presidential nominating process.[44] The contest in Iowa has traditionally tended to winnow out candidates who are rejected by the party faithful. The New Hampshire primary, generally held one week later, tests the Iowa front-runners' appeal to ordinary party voters, which foreshadows their likely strength in the general election. Iowa held its 2008 caucuses on January 3 to be first to select delegates. New Hampshire followed with the nation's first primary on January 8.

To combat the pressures of front-loading in 2008, the Democratic National Committee passed a rule in July 2006 allowing only Iowa, New Hampshire, Nevada, and South Carolina to hold primaries before the February 5 Super Tuesday primaries. The major Democratic candidates pledged not to campaign in states that violated the new party rules.

Two key states—Michigan and Florida—defied the party rules. In response, the DNC initially vowed not to seat Michigan's and Florida's delegates at the party's convention, sparking hot controversy between the

front-loading States' practice of moving delegate selection primaries and caucuses earlier in the calendar year to gain media and candidate attention.

FIRST IN THE NATION

DIXVILLE NOTCH
New Hampshire

2008

JAN 8

REPUBLICAN		DEMOCRATIC	
GIULIANI	1	CLINTON	2
HUCKABEE		EDWARDS	
McCAIN	4	KUCINICH	
PAUL		OBAMA	7
ROMNEY	2	RICHARDSON	1
THOMPSON			

Midnight Madness in New Hampshire

Once every four years, there's something to do after midnight in Dixville Notch, New Hampshire, and in nearby Hart's Landing. Both small towns (each with under forty residents) revel in the tradition of being the first to vote in the nation's first primary. In 2008, Senator Barack Obama crushed his opposition in the Democratic primary, winning seven of the ten votes cast at midnight in Dixville Notch. On the Republican side of the ballot, John McCain picked up four of the seven votes. *(AP Photo/Jim Cole)*

candidates. Hillary Clinton claimed that the delegates she won in both states should be counted at the convention. Barack Obama objected that this would be unfair, as both he and Clinton had signed a pledge supporting the rule. Indeed, Obama's name did not even appear on the ballot in Michigan. Ultimately, the Democratic National Committee decided to seat the delegations in question with only one-half vote per delegate.[45] Without the extra delegates from Florida and Michigan, Clinton had fallen too far behind in the delegate count to beat Obama, so she suspended her campaign. Obama went on to win the nomination and full votes were restored to Michigan and Florida in August. The Republican Party also penalized several states for front-loading primaries by reducing their number of delegates, but it did not affect the outcome of their nomination process.

Requiring prospective presidential candidates to campaign before many millions of party voters in primaries and hundreds of thousands of party activists in caucus states has several consequences:

■ *When no incumbent in the White House is seeking reelection, the presidential nominating process becomes contested in both parties.* This is what occurred in the 2008 elections. With President Bush ineligible to run again in 2008, twelve Republicans and ten Democrats met the Federal Election Committee's requirements for electronic filing of their presidential campaigns.

■ *An incumbent president usually encounters little or no opposition for renomination with the party.* That is what happened in 2004, but challenges can occur. In 1992, President George Herbert Walker Bush faced fierce opposition for the Republican nomination from Pat Buchanan.

■ *The Iowa caucuses and New Hampshire primaries do matter.* Since the first Iowa caucus in 1972, ten candidates in each party have won presidential nominations. All of the ten Republicans nominees were first in either Iowa or New Hampshire, as were eight of the Democrats.

■ *Candidates favored by most party identifiers usually win their party's nomination.* There have been only two exceptions to this rule since 1936, when poll data first became available: Adlai E. Stevenson in 1952 and George McGovern in 1972.[46] Both were Democrats; both lost impressively in the general election.

■ *Candidates who win the nomination do so largely on their own and owe little or nothing to the national party organization, which usually does not promote a candidate.* In fact, Jimmy Carter won the nomination in 1976 against a field of nationally prominent Democrats, although he was a party outsider with few strong connections in the national party leadership.

Elections

By national law, all seats in the House of Representatives and one-third of the seats in the Senate are filled in a **general election** held in early November in even-numbered years. Every state takes advantage of the national election to also fill some of nearly 500,000 state and local offices across the country, which makes the election even more "general." When the president is chosen every fourth year, the election year is identified as a *presidential election.* The intervening years are known as *congressional, midterm,* or *off-year elections.*

Presidential Elections and the Electoral College

In contrast to almost all other offices in the United States, the presidency does not go automatically to the candidate who wins the most votes. In fact, George W. Bush won the presidency in 2000 despite receiving fewer votes than Al Gore. Instead, a two-stage procedure specified in the Constitution decides elections for president. The president and vice president are chosen by a group of electors representing the states. These electors, known collectively as the electoral college, meet in their respective states to cast their ballots.

general election A national election held by law in November of every even-numbered year.

The Electoral College. The Constitution (Article II, Section 1) says, "Each State shall appoint, in such Manner as the Legislature thereof may direct, a Number of Electors, equal to the whole Number of Senators and Representatives to which the State may be entitled in the Congress." Thus, each state is entitled to one elector for each of its senators (100 total) and one for each of its representatives (435 votes total), totaling 535 electoral votes. In addition, the Twenty-third Amendment to the Constitution awarded three electoral votes to the District of Columbia, although it elects no voting members of Congress. So the total number of electoral votes is 538. The Constitution specifies that a candidate needs a majority of electoral votes, or 270 today, to win the presidency. If no candidate receives a majority when the electoral college votes, the election is thrown into the House of Representatives. The House votes by state, with each state casting one vote.*

The 538 electoral votes are apportioned among the states according to their representation in Congress, which depends on their population. Because of population changes recorded by the 2000 census, the distribution of electoral votes among the states changed between the 2000 and 2004 presidential elections. Figure 6.4 shows the distribution of electoral votes for the 2004 and 2008 elections.

The presidential election is a *federal* election. A candidate is not chosen president by national popular vote but by a majority of the states' electoral votes. In forty-eight states, the candidate who wins a plurality of its popular vote—whether by 20 votes or by 20,000—wins all of the state's electoral votes. (The two exceptions are Maine and Nebraska, where two and three of the states' electoral votes, respectively, are awarded by congressional district. The presidential candidate who carries each district wins a single electoral vote, and the statewide winner gets two votes.)

Abolish the Electoral College?   Following the 2000 election, letters flooded into newspapers urging that the electoral college system be changed. To evaluate the criticisms, one must first distinguish between the electoral "college" and the "system" of electoral votes. The electoral college is merely the set of individuals empowered to cast a state's electoral votes. In a presidential election, voters do not actually vote for a candidate; they vote for a slate of little-known electors (their names are rarely even on the ballot) pledged to one of the candidates. On rare occasions "faithless electors" break their pledges when they assemble to cast their written ballots at their state capitol in December. This happened in 2004 when a Democratic elector in Minnesota voted for John Edwards for both president and vice president, rather than casting the presidential vote for John Kerry. Such aberrations make for historical footnotes, but they do not affect outcomes.

---

*The candidates in the House election are the top three finishers in the general election. A presidential election has gone to the House only twice in American history, in 1800 and 1824, before a stable two-party system had developed.

FIGURE 6.4   State Population Change and the Electoral College

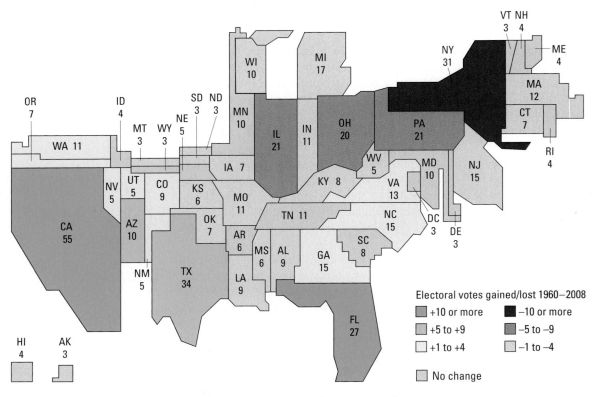

Electoral votes gained/lost 1960–2008

- ▮ +10 or more
- ▮ +5 to +9
- ▯ +1 to +4
- ▮ −10 or more
- ▮ −5 to −9
- ▯ −1 to −4
- ▯ No change

If the states were sized according to their electoral votes, the nation might resemble this map, on which the states are drawn according to their population, based on the census. Each state has as many electoral votes as its combined representation in the Senate (always two) and the House (which depends on population). Although New Jersey is much smaller in area than Montana, it has far more people and is thus bigger in terms of "electoral geography." The coloring on this map shows the states that have gained or lost electoral votes since 1960 due to changing population patterns.

The more troubling criticism centers on the electoral vote *system*, which makes for a federal rather than a national election. Many reformers favor a majoritarian method for choosing the president: a nationwide direct popular vote. They argue that it is simply wrong to have a system that allows a candidate who wins the most popular votes nationally to lose the election. Until 2000, that situation had not happened since 1888. In fact, the electoral vote generally operated to magnify the margin of victory in the popular vote.

The 2000 election proved that a federal election based on electoral votes does not necessarily yield the same outcome as a national election based on the popular vote. However, three lines of argument support selecting a president by electoral votes rather than by popular vote. First, if one supports a federal form of government as embodied within the Constitution, then one may defend the electoral vote system because it gives small states more weight in the vote: they have two senators, the same as large states. Second, if one favors presidential candidates' campaigning on foot and in rural areas (needed to win most states) rather than campaigning via television to the one hundred most populous market areas, then one might favor the electoral vote system.[47] Third, if one does not want to see a *nationwide* recount in a close election (multiplying by fifty the counting problems in Florida after the 2000 election), then one might want to keep the current system. So switching to selecting the president by popular vote has serious implications, which explains why Congress has not moved quickly to amend the Constitution.

Congressional Elections

The candidates for the presidency are listed at the top of the ballot in a presidential election, followed by the candidates for other national offices and for state and local offices. Voters are said to vote a **straight ticket** when they choose one party's candidates for all the offices. A voter who chooses candidates from different parties is said to vote a **split ticket**. About half of all voters say they split their tickets.[48] A common pattern in the 1970s and 1980s was to elect a Republican as president but send mostly Democrats to Congress, producing divided government (see Chapter 9). This pattern was reversed in the 1994 election, when voters elected a Republican Congress to face a Democratic president. Though Republican president George W. Bush enjoyed a unified government for more than half of his presidency, the 2006 midterm elections brought Democratic majorities to both the House and the Senate.

Heading into the 2008 congressional elections, Republicans feared further losses in both houses of Congress. President Bush's approval rate had plummeted, the economy was in steep decline, and the war in Iraq cost more in American lives and money. By early spring, twenty-nine Republican incumbents in the House and six in the Senate had announced their retirement, compared to only five Democrats in the House and none in the Senate.[49] Seats without incumbents are much easier to win. Republican fears were justified. Democrats established a strong majority in the Senate so they would no longer need to depend upon votes from independent senators Bernie Sanders and Joseph Lieberman to pass legislation. Democrats in the House increased their majority by almost two dozen seats.

straight ticket In voting, a single party's candidates for all the offices.

split ticket In voting, candidates from different parties for different offices.

DO IT!

Pick a party at www.politics1
.com/parties.htm and get
involved in political
campaigns.

Campaigns

Political scientists Barbara Salmore and Stephen Salmore have developed an analytical framework that emphasizes the political context of an election campaign, the financial resources available for conducting the campaign, and the strategies and tactics that underlie the dissemination of information about the candidate.[50]

The Political Context

The two most important structural factors that face each candidate planning a campaign are the office the candidate is seeking and whether he or she is the *incumbent* (the current officeholder, running for reelection) or the *challenger* (who seeks to replace the incumbent). Alternatively, the candidate can be running in an **open election**, which lacks an incumbent as a result of resignation or death. Incumbents usually enjoy great advantages over challengers, especially in elections to Congress.

Every candidate organizing a campaign must also examine the characteristics of the district, including its physical size and the sociological makeup of its electorate. In general, the bigger and more populous the district and the more diverse the electorate, the more complicated and costly is the campaign.

The party preference of the electorate is an important factor in the context of a campaign. It is easier for candidates to get elected when their party matches the electorate's preference, in part because raising the money needed to conduct a winning campaign is easier. Finally, significant political issues, such as economic recession, personal scandals, and war, not only affect a campaign but also can dominate it and even negate such positive factors as incumbency and the normal inclinations of the electorate.

Financing

Former House Speaker Thomas ("Tip") O'Neill once said, "As it is now, there are four parts to any campaign. The candidate, the issues of the candidate, the campaign organization, and the money to run the campaign with. Without money you can forget the other three."[51] Money will buy the best campaign managers, equipment, transportation, research, and consultants, making the quality of the organization largely a function of money.[52] Campaign financing is now heavily regulated by national and state governments, and regulations vary according to the level of the office—national, state, or local. At the national level, new legislation now governs raising and spending money for election campaigns.

Regulating Campaign Financing. In 1971, during a period of party reform, Congress passed the Federal Election Campaign Act (FECA), which imposed stringent new rules for full reporting of campaign contri-

open election An election that
lacks an incumbent.

butions and expenditures. FECA has been strengthened several times since 1971. A 1974 amendment created the **Federal Election Commission (FEC)** to enforce limits on financial contributions to national campaigns, require full disclosure of campaign spending, and administer the public financing of presidential campaigns, which began with the 1976 election.

The 1974 legislation imposed limits on contributions by individuals and organizations to campaigns for Congress and the presidency. The FECA called direct donations to individual candidates **hard money** and imposed limits on these donations (for example, no person could give more than $1,000 per candidate for federal office in a given election).

In reviewing the law, the Supreme Court ruled that wealthy candidates could spend their own money without limit. Wall Street investor and Democrat Jon S. Corzine spent $65 million to win the 2000 New Jersey Senate race, spending about $20 for each of his 1.3 million votes.[53] Corzine spent another $42 million to win the governor's seat in New Jersey in 2005 and left the Senate before the end of his first term.[54]

After his run for the 2000 Republican presidential nomination, Senator John McCain (Ariz.) pressed for the bill he had cosponsored with Senator Russell Feingold (D-Wis.) to ban soft-money contributions and issue-advocacy ads that favored a given candidate. In March 2002, Congress passed the **Bipartisan Campaign Reform Act (BCRA)**, known informally as the McCain-Feingold bill.[55] BCRA was fiercely challenged from several sources, but it was upheld by the Supreme Court in 2003 and took effect for the 2004 election.

In general, BCRA raised the old limits on individual contributions in the 1974 act from $1,000 per federal candidate in an election to $2,000 and indexed it for inflation in future years. However, the 2002 law did not raise the $5,000 contribution limit for PACs and did not index PAC contributions for inflation. Here are the major limitations on *individual* contributions for 2007–2008 under BCRA:

- $2,300 to a specific candidate in a separate election during a two-year cycle (primaries, general, and runoff elections count as separate elections)

- $10,000 per year to state, district, and local party committees (combined limit)

- $28,500 per year to any national party committee

- an aggregate limit of $108,200 over a two-year cycle, based on limits to individual candidates and committees

One element of BCRA that did not withstand scrutiny by the Supreme Court was a limitation it placed on advertisements run by corporations and unions. Under BCRA, corporations and unions were banned from spending funds from their general treasuries on advertisements mentioning candidates in the days leading up to an election. In 2007, the Supreme

Federal Election Commission (FEC) A bipartisan federal agency that oversees the financing of national election campaigns.

hard money Financial contributions given directly to a congressional or presidential campaign.

Bipartisan Campaign Reform Act (BCRA) A law passed in 2002 governing campaign financing; the law took effect with the 2004 election.

Court ruled that this broad prohibition was impermissible in all cases except those directly calling for the election or defeat of the candidates.[56] A second provision struck down by the court was the so-called Millionaire's Amendment, which authorized candidates facing wealthy, self-financing opponents to accept substantially larger campaign contributions than was generally allowed.[57]

Public Financing of Presidential Campaigns.   The 1974 campaign finance law provided public funds for presidential candidates who agreed to abide by an overall campaign spending limit and raised at least $5,000 (in private donations of no more than $250 each) in each of twenty states. The FEC matches these donations up to one-half of a preset spending limit for the primary election campaign. By 2008, the inflation-adjusted spending limit for primary election expenditures had risen to $42.05 million. Candidates who raised up to $21.025 million in private funds would have that amount matched by up to $21.025 million in public funds, subject to the limitation that they could not spend more than $42.05 million in their primary campaigns.

From 1976 through 1992, all major candidates seeking their party's presidential nomination accepted public matching funds for their primary election campaigns and thus adhered to the spending limits. Wealthy publisher Steve Forbes was the first to opt out of the system in 1996. In 2004, Democratic hopefuls Howard Dean and John Kerry and incumbent president George W. Bush (who faced no meaningful opposition for renomination) declined public matching funds and chose to raise their own funds for the primary campaigns, avoiding the spending cap.[58] In 2008, only six of the nineteen candidates who participated in either party's primary debates relied on matching funds.[59] Both Barack Obama and John McCain refused federal matching funds during the primary season, relying on private donations instead. Through March 2008, Obama alone had spent $183 million—far more than the $42 million limit imposed by accepting public funds.

The public funding program for presidential elections in November operates somewhat differently. The campaign spending limit for the general election was roughly $84.1 million in 2008, twice the limit for primary elections. Candidates who accept public funds have no need to raise matching funds privately. They are simply reimbursed by the government up to the spending limit.

From 1976 to 2004, every major party nominee for president accepted public funds and spending limits for the general election. In 2008 Republican John McCain agreed to accept public funds and limit his campaign spending in the general election to $84.1 million. The Democratic nominee, Barack Obama, refused public funds for the general election, becoming the first candidate to do so since the system was established over thirty years earlier. He raised $150 million in September 2008 alone. If McCain—coauthor of the McCain-Feingold campaign finance reform law (BCRA)—had not been so closely identified with limiting the role of private money in campaigns, he might also have declined public funding and the spending limit it imposed.

The Politics of Campaign Finance.   In the 1980s, both parties began to exploit a loophole in the law that allowed them to raise a virtually unlimited amount of **soft money:** funds to be spent on party mailings, voter registration, and get-out-the-vote campaigns. Beginning in 2004, BCRA banned the practice of raising soft money by national party committees, which could now raise and spend only hard money for specific campaigns. However, this ban did not extend to state parties, and BCRA also allowed issue-advocacy groups—called **527 committees** after Section 527 of the Internal Revenue Code, which makes them tax exempt—to raise unlimited amounts of soft money to spend on television commercials and other forms of advertising, as long as they did not expressly advocate a candidate's election or defeat. Scholars studying campaign spending by 527 committees after BCRA found that their contributions increased from $151 million in 2002 to $424 million in 2004.[60]

Strategies and Tactics

In an election campaign, strategy is the broad approach used to persuade citizens to vote for a candidate, and tactics determine the content of the messages and the way they are delivered. There are three basic strategies, which campaigns may blend in different mixes.[61] A *party-centered strategy* relies heavily on voters' partisan identification as well as on the party's organization to provide the resources necessary to wage the campaign. An *issue-oriented strategy* seeks support from groups that feel strongly about various policies. A *candidate-oriented strategy* depends on the candidate's perceived personal qualities, such as experience, leadership ability, integrity, independence, and trustworthiness.

The campaign strategy must be tailored to the political context of the election. Research suggests that a party-centered strategy is best suited to voters with little political knowledge.[62] How do candidates learn what the electorate knows and thinks about politics, and how can they use this information? Candidates today usually turn to pollsters and political consultants, of whom there are hundreds.[63] Professional campaign managers can use information from such sources to settle on a strategy that mixes party affiliation, issues, and images in its messages.[64] In major campaigns, the mass media disseminate these messages to voters in news coverage, advertising, and the Internet.

Making the News.   Campaigns value news coverage by the media for two reasons: the coverage is free, and it seems objective to the audience. If news stories do nothing more than report a candidate's name, that is important, for name recognition by itself often wins elections. Getting free news coverage is yet another advantage that incumbents enjoy over challengers,

soft money Funds raised by parties to be spent on party mailings, voter registration, and get-out-the-vote campaigns rather than for a specific federal election campaign.

527 committees Political organizations that are organized under Section 527 of the Internal Revenue Code; they enjoy tax-exempt status and may accept unlimited funds from unlimited sources but cannot expressly advocate a candidate's election or defeat.

for incumbents can command attention simply by announcing political decisions.

Advertising the Candidate.   In all elections, the first objective of paid advertising is name recognition. The next is to promote the candidates by extolling their virtues. Campaign advertising also can have a negative objective: attacking one's opponent. But name recognition is the most important. Studies show that many voters cannot recall the names of their U.S. senators or representatives but can recognize those names on a list—as on a ballot. Researchers attribute the high reelection rate for members of Congress mainly to high name recognition (see Chapter 8).

At one time, candidates for national office relied heavily on newspaper advertising; today they overwhelmingly use the electronic media.[65] The media often inflate the effects of prominent ads by reporting them as news, which means that citizens are about as likely to see controversial ads during the news as in the ads' paid time slots.

Using the Internet.   The Internet has emerged as a significant tool for fundraising and communicating, particularly with the party faithful.[66] Of the two purposes, fundraising has taken the front seat. In January 2008, the month Barack Obama won contests in Iowa and South Carolina, he raised $32 million from 170,000 new contributors, mostly online.[67] However, candidates need not win stunning victories to raise large sums on the Internet. Republican Ron Paul, who trailed in the polls, raised $4 million online in a single day.[68]

It is more difficult to measure the impact of the Internet in campaign communications. A national survey in late December 2007 asked respondents to name two sources for "most of" their news about the presidential campaign. Most people (71 percent) named television, nearly one-third (30 percent) cited newspapers, and only one-quarter (26 percent) said the Internet.[69] Because Internet users seek out what they want to view, the best way to reach average voters is still through local broadcast television.[70]

 # Explaining Voting Choice

Why do people choose one candidate over another? The answer is not easy to determine, but there are ways to approach the question. Individual voting choices may be viewed as products of both long-term and short-term forces. Long-term forces operate throughout a series of elections, predisposing voters to choose certain types of candidates. Short-term forces are associated with particular elections; they arise from a combination of the candidates and the issues at that time. Party identification is by far the most important long-term force affecting U.S. elections. The most important short-term forces are candidates' attributes and their policy positions.

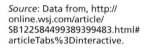 **FIGURE 6.5** Effect of Party Identification on the Vote, 2008

The 2008 election showed that party identification still plays a key role in voting behavior, even with an independent candidate in the contest. The chart shows the results of exit polls of thousands of voters as they left hundreds of polling places across the nation on election day. Voters were asked what party they identified with and how they voted for president. Those who identified with one of the two parties voted strongly for their party's candidate.

Source: Data from, http://online.wsj.com/article/SB122584499389399483.html#articleTabs%3Dinteractive.

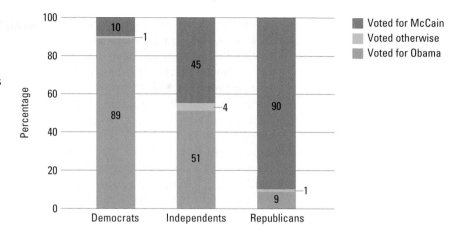

Despite frequent comments in the media about the decline of partisanship in voting behavior, party identification continues to have a substantial effect on the presidential vote, as Figure 6.5 shows. Typically, the winner holds nearly all the voters who identify with his party. The loser holds most of his fellow Democrats or Republicans, but some percentage defects to the winner, a product of short-term forces—the candidates' attributes and the issues—surrounding the election. The winner usually gets most of the independents, who split disproportionately for him, also because of short-term forces.

Candidates' attributes are especially important to voters who lack good information about a candidate's past performance and policy stands—which means most of us. Without such information, voters search for clues about the candidates to try to predict their behavior in office.[71] Some fall back on their personal beliefs about religion, gender, and race in making political judgments. Such stereotypical thinking accounts for the patterns of opposition and support met by a Catholic candidate for president (John Kennedy in 1960) and a woman candidate for vice president (Geraldine Ferraro in 1984). In 2008 Barack Obama tested the stereotype when he became the first African American nominee of a major party.[72]

Voters who choose candidates on the basis of their policies are voting on the issues. Unfortunately for democratic theory, many studies of presidential elections show that issues are less important than either party identification or the candidate's attributes when people cast their ballots. Only in 1972, when voters perceived George McGovern as too liberal for their tastes, did issue voting exceed party identification in importance.[73]

Although party voting has declined somewhat since the 1950s, the relationship between voters' positions on the issues and their party identification is clearer today. For example, Democratic Party identifiers are now more likely than Republican identifiers to describe themselves as liberal, and they are more likely than Republican identifiers to favor government spending for social security and health care. The more closely party identification is aligned with ideological orientation, the more sense it makes to vote by party. When citizens see differences between parties, they are less likely to vote for incumbents and more likely to justify their voting choice.[74] Similarly, in the absence of detailed information about candidates' positions on the issues, party labels are a handy indicator of those positions.[75]

If party identification is the most important factor in the voting decision and also is resistant to short-term changes, there are definite limits to the capacity of a campaign to influence the outcome of elections.[76] In a close election, however, changing a modest percentage of the votes means the difference between victory and defeat, so a campaign can be decisive even if it has little overall effect.

Campaigns, Elections, and Parties

Election campaigns today tend to be highly personalized, candidate centered, and conducted outside the control of party organizations. The increased use of electronic media, especially television, has encouraged candidates to personalize their campaign messages; at the same time, the decline of party identification has decreased the power of party-related appeals. Although the party affiliations of the candidates and the party identifications of the voters jointly explain a good deal of electoral behavior, party organizations are not central to elections in America, and this has implications for democratic government.

Parties and the Majoritarian Model

According to the majoritarian model of democracy, parties link people with their government by making government responsive to public opinion. The Republican and Democratic parties follow the model in that they formulate different platforms and tend to pursue their announced policies when in office. The weak links in this model of responsible party government have been those that connect candidates to voters through campaigns and elections.

You have not read much about the role of the party platform in nominating candidates, conducting campaigns, or explaining voters' choices. Certainly a presidential candidate who wins enough convention delegates through the primaries will be comfortable with any platform that her or his delegates adopt. But House and Senate nominations are rarely fought over the party platform. And thoughts about party platforms usually are absent from campaigning and from voters' minds when they cast their ballots.

Parties and the Pluralist Model

The way parties in the United States operate is more in keeping with the pluralist model of democracy than with the majoritarian model. Our parties are not the basic mechanism through which citizens control their government; instead, they function as two giant interest groups. The parties' interests lie in electing and reelecting their candidates, in enjoying the benefits of public office. Except in extreme cases, the parties care little about the positions or ideologies favored by their candidates for Congress and statewide offices.

Some scholars believe that stronger parties would strengthen democratic government even if they could not meet all the requirements of the responsible party model. Our parties already perform valuable functions in structuring the vote along partisan lines and proposing alternative government policies, but stronger parties might also be able to play a more important role in coordinating government policies after elections. At present, the decentralized nature of the nominating process and campaigning for office offers many opportunities for organized groups outside the party to identify and back candidates who favor their interests. Although this is in keeping with pluralist theory, it is certain to frustrate majority interests on occasion.

Summary

Nevertheless, both parties are still very decentralized compared with parties in other countries.

Campaigning has evolved from a party-centered to a candidate-centered process. The successful candidate for public office usually must campaign first to win the party nomination, then to win the general election. A major factor in the decentralization of American parties is their reliance on primary elections to nominate candidates. Democratic and Republican nominations for president tend not to be decided in the parties' national conventions but are determined in advance through the complex process of selecting delegates pledged to particular candidates. Today winners can legitimately say that they captured the nomination through their own efforts and that they owe little to the party organization.

The need to win a majority of votes in the electoral college structures presidential elections. Although a candidate can win a majority of the popular vote but lose in the electoral college, the 2000 election was the first time in more than a century that this occurred. The electoral college typically magnifies the victory margin of the winning candidate.

In the general election, candidates usually retain the same staffs that helped them win the nomination. The dynamics of campaign financing also force candidates to rely mainly on their own resources or—in the case of presidential elections—on public funds. Party organizations now often contribute money to congressional candidates, but the candidates must raise most of the money themselves. Money is essential in running a modern campaign for major office—for conducting polls and advertising the candidate's name, qualifications, and positions on issues through the media. Candidates seek free news coverage whenever possible, but most must rely on paid advertising to get their messages across. Ironically, voters also get most of their campaign information from advertisements.

Voting choice is influenced by party identification, candidates' attributes, and policy positions. Party identification is still the most important long-term factor in shaping the voting decision, but few candidates rely on it in campaigns.

The way that nominations, campaigns, and elections are conducted in the United States is out of keeping with the ideals of responsible party government that fit the majoritarian model of democracy. In particular, campaigns and elections do not function to link parties strongly to voters as the model posits. American parties are better suited to the pluralist model of democracy, which sees them as major interest groups competing with lesser groups to further their own interests. At least political parties aspire to the noble goal of representing the needs and wants of most of the people. As we see in the next chapter, interest groups do not even pretend as much.

CL **Resources:** Videos, Simulations, News, Timelines, Primary Sources

Interest Groups

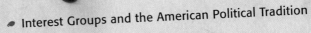

- Interest Groups and the American Political Tradition
- How Interest Groups Form
- Interest Group Resources
- Lobbying Tactics
- Is the System Biased?

This icon will direct you to resources and activities on the website: www.cengage.com/polisci/janda/chall_dem_brief/7e

IT TOOK ONLY THIRTY-TWO YEARS. Before the 2007 law, the last time Congress enacted an automobile fuel efficiency bill was 1975. Given that energy prices have soared during that period while concern over global warming mounted, Congress might have been expected to pass legislation to reduce carbon dioxide emissions. In particular, automobile pollution has grown worse as more cars being driven more miles have sent more greenhouse gases into the atmosphere. Although high-mileage, low-polluting cars are widely available, American consumers have only slowly embraced them.

Although many people agree that the United States should do more to decrease its carbon footprint, interest groups have very different ideas about how to solve this problem. Environmental groups have been ardent advocates of raising the average fuel economy standard from the minimum of 25 miles per gallon, but they have until recently been effectively blocked by American automobile manufacturers. Since American companies, notably General Motors and Ford, depended on the sale of low-mileage vehicles, they made a strong argument that raising fuel standards would put American workers out of a job while helping those foreign companies, such as Toyota and Honda, that excel at manufacturing small, fuel-efficient cars. Both Republicans preferring free market to regulatory solutions and Democrats hailing from car-producing states kept legislation aimed at improving gas mileage from passing. Environmental groups and car companies were not the only interest groups involved in this debate. Groups representing farmers wanted energy-related legislation to include a mandate for using more ethanol, a corn-based gasoline substitute. Green energy companies, such as firms that manufacture solar equipment, also pressed Congress for tax incentives to promote the industry. Appliance makers and light bulb manufacturers were active too.

After considerable negotiations among these groups, both parties in Congress, and the White House, legislation designed to raise the average fuel economy to 35 miles per gallon by the year 2020 was finally enacted. Under this bill, ethanol use is to be increased, appliances made more energy efficient, and the old-fashioned incandescent light bulb will be phased out in favor of compact fluorescents. Despite these mandates, many Americans were disappointed that Congress had not done more to reduce Americans' dependence on carbon fuels.[1]

In this chapter, we look at the central dynamic of pluralist democracy: the interaction of interest groups and government. In analyzing the process by which interest groups and lobbyists come to speak on behalf of different groups, we focus on several questions. How do interest groups form? Whom do they represent? What tactics do they use to convince policymakers that their views are best for the nation? Is the interest group system biased to favor certain types of people? If it is, what are the consequences?

Interest Groups and the American Political Tradition

An **interest group** is an organized body of individuals who share some political goals and try to influence public policy decisions. Among the most prominent interest groups in the United States are the AFL-CIO (representing labor union members), the American Farm Bureau Federation (representing farmers), the Business Roundtable (representing big business), and Common Cause (representing citizens concerned with reforming government). Interest groups are also called *lobbies,* and their representatives are referred to as **lobbyists.**

Interest Groups: Good or Evil?

A recurring debate in American politics concerns the role of interest groups in a democratic society. Are interest groups a threat to the well-being of the political system, or do they contribute to its proper functioning? Alexis de Tocqueville, a French visitor to the United States in the early nineteenth century, marveled at the array of organizations he found. He later wrote that "Americans of all ages, all conditions, and all dispositions, constantly form associations."[2] Tocqueville was suggesting that the ease with which we form organizations reflects a strong democratic culture.

Yet other early observers were concerned about the consequences of interest group politics. Writing in the *Federalist* papers, James Madison warned of the dangers of "factions," the major divisions in American society. In *Federalist* No. 10, written in 1787, Madison said that it was inevitable that substantial differences would develop between factions and that each faction would try to persuade government to adopt policies that favored it at the expense of others.[3] Madison, however, argued against trying to suppress factions. He concluded that they can be eliminated only by removing our freedoms, because "liberty is to faction what air is to fire."[4]

Madison suggested that relief from the self-interested advocacy of factions should come only through controlling the effects of that advocacy. This relief would be provided by a democratic republic in which government would mediate between opposing factions. The size and diversity of the nation as well as the structure of government would also ensure that even a majority faction could never come to suppress the rights of others.[5]

How we judge interest groups—as "good" or "evil"—may depend on how strongly we are committed to freedom or equality (see Chapter 1). In a survey of the American public, almost two-thirds of those polled regarded lobbying as a threat to American democracy.[6] Yet as we will demonstrate, interest groups have enjoyed unparalleled growth in recent years. Apparently we distrust interest groups as a whole, but we like those that speak on our behalf.

interest group An organized group of individuals that seeks to influence public policy. Also called a *lobby.*

lobbyist A representative of an interest group.

The Roles of Interest Groups

The "evil" side of interest group politics is all too apparent: each group pushes its own selfish interests, which, despite the group's claims to the contrary, are not always in the best interest of other Americans. The "good" side of interest group advocacy may not be as clear. How do the actions of interest groups benefit our political system?[7]

Representation.   Interest groups represent people before their government. Just as a member of Congress represents a particular constituency, so does a lobbyist. A lobbyist for the National Association of Broadcasters, for example, speaks for the interests of radio and television broadcasters when Congress or a government agency is considering a relevant policy decision.

Whatever the political interest—the cement industry, social security, endangered species—it is helpful to have an active lobby operating in Washington. Members of Congress represent a multitude of interests, some of them conflicting, from their own districts and states. Government administrators too are pulled in different directions and have their own policy preferences. Interest groups articulate their members' concerns, presenting them directly and forcefully in the political process.

Participation.   Interest groups are also vehicles for political participation. They provide a means by which like-minded citizens can pool their resources and channel their energies into collective political action. One farmer fighting against a new pesticide proposal in Congress probably will not get very far. Thousands of farmers united in an organization will stand a much better chance of getting policymakers to consider their needs.

Education.   As part of their efforts to lobby and increase their membership, interest groups try to educate their members, the public at large, and government officials. High-tech companies were slow to set up lobbying offices in Washington and to develop a mind-set within the corporate structure that communicating with people in government was part of their job. As more and more issues affecting the industry received attention from government, high-tech executives began to realize that policymakers did not have a sufficient understanding of the rapidly changing industry. For example, as it began to grow, the Internet search engine Google found it useful to open a Washington office and to hire an outside law firm to help represent its interests before government. To gain the attention of the policymakers they are trying to educate, interest groups need to provide them with information that is not easily obtained from other sources.[8]

agenda building The process by which new issues are brought into the political limelight.

Agenda Building.   In a related role, interest groups bring new issues into the political limelight through a process called **agenda building**. American society has many problem areas, but public officials are not addressing all of

FIGURE 7.1   Labor Pains

Over the years, many manufacturing jobs in the United States have "migrated" overseas to developing countries with lower wages. That may be good for consumers (cheaper wages mean lower-cost products) but it has been bad for labor unions as workers in heavy industry are the most likely to be unionized. Service sector workers (such as restaurant employees) have been much harder for unions to organize.

Source: Bureau of Labor Statistics, "Union Members (Annual)," available at www.bls.gov/schedule/archives/all_nr.htm#UNION2.

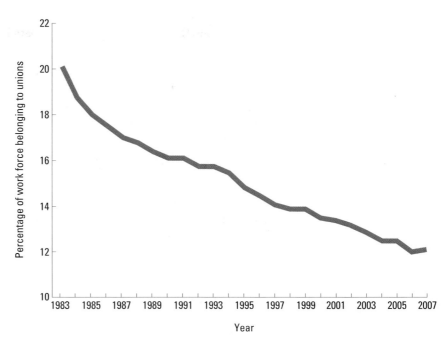

them. Through their advocacy, interest groups make the government aware of problems and then try to see that something is done to solve them. Labor unions, for example, have played a key role in gaining attention for problems that were being systematically ignored. As Figure 7.1 shows, however, union membership has declined significantly over the years.

Program Monitoring.   Finally, interest groups engage in **program monitoring.** Lobbies follow government programs that are important to their constituents, keeping abreast of developments in Washington and in the communities where the policies are implemented. When a program is not operating as it should, concerned interest groups push administrators to resolve problems in ways that promote the group's goals. They draw attention to agency officials' transgressions and even file suit to stop actions they consider unlawful.

Interest groups do play some positive roles in their pursuit of self-interest. But we should not assume that the positive side of interest groups neatly balances the negative. Questions remain about the overall influence of interest groups on public policy making. Are the effects of interest group advocacy being controlled, as Madison believed they should be?

program monitoring Keeping track of government programs, usually by interest groups.

How Interest Groups Form

Do some people form interest groups more easily than others? Are some factions represented while others are not? Pluralists assume that when a political issue arises, interest groups with relevant policy concerns begin to lobby. Policy conflicts are ultimately resolved through bargaining and negotiation between the involved organizations and the government. Unlike Madison, who dwelled on the potential for harm by factions, pluralists believe that interest groups are a good thing: they further democracy by broadening representation within the system.

Disturbance Theory

An important part of pluralism is the belief that new interest groups form as a matter of course when the need arises. David Truman outlines this idea in his classic work, *The Governmental Process*.[9] He says that when individuals are threatened by change, they band together in an interest group. For example, if government threatens to regulate a particular industry, the firms that compose that industry will start a trade association to protect their financial well-being. Truman sees a direct cause-and-effect relationship: existing groups stand in equilibrium until some type of disturbance (such as falling wages or declining farm prices) forces new groups to form.

Truman's *disturbance theory* paints an idealized portrait of interest group politics in America. In real life, people do not automatically organize when they are adversely affected by some disturbance. A good example of such "nonorganization" can be found in Herbert Gans's book *The Urban Villagers*.[10] Gans, a sociologist, moved into the West End, a low-income neighborhood in Boston, during the late 1950s. The neighborhood had been targeted for urban redevelopment. This meant that the people living there, primarily poor Italian Americans who very much liked their neighborhood, had to move. The people of the West End barely put up a fight to save their neighborhood. They started an organization, but it attracted little support. Despite the threat of eviction, residents remained unorganized. Soon they were moved out, and buildings were demolished.

Disturbance theory fails to explain what happened (or did not happen) in Boston's West End. An adverse condition or change does not automatically result in the formation of an interest group. What, then, is the missing ingredient? Political scientist Robert Salisbury says that the quality of interest group leadership may be the crucial factor.[11]

Interest Group Entrepreneurs

Salisbury likens the role of an interest group leader to the role of an entrepreneur in the business world. A business entrepreneur is someone who starts new enterprises, usually at considerable personal financial risk.

Salisbury says that an **interest group entrepreneur,** or organizer, succeeds or fails for many of the same reasons a business entrepreneur succeeds or fails. The interest group entrepreneur must have something attractive to "market" in order to convince people to join the group.[12] Potential members must be persuaded that the benefits of joining outweigh the costs.

The development of the United Farm Workers shows the importance of leadership in the formation of an interest group. Members of this union are men and women who pick crops in California and other parts of the country. They are predominantly poor, uneducated Mexican Americans. Throughout the twentieth century, various unions tried to organize the pickers, and for many reasons—including distrust of union organizers, intimidation by employers, and lack of money to pay union dues—all failed. Then in 1962, the late Cesar Chavez, a poor Mexican American, began to crisscross the Central Valley of California, talking to workers and planting the idea of a union.

After a strike against grape growers failed in 1965, Chavez changed his tactics of trying to build a strong union merely by recruiting more and more members. Copying the civil rights movement, Chavez and his followers marched 250 miles to the California state capitol in Sacramento to demand help from the governor. This march and other nonviolent tactics began to draw sympathy from people who had no direct involvement in farming. With his stature increased by that support, Chavez called for a grape boycott, and a small but significant number of Americans stopped buying grapes. The growers, who had bitterly fought the union, were hurt economically. Under this and other economic pressures, they eventually agreed to recognize and bargain with the United Farm Workers.

Who Is Being Organized?

Cesar Chavez's success is a good example of the importance of leadership in the formation of a new interest group. But another important element is at work in the formation of interest groups. The residents of Boston's West End and the farm workers in California were economically poor, uneducated or undereducated, and politically inexperienced—factors that made it extremely difficult to organize them into interest groups. If they had been well-off, well educated, and politically experienced, they probably would have banded together immediately. People who have money, education, and knowledge of how the system operates are more confident that their actions can make a difference.

Every existing interest group has its own history, but the three variables just discussed can help explain why groups may or may not become fully organized. First, a disturbance or adverse change can heighten people's awareness that they need political representation. However, awareness alone does not ensure that an organization will form, and organizations may form in the absence of a disturbance. Second, the quality of leadership is critical to the organization of interest groups. Third, the higher the

interest group entrepreneur
An interest group organizer.

socioeconomic level of potential members, the more likely they are to know the value of interest groups and to join them.

The question that remains, then, is *how well* various opposing interests are represented. Or, in terms of Madison's premise in *Federalist* No. 10, are the effects of faction—in this case, the advantages of the wealthy and well educated—being controlled? Before we can answer this question, we need to turn our attention to the resources available to interest groups.

 # Interest Group Resources

The strengths, capabilities, and influence of an interest group depend in large part on its resources. A group's most significant resources are its members, lobbyists, and money, including funds that can be contributed to political candidates. The sheer quantity of a group's resources is important, and so is the wisdom with which its resources are used.

Members

One of the most valuable resources an interest group can have is a large, politically active membership. If a lobbyist is trying to persuade a legislator to support a particular bill, having a large group of members who live in the legislator's home district or state is tremendously helpful. A legislator who has not already taken a firm position on a bill might be swayed by the knowledge that interest groups are keeping voters back home informed of his or her votes on key issues.

Members give an organization not only the political muscle to influence policy but also financial resources. The more money an organization can collect through dues and contributions, the more people it can hire to lobby government officials and monitor policymaking. Greater resources also allow the organization to communicate with its members more and to inform them better. And funding helps the group maintain its membership and attract new members.

Maintaining Membership.   To keep the members it already has, an organization must persuade them that it is a strong, effective advocate. Most lobbies use a newsletter to keep members apprised of developments in government that relate to issues of concern and to inform them about steps the organization is taking to protect their interests.

Business, professional, and labor associations generally have an easier time retaining members than do citizen groups—groups whose basis of organization is a concern for issues not directly related to their members' jobs. In many companies, corporate membership in a trade group constitutes only a minor business expense. Labor unions are helped in states that require workers to affiliate with the union that is the bargaining agent with their employer. In contrast, citizen groups base their appeal on members' ideological sentiments. These groups face a difficult challenge: issues can blow hot and cold, and a particularly hot issue one year may not hold the same interest to citizens the next.

Attracting New Members. All membership groups are constantly looking for new members to expand their resources and clout. Groups that rely on ideological appeals have a special problem because the competition in most policy areas is intense. People concerned about the environment, for example, can join a seemingly infinite number of local, state, and national groups that lobby on environmental issues. One common method of attracting new members is *direct mail*—letters sent to a selected audience to promote the organization and appeal for contributions. The main drawbacks to direct mail are its expense and low rate of return.

The Internet is also a tool for building a membership and even building new advocacy organizations. People with hemophilia (their blood does not clot adequately, and thus they are at serious risk from bleeding) were traditionally represented by the National Hemophilia Foundation (NHF). The NHF has a close relationship with drug manufacturers, which provide significant financial support to the group. This close relationship inhibited the organization from lobbying the government to force a reduction in drug prices. Through the Internet, the small and geographically dispersed community of hemophiliacs was able to organize its own independent organizations.[13]

The Free-Rider Problem. The need for aggressive marketing by interest groups suggests that getting people who sympathize with a group's goals to support the group with contributions is difficult. Economists call this difficulty the **free-rider problem,** but we might call it, more colloquially, the "let-George-do-it" problem.[14] Funding for public television stations illustrates this dilemma. Only a fraction of those who watch public television contribute on a regular basis. Why? Because a free rider has the same access to public television as a contributor.

The same problem troubles interest groups. When a lobbying group wins benefits, those benefits are often not restricted to members of the organization. For instance, if the U.S. Chamber of Commerce convinces Congress to enact a policy benefiting business, all businesses will benefit, not just those that pay membership dues to the lobbying group. Thus, some executives may feel that their corporation does not need to spend the money to join the Chamber of Commerce, even though they might benefit from the group's efforts; they prefer to let others shoulder the financial burden.

The free-rider problem increases the difficulty of attracting paying members. Nevertheless, millions of Americans contribute to interest groups because they are concerned about an issue or feel a responsibility to help organizations that work on their behalf. Also, many organizations offer membership benefits that have nothing to do with politics or lobbying. **Trade associations,** for example, are a source of information about industry

free-rider problem The situation in which people benefit from the activities of an organization (such as an interest group) but do not contribute to those activities.

trade association An organization that represents firms within a particular industry

trends and effective management practices; they organize conventions at which members can learn, socialize, and occasionally find new customers or suppliers.

Lobbyists

Interest groups use part of the money they raise to pay lobbyists, who represent the organizations before the government. Lobbyists make sure that people in government know what their members want and that their organizations know what the government is doing.[15] Lobbyists can be full-time employees of an interest group or employees of public relations or law firms hired on retainer. When hiring a lobbyist, an interest group looks for someone who knows his or her way around Washington. Billy Tauzin, a Republican from Louisiana who chaired the House Energy and Commerce Committee, went from that position to head the Pharmaceutical Research and Manufacturers of America, the trade group for the drug industry. Tauzin's experience as head of the committee that oversaw the drug industry and his ties to members in the House made him a prize catch for the trade group. His initial salary was reported to be around $2 million a year.[16]

Lobbyists are valued for their experience and their knowledge of how government operates. Often they are people who have served in the legislative or executive branches and have firsthand experience with government. Many lobbyists have law degrees and find their legal backgrounds useful in bargaining and negotiating over laws and regulations. Because of their

The Two Million Dollar Man
It's understandable that many members of Congress become lobbyists when they leave the House or Senate. Former representative Billy Tauzin's estimated salary of $2 million a year as a lobbyist for the Pharmaceutical Research and Manufacturers of America (PhRMA) is considerably more than the current $169,300 salary for legislators. Given the enormous stakes for drug companies in health care legislation, it's understandable that PhRMA believes that having someone with the knowledge, skill, and connections of Tauzin is well worth the large salary.
(AP/Wide World Photos)

location, many Washington law firms are drawn into lobbying. Corporations without Washington offices rely heavily on these law firms to lobby for them before the national government.

The stereotype of lobbyists portrays them as people of dubious ethics because they trade on their connections and may hand out campaign donations to candidates for office. To enhance their access, many lobbyists also raise money for legislators. However, the lobbyist's primary job is not to trade on favors or campaign contributions but to pass on information to policymakers. Lobbyists provide government officials and their staffs with a constant flow of data that support their organizations' policy goals. Lobbyists also try to build a compelling case for their goals, showing that the "facts" dictate that a particular change be made or avoided. What lobbyists are really trying to do, of course, is to convince policymakers that their data deserve more attention and are more accurate than the data presented by other lobbyists.

PACs and 527s

One of the organizational resources that can make a lobbyist's job easier is a **political action committee (PAC)**. PACs pool campaign contributions from group members and donate those funds to candidates for political office. Under federal law, a PAC can give as much as $5,000 to a candidate for Congress for each separate election. PACs have grown much more prevalent since the early 1970s. In the 2005–2006 election cycle, they contributed more than $372 million to candidates, and more than 4,200 were active in the 2007–2008 election cycle.[17]

The greatest growth came from corporations, most of which had been legally prohibited from operating PACs. There was also rapid growth in the number of nonconnected PACs, largely ideological groups that have no parent lobbying organization and are formed solely for the purpose of raising and channeling campaign funds. Thus, a PAC can be the campaign-wing affiliate of an existing interest group or a wholly independent, unaffiliated group. Although most PACs give less than $50,000 in total contributions during a two-year election cycle, some contribute millions of dollars to campaigns. During the 2005–2006 election cycle, for example, the National Beer Wholesalers' PAC gave approximately $3 million to congressional campaigns, and the National Association of Realtors' PAC disbursed almost $9 million in contributions to candidates, other PACs, and independent election-related expenditures.[18]

Why do interest groups form PACs? Lobbyists believe that campaign contributions help significantly when they are trying to gain an audience with a member of Congress. Members of Congress and their staffers generally are eager to meet with representatives of their constituencies, but their time is limited. However, a member of Congress or a staffer would find it difficult to turn down a lobbyist's request for a meeting if the PAC of the lobbyist's organization had made a significant campaign contribution in the previous election.

DO IT!
What are the organizations on your campus that lobby the school's administration? Think about joining one of them to press an issue that is important to you.

political action committee (PAC) An organization that pools campaign contributions from group members and donates those funds to candidates for political office.

FIGURE 7.2   Friendship Is a Wonderful Thing

Political action committees are more practical than ideological, primarily directing their contributions to incumbents. A modest exception to this trend are so-called nonconnected PACs. These tend to be ideological citizen groups whose primary concern is promoting a broad liberal or conservative perspective. But even nonconnected PACs give almost 60 percent of their contributions to incumbents.

Source: Federal Election Commission, "PAC Activity Continues to Climb in 2006," October 5, 2007.

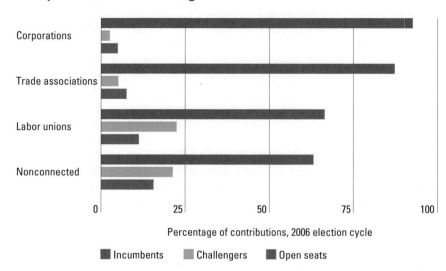

Percentage of contributions, 2006 election cycle

■ Incumbents ■ Challengers ■ Open seats

Typically, PACs, like most other interest groups, are highly pragmatic organizations; pushing a particular political philosophy takes second place to achieving immediate policy goals. As one lobbyist put it, "Politics are partisan; policy is bipartisan."[19] In recent elections, corporate PACs as a group have given as much as 92 percent of their contributions to incumbents (see Figure 7.2).[20] At the same time, different sectors of the PAC universe may strongly favor one party or the other. Approximately nine out of every ten dollars that unions give go to Democrats, whether they be incumbents, challengers, or open seat candidates.[21]

Critics charge that members of Congress cannot help but be influenced by the PAC contributions they receive. Political scientists, however, have not been able to document any consistent link between campaign donations and the way members of Congress vote on the floor of the House and Senate.[22] The problem is this: Do PAC contributions influence votes in Congress, or are they really just rewards for ideologically like-minded legislators who would vote for the group's interests anyway? Some sophisticated research does show that PACs have an advantage in the committee process and appear to gain influence because of the additional access they receive.[23]

During the 2004 election, a form of interest group called **527 committees** became highly involved in the campaign. These groups may take a stand on an issue but may not directly contribute to candidates, may not explicitly endorse candidates, and may not ask voters to vote against a specific candidate. They are different from PACs in another important way: they can

527 committees Political organizations that are organized under Section 527 of the Internal Revenue Code; they enjoy tax-exempt status and may accept unlimited funds from unlimited sources but cannot expressly advocate a candidate's election or defeat.

accept contributions of unlimited size. In the 2004 election, financier George Soros contributed $23.3 million to liberal 527s.[24] Although they may not endorse a candidate, 527s can indirectly criticize candidates they do not like by emphasizing an issue that draws out the differences among candidates. A 527's preferences are often hard to miss. In the 2008 presidential election 527s were again active and appear likely to remain as a significant and controversial participant in campaigns.

Lobbying Tactics

Keep in mind that lobbying extends beyond the legislative branch. Groups can seek help from the courts and administrative agencies as well as from Congress. Moreover, interest groups may have to shift their focus from one branch of government to another. After a bill becomes a law, for example, a group that lobbied for the legislation will probably try to influence the administrative agency responsible for implementing the new law. Some policy decisions are left unresolved by legislation and are settled through regulations. Interest groups try to influence policy through the courts as well, though litigation can be expensive and opportunities to go to court may be narrowly structured.

We discuss three types of lobbying tactics here: those aimed at policymakers and implemented by interest group representatives (direct lobbying), those that involve group members (grassroots lobbying), and those directed toward the public (information campaigns). We also examine the use of new high-tech lobbying tactics as well as cooperative efforts of interest groups to influence government through coalitions.

Direct Lobbying

Direct lobbying relies on personal contact with policymakers. One survey of Washington lobbyists showed that 98 percent use direct contact with government officials to express their group's views.[25] This interaction takes place when a lobbyist meets with a member of Congress, an agency official, or a staff member. In their meetings, lobbyists usually convey their arguments by providing data about a specific issue. If a lobbyist from, for example, a chamber of commerce meets with a member of Congress about a bill the organization backs, the lobbyist does not say (or even suggest), "Vote for this bill, or our people in the district will vote against you in the next election." Instead, the lobbyist might say, "If this bill is passed, we're going to see hundreds of new jobs created back home." The representative has no trouble at all figuring out that a vote for the bill can help in the next election.

Personal lobbying is a day-in, day-out process. Lobbyists must maintain contact with congressional and agency staffers, constantly providing them with pertinent data. One lobbyist described his strategy in personal

direct lobbying Attempts to influence a legislator's vote through personal contact with the legislator.

meetings with policymakers as rather simple and straightforward: "Providing information is the most effective tool. People begin to rely on you."[26] In their meetings with policymakers, lobbyists also try to frame issues in terms most beneficial to their point of view. Is a gun control bill before the Congress a policy that would make streets and schools safer from violent individuals who should not have access to guns, or is it a bill aimed at depriving law-abiding citizens of their constitutional right to bear arms? Research has shown that once an issue emerges, it is very difficult for lobbyists to reframe it—that is, to influence journalists and policymakers alike to view the issue in a new light.[27]

A tactic related to direct lobbying is testifying at committee hearings when a bill is before Congress. This tactic allows the interest group to put its views on record and make them widely known when the hearing testimony is published. Although testifying is one of the most visible parts of lobbying, it is generally considered window dressing. Most lobbyists believe that testimony usually does little by itself to persuade members of Congress.

Another direct but somewhat different approach is legal advocacy. Using this tactic, a group tries to achieve its policy goals through litigation. Claiming some violation of law, a group will file a lawsuit and ask that a judge make a ruling that will benefit the organization. When the Army Corps of Engineers announced plans to permit coal companies to blast off the top of mountains to facilitate their mining, environmental groups went to court alleging a violation of the Clean Water Act. The judge agreed, since the coal companies' actions would leave waste and rock deposits in adjoining streams.[28]

Grassroots Lobbying

Grassroots lobbying involves an interest group's rank-and-file members and may also include people outside the organization who sympathize with its goals. Grassroots tactics, such as letter-writing campaigns and protests, are often used in conjunction with direct lobbying by Washington representatives. Policymakers are more concerned about what a lobbyist says when they know that constituents are really watching their decisions.

The Internet facilitates mobilization; an interest group office can communicate instantaneously with its members and followers through e-mail at virtually no cost. It also makes it easy for interest groups to communicate with each other, easing some of the costs in time and money to forming and maintaining coalitions. Still, it is not clear whether the Internet has fundamentally changed interest group politics in any way. Interest groups of all kinds use high-tech lobbying, so there is no unique advantage that has accrued to any one segment of the interest group world.

If people in government seem unresponsive to conventional lobbying tactics, a group might resort to some form of political protest. A protest or demonstration, such as picketing or marching, is designed to attract media attention to an issue. The main drawback to protesting is that policymak-

grassroots lobbying Lobbying activities performed by rank-and-file interest group members and would-be members.

ing is a long-term, incremental process, but a demonstration is only short-lived. It is difficult to sustain anger and activism among group supporters—to keep large numbers of people involved in protest after protest. A notable exception was the civil rights demonstrations of the 1960s, which were sustained over a long period. The protests were a major factor in stirring public opinion, which hastened passage of the Civil Rights Act of 1964 and the Voting Rights Act of 1965.

Information Campaigns

Interest groups generally feel that public backing strengthens their lobbying efforts. They believe that they will get that backing if they can make the public aware of their position and the evidence supporting it. To this end, interest groups launch **information campaigns,** organized efforts to gain public backing by bringing a group's views to the public's attention. Various means are used. Some are directed at the larger public, others at smaller audiences with long-standing interest in an issue.

Public relations is one information campaign tactic. A public relations campaign might send speakers to meetings in various parts of the country, produce pamphlets and handouts, take out newspaper advertising, or establish websites. Recently labor unions and progressives initiated a campaign critical of Wal-Mart. The huge retailer pays relatively low wages, offers limited benefits, and aggressively fights any efforts to unionize its work force. Both Wake Up Wal-Mart and Wal-Mart Watch have publicized Wal-Mart's record on its treatment of employees. In turn, Wal-Mart has fought back with a concerted public relations campaign designed to demonstrate that it is a responsible citizen in the communities where its stores are located. The company's extensive efforts to provide water and other supplies to victims of Hurricane Katrina were particularly effective at burnishing its image.[29]

Sponsoring research is another way interest groups press their cases. When a group believes that evidence has not been fully developed in a certain area, it may commission research on the subject. In the controversy over illegal immigration studies have proliferated as interest groups push their positions forward. Lobbies on opposing sides of the issue have publicized research on matters such as the impact of illegal immigration on the overall economy, whether immigrants drive down wages, and whether undocumented aliens take jobs away from citizens who would otherwise fill them.

Coalition Building

A final aspect of lobbying strategy is **coalition building,** in which several organizations band together for the purpose of lobbying. Such joint efforts conserve or make more effective use of the resources of groups with similar views. Most coalitions are informal, ad hoc arrangements that exist only for the purpose of lobbying on a single issue.

information campaign An organized effort to gain public backing by bringing a group's views to public attention.

coalition building The banding together of several interest groups for the purpose of lobbying.

Coalitions form most often among groups that work in the same policy area and have similar constituencies, such as environmental groups or feminist groups. Yet coalitions often extend beyond organizations with similar constituencies and similar outlooks. Some business groups support the same goals as environmental lobbies, because doing so is in their self-interest. For example, companies in the business of cleaning up toxic waste sites have worked with environmental groups.[30] Lobbyists see an advantage in having a diverse coalition. In the words of one lobbyist, "You can't do anything in this town without a coalition. I mean the first question [from policymakers] is, 'Who supports this?'"[31]

 ## Is the System Biased?

As we noted in Chapter 1, our political system is more pluralist than majoritarian. Policymaking is determined more by the interaction of groups with government than by elections. Indeed, among Western democracies, the United States is one of the most pluralistic governments (see "Compared with What? Pluralism Worldwide"). How, then, do we determine whether policy decisions in a pluralist system are fair?

There is no precisely agreed-on formula, but most people would agree with the following two simple notions. First, all significant interests in the population should be adequately represented by lobbying groups. Second, government should listen to the views of all major interests as it develops policy. We should also recognize that elections inject some of the benefits of majoritarianism into our system, because the party that wins an election will have a larger voice in the making of public policy than its opponent.

Membership Patterns

Those who work in business or in a profession, those with a high level of education, and those with high incomes are the most likely to belong to interest groups. Even middle-income people are much more likely to join interest groups than people who are poor.

A recent survey of interest groups is revealing, finding that "the 10 percent of adults who work in an executive, managerial, or administrative capacity are represented by 82 percent" of the organizations that in one way or another engage in advocacy on economic issues. In contrast, "organizations of or for the economically needy are a rarity." In terms of membership in interest groups, there is a profound bias in favor of those who are well off financially.[32]

Citizen Groups

Before we reach the conclusion that the interest group system is biased, we should examine another set of data. The actual population of interest groups

Compared with What?

Pluralism Worldwide

Astudy of democracies around the world measured the degree to which interest groups operated independent of any formal link to government. Interest groups in political systems with low scores in this chart (such as Norway) run the risk of being co-opted by policymakers because of their partnerships with government. These coun-tries tend to have fewer groups, but those groups are expected to work with government in a coordinated fashion. High scores indicate that the interest groups in those systems are clearly in a competitive position with other groups. Thus, countries with high scores (such as the United States) are the most pluralistic.

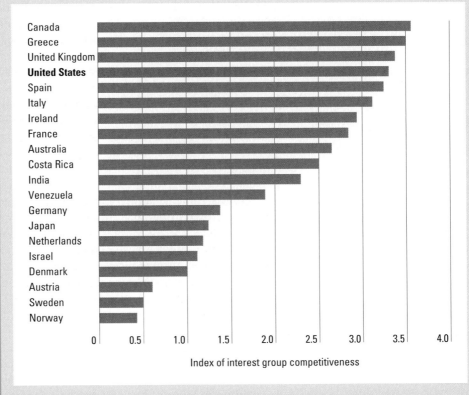

Source: Arend Lijphart, *Patterns of Democracy* (New Haven, Conn.: Yale University Press, 1999), p. 177.

in Washington surely reflects a class bias in interest group membership, but that bias may be modified in an important way. Some interest groups derive support from sources other than their membership. Thus, although the Center for Budget and Policy Priorities and the Children's Defense Fund have no welfare recipients among their members, they are highly respected Washington lobbies working on the problems of poor people. Poverty groups gain their financial support from philanthropic foundations, government grants, corporations, and wealthy individuals. Such groups have played an important role in influencing policy on poor people's programs. In short, some bias exists in the representation of the poor, but it is not nearly as bad as membership patterns suggest.

Another part of the problem of membership bias has to do with free riders. The interests that are most affected by free riders are broad societal problems, such as the environment and consumer protection, in which literally everyone can be considered as having a stake in the outcome. The greater the number of potential members of a group, the more likely it is that individuals will decide to be free riders, because they believe that plenty of others can offer financial support to the organization.

Environmental and consumer interests have been chronically underrepresented in the Washington interest group community. In the 1960s, however, a strong citizen group movement emerged. **Citizen groups** are lobbying organizations built around policy concerns unrelated to members' vocational interests. People who join Environmental Defense do so because they care about the environment, not because it lobbies on issues related to their profession. If that group fights for stricter pollution control requirements, it does not further the financial interests of its members. The benefits to members are largely ideological and aesthetic. In contrast, a corporation fighting the same stringent standards is trying to protect its economic interests.

Organizations pursuing environmental protection, consumer protection, good government, family values, and equality for various groups in society have grown in number and collectively attracted millions of members. The national press gives them considerable coverage, reinforcing the ability of these groups to get their issues on the national agenda. One study showed that citizen groups received almost half of all TV network news coverage of interest groups, even though they are a much smaller portion of the interest group universe.[33]

INTERACTIVE 7.1

War Over the Arctic National Wildlife Refuge

Business Mobilization

Because a strong public interest movement has become an integral part of Washington politics, an easy assumption is that the bias in interest group representation in favor of business has been largely overcome. What must be factored in is that business has become increasingly mobilized as well.[34] The 1970s and 1980s saw a vast increase in the number of business lobbies in Washington. Many corporations opened Washington lobbying offices,

citizen group Lobbying organization built around policy concerns unrelated to members' vocational interests.

Sanchez Reaches Out
Usually we think of lobbying as a process where groups approach a government official. But sometimes the reverse is true: a policymaker might approach an interest group to try to gain its support for a specific proposal or just to promote a good working relationship. Here, Representative Loretta Sanchez (D-Calif.) works the room at a meeting of the Hispanic Leadership Summit. (© *Ted Soqui/Corbis*)

and many trade associations headquartered elsewhere either moved to Washington or opened branch offices there.

This mobilization was partly a reaction to the success of the liberal public interest movement, which business tended to view as hostile to the free-enterprise system. The reaction of business also reflected the expanded scope of the national government. As the Environmental Protection Agency, the Consumer Product Safety Commission, the Occupational Safety and Health Administration, and other regulatory agencies were created, many more companies found they were affected by federal regulations.

The health-care industry is a case in point. As government regulation has become an increasingly important factor in determining health-care profits, more and more health-care trade associations have opened offices in Washington so that they can make more of an effort to influence the government. In 1979 there were roughly one hundred health-care lobbies in Washington. A little over a decade later, there were over seven hundred. Another decade later, the number had passed one thousand.[35]

The advantages of business are enormous. As Figure 7.3 illustrates, there are more business lobbies (corporations and trade associations) than any other type. Professional associations, such as the American Dental Association, tend to represent business interests as well. Beyond the numbers of groups are the superior resources of business including lobbyists, researchers, campaign contributions, and well-connected CEOs. Whereas citizen groups can try to mobilize their individual members, trade associations can mobilize the corporations that are members of the organization.

Yet the resource advantages of business make it easy to overlook the obstacles business faces in the political arena. To begin with, business is

Who Lobbies?

One large-scale study of lobbying in Washington documented the pattern of participation by interest groups on close to one hundred issues before the federal government. Business-related groups (corporations and trade associations) made up the largest segment of all lobbies, while citizen groups constituted roughly a quarter of all organizations.

Source: Frank R. Baumgartner, Jeffrey M. Berry, Marie Hojnacki, David C. Kimball, Beth L. Leech, *Advocacy and Policy Change* (forthcoming).

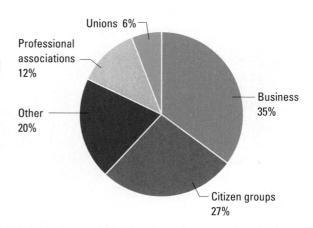

Unions 6%
Professional associations 12%
Other 20%
Business 35%
Citizen groups 27%

often divided, with companies and industries competing with one another. Cable companies and phone companies have frequently tangled over who will have access to what markets. And even if an industry is unified, it may face strong opposition from labor or citizen groups—sectors that have substantial resources too, even if they do not match up to businesses.[36]

Reform

In an economic system marked by great differences in income, great differences in the degree to which people are organized are inevitable. Moreover, as Madison foresaw, limiting interest group activity is difficult without limiting fundamental freedoms. The First Amendment guarantees Americans the right to petition their government, and lobbying, at its most basic level, is a form of organized petitioning.

Still, if it is felt that the advantages of some groups are so great that they affect the equality of people's opportunity to be heard in the political system, then restrictions on interest group behavior can be justified on the ground that the disadvantaged must be protected. Pluralist democracy is justified on exactly these grounds: all constituencies must have the opportunity to organize, and the competition between groups as they press their case before policymakers must be fair.

Some critics charge that a system of campaign finance that relies so heavily on PACs undermines our democratic system. Around two-thirds of PAC contributions come from corporations, business trade associations, and professional associations.[37] It is not merely a matter of wealthy interest groups showering incumbents with donations; members of Congress aggressively solicit donations from PACs. Although observers disagree on whether PAC money actually influences policy outcomes, agreement is widespread that PAC donations give donors better access to members of Congress.

In 2002 the Congress enacted a major campaign finance reform. Until passage of the Bipartisan Campaign Reform Act (BCRA), corporations, labor unions, and other organizations could donate unlimited amounts of so-called soft money to the political parties. Before BCRA, a company or union with issues before government could give a six-figure gift to the Democratic or Republican Party, even though the company or union PAC could make only a modest contribution to individual candidates. The new legislation bans soft money contributions to national party committees. Yet 527s have emerged to present a different challenge to the campaign finance system. Although they do not contribute directly to candidates or parties, these organizations are playing an increasingly significant role in elections. As a percentage of all campaign funds, expenditures by 527s are increasing, while party contributions are declining.[38] This is a disturbing trend for those who would like to see our political system move more toward the majoritarian influence of parties and away from interest group-based pluralism.

A second element of reform in BCRA was a ban on "electioneering communications" by corporations and unions. In an effort to prevent these organizations from running sham issue ads that were really intended to support or oppose candidates, BCRA prohibited corporations and unions from using their general treasuries to run advertisements discussing federal candidates in the days before an election. In *Federal Election Commission* v. *Wisconsin Right to Life, Inc.* (2007) the U.S. Supreme Court declared this limitation an impermissible violation of the First Amendment in all cases except those expressly advocating the election or defeat of a candidate.[39]

Pressure on Congress to tighten its lobbying rules mounted after a series of scandals involving a lobbyist named Jack Abramoff surfaced. Abramoff and his law firm serviced several different clients and he was known for his access to lawmakers. Among other things, Abramoff paid for a golf trip to Scotland that included former Republican majority leader Tom DeLay and his wife. The lobbyist's many transgressions led to an indictment and Abramoff is currently serving six years in jail. Congress responded with a tightening of its ethical rules and legislation passed in 2007 bans gifts and travel and meals paid for by lobbyists. Lobbyists must also now disclose campaign contributions that they solicit on behalf of candidates.[40]

Summary

Interest groups play many important roles in our political process. They are a means by which citizens can participate in politics, and they communicate their members' views to those in government. Interest groups differ greatly in the resources at their disposal and in the tactics they use to influence government.

The number of interest groups has grown sharply in recent years. Despite the growth and change in the nature of interest groups, the fundamental problem that Madison identified more than two hundred years ago endures: in a free and open society, groups form to pursue policies that favor themselves at the expense of the broader national interest. Madison hoped that the solution to the problem would come from the diversity of the population and the structure of our government. And to a certain extent, Madison's expectations have been borne out. The natural differences between groups have prevented a tyranny of any one faction. Yet the interest group system remains unbalanced, with some segments of society (particularly business, the wealthy, and the educated) considerably better organized than others. The growth of citizen groups has reduced the disparity somewhat, but significant inequalities remain in how well different interests are represented in Washington.

The inequities point to flaws in pluralist theory. There is no mechanism to automatically ensure that interest groups will form to speak for those who need representation. Likewise, when an issue arises and policymakers meet with interest groups that have a stake in the outcome, those groups may not equally represent all the constituencies that the policy changes will affect. The interest group system clearly compromises the principle of political equality stated in the maxim "one person, one vote." Formal political equality is certainly more likely to occur outside interest group politics, in elections between candidates from competing political parties, which better fit the majoritarian model of democracy. Despite the inequities of the interest group system, little direct effort has been made to restrict interest group activity. Madison's dictum to avoid suppressing political freedoms, even at the expense of permitting interest group activity that promotes the selfish interests of narrow segments of the population, has generally guided public policy. Yet as the problem of PACs and 527 committees demonstrates, government has had to set some restrictions on interest groups. Where to draw the line on PAC and 527 activity remains a thorny issue, because there is little consensus on how to balance the conflicting needs of our society.

Congress is one institution that must try to balance our diverse country's conflicting interests. In the next chapter, we will see how difficult this part of Congress's job is.

CL Resources: Videos, Simulations, News, Timelines, Primary Sources

Congress

This icon will direct you to resources and activities on the website: www.cengage.com/polisci/janda/chall_dem_brief/7e

CL

CONTROL OF CONGRESS DOES
not change hands very often. Yet against improbable odds the Democrats gained enough seats in the 2006 congressional election to oust the Republicans and take majority control of both the House and the Senate. The Democrats had not controlled the House of Representatives since 1994. In the wake of the election, California Democrat Nancy Pelosi became the first woman to become Speaker of the House.

The dominant issue in the campaign was the war in Iraq. A majority of the public had turned against the war, believing that American casualties and the cost of the war were far too high. What's more, many voters did not see an end in sight, as President Bush emphasized that the nation needed to stay the course.

Many Democrats ran on platforms opposing the war and promised to legislate an end to the country's participation in the conflict. Although Republican candidates generally sided with President Bush, the Democratic sweep suggested that the new majority in the Congress would bring an end to American military involvement in Iraq.

In theory, at least, that's how majoritarian government should work. The parties present a clear choice on a key issue and the voters choose one or the other. The winning party then implements its policy objectives. In practice, however, majority preferences can sometimes be thwarted.

To begin with, divisions existed within the Democratic Party, and some in the party were apprehensive about legislating an end to the war. The party had only a two-vote margin in the Senate, so finding common ground that all Democrats could stand on was of paramount importance. But a softer position, such as merely calling for benchmarks for the Iraqi government to meet, risked rejection by those Democrats most fiercely opposed to the war itself.

Pelosi and her Senate counterpart, Majority Leader Harry Reid of Nevada, managed to hold their party together and were able to pass one bill ending funding for the war. However, President Bush promptly vetoed the bill. Bush knew that while the public wanted an end to the war, there was little consensus on how to end American involvement. The Democrats could not muster the votes to overcome a Republican filibuster in the Senate. Democratic representative David Obey of Wisconsin said, "There has never been a snowball's chance in Hades that Congress would cut off those funds to those troops in the field."[1]

Many rank-and-file Democratic voters across the country were disappointed in the Democratic Congress. They were frustrated that the electoral majorities could not be translated into a policy change. Throughout 2008 President Bush held firm on his Iraq policy and many Democrats looked to the president-elect, Barack Obama, with the hope that after the inauguration he would lead the country out of the war in Iraq.

In this chapter we examine majoritarian politics through the prism of the two congressional parties, looking at how the forces of pluralism work against majoritarian policymaking. We then explore the procedures and norms that facilitate bargaining and compromise in the Congress. We will also focus on Congress's relations with the executive branch and analyze how the legislative process affects public policy. A starting point is to ask how the framers envisioned Congress.

The Origin and Powers of Congress

The framers of the Constitution wanted to prevent the concentration of power in the hands of a few, but they also wanted to create a union strong enough to overcome the weaknesses of the government created by the Articles of Confederation. They argued passionately about the structure of the new government and in the end produced a legislative body that was as much of an experiment as the new republic itself.

The Great Compromise

The U.S. Congress has two separate and powerful chambers: the House of Representatives and the Senate. A bill cannot become law unless it is passed in identical form by both chambers. When the framers were drafting the Constitution during the summer of 1787, "the fiercest struggle for power" centered on representation in the legislature.[2] The small states wanted all the states to have equal representation. The more populous states wanted representation based on population; they did not want their power diluted. The Great Compromise broke the deadlock: the small states would receive equal representation in the Senate, but the number of each state's representatives in the House would be based on population, and the House would have the sole right to originate revenue-related legislation.

As the Constitution specifies, each state has two senators, and senators serve six-year terms of office. Terms are staggered, so that one-third of the Senate is elected every two years. When it was ratified, the Constitution directed that senators should be chosen by the state legislatures. However, the Seventeenth Amendment, adopted in 1913, provided for the direct election of senators by popular vote. From the beginning, the people have directly elected members of the House of Representatives. They serve two-year terms, and all House seats are up for election at the same time.

There are 435 members in the House of Representatives. Because each state's representation in the House is in proportion to its population, the Constitution provides for a national census every ten years. Population shifts are handled by the **reapportionment** (redistribution) of seats among the states after each census is taken. Since recent population growth has been centered in the Sunbelt, California, Texas, and Florida have gained seats, and the Northeast and Midwest states like New York and Illinois have lost them. Each representative is elected from a particular congressional district within his or her state, and each district elects only one representative. The districts within a state must be roughly equal in population.

reapportionment Redistribution of representatives among the states, based on population change. Congress is reapportioned after each census.

Duties of the House and Senate

Although the Great Compromise provided for considerably different schemes of representation for the House and Senate, the Constitution gives them essentially similar legislative tasks. They share many important powers, among them the powers to declare war, raise an army and navy, borrow and coin money, regulate interstate commerce, create federal courts, establish rules for the naturalization of immigrants, and "make all Laws which shall be necessary and proper for carrying into Execution the foregoing Powers."

Of course, the constitutional duties of the two chambers are different in at least a few important ways. As noted earlier, the House alone has the right to originate revenue bills, a right that apparently was coveted at the Constitutional Convention. In practice, this power is of limited consequence because both House and Senate must approve all bills, including revenue bills. The House also has the power of **impeachment**: the power to charge the president, vice president, or other "civil Officers" of the national government with "Treason, Bribery, or other high Crimes and Misdemeanors." The Senate is empowered to act as a court to try impeachments; a two-thirds majority vote of the senators present is necessary for conviction. Prior to President Clinton's impeachment in 1998, only one president, Andrew Johnson, had been impeached, and in 1868 the Senate came within a single vote of finding him guilty. Clinton was accused of both perjury and obstruction of justice concerning his relationship with a White House intern, Monica Lewinsky, but was acquitted by the Senate as well. The House Judiciary Committee voted to impeach President Richard Nixon for his role in the Watergate scandal, but he resigned (in August 1974) before the full House could vote.

The Constitution gives the Senate the power to approve major presidential appointments (such as to federal judgeships, ambassadorships, and cabinet posts) and treaties with foreign nations. The president is empowered to make treaties, but he must submit them to the Senate for approval by a two-thirds majority. Because of this requirement, the executive branch generally considers the Senate's sentiments when it negotiates a treaty.[3]

Despite the long list of congressional powers in the Constitution, the question of what powers are appropriate for Congress has generated substantial controversy. For example, although the Constitution gives Congress the sole power to declare war, many presidents have initiated military action on their own. And at times, the courts have found that congressional actions have usurped the rights of the states.

Electing the Congress

If Americans are not happy with the job Congress is doing, they can use their votes to say so. With a congressional election every two years, the voters have frequent opportunities to express themselves.

impeachment The formal charging of a government official with "treason, bribery, or other high crimes and misdemeanors."

FIGURE 8.1   Incumbents: Life Is Good

Despite the public's dissatisfaction with Congress in general, incumbent representatives win reelection at an exceptional rate. Incumbent senators are not quite as successful but still do well in reelection races. Voters seem to believe that their own representatives and senators do not share the same foibles that they attribute to the other members of Congress.

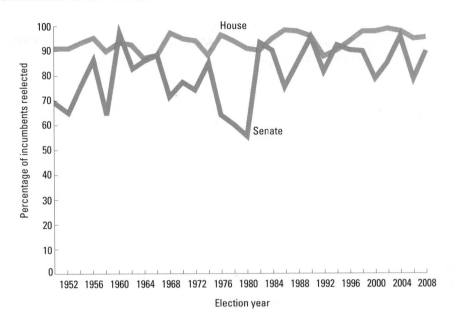

Sources: Norman J. Ornstein, Thomas E. Mann, and Michael J. Malbin, *Vital Statistics on Congress, 2001–2002* (Washington, D.C.: American Enterprise Institute, 2002), pp. 69–70; David Nather with John Cochran, "Still-Thin Edge Leaves GOP with a Cautious Mandate," *CQ Weekly,* 9 November 2002, pp. 2888–2893; "The 2006 Election: Congress," *New York Times,* 9 November 2006, pp. P8–P9.

The Incumbency Effect

Congressional elections offer voters a chance to show their approval of Congress's performance by reelecting **incumbents** or to demonstrate their disapproval by "throwing the rascals out." The voters seem to do more reelecting than rascal throwing. The reelection rate is astonishingly high; in the majority of elections since 1950, more than 90 percent of all House incumbents have held on to their seats (see Figure 8.1). In the 2006 congressional elections, twenty-three incumbents in the House of Representatives were defeated by challengers.[4] Most House elections are not even close; in recent elections, many House incumbents have faced weak, poorly funded opponents. Senate elections are usually somewhat more competitive, but incumbents still have a high reelection rate.[5] In the 2006 Senate races, six of the twenty-nine incumbents running for reelection were defeated. All six were Republicans.

These findings may seem surprising, since the public does not hold Congress as a whole in particularly high esteem. In the past few years Americans have been particularly critical of the Congress and some polls have showed less than one in five approving its performance (see Figure 8.2). One reason

incumbent A current officeholder.

FIGURE 8.2   We Love Our Incumbents . . . but Not the Congress

Despite the reelection rate of incumbents reflected in Figure 8.1, public approval of Congress is far less positive. Confidence scores have never been particularly high, but opinion has turned decidedly negative in recent years. Citizens do not believe that the House and Senate are addressing the nation's problems.

Source: NBC News/*Wall Street Journal* polls, accessed at http://pollingreport.com. The question used asks respondents, "In general, do you approve or disapprove of the job that Congress is doing?"

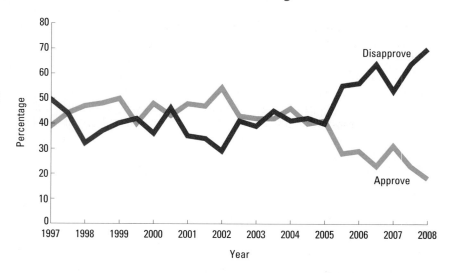

Congress is held in disdain is that Americans regard it as overly influenced by interest groups. A declining economy, the war in Iraq, and persistent partisan disagreements within the Congress have also reduced the people's confidence in the institution. In short, voters tend to support their own representatives while being contemptuous of the rest of the membership.

Redistricting.   One explanation for the incumbency effect centers on redistricting—the way House districts are redrawn by state legislatures after a census-based reapportionment. It is entirely possible for them to draw the new districts to benefit the incumbents of one or both parties. Altering district lines for partisan advantage is commonly called **gerrymandering.** Of course, a state legislature can redraw district boundaries to harm incumbents as well. Of the seven incumbents in the U.S. House of Representatives who lost their seats on Election Day in 2004, four were Texas Democrats whose districts' boundaries had been altered in a controversial redistricting plan supported by Republicans in the state legislature.[6]

Gerrymandering contributes to the increasing pattern of polarization between the two parties in the House. In a district with a disproportionate number of liberals or conservatives, the representative will be pulled more toward a pole of the ideological spectrum than the moderate center.[7]

gerrymandering Redrawing a congressional district to intentionally benefit one political party.

Name Recognition.   Holding office brings with it some important advantages. First, incumbents develop significant name recognition among voters simply by being members of Congress. Congressional press secretaries promote name recognition through their efforts to get publicity for the activities and speeches of their bosses. The primary focus of such publicity seeking is on the local media back in the home district, where the votes are.[8] The local press, in turn, is eager to cover what members of Congress are saying about the issues.

Another resource available to members of Congress is the *franking privilege*—the right to send mail free of charge. Mailings work to make constituents aware of their legislators' names, activities, and accomplishments. In 2006 House members sent out 116 million pieces of mail, "many of them glossy productions filled with flattering photos and lists of the latest roads and bridges the lawmaker has brought home to the district."[9] The individual websites of legislators can be best described as exercises in narcissism: long on public relations but short on information on how the legislator voted on recent or past legislation.[10]

Casework.   Much of the work performed by the large staffs of members of Congress is **casework**—services for constituents such as tracking down a social security check or directing the owner of a small business to the appropriate federal agency. Legislators devote much of their office budget to casework because they assume that when they provide assistance to a constituent, that constituent will be grateful. Not only will this person probably vote for the legislator next time, he or she will be sure to tell family members and friends how helpful the representative or senator was.

Campaign Financing.   Anyone who wants to challenge an incumbent needs solid financial backing. But here too the incumbent has the advantage. In the preelection phase of the 2005–2006 campaign cycle, House incumbents running for reelection received approximately 70 percent of all money contributed to congressional races. Challengers received only 19 percent of the contributions, with the remainder going to candidates in open races where there was no incumbent running for reelection.[11] Challengers find raising campaign funds difficult because they have to overcome contributors' doubts about whether they can win. PACs show a strong preference for incumbents (see Chapter 7). They tend not to want to risk offending an incumbent by giving money to a long-shot challenger.

Successful Challengers.   Clearly the deck is stacked against challengers to incumbents. Yet some challengers do beat incumbents. How? The opposing party and unsympathetic PACs may target incumbents who seem vulnerable because of age, lack of seniority, a scandal, or unfavorable redistricting.

Senate challengers have a higher success rate than House challengers, in part because they are generally higher-quality candidates. Often they are governors or members of the House who enjoy high name recognition and can attract significant campaign funds because they are regarded as credible candidates.[12]

casework Solving problems for constituents, especially problems involving government agencies.

The party controlling the White House almost always loses House seats in the midterm election as voters take out their disappointments with the president on candidates from his party. The president's party usually loses seats in the Senate too. This was the case in 2006, when the Republicans lost enough seats to give the Democrats control of both the House and the Senate.

2008 Election

A similar pattern emerged in 2008. In the months leading up to the election, the nation's financial markets were shaken by the collapse of major brokerages and a virtual freeze in mortgages and credit. After intense pressure from the administration, Congress enacted a $700 billion plan to prop up the financial services industry, and the government purchased a share in nine of the nation's largest banks. Voters reacted with concern. With President Bush's public support at an all-time low, Democrats picked up seats in both the House and the Senate, solidifying their majorities. Though they did not reach sixty seats in the Senate (the number of votes required to end a filibuster), Democrats emerged well positioned to enact legislation with President Obama.

Whom Do We Elect?

The people we elect (and then reelect) to Congress are not a cross-section of American society. Most members of Congress are professionals—primarily lawyers and businesspeople.[13] Although nearly a third of the American labor force works in blue-collar jobs, a person employed as a blue-collar worker rarely wins a congressional nomination. Women and minorities also have long been underrepresented in elective office, although both groups have recently increased their representation in Congress significantly. In the 110th Congress, elected in November 2006, seventy-one representatives and sixteen senators were women, forty-two representatives and one senator were African Americans, and twenty-three representatives and three senators were Hispanic.[14] Yet many women and minorities believe that only members of their own group—people who have experienced what they have experienced—can truly represent their interests. This is a belief in **descriptive representation**—the view that a legislature should resemble the demographic characteristics of the population it represents.[15]

When Congress amended the Voting Rights Act in 1982, it encouraged the states to draw districts that concentrated minorities together so that African Americans and Hispanic Americans would have a better chance of being elected to office. Supreme Court decisions also pushed the states to concentrate minorities in House districts.[16] After the 1990 census, states redrew House boundaries with the intent of creating districts with majority or near-majority minority populations. Some districts were very oddly shaped, snaking through their state to pick up black neighborhoods in various cities but leaving adjacent white neighborhoods to other districts.

descriptive representation
A belief that constituents are most effectively represented by legislators who are similar to them in such key demographic characteristics as race, ethnicity, religion, or gender.

This effort led to a roughly 50 percent increase in the number of blacks elected to the House.

The effort to draw boundaries to promote the election of minorities has been considerably less effective for Hispanics. Hispanic representation is only about two-thirds that of African Americans, even though there are slightly more Hispanics in the United States than African Americans.[17] Part of the reason for this inequity is that Hispanics tend not to live in such geographically concentrated areas as do African Americans. This makes it harder to draw boundaries that will likely lead to the election of a Hispanic.

In a decision that surprised many, the Supreme Court ruled in 1993 that states' efforts to increase minority representation through **racial gerrymandering** could violate the rights of whites. In *Shaw v. Reno*, the majority ruled in a split decision that a North Carolina district that meandered 160 miles from Durham to Charlotte was an example of "political apartheid." In effect, the Court ruled that racial gerrymandering segregated blacks from whites instead of creating districts built around contiguous communities.[18] In a later decision, the Supreme Court ruled that the "intensive and pervasive use of race" to protect incumbents and promote political gerrymandering violated the Fourteenth Amendment and Voting Rights Act of 1965.[19] In 2001, just before the redistricting from the 2000 census was to begin in the individual states, the Court modified its earlier decisions by declaring that race was not an illegitimate consideration in drawing congressional boundaries as long as it was not the "dominant and controlling" factor.[20]

Although this movement over time to draw districts that work to elect minorities has clearly increased the number of black and Hispanic legislators, almost all of whom are Democrats, it has also helped the Republican Party. As more Democratic voting minorities have been packed into selected districts, their numbers in other districts have fallen. This has left the remaining districts not merely "whiter" but also more Republican than they would have otherwise been.[21]

How Issues Get on the Congressional Agenda

The formal legislative process begins when a member of Congress introduces a *bill*—a proposal for a new law. In the House, members drop new bills in the "hopper," a mahogany box near the rostrum where the Speaker presides. Senators give their bills to one of the Senate clerks or introduce them from the floor.[22] But before a bill can be introduced to solve a problem, someone must perceive that a problem exists or that an issue needs to be resolved. In other words, the problem or issue somehow must find its way onto the congressional agenda. Many of the issues Congress is working on at any one time seem to have been around forever, yet all issues have a beginning point. Foreign aid, the national debt, and social security have come up in just about every recent session of Congress. Other issues emerge

racial gerrymandering The drawing of a legislative district to maximize the chances that a minority candidate will win election.

more suddenly, especially those that are the product of technological change.[23] Genetically altered foods have become a controversial issue. In the Congress, consumer advocates have introduced legislation to require labeling of bioengineered food products. Members from farm areas have commissioned reports to show that such foods are safe. Once the technology was used to alter crops and food products, it was inevitable that Congress would have to place such a controversial issue on its agenda.[24]

Sometimes a highly visible event focuses national attention on a problem. When it became evident that the September 11 hijackers had little trouble bringing box cutters that they would use as weapons on board the planes, Congress quickly took up the issue of airport screening procedures. It decided to create a federal work force to conduct passenger and luggage screening at the nation's airports. Presidential support can also move an issue onto the agenda quickly. Media attention gives the president enormous opportunity to draw the nation's attention to problems he believes need some form of governmental action.

Within Congress, party leaders and committee chairs have the opportunity to influence the political agenda. At times, the efforts of an interest group spark awareness of an issue.

The Dance of Legislation: An Overview

The process of writing bills and getting them passed is relatively simple, in the sense that it follows a series of specific steps. What complicates the process is the many different ways legislation can be treated at each step. Here, we examine the straightforward process by which laws are made. In the next few sections, we discuss some of the complexities of that process.

After a bill is introduced in either house, it is assigned to the committee with jurisdiction over that policy area (see Figure 8.3). A banking bill, for example, is assigned to the Banking and Finance Services Committee in the House or the Banking, Housing, and Urban Affairs Committee in the Senate. When a committee actively considers a piece of legislation assigned to it, the bill is usually referred to a specialized subcommittee. The subcommittee may hold hearings, and legislative staffers may do research on the bill. The original bill usually is modified or revised. If passed in some form, it is sent to the full committee. A bill approved by the full committee is reported (that is, sent) to the entire membership of the chamber, where it may be debated, amended, and either passed or defeated.

Bills coming out of House committees go to the Rules Committee before going before the full House membership. The Rules Committee attaches a rule to the bill that governs the coming floor debate, typically specifying the length of the debate and the types of amendments House members may offer. The Senate does not have a comparable committee, although restrictions on the length of floor debate can be reached through unanimous consent agreements (see the "Rules of Procedure" section later in the chapter).

FIGURE 8.3   The Legislative Process

The process by which a bill becomes law is subject to much variation. This diagram depicts the typical path a bill might follow. It is important to remember that a bill can fail at any stage because of lack of support.

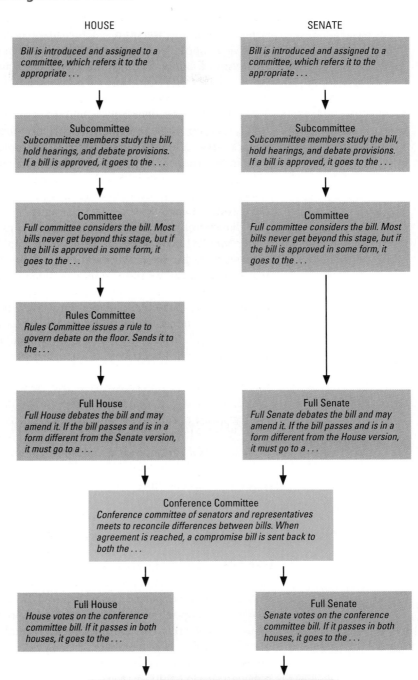

HOUSE

Bill is introduced and assigned to a committee, which refers it to the appropriate . . .

Subcommittee
Subcommittee members study the bill, hold hearings, and debate provisions. If a bill is approved, it goes to the . . .

Committee
Full committee considers the bill. Most bills never get beyond this stage, but if the bill is approved in some form, it goes to the . . .

Rules Committee
Rules Committee issues a rule to govern debate on the floor. Sends it to the . . .

Full House
Full House debates the bill and may amend it. If the bill passes and is in a form different from the Senate version, it must go to a . . .

SENATE

Bill is introduced and assigned to a committee, which refers it to the appropriate . . .

Subcommittee
Subcommittee members study the bill, hold hearings, and debate provisions. If a bill is approved, it goes to the . . .

Committee
Full committee considers the bill. Most bills never get beyond this stage, but if the bill is approved in some form, it goes to the . . .

Full Senate
Full Senate debates the bill and may amend it. If the bill passes and is in a form different from the House version, it must go to a . . .

Conference Committee
Conference committee of senators and representatives meets to reconcile differences between bills. When agreement is reached, a compromise bill is sent back to both the . . .

Full House
House votes on the conference committee bill. If it passes in both houses, it goes to the . . .

Full Senate
Senate votes on the conference committee bill. If it passes in both houses, it goes to the . . .

President
President signs or vetoes the bill. Congress can override a veto by a two-thirds majority vote in both the House and Senate.

Even if both houses of Congress pass a bill on the same subject, the Senate and House versions usually differ. In that case, a conference committee, composed of legislators from both houses, works out the differences and develops a compromise version. This version goes back to each house for another floor vote. If both chambers approve the bill, it is then sent to the president for his signature (approval) or **veto** (rejection).

When the president signs a bill, it becomes law. If the president vetoes a bill, it is sent back to Congress with his reasons for rejecting it. The bill becomes law only if Congress overrides the president's veto by a two-thirds vote in each house. If the president neither signs nor vetoes the bill within ten days of receiving it (Sundays excepted), the bill becomes law. But if Congress adjourns within that ten-day period, the president can let the bill die through a **pocket veto** by not signing it.

The content of a bill can be changed at any stage of the process and in either house. Lawmaking (and thus policymaking) in Congress has many access points for those who want to influence legislation. This openness tends to fit within the pluralist model of democracy. As a bill moves through the Congress, it is amended again and again, in a search for a consensus that will get it passed and signed into law. The process can be tortuously slow, and it often is fruitless. Derailing legislation is much easier than enacting it. The process gives groups frequent opportunities to voice their preferences and, if necessary, thwart their opponents.

Committees: The Workhorses of Congress

Woodrow Wilson once observed that "Congress in session is Congress on public exhibition, whilst Congress in its committee-rooms is Congress at work."[25] The real nuts and bolts of lawmaking goes on in congressional committees.

The Division of Labor Among Committees

The House and Senate are divided into committees for the same reason that other large organizations are broken into departments or divisions: to develop and use expertise in specific areas. For example, congressional decisions on weapons systems require special knowledge that is of little relevance to decisions on reimbursement formulas for health insurance. It makes sense for some members of Congress to spend more time examining defense issues, becoming increasingly expert as they do so, while others concentrate on health matters.

Eventually all members of Congress have to vote on each bill that emerges from the committees. Those who are not on a particular committee depend on committee members to examine the issues thoroughly, make compromises as necessary, and bring forward a sound piece of legislation

veto The president's disapproval of a bill that has been passed by both houses of Congress. Congress can override a veto with a two-thirds vote in each house.

pocket veto A means of killing a bill that has been passed by both houses of Congress, in which the president does not sign the bill and Congress adjourns within ten days of the bill's passage.

that has a good chance of being passed. Each member decides individually on a bill's merits. But once it reaches the House or Senate floor, members may get to vote on only a handful of amendments (if any at all) before they must cast their yea or nay for the entire bill.

Standing Committees.

There are several different kinds of congressional committees, but the **standing committee** is predominant. Standing committees are permanent committees that specialize in a particular area of legislation—for example, the House Judiciary Committee or the Senate Environment and Public Works Committee. Most of the day-to-day work of drafting legislation takes place in the sixteen standing Senate committees and twenty standing House committees. Typically from sixteen to twenty senators serve on each standing Senate committee, and on average forty-two members serve on each standing committee in the House. The proportion of Democrats and Republicans on a standing committee generally reflects party proportions in the full Senate or House.

With a few exceptions, standing committees are further broken down into subcommittees. The House Agriculture Committee, for example, has five subcommittees, among them one on specialty crops and another on livestock and horticulture.

Other Congressional Committees.

Members of Congress can also serve on joint, select, and conference committees. **Joint committees** are made up of members of both House and Senate. Like standing committees, they are concerned with particular policy areas. The Joint Economic Committee, for instance, analyzes the country's economic policies. Joint committees are much weaker than standing committees because they are almost always restricted from reporting bills to the House or Senate.

A **select committee** is usually a temporary committee created for a specific purpose. Congress establishes select committees to deal with special circumstances or with issues that either overlap or fall outside the areas of expertise of standing committees. The Senate committee that investigated the Watergate scandal was a select committee, created for that purpose only. These committees typically disband after their work is completed. However, some select committees, such as the Senate Select Committee on Intelligence and the House Permanent Select Committee on Intelligence, are granted permanent status and function like standing committees.

A **conference committee** is also a temporary committee, created to work out differences between House and Senate versions of a specific piece of legislation. Its members are appointed from the standing committees or subcommittees from each house that originally handled and reported the legislation. Depending on the nature of the differences and the importance of the legislation, a conference committee may meet for hours or for weeks on end. When the conference committee agrees on a compromise, it reports the bill to both houses, which must then either approve or disapprove the compromise; they cannot amend or change it in any way. Conference

standing committee
A permanent congressional committee that specializes in a particular legislative area.

joint committee A committee made up of members of both the House and the Senate.

select committee A congressional committee created for a specific purpose and, usually, for a limited time.

conference committee
A temporary committee created to work out differences between the House and Senate versions of a specific piece of legislation.

committees are not always used, however, to reconcile differing bills. Often, informal negotiations between committee leaders in the House and Senate resolve differences. The increasing partisan conflict between Democrats and Republicans has often resulted in a compromise bill devised solely by the majority party (when a single party controls both chambers).

Congressional Expertise and Seniority

Once appointed to a committee, a representative or senator has great incentive to remain on it in order to gain increasing expertise and influence. Influence also grows in a more formal way—with **seniority** or years of consecutive service on a committee. In their quest for expertise and seniority, members tend to stay on the same committees. However, sometimes they switch places when they are offered the opportunity to move to one of the high-prestige committees (such as Ways and Means in the House or Finance in the Senate) or to a committee that handles legislation of vital importance to their constituents.

Within each committee, the senior member of the majority party usually becomes the committee chair. Other senior members of the majority party become subcommittee chairs; their counterparts from the minority party gain influence as ranking minority members. The numerous subcommittees in the House and Senate offer multiple opportunities for power and status.

After the Republicans gained control of the House in 1994, the seniority norm was weakened. The party leadership established six-year term limits for committee and subcommittee chairs, a sharp break with the tradition of unlimited tenure as a committee chair. The Speaker of the House at that time, Newt Gingrich, also rejected three Republicans who were in line to become committee chairs in favor of other committee members who he thought would best promote the Republican program. Speakers had not appointed House committee chairs in this fashion since "Uncle Joe" Cannon ruled the chamber with an iron fist as Speaker from 1903 to 1911.[26] After the Democrats won control of the House in 2006, new Speaker Nancy Pelosi decided not to reappoint sometimes-rival Jane Harman (D-Calif.) to the House Permanent Select Committee on Intelligence. As the senior Democrat on that committee, Harmon would have been first in line to serve as chair. Pelosi also bypassed number two in seniority, Alcee Hastings, whose impeachment from the federal judiciary made him a controversial candidate. In the end, Pelosi appointed Silvestre Reyes from Texas to chair the intelligence committee, despite his lack of tenure.[27]

The way in which committees and subcommittees are led and organized within Congress is significant because much public policy decision making takes place there. The first step in drafting legislation is to collect information on the issue. Committee staffers research the problem, and hearings may be held to take testimony from witnesses who have special knowledge on the subject.

seniority Years of consecutive service on a particular congressional committee.

The meetings at which subcommittees and committees actually debate and amend legislation are called *markup sessions*. The process by which committees reach decisions varies. In many committees, there is a strong tradition of decision by consensus. The chair, the ranking minority member, and others on these committees work hard, in formal committee sessions and in informal negotiations, to find a middle ground on issues that divide committee members. In other committees, members exhibit strong ideological and partisan sentiments. However, committee and subcommittee leaders prefer to find ways to overcome inherent ideological and partisan divisions so that they can build compromise solutions that will appeal to the broader membership of their house. The skill of committee leaders in assembling coalitions that produce legislation that can pass on the floor of their house is critically important.

Oversight: Following Through on Legislation

It is often said in Washington that "knowledge is power." For Congress to retain its influence over the programs it creates, it must be aware of how the agencies responsible for them are administering them. To that end, legislators and their committees engage in **oversight,** the process of reviewing agency operations to determine whether the agency is carrying out policies as Congress intended.

Congress performs its oversight function in several different ways. The most visible is the hearing. Hearings may be part of a routine review or the byproduct of information that reveals a major problem with a program or with an agency's administrative practices. After the disastrous federal response to Hurricane Katrina, a storm that destroyed much of New Orleans, congressional committees held hearings to understand why the government failed. Another way Congress keeps track of what departments and agencies are doing is by requesting reports on specific agency practices and operations. After the Democrats captured the Congress in the 2006 election, committees in both houses became much more aggressive in investigating activities in the Bush administration. A good deal of congressional oversight takes place informally. There is ongoing contact between committee and subcommittee leaders and agency administrators and between committee staffers and top agency staffers.

Oversight is often stereotyped as a process in which angry legislators bring some administrators before the television cameras at a hearing and proceed to dress them down for some recent scandal or mistake. Some of this does go on, but at least some members of a committee are advocates of the programs they oversee because those programs serve their constituents back home. Members of the House and Senate agriculture committees, for example, both Democrats and Republicans, want farm programs to succeed. Most oversight is aimed at finding ways to improve programs, not discredit them.[28] In the last analysis, Congress engages in oversight because it is an extension of its efforts to control public policy.[29]

oversight The process of reviewing the operations of an agency to determine whether it is carrying out policies as Congress intended.

Mukasey Under Fire
At times, committee hearings are more theatrical than informational, to draw public attention to them. Still, hearings can be quite revealing. When President Bush nominated Judge Michael Mukasey to be attorney general, his confirmation hearings turned into a tense discussion of "water boarding," an interrogation technique that had been used by the CIA to force three recalcitrant enemy combatants to reveal secrets. Many believe that water boarding is a form of torture, forbidden by the Geneva Convention. The Bush administration believed that it needed the flexibility in interrogation techniques to fight terrorism. Under sharp questioning from Democrats on the Senate Judiciary Committee, Mukasey said he did not know if water boarding actually constituted torture. Nevertheless, Mukasey won confirmation. *(Chip Somodevilla/Getty Images)*

Majoritarian and Pluralist Views of Committees

Government by committee vests a tremendous amount of power in the committees and subcommittees of Congress, and especially in their leaders. This is particularly true of the House, which has more decentralized patterns of influence than the Senate and is more restrictive about letting members amend legislation on the floor. Committee members can bury a bill by not reporting it to the full House or Senate. The influence of committee members extends even further, to the floor debate. Many of them also make up the conference committees charged with developing compromise versions of bills.

In some ways, the committee system enhances the force of pluralism in American politics. Representatives and senators are elected by the voters in particular districts and states, and they tend to seek membership on the committees that make the decisions most important to their constituents. Members from farm areas, for example, want membership on the House and Senate agriculture committees. As a result, committees with members who represent constituencies with an unusually strong interest in their policy area are predisposed to write legislation favorable to those constituencies.

The committees have a majoritarian aspect as well. The membership of most committees tends to resemble the general ideological profiles of the two parties' congressional contingents. Even if a committee's views are not in line with the views of the full membership, the committee is constrained in the legislation it writes because bills cannot become law unless they are passed by the parent chamber and the other house. Consequently, in formulating legislation, committees anticipate what other representatives and senators will accept. The parties within each chamber also have means of rewarding the members who are most loyal to party priorities. Party committees and the party leadership within each chamber make committee assignments and respond to requests for transfers from less prestigious to more prestigious committees. Those whose voting is most in line with the party get the best assignments.[30]

Leaders and Followers in Congress

Above the committee chairs is another layer of authority in the organization of the House and Senate. The Democratic and Republican leaders in each house work to maximize the influence of their own party while trying to keep their chamber functioning smoothly and efficiently. The operation of the two houses is also influenced by the rules and norms that each chamber has developed over the years.

The Leadership Task

Each of the two parties elects leaders in each of the two houses. In the House of Representatives, the majority party's leader is the **Speaker of the House,** who, gavel in hand, chairs sessions from the ornate rostrum at the front of the chamber. The Speaker's counterpart in the opposing party is the House *minority leader.* The Speaker is a constitutional officer, but the Constitution does not list the Speaker's duties. The majority party in the House also has a majority leader, who helps the Speaker guide the party's policy program through the legislative process, and a majority whip, who keeps track of the vote count and rallies support for legislation on the floor. The minority party is led by a minority leader who is assisted by the minority whip.

The Constitution makes the vice president of the United States the president of the Senate. But in practice, the vice president rarely visits the Senate chamber unless there is a possibility of a tie vote, in which case he can break the tie. The *president pro tempore* (president "for the time"), elected by the majority party, is supposed to chair the Senate in the vice president's absence. By custom this constitutional position is entirely honorary and occupied by the senator of the majority party with the longest continuous tenure. The real power in the Senate resides with the **majority leader.** The top position in the opposing party is Senate *minority leader.* Technically, the majority leader does not preside over Senate sessions (members rotate in the president pro tempore's chair). But the majority leader does schedule legislation in consultation with the minority leader.

Party leaders play a critical role in getting bills through Congress. Their most significant function is steering the bargaining and negotiating

Speaker of the House The presiding officer of the House of Representatives.

majority leader The head of the majority party in the Senate; the second-highest-ranking member of the majority party in the House.

over the content of legislation. When an issue divides their party, their house, the two houses, or their house and the White House, the leaders must take the initiative to work out a compromise. Day in and day out, much of what they do is to meet with other members of their house to try to strike deals that will yield a majority on the floor. Beyond trying to engineer tradeoffs that will win votes, the party leaders must persuade others (often powerful committee chairs) that theirs is the best deal possible. Former Speaker of the House Dennis Hastert used to say, "They call me the Speaker, but . . . they really ought to call me the Listener."[31]

It is often difficult for party leaders to control rank-and-file members because they have independent electoral bases in their districts and states and receive the vast bulk of their campaign funds from nonparty sources. Contemporary party leaders are coalition builders, not autocrats. Yet party leaders can be aggressive about enforcing party discipline. When an energy bill was being developed in the House in 2007, Speaker Pelosi found herself at odds with Michigan Democrat John Dingell, chair of the Energy and Commerce Committee. Dingell believed that a proposed increase in fuel consumption standards would be bad for the automobile industry, key to his home state's economy. Advised of an initiative pushing for high fuel economy standards, the gruff Dingell dismissed it. "Let them try," he said. But Pelosi persuaded enough members of the committee to go against Dingell and the chastised chair was forced to go along with the Speaker's wishes.[32]

Rules of Procedure

The operations of the House and Senate are structured by both formal rules and informal norms of behavior. Rules in each chamber are mostly matters of parliamentary procedure. For example, they govern the scheduling of legislation, outlining when and how certain types of legislation can be brought to the floor.

An important difference between the two chambers is the House's use of its Rules Committee to govern floor debate. Lacking a similar committee to act as a "traffic cop" for legislation approaching the floor, the Senate relies on unanimous consent agreements to set the starting time and length of the debate. If only one senator objects to an agreement, it does not take effect. Senators do not routinely object to unanimous consent agreements, however, because they know they will need them when bills of their own await scheduling by the leadership.

A senator who wants to stop a bill badly enough may start a **filibuster** and (in its classic form) try to talk the bill to death. By historical tradition, the Senate gives its members the right of unlimited debate. The record for holding the floor belongs to the late Republican senator Strom Thurmond of South Carolina, for a twenty-four-hour, eighteen-minute marathon.[33] In the House, no member is allowed to speak for more than an hour without unanimous consent.

INTERACTIVE 8.1

AP | *Filibuster Fight*

filibuster A delaying tactic, used in the Senate, that often involves speech making to prevent action on a piece of legislation.

After a 1917 filibuster by a small group of senators killed President Wilson's bill to arm merchant ships, a bill favored by a majority of senators, the Senate finally adopted **cloture,** a means of limiting debate. A petition signed by sixteen senators initiates a cloture vote. It now takes the votes of sixty senators to invoke cloture, which creates a time limit for the debate. Since the 1960s the filibuster has taken on a variety of new forms that do not actually require a senator to occupy the floor and speak continuously. Today the term *filibuster* is also applied to a parliamentary device in the Senate that blocks action on a bill (as if a senator were speaking), but still allows business on other issues to take place. Because a senator can now filibuster without actually occupying the floor and speaking continuously about a bill, it is much easier to maintain filibusters, and they have become much more common. Filibusters have also raised considerable controversy, particularly when senators prevented votes on several nominees for the federal judiciary during the administrations of Bill Clinton and George W. Bush. Several proposals have emerged that would reduce the number of votes required for cloture on judicial appointments.

Norms of Behavior

Both houses have codes of behavior that help keep them running. These codes are largely unwritten norms, although some have been formally adopted as rules. Members of Congress recognize that they must eliminate personal conflict, lest Congress dissolve into bickering factions unable to work together. One of the most celebrated norms is that members show respect for their colleagues in public deliberations. During floor debate, bitter opponents have traditionally referred to one another in such terms as "my good friend, the senior senator from . . ." or "my distinguished colleague." There are no firm measures of civility in Congress, but it seems to have declined in recent years.[34]

Probably the most important norm of behavior in Congress is that individual members should be willing to bargain with one another. Policy-making is a process of give-and-take; it demands compromise. Members of Congress are not expected to violate their consciences on policy issues simply to strike a deal. Rather, they are expected to listen to what others have to say and to make every effort to reach a reasonable compromise. Obviously, if they all stick rigidly to their own views, they will never agree on anything. Moreover, few policy matters are so clear-cut that compromise destroys one's position.

Some important norms have changed in recent years, most notably the notion that junior members of the House and Senate should serve apprenticeships and defer to their party and committee elders during their first couple of years in Congress. Aggressive, impatient, and ambitious junior legislators of both parties chafed under this norm, and it has weakened considerably in the past few decades.

cloture The mechanism by which a filibuster is cut off in the Senate.

The Legislative Environment

In this section, we examine the broader legislative environment that affects decision making in Congress. More specifically, we look at the influence on legislators of political parties, the president, constituents, and interest groups. The first two influences push Congress toward majoritarian democracy. The other two are pluralist influences on congressional policymaking.

Political Parties

The national political parties might appear to have limited resources at their disposal to influence lawmakers. They do not control the nominations of House and Senate candidates. Candidates receive the bulk of their funds from individual contributors and political action committees, not from the national parties. Nevertheless, the parties are strong forces in the legislative process. The party leaders and various party committees within each house can help or hinder the efforts of rank-and-file legislators to get on the right committees, get their bills and amendments considered, and climb onto the leadership ladder themselves. Moreover, party members on a committee tend to act as agents of their party as they search for solutions to policy problems.[35]

The most significant reason that the parties are important in Congress is that Democrats and Republicans have different ideological views. Both parties have diversity, but as Figure 8.4 illustrates, Democrats increasingly tend to vote one way and Republicans the other. The main reason that partisanship has been rising is that each party is becoming more homogeneous.[36] The liberal wing of the Republican Party has practically disappeared, and the party is unified around a conservative agenda for America. Likewise, the conservative wing of the Democratic Party has declined. Republicans tend to be dominant in the South and West; Democrats control more seats in the Northeast and West Coast.

Majoritarianism was clearly at work when Congress convened after the 2006 election. Democrats have been largely united around their priorities, such as ending the war in Iraq, promoting child health care, and refusing to extend tax cuts that were enacted earlier in President Bush's tenure. Conversely, Republicans have stood fast, backing the administration's priorities, especially the American troop surge in Iraq.

The President

Unlike members of Congress, the president is selected by voters across the entire nation. The president has a better claim, then, to representing the nation than does any single member of Congress. But it can also be argued that Congress as a whole has a better claim than the president to representing the majority of voters. Nevertheless, presidents capitalize on their national constituency and usually act as though they are speaking for the majority.

FIGURE 8.4   Rising Partisanship

Congress long relied on bipartisanship—the two parties working together—in policymaking. This often meant that the moderates of both parties were central to the development of legislation as they coalesced around the most workable compromise. More recently, behavior has turned more partisan. Increasingly, members of each party vote with each other and against the position of the other party.

Source: "United We Stand Opposed," *CQ Weekly,* 14 January 2008, p. 144.

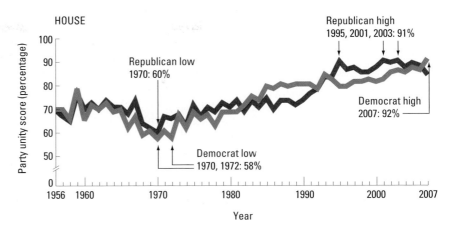

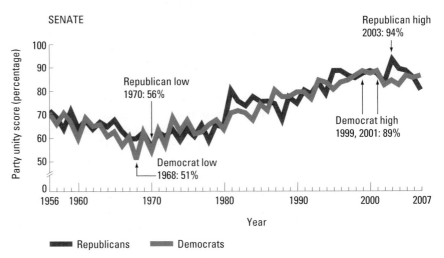

During the twentieth century, public expectations of what the president can accomplish in office grew enormously. We now expect the president to be our chief legislator: to introduce legislation on major issues and use his influence to push bills through Congress.[37] This is much different from our early history, when presidents felt constrained by the constitutional doctrine of separation of powers and had to have members of Congress work confidentially for them during legislative sessions.[38]

Today the White House is openly involved not only in the writing of bills but also in their development as they wind their way through the legislative process. If the White House does not like a bill, it tries to work out a compromise with key legislators to have the legislation amended. On issues of the greatest importance, the president himself may meet with individual legislators to persuade them to vote a certain way. In the Bush White House, Vice President Cheney was also used to lobby wayward Republicans, making every effort to persuade them to support the president's policies. To monitor daily congressional activities and lobby for the administration's policies, there are hundreds of legislative liaison personnel who work for the executive branch.

Although members of Congress grant presidents a leadership role in proposing legislation, they jealously guard the power of Congress to debate, shape, and pass or defeat any legislation the president proposes. Congress often clashes sharply with the president when his proposals are seen as ill advised.

Constituents

Constituents are the people who live and vote in a legislator's district or state. As much as members of Congress want to please their party's leadership or the president by going along with their preferences, they have to think about what the voters back home want. If the way members vote displeases enough people, they might lose their seats in the next election.

Constituents' influence contributes to pluralism, because the diversity of America is mirrored in the geographical basis of representation in the House and Senate. A representative from Los Angeles, for instance, may need to be sensitive to issues of particular concern to constituents whose backgrounds are Korean, Vietnamese, Hispanic, Indian, African American, or Jewish. A representative from Montana will have few such constituents but must pay particular attention to issues involving minerals and mining. A senator from Nebraska will give higher priority to agricultural issues than to urban issues. Conversely, a senator from New York will be hypersensitive to issues related to cities. All these constituencies, enthusiastically represented by legislators who want to do a good job for the people back home, push and pull Congress in many different directions.

Interest Groups

As we pointed out in Chapter 7, interest groups offer constituents one way to influence Congress. Because they represent a vast array of vocational, regional, and ideological groupings within the population, interest groups exemplify pluralist politics. They press members of Congress to take a particular course of action, believing sincerely that what they prefer is also best for the country. Legislators, in turn, are attentive to interest groups because these organizations represent citizens, some of whom live in their home district or state. Lobbies are also sources of useful information and potentially of political support (and, in some instances, campaign contributions) for members of Congress.

DO IT!

Find out who your U.S. Representative is on the House's website: https://forms.house.gov/wyr/welcome.shtml.

constituents People who live and vote in a government official's district or state.

With all these strong forces pushing and constraining legislators, it is easy to believe that they function solely in response to these external pressures. Legislators, however, bring their own views and own life experiences to Congress. The issues they choose to work on and the way they vote reflect these personal values too.[39] But to the degree that the four external sources of influence on Congress—parties, the president, constituents, and interest groups—do influence legislators, they push them in both majoritarian and pluralist directions. We will return to the conflict between pluralism and majoritarianism at the end of this chapter.

The Dilemma of Representation: Trustees or Delegates?

When candidates for the House and Senate campaign for office, they routinely promise to work hard for their district's or state's interests. When they get to Washington, though, they all face a troubling dilemma: what their constituents want may not be what the people across the nation want. Members of Congress are often criticized for being out of touch with the people they are supposed to represent. This charge does not seem justified. A typical week in the life of a representative means working in Washington, then boarding a plane and flying back to the home district. There the representative spends time meeting with individual constituents and talking to civic groups, church gatherings, business associations, labor unions, and the like. A survey of House members during a nonelection year showed that each made an average of thirty-five trips back to his or her district, spending an average of 138 days there.[40] Legislators work extraordinarily hard at keeping in touch with voters and finding out what is on their constituents' minds. The problem is how to act on that knowledge.

Are members of Congress bound to vote the way their constituents want them to vote, even if doing so means voting against their consciences? Some say no. They argue that legislators must be free to vote in line with what they think is best. This view is associated with the English political philosopher Edmund Burke (1729–1797). Burke, who served in Parliament, told his constituents in Bristol that "you choose a member, indeed; but when you have chosen him, he is not a member of Bristol, but he is a member of *Parliament.*"[41] Burke reasoned that representatives are sent by their constituents to vote as they think best. As **trustees,** representatives are obligated to consider the views of constituents, but they are not obligated to vote according to those views if they think they are misguided.

Others disagree. They hold that legislators are duty-bound to represent the majority view of their constituents. They maintain that legislators are **delegates** with instructions from the people at home on how to vote on critical issues, and they insist that delegates, unlike trustees, must be prepared to vote against their own policy preferences.

trustee A representative who is obligated to consider the views of constituents but is not obligated to vote according to those views if he or she believes they are misguided.

delegate A legislator whose primary responsibility is to represent the majority view of his or her constituents, regardless of his or her own view.

Although the interests of their districts encourage them to act as delegates, their interpretation of the larger national interest calls on them to be trustees.[42] Given these conflicting role definitions, it is not surprising that Congress is not clearly either a body of delegates or a body of trustees. Research has shown, however, that members of Congress are most likely to assume the delegate role on issues that are of great concern to their constituents.[43] But much of the time, what constituents really want is not clear. Many issues are not highly visible back home, they cut across the constituency to affect it in different ways, or constituents only partially understand them. For such issues, no delegate position is obvious.

Pluralism, Majoritarianism, and Democracy

The dilemma that individual members of Congress face in adopting the role of either delegate or trustee has broad implications for the way our country is governed. If legislators tend to act as delegates, congressional policymaking is more pluralistic, and policies reflect the bargaining that goes on among lawmakers who speak for different constituencies. If, instead, legislators tend to act as trustees and vote their consciences, policymaking becomes less tied to the narrower interests of districts and states. But even here there is no guarantee that congressional decision making reflects majority interests.

We end this chapter with a short discussion of pluralism versus majoritarianism in Congress. But first, to establish a frame of reference, we need to take a quick look at a more majoritarian type of legislature: the parliament.

Parliamentary Government

In our system of government, the executive and legislative functions are divided between a president and a congress, each elected separately. Most other democracies—for example, Britain and Japan—have parliamentary governments. In a **parliamentary system,** the chief executive is the legislative leader whose party holds the most seats in the legislature after an election, or whose party forms a major part of the ruling coalition. For instance, in Great Britain, voters do not cast a ballot for prime minister. They vote only for their member of Parliament and thus influence the choice of prime minister only indirectly, by voting for the party they favor in the local district election. Parties are unified, and in Parliament, legislators vote for their party's position, giving voters a strong and direct means of influencing public policy. Where there is a multiple party system (as opposed to just two parties), a governing coalition must sometimes be formed out of an alliance of several parties. (See "Politics of Global Change: A Multi Multi-Party Parliament").

In a parliamentary system, government power is highly concentrated in the legislature, because the leader of the majority party is also the head

parliamentary system A system of government in which the chief executive is the leader whose party holds the most seats in the legislature after an election or whose party forms a major part of the ruling coalition.

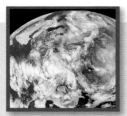

Politics of Global Change

A Multi Multi-Party Parliament

As India has modernized, cultural fragmentation has become more pronounced. At the root of this fragmentation are the forces of religion, ethnicity, language, and regionalism.

These influences are manifested in the Indian Parliament, which is nothing if not diverse. The 545-seat *Lok Sabha* (House of the People) is governed by a coalition of more than a dozen parties. The ruling coalition is known as the United Progressive Alliance. Overall, the country has fifty officially recognized parties and countless others too small to gain official recognition. The electoral trend is clear: in 1984 regional parties won just 13 percent of the national vote but in the 2004 election they won fully one-third of the vote.

The Indian party system is not dominated by a liberal-conservative disagreement between two major parties. The two largest parties, Congress and the Bharatiya Janata Party (BJP) are quite different. The BJP is a Hindu nationalist party, while Congress, which worked for independence from Great Britain during the colonial period, is a centrist party. Congress is the lead party in the current government but its coalition partners are a rich stew of varying political flavors. In India joining a coalition in Parliament is not tied to ideological compatibility but to horse trading between the lead party and those willing to join an alliance if their demands are met.

One of the parties that joined the United Progressive Alliance is the *Telangana Rashtra Samiti* (TRS) party, which won five seats in the *Lok Sabha* in the 2004 election. Its primary objective is statehood for the Telangana region in the southeastern part of the country. The TRS formally left the coalition in 2006 because the government had not been working for Telangana statehood.

The great disadvantage of coalition governments is that small parties have great leverage over the more broadly popular parties. As the United Progressive Alliance tried to negotiate an agreement with the United States concerning nuclear power, it was bedeviled by internal dissension among its member parties.

Regional parties have also prospered because they have proven to be more dynamic and more aggressive in adapting to the world economy. Regional governments paved the way for "outsourcing" in information technology and other fields. When you call for help about a computer problem, it really does not matter where the person on the other end of the line is located, so long as he or she can solve your problem. The lower wages and highly trained work force in India have made it a striking success in the business of outsourcing. Many American firms outsource to India for their telephone help desks and for the processing of high volumes of mundane office paperwork.

of the government. Moreover, parliamentary legislatures are usually composed of only one house or have a second chamber that is much weaker than the other. And parliamentary governments usually do not have a court that can invalidate acts of the parliament. Under such a system, the government is in the hands of the party that controls the parliament. Overall, these governments fit the majoritarian model of democracy to a much greater extent than a separation-of-powers system.

Pluralism Versus Majoritarianism in Congress

The U.S. Congress is often criticized for being too pluralistic and not majoritarian enough. The federal budget deficit provides a case in point. Americans are deeply concerned about the big deficits that have plagued national budgets in recent years. And both Democrats and Republicans in Congress have repeatedly called for reductions in those deficits. But when spending bills come before Congress, legislators' concerns turn to what the bills will or will not do for their district or state. Appropriations bills usually include **earmarks**, pork barrel projects that benefit specific districts or states and further add to any deficit. Recent earmarks include $135,000 for a library and museum honoring the nation's first ladies (presidents' wives); $100,000 for a science education program that takes children out onto the ocean aboard a catamaran off California's Monterey coast; and $350,000 for a study of the relationship between carpets and indoor air quality. More expensive earmarks abound too. Representative John Murtha (D-Pa.) secured over $600 million in earmarks (mostly contracts for area firms in his district) during a four-year period.[44]

Projects such as these get into the budget through bargaining among members. Members of Congress try to win projects and programs that will benefit their constituents and thus help them at election time. To win approval of such projects, members must be willing to vote for other legislators' projects in turn. Such a system obviously promotes pluralism (and spending).

It is easy to conclude that the consequence of pluralism in Congress is a lot of unnecessary spending and tax loopholes. Yet many different constituencies are well served by an appropriations process that takes pluralism into account. When Congress included $50 million for the Iowa Environmental/Education Project, was it one more example of frivolous pork barrel spending? The Iowa economy has been hit hard in recent years, and the new tourist attraction is to be built on a former industrial site in Coralville. When it is finished, tourists will be able to enter replicas of different ecosystems, including a 4.5-acre indoor rain forest. One estimate—possibly optimistic—is that when it is up and running, the new facility will generate $120 million a year for the state's economy. It will provide jobs too, replacing at least some of those lost when factories shut down.[45] The people of Iowa pay taxes to Washington, so shouldn't Washington send

earmarks Federal funds appropriated by Congress for use on specific local projects.

Earmark Question Mark
Distributional policies allocate resources to a specific constituency, sometimes through congressional earmarks. One such earmark went to support the Drake Well Museum in Venango County, Pennsylvania. The museum contains artifacts of the oil discovery there in 1859, including the oil rig pictured here. Earmarks such as these are controversial as many believe that they're a poor use of taxpayer money.
(Superstock)

some of that money back to the district in the form of economic development projects?

Proponents of pluralism also argue that the makeup of Congress generally reflects that of the nation, that different members of Congress represent farm areas, oil and gas areas, low-income inner cities, industrial areas, and so on. They point out that America itself is pluralistic, with a rich diversity of economic, social, religious, and racial groups, and that even if one's own representatives and senators do not represent one's particular viewpoint, it is likely that someone else in Congress does.[46]

Whatever the shortcomings of pluralism, broad-scale institutional reform aimed at reducing legislators' concern for individual districts and states is difficult. Members of Congress resist any structural changes that might weaken their ability to gain reelection. Certainly, maintaining the prerogatives of the committee system and the dominant influence of committees over legislation and pork barrel spending has proven stubbornly resistant to significant reform.[47] Nevertheless, the growing partisanship in the Congress illustrated in Figure 8.3 represents a trend toward greater majoritarianism. As noted earlier, as both parties have become more ideologically homogeneous, there is greater unity around policy preferences. To the degree that voters correctly recognize the differences between the parties and are willing to cast their ballots on that basis, the more majoritarianism will act as a constraint on pluralism in the Congress. Ironically, once in office, legislators can weaken the incentive for their constituents to vote on the basis of ideology. The congressional system is structured to facilitate casework for voters with a problem and to fund a certain amount of pork barrel spending. Both of these characteristics of the modern Congress work to boost each legislator's reputation in his or her district or state.

In short, the modern Congress is characterized by strong elements of both majoritarianism and pluralism.

Summary

Congress writes the laws of the land and attempts to oversee their implementation. It helps to educate us about new issues as they appear on the political agenda. Most important, members of Congress represent us, working to see to it that interests from home and from around the country are heard throughout the policymaking process.

We count on Congress to do so much that criticism about how well it does some things is inevitable. However, certain strengths are clear. The committee system fosters expertise; representatives and senators who know the most about particular issues have the most influence over them. And the structure of our electoral system keeps legislators in close touch with their constituents.

Bargaining and compromise play important roles in congressional policymaking. Some find this disquieting. They want less deal making and more adhering to principle. This thinking is in line with the desire for a more majoritarian democracy. Others defend the current system, arguing that the United States is a large, complex nation and the policies that govern it should be developed through bargaining among various interests.

There is no clear-cut answer on whether a majoritarian or a pluralist legislative system provides better representation for voters. Our system is a mix of pluralism and majoritarianism. It serves minority interests that might otherwise be neglected or even harmed by an unthinking or uncaring majority. At the same time, congressional parties work to represent the broader interests of the American people.

CL **Resources:** Videos, Simulations, News, Timelines, Primary Sources

The Presidency

This icon will direct you to resources and activities on the website: www.cengage.com/polisci/janda/chall_dem_brief/7e

BARACK OBAMA RAN FOR president using the motto "change we can believe in" and won an historic victory to serve as the first African American president of the United States. While Obama won a landslide victory over John McCain in the electoral college, it was clear he would not enter office with a clean slate. Obama inherited a country at war in Iraq and Afghanistan and facing vexing economic problems. To understand the challenges facing President Obama, it is necessary to consider how they developed.

In November 2000, Bush became president in a closely divided and bitterly disputed election in which Democrat Al Gore won half a million more popular votes and Bush won a bare majority of the electoral college vote. Many Democrats believed that the 2000 election was stolen, first by the Republican Party in Florida and then by a partisan Supreme Court.[1]

The fight against terrorism and the ongoing war in Iraq were the defining issues of the Bush presidency. Within days of the September 11, 2001, terrorist attacks, Bush's popularity rose to 90 percent, the highest rating received by a president since Gallup started conducting popularity polls in the 1950s. Within a month, Bush sent troops to Afghanistan to topple the Taliban regime, which provided support to terrorist organizations like Al Qaeda. In March 2003 he ordered U.S. troops to Iraq to force Iraqi president Saddam Hussein from power, arguing that Iraq was building weapons of mass destruction. Bush worked with a Republican Congress to pass major legislation such as tax cuts, the "No Child Left Behind" education law, and funding for fighting AIDS around the world.[2]

Though Bush was reelected to a second term, his approval ratings fell steadily as the wars in Iraq and Afghanistan worsened and

Americans learned more about the poor quality of intelligence leading up to the war in Iraq.[3] The Taliban regime was removed from power in Afghanistan, but the war did not succeed at eliminating terrorist activity. Over five hundred American soldiers have been killed in and around Afghanistan, and over 2,200 have been wounded in action. U.S. troops never uncovered clear evidence that Iraq possessed weapons of mass destruction. A commission created to look into the September 11 attacks concluded that there was no "collaborative relationship" between Iraq and the Al Qaeda terrorist organization. Over four thousand Americans have been killed in Iraq; over 30,000 American soldiers have been wounded in action.[4]

With public approval declining, President Bush pushed to expand presidential power.[5] He authorized the National Security Agency to eavesdrop—without a warrant—on the international telecommunications of U.S. citizens. His administration declared that the president could decide how to detain and interrogate suspected terrorists. Without seeking congressional authorization, they established military commissions to try suspects captured in Afghanistan and Iraq and held at a naval base at Guantánamo Bay, Cuba, until the Supreme Court ruled this impermissible without congressional authorization.

Bush's bold assertions of executive power and discontent with his foreign policy left him ineffective in his second term, particularly after Democrats regained control of Congress in the 2006 midterm elections.[6] Bush issued several vetoes but did not steer any major legislation through Congress. As the economy declined, his approval ratings hovered around 30 percent and over three-quarters of Americans declared that the country was on the "wrong track."[7]

George W. Bush's experience as president was unique, but all presidents face challenges. American presidents are expected to offer solutions to national problems, whether fighting crime or reviving a failing economy. As the nation's major foreign diplomat and commander in chief of the armed forces, they are held responsible for the security and status of America in the world. Our presidents are the focal point for the nation's hopes and disappointments.

This chapter analyzes presidential leadership, looking at how presidents try to muster majoritarian support for their domestic goals and how presidents must function today as global leaders. What are the powers of the presidency? How is the president's advisory system organized? What are the ingredients of strong presidential leadership: character, public relations, or a friendly Congress? Finally, what are the issues and problems that presidents face in foreign affairs?

The Constitutional Basis of Presidential Power

When the presidency was created, the thirteen former colonies had just fought a war of independence; their reaction to British domination had focused on the autocratic rule of King George III. Thus, delegates to the Constitutional Convention were extremely wary of unchecked power and were determined not to create an all-powerful, dictatorial presidency. The delegates' fear of a powerful presidency was counterbalanced by their desire for strong leadership. The Articles of Confederation, which did not provide for a single head of state, had failed to bind the states together into a unified nation (see Chapter 2). The delegates knew they had to create some type of effective executive office. Their task was to provide national leadership without allowing any opportunity for tyranny.

Initial Conceptions of the Presidency

Debates over the nature of the office began. Should there be one president or a presidential council or committee? Should the president be chosen by Congress and remain subservient to that body?

The final structure of the presidency reflected the "checks and balances" philosophy that shaped the entire Constitution. The delegates believed they had imposed important limits on the presidency through the powers specifically delegated to Congress and the courts. Those counterbalancing powers would act as checks, or controls, on presidents who might try to expand the office beyond its proper bounds.

Mourning Ford

Gerald Ford, who served as president between 1974 and 1977, died in December 2006. All living former presidents and first ladies attended a funeral service at the National Cathedral in Washington, D.C. Ford became Richard Nixon's vice president when Spiro Agnew resigned over questions about possible income tax evasion. He then assumed the presidency when Nixon resigned over the Watergate scandal. He was the only president who was never elected vice president or president. His most controversial act was to pardon Nixon for any crimes that he may have committed. After the pardon, Ford's approval ratings plummeted and he lost the 1976 election to Jimmy Carter. *(© Mark Wilson/Getty Images)*

The Powers of the President

The requirements for the presidency are set forth in Article II of the Constitution. The president must be a U.S.-born citizen, at least thirty-five years old, who has lived in the United States for a minimum of fourteen years. Article II also sets forth the responsibilities of presidents. In view of the importance of the office, the constitutional description of the president's duties is surprisingly brief and vague. This vagueness has led to repeated conflict about the limits of presidential power.

The major presidential duties and powers listed in the Constitution can be summarized as follows:

■ *Serve as administrative head of the nation.* The Constitution gives little guidance on the president's administrative duties. It states merely that "the executive Power shall be vested in a President of the United States of America" and that "he shall take Care that the Laws be faithfully executed." These imprecise directives have been interpreted to mean that the president is to supervise and offer leadership to various departments, agencies, and programs created by Congress. In practice, a chief executive spends much more time making policy decisions for his cabinet departments and agencies than enforcing existing policies.

■ *Act as commander in chief of the military.* In essence, the Constitution names the president as the highest-ranking officer in the armed forces. But it gives Congress the power to declare war. The framers no doubt intended Congress to control the president's military power; nevertheless, presidents have initiated military action without the approval of Congress.[8]

 INTERACTIVE 9.1

U.S. Military Intervention Since the 1950s

- *Convene Congress.* The president can call Congress into special session on "extraordinary Occasions," although this has rarely been done. He must also periodically inform Congress of "the State of the Union."

- *Veto legislation.* The president can **veto** (disapprove) any bill or resolution enacted by Congress, with the exception of joint resolutions that propose constitutional amendments. Congress can override a presidential veto with a two-thirds vote in each house.

- *Appoint various officials.* The president has the authority to appoint federal court judges, ambassadors, cabinet members, other key policymakers, and many lesser officials. Many appointments are subject to Senate confirmation.

- *Make treaties.* With the "Advice and Consent" of at least two-thirds of those senators voting at the time, the president can make treaties with foreign powers. The president is also to "receive Ambassadors," a phrase that presidents have interpreted to mean the right to formally recognize other nations.

- *Grant pardons.* The president can grant pardons to individuals who have committed "Offenses against the United States, except in Cases of Impeachment."

The Expansion of Presidential Power

The framers' limited conception of the president's role has given way to a considerably more powerful interpretation. In this section, we discuss how presidential power has expanded as presidents have exercised their explicit constitutional responsibilities and boldly interpreted the ambiguities of the Constitution. First, we look at the ways in which formal powers, such as the veto power, have been increasingly used over time. Second, we turn to claims that presidents make about "inherent" powers implicit in the Constitution. Finally, we discuss congressional grants of power to the executive branch.

Formal Powers

The Constitution clearly involves the president in the policymaking process through his veto power, ability to report to Congress on the state of the union, and role as commander in chief. Over time, presidents have been increasingly aggressive in their use of these formal powers. Vetoes,

veto The president's disapproval of a bill that has been passed by both houses of Congress. Congress can override a veto with a two-thirds vote in each house.

for instance, have become much more frequent, particularly when presidents face a Congress dominated by the opposing political party. The first sixteen presidents, from Washington to Lincoln, issued a total of 59 vetoes. Dwight Eisenhower issued 181 vetoes over the course of his two terms in office; Ronald Reagan vetoed legislation 78 times.[9] George W. Bush vetoed a very small number of bills. Yet the ability to veto legislation gives the president power even when he does not issue many vetoes. Veto threats shape legislation because members of Congress anticipate vetoes and modify legislation to avoid them.[10]

Modern presidents have also taken a much more active role in setting the nation's policy agenda. The Constitution states that the president shall give Congress information on the state of the Union "from time to time." For the most part, nineteenth-century presidents sent written messages to Congress and did not publicly campaign for the passage of legislation.[11] Early twentieth-century presidents like Woodrow Wilson began to deliver their State of the Union speeches in person before Congress, personalizing and fighting for their own policy agenda. It is now expected that the president will enter office with clear policy goals and work with his party in Congress to pass legislation.

Modern presidents have used their power as commander in chief to enter into foreign conflicts without appealing to Congress for a formal declaration of war.[12] The entire Vietnam War was fought without a congressional declaration of war. When President Bush ordered retaliatory military strikes and the bombing of Taliban strongholds in Afghanistan after the September 11 terrorist attacks, Congress never formally declared war. In 2002 the House and Senate passed a joint resolution authorizing President Bush to use military force "as he determined necessary and appropriate" in order to enforce United Nations Security Council resolutions regarding Iraq, but they did not declare war.[13]

The Inherent Powers

Several presidents have expanded the power of the office by taking actions that exceeded commonly held notions of the president's proper authority. These men justified what they had done by saying that their actions fell within the **inherent powers** of the presidency. From this broad perspective, presidential power derives not only from those duties clearly outlined in Article II but also from inferences that may be drawn from the Constitution.

When a president claims a power that has not been considered part of the chief executive's authority, he forces Congress and the courts to either acquiesce to his claim or restrict it. For instance, President Bush unilaterally established a military commission to try alleged enemy combatants held at the U.S. naval base at Guantánamo Bay, Cuba. In 2006, the U.S. Supreme Court ruled that the military commissions as established were illegal. The Bush administration was forced to go to Congress for the authorization to establish new commissions with new trial procedures.[14]

inherent powers Authority claimed by the president that is not clearly specified in the Constitution. Typically these powers are inferred from the Constitution.

Claims of inherent powers often come at critical points in the nation's history. During the Civil War, for example, Abraham Lincoln issued several orders that exceeded the accepted limits of presidential authority and usurped powers constitutionally conferred on Congress. Lincoln said the urgent nature of the South's challenge to the Union forced him to act without waiting for congressional approval. His rationale was simple: "Was it possible to lose the nation and yet preserve the Constitution?"[15] In other words, Lincoln circumvented the Constitution in order to save the nation. Subsequently, Congress and the Supreme Court approved Lincoln's actions. That approval gave added legitimacy to the theory of inherent powers, a theory that has transformed the presidency over time.

Today presidents routinely issue **executive orders**, presidential directives that carry the force of law.[16] The Constitution does not explicitly grant the president the power to issue an executive order. Sometimes presidents use them to see that the laws are "faithfully executed." This was the case when Dwight Eisenhower ordered the Arkansas National Guard into service in Little Rock, Arkansas, to enforce court orders to desegregate the schools. But many times presidents issue executive orders by arguing that they may take actions in the best interest of the nation so long as the law does not directly prohibit these actions. Executive orders are issued for a wide variety of purposes, from administrative reorganization to civil rights.

Executive orders have become an important policymaking tool for presidents because they allow the president to act quickly and decisively, without seeking the agreement of the Congress. However, it is possible, though rare, for congressional bills and court challenges to overturn executive orders. If an executive order requires federal funds, then Congress can set the terms by which funds are appropriated.

Congressional Delegation of Power

Presidential power grows when presidents successfully challenge Congress, but in many instances, Congress willingly delegates power to the executive branch. As the American public pressures the national government to solve various problems, Congress, through a process called **delegation of powers**, gives the executive branch more responsibility to administer programs that address those problems. One example of delegation of congressional power occurred in the 1930s, during the Great Depression, when Congress gave Franklin Roosevelt's administration wide latitude to do what it thought was necessary to solve the nation's economic ills.

When Congress concludes that the government needs flexibility in its approach to a problem, the president is often given great freedom in how or when to implement policies. Richard Nixon was given discretionary authority to impose a freeze on wages and prices in an effort to combat escalating inflation. If Congress had been forced to debate the timing of this freeze, merchants and manufacturers would surely have raised their prices in anticipation of it. Instead, Nixon was able to act suddenly, and the

executive orders Presidential directives to the executive branch that create or modify public policies, without the direct approval of Congress.

delegation of powers The process by which Congress gives the executive branch the additional authority needed to address new problems.

freeze was imposed without warning. (We discuss congressional delegation of authority to the executive branch in more detail in Chapter 10.)

At other times, Congress believes that too much power has accumulated in the executive branch, and it enacts legislation to reassert congressional authority. During the 1970s, many representatives and senators agreed that presidents were exercising power that rightfully belonged to the legislative branch and that Congress's role in the American political system was declining. The most notable reaction was passage of the War Powers Resolution (1973), directed toward ending the president's ability to pursue armed conflict without explicit congressional approval.

The Executive Branch Establishment

Although we elect a single individual as president, it would be a mistake to ignore the extensive staff and other resources of the executive branch of government. The president has a White House staff that helps him formulate policy. The vice president is another resource; his duties within the administration vary according to his relationship with the president. The president's cabinet secretaries—the heads of the major departments of the national government—play several roles, including the critical function of administering the programs that fall within their jurisdictions.

The Executive Office of the President

The president depends heavily on his key aides. They advise him on crucial political choices, devise the general strategies the administration will follow in pursuing congressional and public support, and control access to the president to ensure that he has enough time for his most important tasks. Consequently, he needs to trust and respect these top staffers; many in a president's inner circle of assistants are long-time associates. The president's personal staff constitutes the White House Office.

Presidents typically have a chief of staff, who may be first among equals or, in some administrations, the unquestioned leader of the staff. There also is a national security adviser to provide daily briefings on foreign and military affairs and longer-range analyses of issues confronting the administration. Similarly, the Council of Economic Advisers advises the president on the best way to promote economic growth. Senior domestic policy advisers help determine the administration's basic approach to such areas as health, education, and social services.

Below these top aides are the large staffs that serve them and the president. For example, the national security adviser to President George W. Bush, Stephen Hadley, oversaw the National Security Council staff, which provides analysis and logistical support to the president on foreign affairs. These staffs are organized around certain specialties. Some staff members work on political matters, such as liaison with interest groups, relations with ethnic and religious minorities, and party affairs. One staff deals exclusively with the media, and a legislative liaison staff lobbies Congress for the administration. The large Office of Management and Budget (OMB) analyzes budget requests, is involved in the policymaking process, and also examines agency management practices. This extended White House executive establishment, including the White House Office, is known as the **Executive Office of the President (EOP)**. The Executive Office employs close to 1,700 individuals and has an annual budget outlay of approximately $2.7 billion.[17]

No one agrees about a "right way" for a president to organize his White House staff, but scholars have identified three major advisory styles.[18] Franklin Roosevelt exemplified the first system: a competitive management style. He organized his staff so that his advisers had overlapping authority and differing points of view. Roosevelt used this system to ensure that he would get the best possible information, hear all sides of an argument, and still be the final decision maker in any dispute. Dwight Eisenhower, a former general, best exemplifies a hierarchical staff model. His staff was arranged with clear lines of authority and a hierarchical structure that mirrored a military command. This places fewer demands on presidential time and energy, since the president does not participate in the details of policy discussion. Bill Clinton had more of a collegial staffing arrangement, a loose staff structure that gave many top staffers direct access to him, particularly early in his first administration. Clinton himself was immersed in the details of the policymaking process, brainstorming with his advisers. He was much less likely to delegate authority to others. Presidents tend to choose the advisory systems that best suit their personality. Most presidents use a combination of styles, learning from their predecessors.

Above all, a president must ensure that staff members feel comfortable telling him things he may not want to hear. Telling the president of the United States he is misguided on something is not an easy thing to do. The term *groupthink* has been used to refer to situations in which staffers reach consensus without properly considering all sides of an issue.[19] Several analysts have argued that the Johnson administration suffered from groupthink when making decisions about the Vietnam War.

The Vice President

The vice president's most important duty is to take over the presidency in the event of presidential death, disability, impeachment, or resignation. Traditionally, vice presidents were not used in any important advisory capacity. Instead, presidents tended to give them political chores: campaigning, fundraising, and "stroking" the party faithful. This is often the case because vice-presidential candidates are chosen for reasons that have more to do with the political campaign than with governing the nation. Presidential candidates often choose vice-presidential candidates who appeal to

Executive Office of the President (EOP) The president's executive aides and their staffs; the extended White House executive establishment.

Next in Line
Barack Obama tapped Delaware senator Joe Biden as his running mate in 2008. Biden had run unsuccessfully for the Democratic presidential nomination himself. As a thirty-five-year veteran of the Senate and Chair of the Senate Committee on Foreign Relations, Biden brought deep foreign policy expertise to the Democratic ticket. *(Brendan Smlalowski/ Getty Images)*

a different geographic region or party coalition. Sometimes they even join forces with a rival from their political primary campaign. New Englander John Kennedy chose Texan Lyndon Johnson. Conservative Ronald Reagan selected George H. W. Bush, his more moderate rival in the Republican primaries. Texas governor George W. Bush chose Washington insider Dick Cheney as his vice-presidential running mate, who brought experience as a former member of the House of Representatives, presidential chief of staff to Richard Nixon, and secretary of defense to Bush's father.[20]

The Cabinet

The president's **cabinet** is composed of the heads of the departments in the executive branch and a small number of other key officials, such as the head of the Office of Management and Budget and the U.S. Trade Representative. The cabinet has expanded greatly since George Washington formed his first cabinet: an attorney general and the secretaries of state, treasury, and war. Clearly, the growth of the cabinet to fifteen departments reflects the growth of government responsibility and intervention in areas such as energy, housing, and, most recently, homeland security.

In theory, the members of the cabinet constitute an advisory body that meets with the president to debate major policy decisions. In practice, however, cabinet meetings have been described as "vapid non-events in which there has been a deliberate non-exchange of information as part of a process of mutual non-consultation."[21] Why is this so?

cabinet A group of presidential advisers; the heads of the executive department and other key officials.

First, the cabinet has become rather large. Counting department heads, other officials of cabinet rank, and presidential aides, it is a body of at least twenty people—a size that many presidents find unwieldy for the give-and-take of political decision making. Second, most cabinet members have limited areas of expertise and cannot contribute much to deliberations in policy areas they know little about. The secretary of defense, for example, would probably be a poor choice to help decide important issues of agricultural policy. Third, although cabinet members have impressive backgrounds, they may not be personally close to the president or easy for him to work with. The president often chooses cabinet members because of their reputations, or he may be guided by a need to give his cabinet some racial, ethnic, geographic, sexual, or religious balance.

Finally, modern presidents do not rely on the cabinet to make policy because they have such large White House staffs, which offer most of the advisory support they need. And in contrast to cabinet secretaries, who may be pulled in different directions by the wishes of the president and those of their clientele groups, staffers in the White House Office are likely to see themselves as being responsible to the president alone. Thus, despite periodic calls for the cabinet to be a collective decision-making body, cabinet meetings seem doomed to be little more than academic exercises. In practice, presidents prefer the flexibility of ad hoc groups, specialized White House staffs, and the advisers and cabinet secretaries with whom they feel most comfortable.

More broadly, presidents use their personal staffs and the large Executive Office of the President to centralize control over the entire executive branch. The vast size of the executive branch and the number and complexity of decisions that must be made each day pose a challenge for the White House. Each president must be careful to appoint to top administrative positions people who are passionate about the president's goals and skillful enough to lead others in the executive branch to fight for the president's program instead of for their own agendas.[22]

Presidential Leadership

A president's influence in office comes not only from his assigned responsibilities but also from his political skills and from how effectively he uses the resources of his office. His leadership also depends on perceptions of his character and the political environment in which he finds himself. Table 9.1 provides a ranking of presidents based on a C-SPAN survey of fifty-eight prominent historians and professional observers of the presidency. The final score of each president is based on evaluations of characteristics such as crisis leadership, public persuasion, and administrative skill. In this section, we look at the factors that affect presidential performance. Why do some presidents rank higher than others?

TABLE 9.1   Presidential Greatness

This table provides one possible ranking of American presidents from George Washington to Bill Clinton. Survey participants were historians or observers of the presidency who rated presidents on ten scales: public persuasion, crisis leadership, economic management, moral authority, international relations, administrative skills, relations with Congress, vision/setting an agenda, pursuit of equal justice for all, and performance within the context of their time. Each subscale ranged from 0 to 100, so that the final score ranges from the lowest possible score of 0 to a perfect score of 1000

Rank	President	Score	Rank	President	Score
1	Abraham Lincoln	900	22	Jimmy Carter	518
2	Franklin Delano Roosevelt	876	23	Gerald Ford	495
3	George Washington	842	24	William Howard Taft	491
4	Theodore Roosevelt	810	25	Richard Nixon	477
5	Harry S. Truman	753	26	Rutherford B. Hayes	477
6	Woodrow Wilson	723	27	Calvin Coolidge	451
7	Thomas Jefferson	711	28	Zachary Taylor	447
8	John F. Kennedy	704	29	James Garfield	444
9	Dwight D. Eisenhower	699	30	Martin Van Buren	429
10	Lyndon Baines Johnson	655	31	Benjamin Harrison	426
11	Ronald Reagan	634	32	Chester Arthur	423
12	James K. Polk	632	33	Ulysses S. Grant	403
13	Andrew Jackson	632	34	Herbert Hoover	400
14	James Monroe	602	35	Millard Fillmore	395
15	William McKinley	601	36	John Tyler	369
16	John Adams	598	37	William Henry Harrison	329
17	Grover Cleveland	576	38	Warren G. Harding	326
18	James Madison	567	39	Franklin Pierce	286
19	John Quincy Adams	564	40	Andrew Johnson	280
20	George H. W. Bush	548	41	James Buchanan	259
21	Bill Clinton	539			

Source: C-SPAN survey of Presidential Leadership 2000, www.americanpresidents .org/survey/historians/overall.asp. Copyright 2000 C-SPAN.

Presidential Character

How does the public assess which presidential candidate has the best judgment and a character suitable to the office? Americans must make a broad evaluation of the candidates' personalities and leadership styles. Although it is difficult to judge, character matters. One of Lyndon Johnson's biographers argues that Johnson had trouble extricating the United States from Vietnam because of insecurities about his masculinity. Johnson wanted to make sure he "was not forced to see himself as a coward, running away from Vietnam."[23] It is hard to know for sure whether this psychological interpretation is valid. Clearer, surely, is the tie between President Nixon's character and Watergate. Nixon had such an exaggerated fear of what his "enemies" might try to do to him that he created a climate in the White House that nurtured the Watergate break-in and subsequent cover-up.

Presidential character was at the forefront of national politics when it was revealed that President Clinton engaged in a sexual relationship with Monica Lewinsky, a White House intern half his age.[24] Many argued that presidential authority is irreparably damaged when the president is perceived as personally untrustworthy or immoral. Yet despite the disgust and anger that Clinton's actions provoked among many Americans, most remained unconvinced that his behavior constituted an impeachable offense. The buoyant economy and the public's general satisfaction with Clinton's leadership strongly influenced the country's views on the matter. A majority of the House of Representatives voted to impeach him, on the grounds that he had committed perjury when testifying before a federal grand jury and that he had obstructed justice by concealing evidence and encouraging others to lie about his relationship with Lewinsky. But the Senate did not have the two-thirds majority necessary to convict Clinton, so he remained in office.

Scholars have identified personality traits such as strong self-esteem and emotional intelligence that are best suited to leadership positions like the American presidency.[25] In the media age, it often proves difficult to evaluate a candidate's personality when everyone tries to present himself or herself in a positive light. Even so, voters repeatedly claim that they care about traits such as leadership, integrity, and competence when casting their ballots.[26]

The President's Power to Persuade

In addition to desirable character traits, individual presidents must have the interpersonal and practical political skills to get things done. A classic analysis of the use of presidential resources is offered by Richard Neustadt in his book *Presidential Power*, which discusses how presidents gain, lose, or maintain their influence. Neustadt's initial premise is simple: "Presidential power is the power to persuade."[27] Presidents, for all their resources—a skilled staff, extensive media coverage of presidential actions, the great respect the country holds for the office—must depend on others' cooperation to get things done. Harry Truman echoed Neustadt's premise when he said, "I sit here all day trying to persuade people to do the things they ought to have sense enough to do without my persuading them. . . . That's all the powers of the President amount to."[28]

Ability in bargaining, dealing with adversaries, and choosing priorities, according to Neustadt, separates above-average presidents from mediocre ones. A president must make wise choices about which policies to push and which to put aside until he can find more support. He must decide when to accept compromises and when to stand on principles. He must know when to go public and when to work behind the scenes.

A president's political skills can be important in affecting outcomes in Congress. The chief executive cannot intervene in every legislative struggle. He must choose his battles carefully, then try to use the force of his personality and the prestige of his office to forge an agreement among differing factions. In terms of getting members to vote a certain way, presidential influence is best described as taking place "at the margins." Presidents do not have the power to consistently move large numbers of votes one way or the other. They can, however, affect some votes—possibly enough to affect the fate of a closely fought piece of legislation.[29] Neustadt stresses that a president's influence is related to his professional reputation and public prestige. When a president pushes hard for a bill that Congress eventually defeats or emasculates, the president's reputation is hurt. The public perceives him as weak or as showing poor judgment, and Congress becomes even less likely to cooperate with him in the future.

The President and the Public

Neustadt's analysis suggests that a popular president is more persuasive than an unpopular one. A popular president has more power to persuade because he can use his public support as a resource in the bargaining process.[30] Members of Congress who know that the president is highly popular back home have more incentive to cooperate with the administration.

A familiar aspect of the modern presidency is the effort presidents devote to mobilizing public support for their programs. A president uses televised addresses (and the press coverage surrounding them), remarks to reporters, and public appearances to speak directly to the American people and convince them of the wisdom of his policies. Scholars have coined the phrase "going public" to describe situations where the president "forces compliance from fellow Washingtonians by going over their heads to appeal to their constituents."[31] Rather than bargain exclusively with a small number of party and committee leaders in Congress, the president rallies broad coalitions of support as though undertaking a political campaign.

Since public opinion is a resource for modern presidents, they pay close attention to their standing in the polls. Presidential popularity is typically at its highest during a president's first year in office. This "honeymoon period" affords the president a particularly good opportunity to use public support to get some of his programs through Congress.[32]

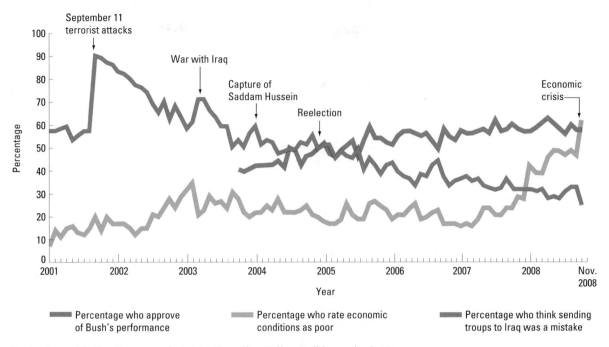

FIGURE 9.1   Peace, Prosperity, and Presidential Approval

Legend:
- Percentage who approve of Bush's performance
- Percentage who rate economic conditions as poor
- Percentage who think sending troups to Iraq was a mistake

Beginning with the Truman administration, the Gallup Poll has asked, "Do you approve or disapprove of the way [the current president] is handling his job as president?" This graph presents the percentages of Americans approving of President George W. Bush throughout his two terms in office. The graph also shows the percentage of Americans who rated economic conditions as poor. Beginning in 2003, a third line shows the percentages of Americans who agreed that it was a mistake to send troops to Iraq.

While Bush's ratings clearly rallied in response to foreign policy crises such as the September 11, 2001, terrorist attacks and the war with Iraq in March 2003, his approval declined in the long run as the economy worsened and casualties mounted.

Source: Data from www.gallup.com.

Several factors generally explain the rise and fall in presidential popularity. First, public approval of the job done by a president is affected by economic conditions, such as inflation and unemployment. Second, a president is affected by unanticipated events of all types that occur during his administration.[33] A third factor that affects approval ratings, however, is that presidents typically lose popularity when involved in a war with heavy casualties.[34]

Figure 9.1 graphs George W. Bush's monthly job approval ratings as well as the percentage of Americans who believed that the Iraq war was a mistake and the percentage of Americans who rated economic conditions as poor. The effect of events is clear. In early September 2001, only 51 percent of respondents in a Gallup poll approved of the way George W. Bush was handling his job as president. After September 11, Bush's approval rate soared to 90 percent, the highest rating in Gallup's history.[35] There was a boost or "rally around the flag effect" from the March 2003 start of the war in Iraq. It is also clear that Bush's approval ratings were highly correlated with public views of the health of the economy and the war in Iraq. As the public soured on the economy and the war, they lost faith in the president.

The strategy of leading by courting public opinion, however, poses considerable risks. It is not easy to move public opinion, and presidents who plan to use it as leverage in dealing with Congress are left highly vulnerable if public support for their position does not materialize. When Bill Clinton came into office, he was strongly predisposed toward governing by leading public opinion. His strategy worked poorly, though, because he was frequently unsuccessful in rallying the public to his side on issues crucial to his administration. Communicating with the public is crucial to a modern president's success, but so too is an ability to form bipartisan coalitions in Congress and broad interest group coalitions.

Presidents' obsessive concern with public opinion can be defended as a means of furthering majoritarian democracy: the president tries to gauge what the people want so that he can offer policies that reflect popular preferences. Responsiveness to the public's views is a bedrock principle of democracy, and presidents should respond to public opinion as well as try to lead it.[36] Some believe that presidents are too concerned about their popularity and are unwilling to champion unpopular causes or take principled stands that may affect their poll ratings. Commenting on the presidential polls that first became widely used during his term, Harry Truman said, "I wonder how far Moses would have gone if he'd taken a poll in Egypt?"[37]

The Political Context

Although character and political skill are important, the president's popularity and legislative success also depend on the wider political environment.

Partisans in Congress.   Presidents vary considerably in their ability to convince Congress to enact the legislation they send to Capitol Hill. Generally presidents have their greatest success in Congress during the period immediately following their inauguration, which we noted is also the peak of their popularity. One of the best predictors of presidential success in Congress is the number of fellow partisans in Congress, particularly whether the president's party has a majority in each chamber.[38]

Presidential success in Congress is measured as how often the president wins his way on congressional roll call votes on which he takes a clear position. During the first two years of his term, Bill Clinton won 86 percent of the time; after the Democrats lost control of Congress in the 1994 midterm elections, his success rate plummeted to 36 percent. George W. Bush suffered a similar fate. His success rate hovered around 75 percent during his first six years in office with a Republican Congress. After the Democrats won control of Congress in 2006, his success rate fell to 38 percent.[39]

The American political system poses a challenge for presidents and their policy agendas because the president is elected independent of Congress. Often this leads to **divided government,** with one party controlling the White House and the other party controlling at least one house of Congress. This outcome may seem politically schizophrenic, with the electorate saying one thing by electing a president and another by electing a majority in Congress that opposes his policies. But it does not appear to bother the American people. Polls often show that the public feels it is desirable for control of the government to be divided between Republicans and Democrats.[40]

Voters appear to use quite different criteria when choosing a president than they do when choosing congressional representatives. As one scholar has noted, "Presidential candidates are evaluated according to their views on national issues and their competence in dealing with national problems. Congressional candidates are evaluated on their personal character and experience and on their devotion to district services and local issues."[41] This congressional independence is another reason that contemporary presidents work so hard to gain public support for their policies.[42]

Scholars have different opinions on the impact of divided government. One study showed that just as much significant legislation gets passed and signed into law when there is divided government as when one party controls both the White House and Congress.[43] Using different approaches, other scholars have shown that divided governments are in fact less productive than unified ones.[44] Despite these differences in the scholarly literature, political scientists generally do not believe that divided government produces **gridlock,** a situation in which government is incapable of acting on important policy issues.[45] A strong tradition of bipartisan policymaking in Congress facilitates cooperation when the government is divided. Although rising partisanship in Congress may make divided government more of a problem (recall Figure 8.4), favorable public opinion can also help a president build consensus in a highly independent legislative branch.[46]

Elections.   In his farewell address, Jimmy Carter lashed out at the interest groups that had plagued his presidency. Interest groups, he said, "distort our purposes because the national interest is not always the sum of all our single or special interests." Carter noted the president's singular responsibility: "The president is the only elected official charged with representing all the people."[47] Like all other presidents, Carter quickly recognized the dilemma of majoritarianism versus pluralism after he took office. The president must try to please countless separate constituencies while trying to do what is best for the whole country.

It is easy to stand on the sidelines and say that presidents should always try to follow a majoritarian path, pursuing policies that reflect the preferences of most citizens. However, simply by running for office, candidates align themselves with particular segments of the population. As a

divided government The situation in which one party controls the White House and the other controls at least one house of Congress.

gridlock A situation in which government is incapable of acting on important issues, usually because of divided government.

result of their electoral strategy, their identification with activists in their party, and their own political views, candidates come into office with an interest in pleasing some constituencies more than others.

Each candidate tries to win votes from different groups of voters through his stand on various issues. Because issue stances can cut both ways—attracting some voters but driving others away—candidates may try to finesse an issue by being deliberately vague. However, a candidate who is noncommittal on too many issues appears wishy-washy. And future presidents do not build their political careers without working strongly for and becoming associated with important issues and constituencies. Moreover, after the election is over, the winning candidate wants to claim that he has been given a **mandate,** or endorsement, by the voters to carry out the policies he campaigned on. New presidents try to make a majoritarian interpretation of the election, claiming that their victory is an expression of the direct will of the people. Candidates who win by large margins are more likely to claim mandates and ask for major policy changes.

Barack Obama won an overwhelming majority in the electoral college in 2008, largely because of voters who were looking for new leadership on the economy. Obama interpreted this as a mandate to enact his economic, domestic, and foreign policy goals. While voters were receptive to the Obama campaign's mantra of change, he needs to convince the Congress that the public also supports his specific policy proposals.

Political Party Systems.   American political history is marked by eras in which one of the major political parties tends to dominate national-level politics, consistently capturing the presidency and majorities in the Senate and House of Representatives. Political scientist Stephen Skowronek argues that leadership depends on the president's place in the cycle of rising and falling political party regimes or governing coalitions.[48] Presidential leadership is determined in part by whether the president is a member of the dominant political party and whether the public policies and political philosophy associated with his party have widespread support. A president will have a greater opportunity to change public policy when he is in the majority and the opposing political party is perceived as unable to solve major national problems.

Presidents who come to power right after critical elections have the most favorable environment for exerting strong presidential leadership. Franklin Roosevelt, for instance, came to office when the Republican Party was unable to offer solutions to the economic crisis of the Great Depression. He enjoyed a landslide victory and large Democratic majorities in Congress, and he proposed fundamental changes in government and public policy. The weakest presidents are those, like Herbert Hoover, who are constrained by their affiliation with a political party that is perceived to stand for worn-out ideas.

Some presidents inherit a political climate ripe for change; others do not. As Skowronek notes, "The political conditions for presidential action

mandate An endorsement by voters. Presidents sometimes argue they have been given a mandate to carry out policy proposals.

can shift radically from one administration to the next, and with each change the challenge of exercising political leadership will be correspondingly altered."[49] Our evaluations of presidential greatness and success need to take the political context into account; personality and skill may be less important than historical fate.

The President as National Leader

With an election behind him and the resources of his office at hand, a president is ready to lead the nation. Each president enters office with a general vision of how government should approach policy issues. During his term, he spends much of his time trying to get Congress to enact legislation that reflects his general philosophy and specific policy preferences.

From Political Values ...

Presidents differ greatly in their views of the role of government. Lyndon Johnson had a strong liberal ideology concerning domestic affairs. He believed that government has a responsibility to help disadvantaged Americans. In describing his vision of justice in his inaugural address, Johnson used the words *justice* and *injustice* as code words for *equality* and *inequality*. They were used six times in his speech; *freedom* was used only twice. Johnson used his popularity, his skills, and the resources of his office to press for a "just" America—a "Great Society."[50]

To achieve his Great Society, Johnson sent Congress an unprecedented package of liberal legislation. He launched such projects as the Job Corps (which created centers and camps offering vocational training and work experience to youths aged sixteen to twenty-one), Medicare (which provided medical care for the elderly), and the National Teacher Corps (which paid teachers to work in impoverished neighborhoods). Supported by huge Democratic majorities in Congress during 1965 and 1966, he had tremendous success in getting his proposals through. Liberalism was in full swing.

In 1985, exactly twenty years after Johnson's inaugural speech, Ronald Reagan took his oath of office for the second time. Addressing the nation, Reagan reasserted his conservative philosophy. He emphasized *freedom,* using the term fourteen times, and failed to mention justice or equality even once. He turned Johnson's philosophy on its head, declaring that "government is not the solution to our problem. Government is the problem." During his presidency, Reagan worked to undo many welfare and social service programs, and he cut funding for such programs as the Job Corps and food stamps. By the end of his term, there had been a fundamental shift in federal spending, with sharp increases in defense spending and "decreases in federal social programs [which] served to defend Democratic interests and constituencies."[51]

DO IT!

Find a local volunteering opportunity through the White House's USA Freedom Corps website at www.usafreedomcorps.gov.

. . . to Policy Agenda

The roots of particular policy proposals can be traced to the more general political ideology of the president. Presidential candidates outline that philosophy of government during their campaigns for the White House. But when the hot rhetoric of the presidential campaign meets the cold reality of what is possible in Washington, the newly elected president must make some hard choices about what to push for during the coming term. These choices are reflected in the bills the president submits to Congress, as well as in the degree to which he works for their passage. The president's bills, introduced by his allies in the House and Senate, always receive a good deal of initial attention. In the words of one Washington lobbyist, "When a president sends up a bill, it takes first place in the queue. All other bills take second place."[52]

The president's role in legislative leadership began primarily in the twentieth century. Not until the Budget and Accounting Act of 1921 did executive branch departments and agencies have to clear their proposed budget bills with the White House. Before this, the president did not even coordinate proposals for how much the executive branch would spend on all the programs it administered. Later, Franklin D. Roosevelt required that the White House clear all major legislative proposals by an agency or department. No longer could a department submit a bill without White House support.[53]

Roosevelt's influence on the relationship between the president and Congress went far beyond this new administrative arrangement. With the nation in the midst of the Great Depression, Roosevelt began his first term in 1933 with an ambitious array of legislative proposals. During the first hundred days Congress was in session, it enacted fifteen significant laws, including the Agricultural Adjustment Act, the act creating the Civilian Conservation Corps, and the National Industrial Recovery Act. Never before had a president demanded—and received—so much from Congress. Roosevelt's legacy was that the president would henceforth provide aggressive leadership for Congress through his own legislative program.

Chief Lobbyist

When Franklin D. Roosevelt and Harry Truman first became heavily involved in preparing legislative packages, political scientists typically described the process as one in which "the president proposes and Congress disposes." In other words, once the president sends his legislation to Capitol Hill, Congress decides on its own what to do with it. Over time, though, presidents have become increasingly active in all stages of the legislative process. The president is expected not only to propose legislation but also to make sure that it passes.

The president's efforts to influence Congress are reinforced by the work of his legislative liaison staff. All departments and major agencies have legislative specialists who work with the White House liaison staff to coordinate the administration's lobbying on major issues. The **legislative liaison staff** is the communications link between the White House and Congress. As a bill slowly makes its way through Congress, liaison staffers advise the president on the problems that emerge. They specify what parts of a bill are in trouble and may have to be modified or dropped. They tell their boss what amendments are likely to be offered, which members of Congress need to be lobbied, and what the bill's chances for passage are with or without certain provisions. Decisions on how the administration will respond to such developments must then be reached. For example, when the Reagan White House realized that it was still a few votes short of victory on a budget bill in the House, it reversed its opposition to a sugar price support bill. This attracted the votes of representatives from Louisiana and Florida, two sugar-growing states, for the budget bill. The White House would not call what happened a deal, but it noted that "adjustments and considerations" had been made.[54]

A certain amount of the president's job consists of stereotypical arm twisting—pushing reluctant legislators to vote a certain way. Yet most day-in, day-out interactions between the White House and Congress tend to be more subtle, with the liaison staff trying to build consensus by working cooperatively with legislators. The White House also works directly with interest groups in its efforts to build support for legislation.[55] Interest groups can quickly reach the constituents who are most concerned about a bill, using their communications network to quickly mobilize members to write, call, or email their members of Congress.

Although much of the liaison staff's work with Congress is done in a cooperative spirit, agreement cannot always be reached. When Congress passes a bill that the president opposes, he may veto it and send it back to Congress. As we noted earlier, Congress can override a veto with a two-thirds majority of those voting in each house. Presidents use their veto power sparingly, but the threat that a president will veto an unacceptable bill increases his bargaining leverage with members of Congress. We have also seen that a president's leverage with Congress is enhanced when he is riding high in the public opinion polls and hindered when the public is critical of his performance.[56]

Party Leader

Part of the president's job is to lead his party. This is very much an informal duty, with no prescribed tasks. In this respect, American presidents are considerably different from European prime ministers, who are the formal leader of their party in the national legislature, as well as the head of their government. In the American system, a president and members of his party in Congress can clearly take very different positions on the issues before them. Because political parties in Europe tend to have strong national organizations, prime ministers have more reason to lead the party organization. In the United States, national party committees play a relatively minor role

legislative liaison staff Those people who compose the communications link between the White House and Congress, advising the president or cabinet secretaries on the status of pending legislation.

in national politics, although they are active in raising money for their congressional candidates.

The president himself has become the "fundraiser in chief" for his party. Since presidents have a vital interest in more members of their party being elected to the House and Senate, they have a strong incentive to spend time raising money for congressional candidates. All incumbent presidents travel frequently to fundraising dinners in different states where they are the main attraction. In addition to helping elect more members of his party, the president gains the gratitude of legislators. It is a lot harder to say no to a president's request for help on a bill when he spoke at your fundraiser during the previous election.

The President as World Leader

The president's leadership responsibilities extend beyond Congress and the nation into the international arena. Each administration tries to advance what it sees as the country's best interests in its relations with allies, adversaries, and the developing countries of the world. In this role, the president must be ready to act as diplomat and crisis manager.

Foreign Relations

From the end of World War II until the late 1980s, presidents were preoccupied with containing communist expansion around the globe. After the collapse of communism in the Soviet Union and Eastern Europe, American presidents entered a new era in international relations, but they are still concerned with four fundamental objectives.

First is national security: the direct protection of the United States and its citizens from external threats. National security has been highlighted since the September 11 terrorist attacks. Indeed, George W. Bush called the global war against terrorism his number one priority, sending military troops to both Afghanistan and Iraq.[57]

Second, and related, is fostering a peaceful international environment. Presidents work with international organizations like the United Nations and the North Atlantic Treaty Organization (NATO) to seek an end to regional conflicts throughout the world.

A third objective is the protection of U.S. economic interests. The new presidential job description places much more emphasis on managing economic relations with the rest of the world. Trade relations are an especially difficult problem, because presidents must balance the conflicting interests of foreign countries (many of them U.S. allies), the interests of particular American industries, the overall needs of the American economy, and the demands of the legislative branch.

Finally, American presidents make foreign policy on the basis of humanitarian concerns and the promotion of democracy throughout the world. President George W. Bush pledged support for UN peacekeeping

From Peanuts to the Peace Prize

Former president and peanut farmer Jimmy Carter won the Nobel Peace Prize in 2002 for his continuing efforts to "find peaceful solutions to international conflicts, to advance democracy and human rights, and to promote economic and social development." Since leaving office, he has participated in activities such as election watches and the fight against tropical diseases in developing countries. Carter maintained an average approval rating of only 45 percent during his term. A little more than twenty years later, 60 percent of the public claimed to retrospectively approve of his job while in office. The long-term reputations of presidents do not settle until well after their time in office. *(Bjoern Sigardsoen/AP/Wide World Photos)*

troops to oversee a peaceful transition of power in Liberia, a nation torn by years of civil war. Each president must decide the extent to which the United States should use its power to promote American ideals abroad.

A Case Study: War in Iraq

The United States' relationship with Iraq illustrates the choices presidents must make when balancing these multiple foreign policy objectives.[58] Both George H. W. Bush and George W. Bush sent troops to Iraq, yet their objectives and the outcomes that followed differed dramatically. When George H. W. Bush was elected in 1988, Iraqi president Saddam Hussein had a record of human rights violations and was thought to possess chemical and biological weapons. In August 1990, the Iraqi military invaded and occupied Kuwait. The United Nations Security Council, NATO, and the Arab League immediately condemned the invasion. The UN Security Council imposed an economic embargo.

For President George H. W. Bush, Iraq's invasion of Kuwait was a clear violation of international law. The United States also had a clear interest in fostering stability in the Middle East, a region that is a major oil producer. President Bush rallied the international community to punish Iraq for its behavior. He used the United Nations as a forum for taking action against Iraq. He worked the phones to get Western and Arab leaders to join the United States in a coordinated military buildup in the area around Kuwait.

The UN Security Council passed a resolution to allow its members to "use all necessary means" to force Iraq from Kuwait. Bush also went to the U.S. Congress for a resolution authorizing the use of force. When Iraq did not leave Kuwait by the UN-mandated deadline, the United States launched massive air strikes, followed by a ground war one month later. Iraq was driven out of Kuwait and a cease-fire was reached within a hundred hours of the beginning of the introduction of ground troops. The Persian Gulf War was viewed as one of the major accomplishments of Bush's presidency.

Ten years later, Iraq resurfaced as a major foreign policy issue. Four months after the 2001 terrorist attacks, President George W. Bush charged that states such as Iraq, Iran, and North Korea "and their terrorist allies constitute an axis of evil, arming to threaten the peace of the world. By seeking weapons of mass destruction, these regimes pose a grave and growing danger. They could provide these arms to terrorists, giving them the means to match their hatred." At the time of Bush's speech, Iraq had not been cooperating with UN weapons inspectors for almost four years. Bush repeatedly demanded proof that Iraq had destroyed all weapons of mass destruction. The U.S. Congress passed a resolution authorizing Bush to use military force if necessary to enforce compliance with UN resolutions concerning weapons inspections. The UN Security Council threatened "serious consequences" if Iraq did not cooperate. Iraq finally allowed weapons inspections to resume.

Despite the return of weapons inspectors, the Bush administration argued that Hussein was not fully cooperating. President Bush sought a UN resolution authorizing the use of force against Iraq. Several countries and key members of the UN Security Council—including France, Germany, Russia, and China—wanted to give weapons inspections more time and strongly opposed the use of force without UN approval. NATO was similarly divided, with the United States, Britain, and Spain pitted against Germany and France. Bush's threats of war with Iraq were greeted with mass popular protests at home and abroad.

Dissent in the international community and popular protest at home did not deter the Bush administration. When the UN Security Council would not authorize the use of force, the United States, Great Britain, and a small number of allies pursued military action on their own. In March 2003, U.S. and British forces invaded Iraq and forced Saddam Hussein from power. President Bush justified his actions against Iraq as necessary for the national security of the United States and the human rights of Iraqi citizens. As we noted at the beginning of the chapter, this second war in Iraq did not go smoothly. As the war dragged on, international public opinion turned against the United States (see "Politics of Global Change: International Support for the War on Terror").[59]

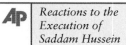

INTERACTIVE 9.2

Reactions to the Execution of Saddam Hussein

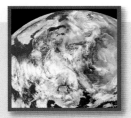

Politics of Global Change

International Support for the War on Terror

All presidents inherit the legacy of their predecessor's actions in the world. President Barack Obama takes office at a time when other countries are skeptical of U.S.-led efforts to fight terrorism. In 2002, a little more than six months after the September 11, 2001, terrorist attacks and the start of the war in Afghanistan, the Pew Global Attitudes Project asked respondents in fifteen countries whether they favored or opposed U.S.-led efforts to fight terrorism. The same question was asked again in spring 2007, four years after the start of the war in Iraq. The figure here lists the results of both surveys. Public opinion in Middle Eastern countries has hardly changed; most respondents in these countries did not respond favorably before the start of the war in Iraq. Support among respondents in European countries has dramatically declined over time. Only Israelis show consistently high support for U.S. efforts.

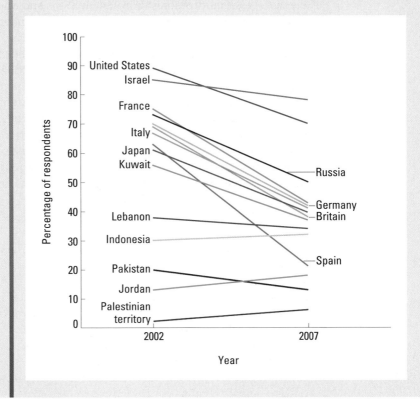

Crisis Management

Periodically the president faces a grave situation in which conflict is imminent or a small conflict threatens to explode into a larger war. Handling such episodes is a critical part of the president's job. Thus, citizens may vote for candidates who project careful judgment and intelligence.

A president must be able to exercise good judgment and remain cool in crisis situations. John Kennedy's behavior during the Cuban missile crisis of 1962 has become a model of effective crisis management. When the United States learned that the Soviet Union had placed missiles containing nuclear warheads in Cuba, Kennedy sought the advice of a group of senior aides, Pentagon officials, cabinet secretaries, and other trusted advisers. An armed invasion of Cuba and air strikes against the missiles were two options considered. In the end, Kennedy decided on a more flexible response: a naval blockade of Cuba. Faced with this challenge and a secret, back-channel overture from Kennedy, the Soviet Union agreed to remove its missiles. For a short time, though, the world held its breath over the very real possibility of a nuclear war.

What guidelines determine what a president should do in times of crisis? Drawing on a range of advisers and opinions is one.[60] Not acting in unnecessary haste is another. A third is having a well-designed, formal review process that promotes thorough analysis and open debate.[61] A fourth guideline is rigorously examining the reasoning underlying each option to ensure that its assumptions are valid. Still, these are rather general rules and provide no assurance that mistakes will not be made. Each crisis is a unique event. In the crisis after September 11, 2001, President Bush resisted calls for immediate retaliation. Instead, he planned a concerted attack against the Al Qaeda terrorist network in Afghanistan. The first air strikes, conducted jointly with Britain, did not occur until October 7. Two months later, the defeated Taliban government surrendered its last stronghold. Though coalition allies praised Bush's patience, they levied criticism when he named North Korea, Iran, and Iraq terrorist regimes that constitute an "axis of evil." They feared where Bush was heading.

Summary

When the delegates to the Constitutional Convention met to design the government of this new nation, they had trouble shaping the office of the president. They struggled to find a balance between an office that was powerful enough to provide unified leadership but not so strong that presidents could use their powers to become tyrants or dictators. The initial conceptions of the presidency have slowly been transformed as presidents have adapted the office to meet the nation's changing needs. The trend has been to expand presidential power. Some of this expansion has come from presidential actions taken under claims of inherent powers. Congress has also delegated a great deal of power to the executive branch, further expanding the role of the president.

The executive branch establishment has grown rapidly, and the White House has become a sizable bureaucracy. New responsibilities of the presidency are particularly noticeable in the area of legislative leadership. Now a president is expected to be a policy initiator for Congress, as well as a lobbyist who guides his bills through the legislative process.

The presidential "job description" for foreign policy has changed considerably. After World War II, presidents were preoccupied with containing the spread of communism. But since the collapse of communism in the Soviet Union and Eastern Europe, presidents pay more attention to international economic relations and security issues like terrorism.

Finally, presidential leadership is shaped by the president's ability to bargain, persuade, and make wise choices. His influence is related to his popularity with the public because he can use his support to gain leverage with members of Congress. The president's legislative success also depends on his political party's numerical strength in Congress. Presidents who are part of a strong majority party will have more resources to make bold policy changes.

CL **Resources:** Videos, Simulations, News, Timelines, Primary Sources

CHAPTER 10

The Bureaucracy

This icon will direct you to resources and activities on the website: www.cengage.com/polisci/janda/ chall_dem_brief/7e

PRESIDENT GEORGE W. BUSH
offered a powerful rationale for invading Iraq, asserting that its unpredictable dictator, Saddam Hussein, possessed chemical and biological weapons that could be used to inflict catastrophic harm. In the wake of the September 11, 2001, attacks against the United States, such threats of terrorism could not be taken lightly. How could we tell whether Saddam had weapons of mass destruction? That was the task of the intelligence community, a set of bureaucracies that serve the commander in chief.

To make its case that invading Iraq was imperative, the Bush administration maintained that there was a tie between Al Qaeda, the terrorist organization behind the four plane hijackings on September 11, and Iraq. One of the most alarming bits of intelligence leaked to the press was that one of the September 11 hijackers, Mohammed Atta, had met secretly in the Czech Republic with Iraqi officials.

As we later learned, no such meeting ever took place. The report of a meeting emanated from the Department of Defense's Office of Special Plans. Run by Undersecretary of Defense Douglas Feith, this small bureaucracy reviewed raw data collected by the Central Intelligence Agency (CIA), the government's central foreign intelligence–gathering bureaucracy. The CIA had been unable to find any reliable evidence of weapons of mass destruction or of an Al Qaeda–Iraq link, but Feith and his assistants aggressively sought to find ways of supporting the administration's contentions about Al Qaeda and Iraqi weapons of mass destruction. Feith's office passed many of their intelligence assessments on to the White House, which then leaked some of them to selected reporters with the stipulation that the source not be identified.

No weapons of mass destruction were uncovered by U.S. troops in the aftermath of the war. Although Iraq had used nerve gas in the past, it apparently had abandoned such weapons some years back. A bipartisan commission discovered no meaningful ties between Al Qaeda and Iraq before the war.[1] As opposition to the war grew over time, criticism of the administration mounted. The Bush White House blamed the bureaucracy, saying the intelligence gathering was weak and it was not provided with the kind of information it needed.

Surely the intelligence on Iraq could have been better, but the culprit was not just the bureaucracy. Rather, it was leadership of the bureaucracy. The White House let the CIA's director, George Tenet, know that a key presentation to President Bush was inadequate because he did not demonstrate that Iraq had weapons of mass destruction. Feith, from the Defense Department, delivered to the White House what it wanted to hear. But a 2007 Pentagon review of what had gone wrong concluded that Feith's office "was predisposed to finding a significant relationship between Iraq and al Qaeda."[2] Moreover, it determined that Feith and his associates had produced and disseminated assessments "inconsistent" with what the rest of the intelligence community had determined.

Bureaucracies are vital; our way of life depends on their proper functioning. But bureaucracies require leaders who make sure that they operate appropriately. In the case of the buildup to the Iraq war, the intelligence process was corrupted by leaders who mismanaged those organizations.[3]

Despite the shortcomings of bureaucracies, we must rely on them to administer government. In this chapter we examine how bureaucracies operate and address many of the central dilemmas of American political life. Bureaucracies represent what Americans dislike about government, yet our interest groups lobby them to provide us with more of the services we desire. We say we want smaller, less intrusive government, but different constituencies value different agencies of government and fight fiercely to protect those bureaucracies' budgets. This enduring conflict once again represents the majoritarian and pluralist dimensions of American politics.

Organization Matters

In the American system, the legislative branch passes laws, but it does not actually administer them. A nation's laws and policies are administered, or put into effect, by a variety of executive branch departments, agencies, bureaus, offices, and other government units that together are known as the *bureaucracy*. **Bureaucracy** actually means any large, complex organization in which employees have very specific job responsibilities and work within a hierarchy of authority. The employees of these government units have become known, somewhat derisively, as **bureaucrats.**

Bureaucracies play a central role in the governments of modern societies. In fact, organizations are a crucial part of any society. The organization of modern governmental bureaucracies reflects their need to survive. The environment of modern bureaucracies is filled with conflicting political demands and the ever-present threat of budget cuts. The way a given government bureaucracy is organized also reflects the needs of its clients. The bottom line, however, is that the manner in which any bureaucracy is organized affects how well it can accomplish its tasks.

Unfortunately, "if organization matters, it is also the case that there is no one best way of organizing."[4] Although centralizing the control and analysis of information might improve the ability of the intelligence community to detect potential attacks, that might not be the best approach to solving every bureaucratic performance problem. A common complaint against Washington bureaucracies is that they devise one-size-fits-all solutions to problems. The study of bureaucracy, then, centers around finding solutions to the many different kinds of problems that large government organizations face.

bureaucracy A large, complex organization in which employees have specific job responsibilities and work within a hierarchy of authority.

bureaucrat An employee of a bureaucracy, usually meaning a government bureaucracy.

The Development of the Bureaucratic State

A common complaint voiced by Americans is that the national bureaucracy is too big and tries to accomplish too much. To the average citizen, the federal government may seem like an octopus—its long arms reach just about everywhere. Ironically, compared to other Western democracies, the size of the U.S. government is proportionally smaller (see "Compared with What? Not So Big by Comparison").

The Growth of the Bureaucratic State

American government seems to have grown unchecked during the twentieth century. As one observer noted wryly, "The assistant administrator for water and hazardous materials of the Environmental Protection Agency presided over a staff larger than Washington's entire first administration."[5] Yet even during George Washington's time, bureaucracies were necessary. No one argued then about the need for a postal service to deliver mail or a treasury department to maintain a system of currency.

However, government at all levels (national, state, and local) grew enormously in the twentieth century.[6] There are several major reasons for this growth. A principal cause of government expansion is the increasing complexity of society. George Washington did not have an assistant administrator for water and hazardous materials because there was no need for one. A National Aeronautics and Space Administration (NASA) was not necessary until rockets were invented.

Another reason government has grown is that the public's attitude toward business has changed. Throughout most of the nineteenth century, business was generally autonomous, and government intervention in the economy that might limit that autonomy was considered inappropriate. This attitude began to change toward the end of the nineteenth century, as more Americans became aware that a laissez-faire approach did not always create competitive markets that benefited consumers. Gradually government intervention came to be accepted as necessary to protect the integrity of markets.[7] And if government was to police unfair business practices effectively, it needed administrative agencies.

During the twentieth century, new bureaucracies were organized to regulate specific industries. Among them are the Securities and Exchange Commission (SEC), which oversees securities trading, and the Food and Drug Administration (FDA), which tries to protect consumers from unsafe food, drugs, and cosmetics. Through bureaucracies such as these, government has become a referee in the marketplace, developing standards of fair trade, setting rates, and licensing individual businesses for operation. As new problem areas have emerged, government has added new agencies, further expanding the scope of its activities.

General attitudes about government's responsibilities in the area of social welfare have changed too. An enduring part of American culture is the belief in self-reliance. People are expected to overcome adversity on their own, to succeed because of their own skills and efforts. Yet certain segments of our population are believed to deserve government support, because we so value their contribution to society or have come to believe that they cannot realistically be expected to overcome adversity on their own.[8] This belief dates back to the nineteenth century. The government provided

Compared with What?

Not So Big by Comparison

When the United States is viewed against the other Western democracies, our government turns out to be relatively small. Measuring the size of government is difficult, but one way is to calculate the proportion of all of a nation's workers who are employed by their government.

The primary reason that the size of the bureaucracies in other democracies is larger in comparison to the United States is that they offer a much more extensive array of welfare and social service benefits to their citizens. These countries tend to have generous pension, health, and unemployment benefits. These benefits do not come cheaply, however; residents of the other advanced industrialized countries tend to pay much higher taxes than do Americans. There is no free lunch. In recent years, budget pressures have forced European governments to try to trim their spending.

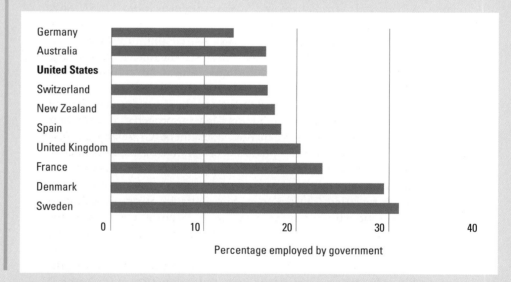

Percentage employed by government

Source: Alan R. Ball and B. Guy Peters, *Modern Politics and Government,* 7th ed. (New York: Palgrave Macmillan, 2005), p. 231.

pensions to Civil War veterans. Later, programs to help mothers and children were developed.[9] In the wake of the Great Depression, the Social Security Act became law, creating a fund that workers pay into and then collect income from during old age. In the 1960s, the government created programs designed to help minorities. As the government made these new commitments, it also created new bureaucracies or expanded existing ones.

Also, government has grown because ambitious, entrepreneurial agency officials have expanded their organizations and staffs to take on added responsibilities. Each new program that is developed leads to new authority. Larger budgets and staffs, in turn, are necessary to support that authority.

Can We Reduce the Size of Government?

Even incumbent candidates for Congress and the presidency typically "run against the government." Government is unpopular: most Americans have little confidence in its capabilities and feel that it wastes money and is out of touch with ordinary people. Americans want a smaller government that costs less and performs better.

If government is to become smaller, bureaucracies will have to be eliminated or reduced in size. Serious budget cuts also require serious reductions in programs. Not surprisingly, presidents and members of Congress face a tough job when they try to cut specific programs. One strategy the national government uses is to modestly reduce the number of bureaucrats (which is popular) without reducing government programs (which is politically risky). This is done by hiring nonprofit or private contractors who do the same job as bureaucrats but are not technically government employees.[10]

Efforts to contract the bureaucracy have varied considerably. During the 1980s, President Reagan preached smaller government and made a concerted effort to reduce domestic social programs. He had only modest success, and his most ambitious proposals, like abolishing the Department of Education, did not come close to passage by Congress. In contrast, liberal Bill Clinton wanted to expand government through a health reform plan (ultimately unsuccessful) designed to broaden access to health care for many previously uninsured. To Reagan small government enhanced personal freedom; to Clinton a larger government was a means of promoting equality.

The presidency of George W. Bush did not fit this traditional pattern. Though a conservative, Bush worked to enlarge the government. Most significant, the attacks on September 11 and the continuing threat of terrorism led to the creation of the Department of Homeland Security and the expansion of defense and other security-related agencies. But the new programs and bureaucracies went far beyond security threats. Accounting scandals that inflated corporate profits and misled investors at large companies such as Enron and WorldCom led to the new Public Company Accounting Oversight Board. Most surprising is that Bush worked to expand social welfare through a prescription drug benefit for senior citizens. Bush was certainly conservative but he understood that it was not always good politics to try to downsize government.

The tendency for big government to endure reflects the tension between majoritarianism and pluralism. Even when the public as a whole wants a smaller national government, that sentiment can be undermined by the strong desire of different segments of society for government to continue performing some valuable function for them. Lobbies that represent these segments work strenuously to convince Congress and the administration that certain agencies' funding is vital and that any cuts ought to come out of other agencies' budgets.

Bureaus and Bureaucrats

We often think of the bureaucracy as a monolith. In reality, the bureaucracy in Washington is a disjointed collection of departments, agencies, bureaus, offices, and commissions, each a bureaucracy in its own right.

The Organization of Government

By examining the basic types of government organizations, we can better understand how the executive branch operates. In our discussion, we pay particular attention to the relative degree of independence of these organizations and to their relationship with the White House.

Departments. **Departments** are the biggest units of the executive branch, covering broad areas of government responsibility. As noted in Chapter 9, the secretaries (heads) of the departments, along with a few other key officials, form the president's cabinet. The current cabinet departments are State, Treasury, Defense, Interior, Agriculture, Justice, Commerce, Labor, Health and Human Services, Housing and Urban Development, Transportation, Energy, Education, Veterans Affairs, and Homeland Security. Each of these massive organizations is broken down into subsidiary agencies, bureaus, offices, and services. The largest of the cabinet-level departments is the Department of Defense, with approximately 680,000 civilian employees supporting and providing policy direction for over 1.4 million active duty military personnel.[11] (See Figure 10.1.)

Independent Agencies. Within the executive branch, there are also many **independent agencies,** which are not part of any cabinet department. They stand alone and are controlled to varying degrees by the president. Some, among them the CIA, are under the president's control. Others, such as the Federal Communications Commission, are structured as **regulatory commissions.** Each commission is run by a small number of commissioners appointed to fixed terms by the president. Some commissions were formed to guard against unfair business practices. Others were formed to protect the public from unsafe products. Although presidents do not have

department The biggest unit of the executive branch, covering a broad area of government responsibility. The heads of the departments, or secretaries, form the president's cabinet.

independent agency An executive agency that is not part of a cabinet department.

regulatory commission An agency of the executive branch of government that controls or directs some aspect of the economy.

FIGURE 10·1   **Bureaucrats at Work**

The size of cabinet departments varies dramatically. As
this graph indicates, the
Department of Defense is by
far the largest cabinet-level
bureaucracy within the
federal government. That
more than 1 million civilian
workers are employed in the
departments of Defense,
Veterans Affairs, and Homeland Security is a reflection
of the centrality of national
security and war in recent
American history. At the
opposite end of the spec-
trum is the tiny Department
of Education, with fewer
than 5,000 employees.

*Source: Statistical Abstract of the
United States, 2008,* available at
www.census.gov/compendia/
statab/tables/08s0485.xls.

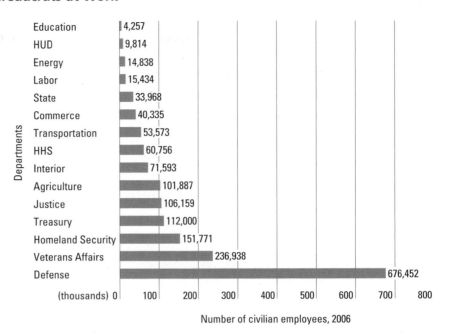

Department	Number of civilian employees, 2006
Education	4,257
HUD	9,814
Energy	14,838
Labor	15,434
State	33,968
Commerce	40,335
Transportation	53,573
HHS	60,756
Interior	71,593
Agriculture	101,887
Justice	106,159
Treasury	112,000
Homeland Security	151,771
Veterans Affairs	236,938
Defense	676,452

(thousands) 0   100   200   300   400   500   600   700   800

Number of civilian employees, 2006

direct control over these regulatory commissions, they can strongly influence their direction through their appointments of new commissioners.

Government Corporations.   Congress has created a small number of
government corporations. In theory, the services these executive branch agencies perform could be provided by the private sector, but Congress has decided that the public will be better served if these organizations have some
link with the government. For example, the national government maintains the postal service as a government corporation because it feels that
Americans need low-cost, door-to-door service for all kinds of mail, not
just for profitable routes or special services. In some instances, the private
sector does not have enough financial incentive to provide an essential service. This is the case with the financially troubled Amtrak train line.[12]

The Civil Service

The national bureaucracy is staffed by about 2.7 million civilian employees, who account for about 2 percent of the U.S. work force.[13] Most of those
government workers are hired under the requirements of the **civil service.**

government corporation
A government agency that performs services that might be provided by the private sector but that
involve either insufficient financial
incentive or are better provided
when they are somehow linked
with government.

civil service The system by
which most appointments to the
federal bureaucracy are made, to
ensure that government jobs are
filled on the basis of merit and that
employees are not fired for
political reasons.

The civil service was created by the Pendleton Act (1883). The objective of the act was to reduce *patronage*—the practice of filling government positions with the president's political allies or cronies. The civil service fills jobs on the basis of merit and sees to it that workers are not fired for political reasons.

The vast majority of the national government's workers are employed outside Washington. One reason for this decentralization is to make government offices accessible to the people they serve. Decentralization is also a way to distribute jobs and income across the country. Members of Congress, of course, are only too happy to place some of this "pork" back home, so that their constituents will credit them with the jobs and money that government installations create.

Presidential Control Over the Bureaucracy

Civil service and other reforms have effectively insulated the vast majority of government workers from party politics. An incoming president can appoint only about seven thousand people to jobs in the administration, less than 1 percent of all executive branch employees. Still, presidential appointees fill the top policymaking positions in government, and about eight hundred of his appointees require Senate confirmation.[14] Each new president establishes an extensive personnel review process to find appointees who are both politically compatible and qualified in their field. Although the president selects some people from his campaign staff, cabinet secretaries, assistant secretaries, and agency heads tend to be drawn directly from business, universities, and government itself.

Presidents find that the bureaucracy is not always as responsive as they might like, for several reasons. Principally, pluralism can pull agencies in a direction other than that favored by the president. The Department of Transportation may want to move toward more support for mass transit, for example, but politically it cannot afford to ignore the preferences of highway builders. An agency administrator must often try to broker a compromise between conflicting groups rather than pursue a position that holds fast and true to the president's ideology. Bureaucracies must also follow—at least in general terms—the laws governing the programs they are entrusted with, even if the president does not agree with some of those statutes.

Congress always has the prerogative to pass news laws overriding regulations that it feels distort its intent. Whatever party controls Congress, the White House and agency administrators have an incentive to consult with committee chairs to minimize conflict and gain a sense of what might provoke a hostile response on the part of a committee overseeing a particular agency.[15] A committee can punish an agency by cutting its budget, altering a key program, or (for Senate committees) holding up confirmation of a nominee to a top agency post.

Administrative Policymaking: The Formal Processes

Many Americans wonder why agencies sometimes make policy rather than merely carry it out. Administrative agencies are, in fact, authoritative policymaking bodies, and their decisions on substantive issues are legally binding on the citizens of this country.

Administrative Discretion

What are executive agencies set up to do? Cabinet departments, independent agencies, and government corporations are creatures of Congress. Congress creates a new department or agency by enacting a law that describes the organization's mandate, or mission. As part of that mandate, Congress grants to the agency the authority to make certain policy decisions. Congress long ago recognized that it has neither the time nor the technical expertise to make all policy decisions. Ideally, it sets general guidelines for policy and expects agencies to act within those guidelines. The latitude that Congress gives agencies to make policy in the spirit of their legislative mandate is called **administrative discretion.**

Critics of the bureaucracy frequently complain that agencies are granted too much discretion.[16] Congress often is vague about its intent when setting up a new agency or program. At times a problem is clear cut but the solution is not, yet Congress is under pressure to act. So Congress creates an agency or program to show that it is concerned and responsive, but it leaves the development of specific solutions to agency administrators. For example, the 1934 enabling legislation that established the Federal Communications Commission (FCC) recognized a need for regulation in the burgeoning radio industry. But Congress avoided tackling several sticky issues by giving the FCC the ambiguous directive that broadcasters should "serve the public interest, convenience, and necessity."[17] In other cases, several obvious solutions to a problem may be available, but lawmakers cannot agree on which one is best. Compromise wording is thus often ambiguous, papering over differences and ensuring conflict over administrative regulations as agencies try to settle lingering policy disputes.

The broadest discretion granted by Congress is to those agencies involved in domestic and global security. Both the FBI and the CIA have enjoyed a great deal of freedom from formal and informal congressional constraints because of the legitimate need for secrecy in their operations. The National Security Agency (NSA) also monitors foreign communications. After September 11, President Bush directed the NSA to wiretap telephone conversations between people within the United States and people overseas who have suspected links with terrorists, without first obtaining a warrant as required by the 1978 Foreign Intelligence Surveillance Act.

IDEAlog.org

One of the questions in the IDEAlog program that accompanies this textbook deals with the issue of government regulation of cable television content. How did you answer that question in the self-test?

administrative discretion
The latitude that Congress gives agencies to make policy in the spirit of their legislative mandate.

NSA bureaucrats followed the secret orders of the president, often without the knowledge of most members of Congress.[18] Congress has since amended the law, actually expanding the authority of the government to eavesdrop.[19]

The wide latitude Congress gives administrative agencies often leads to charges that the bureaucracy is out of control. But such claims are frequently exaggerated. Congress has the power to express its displeasure by reining in agencies with additional legislation. If Congress is unhappy with an agency's actions, it can pass laws invalidating specific policies, reducing discretion, or providing more guidance to the bureaucracy.[20] A second powerful tool is Congress's control over the budget. Congress can threaten an agency through its power to cut budgets and can reorder agency priorities through its detailed appropriations legislation.

Rule Making

Agencies make policy through formal administrative procedures, usually **rule making,** the administrative process that results in regulations.[21] **Regulations** are rules that govern the operation of government programs. When an agency issues regulations, it is using the discretionary authority granted to it by Congress to implement a program or policy.

Rule making itself follows procedural guidelines requiring that proposed regulations first be published so that interested parties—typically interest groups—have a chance to comment on them, making any recommendations they see as appropriate.[22]

Because they are authorized by congressional statutes, regulations have the effect of law. For example, since 1935, Congress has given the executive branch the authority to write regulations to set standards for the trucking industry. Trucks are now regulated by the Federal Motor Carrier Safety Administration, which is part of the Department of Transportation.

Industry executives have pushed for rule making to reduce regulatory restrictions on truck drivers that they find burdensome. Limits on how many hours an employee can drive reduce efficiency because once the maximum is reached, he or she must pull off the road for a period of time. That in turn reduces profits and raises shipping costs for both vendors and consumers. Recently, the agency issued new rules that increased the number of hours an individual can drive a truck from a maximum sixty hours over seven days to seventy-seven hours over seven days. The agency said safety would not be compromised because the extended hours would keep the companies from having to hire additional, inexperienced drivers. In the few years since the new regulations were put into effect the number of fatalities resulting from truck accidents has gone up slightly.[23]

The regulatory process is controversial because regulations often require individuals and corporations to act against their own self-interest. The trucking regulations are a classic case of freedom versus order. The trucking companies believed they needed the greater freedom to conduct

rule making The administrative process that results in the issuance of regulations by government agencies.

regulations Administrative rules that guide the operation of a government program.

business in a way that they found most efficient. Safety groups preferred that the government put more emphasis on maintaining order (keeping the highways safe). Administrative rule making gives agencies the flexibility as they try to find a balance between conflicting pressures.

Administrative Policymaking: Informal Politics

When an agency is considering a new regulation and all the evidence and arguments have been presented, how does an administrator reach a decision? Because policy decisions typically address complex problems that lack a single satisfactory solution, they rarely exhibit mathematical precision and efficiency.

The Science of Muddling Through

In his classic analysis of policymaking, "The Science of Muddling Through," Charles Lindblom compared the way policy might be made in the ideal world with the way it is formulated in the real world.[24] The ideal rational decision-making process, according to Lindblom, would begin with an administrator tackling a problem by ranking values and objectives. After the objectives were clarified, the administrator would thoroughly consider all possible solutions to the problem. The administrator would comprehensively analyze alternative solutions, taking all relevant factors into account. Finally, the administrator would choose the alternative that is seen as the most effective means of achieving the desired goal and solving the problem.

Lindblom claims that this "rational-comprehensive" model is unrealistic. Policymakers have great difficulty defining precise values and goals. Administrators at the U.S. Department of Energy, for example, want to be sure that supplies of home heating oil are sufficient each winter, but at the same time they want to reduce dependence on foreign oil. Obviously the two goals are not fully compatible. How do administrators decide which is more important? And how do they relate those goals to the other goals of the nation's energy policy?

Real-world decision making parts company with the ideal in another way: the policy selected cannot always be the most effective means to the desired end. Even if a tax at the pump is the most effective way to reduce gasoline consumption during a shortage, motorists' anger would make this theoretically "right" decision politically difficult. The "best" policy is often the one on which most people can agree. However, political compromise may mean that the government is able to solve only part of a problem.

Finally, critics of the rational-comprehensive model point out that policymaking can never be based on truly comprehensive analysis. Time is of the essence, and many problems are too pressing to wait for a complete study.

INTERACTIVE 10.1

 Oil Dependency

In short, policymaking tends to be characterized by **incrementalism**: policies and programs change bit by bit, step by step.[25] Decision makers are constrained by competing policy objectives, opposing political forces, incomplete information, and the pressures of time. They choose from a limited number of feasible options that are almost always modifications of existing policies rather than wholesale departures from them. Although Lindblom offered a more realistic portrayal of the policymaking process, incrementalism is not ubiquitous. There are a minority of cases in which decisions are made that move a policy in a significantly new direction. It is certainly true that virtually all policy changes have antecedents in current policy, but some changes are considerable in scope.[26]

The Culture of Bureaucracy

How an agency makes decisions and performs its tasks is greatly affected by the people who work there: the bureaucrats. Americans often find their interactions with bureaucrats frustrating because bureaucrats are inflexible (they go by the book) or lack the authority to get things done. Top administrators too can also become frustrated with the bureaucrats who work for them.

Why do people act bureaucratically? Individuals who work for large organizations cannot help but be affected by the culture of bureaucracy.[27] Modern bureaucracies develop explicit rules and standards in order to make operations more efficient and to guarantee fair treatment of their clients. Within each organization, **norms** (informal, unwritten rules of behavior) also develop and influence the way people act on the job.

Bureaucracies are often influenced in their selection of policy options by the prevailing customs, attitudes, and expectations of the people working within them. Departments and agencies commonly develop a sense of mission, which emphasizes a particular objective. The Army Corps of Engineers, for example, is dominated by engineers who define the agency's objective as protecting citizens from floods by building dams. There could be other objectives, and there are other methods of achieving flood protection, but the engineers promote the solutions that fit their conception of what the agency should be doing. Bureaucrats are often criticized for being rigid, for going by the book when some flexibility might be a better option. Bureaucrats go by the book because the "book" is actually the law they administer, and they are obligated to enforce the law. The regulations under those laws are often broad standards intended to cover a range of behaviors. Bureaucratic caution and close adherence to agency rules ensure a measure of consistency. It would be unsettling if government employees interpreted rules as they pleased. Americans expect to be treated equally before the law, and bureaucrats work with that expectation in mind.

incrementalism Policymaking characterized by a series of decisions, each instituting modest change.

norms An organization's informal, unwritten rules that guide individual behavior.

Problems in Implementing Policy

The development of policy in Washington marks the end of one phase of the policymaking cycle and the beginning of another. After policies are developed, they must be implemented. **Implementation** is the process of putting specific policies into operation. It is important to study implementation because policies do not always do what they were designed to do.

Implementation may be difficult because the policy to be carried out is not clearly stated. Policy directives to bureaucrats sometimes lack specificity and leave them with too much discretion.

Implementation can also be problematic because of the complexity of some government endeavors. Toxic cleanups, for example, pose complicated engineering, political, and financial problems. Inevitably, regional Environmental Protection Agency (EPA) offices and key actors at the local level engage in intense negotiations at each stage of the process.[28] The federal response to Hurricane Katrina in late August 2005 illustrates the difficulties of policy implementation, particularly when bureaucracy must respond rapidly to a crisis.[29]

Though the Bush administration was warned about the impending hurricane, senior officials failed to appoint an executive branch officer to take charge of the disaster before the storm hit the coast.[30] With no clear chain of command, bureaucrats at all levels of government—state, local, and federal—had a difficult time sharing information about storm damage and coordinating relief. Responsibility for natural disaster relief falls within the jurisdiction of the Federal Emergency Management Agency (FEMA). Three days after the storm, Department of Homeland Security Secretary Michael Chertoff could not find out how many people were stranded in

INTERACTIVE 10.2

 How Would You Respond to a Disaster?

implementation The process of putting specific policies into operation.

the Ernest N. Morial Convention Center in downtown New Orleans. Estimates ranged from 1,500 to 15,000. Nor could he find out how many buses had evacuated people seeking refuge at the Superdome. State and local officials had trouble locating FEMA chief Michael Brown by phone or e-mail in the days after the disaster. The more organizations and levels of government that are involved in handling anything, the more difficult it is to coordinate implementation.

Obstacles to effective implementation can create the impression that nothing the government does succeeds, but programs can and do work. Problems in implementation demonstrate why patience and continual analysis are necessary ingredients of successful policymaking. Implementation is an *incremental* process in which trial and error eventually lead to policies that work.

Reforming the Bureaucracy: More Control or Less?

As we saw at the beginning of this chapter, organization matters. How bureaucracies are designed directly affects how effective they are in accomplishing their tasks.[31] Administrative reforms have taken many different approaches in recent years as the criticism of government has mounted.

Deregulation

Many people believe that government is too involved in **regulation,** intervention in the natural workings of business markets to promote some social goal. For example, government might regulate a market to ensure that products pose no danger to consumers. Through **deregulation,** the government reduces its role and lets the natural market forces of supply and demand take over.

Considerable deregulation took place in the 1970s and 1980s, notably in the airline, trucking, financial services, and telecommunications industries. In telecommunications, for example, consumers before 1982 had no choice of long-distance vendors: they could call on AT&T's Bell System or not call at all. After an out-of-court settlement broke up the Bell System in 1982, AT&T was awarded the right to sell the long-distance services that Bell had been providing, but it now had to face competition from other long-distance carriers, such as MCI and Sprint. Consumers have benefited from the competition for long-distance phone calls, and competition has since opened up for local service as well.

Deciding on an appropriate level of deregulation is particularly difficult for health and safety issues. Companies within an industry may legitimately claim that health and safety regulations are burdensome, making it difficult for them to earn sufficient profits or compete effectively with for-

regulation Government intervention in the workings of business to promote some socially desired goal.

deregulation A bureaucratic reform by which the government reduces its role as a regulator of business.

The Return of Thalidomide
The United States was spared this disaster because of the skepticism of Frances Kelsey, a Food and Drug Administration doctor who refused to allow thalidomide to be prescribed here. In 1997, the FDA reversed course and decided to permit the use of thalidomide to treat leprosy, but the dangers to pregnant women remain. To avert a catastrophe, the FDA includes stickers on the drug's packaging to warn women of the consequences of taking this drug during pregnancy. Shown here is an adult thalidomide victim. *(© Don Jones)*

eign manufacturers. But the drug-licensing procedures used by the FDA illustrate the potential danger of deregulating in such policy areas. The thorough and lengthy process the FDA uses to evaluate drugs has as its ultimate validation the thalidomide case in the 1960s. Dr. Frances Kelsey, who was assigned to evaluate the sedative, demanded that all FDA drug-testing requirements be met, despite the fact that the drug was already in use in other countries. Before the tests were completed, news came pouring in from Europe that some women who had taken thalidomide during pregnancy were giving birth to babies without arms, legs, or ears. Strict adherence to FDA regulation protected Americans from the same tragic consequences.

Some agencies have tried to move beyond rules that simply increase or decrease the amount of government control to regulatory processes that offer firms flexibility in meeting standards while at the same time protecting health and safety concerns. For example, the Environmental Protection Agency (EPA) has instituted flexible caps on air pollution at some manufacturing plants. Instead of having to request permits on new equipment and processes, plants are given an overall pollution cap and can decide on their own how to meet that limit. Although such "cap and trade" provisions for power plants were struck down by a federal appeals court in 2008, they illustrate the creativity that bureaucracies can at times bring to the regulatory process.[32]

Another regulatory approach gaining favor is the effort to make organizations, typically corporations, more transparent and accountable in their actions. For example, food manufacturers are now required to disclose the quantity of trans-fats in a product on its label. Regulations do not limit the

DO IT!

Before you buy that new electronic product, check out the Environmental Protection Agency's ENERGY STAR website: www.energystar.gov/index.cfm?fuseaction=find_a_product. ENERGY STAR products "use less energy, save money, and help protect the environment."

amount of trans-fatty acids but, rather, give consumers the information and then let them decide how much is too much.[33]

As noted in the case of rules governing truck drivers, the conflict over how far to take deregulation reflects the traditional dilemma of choosing between freedom and order. A strong case can be made for deregulated business markets, in which free and unfettered competition benefits consumers and promotes productivity. The strength of capitalist economies comes from the ability of individuals and firms to compete freely in the marketplace, and the regulatory state places restrictions on this freedom. But without regulation, nothing ensures that marketplace participants will act responsibly.

Competition and Outsourcing

Conservative critics of government have long complained that bureaucracies should act more like businesses, meaning they should try to emulate private sector practices that promote efficiency and innovation. Many recent reformers advocate something more drastic: unless bureaucracies can demonstrate that they are as efficient as the private sector, turn those agencies' functions over to the private sector. Underlying this idea is the belief that competition will make government more dynamic and more responsive to changing environments.[34]

One widespread adaptation of competitive bidding to administer government programs has come in the area of social services. Over time

---

FIGURE 10.2   **Contracting Out**

An explosive growth in contracting out government programs and services to nonprofits and for-profit organizations is changing the face of government. In a recent six-year period, contracting out almost doubled. Although competitive bidding theoretically gives the government the lowest prices, only half of all contracts are subject to full and open competition. Government officials claim that national security concerns often lead it to seek out a single contractor rather opening the process to all potential bidders.

Source: Scott Shane and Ron Nixon, "In Washington, Contractors Take On Biggest Role Ever," *New York Times,* 4 February 2007, p. 1.

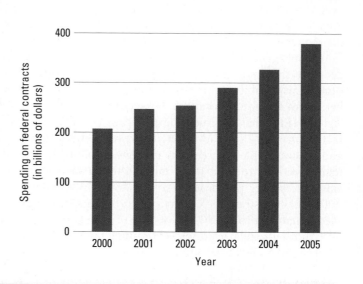

government welfare programs have increasingly emphasized social services—giving people training and noncash support—rather than income maintenance (cash support). State and local governments have found it efficient to outsource programs to nonprofit organizations like community health centers and elderly day-care centers. Recently, for-profit companies have started to compete for the grants and contracts that the government awards through competitive grants or bidding.[35] This movement toward **competition and outsourcing** continues to grow. More and more government jobs are open to bidding from nongovernment competitors and sometimes a government bureau or office competes for the jobs and programs that they used to "own." (See Figure 10.2.)

Performance Standards

Another approach to improving the bureaucracy's performance is to hold it accountable for reaching quantifiable goals each year or budget cycle. A major initiative to hold agencies accountable for their performance is the **Government Performance and Results Act**. This law requires each agency to identify specific goals, adopt a performance plan, and develop quantitative indicators of agency progress in meeting its goals.[36] Beginning in 2000, the law required that agencies begin to publish reports with performance data on each measure established.

This is no small challenge. A case in point is the Healthy Start program funded by the Health Resources and Services Administration (HRSA) and intended to improve infant mortality rates and infant health generally. Among the specific goals are increasing the number of mothers receiving prenatal care during the first trimester and reducing the number of low-weight births. These are measurable and the hospitals and health centers receiving federal funding for Healthy Start must report the appropriate data to HRSA. More complicated is the degree to which these various programs make a difference since infant health can be influenced by many different factors.[37]

Despite the value of improved accountability, performance management is not without problems. Since agencies set their own goals and know they will be judged on meeting them, they may select indicators where they know they'll do best. Should an agency running a job training program emphasize its success in the number of people it enrolls or the success rate of its graduates? If it chooses the success rate of its graduates, will the agency be tempted to be more selective in whom it takes into the program? That is, would it reject those with the most problematic record but who are most in need of assistance? In short, performance-based management runs the risk of perverting an agency's incentives toward what it can achieve rather than what would be most valuable to achieve.[38]

Despite the relative appeal of these different approaches to improving the bureaucracy, each has serious shortcomings. The commitment of the government to solve a problem is far more important than management

competition and outsourcing Procedures that allow private contractors to bid for jobs previously held exclusively by government employees.

Government Performance and Results Act A law requiring each government agency to implement quantifiable standards to measure its performance in meeting stated program goals.

techniques.[39] Still, to return to a theme that we began with, organization does matter. Trying to find ways of improving the bureaucracy is important because bureaucracies affect people's lives and enhancing their performance, even at the margins, has real consequences.

Summary

As the scope of government activity has grown during the twentieth and early twenty-first centuries, so too has the bureaucracy. The executive branch evolved into a complex set of departments, independent agencies, and government corporations. The way in which these various bureaucracies are organized matters a great deal because the way they are structured affects their ability to carry out their tasks.

Through the administrative discretion granted them by Congress, these bodies make policy decisions through rule making and adjudication that have the force of law. In making policy choices, agency decision makers are influenced by their external environment, especially the White House, Congress, and interest groups. Internal norms and the need to work cooperatively with others both inside and outside their agencies also influence decision makers.

The most serious charge facing the bureaucracy is that it is unresponsive to the will of the people. In fact, the White House, Congress, interest groups, and public opinion act as substantial controls on the bureaucracy. Still, to many Americans, the bureaucracy seems too big, too costly, and too intrusive. Reducing the size and scope of bureaucratic activity is difficult because pluralism characterizes our political system. The entire executive branch may appear too large, and each of us can point to agencies that we believe should be reduced or eliminated. Yet each bureaucracy has its supporters. Bureaucracies survive because they provide important services to groups of people, and those people—no matter how strong their commitment to shrinking the government—are not willing to sacrifice their own benefits.

Plans for reforming the bureaucracy to make it work better are not in short supply. Broad-scale reforms include deregulation, competition and outsourcing, total quality management, and performance standards. Each has merits and offers plausible mechanisms for improving government efficiency and responsiveness. Each has shortcomings as well, and advocates often overlook the tradeoffs and problems associated with these reforms. Yet it is important to keep trying to find ways of improving government because most people continue to believe that the overall management of bureaucracies is poor and that government needs to be more customer driven.

CL **Resources:** Videos, Simulations, News, Timelines, Primary Sources

The Courts

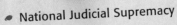

- National Judicial Supremacy
- The Organization of Courts
- The Supreme Court
- Judicial Recruitment
- The Consequences of Judicial Decisions
- The Courts and Models of Democracy

This icon will direct you to resources and activities on the website: www.cengage.com/polisci/janda/ chall_dem_brief/7e

WHEN CHIEF JUSTICE FRED M. Vinson died unexpectedly in September 1953, his colleague Associate Justice Felix Frankfurter commented, "This is the first solid piece of evidence I've ever had that there really is a God."[1] Frankfurter despised Vinson as a leader and disliked him as a person. Vinson's sudden death would bring a new colleague—and perhaps new hope—to the school desegregation cases known collectively as *Brown* v. *Board of Education.* The issue of segregated schools had arrived in the Supreme Court in late 1951. Although the Court had originally scheduled oral argument for October 1952, the justices elected a postponement until December and merged several similar cases. When a law clerk expressed puzzlement at the delay, Frankfurter explained that the Court was holding the cases for the outcome of the national election in 1952. "I thought the Court was supposed to decide without regard to elections," declared the clerk. "When you have a major social political issue of this magnitude," replied Frankfurter, "we do not think this is the time to decide it."[2]

The justices were at loggerheads following the December argument, with Vinson unwilling to invalidate racial segregation in public education. Because the justices were not ready to reach a decision, they scheduled the cases for reargument the following year. The justices asked the attorneys to address the history of the Fourteenth Amendment and the potential remedies if the Court ruled against segregation.

Frankfurter's caustic remark about Vinson's death reflected the critical role Vinson's replacement would play when the Court again tackled the desegregation issue. In his first appointment to the nation's highest court, President Dwight D. Eisenhower chose California's Republican governor, Earl Warren, as chief justice. The president would later regret his choice.

When the Court heard the reargument of *Brown* v. *Board of Education* in late 1953, the

The power of the courts to shape public policy creates a difficult problem for democratic theory. According to that theory, the power to make law and the power to determine the outcome of elections reside only in the people or their elected representatives.

Court rulings—especially Supreme Court rulings—extend far beyond any particular case. Judges are students of the law, but they remain human beings. They have their own opinions about the values of freedom, order, and equality. And although all judges are constrained by statutes and precedents from expressing their personal beliefs in their decisions, some judges are more prone than others to interpret laws in the light of those beliefs. America's courts are deeply involved in the life of the country and its people. Some courts, such as the Supreme Court, make fundamental policy decisions vital to the preservation of freedom, order, and equality. Through

new chief justice led his colleagues from division to unanimity on the issue of public school segregation. Unlike his predecessor, Warren began the secret conference to decide the segregation issue with a strong statement: that segregation was contrary to the Thirteenth, Fourteenth, and Fifteenth Amendments to the Constitution. "Personally," remarked the new chief justice, "I can't see how today we can justify segregation based solely on race."[3] Moreover, if the Court were to uphold segregation, he argued, it could do so only on the theory that blacks were inherently inferior to whites. As the discussion proceeded, Warren's opponents were cast in the awkward position of appearing to support racism.

Five justices were clearly on Warren's side, making six votes; two were prepared to join the majority if Warren's reasoning satisfied them. With only one clear holdout, Warren set about the task of responding to his colleagues' concerns. In the months that followed, he met with them individually in their chambers, reviewing the decision and the justification that would accompany it. Finally, in April 1954, Warren approach Justice Stanley Reed, whose vote would make the opinion unanimous. "Stan," said the Chief Justice, "you're all by yourself in this now. You've got to decide whether it's really the best thing for the country." Ultimately, Reed joined the others. On May 17, 1954, the Supreme Court unanimously ruled against racial segregation in public schools, signaling the end of legally created or government-enforced segregation of the races in the United States.[4]

Judges confront conflicting values in the cases before them, and in crafting their decisions judges—especially Supreme Court justices—make policy. Their decisions become the precedents other judges use to rule in similar cases. One judge in one court makes public policy to the extent that she or he influences other decisions in other courts.

checks and balances, the elected branches link the courts to democracy, and the courts link the elected branches to the Constitution. But does this arrangement work? Can the courts exercise political power within the pluralist model? Or are judges simply sovereigns in black robes, making decisions independent of popular control? This chapter seeks to answer these questions by exploring the role of the judiciary in American political life.

National Judicial Supremacy

Section 1 of Article III of the Constitution creates "one supreme Court." The founders were divided on the need for other national courts, so they deferred to Congress the decision to create a national court system. Those who opposed the creation of national courts believed that such a system would usurp the authority of the state courts.[5] Congress considered the issue in its first session and, in the Judiciary Act of 1789, gave life to a system of federal (that is, national) courts that would coexist with the courts in each state but be independent of them. Federal judges would also be independent of popular influences because the Constitution provided for their virtual lifetime appointment.

In the early years of the Republic, the federal judiciary was not a particularly powerful branch of government. It was especially difficult to recruit and keep Supreme Court justices. They spent much of their time as individual traveling judges ("riding circuit"), and disease and transportation were everyday hazards. The justices met as the Supreme Court for only a few weeks in February and August.[6] John Jay, the first chief justice, refused to resume his duties in 1801 because he concluded that the Court could not muster the "energy, weight, and dignity" to contribute to national affairs.[7] But a period of profound change began in 1801 when President John Adams appointed his secretary of state, John Marshall, to the position of chief justice.

Judicial Review of the Other Branches

Shortly after Marshall's appointment, the Supreme Court confronted a question of fundamental importance to the future of the new republic: If a law enacted by Congress conflicts with the Constitution, which should prevail? The question arose in the case of *Marbury* v. *Madison* (1803), which involved a controversial series of last-minute political appointments.

The case began in 1801, when an obscure Federalist, William Marbury, was designated a justice of the peace in the District of Columbia. Marbury and several others were appointed to government posts created by Congress in the last days of John Adams's presidency, but the appointments were never completed. Though the Senate had approved their appointment, the official documents of appointment were not delivered to several of the judicial appointments, including Marbury. The newly arrived Jefferson administration had little interest in delivering the required documents; qualified Jeffersonians would welcome the jobs.

To secure their jobs, Marbury and the other disgruntled appointees invoked an act of Congress to obtain the papers. The act authorized the Supreme Court to issue orders against government officials. Marbury and the others sought such an order in the Supreme Court against the new secretary of state, James Madison, who held the crucial documents.

Chief Justice John Marshall observed that the act of Congress that Marbury invoked to sue in the Supreme Court conflicted with Article III of the U.S. Constitution, which did not authorize such suits. In February 1803, the Court delivered its opinion.

Must the Supreme Court follow the law or the Constitution? The Court held, in Marshall's forceful argument, that the Constitution was "the fundamental and paramount law of the nation" and that "an act of the legislature repugnant to the constitution is void." In other words, when an act of the legislature conflicts with the Constitution—the nation's highest law—that act is invalid. Marshall's argument vested in the judiciary the power to weigh the validity of congressional acts:

> It is emphatically the province and duty of the judicial department to say what the law is. Those who apply the rule to particular cases, must of necessity expound and interpret that rule. . . . If a law be in opposition to the constitution, if both the law and the constitution apply to a particular case, so that the court must either decide that case conformably to the law, disregarding the constitution; or conformably to the constitution, disregarding the law; the court must determine which of these conflicting rules governs the case. This is the very essence of judicial duty.[8]

The decision in *Marbury* v. *Madison* established the Supreme Court's power of **judicial review**—the power to declare congressional acts invalid if they violate the Constitution.* Subsequent cases extended the power to cover presidential acts as well.[9]

Marshall expanded the potential power of the Supreme Court to equal or exceed the power of the other branches of government. Should a congressional act (or, by implication, a presidential act) conflict with the Constitution, the Supreme Court claimed the power to declare the act void. The judiciary would be a check on the legislative and executive branches, consistent with the principle of checks and balances embedded in the Constitution. Judicial review gave the Supreme Court the final word on the meaning of the Constitution.

The exercise of judicial review—an appointed branch's checking of an elected branch in the name of the Constitution—appears to run counter to democratic theory. But in nearly two hundred years of practice, the Supreme Court has invalidated only about 160 provisions of national law. Only a small number have had great significance for the political system.[10] Moreover, there are mechanisms to override judicial review (constitutional amendment) and to control the excesses of the justices (impeachment). In addition, the Court can respond to the continuing struggle among competing interests (a struggle that is consistent with the pluralist model) by reversing itself.

Judicial Review of State Government

The establishment of judicial review of national laws made the Supreme Court the umpire of the national government. When acts of the national government conflict with the Constitution, the Supreme Court can declare those acts invalid. But suppose state laws conflict with the Constitution,

---

*The Supreme Court had earlier upheld an act of Congress in *Hylton* v. *United States,* 3 Dallas 171 (1796). *Marbury* v. *Madison* was the first exercise of the power of a court to invalidate an act of Congress.

judicial review The power to declare congressional and presidential acts invalid because they violate the Constitution.

national laws, or federal treaties? Can the U.S. Supreme Court invalidate them as well?

The Court answered in the affirmative in 1796. The case involved a British creditor who was trying to collect a debt from the state of Virginia.[11] Virginia law canceled debts owed British subjects, yet the Treaty of Paris (1783), in which Britain formally acknowledged the independence of the colonies, guaranteed that creditors could collect such debts. The Court ruled that the Constitution's supremacy clause (Article VI), which embraces national laws and treaties, nullified the state law.

The states continued to resist the yoke of national supremacy. Advocates of strong states' rights conceded that the supremacy clause obligates state judges to follow the Constitution when state law conflicts with it; however, they maintained that the states were bound only by their own interpretation of the Constitution. The Supreme Court said no, ruling that it had the authority to review state court decisions that called for the interpretation of national law.[12] National supremacy required the Supreme Court to impose uniformity on federal law; otherwise, the Constitution's meaning would vary from state to state. The people, not the states, had ordained the Constitution, and the people had subordinated state power to it in order to establish a viable national government. In time, the Supreme Court would use its judicial review power in nearly 1,300 instances to invalidate state and local laws on issues as diverse as abortion, the death penalty, the rights of the accused, and reapportionment.[13]

The Exercise of Judicial Review

These early cases, coupled with other historic decisions, established the components of judicial review:

- The power of the courts to declare national, state, and local laws invalid if they violate the Constitution

- The supremacy of national laws or treaties when they conflict with state and local laws

- The role of the Supreme Court as the final authority on the meaning of the Constitution

This political might—the power to undo decisions of the representative branches of the national and state governments—lay in the hands of appointed judges, people not accountable to the electorate. Did judicial review square with democratic government?

Alexander Hamilton had foreseen and tackled the problem in *Federalist* No. 78. Writing during the ratification debates surrounding the adoption of the Constitution (see Chapter 2), Hamilton maintained that despite the power of judicial review, the judiciary would be the weakest of the three branches of government because it lacked "the strength of the sword or the purse." The judiciary, wrote Hamilton, had "neither force nor will, but only judgment."

Although Hamilton was defending legislative supremacy, he argued that judicial review was an essential barrier to legislative oppression.[14] He recognized that the power to declare government acts void implied the superiority of the courts over the other branches. But this power, he contended, simply reflects the will of the people declared in the Constitution as opposed to the will of the legislature expressed in its statutes. Judicial independence, guaranteed by lifetime tenure and protected salaries, frees judges from executive and legislative control, minimizing the risk of their deviating from the law established in the Constitution. If judges make a mistake, the people or their elected representatives have the means to correct the error, through constitutional amendments and impeachment.

Nevertheless, lifetime tenure does free judges from the direct influence of the president and Congress. And although mechanisms to check judicial power are in place, they require extraordinary majorities and are rarely used. When judges exercise the power of judicial review, then, they can and occasionally do operate counter to majoritarian rule by invalidating the actions of the people's elected representatives.

The Organization of Courts

The American court system is complex, partly as a result of our federal system of government. Each state runs its own court system, and no two states' courts are identical. In addition, we have a system of courts for the national government. The national, or federal, courts coexist with the state courts (see Figure 11.1). Individuals fall under the jurisdiction of both court systems. They can sue or be sued in either system, depending mostly on what their case is about. Litigants file nearly all cases (99 percent) in the state courts.[15]

Some Court Fundamentals

Criminal and Civil Cases. A crime is a violation of a law that forbids or commands an activity. Criminal laws are set forth in each state's penal code, as are punishments for violations. Because crime is a violation of public order, the government prosecutes **criminal cases**. Maintaining public order through the enforcement of criminal law is largely a state and local function. Criminal cases brought by the national government represent only a small fraction of all criminal cases prosecuted in the United States.

Courts decide both criminal and civil cases. **Civil cases** stem from disputed claims to something of value. Disputes arise from accidents, contractual obligations, and divorce, for example. Often the parties disagree over

criminal case A court case involving a crime, or violation of public order.

civil case A court case that involves a private dispute arising from such matters as accidents, contractual obligations, and divorce.

FIGURE 11.1 The Federal and State Court Systems, 2006–2007

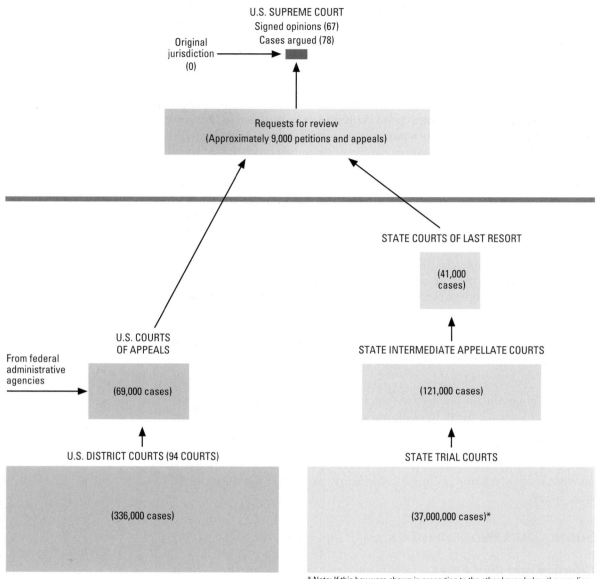

U.S. SUPREME COURT
Signed opinions (67)
Cases argued (78)

Original jurisdiction (0)

Requests for review
(Approximately 9,000 petitions and appeals)

STATE COURTS OF LAST RESORT

(41,000 cases)

U.S. COURTS OF APPEALS

From federal administrative agencies

(69,000 cases)

STATE INTERMEDIATE APPELLATE COURTS

(121,000 cases)

U.S. DISTRICT COURTS (94 COURTS)

(336,000 cases)

STATE TRIAL COURTS

(37,000,000 cases)*

* Note: If this box were shown in proportion to the other boxes below the gray line, the actual size would be approximately 3 feet wide × 1 foot high.

The federal courts have three tiers: district courts, courts of appeals, and the Supreme Court. The Supreme Court was created by the Constitution; all other federal courts were created by Congress. State courts dwarf federal courts, at least in terms of case load. There are more than one hundred state cases for every federal case filed. The structure of state courts varies from state to state; usually there are minor trial courts for less serious cases, major trial courts for more serious cases, intermediate appellate courts, and supreme courts. State courts were created by state constitutions.

Sources: John Roberts, "The 2007 Year-End Report on the Federal Judiciary," 1 January 2008, available at www.supremecourtus.gov/publicinfo/year-end/2007year-endreport.pdf; Federal Court Management Statistics 2007, available at www.uscourts.gov/fcmstat/index.html; Court Statistics Project, State Court Caseload Statistics, 2006 (National Center for State Courts, 2007), available at www.ncsconline.org/D_Research/csp/CSP_Main_Page.html.

tangible issues (possession of property, custody of children), but civil cases can involve more abstract issues too (the right to equal accommodations, damages for pain and suffering). The government can be a party to civil disputes, called on to defend its actions or to allege wrongdoing.

Procedures and Policymaking. Most civil and criminal cases never go to trial. In a criminal case, a defendant's lawyer and the prosecutor might **plea-bargain**, which means they negotiate about the severity and number of charges facing the accused. The defendant pleads guilty to a lesser charge in exchange for the promise of less severe punishment. In a civil case, one side may use a lawsuit as a threat to exact a concession from the other. Often the parties settle their dispute. When parties do not settle, cases end with *adjudication*, a court judgment resolving the parties' claims and ultimately enforced by the government. When trial judges adjudicate cases, they may offer written reasons to support their decisions. When the issues or circumstances of cases are novel, judges may publish *opinions*, explanations justifying their rulings.

Judges make policy in two different ways. Occasionally, in the absence of legislation, they use rules from prior decisions. We call this body of rules **common**, or **judge-made, law**. The roots of common law lie in the English legal system. Contracts, property, and torts (an injury or wrong to the person or property of another) are common law domains. The second area of judicial lawmaking involves the application of statutes enacted by legislatures. The judicial interpretation of legislative acts is called *statutory construction*. To determine how a statute should be applied, judges look for the legislature's intent, reading reports of committee hearings and debates. If these sources do not clarify the statute's meaning, the court does so. With or without legislation to guide them, judges look to the relevant opinions of higher courts for authority to decide the issues before them.

The federal courts are organized in three tiers, as a pyramid. At the bottom of the pyramid are **U.S. district courts**, where litigation begins. In the middle are **U.S. courts of appeals**. At the top is the Supreme Court of the United States. To *appeal* means to take a case to a higher court. The courts of appeals and the Supreme Court are appellate courts; with few exceptions, they review only cases already decided in lower courts.

The U.S. District Courts

There are ninety-four federal district courts in the United States. Each state has at least one district court, and no district straddles more than one state.[16] In 2007 there were 678 authorized federal district judgeships with 647 active judges.[17] These judges received approximately 326,000 new criminal and civil cases.[18]

The district courts are the entry point to the federal court system. When trials occur in the federal system, they take place in the federal district

plea-bargain A defendant's admission of guilt in exchange for a less severe punishment.

common (judge-made) law Legal precedents derived from previous judicial decisions.

U.S. district court A court within the lowest tier of the three-tiered federal court system; the trial court in which litigation begins.

U.S. court of appeals A court within the second tier of the three-tiered federal court system, to which decisions of the district courts and federal agencies may be appealed for review.

courts. Here is where witnesses testify, lawyers conduct cross-examinations, and judges and juries decide the fate of litigants. More than one judge may sit in each district court, but each case is tried by a single judge, sitting alone. Federal magistrates assist district judges, but they lack independent judicial authority. In 2007 there were 505 full-time magistrate positions and 45 part-time magistrate positions.[19]

Sources of Litigation.   Today the authority of U.S. district courts extends to the following types of cases:

- Federal criminal cases as defined by national law (for example, robbery of a federally insured bank or interstate transportation of stolen securities)

- Civil cases brought by individuals, groups, or government alleging violation of national law (for example, failure of a municipality to implement pollution-control regulations required by a national agency)

- Civil cases brought against the national government (for example, a vehicle manufacturer sues the motor pool of a government agency for its failure to take delivery of a fleet of new cars)

- Civil cases between citizens of different states when the amount in controversy exceeds $75,000 (for example, when a citizen of New York sues a citizen of Alabama in a U.S. district court in Alabama for damages stemming from an auto accident that occurred in Alabama)

The U.S. Courts of Appeals

All cases resolved in a U.S. district court and all decisions of federal administrative agencies can be appealed to one of the twelve regional U.S. courts of appeals. These courts, with 167 authorized judgeships, received over 58,000 thousand new cases in 2007.[20] Each appeals court hears cases from a geographic area known as a *circuit*. The United States is divided into twelve circuits.*

Appellate Court Proceedings.   Appellate court proceedings are public, but they usually lack courtroom drama. There are no jurors, witnesses, or cross-examinations; these are features of the trial courts. Appeals are based strictly on the rulings made and procedures followed in the trial courts.

Suppose that in the course of a criminal trial, a U.S. district judge allows the introduction of evidence that convicts a defendant but was ob-

---

*A thirteenth court, the U.S. Court of Appeals for the Federal Circuit, is not a regional court. It specializes in appeals involving patents, contract claims against the national government, and federal employment cases.

tained under questionable circumstances. The defendant can appeal on the grounds that the evidence was obtained in the absence of a valid search warrant and so was inadmissible. The issue on appeal is the admissibility of the evidence, not the defendant's guilt or innocence. If the appellate court agrees with the trial judge's decision to admit the evidence, the conviction stands. If the appellate court disagrees with the trial judge and rules that the evidence is inadmissible, the defendant must be retried without the incriminating evidence or must be released.

It is common for litigants to try to settle their dispute while it is on appeal. Occasionally litigants abandon their appeals for want of resources or resolve. Most of the time, however, appellate courts adjudicate the cases.

The courts of appeals are regional courts. They usually convene in panels of three judges to render judgments. The judges receive written arguments known as *briefs* (which are also sometimes submitted in trial courts). Often the judges hear oral arguments and question the lawyers to probe their arguments.

Precedents and Making Decisions. When an appellate opinion is published, its influence can reach well beyond the immediate case. For example, a lawsuit turning on the meaning of the Constitution produces a ruling that serves as a **precedent** for subsequent cases—that is, the decision becomes a basis for deciding similar cases in the same way. At the appellate level, precedent requires that opinions be written.

Making decisions according to precedent is central to the operation of our legal system, providing continuity and predictability. The bias in favor of existing decisions is captured by the Latin expression ***stare decisis,*** which means "let the decision stand." But the use of precedent and the principle of *stare decisis* do not make lower-court judges cogs in a judicial machine. "If precedent clearly governed," remarked one federal judge, "a case would never get as far as the Court of Appeals: the parties would settle."[21]

Judges on courts of appeals direct their energies to correcting errors in district court proceedings and interpreting the law (in the course of writing opinions). When judges interpret the law, they often modify existing laws. In effect, they are making policy. Judges are politicians in the sense that they exercise political power, but the black robes that distinguish judges from other politicians signal constraints on their exercise of power.

Uniformity of Law. Decisions by the courts of appeals ensure a measure of uniformity in the application of national law. The courts of appeals harmonize the decisions of district judges within their region so that laws are applied uniformly.

Nevertheless, the regional character of the courts of appeals undermines uniformity somewhat because the courts are not bound by the decisions of other circuits. The percolation of cases up through the federal system of courts practically guarantees that at some point, two or more

precedent A judicial ruling that serves as the basis for the ruling in a subsequent case.

stare decisis Literally, "let the decision stand"; decision making according to precedent.

courts of appeals, working with similar sets of facts, are going to interpret the same law differently. However, the problem of conflicting decisions in the intermediate federal courts can be corrected by review in the Supreme Court, where policymaking, not error correction, is the paramount goal.

 ## The Supreme Court

Above the west portico of the Supreme Court Building are inscribed the words EQUAL JUSTICE UNDER LAW. At the opposite end of the building, above the east portico, are the words JUSTICE THE GUARDIAN OF LIBERTY. These mottoes reflect the Court's difficult task: achieving a just balance among the values of freedom, order, and equality. Consider how those values came into conflict in two controversial issues the Court has faced: flag burning and school desegregation.

INTERACTIVE 11.1

 Flag Fight: Free Speech or Felony?

Flag burning as a form of political protest pits the value of order, or the government's interest in maintaining a peaceful society, against the value of freedom, including the individual's right to vigorous and unbounded political expression. In two flag-burning cases, the Supreme Court affirmed constitutional protection for unbridled political expression, including the emotionally charged act of desecrating a national symbol.[22]

School desegregation pits the value of equality against the value of freedom. In *Brown* v. *Board of Education*, the Supreme Court carried the banner of racial equality by striking down state-mandated segregation in public schools. The justices recognized the disorder their decision would create in a society accustomed to racial bias, but in this case, equality

The Supreme Court, 2008 Term: The Lineup

The justices of the Supreme Court of the United States. Seated are *(left to right)* Anthony Kennedy, John Paul Stevens, Chief Justice John Roberts, Antonin Scalia, and David Souter. Standing are Stephen Breyer, Clarence Thomas, Ruth Bader Ginsburg, and Samuel Alito. *(© Brooks Kraft/Corbis)*

clearly outweighed freedom. Twenty-four years later, the Court was still embroiled in controversy over equality when it ruled that race could be a factor in university admissions (to diversify the student body), in *Regents of the University of California* v. *Bakke* (1978).[23] Having secured equality for blacks, the Court in 2003 faced the charge by white students who sought admission to the University of Michigan that it was denying whites the freedom to compete for admission. A slim Court majority concluded that the equal protection clause of the Fourteenth Amendment did not prohibit the narrowly tailored use of race as a factor in law school admissions but rejected the automatic use of racial categories to award fixed points toward undergraduate admissions.[24]

The use of race in assigning students to public schools was narrowed significantly in *Parents Involved in Community Schools* v. *Seattle School Dist. No. 1* (2007). In a deeply divided decision that addressed parallel cases in Seattle, Washington, and Louisville, Kentucky, the Court struck down two desegregation plans that classified students by race and used that information to determine where students would go to school to achieve racial balance. Though the plans were intended to integrate students rather than segregate them, the majority ruled that race was inappropriately used by the school district in plans that were not narrowly tailored. Though district administrators may consider race in the context of broader goals and issues, the broad and blunt use of race as a determining factor was struck down.[25]

The Supreme Court makes national policy. Because its decisions have far-reaching effects on all of us, it is vital that we understand how it reaches those decisions.

Access to the Court

There are rules of access that must be followed to bring a case to the Supreme Court. Also important is sensitivity to the justices' policy and ideological preferences. The notion that anyone can take a case all the way to the Supreme Court is true only in theory, not in fact.

The Supreme Court's cases come from two sources. A few arrive under the Court's **original jurisdiction,** conferred by Article III, Section 2, of the Constitution, which gives the Court the power to hear and decide "all Cases affecting Ambassadors, other public Ministers and Consuls, and those in which a State shall be a Party." Cases falling under the Court's original jurisdiction are tried and decided in the Court itself; the cases begin and end there. For example, the Court is the first and only forum in which legal disputes between states are resolved. Most cases enter the Supreme Court from the U.S. courts of appeals or the state courts of last resort. These cases are within the Court's **appellate jurisdiction.** They have been tried, decided, and reexamined as far as the law permits in other federal or state courts. The Supreme Court exercises judicial power under its appellate jurisdiction because Congress gives it the authority to do so. Congress

original jurisdiction The authority of a court to hear a case before any other court does.

appellate jurisdiction The authority of a court to hear cases that have been tried, decided, or reexamined in other courts.

may change (and perhaps eliminate) the Court's appellate jurisdiction. This is a powerful but rarely used weapon in the congressional arsenal of checks and balances.

Litigants in state cases who invoke the Court's appellate jurisdiction must satisfy two conditions. First, the case must reach the end of the line in the state court system. Litigants cannot jump at will from state to federal arenas of justice. Second, the case must raise a **federal question,** an issue covered under the Constitution, federal laws, or national treaties. However, even most cases that meet these conditions do not reach the Supreme Court.

Since 1925, the Court has exercised substantial (today, nearly complete) control over its **docket,** or agenda. The Court selects a handful of cases (fewer than one hundred) for consideration from the seven thousand or more requests filed each year. These requests take the form of petitions for *certiorari,* in which a litigant seeking review asks the Court "to become informed" of the lower-court proceedings. For the vast majority of cases, the Court denies the petition for *certiorari,* leaving the decision of the lower court undisturbed. No explanations accompany cases that are denied review, so they have little or no value as Court rulings.

The Court grants a review only when four or more justices agree that a case warrants full consideration. This unwritten rule is known as the **rule of four.** With advance preparation by their law clerks, who screen petitions and prepare summaries, all nine justices make these judgments at conferences held twice a week.[26] During these conferences, justices vote on previously argued cases and consider which new cases to add to the docket.

Business cases represent a substantial portion of the Court's docket, though they receive far less attention than cases addressing social issues such as the death penalty, affirmative action, or school prayer. Business disputes are less emotional and the issues more technical. But business cases involve billions of dollars, have enormous consequences for the economy, and affect people's lives more often than the social issues that tend to dominate public debate and discussion.[27]

The Solicitor General

Why does the Court decide to hear certain cases but not others? The best evidence scholars have adduced suggests that agenda setting depends on the individual justices, who vary in their decision-making criteria and the issues raised by the cases. Occasionally justices weigh the ultimate outcome of a case when granting or denying review. At other times, justices grant or deny review based on disagreement among the lower courts or because delay in resolving the issues would impose alarming economic or social costs.[28] The solicitor general plays a vital role in the Court's agenda setting.

The **solicitor general** represents the national government before the Supreme Court. Appointed by the president, the solicitor general is the third-highest-ranking official in the U.S. Department of Justice (after the attorney general and the deputy attorney general). The solicitor general's duties in-

federal question An issue covered by the U.S. Constitution, national laws, or U.S. treaties.

docket A court's agenda.

rule of four An unwritten rule that requires at least four justices to agree that a case warrants consideration before it is reviewed by the Supreme Court.

solicitor general The third-highest-ranking official of the U.S. Department of Justice, and the one who represents the national government before the Supreme Court.

clude determining whether the government should appeal lower-court decisions; reviewing and modifying, when necessary, the briefs filed in government appeals; and deciding whether the government should file an **amicus curiae brief*** in any appellate court.[29] The objective is to create a cohesive program for the executive branch in the federal courts. Solicitors general are a "formidable force" in the setting of the Supreme Court's agenda.[30] Their influence in bringing cases to the Court and arguing them there has earned the solicitor general the informal title of "the tenth justice."

Decision Making

Once the Court grants review, attorneys submit written arguments (briefs). Oral arguments, limited to thirty minutes for each side, usually follow. From October through April, the justices spend four hours a day, five or six days a month, hearing arguments. They reach no collective decision at oral argument. A tentative decision is reached only after they have met in conference.

Only the justices attend the Court's Wednesday and Friday conferences. After the justices shake hands, the chief justice begins the presentation of each case with a discussion of it and his vote, which is followed by a discussion and vote from each of the other justices, in order of their seniority on the Court. As Justice Antonin Scalia once remarked, "To call our discussion of a case a conference is really something of a misnomer. It's much more a statement of the views of each of the nine Justices, after which the totals are added and the case is assigned" for an opinion.[31] Votes remain tentative until the opinion announcing the Court's judgment is issued.

Judicial Restraint and Judicial Activism. How do the justices decide how to vote on a case? According to some scholars, legal doctrines and past decisions explain their votes. This explanation, which is consistent with the majoritarian model, anchors the justices closely to the law and minimizes the contribution of their personal values. This view is embodied in the concept of **judicial restraint**, which maintains that legislators, not judges, should make the laws. Judges are said to exercise judicial restraint when they hew closely to statutes and previous cases in reaching their decisions. Other scholars contend that the value preferences and resulting ideologies of the justices provide a more powerful interpretation of their voting.[32] This view is embodied in the concept of **judicial activism,** which maintains that judges should interpret laws loosely, using their power to promote their preferred social and political goals. Judges are said to exercise judicial activism when they seem to interpret existing laws and rulings

amicus curiae brief A brief filed (with the permission of the court) by an individual or group that is not a party to a legal action but has an interest in it.

judicial restraint A judicial philosophy whereby judges adhere closely to statutes and precedents in reaching their decisions.

judicial activism A judicial philosophy whereby judges interpret existing laws and precedents loosely and interject their own values in court decisions.

---

*Amicus curiae is Latin for "friend of the court." Amicus briefs can be filed with the consent of the Court. They allow groups and individuals who are not parties to the litigation but have an interest in it to influence the Court's thinking and, perhaps, its decision.

with little regard to precedent and to interject their own values into court decisions. Judicial activism, which is consistent with the pluralist model, sees the justices as actively promoting their value preferences.

Judgment and Argument.   The voting outcome is the **judgment**, the decision on who wins and who loses. The justices often disagree, not only on winners and losers but also on the reasons for their judgments. After voting, a justice in the majority must draft an opinion setting out the reasons for their decision. The **argument** is the kernel of the opinion—its logical content, as distinct from facts, rhetoric, and procedure. If all justices agree with the judgment and the reasons supporting it, the opinion is unanimous. Agreement with a judgment for reasons different from those set forth in the majority opinion is called a **concurrence**. Or a justice can **dissent** if she or he disagrees with a judgment. Both concurring and dissenting opinions may be drafted in addition to the majority opinion.

The Opinion.   After the conference, the chief justice writes the majority opinion or assigns that responsibility to another justice in the majority. If the chief justice is not in the majority, the writing or assigning responsibility rests with the most senior associate justice in the majority. An opinion may have to be rewritten several times to accommodate colleagues who remain unpersuaded by the draft. Justices can change their votes, and perhaps alter the judgment, at any time before the decision is officially announced.

Justices in the majority frequently try to muffle or stifle dissent in order to encourage institutional cohesion. Since the mid-1940s, however, unity has been more difficult to obtain.[33] Gaining agreement from the justices today is akin to negotiating with nine separate law firms. Nevertheless, the justices must be keenly aware of the slender foundation of their authority, which rests largely on public respect. That respect is tested whenever the Court ventures into areas of controversy. Freedom of speech and religion, racial equality, the right to privacy, and the extent of presidential power have led the Court into controversy in the past half-century.

Strategies on the Court

judgment The judicial decision in a court case.

argument The heart of a judicial opinion; its logical content separated from facts, rhetoric, and procedure.

concurrence The agreement of a judge with the court's majority decision, for a reason other than the majority reason.

dissent The disagreement of a judge with a majority decision.

If we start with the assumption that the justices attempt to stamp their own policy views on the cases they review, we should expect typical political behavior from them. Because the justices are grappling with conflict on a daily basis, they probably have well-defined ideologies that reflect their values.

Scholars and journalists have attempted to pierce the veil of secrecy that shrouds the Court from public view and analyze the justices' ideologies.[34] The beliefs of most justices can be located on the two-dimensional model of political values discussed in Chapter 1 (see Figure 1.2). Liberal justices, such as John Paul Stevens and Ruth Bader Ginsburg, choose freedom over order and equality over freedom. Conservative justices—Antonin Scalia and Clarence Thomas, for example—choose order over freedom and freedom over equality. These choices translate into policy preferences as the justices struggle to win votes or retain coalitions.

As in any other group of people, the justices also vary in intellectual ability, advocacy skills, social graces, temperament, and other characteristics. They argue for the support of their colleagues, offering information in the form of drafts and memoranda to explain the advantages and disadvantages of voting for or against an issue. And the justices make occasional, if not regular, use of friendship, ridicule, and appeals to patriotism to mold their colleagues' views.

The Chief Justice

The chief justice is only one of nine justices, but he has several important functions based on his authority. Apart from his role in forming the docket and directing the Court's conferences, the chief justice can also be a social leader, generating solidarity within the group. Sometimes a chief justice can embody intellectual leadership. The chief justice also can provide policy leadership, directing the Court toward a general policy position.

When presiding at the conference, the chief justice can control the discussion of issues, although independent-minded justices are not likely to acquiesce to his views. Moreover, justices today rarely engage in a debate of the issues in the conference. Rather, they use their law clerks as ambassadors between justices' chambers and, in effect, "run the Court without talking to one another."[35]

 Judicial Recruitment

Neither the Constitution nor national law imposes formal requirements for appointment to the federal courts. Once appointed, district court and appeals judges must reside in the district or circuit to which they are appointed. The president appoints judges to the federal courts, and all nominees must be confirmed by the Senate. Congress sets, but cannot lower, a judge's compensation.

State courts operate somewhat similarly. Governors appoint judges in more than half the states, often in consultation with judicial nominating commissions. In many of these states, voters decide whether judges should be retained in office. In some states, nominees must be confirmed by the state legislature. Contested elections for judgeships are relatively unusual, but in 2006 eleven states had contested elections for their supreme courts. Ten of these states allowed television advertising by their supreme court candidates. Candidates for the Alabama Supreme Court alone raised some $13.4 million in campaign funds. In 2008, there were twenty-six state supreme court seats up for grab in contestable elections throughout the United States. Given the emphasis in federal courts on an independent judiciary

DO IT!

Thirty-eight states hold some type of election for state high court judges. What about your state? How much money do judicial candidates spend? Find out at www.followthemoney.org/database/graphs/judicial/index.phtml.

free of electoral pressures and perceived conflicts of interest, it should come as no surprise that there are many critics of state judicial elections.[36]

The Appointment of Federal Judges

The Constitution states that federal judges hold their commission "during good Behaviour," which in practice means for life.* A president's judicial appointments, then, are likely to survive his administration, providing a kind of political legacy. The appointment power assumes that the president is free to identify candidates and appoint judges who favor his policies.

Judicial vacancies occur when sitting judges resign, retire, or die. Vacancies also arise when Congress creates new judgeships to handle increasing caseloads. In both cases, the president nominates a candidate, who must be confirmed by the Senate. The president has the help of the Justice Department, which screens candidates before the formal nomination, subjecting serious contenders to FBI investigation. The White House and the Justice Department have formed a Judicial Selection Committee as part of this vetting process. The White House and the Senate vie for control in the appointment of district and appeals judges.

The "Advice and Consent" of the Senate. For district and appeals vacancies, a practice called **senatorial courtesy** forces presidents to share the nomination power with members of the Senate. The Senate will not confirm a nominee who is opposed by the senior senator from the nominee's state if that senator is a member of the president's party. The Judicial Selection Committee searches for acceptable candidates and polls the appropriate senator for her or his reaction to them. The Senate does not actually reject the candidate. Instead, the chairman of the Senate Judiciary Committee, which reviews all judicial nominees, will not schedule a confirmation hearing, effectively killing the nomination.

The Senate Judiciary Committee conducts a hearing for each judicial nominee. The chairperson exercises a measure of control in the appointment process that goes beyond senatorial courtesy. If a nominee is objectionable to the chair, he or she can delay a hearing or hold up other appointments until the president and the Justice Department find an alternative.

The American Bar Association. The American Bar Association (ABA), the biggest organization of lawyers in the United States, has been involved in evaluating candidates for the federal bench since 1946.[37] Its role is defined by custom, not law. The ABA's Standing Committee on the Federal Judiciary routinely rates the professional qualifications of prospective appointees, using a three-value scale: "well qualified," "qualified," and

senatorial courtesy A practice whereby the Senate will not confirm for a lower federal court judgeship a nominee who is opposed by the senior senator in the president's party in the nominee's state.

---

*Only twelve federal judges have been impeached. Of these, seven were convicted in the Senate and removed from office. Three judges were impeached by the Senate in the 1980s. In 1992, Alcee Hastings became the first such judge to serve in Congress.

Justice Thomas & Company
Justice Clarence Thomas meets with his law clerks in his chambers at the Supreme Court. Justices assign a range of responsibilities to their clerks, from memo preparation to opinion drafting. The typical clerkship lasts a year, though it may seem longer at times because of the demanding work schedule. Despite the absence of overtime pay, there is no shortage of applications from the best graduates of the best law schools. *(© David Hume Kennerly/Getty Images)*

"not qualified." The association no longer has advance notice of possible nominees. The George W. Bush administration considered the ABA too liberal, posing an unnecessary impediment to the confirmation of conservative judges.[38] Nonetheless, the ABA continues to evaluate the professional qualifications of nominees after they have been nominated.

Recent Presidents and the Federal Judiciary

Since the presidency of Jimmy Carter, presidents have tended to make appointments to the federal courts that are more diverse in racial, ethnic, and gender terms than in previous administrations. President Bill Clinton took the lead on diversity. For the first time in history, more than half of a president's judicial appointments were women or minorities. In his first term in office, George W. Bush appointed more Hispanics to the bench (9 percent) than any of his predecessors. Twenty-two percent of the president's confirmed judicial nominees were women.[39]

The racial and ethnic composition of the parties themselves helps to explain much of the variation between the appointments of presidents of different parties. It seems clear that political ideology, not demographics, lies at the heart of judicial appointments. A review of more than 25,000 federal court decisions from 1968 to 1995 concluded that Carter-appointed judges were the most liberal, whereas judges appointed by Ronald Reagan and George H. W. Bush were the least liberal.[40] George W. Bush's judges are among the most conservative when it comes to civil rights and civil liberties.[41] One general rule seems clear: presidents like to appoint judges who share similar values.

Appointment to the Supreme Court

The president is not shackled by senatorial courtesy when it comes to nominating a Supreme Court justice. However, appointments to the Court attract more intense public scrutiny than do lower-level appointments, effectively narrowing the president's options and focusing attention on the Senate's advice and consent.

Presidents have sent the Senate 158 nominations for the Supreme Court, including nominations for the chief justice. Of these nominations, 122 were confirmed by the Senate (though seven of those ultimately declined to serve). Eleven names were withdrawn, and the other twenty-five failed to receive Senate confirmation.[42] The most important factor in the rejection of a nominee is partisan politics.

Eighteen of the twenty-four successful Supreme Court nominees since 1950 have had prior judicial experience in federal or state courts. This tendency toward "promotion" from within the judiciary may be based on the idea that judges' previous opinions are good predictors of their future opinions on the Supreme Court. After all, a president is handing out a powerful lifetime appointment; it makes sense to want an individual who is sympathetic to his views.

When Sandra Day O'Connor announced her retirement in 2005, President Bush nominated John G. Roberts to replace her. Roberts had served for two years on the U.S. Court of Appeals for the District of Columbia. Prior to Roberts's confirmation hearings, Chief Justice William Rehnquist died. Bush withdrew the Roberts nomination for associate justice and nominated him to fill Rehnquist's seat instead. He was confirmed by the Senate and joined the Court in 2005. Bush's second nomination to serve as associate justice was Harriet Miers, Counsel to the President on the White House staff. Though a distinguished corporate lawyer, Miers had not previously served as a judge. After contentious debates, Bush withdrew her nomination and nominated a third individual to fill the seat O'Connor was vacating. This nominee, Samuel A. Alito, had the judicial credentials Miers lacked, having served on the Third Circuit Court of Appeals for fifteen years. Alito was confirmed by the Senate and joined the court as the 110th justice in 2006.

The results of the Roberts and Alito appointments were soon apparent. In the 2006 term—the first full term with Roberts and Alito on the bench—the Court moved in a decidedly conservative direction. One-third of all the cases were decided by a vote of 5–4, almost triple the proportion of close votes from the previous term. In each case, Justice Anthony Kennedy cast the deciding vote. He joined the majority in all twenty-four 5–4 decisions, siding more often with his conservative colleagues (see Figure 11.2).

FIGURE 11.2   Courting the Justice in the Middle

If you wondered who casts the deciding vote today in the Supreme Court, you need look no further than Justice Anthony Kennedy. In all the closely divided cases in the 2006 term (October 2006 through June 2007), Kennedy was the single justice in the majority for every case. It is no surprise that attorneys pitch their arguments to him. Their cases are likely to prevail or fail depending on his vote.

Source: "Roberts Court Unites on Business," *Wall Street Journal,* 30 June and 1 July 2007, p. A5.

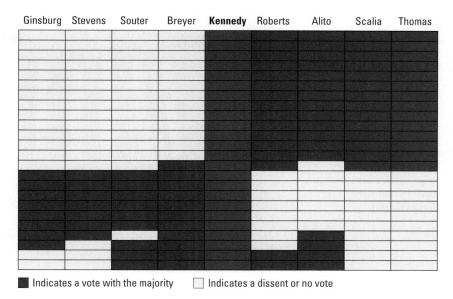

■ Indicates a vote with the majority   □ Indicates a dissent or no vote

The Consequences of Judicial Decisions

Of all the lawsuits begun in the United States, the overwhelming majority end without a court judgment. Many civil cases are settled, or the parties give up, or the courts dismiss the suits because they are beyond the legitimate bounds of judicial resolution. Most criminal cases end with a plea bargain, the defendant's admission of guilt in exchange for a less severe punishment. Only about 10 percent of criminal cases in the federal district courts are tried; an equally small percentage of civil cases are adjudicated.

Furthermore, the fact that a judge sentences a criminal defendant to ten years in prison or a court holds a company liable for $11 billion in damages does not guarantee that the defendant will lose his or her freedom or the company will give up any assets. In the cases of criminal defendants, the road of appeal following trial and conviction is well traveled, and if it accomplishes nothing else, an appeal delays the day when a defendant must go to prison. In civil cases as well, an appeal may be filed to delay the day of reckoning.

Supreme Court Rulings: Implementation and Impact

When the Supreme Court makes a decision, it relies on others to implement it, to translate policy into action. How a judgment is implemented

Deal
Chief Justice John G. Roberts Jr. greets newest colleague, Associate Justice Samuel A. Alito. Both Roberts and Alito possess strong conservative credentials. Their appointments were a consequence of Republican victories in the 2004 elections. The Court has shifted in a more conservative direction. *(© Tim Sloan/AFP/ Getty Images)*

rests in good measure on how it was crafted. Remember that the justices, in preparing their opinions, must work to hold their majorities together to gain greater, if not unanimous, support for their arguments. This forces them to compromise in their opinions and to moderate their arguments, and it introduces ambiguity into many of the policies they articulate. Ambiguous opinions affect the implementation of policy. For example, when the Supreme Court issued its order in 1955 to desegregate public school facilities "with all deliberate speed,"[43] judges who opposed the Court's policy dragged their feet in implementing it.

Because the Supreme Court confronts issues freighted with deeply felt social values or fundamental political beliefs, its decisions have an impact beyond the immediate parties in a dispute. The Court's decision in *Roe* v. *Wade* legalizing abortion generated heated public reaction. Groups opposing abortion vowed to overturn the decision; groups favoring the freedom to obtain an abortion moved to protect the right they had won. Within eight months of the decision, more than two dozen constitutional amendments had been introduced in Congress, although none managed to carry the extraordinary majority required for passage.

Public Opinion and the Supreme Court

Democratic theorists have a difficult time reconciling a commitment to representative democracy with a judiciary that is not accountable to the electorate yet has the power to undo legislative and executive acts. This difficulty may simply be a problem for theorists, however. Policies coming from the Supreme Court, though lagging years behind public opinion, rarely seem out of line with the public's ideological choices.[44] Surveys in several controversial areas reveal that the Court seldom departs from majority sentiment or trends.[45] The evidence squarely supports the view that the Supreme Court reflects public opinion at least as often as other elected institutions do.[46]

There are at least three explanations for the Court's reflecting majority sentiment. First, the modern Court has shown deference to national laws and policies, which typically echo national public opinion. Second, the Court moves closer to public opinion during periods of crisis. Third, rulings that reflect the public view are subject to fewer changes than rulings that depart from public opinion. The fit is not perfect, however, and the Court occasionally steps into a minefield of criticism. In 2005 the Court ruled that the Constitution did not forbid a city from taking private property for private development.[47] The outrage across the ideological spectrum was enormous and immediate. State legislatures and courts acted swiftly to give greater protection to private property. This was strong evidence that the Court's measured opinion was out of step with conventional wisdom.

Following the 2000 presidential election, polling organizations documented a large gap in the Court's approval ratings between Democrats and Republicans. But time seems to have healed that wound, and today there is virtually no difference in support for the Court across political party affiliation. So despite the barrage of criticism, the Court weathered the controversial 2000 presidential election with no sustainable damage to its integrity.[48]

The evidence also supports the view that the Court seldom influences public opinion. The Court enjoys only moderate popularity, and its decisions are not much noticed by the public. With few exceptions, there is no evidence of shifting public opinion after a Supreme Court ruling.[49]

The Courts and Models of Democracy

How far should judges stray from existing statutes and precedents? Supporters of the majoritarian model argue that judges must refrain from injecting their own values into their decisions. If the law places too much (or not enough) emphasis on equality or order, the elected legislature, not the courts, can change the law. In contrast, those who support the pluralist model maintain that the courts are a policymaking branch of government. It is thus legitimate for the individual values and interests of judges to mirror group interests and preferences and for judges to consciously attempt to advance group interests as they see fit. However, when, where, and how to proceed are difficult for judges at all levels to determine (see "Politics of Global Change: The Right to Die").

The argument that our judicial system fits the pluralist model gains support from a legal procedure called a **class action**. A class action is a device

class action A procedure by which similarly situated litigants may be heard in a single lawsuit.

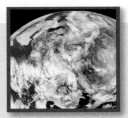

Politics of Global Change

The Right to Die

In June 1997, the Supreme Court ended its long silence on the constitutionality of a right to suicide, rejecting two separate challenges to state laws prohibiting assisted suicide. In 1996, the U.S. Court of Appeals for the Ninth Circuit relied on the Supreme Court's abortion decisions to strike down a Washington State law against aiding or abetting suicide. The circuit court reasoned from the High Court's abortion rulings that the Fourteenth Amendment's due process clause protects the individual's right "to define one's own concept of existence, of meaning, of the universe, and of the mystery of life." The Supreme Court, however, in *Washington* v. *Glucksberg*, unanimously rejected the circuit court's reasoning, in no uncertain terms stressing that suicide is not a "fundamental right" that is "deeply rooted in our legal tradition." Unlike abortion, suicide has been all but universally condemned in the law.

In another 1996 decision, the U.S. Court of Appeals for the Second Circuit adopted a different line of reasoning to invalidate a New York law banning physician-assisted suicide. The court held that the law violated the Fourteenth Amendment's equal protection clause because it treated those who needed a physician's help to administer lethal doses of prescription drugs (which is criminalized by law) differently from those who can demand removal of life-support systems (which is allowed under prior Supreme Court cases). In June 1997, the Supreme Court unanimously rejected this argument in *Vacco* v. *Quill*. The Court held that the New York law does not result in similar cases being treated differently. "The distinction between letting a patient die and making that patient die is important, logical, rational, and well established," the majority declared.

The Supreme Court displayed an acute awareness of the ongoing debate in the states about assisted suicide. Because the Court determined only that the U.S. Constitution does not protect a right to assisted suicide, the states may still establish such a right by statute or state constitutional amendments.

for assembling the claims or defenses of similarly situated individuals so that they can be tried in a single lawsuit. A class action makes it possible for people with small individual claims and limited financial resources to aggregate their claims and resources in order to make a lawsuit viable. Since the 1940s, class action suits have been the vehicles through which groups have asserted claims involving civil rights, legislative apportionment, and environmental problems. For example, schoolchildren have

In 2008 voters in the state of Washington established a limited right to assisted suicide. Prior to this, only Oregon recognized such a right. Modeled after Oregon's Death with Dignity Act, the Washington law sets out a detailed set of conditions that terminally ill individuals and their doctors must follow in order to implement physician assisted suicide. From 1998 through 2007, 341 people in Oregon have died in this fashion.

In a much more complicated case, the Supreme Court spoke through its silence. In 1990, Terri Schiavo suffered cardiac arrest that led to irreversible brain damage. In the ensuing fifteen years, she was aided by a feeding tube to provide nutrition and hydration. Her husband (and legal guardian) received state court approval to remove the tube and hasten her death. The U.S. Supreme Court refused to get involved after a federal court turned down a plea by her family to reinsert the feeding tube. The Florida governor, the Florida legislature, the U.S. Congress, and President George W. Bush all sought to intervene and encroach on judicial authority, but to no avail. Schiavo died without regaining consciousness.

Other industrial democracies have tacked in a different direction by decriminalizing euthanasia, as assisted suicide is sometimes called. The Netherlands, Belgium, and Switzerland have adopted distinct laws that regulate the right to a mercy death. Physician-assisted suicide is legal in the Netherlands, whereas Swiss law decriminalizes assisted suicide only when physicians are not involved. The Swiss legislation on assisted suicide is one of the most liberal in the world, and "many terminally ill foreigners . . . now travel to Switzerland to commit suicide." Since 2005, in Belgium pharmacists can supply doctors with fatal doses of medicines permitting assisted suicide.

Sources: Washington v. *Glucksberg,* 521 U.S. 793 (1997); *Vacco* v. *Quill,* 521 U.S. 702 (1997); *Compassion in Dying* v. *Washington,* 79 F.3d 790 (9th Cir. 1996); *Quill* v. *Vacco,* 80 F.3d 716 (2d Cir. 1996); *Tenth Annual Report on Oregon's Death with Dignity Act,* March 2008, available at http://egov.oregon.gov/DHS/ph/pas/docs/year10.pdf; K. L. Cerminara and K. W. Goodman, *Key Events in the Case of Theresa Marie Schiavo,* available at www.miami.edu/ethics/schiavo/timeline.htm; "Schiavo Parents Back in Federal Court. Supreme Court, State Judge Deny Appeals to Resume Feeding," *CNN On Line,* 25 March 2005, available at www.cnn.com/2005/LAW/03/24/schiavo; Ursula Smartt, "Euthanasia and the law," BBC News, 21 February 2007, available at http://news.bbc.co.uk/1/hi/health/2600923.stm.

sued (through their parents) under the banner of class action to rectify claimed racial discrimination by school authorities, as in *Brown* v. *Board of Education.*

Abetting the class action is the resurgence of state supreme courts' fashioning policies consistent with group preferences. State courts may serve as the staging areas for legal campaigns to change the law in the nation's highest court. They also exercise substantial influence over policies that affect citizens daily, including the rights and liberties enshrined in their state constitutions, statutes, and common law.[50]

Furthermore, a state court can avoid review by the U.S. Supreme Court by basing its decision solely on state law or by plainly stating that its decision rests on both state and federal law. If a state court chooses to rely solely on national law in deciding a case, that case is reviewable by the U.S. Supreme Court. If the U.S. Supreme Court is likely to render a restrictive view of a constitutional right and the judges of a state court are inclined toward a more expansive view, the state judges can use the state ground to avoid Supreme Court review. In a period when the nation's highest court is moving in a conservative direction, some state courts have become safe havens for liberal values.

When judges reach decisions, they pay attention to the views of other courts, and not just courts above them in the judicial hierarchy. State and federal court opinions are the legal storehouse from which judges regularly draw their ideas. Often the issues that affect individual lives—property, family, contracts—are grist for state courts, not federal courts. State courts have become arenas for political conflict with litigants, individually or in groups, vying for their preferred policies. The multiplicity of the nation's court system, with overlapping state and federal responsibilities, provides alternative points of access for individuals and groups to present and argue their claims. This description of the courts fits the pluralist model of government.

Summary

The power of judicial review, claimed by the Supreme Court in 1803, placed the judiciary on an equal footing with Congress and the president. The principle of checks and balances can restrain judicial power through several means, such as constitutional amendments and impeachment. But restrictions have been infrequent, and the federal courts exercise considerable influence through judicial review and statutory construction.

The federal court system has three tiers. At the bottom are district courts, where litigation begins and most disputes end. In the middle are courts of appeals. At the top is the Supreme Court. The ability of judges to make policy increases as they move up the pyramid from trial courts to appellate courts to the Supreme Court.

The Supreme Court, free to draft its agenda through the discretionary control of its docket, harmonizes conflicting interpretations of national law and articulates constitutional rights. It is helped at this crucial stage by the solicitor general, who represents the executive branch of government before the Court. The solicitor general's influence affects the justices' choice of cases to review.

Political allegiance and complementary values are necessary conditions for appointment by the president to the coveted position of judge. The president and senators from the president's party share the power of appointment of federal district and appellate judges. The president has more leeway in the nomination of Supreme Court justices, although all nominees must be confirmed by the Senate.

Courts inevitably fashion policy for each of the states and for the nation. They provide multiple points of access for individuals to pursue their preferences and so fit the pluralist model of democracy. Furthermore, the class action enables people with small individual claims and limited financial resources to pursue their goals in court, reinforcing the pluralist model.

Judges confront both the original and the modern dilemmas of government. The impact of their decisions can extend well beyond a single case. Some democratic theorists are troubled by the expansion of judicial power. But today's courts fit within the pluralist model and usually are in step with what the public wants.

As the U.S. Supreme Court heads in a more conservative direction, some state supreme courts have become safe havens for liberal policies on civil rights and civil liberties. State court systems have overlapping state and national responsibilities, offering groups and individuals many access points to present and argue their claims.

CL **Resources:** Videos, Simulations, News, Timelines, Primary Sources

CHAPTER 12

Order and Civil Liberties

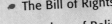

- The Bill of Rights
- Freedom of Religion
- Freedom of Expression
- The Right to Bear Arms
- Applying the Bill of Rights to the States
- The Ninth Amendment and Personal Autonomy

This icon will direct you to resources and activities on the website: www.cengage.com/polisci/janda/chall_dem_brief/7e

IN SEPTEMBER 2006, THE
Bayonne, New Jersey, public school system established a mandatory uniform policy for students from kindergarten through eighth grade. The school board expressed concern that some clothing might pose health or safety issues, create disorder, or prove disruptive to the educational process. The policy mandated that boys and girls wear a prescribed uniform each day.

Two fifth-graders, Michael DePinto and Anthony LaRocco, decided to protest the policy. They came to school sporting buttons depicting a photograph of a Hitler Youth group with a superimposed red circle plus slash and the phrase "No School Uniforms." The principal threatened suspension if the buttons were not removed. The parents sought an injunction in federal court to prevent the suspensions, arguing that suspension would infringe on the students' freedom of expression. Given the age of the protesters, the school district maintained that it could prohibit the wearing of the buttons.

Can school officials suppress student expression? (The answer will come later in this chapter.) More generally, how well do the courts respond to clashes that pit freedom against order in some cases and freedom against equality in others? Are freedom, order, or equality ever unconditional? In this chapter, we explore some value conflicts that the judiciary has resolved. You will be able to judge from the decisions in these cases whether American government has met the challenge of democracy by finding the appropriate balance between freedom and order and between freedom and equality.

The value conflicts described in this chapter revolve around claims or entitlements that rest on law. Although we concentrate on conflicts over constitutional issues, the Constitution is not the only source of people's rights. Government at all levels can—and does—create rights through laws written by legislatures and regulations issued by bureaucracies.

We begin this chapter with the Bill of Rights and the freedoms it protects. Then we take a closer look at the role of the First Amendment in the original conflict between freedom and order. Next we explore how the Bill of Rights applies to the states under the Fourteenth Amendment. Then we examine the Ninth Amendment and its relationship to issues of personal autonomy.

The Bill of Rights

You may remember from Chapter 2 that the omission of a bill of rights was the most important obstacle to the adoption of the Constitution by the states. Eventually the First Congress approved twelve amendments and sent them to the states for ratification. In 1791, ten were ratified, and the nation had a bill of rights.

Compared with What?

Britain's Bill of Rights

Britain does not have a written constitution, that is, a deliberate scheme of government formally adopted by the people and specifying special processes for its amendment. In Britain, no single document or law is known as "the constitution." Instead, Britain has an "unwritten constitution," an amalgam of important documents and laws passed by Parliament (the British legislature), court decisions, customs, and conventions. Britain's "constitution" has no existence apart from ordinary law. In contrast to the American system of government, Britain's Parliament may change, amend, or abolish its fundamental laws and conventions at will. No special proce-

dures or barriers must be overcome to enact such changes.

According to government leaders, Britain has done very well without a written constitution. Or at least that was the position of Prime Minister Margaret Thatcher when she was presented with a proposal for a written constitution in 1989. Thatcher observed that despite Britain's lack of a bill of rights and an independent judiciary, "our present constitutional arrangements continue to serve us well. . . . Furthermore, the government does not feel that a written constitution in itself changes or guarantees anything."

In 1995, a nationwide poll revealed that the British people held a

---

The Bill of Rights imposed limits on the national government but not on the state governments.* During the next seventy-seven years, litigants pressed the Supreme Court to extend the amendments' restraints to the states, but the Court refused until well after the adoption of the Fourteenth Amendment in 1868. Before then, protection from repressive state government had to come from state bills of rights.

The U.S. Constitution guarantees Americans numerous liberties and rights. In this chapter, we explore several of them. We will define and distinguish between *civil liberties* and *civil rights* (although on some occasions, we use the terms interchangeably). **Civil liberties** are freedoms that are guar-

---

*Congress considered more than one hundred amendments in its first session. One that was not approved would have limited the power of the states to infringe on the rights on conscience, speech, press, and jury trial in criminal cases. James Madison thought this amendment was the "most valuable" of the list, but it failed to muster a two-thirds vote in the Senate.

civil liberties Freedoms guaranteed to individuals.

different view. Three-fourths of British adults thought that it was time for a written constitution, and even more maintained that the country needed a written bill of rights. These high levels of public support and the election of a new government in 1997 helped to build momentum for important changes. In October 2000, England formally began enforcing the Human Rights Act, a key component of the government's political program, which incorporated into British law sixteen guarantees of the European Convention on Human Rights. Thus, the nation that has been the source of some of the world's most significant ideas concerning liberty and individual freedom finally put into writing guarantees to ensure these fundamental rights for its own citizens. Legal experts hailed the edict as the largest change to British law in three centuries.

It remains to be seen whether the Human Rights Act will, in the words of one former minister in the Thatcher government, "rob us of freedoms we have had for centuries" or, as British human rights lawyer Geoffrey Robertson sees it, "help produce a better culture of liberty." Perhaps the track record of the United States and its nearly 220 years of experience with the Bill of Rights will prove useful to our British "cousins," who appear ready to alter their system of unwritten rules.

Sources: Andrew Marr, *Ruling Britannia: The Failure and Future of British Democracy* (London: Michael Joseph, 1995); Will Hutton, *The State We're In* (London: Cape, 1995); Fred Barbash, "The Movement to Rule Britannia Differently," *Washington Post,* 23 September 1995, p. A27; "Bringing Rights Home," *The Economist,* 26 August 2000, pp. 45–46; Sarah Lyall, "209 Years Later, the English Get American-Style Bill of Rights," *New York Times,* 2 October 2000, p. A3; Suzanne Kapner, "Britain's Legal Barriers Start to Fall," *New York Times,* 4 October 2000, p. W1.

anteed to the individual. The guarantees take the form of restraints on government. For example, the First Amendment declares that "Congress shall make no law . . . abridging the freedom of speech." Civil liberties declare what the government cannot do. In contrast, civil rights declare what the government must do or provide.

Civil rights are powers or privileges that are guaranteed to the individual and protected against arbitrary removal at the hands of the government or other individuals. The right to vote and the right to a jury trial in criminal cases are civil rights embedded in the Constitution. Today, civil rights also embrace laws that further certain values. The Civil Rights Act of 1964, for example, furthered the value of equality by establishing the right to nondiscrimination in places of public accommodation and the right to equal employment opportunity.

The Bill of Rights lists both civil liberties and civil rights. When we refer to the "rights and liberties" of the Constitution, we mean the protections enshrined in the Bill of Rights and the first section of the Fourteenth

civil rights Powers or privileges guaranteed to individuals and protected from arbitrary removal at the hands of government or individuals.

Amendment.[1] The list includes freedom of religion, freedom of speech and of the press, the right to assemble peaceably and to petition the government, the right to bear arms, the rights of the criminally accused, the requirement of due process, and the equal protection of the laws.

The idea of a written enumeration of rights seems entirely natural to Americans today. Lacking a written constitution, Great Britain has started to provide written guarantees for human rights (see "Compared with What? Britain's Bill of Rights").

Freedom of Religion

> Congress shall make no law respecting an establishment of religion, or prohibiting the free exercise thereof.

Religious freedom was very important to the colonies, and later to the states. That importance is reflected in its position in the Bill of Rights: the first amendment. The First Amendment guarantees freedom of religion in two clauses: the **establishment clause** prohibits laws establishing religion, and the **free-exercise clause** prevents the government from interfering with the exercise of religion. Together they ensure that the government can neither promote nor inhibit religious beliefs or practices.

At the time of the Constitutional Convention, many Americans, especially in New England, maintained that government could and should foster religion, specifically Protestantism. However, many more Americans agreed that this was an issue for state governments; the national government had no authority to meddle in religious affairs. The religion clauses were drafted in this spirit.[2]

The Supreme Court has refused to interpret the religion clauses definitively. The result is an amalgam of rulings, the cumulative effect of which is the idea that freedom to believe is unlimited but freedom to practice a belief can be limited. Religion cannot benefit directly from government actions (for example, government cannot make contributions to churches or synagogues), but it can benefit indirectly from government actions (for example, government can supply books on secular subjects for use in all schools—public, private, and parochial).

The Establishment Clause

establishment clause The first clause in the First Amendment, which forbids government establishment of religion.

free-exercise clause The second clause in the First Amendment, which prevents the government from interfering with the exercise of religion.

The provision that "Congress shall make no law respecting an establishment of religion" bars government sponsorship or support of religious activity. The Supreme Court has consistently held that the establishment clause requires government to maintain a position of neutrality toward religions and maintain that position in cases that involve choices between religion and nonreligion. However, the Court has never interpreted the clause as barring all assistance that incidentally aids religious institutions.

Government Support of Religion. In 1879, the Supreme Court contended, quoting Thomas Jefferson, that the establishment clause erected "a wall of separation between church and state."[3] That wall was breached somewhat in 1947, when the justices upheld a local government program that provided free transportation to parochial school students.[4] The breach seemed to widen in 1968, when the Court held constitutional a government program in which parochial school students borrowed state-purchased textbooks.[5] The objective of the program, reasoned the majority, was to further educational opportunity. The students, not the schools, borrowed the books, and the parents, not the church, realized the benefits.

But in 1971, in *Lemon* v. *Kurtzman,* the Court struck down a state program that would have helped pay the salaries of teachers hired by parochial schools to give instruction in secular subjects.[6] The justices proposed a three-pronged test for determining the constitutionality of government programs and laws under the establishment clause:

- They must have a secular purpose (such as lending books to parochial school students).

- Their primary effect must not be to advance or inhibit religion.

- They must not entangle the government excessively with religion.

A program or law missing any prong would be unconstitutional.

The program at issue in *Lemon* failed on the last ground. To be sure that the secular teachers did not include religious instruction in their lessons, the government would have needed to constantly monitor them. However, in a 1997 test of the establishment clause, the Court held that "a federally funded program providing supplemental, remedial instruction to disadvantaged children on a neutral basis is not invalid under the Establishment Clause when such instruction is given on the premises of sectarian schools by government employees pursuant to a program containing safeguards," such as that of a New York program that, in the eyes of the Court, did not "run afoul of the three primary criteria" cited in *Lemon.*[7]

The issue of neutrality has taken on great significance in recent years. Writing for the Court in *Zelman* v. *Simmons-Harris* (2002), Chief Justice William Rehnquist summarized this principle:

> Where a government aid program is neutral with respect to religion, and provides assistance directly to a broad class of citizens who, in turn, direct government aid to religious schools wholly as a result of their own genuine and independent private choice, the program is not readily subject to challenge under the Establishment Clause.[8]

Using this logic, the Court ruled that it was constitutional for the state of Ohio to provide poor students with tuition vouchers they could use at the school of their choice. In fact, a large number of voucher recipients chose to use the state funds to attend parochial schools, but this was merely an option along with public schools, magnet schools, community schools, and secular private schools.

School Prayer.   The Supreme Court has consistently equated organized prayer in public schools with government support of religion. In *Engel* v. *Vitale* (1962), it struck down the daily reading of a twenty-two-word nondenominational prayer in New York's public schools. In the years since that decision, new challenges on the issue of school prayer have continued to find their way to the Supreme Court. In 1985, the Court struck down a series of Alabama statutes requiring a moment of silence for meditation or voluntary prayer in elementary schools.[9] In 1992, the Court ruled 5–4 that public schools may not include nondenominational prayers in graduation ceremonies.[10] By a 6–3 vote, the Court went further in 2000 by striking down the practice of organized, student-led prayer at public high school football games.[11]

Religious training during public school is out of bounds, but this does not mean that students may not participate in religious activities on school property. In 2001 the Supreme Court ruled that public schools must open their doors to after-school religious activities on the same basis as other after-school programs such as the debate club.[12] To do otherwise would constitute viewpoint discrimination in violation of the free speech clause of the First Amendment.

The establishment clause creates a problem for government. Support for all religions at the expense of nonreligion seems to pose the least risk to social order. Tolerance of the dominant religion at the expense of other religions risks minority discontent, but support for no religion (neutrality between religion and nonreligion) risks majority discontent.

The Free-Exercise Clause

The free-exercise clause of the First Amendment states that "Congress shall make no law . . . prohibiting the free exercise [of religion]." The Supreme Court has struggled to avoid absolute interpretations of this restriction so as not to violate its complement, the establishment clause. An example: suppose Congress grants exemptions from military service to individuals who have religious scruples against war. These exemptions could be construed as a violation of the establishment clause because they favor some religious groups over others. But if Congress forces conscientious objectors to fight—to violate their religious beliefs—the government would run afoul of the free-exercise clause. In fact, Congress has granted military draftees such exemptions. But the Supreme Court has avoided a conflict between the establishment and free-exercise clauses by equating religious objection to war with any deeply held humanistic opposition to it.[13]

In the free-exercise cases, the justices have distinguished religious beliefs from actions based on those beliefs. Beliefs are inviolate, beyond the reach of government control. But the First Amendment does not protect

The Eyes Have It
In 2003, Sultaana Freeman wore a veil for her Florida driver's license photo. When Florida officials denied her a license, she took her case to court. Freeman contended that government interfered with her free exercise of religion, since her Muslim faith requires the wearing of the veil. Florida argued, and prevailed, that government has a compelling interest in identifying drivers.
(© AP/Wide World Photos)

antisocial actions. Consider conflicting values about working on the Sabbath and using drugs in religious sacraments.

Working on the Sabbath. The modern era of free-exercise thinking begins with *Sherbert* v. *Verner* (1963). Adeil Sherbert was a Seventh-Day Adventist who was disqualified from receiving unemployment benefits after declining a job that required working on Saturday, which is the Adventist Sabbath. In a 7–2 decision, the Supreme Court ruled that the disqualification imposed an impermissible burden on Sherbert's free exercise of religion. The First Amendment, declared the majority, protected observance as well as belief. A neutral law that burdens the free exercise of religion is subject to **strict scrutiny**. This means the law may be upheld only if the government can demonstrate that the law is justified by a "compelling governmental interest," must be narrowly tailored, and must be the least restrictive means for achieving that interest.[14]

Using Drugs as Religious Sacraments. Partaking of illegal substances as part of a religious sacrament forces believers to violate the law. For example, Rastafarians and members of the Ethiopian Zion Coptic Church smoke marijuana in the belief that it is the body and blood of Christ. Taken to an extreme the freedom to practice religion can result in

INTERACTIVE 12.1

 Understanding Islam

strict scrutiny A standard used by the Supreme Court in deciding whether a law or policy is to be adjudged constitutional. To pass strict scrutiny, the law or policy must be justified by a "compelling governmental interest," must be narrowly tailored, and must be the least restrictive means for achieving that interest.

license to engage in illegal conduct. The inevitable result is a clash between religious freedom and social order.

The courts used the compelling-government-interest test for many years and on that basis invalidated most laws restricting free exercise. But in 1990, the Supreme Court abruptly and unexpectedly rejected its long-standing rule, tipping the balance in favor of social order. In *Employment Division* v. *Smith,* two members of the Native American Church sought an exemption from an Oregon law that made the possession or use of peyote a crime.[15] (Peyote is a cactus that contains the hallucinogen mescaline. Native Americans have used it for centuries in their religious ceremonies.) Oregon rejected the two church members' applications for unemployment benefits after they were dismissed from their drug-counseling jobs for using peyote. Oregon believed it had a compelling interest in proscribing the use of certain drugs according to its own drug laws.

Justice Antonin Scalia, writing for the 6–3 majority, examined the conflict between freedom and order through the lens of majoritarian democratic thought. He observed that the Court has never held that an individual's religious beliefs excuse him or her from compliance with an otherwise valid law prohibiting conduct that government is free to regulate. Allowing exceptions to every state law or regulation affecting religion "would open the prospect of constitutionally required exemptions from civic obligations of almost every conceivable kind." Scalia cited as examples compulsory military service, payment of taxes, vaccination requirements, and child-neglect laws. The Court ruled that laws indirectly restricting religious practices are acceptable; only laws aimed at religious groups are constitutionally prohibited.

The political response to *Employment Division* v. *Smith* was an example of pluralism in action. An unusual coalition of religious and nonreligious groups (including the National Association of Evangelicals, the American Civil Liberties Union, the National Islamic Prison Foundation, and B'nai B'rith) organized to restore the more restrictive strict scrutiny test. The alliance regained in Congress what it had lost in the Supreme Court. In 1993, President Bill Clinton signed into law the Religious Freedom Restoration Act (RFRA). The law once again required federal, state, and local government to satisfy the strict-scrutiny standard before it could institute measures that interfere with religious practices. However, the Supreme Court struck back in 1997, declaring the act's attempt to impose the strict scrutiny standard on states unconstitutional in *City of Boerne* v. *Flores.* The 6–3 Supreme Court decision means that RFRA no longer binds state and local government actions.[16] However, in a unanimous 2006 opinion, the Court upheld RFRA limitations over federal law. The national government sought to control the sacramental use of a hallucinogenic tea by a small religious sect in New Mexico. The Court held that the government was unable to detail a compelling interest in barring the use of the tea under the strict scrutiny that RFRA imposes on federal laws and regulations.[17]

Freedom of Expression

> Congress shall make no law . . . abridging the freedom of speech, or
> of the press; or the right of the people peaceably to assemble, and to
> petition the government for a redress of grievances.

James Madison introduced the initial versions of the speech clause and the
press clause of the First Amendment in the House of Representatives in
June 1789. One of these proposals was merged with the religion and peaceable
assembly clauses to yield the First Amendment.

The sparse language of the First Amendment seems perfectly clear:
"Congress shall make no law . . . abridging the freedom of speech, or of
the press." Yet a majority of the Supreme Court has never agreed that this
"most majestic guarantee" is absolutely inviolable.[18] Historians have long
debated the framers' intentions regarding these **free-expression clauses.** The
dominant view is that the clauses confer the right to unrestricted discussion of public affairs.[19] Other scholars, examining much the same evidence,
conclude that few, if any, of the framers clearly understood the clause;
moreover, they insist that the First Amendment does not rule out prosecution for seditious statements (statements inciting insurrection).[20]

Careful analysis of the records of the period supports the view that the
press clause prohibited only the imposition of **prior restraint**—censorship
before publication. Publishers could not claim protection from punishment if works that had already been published were later deemed improper,
mischievous, or illegal. Today, however, the clauses are deemed to bar not
only most forms of prior restraint but also after-the-fact prosecution for
political and other discourse.

The Supreme Court has evolved two approaches to the resolution of
claims based on the free-expression clauses. First, government can regulate
or punish the advocacy of ideas, but only if it can prove an intent to promote lawless action and demonstrate that a high probability exists that
such action will occur. Second, government may impose reasonable restrictions on the means for communicating ideas, which can incidentally discourage free expression.

Suppose that a political party advocates nonpayment of personal income taxes. Government cannot regulate or punish that party for advocating nonpayment, because the standards of proof—that the act be directed
to inciting or producing imminent lawless action and that the act be judged
likely to produce such action—do not apply. But government can impose
restrictions on the way the party's candidates communicate what they are
advocating. Government can bar them from blaring messages from loud-
speakers in residential neighborhoods at 3:00 A.M., for example.

DO IT!

Investigate college and university conduct codes at the
Foundation for Individual
Rights in Education website,
www.thefire.org, and decide
for yourself whether constitutional protections are safe or
in jeopardy on your campus.

free-expression clauses
The press and speech clauses of
the First Amendment.

prior restraint Censorship
before publication.

Freedom of Speech

The starting point for any modern analysis of free speech is the **clear and present danger test** formulated by Justice Oliver Wendell Holmes in the Supreme Court's unanimous decision in *Schenck* v. *United States* (1919). Charles T. Schenck and his fellow defendants were convicted under a federal criminal statute for attempting to disrupt World War I military recruitment by distributing leaflets claiming that conscription was unconstitutional. The government believed this behavior threatened the public order. At the core of the Court's opinion, as Holmes wrote, was the view that

> the character of every act depends upon the circumstances in which it is done. . . . The most stringent protection of free speech would not protect a man in falsely shouting fire in a theatre and causing a panic. . . . The question in every case is whether the words used are used in such circumstances and are of such a nature as to create a *clear and present danger* that they will bring about the substantive evils that Congress has a right to prevent. It is a question of proximity and degree. When a nation is at war many things that might be said in time of peace are such a hindrance to its effort that their utterance will not be endured so long as men fight and that no Court could regard them as protected by any constitutional right. [Emphasis added.][21]

Because the actions of the defendants in *Schenck* were deemed to create a clear and present danger to the United States at that time, the Supreme Court upheld the defendants' convictions. The clear and present danger test helps to distinguish the advocacy of ideas, which is protected, from incitement, which is not.

In 1925, the Court issued a landmark decision in *Gitlow* v. *New York*.[22] Benjamin Gitlow was arrested for distributing copies of a "left-wing manifesto" that called for the establishment of socialism through strikes and class action of any form. Gitlow was convicted under a state criminal anarchy law; Schenck had been convicted under a federal law. For the first time, the Court assumed that the First Amendment speech and press provisions applied to the states through the due process clause of the Fourteenth Amendment. Still, a majority of the justices affirmed Gitlow's conviction.

The protection of advocacy faced yet another challenge in 1948, when eleven members of the Communist Party were charged with violating the Smith Act, a federal law making the advocacy of force or violence against the United States a criminal offense. The leaders were convicted, although the government introduced no evidence that they actually had urged people to commit specific violent acts. The Supreme Court mustered a majority for its decision to uphold the convictions under the Smith Act, but it could not get a majority to agree on the reasons in support of that decision. Four justices announced the plurality opinion in 1951, arguing that the government's interest was substantial enough to warrant criminal penalties.[23] The justices interpreted the threat to government to be the gravity of the advo-

clear and present danger test A means by which the Supreme Court has distinguished between speech as the advocacy of ideas, which is protected by the First Amendment, and speech as incitement, which is not protected.

cated action "discounted by its improbability." In other words, a single soap-box orator advocating revolution stands a low chance of success, and a well-organized, highly disciplined political movement advocating revolution in the tinderbox of unstable political conditions stands a greater chance of success. In broadening the meaning of "clear and present danger," the Court held that the government was justified in acting preventively rather than waiting until revolution was about to occur.

By 1969, the pendulum had swung back in the other direction. That year, in *Brandenburg v. Ohio*, a unanimous decision extended the freedom of speech to new limits.[24] Clarence Brandenburg, the leader of the Ohio Ku Klux Klan, had been convicted under a state law for advocating racial strife at a Klan rally. His comments, filmed by a television crew, included threats against government officials. The Court reversed Brandenburg's conviction because the government had failed to prove that the danger was real. The Court went even further and declared that threatening speech is protected by the First Amendment unless the government can prove that such advocacy is "directed to inciting or producing imminent lawless action and is likely to produce such action."

Symbolic Expression. Symbolic expression, or nonverbal communication, generally receives less protection than pure speech. But the courts have upheld certain types of symbolic expression. *Tinker v. Des Moines Independent County School District* (1969) involved three public school students who wore black armbands to school to protest the Vietnam War. Principals in their school district had prohibited the wearing of armbands on the grounds that such conduct would provoke a disturbance; the district suspended the students. The Supreme Court overturned the suspensions. Justice Abe Fortas declared for the majority that the principals had failed to show that the forbidden conduct would substantially interfere with appropriate school discipline:

> Undifferentiated fear or apprehension is not enough to overcome the right to freedom of expression. Any departure from absolute regimentation may cause trouble. Any variation from the majority's opinion may inspire fear. Any word spoken, in class, in the lunchroom, or on the campus, that deviates from the views of another person may start an argument or cause a disturbance. But our Constitution says we must take this risk.[25]

Recall the Bayonne, New Jersey, school uniform protest. In September 2007, federal district court judge Joseph A. Greenaway Jr. issued an injunction to prevent the students' suspension. Citing the *Tinker* case, Greenaway wrote that "a student may not be punished for merely expressing views unless the school has reason to believe that the speech or expression will 'materially and substantially disrupt the work and discipline of the school.'"[26] The Supreme Court does allow school administrators some leeway in limiting expression advocating the use of illegal drugs. In *Morse v.*

Frederick (2007), the Court ruled that a principal had the authority to suspend a student who unfurled a banner reading "Bong Hits 4 Jesus" at a school event. Unlike political speech, advocating illegal drug use in school is not protected by the First Amendment.[27]

Free Speech Versus Order: Obscenity. The Supreme Court has always viewed obscene material—words, music, books, magazines, films—as outside the bounds of constitutional protection, which means that states may regulate or even ban obscenity. However, difficulties arise in determining what is obscene and what is not.

In *Miller* v. *California* (1973), its most recent major attempt to clarify constitutional standards governing obscenity, the Court declared that a work—play, film, or book—is obscene and may be regulated by government if (1) the work taken as a whole appeals to prurient interest ("prurient" means having a tendency to excite lustful thoughts), (2) the work portrays sexual conduct in a patently offensive way, and (3) the work taken as a whole lacks serious literary, artistic, political, or scientific value.[28] Local community standards govern application of the first and second prongs of the *Miller* test.

In 1996, Congress passed the Communications Decency Act, which made it a crime for a person knowingly to circulate "patently offensive" sexual material to Internet sites accessible to those under eighteen years old. Is this an acceptable way to protect children from offensive material, or is it a muzzle on free speech? A federal court quickly declared the act unconstitutional. In an opinion of over two hundred pages, the court observed that "just as the strength of the Internet is chaos, so the strength of our liberty depends on the chaos and cacophony of the unfettered speech the First Amendment protects."[29]

The Supreme Court upheld the lower court's ruling in June 1997 in *Reno* v. *ACLU*.[30] The Court's nearly unanimous opinion was a broad affirmation of free speech rights in cyberspace, arguing that the Internet was more analogous to print media than to television, and thus even indecent material on the Internet was entitled to First Amendment protection. Following the *Reno* decision, Congress enacted the Child Online Protection Act (COPA) to achieve similar goals in a more carefully targeted fashion. District and appellate courts granted a preliminary injunction blocking enforcement of the new law, because the law was not the least restrictive means to protect children. In *Ashcroft* v. *ACLU* (2004), the Supreme Court agreed that COPA did not appear to represent the least restrictive means possible for a compelling governmental interest. The Court remanded the case to the lower courts for further consideration, where in *ACLU* v. *Gonzales*, COPA was declared unconstitutional in March 2007, in part because COPA "prohibits much more speech than is necessary to further Congress' compelling interest."[31] However, in 2008 the Supreme Court upheld a national law established to punish those who offered or sought child pornography, whether pornographic materials actually existed or

not. In a 7–2 decision written by Associate Justice Antonin Scalia, the Court declared, "We hold that offers to provide or requests to obtain child pornography are categorically excluded from the First Amendment."[32]

Freedom of the Press

The First Amendment guarantees that government "shall make no law . . . abridging the freedom . . . of the press." Although it originally was adopted as a restriction on the national government, since 1931 the Supreme Court has held the free press guarantee to apply to state and local governments as well.

The ability to collect and report information without government interference was (and still is) thought to be essential to a free society. The print media continue to use and defend the freedom conferred on them by the framers. However, the electronic media have had to accept some government regulation stemming from the scarcity of broadcast frequencies (see Chapter 4).

Defamation of Character.   Libel is the written defamation of character.* A person who believes his or her name and character have been harmed by false statements in a publication can institute a lawsuit against the publication and seek monetary compensation for the damage. Such a lawsuit can impose limits on freedom of expression; at the same time, false statements impinge on the rights of individuals. In a landmark decision in *New York Times* v. *Sullivan* (1964), the Supreme Court declared that freedom of the press takes precedence—at least when the defamed individual is a public official.[33] The Court unanimously agreed that the First Amendment protects the publication of all statements, even false ones, about the conduct of public officials except when statements are made with actual malice (with knowledge that they are false or in reckless disregard of their truth or falsity). Citing John Stuart Mill's 1859 treatise *On Liberty,* the Court declared that "even a false statement may be deemed to make a valuable contribution to public debate, since it brings about the clearer perception and livelier impression of truth, produced by its collision with error."

Three years later, the Court extended this protection to apply to suits brought by any public figures, whether a government official or not. **Public figures** are people who assume roles of prominence in the affairs of society or thrust themselves to the forefront of public controversy—officials, actors, writers, television personalities, and others. These people must show actual malice on the part of the publisher that prints false statements about them. Because the burden of proof is so great, few plaintiffs prevail.

---

*Slander is the oral defamation of character. The durability of the written word usually means that libel is a more serious accusation than slander.

public figures People who assume roles of prominence in society or thrust themselves to the forefront of public controversy.

Prior Restraint and the Press.   In the United States, freedom of the press has primarily meant protection from prior restraint, or censorship. The Supreme Court's first encounter with a law imposing prior restraint on a newspaper was in *Near* v. *Minnesota* (1931).[34] In Minneapolis, Jay Near published a scandal sheet in which he attacked local officials, charging that they were in league with gangsters.[35] Minnesota officials obtained an injunction to prevent Near from publishing his newspaper under a state law that allowed such action against periodicals deemed "malicious, scandalous, and defamatory."

The Supreme Court struck down the law, declaring that prior restraint is an unacceptable burden on a free press. Chief Justice Charles Evans Hughes forcefully articulated the need for a vigilant, unrestrained press: "The fact that the liberty of the press may be abused by miscreant purveyors of scandal does not make any the less necessary the immunity of the press from previous restraint in dealing with official misconduct." Although the Court acknowledged that prior restraint may be permissible in exceptional circumstances, it did not specify those circumstances, nor has it yet done so.

Consider another case, which occurred during a war, a time when the tension between government-imposed order and individual freedom is often at a peak. In 1971, Daniel Ellsberg, a special assistant in the Pentagon, delivered portions of a classified U.S. Department of Defense study to the *New York Times* and the *Washington Post*. By making the documents public, he hoped to discredit the Vietnam War and thereby end it. The U.S. Department of Justice sought to restrain the *Times* and the *Post* from publishing the documents, contending that publication would prolong the war and embarrass the government. The case was quickly brought before the Supreme Court.

Three days later, in a 6–3 decision in *New York Times* v. *United States* (1971), the Court concluded that the government had not met the heavy burden of proving that immediate, inevitable, and irreparable harm would follow publication.[36] The majority expressed its view in a brief unsigned opinion; individual and collective concurring and dissenting views added nine opinions to the decision. Two justices maintained that the First Amendment offers absolute protection against government censorship, no matter what the situation. But the other justices left the door ajar for the imposition of prior restraint in the most extreme and compelling of circumstances.

Freedom of Expression Versus Maintaining Order.   The courts have consistently held that freedom of the press does not override the requirements of law enforcement. A grand jury called a Louisville, Kentucky, reporter, who had researched and written an article about drug-related activities, and asked him to identify people he had seen in possession of marijuana or in the act of processing it. The reporter refused to testify, maintaining that freedom of the press shielded him from inquiry. In a closely divided decision, the Supreme Court in 1972 rejected this position.[37] The Court declared that no exception exists to the rule that all citizens have a duty to give their government whatever testimony they are capable of giving.[38]

Consider the 1988 case of a St. Louis high school principal who deleted articles on divorce and teenage pregnancy from the school's newspaper on the grounds that the articles invaded the privacy of the individuals who were the focus of the stories.[39] Three student editors claimed that the principal's censorship interfered with the newspaper's function as a public forum, a role protected by the First Amendment. The principal maintained that the newspaper was an extension of classroom instruction and was thus not protected by the First Amendment.

In a 5–3 decision, the Court upheld the principal's actions in sweeping terms. Educators may limit speech within the confines of the school curriculum and speech that might seem to bear the approval of the school, provided their actions serve a "valid educational purpose."

The Rights to Assemble Peaceably and to Petition the Government

The final clause of the First Amendment states that "Congress shall make no law . . . abridging . . . the right of the people peaceably to assemble, and to petition the Government for a redress of grievances." The framers meant that the people have the right to assemble peaceably *in order to* petition the government. Today, however, the right to assemble peaceably is equated with the right of free speech and a free press, independent of whether the government is petitioned. Precedent has merged these rights and made them equally indivisible.[40] Government cannot prohibit peaceful political meetings and cannot brand as criminals those who organize, lead, and attend such meetings.[41]

The Right to Bear Arms

The Second Amendment declares:

> A well-regulated militia being necessary to the security of a free State,
> the right of the people to keep and bear arms shall not be infringed.

Gun-control advocates assert that the amendment protects the right of the states to maintain *collective* militias. Gun-use advocates assert that the amendment protects the right of *individuals* to own and use guns. There are good arguments on both sides.

Federal firearms regulations did not come into being until Prohibition, so the Supreme Court had little to say on the matter. In 1939, however, a unanimous Court upheld a 1934 federal law requiring the taxation and registration of machine guns and sawed-off shotguns. The Court held that the Second Amendment protects a citizen's right to own ordinary militia weapons; sawed-off shotguns did not qualify for protection.[42] Restrictions on gun ownership (for example, registration and licensing) have passed constitutional muster. However, outright prohibitions on gun ownership (for example, a ban on handguns) run afoul of the amendment.

In 2007, the Court considered whether the Second Amendment protects an individual's right to gun ownership or is simply a right tied to service in a militia. Opponents of gun control challenged the strictest gun-control statute in the country, a District of Columbia law that barred private possession of handguns and required the disassembly or use of trigger locks on rifles and shotguns. In *District of Columbia* v. *Heller,* the Supreme Court struck down the District of Columbia's statue, established gun ownership as an individual right, and clarified that the Second Amendment forbids outright bans on gun ownership. Writing for a 5–4 majority, Associate Justice Antonin Scalia declared that the Second Amendment "surely elevates above all other interests the right of law-abiding, responsible citizens to use arms in defense of hearth and home." Despite the expansive sweep of the decision, Scalia was careful to point out that nothing in the decision overturned previous prohibitions on the "possession of firearms by felons and the mentally ill, or laws forbidding the carrying of firearms in sensitive places such as schools and government buildings, or laws imposing conditions and qualifications on the commercial sale of arms."[43]

Applying the Bill of Rights to the States

The major purpose of the Constitution was to structure the division of power between the national government and the state governments. Even before it was amended, the Constitution set some limits on both the nation and the states with regard to citizens' rights. It barred both governments from passing **bills of attainder,** laws that make an individual guilty of a crime without a trial. Both were also prohibited from enacting **ex post facto laws,** laws that declare an action a crime after it has been performed. And it barred both nation and states from impairing the **obligation of contracts,** the obligation of the parties in a contract to carry out its terms.

Although initially the Bill of Rights seemed to apply only to the national government, various litigants pressed the claim that its guarantees also applied to the states. In response to one such claim, Chief Justice John Marshall affirmed that the provisions of the Bill of Rights served only to limit national authority: "Had the framers of these amendments intended them to be limitations on the powers of the state governments," wrote Marshall, "they would have . . . expressed that intention."[44]

Change came with the Fourteenth Amendment, which was adopted in 1868. The due process clause of that amendment is the linchpin that holds the states to the provisions of the Bill of Rights.

The Fourteenth Amendment: Due Process of Law

Section 1 . . .
No State shall make or enforce any law which shall abridge the privileges or immunities of citizens of the United States; nor shall any State

bill of attainder A law that pronounces an individual guilty of a crime without a trial.

ex post facto law A law that declares an action to be criminal after it has been performed.

obligation of contracts The obligation of the parties to a contract to carry out its terms.

deprive any person of life, liberty, or property, without due process of law.

Most freedoms protected in the Bill of Rights today apply as limitations on the states. And many of the standards that limit the national government serve equally to limit state governments. These changes have been achieved through the Supreme Court's interpretation of the due process clause of the Fourteenth Amendment: "nor shall any State deprive any person of life, liberty, or property, without due process of law." The clause has two central meanings. First, it requires the government to adhere to appropriate procedures. Second, it forbids unreasonable government action. The Supreme Court has used the first meaning of the due process clause as a sponge, absorbing or incorporating the procedural specifics of the Bill of Rights and spreading or applying them to the states.

The Fundamental Freedoms

In 1897, the Supreme Court declared that the states are limited by the Fifth Amendment's prohibition on taking private property without providing just compensation.[45] The Court accomplished its goal by absorbing that prohibition into the due process clause of the Fourteenth Amendment, which applies to the states. Thus, one Bill of Rights protection—but only that one—applied to both the states and the national government. In 1925, the Court assumed that the due process clause protected the First Amendment speech and press liberties from impairment by the states.[46]

The inclusion of other Bill of Rights guarantees within the due process clause faced a critical test in *Palko v. Connecticut* (1937).[47] Frank Palko had been charged with homicide in the first degree. He was convicted of second-degree murder, however, and sentenced to life imprisonment. The state of Connecticut appealed and won a new trial; this time Palko was found guilty of first-degree murder and sentenced to death. Palko appealed the second conviction on the grounds that it violated the protection against double jeopardy guaranteed to him by the Fifth Amendment. This protection applied to the states, he contended, because of the Fourteenth Amendment's due process clause.

The Supreme Court upheld Palko's second conviction. Justice Benjamin N. Cardozo, in his opinion for the majority, formulated principles that were to direct the Court's actions for the next three decades. He noted that some Bill of Rights guarantees, such as freedom of thought and speech, are fundamental, and that these fundamental rights are absorbed by the Fourteenth Amendment's due process clause and are therefore applicable to the states. These rights are essential, argued Cardozo, because "neither liberty nor justice would exist if they were sacrificed." Trial by jury and other rights, though valuable and important, are not essential to liberty and justice and therefore are not absorbed by the due process clause. "Few would be so narrow or provincial," Cardozo claimed, "as to maintain that a fair

FIGURE 12.1   **The Incorporation of the Bill of Rights**

The Supreme Court has used the due process clause of the Fourteenth Amendment as a sponge, absorbing most—but not all—of the provisions in the Bill of Rights and applying them to state and local governments. All provisions in the Bill of Rights apply to the national government.

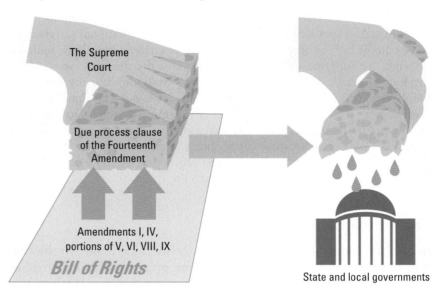

and enlightened system of justice would be impossible" without these other rights. In other words, only some provisions of the Bill of Rights—the "fundamental" provisions—were absorbed into the due process clause and made applicable to the states (see Figure 12.1). Because protection against double jeopardy was not one of them, Palko died in Connecticut's gas chamber in April 1938.

The next thirty years saw slow but perceptible change in the standard for determining whether a Bill of Rights guarantee was fundamental. The reference point changed from the idealized "fair and enlightened system of justice" in *Palko* to the more realistic "American scheme of justice" thirty years later.[48] Case after case tested various guarantees that the Court found to be fundamental. By 1969, when *Palko* was finally overturned, the Court had found most of the Bill of Rights applicable to the states.

Criminal Procedure: The Meaning of Constitutional Guarantees

"The history of liberty," remarked Justice Felix Frankfurter "has largely been the history of observance of procedural safeguards."[49] The safeguards embodied in the Fourth through Eighth Amendments to the Constitution specify how government must behave in criminal proceedings. Their application to the states has reshaped American criminal justice in the previous four decades in two steps. The first step is the judgment that a guarantee asserted in the Bill of Rights also applies to the states. The second step requires that the judiciary give specific meaning to the guarantee. If the rights are fundamental, their meaning cannot vary from state to state. But life is not quite so simple under the U.S. Constitution. The concept of federalism is sewn into the constitutional fabric, and the Supreme Court recognizes that there may be more than one way to prosecute the accused while heeding fundamental rights.

Consider, for example, the right to a jury trial in criminal cases, which is guaranteed by the Sixth Amendment. This right was made obligatory on the states in *Duncan* v. *Louisiana* (1968). The Supreme Court later held that the right applied to all nonpetty criminal cases—those in which the penalty for conviction was more than six months' imprisonment.[50] But the Court did not require that state juries have twelve members, the number required for federal criminal proceedings. The Court permits jury size to vary from state to state, although it set the minimum number at six. Furthermore, it has not imposed on the states the federal requirement of a unanimous jury verdict.

In contrast, the Court left no room for variation in its definition of the fundamental right to an attorney, also guaranteed by the Sixth Amendment. Clarence Earl Gideon was a penniless vagrant accused of breaking into and robbing a pool hall. Because Gideon could not afford a lawyer, he asked the state to provide him with legal counsel for his trial. The state refused, and Gideon was subsequently convicted and sentenced to five years in the Florida State Penitentiary. From his cell, Gideon appealed to the U.S. Supreme Court, claiming that his conviction should be struck down because the state had denied him his Sixth Amendment right to counsel.[51]

In its landmark decision in *Gideon* v. *Wainwright* (1963), the Court set aside Gideon's conviction and extended to the states the Sixth Amendment right to counsel.[52] The state retried Gideon, who this time had the assistance of a lawyer, and the court found him not guilty. In subsequent rulings that stretched over more than a decade, the Court specified at what points in the course of criminal proceedings a defendant is entitled to a lawyer (from arrest to trial, appeal, and beyond). These pronouncements are binding on all states.

During this period, the Court also came to grips with another procedural issue: informing suspects of their constitutional rights. Ernesto Miranda was arrested in Arizona in connection with the kidnapping and rape of an eighteen-year-old woman. After the police questioned him for two hours and the woman identified him, Miranda confessed to the crime. An Arizona court convicted him on the basis of that confession—although he was never told he had the right to counsel and the right not to incriminate himself. Miranda appealed his conviction, which the Supreme Court overturned in 1966.[53]

The Court based its decision in *Miranda* v. *Arizona* on the Fifth Amendment privilege against self-incrimination. According to the Court, warnings are necessary to dispel the coercion that is inherent in custodial interrogation without counsel. The Court does not require warnings if a person is only in custody without questioning or subject to questioning without arrest. But in *Miranda*, the Court found the combination of custody and interrogation sufficiently intimidating to require warnings before questioning. These statements are known today as the *Miranda* **warnings.**

- You have the right to remain silent.

- Anything you say can be used against you in court.

- You have the right to talk to a lawyer of your own choice before questioning.

- If you cannot afford to hire a lawyer, a lawyer will be provided without charge.

In one of its most important cases in 2000, the Court reaffirmed this protection in a 7–2 decision, holding that *Miranda* had "announced a constitutional rule" that Congress could not undermine through legislation.[54] In 2004, the Court underscored this status by ruling unconstitutional a police tactic of questioning suspects before they were informed of their *Miranda* rights, and then, after informing suspects of their rights, questioning them again until they obtained the same answers.[55]

The Fourth Amendment guarantees that "the right of the people to be secure in their persons, houses, papers, and effects, against unreasonable searches and seizures, shall not be violated." The Court made this right applicable to the states in *Wolf* v. *Colorado* (1949).[56] But although the Court found that protection from illegal searches by state and local government was a fundamental right, it refused to apply to the states the **exclusionary rule** that evidence obtained from an illegal search and seizure cannot be used in a trial.

The justices considered the exclusionary rule again in *Mapp* v. *Ohio* (1961).[57] An Ohio court had found Dolree Mapp guilty of possessing obscene materials after an admittedly illegal search of her home for a fugitive. The Ohio Supreme Court affirmed her conviction, and she appealed to the U.S. Supreme Court. In a 6–3 decision, the Court declared, "all evidence obtained by searches and seizures in violation of the Constitution is, by [the Fourth Amendment], inadmissible in a state court." The decision was historic. It placed the exclusionary rule within the confines of the Fourth Amendment and required all levels of government to operate according to the provisions of that amendment.

The struggle over the exclusionary rule took a new turn in 1984, when the Court reviewed *United States* v. *Leon*.[58] In this case, a judge had issued a search warrant without "probable cause" having been firmly established. The police, relying on the warrant, found large quantities of illegal drugs.

The Court, by a 6–3 vote, established the **good faith exception** to the exclusionary rule. The justices held that the state could introduce at trial evi-

Miranda **warnings** Statements concerning rights that police are required to make to a person before he or she is subjected to in-custody questioning.

exclusionary rule The judicial rule that states that evidence obtained in an illegal search and seizure cannot be used in trial.

good faith exception An exception to the Supreme Court exclusionary rule, holding that evidence seized on the basis of a mistakenly issued search warrant can be introduced at trial if the mistake was made in good faith, that is, if all the parties involved had reason at the time to believe that the warrant was proper.

dence seized on the basis of a mistakenly issued search warrant. The exclusionary rule, argued the majority, is not a right but a remedy justified by its ability to deter illegal police conduct. Such a deterrent effect was not a factor in *Leon:* the police acted in good faith. Hence, the Court decided, there is a need for an exception to the rule.

The USA-PATRIOT Act

More than fifty years ago, Justice Robert H. Jackson warned that exceptional protections for civil liberties might convert the Bill of Rights into a suicide pact. The national government decided, after the September 11, 2001, terrorist attacks, to forgo some liberties to secure greater order, through bipartisan passage of the USA-PATRIOT Act. This landmark law greatly expanded the ability of law enforcement and intelligence agencies to tap phones, monitor Internet traffic, and conduct other forms of surveillance in pursuit of terrorists.

Shortly after the bill became law, then attorney general John Ashcroft declared: "Let the terrorists among us be warned: If you overstay your visas, even by one day, we will arrest you. If you violate a local law, we will hope that you will, and work to make sure that you are, put in jail and kept in custody as long as possible. We will use every available statute. We will seek every prosecutorial advantage. We will use all our weapons within the law and under the Constitution to protect life and enhance security for America."[59]

In this shift toward order, civil libertarians worry. "These new and unchecked powers could be used against American citizens who are not under criminal investigation," said Gregory T. Nojeim, associate director of the American Civil Liberties Union's Washington office.[60]

The USA-PATRIOT Act ran over 300 pages. Some parts engendered strong opposition; others were benign. More than 400 communities have passed resolutions denouncing the act as an assault on civil liberties. Consider one of the key provisions: Section 215 dealing with rules for searching private records such as you might find in the library, video store, telephone company, or doctor's office. Prior to the act, the government needed, at minimum, a warrant issued by a judge and probable cause to access such records. Now, under the USA-PATRIOT Act, the government need certify without substantiation only that its search protects against terrorism, which turns judicial oversight into a rubber stamp. To complicate matters, a gag order barred the person turning over the records from disclosing the search to anyone. The USA-PATRIOT Act was reauthorized in 2006, at which time Congress made many of its temporary provisions permanent. The reauthorizing legislation also tightened up the definition of domestic terrorism and modified Section 215 to explicitly allow individuals to consult their attorneys when they receive a request to turn over records to the government.

Detainees and the War on Terrorism

An important debate has arisen over whether suspected terrorists held by the U.S. government overseas are guaranteed access to attorneys and to the judicial system under the Constitution. President Bush maintained that detainees held as "enemy combatants" were not entitled to basic legal requirements such as attorneys or hearings and that his actions could not be reviewed in the courts. In 2004 the Supreme Court handed down two decisions rejecting that view. In *Rasul v. Bush*, the Court ruled that U.S. judges have the jurisdiction to consider the legality of detaining foreign nationals captured abroad and held at the Guantánamo Bay detention facility in Cuba.[61]

INTERACTIVE 12.2

Inside Guantánamo

In *Hamdi v. Rumsfeld*, the Court considered the case of a Saudi Arabian resident who was born in the United States and was thus a citizen. Hamdi was picked up on an Afghan battlefield and detained as an enemy combatant. In the 8–1 vote, the Court declared that he is entitled by the due process clause of the Fifth Amendment to a "meaningful opportunity" to contest the basis for his detention. In blunt language, Justice Sandra Day O'Connor, speaking for herself and three other justices, rebuffed the president's claim: "We have long since made clear that a state of war is not a blank check for the President when it comes to the rights of the Nation's citizens."[62]

The Supreme Court issued a third critical decision in *Hamdan v. Rumsfeld* in July 2006. Hamdan was a Yemeni citizen captured on the battlefield in Afghanistan and held at Guantánamo Bay, Cuba, in anticipation of prosecution before a military commission. In a 5–4 decision, the Court ruled that the military commissions were not authorized by federal law and would violate the Uniform Code of Military Justice and the Geneva Convention because of the lack of procedural rights for the defendants.[63]

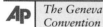

INTERACTIVE 12.3

The Geneva Convention

The detainee debate took on added layers of complexity when President Bush confirmed news accounts that the Central Intelligence Agency (CIA) had been running secret prisons abroad, in which "high-value" terrorism suspects had been kept and interrogated. The president announced the CIA's high-value detainees had been transferred from their secret prisons abroad to Guantanamo Bay to await trial by tribunal. While the ruling in *Hamdan v. Rumsfeld* was initially a setback for the Bush administration, Bush's transfer of the high-value detainees to Guantánamo Bay put the Congress under pressure to explicitly authorize military tribunals.

In October 2006 the Congress passed the Military Commission Act of 2006, authorizing the establishment of the commissions, limiting the use of habeas corpus petitions from noncitizen detainees, eliminating some traditional defendant rights associated with military prosecutions, and authorizing the CIA to continue detainment and tough interrogation techniques.[64] In 2008 the Supreme Court responded by striking down these limits on habeas corpus petitions. In its narrow 5–4 decision in *Boumediene v. Bush*, the Court ruled again that detainees have a right to challenge their imprisonment in courts of law.[65] While the Constitution does allow

Congress to formally (and temporarily) suspend habeas rights "when in Cases of Rebellion or Invasion the public Safety may require it," legislation simply banning federal judges from hearing detainee habeas cases did not meet the constitutional standard.[66]

The Ninth Amendment and Personal Autonomy

> The enumeration in the Constitution, of certain rights, shall not be construed to deny or disparage others retained by the people

The wording and history of the Ninth Amendment remain an enigma. The evidence supports two different views: the amendment may protect rights that are not enumerated, or it may simply protect state governments against the assumption of power by the national government.[67] The meaning of the amendment was not an issue until 1965, when the Supreme Court used it to protect privacy, a right that is not enumerated in the Constitution.

Controversy: From Privacy to Abortion

In *Griswold* v. *Connecticut* (1965), the Court struck down, by a 7–2 vote, a seldom-used Connecticut statute that made the use of birth control devices a crime.[68] Justice William Douglas, writing for the majority, asserted that the "specific guarantees in the Bill of Rights have penumbras [partially illuminated regions surrounding fully lit areas]" that give "life and substance" to broad, unspecified protections in the Bill of Rights. Several specific guarantees in the First, Third, Fourth, and Fifth amendments create a zone of privacy, Douglas argued, and this zone is protected by the Ninth Amendment and is applicable to the states by the due process clause of the Fourteenth Amendment.

Griswold established a zone of personal autonomy, protected by the Constitution, which was the basis of a 1973 case that sought to invalidate state antiabortion laws. In *Roe* v. *Wade* (1973), the Court in a 7–2 decision declared unconstitutional a Texas law making it a crime to obtain an abortion except for the purpose of saving the woman's life.[69]

Justice Harry A. Blackmun, who authored the majority opinion, based the decision on the right to privacy protected by the due process clause of the Fourteenth Amendment. The Court declared that in the first three months of pregnancy, the abortion decision must be left to the woman and her physician. In the interest of protecting the woman's health, states may restrict but not prohibit abortions in the second three months of pregnancy. Finally, in the last three months of pregnancy, states may regulate or even prohibit abortions to protect the life of the fetus except when medical judgment determines that an abortion is necessary to save the woman's life. In all, the Court's ruling affected the laws of forty-six states.

The dissenters—Justices Byron White and William Rehnquist—were quick to assert what critics have frequently repeated since the decision: the Court's judgment was directed by its own dislikes, not by any constitutional compass. In the absence of guiding principles, they asserted, the majority justices simply substituted their views for the views of the state legislatures whose abortion regulations they invalidated.[70]

There was a perceptible shift away from abortion rights in *Webster* v. *Reproductive Health Services* (1989). In *Webster,* the Court upheld the constitutionality of a Missouri law that denied the use of public employees or publicly funded facilities in the performance of an abortion unless the woman's life was in danger.[71] Furthermore, the law required doctors to perform tests to determine whether fetuses twenty weeks and older could survive outside the womb. This was the first time the Court upheld significant government restrictions on abortion.

The Court has since moved cautiously down the road toward greater government control of abortion. In 1990, the justices split on two state parental notification laws. Since then, the Court has reaffirmed *Roe* while tolerating additional restrictions on abortion. In *Planned Parenthood* v. *Casey* (1992), the Court opted for O'Connor's test that restrictions must not place "an undue burden" on a woman's ability to choose an abortion. Although the Court struck down a Nebraska law in 2000 that had banned partial-birth abortions in that state in a 5–4 decision, it upheld a more narrowly tailored federal law banning the procedure in *Gonzales* v. *Carhart* (2007) in another 5–4 vote. The Court remains deeply divided on abortion.[72]

Personal Autonomy and Sexual Orientation

The right-to-privacy cases may have opened a Pandora's box of divisive social issues. Does the right to privacy embrace private homosexual acts between consenting adults? Consider the case of Michael Hardwick, who was arrested in 1982 in his Atlanta bedroom while having sex with another man. In a standard approach to prosecuting homosexuals, Georgia charged him under a state criminal statute with the crime of sodomy, which means oral or anal intercourse. Hardwick sued to challenge the law's constitutionality. He won in the lower courts. However, in a bitterly divided ruling in 1986, the Supreme Court held in *Bowers* v. *Hardwick* that the Constitution does not protect homosexual relations between consenting adults, even in the privacy of their own homes.[73]

Justice White's majority opinion was reconsidered in 2003 when the Supreme Court considered a challenge to a Texas law that criminalized homosexual but not heterosexual sodomy. This time, in *Lawrence and Garner* v. *Texas,* a new coalition of six justices viewed the issue in a different light. Speaking through Justice Kennedy, the Court observed "an emerging awareness that liberty gives substantial protection to adult persons in deciding how to conduct their private lives in matters pertaining to sex." Since the Texas law furthered no legitimate state interest but intruded into the intimate personal choices of individuals, the law was void. Kennedy, along with four other justices, then took the unusual step of reaching back in time to declare that the *Bowers* decision was wrong and therefore should be overruled.[74]

Justice Antonin Scalia, joined by Chief Justice Rehnquist and Justice Clarence Thomas, issued a stinging dissent. Scalia charged the majority with "signing on to the homosexual agenda" aimed at eliminating moral opprobrium traditionally attached to homosexual conduct. The consequence is that the Court would be departing from its role of ensuring that the democratic rules of engagement are observed. He continued:

> What Texas has chosen to do is well within the range of traditional democratic action, and its hand should not be stayed through the invention of a brand-new "constitutional right" by a Court that is impatient of democratic change. It is indeed true that "later generations can see that laws once thought necessary and proper in fact serve only to oppress," . . . and when that happens, later generations can repeal those laws. But it is the premise of our system that those judgments are to be made by the people, and not imposed by a governing caste that knows best.[75]

The challenge of democracy calls for the democratic process to sort out value conflicts whenever possible. And according to Scalia, the Court's majority has moved from its traditional role umpiring the system to favoring one side over another in the struggle between freedom and order.

Issues around sexual orientation have shifted toward the states, where various groups continue to assert their political power. Some states have been innovators in legitimizing homosexuality. In 2000, the Vermont legislature approved same-sex "unions" but not same-sex marriages. Eight other states plus the District of Columbia have followed suit. In 2003, the highest court in Massachusetts mandated that the state legislature acknowledge homosexual marriage as a fundamental right under its state constitution. In 2008, the California Supreme Court followed suit, declaring that under the state constitution marriage is a basic civil right guaranteed to all Californians. Californians reacted by voting six months later to amend the state's constitution to again limit marriage to heterosexual couples. In October 2008, the Connecticut Supreme Court legalized same-sex marriage in that state.[76]

In 2009, twenty-nine states have constitutional amendments barring the recognition of same-sex marriage and confining civil marriage to a union of a man and a woman. Forty-four states now have laws restricting marriage to persons of the opposite sex, including states that recognize same-sex unions.

The pluralist model provides one solution for groups dissatisfied with rulings from the nation's highest court. State courts and state legislatures have demonstrated their receptivity to positions that are probably untenable in the federal courts.

Summary

When the states and the people established the new government of the United States, they compelled the framers, through the Bill of Rights, to protect their freedoms. In their interpretation of the first ten amendments, the courts, especially the Supreme Court, have taken on the task of balancing freedom and order.

The First Amendment protects several freedoms: freedom of religion, freedom of speech and of the press, and the freedom to assemble peaceably and petition the government. The establishment clause demands government neutrality toward religions and between the religious and the nonreligious. According to judicial interpretations of the free-exercise clause, religious beliefs are inviolable, but the Constitution does not protect antisocial actions in the name of religion. Extreme interpretations of the religion clauses could bring the clauses into conflict with each other.

Freedom of expression encompasses freedom of speech, freedom of the press, and the right to assemble peaceably and petition the government. Freedom of speech and freedom of the press have never been held to be absolute, but the courts have ruled that the Bill of Rights gives them far greater protection than other freedoms. Exceptions to free speech protections include some forms of symbolic expression and obscenity. Press freedom has had broad constitutional protection because a free society depends on the ability to collect and report information without government interference. The rights to assemble peaceably and to petition the government stem from the guarantees of freedom of speech and of the press. Each freedom is equally fundamental, but the right to exercise them is not absolute.

The adoption of the Fourteenth Amendment in 1868 extended the guarantees of the Bill of Rights to the states. The due process clause became the vehicle for applying specific provisions of the Bill of Rights—one at a time, case after case—to the states. The designation of a right as fundamental also called for a definition of that right. The Supreme Court has tolerated some variation from state to state in the meaning of certain constitutional rights. The Court has also imposed a duty on governments to inform citizens of their rights so that they are equipped to exercise them.

As it has fashioned new fundamental rights from the Constitution, the Supreme Court has become embroiled in controversy. The right to privacy served as the basis for the right of women to terminate a pregnancy, which in turn suggested a right to personal autonomy. The abortion controversy is still raging, and the justices, relying in part on the logic of the abortion cases, have extended protections against state criminal prosecution of private consensual sexual behavior for homosexuals.

These controversial judicial decisions raise a basic issue. By offering constitutional protection to certain public policies, the courts may be threatening the democratic process, the process that gives the people a voice in government through their elected representatives. One thing is certain: the challenge of democracy requires the constant balancing of freedom and order.

KEY CASES

Lemon v. *Kurtzman*
Engel v. *Vitale*
Sherbert v. *Verner*
Brandenburg v. *Ohio*
Tinker v. *Des Moines Independent County School District*
Miller v. *California*
New York Times v. *Sullivan*
New York Times v. *United States*
District of Columbia v. *Heller*

Palko v. *Connecticut*
Gideon v. *Wainwright*
Miranda v. *Arizona*
Griswold v. *Connecticut*
Roe v. *Wade*
Gonzales v. *Carhart*
Lawrence and Garner v. *Texas*

CL **Resources:** Videos, Simulations, News,
Timelines, Primary Sources

Equality and Civil Rights

This icon will direct you to resources and activities on the website: www.cengage.com/polisci/janda/chall_dem_brief/7e

CL

"WHEN WE WANT YOU, WE'LL CALL you; when we don't, git."[1] A rancher's sentiment toward his Mexican workers summarizes the treatment of illegal immigrants, many of them Mexicans or Latin Americans, who routinely cross our southern border in search of better wages and the possibility of a better life.

The swings of the economy often signal whether illegal immigrants will be welcomed or sent packing. To be sure, illegal immigrants have provided the United States with cheap labor for a hundred years, undertaking tasks that few, if any, Americans would care to shoulder and providing goods and services at a far lower price than we would otherwise have to pay. They pick our fruit and vegetables, butcher our meat and poultry, clean our homes, flip our burgers, and mow our lawns. But illegal immigrants have also taken up jobs and better pay in other trades, including construction and manufacturing. "Better pay" is relative; it may be better for the illegal, but it is likely to drive down wages for everyone else.

All governments provide for the general welfare, which embraces health, education, and fire and police protection. For example, public hospitals cannot decline care, and public schools must admit and educate every student. These services ensure a measure of equality, a floor beneath which no one need fall. But does the floor exist for illegal immigrants and their children? Should illegal immigrants or their children be denied public education or health care?

In this chapter, we will consider the different ideals of equality and the quest to realize them through government action. We begin with the struggle for racial equality, which continues to cast a long shadow in government policies. This struggle has served as a model for the diverse groups that chose to follow in the same path.

Two Conceptions of Equality

Most Americans support **equality of opportunity**—the idea that people should have an equal chance to develop their talents and that effort and ability should be rewarded equitably. This form of equality glorifies personal achievement and free competition, and it allows everyone to play on a level field where the same rules apply to all. Special recruitment efforts aimed at identifying qualified minority or female job applicants, for example, ensure that everyone has the same chance starting out. Low-bid contracting illustrates equality of opportunity because every bidder has the same chance to compete for work.

Americans are far less committed to **equality of outcome**, which means greater uniformity in social, economic, and political power among different

equality of opportunity
The idea that each person is guaranteed the same chance to succeed in life.

equality of outcome
The concept that society must ensure that people are equal, and governments must design policies to redistribute wealth and status to achieve economic and social equality.

social groups. Equality of outcome can occur only with restrictions on the free competition that is the basis of equality of opportunity. For example, schools and businesses aim at equality of outcome when they allocate admissions or jobs on the basis of race, gender, or disability—factors that are unrelated to ability. Some observers refer to these allocations as *quotas;* others call them *goals.* The difference is subtle. A quota *requires* that a specified, proportional share of some benefit go to a favored group. A goal *aims* for a proportional allocation of benefits, but without requiring it. The government seeks equality of outcome when it adjusts the rules to handicap some bidders and favor others. The vast majority of Americans, however, consistently favor low-bid contracting and merit-based admissions and employment over preferential treatment.[2] Quota- or goal-based policies muster only modest support.

Quota policies generate the most opposition because they confine competition. Quotas limit advancement for some individuals and ensure advancement for others by taking into account factors unrelated to ability. Quotas seem to be at odds with individual initiative. In other words, equality clashes with freedom. To understand the ways government resolves this conflict, we have to understand the evolution of civil rights in this country. The struggle of blacks has been a beacon lighting the way for Native Americans, Hispanic Americans, women, and the disabled. Each of these groups has confronted **invidious discrimination**. Discrimination is simply the act of making or recognizing distinctions. When making distinctions among people, discrimination may be benign (that is, harmless) or invidious (harmful).

Remember that **civil rights** are powers or privileges guaranteed to the individual and protected from arbitrary removal at the hands of the government or other individuals. Sometimes people refer to civil rights as "positive rights." In this chapter, we concentrate on the rights guaranteed by the constitutional amendments adopted after the Civil War and by laws passed to enforce those guarantees. Prominent among them is the right to equal protection under the law.

The Civil War Amendments

The Civil War amendments were adopted to provide freedom and equality to black Americans. The Thirteenth Amendment, ratified in 1865, provided that

> neither slavery nor involuntary servitude ... shall exist within the United States, or any place subject to their jurisdiction.

The Fourteenth Amendment, adopted three years later, provides first that freed slaves are citizens:

> All persons born or naturalized in the United States, and subject to the jurisdiction thereof, are citizens of the United States and of the State wherein they reside.

It also prohibits the states from abridging the "privileges or immunities of citizens of the United States" or depriving "any person of life, liberty, or property, without due process of law." The Fourteenth Amendment then goes on to protect equality under the law, declaring that no state shall

> deny to any person within its jurisdiction the equal protection of the laws.

The Fifteenth Amendment, adopted in 1870, added a measure of political equality:

> The right of citizens of the United States to vote shall not be denied or abridged by the United States or by any State on account of race, color, or previous condition of servitude.

American blacks were thus free and politically equal—at least according to the Constitution. But for many years, the courts sometimes thwarted the efforts of other branches to protect these constitutional rights.

Congress and the Supreme Court: Lawmaking Versus Law Interpreting

In the years after the Civil War, Congress went to work to protect the rights of black citizens. In 1866, lawmakers passed a civil rights act that granted all citizens, white and black, the right to make and enforce contracts; sue or be sued; give evidence; and inherit, purchase, lease, sell, hold, or convey property. Later, in the Civil Rights Act of 1875, Congress attempted to guarantee blacks equal access to public accommodations (streetcars, inns, parks, theaters, and the like).

Although Congress enacted laws to protect the civil rights of black citizens, the Supreme Court weakened some of those rights. In 1873, the Court ruled that the Civil War amendments had not changed the relationship between the state and national governments.[3] State citizenship and national citizenship remained separate and distinct. According to the Court, the Fourteenth Amendment did not obligate the states to honor the rights guaranteed by U.S. citizenship. In effect, the Court stripped the amendment of its power to secure for black citizens the freedoms guaranteed by the Bill of Rights.

In 1883, the Court struck down the public accommodations section of the Civil Rights Act of 1875.[4] The justices declared that the national government could prohibit only government action that discriminated against blacks. Private acts of discrimination or acts of omission by a state, they maintained, were beyond the reach of the national government. The Court refused to see racial discrimination as an act that the national government could prohibit. By tolerating racial discrimination, the justices abetted **racism**, the belief that there are inherent differences among the races that determine people's achievement and that one's own race is superior to, and thus has a right to dominate, others.

The Court's decisions gave the states ample room to maneuver around civil rights laws. In the matter of voting rights, for example, states that

racism A belief that human races have distinct characteristics such that one's own race is superior to, and has a right to rule, others.

wanted to bar black men from the polls simply used nonracial means to do so. One popular tool was the **poll tax**, first imposed by Georgia in 1877. This was a tax of $1 or $2 on every citizen who wanted to vote. The tax was not a burden for most whites. But many blacks were tenant farmers who did not have any extra money for voting. Other bars to black suffrage included literacy tests, minimum education requirements, and a grandfather clause that restricted suffrage to men who could establish that their grandfathers were eligible to vote before 1867 (three years before the Fifteenth Amendment declared that race could not be used to deny individuals the right to vote).[5] Intimidation and violence were also used to keep blacks from the polls.

The Roots of Racial Segregation

Well before the Civil War, **racial segregation** was a way of life in the South: blacks lived and worked separately from whites. After the war, southern states began to enact Jim Crow laws that enforced segregation (*Jim Crow* was a derogatory term for a black person). Once the Supreme Court took the teeth out of the Civil Rights Act of 1875, such laws proliferated. They required blacks to live in separate (generally inferior) areas and restricted them to separate sections of hospitals, separate cemeteries, separate schools, and separate sections of streetcars, trains, jails, and parks. Each day, in countless ways, blacks were reminded of the inferior status accorded them by white society.

In 1892, Homer Adolph Plessy, who was seven-eighths Caucasian, took a seat in a "whites only" car of a Louisiana train. He refused to move to the car reserved for blacks and was arrested. Plessy argued that Louisiana's law mandating racial segregation on its trains was an unconstitutional infringement on the privileges and immunities guaranteed by the Fourteenth Amendment and its equal protection clause. The Supreme Court disagreed. The majority in *Plessy* v. *Ferguson* (1896) upheld state-imposed racial segregation.[6] They based their decision on the **separate-but-equal doctrine**, which held that separate facilities for blacks and whites satisfied the Fourteenth Amendment so long as they were equal. The lone dissenter, Justice John Marshall Harlan, who envisioned a "color-blind Constitution," wrote this in his dissenting opinion:

> We boast of the freedom enjoyed by our people above all other peoples. But it is difficult to reconcile that boast with a state of the law which, practically, puts the brand of servitude and degradation upon a large class of our fellow citizens—our equals before the law. The thin disguise of "equal" accommodations for passengers in railroad coaches will not mislead any one, nor atone for the wrong this day done.[7]

Three years later, the Supreme Court extended the separate-but-equal doctrine to schools.[8] The justices ignored the fact that black educational

poll tax A tax of $1 or $2 on every citizen who wished to vote, first instituted in Georgia in 1877. Although it was no burden on most white citizens, it effectively disenfranchised blacks.

racial segregation Separation from society because of race.

separate-but-equal doctrine The concept that providing separate but equivalent facilities for blacks and whites satisfies the equal protection clause of the Fourteenth Amendment.

facilities (and most other "colored-only" facilities) were far from equal to those reserved for whites.

By the end of the nineteenth century, racial segregation was firmly and legally entrenched in the American South. Although constitutional amendments and national laws to protect equality under the law were in place, the Supreme Court's interpretation of those amendments and laws rendered them ineffective. Several decades passed before any change was discernible.

The Dismantling of School Segregation

By the middle of the twentieth century, public attitudes toward race relations were slowly changing. Black troops had fought with honor, albeit in segregated military units, in World War II. Blacks and whites were working together in unions and in service and religious organizations. Social change and court decisions suggested that government-imposed segregation was vulnerable.

President Harry S Truman risked his political future with his strong support of blacks' civil rights. In 1947, he established the President's Committee on Civil Rights. The committee's report, issued later that year, became the agenda for the civil rights movement over the next two decades. It called for national laws prohibiting racially motivated poll taxes, segregation, and brutality against minorities and for guarantees of voting rights and equal employment opportunity. In 1948, Truman ordered the **desegregation** (the dismantling of authorized racial segregation) of the armed forces.

In 1947, the U.S. Department of Justice had begun to submit briefs to the courts in support of civil rights. Perhaps the department's most important intervention came in *Brown* v. *Board of Education*.[9] This case was the culmination of twenty years of planning and litigation by the National Association for the Advancement of Colored People (NAACP) to invalidate racial segregation in public schools.

Linda Brown was a black child whose father tried to enroll her in a white public school in Topeka, Kansas. Brown's request was refused because of Linda's race. A federal district court found that the black public school was, in all major respects, equal in quality to the white school; therefore, according to the *Plessy* doctrine, Linda was required to go to the black public school. Brown appealed the decision.

Brown v. *Board of Education* reached the Supreme Court in late 1951. The justices delayed argument on the sensitive race issue, placing the case beyond the 1952 national election. *Brown* was merged with four similar cases into a class action (see Chapter 11). The class action was supported by the NAACP and coordinated by Thurgood Marshall, who later became the first black justice to sit on the Supreme Court. The five cases squarely challenged the separate-but-equal doctrine. By all tangible measures (standards for teacher licensing, teacher-pupil ratios, library facilities), the two

desegregation The ending of authorized segregation, or separation by race.

school systems in each case—one white, the other black—were equal. The issue was legal separation of the races.

On May 17, 1954, Chief Justice Earl Warren, who had recently joined the Court, delivered a single opinion covering four of the cases. Warren spoke for a unanimous Court when he declared that "in the field of public education the doctrine of 'separate but equal' has no place. Separate educational facilities are inherently unequal,"[10] depriving the plaintiffs of the equal protection of the laws. Segregated facilities generate in black children "a feeling of inferiority . . . that may affect their hearts and minds in a way unlikely ever to be undone."[11] In short, the nation's highest court found that state-imposed public school segregation violated the equal protection clause of the Fourteenth Amendment.

The Court deferred implementation of the school desegregation decisions until 1955. Then, in *Brown* v. *Board of Education II*, it ruled that school systems must desegregate "with all deliberate speed," and it assigned the process of supervising desegregation to the lower federal courts.[12]

Some states quietly complied with the *Brown* decree. Others did little to desegregate their schools. Many communities in the South defied the Court, sometimes violently. This resistance, along with the Supreme Court's "all deliberate speed" order, placed a heavy burden on federal judges to dismantle what was the fundamental social order in many communities.[13] Gradual desegregation under *Brown* was in some cases no desegregation at all. By 1969, a unanimous Supreme Court ordered that the operation of segregated school systems must stop "at once."[14]

Two years later, the Court approved several remedies to achieve integration, including busing, racial quotas, and the pairing or grouping of noncontiguous school zones. But these remedies applied only to **de jure segregation,** government-imposed segregation (for example, government assignment of whites to one school and blacks to another within the same community). Court-imposed remedies did not apply to **de facto segregation,** segregation that is not the result of government influence (for example, racial segregation resulting from residential patterns).

Public opinion strongly opposed the busing approach, and Congress sought limits on busing as a remedy. In 1974, a closely divided Court ruled that lower courts could not order busing across school district boundaries unless each district had practiced racial discrimination or unless school district lines had been deliberately drawn to achieve racial segregation.[15]

The Civil Rights Movement

The NAACP concentrated on school desegregation but made headway in other areas as well. The Supreme Court responded to NAACP efforts in the late 1940s by outlawing the whites-only primary elections in the South, declaring them to be in violation of the Fifteenth Amendment. The Court also declared segregation on interstate bus routes to be unconstitutional, and it

---

INTERACTIVE 13.1

 Brown v. Board of Education

INTERACTIVE 13.2

 Black History Month

INTERACTIVE 13.3

 Montgomery: A Victory for Civil Rights

de jure segregation
Government-imposed segregation.

de facto segregation
Segregation that is not the result of government influence.

desegregated restaurants and hotels in the District of Columbia. Despite these and other decisions that chipped away at existing barriers to equality, the realization of equality required the political mobilization of the people—black and white—into what is now known as the **civil rights movement**.

Civil Disobedience

Rosa Parks, a black woman living in Montgomery, Alabama, sounded the first call to action. That city's Jim Crow ordinances required blacks to sit in the back of the bus and empowered drivers to order blacks to vacate an entire row of seats to make room for one white or to order blacks to stand even when some seats were vacant. In December 1955, Parks boarded a city bus on her way home from work and took an available seat near the front of the bus. She refused to give up her seat when the driver asked her to do so and was arrested and fined $10 for violating the city ordinance.

Under the leadership of a charismatic twenty-six-year-old Baptist minister named Martin Luther King Jr., Montgomery's black community responded to Parks's arrest with a boycott of the city's bus system. A **boycott** is a refusal to do business with a company or individual, as an expression of disapproval or a means of coercion. A year after the boycott began, the federal courts ruled that segregated transportation systems violated the equal protection clause of the Constitution.

In 1957, King helped organize the Southern Christian Leadership Conference (SCLC) to coordinate civil rights activities. King was totally committed to nonviolent action to bring racial issues into the light. To that end, he advocated **civil disobedience**, the willful but nonviolent breach of unjust laws.

Martin Luther King Jr. had risen to worldwide prominence by August 1963, when he joined in a march on Washington, D.C., called "A March for Jobs and Freedom." More than 250,000 people, black and white, gathered peaceably at the Lincoln Memorial to hear King speak. "I have a dream," he told them, "that my little children will one day live in a nation where they will not be judged by the color of their skin but by the content of their character."[16]

The Civil Rights Act of 1964

President Lyndon B. Johnson considered civil rights his top legislative priority. Within months after he assumed office, Congress passed the Civil Rights Act of 1964, the most comprehensive legislative attempt ever to erase racial discrimination in the United States. Among its many provisions, the act:

- Entitled all persons to "the full and equal enjoyment" of goods, services, and privileges in places of public accommodation without discrimination on the grounds of race, color, religion, or national origin

INTERACTIVE 13.4

 "I Have a Dream"

civil rights movement The mass mobilization during the 1960s that sought to gain equality of rights and opportunities for blacks in the South and to a lesser extent in the North, mainly through nonviolent unconventional means of participation. Martin Luther King Jr. was the leading figure and symbol of the civil rights movement, but it was powered by the commitment of great numbers of people, black and white, of all sorts and stations in life.

boycott A refusal to do business with a firm, individual, or nation as an expression of disapproval or as a means of coercion.

civil disobedience The willful but nonviolent breach of laws that are regarded as unjust.

A Modern-Day Moses

Martin Luther King Jr. was a Baptist minister who believed in the principles of nonviolent protest practiced by India's Mohandas ("Mahatma") Gandhi. This photograph, taken in 1963 in Baltimore, captures the crowd's affection for King, the man many thought would lead them to a new Canaan of racial equality. King, who won the Nobel Peace Prize in 1964, was assassinated in 1968 in Memphis, Tennessee. (© Leonard Freed/Magnum Photos)

- Established the right to equality in employment opportunities

- Strengthened voting rights legislation

- Created the Equal Employment Opportunity Commission (EEOC) and charged it with hearing and investigating complaints of job discrimination*

- Provided that funds could be withheld from federally assisted programs that were administered in a discriminatory manner

President Johnson's goal was a "great society." Soon a constitutional amendment and a series of civil rights laws were in place to help him meet his goal:

- The Twenty-fourth Amendment, ratified in 1964, banned poll taxes in primary and general elections for national office.

- The Economic Opportunity Act of 1964 focused on education and training to combat poverty.

- The Voting Rights Act of 1965 empowered the attorney general to send voter registration supervisors to areas in which fewer than half the eligible minority voters had been registered. This act has been

---

*Since 1972, the EEOC has had the power to institute legal proceedings on behalf of employees who allege that they have been victims of illegal discrimination.

credited with doubling black voter registration in the South in only five years.[17]

■ The Fair Housing Act of 1968 banned discrimination in the rental or sale of most housing.

The Continuing Struggle Over Civil Rights

Civil rights laws on the books do not ensure civil rights in action. While Congress has tried to expand civil rights enforcement, the Supreme Court has weakened it in recent years. In 1989, the Court restricted minority contractor set-asides of state public works funds, an arrangement it had approved in 1980. (A *set-aside* is a purchasing or contracting provision that reserves a certain percentage of funds for minority-owned contractors.) The five-person majority held that past societal discrimination alone cannot serve as the basis for rigid quotas.[18]

Buttressed by Republican appointees, the Supreme Court continued to narrow the scope of national civil rights protections in a string of decisions that suggested the ascendancy of a new conservative majority concerned more with freedom than with equality.[19] To counter the Court's changing interpretations of civil rights laws, liberals turned to Congress to restore and enlarge earlier Court decisions by writing them into law. The result was a comprehensive new civil rights bill. The Civil Rights Act of 1991 reversed or altered twelve Court decisions that had narrowed civil rights protections. The new law clarified and expanded earlier legislation and increased the costs to employers for intentional, illegal discrimination. Continued resentment generated by equal outcomes policies moved the battle back to the courts, however.

 # Civil Rights for Other Minorities

Recent civil rights laws and court decisions protect members of all minority groups. The Supreme Court underscored the breadth of this protection in an important decision in 1987.[20] The justices ruled unanimously that the Civil Rights Act of 1866 (known today as "Section 1981") offered broad protection against discrimination to all minorities. Previously, members of white ethnic groups could not invoke the law in bias suits. The 1987 decision allows members of *any* ethnic group—Italian, Iranian, Norwegian, or Chinese, for example—to recover money damages if they prove they were denied a job, excluded from rental housing, or subjected to another form of discrimination prohibited by the law. The 1964 Civil Rights Act offers similar protections but specifies strict procedures for filing suits that tend to discourage litigation.

Clearly the civil rights movement has had an effect on all minorities. Here we examine the civil rights struggles of three groups: Native Americans, immigrant groups, and the disabled.

Native Americans

During the eighteenth and nineteenth centuries, the U.S. government took Indian lands, isolated Native Americans on reservations, and denied them political and social rights. The government's dealings with the Indians were often marked by violence and broken promises. The agencies responsible for administering Indian reservations kept Native Americans poor and dependent on the national government.

The national government switched policies at the beginning of the twentieth century, promoting assimilation instead of separation. The government banned the use of native languages and religious rituals; it sent Indian children to boarding schools and gave them non-Indian names. In 1924, Indians received U.S. citizenship. Until that time, they were considered members of tribal nations whose relations with the U.S. government were determined by treaties. The agencies responsible for administering Indian reservations kept Native Americans poor and dependent on the national government. And Indian lands continued to shrink through the 1950s and into the 1960s—despite signed treaties and the religious significance of portions of the lands they lost.

Anger bred of poverty, unemployment, and frustration with an uncaring government exploded into militant action in November 1969, when several Indians seized Alcatraz Island, an abandoned island in San Francisco Bay. The group cited an 1868 Sioux treaty that entitled them to unused federal lands; they remained on the island for a year and a half. In 1973, armed members of the American Indian Movement seized eleven hostages at Wounded Knee, South Dakota, the site of an 1890 massacre of two hundred Sioux (Lakota) by U.S. cavalry troops. They remained there, occasionally exchanging gunfire with federal marshals, for seventy-one days until the government agreed to examine the treaty rights of the Oglala Sioux.[21]

In 1946, Congress enacted legislation establishing an Indian claims commission to compensate Native Americans for land that had been taken from them. In the 1970s, the Native American Rights Fund and other groups used that legislation to win important victories in the courts. The tribes won the return of lands in the Midwest and in the states of Oklahoma, New Mexico, and Washington. In 1980, the Supreme Court ordered the national government to pay the Sioux $117 million plus interest for the Black Hills of South Dakota, which had been stolen from them a century before. Other cases, involving land from coast to coast, are still pending.

The special status accorded Indian tribes in the Constitution has proved attractive to a new kind of Indian leaders. Some of the 557 recognized tribes have successfully instituted casino gambling on their reservations, even in the face of state opposition. Congress allows these developments provided that the tribes spend their profits on Indian assistance programs. The wealth created by casino gambling and other ventures funded with gambling profits may prove to be Native Americans' most effective weapon for retaining and regaining their heritage.

DO IT!

Educate yourself about Native Americans at the library or a campus group. Remember, no single organization speaks for all tribes or individuals. Identify the range of ideas to promote greater equality for native peoples.

Laboring Without Illegals
On May 1, 2007, mothers and babies took to the streets in seventy-five cities across the United States to march for immigrant and labor rights. Demonstrations like this are intended to convey many messages. One aim of this Labor Day march was to stress the importance of immigrant labor to the lives of Americans. Another was to support a public policy of legalization rather than deportation for undocumented workers. The strollers reminded spectators that children born in the United States are U.S. citizens, regardless of their parents' status. *(© J. Emilio Flores/Corbis)*

Immigrant Groups

For most of the first half of the twentieth century, immigration rules established a strict quota system that gave a clear advantage to Northern and Western Europeans and guaranteed that few Southern or Eastern Europeans, Asians, Africans, and Jews would enter the country by legal means. In 1965, President Lyndon Johnson signed a new immigration bill into law. Henceforth, the invidious quota system was gone; everyone was supposed to have an equal chance of immigrating to the United States. One purpose of the new law was to reunite families. Another provision gave preference in much smaller numbers to immigrants with needed skills, such as doctors and engineers.

The demand for cheap labor in agriculture and manufacturing proved an enticing lure to many of the poor with access to America's southern border. The personal risk in crossing the border illegally was often outweighed by the possible gain in employment and a new, though illegal, start. In 1986 Congress placed the burden of enforcement on employers by imposing fines for hiring undocumented workers and then by offering amnesty to resident illegal immigrants who were in the United States for at least five years.

Many Latinos have a rich and deep-rooted heritage in America, but until the 1920s that heritage was largely confined to the southwestern states and California. Then unprecedented numbers of Mexican and Puerto Rican immigrants came to the United States in search of employment and a better life. Businesspeople who saw in them a source of cheap labor welcomed them. Many Mexicans became farm workers, but both groups settled mainly in crowded low-rent, inner-city districts: Mexicans in the Southwest and Puerto Ricans primarily in New York City. Like blacks who had migrated to northern cities, most of them met poverty and discrimination. During the Great Depression in the 1930s, about one-third of the Mexican American population (mainly those who had been migratory farm workers) returned to Mexico.

World War II gave rise to another influx of Mexicans, this time primarily courted to work on farms in California. But by the late 1950s, most farm workers—blacks, whites, and Hispanics—were living in poverty. Hispanic Americans who lived in cities fared little better. Yet millions of Mexicans continued to cross the border into the United States, both legally and illegally. The effect was to depress wages for farm labor in California and the Southwest.

The Hispanic American population continues to grow. The 20 million Hispanics living in the United States in the 1970s were still mainly Puerto Rican and Mexican American, but they were joined by immigrants from the Dominican Republic, Colombia, Cuba, Ecuador, and elsewhere. Although civil rights legislation helped them to some extent, they are among the poorest and least-educated groups in the United States.

One effect of the language barrier is that voter registration and voter turnout among Hispanic citizens are lower than among other groups. Also, voter turnout depends on effective political advertising, and Hispanics are not targeted as often as other groups with political messages that they can understand. But despite these stumbling blocks, Latinos have started to exercise a measure of political power.

Hispanics or Latinos constitute approximately 15 percent of the population and 5 percent of the Congress. The 110th Congress (2007–2009) convened with a group of twenty-six Hispanic House members (twenty-two Democrats and four Republicans) and three Hispanic senators (two Democrats and one Republican). Eight members are of Asian, Native Hawaiian, or Pacific Island heritage, six in the House (five Democrats and one Republican) and two in the Senate (both Democrats). Eleven U.S. representatives and one senator were born outside the United States.[22]

Disabled Americans

Minority status is not confined to racial and ethnic groups. Forty-three million disabled Americans gained recognition in 1990 as a protected minority with the enactment of the Americans with Disabilities Act (ADA). The law extends the protections embodied in the Civil Rights Act of 1964 to people with physical or mental disabilities, including people with AIDS, recovering alcoholics, and drug abusers. It guarantees them access to employment, transportation, public accommodations, and communication services.

Advocates for the disabled found a ready model in the existing civil rights laws. Opponents argued that the changes mandated by the 1990 law (such as access for those confined to wheelchairs) could cost billions of dollars, but supporters replied that the costs would be offset by an equal or greater reduction in federal aid to disabled people, who would rather be working.

The law's enactment set off an avalanche of job discrimination complaints filed with the national government's discrimination watchdog agency, the Equal Employment Opportunity Commission (EEOC). By 2007, the EEOC had received over 253,000 ADA-related complaints. Most complaints charged that employers failed to provide reasonable accommodations as required by the law.[23]

A change in the law, no matter how welcome, does not ensure a change in attitudes. Laws that end racial discrimination do not extinguish racism, and laws that ban biased treatment of the disabled cannot mandate their acceptance. But civil rights advocates predict that bias against the disabled, like similar attitudes toward other minorities, will wither away as they become full participants in society.

Gender and Equal Rights: The Women's Movement

The Supreme Court has expanded the array of legal weapons available to all minorities to help them achieve social equality. Women, too, have benefited from this change.

Political Equality for Women

Until the early 1970s, laws that affected the civil rights of women were based on traditional views of the relationship between men and women. At the heart of these laws was **protectionism**—the notion that women must be sheltered from life's harsh realities. And protected they were, through laws that discriminated against them in employment and other areas. With few exceptions, women were also "protected" from voting until early in the twentieth century.

In 1878, Susan B. Anthony, a women's rights activist, persuaded a U.S. senator from California to introduce a constitutional amendment requiring that "the right of citizens of the United States to vote shall not be denied or abridged by the United States or by any State on account of sex." The amendment was introduced and voted down a number of times over the next twenty years. Meanwhile, a number of states, primarily in the Midwest and West, granted limited suffrage to women.

By the early 1900s, the movement for women's suffrage had become a political battle to amend the Constitution. The battle was won in 1920 when the **Nineteenth Amendment** gave women the right to vote in the wording first suggested by Anthony.

protectionism The notion that women must be protected from life's cruelties, the basis, until the 1970s, for laws affecting women's civil rights.

Nineteenth Amendment The amendment to the Constitution, adopted in 1920, that assures women of the right to vote.

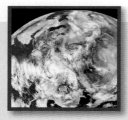

Politics of Global Change

Gender Quotas for Representatives in Lower Legislative Houses

One way to assure the election of women to public office is to mandate it. Several countries have taken such action, with mixed results. One approach is to establish a quota system requiring that women must constitute a certain percentage or number of elective positions. The philosophical justifi-

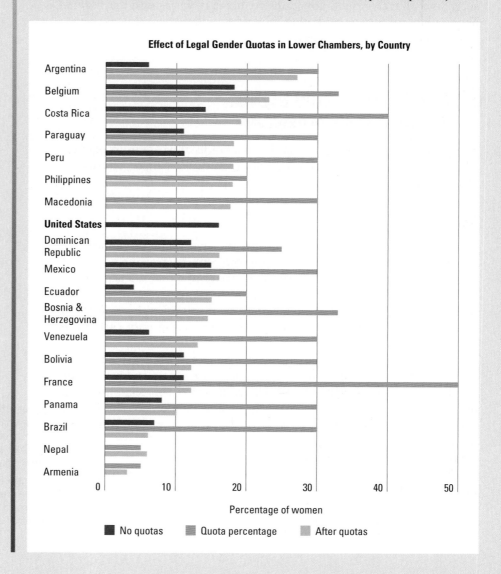

Effect of Legal Gender Quotas in Lower Chambers, by Country

Argentina
Belgium
Costa Rica
Paraguay
Peru
Philippines
Macedonia
United States
Dominican Republic
Mexico
Ecuador
Bosnia & Herzegovina
Venezuela
Bolivia
France
Panama
Brazil
Nepal
Armenia

Percentage of women

0   10   20   30   40   50

■ No quotas   ▨ Quota percentage   ▨ After quotas

cation behind this idea is the notion of equality of outcome. While women constitute 50 percent of the population, they hold far fewer political offices than do men. The establishment of legal quotas aims at solving this disparity.

There are different mechanisms to pursue such a result. Some nations include quotas in their constitutions, such as Nepal and the Philippines; others do so in their electoral laws, such as most of Latin America; and in some cases several political parties advance a voluntary quota system regardless of their country's legislation, such as in Germany, Italy, Norway, and Sweden. Gender quota systems also vary according to the level in which they are applied. In some cases they regulate the number of female candidates, whereas in others they mandate the number or percent of elected positions held by women.

Have these quota systems achieved their desired level of gender equality? The figure on the left identifies eighteen countries with gender quota systems (and the United States, which lacks such a system), their gender goals, and in thirteen cases the pre- and post-quota results. In no case have actual electoral results lived up to the established quota, and there is great variance regarding the ultimate effectiveness of gender quotas. Women's representation increased significantly in some countries such as Argentina; but in most countries, the result is not as spectacular. The figure on the right offers a partial explanation for the disparity. The main reason is the electoral system itself. Quotas are most effective in proportional representation systems with closed lists of candidates and least effective in majoritarian electoral systems.

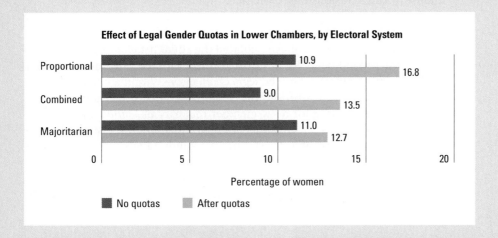

Effect of Legal Gender Quotas in Lower Chambers, by Electoral System

Electoral System	No quotas	After quotas
Proportional	10.9	16.8
Combined	9.0	13.5
Majoritarian	11.0	12.7

Percentage of women

■ No quotas   ■ After quotas

The right of women to vote does not assure that women representatives will be elected to public office. Beginning in the 1990s, several countries sought to assure elected representation of women by the use of gender quotas. The results have been mixed. (See "Politics of Global Change: Gender Quotas for Representatives in Lower Legislative Houses.")

Prohibiting Sex-Based Discrimination

The movement to provide equal rights to women advanced a step with the passage of the Equal Pay Act of 1963. That act requires equal pay for men and women doing similar work. However, to remove the restrictions of protectionism, women needed equal opportunity for employment. They got it in the Civil Rights Act of 1964 and later legislation. The EEOC, which had been created by that law, was empowered to act on behalf of victims of invidious sex discrimination, or **sexism**.

Stereotypes Under Scrutiny

After nearly a century of protectionism, the Supreme Court began to take a closer look at gender-based distinctions. In 1971, it struck down a state law that gave men preference over women in administering the estate of a person who died without naming an administrator.[24] Two years later, the justices declared that paternalism operated to "put women not on a pedestal, but in a cage."[25] They then proceeded to strike down several gender-based laws that either prevented or discouraged departures from "proper" sex roles. In 1976, the Court finally developed a workable standard for reviewing these kinds of laws. Gender-based distinctions are justified only if they serve some important government purpose.[26]

The courts have not been reluctant to extend to women the constitutional guarantees won by blacks. In 1994, the Supreme Court extended the Constitution's equal protection guarantee by forbidding the exclusion of potential jurors on the basis of their sex.[27] The 1994 decision completed a constitutional revolution in jury selection that began in 1986 with a bar against juror exclusions based on race.

In 1996, the Court spoke with uncommon clarity when it declared that the men-only admissions policy of the Virginia Military Institute (VMI), a state-supported military college, violated the equal protection clause of the Fourteenth Amendment. In an effort to meet women's demands to enter VMI—and to stave off continued legal challenges—Virginia had established a separate-but-equal institution, the Virginia Women's Institute for Leadership (VWIL). Writing for a six-member majority in *United States* v. *Virginia,* Justice Ruth Bader Ginsburg applied a demanding test she labeled "skeptical scrutiny" to official acts that deny individuals rights or responsibilities based on their sex. "Parties who seek to defend gender-based government action," she wrote, "must demonstrate an 'exceedingly persuasive justification' for that action." Ginsburg declared that "women seeking and

sexism Invidious sex discrimination.

fit for a VMI-quality education cannot be offered anything less, under the State's obligation to afford them genuinely equal protection."[28] The upshot is that distinctions based on sex are now almost as suspect as distinctions based on race.

The Equal Rights Amendment

Policies protecting women, based largely on sexual stereotypes, have been woven into the legal fabric of American life. This protectionism has limited the freedom of women to compete with men socially and economically on an equal footing.

The **equal rights amendment (ERA)** was introduced in 1923. It declared that "equality of rights under the law shall not be denied or abridged by the United States or any State on account of sex." A national coalition of women's rights advocates generated enough support to get the ERA through Congress in 1972. However, the amendment died on July 1, 1982, three states short of adoption.

Despite the failure of the proposed amendment, some scholars argue that for practical purposes, the Supreme Court has implemented the ERA through its decisions. It has struck down distinctions based on sex and held that stereotyped generalizations of sexual differences must fall.[29] In recent rulings, the Court has held that states may require employers to guarantee job reinstatement to women returning from maternity leave, sexual harassment in the workplace is illegal, and a hostile work environment will be judged by a reasonable perception of abuse rather than a demonstration of psychological injury.[30]

Affirmative Action: Equal Opportunity or Equal Outcome?

In his vision of the Great Society, President Johnson linked economic rights with civil rights and equality of outcome with equality of opportunity. "Equal opportunity is essential, but not enough," he declared. "We seek not just legal equity but human ability, not just equality as a right and a theory but equality as a fact and equality as a result."[31] This commitment led to affirmative action programs to expand opportunities for women, minorities, and those who are disabled.

Affirmative action is a commitment by a business, employer, school, or other public or private institution to expand opportunities for women, blacks, Hispanic Americans, and members of other minority groups. It embraces a range of public and private programs, policies, and procedures, including special recruitment, preferential treatment, and quotas in job training and professional education, employment, and the awarding of government contracts. The point of these programs is to move beyond equality of opportunity to equality of outcome.

equal rights amendment (ERA) A failed constitutional amendment introduced by the National Women's Party in 1923, declaring that "equality of rights under the law shall not be denied or abridged by the United States or any State on account of sex."

affirmative action Any of a wide range of programs, from special recruitment efforts to numerical quotas, aimed at expanding opportunities for women and minority group.

Arguments for affirmative action programs (from increased recruitment efforts to quotas) tend to use the following reasoning. Certain groups have historically suffered invidious discrimination, denying them educational and economic opportunities. To eliminate the lasting effects of such discrimination, the public and private sectors must take steps to provide access to good education and jobs. If the majority once used discrimination to hold groups back, discriminating to benefit those groups is fair. Therefore, quotas are a legitimate means to provide a place on the ladder of success.[32]

Affirmative action opponents maintain that quotas for designated groups necessarily create invidious discrimination (in the form of reverse discrimination) against individuals who are themselves blameless. Moreover, they say, quotas lead to admission, hiring, or promotion of the less qualified at the expense of the well qualified. In the name of equality, such policies thwart individuals' freedom to succeed.

Reverse Discrimination

The Supreme Court confronted an affirmative action quota program for the first time in *Regents of the University of California* v. *Bakke.*[33] Allan Bakke, a thirty-five-year-old white man, had twice applied for admission to the University of California Medical School at Davis. He was rejected both times. The school had reserved sixteen places in each entering class of one hundred for qualified minority applicants as part of the university's affirmative action program. Bakke's qualifications (college grade point average and test scores) exceeded those of any of the minority students admitted in the two years his applications were rejected. Bakke contended, first in the California courts and then in the Supreme Court, that he was excluded from admission solely on the basis of race. He argued that the equal protection clause of the Fourteenth Amendment and the Civil Rights Act of 1964 prohibited this reverse discrimination.

The Court's decision in *Bakke* contained six opinions and spanned 154 pages. But even after careful analysis of the decision, discerning what the Court had decided was difficult. No opinion had a majority. One bloc of four justices opposed the medical school's plan; a second bloc of four justices supported the plan. Justice Lewis F. Powell Jr. agreed with parts of both arguments. With the first bloc, he argued that the school's rigid use of racial quotas violated the equal protection clause of the Fourteenth Amendment. With the second bloc, he contended that the use of race was permissible as one of several admissions criteria. Powell cast the deciding vote ordering the medical school to admit Bakke. Despite the confusing multiple opinions, the Court signaled its approval of affirmative action programs in education that use race as a *plus* factor (one of many such factors) but not as *the* factor (one that alone determines the outcome).

True to the pluralist model, groups opposed to affirmative action continued their opposition in federal courts and state legislatures. They met with some success. In 1995, the Supreme Court struck down government mandated set-aside programs in the U.S. Department of Transportation, declaring that such programs must be subject to the most searching judicial inquiry ("strict scrutiny") and must be "narrowly tailored" to achieve a "compelling government interest."[34]

By 2003, twenty-five years after *Bakke*, the Supreme Court was ready to weigh in again on affirmative action in two cases that challenged aspects of the University of Michigan's racial preference policies. In *Gratz* v. *Bollinger*, the Court considered the university's undergraduate admissions policy, which conferred 20 points automatically to members of favored groups (100 points guaranteed admission). In a 6–3 opinion, Chief Justice William H. Rehnquist argued that such a policy violated the equal protection clause because it lacked the narrow tailoring required for permissible racial preferences and it failed to provide for individualized consideration of each candidate.[35] In the second case, *Grutter* v. *Bollinger*, the Court considered the University of Michigan's law school admissions policy, which gave preference to minority applicants. The school defended its policy on the ground that it served a "compelling interest in achieving diversity among its student body." This time, the Court, in a 5–4 decision, held that the equal protection clause did not bar the school's narrowly tailored use of racial preferences to further a compelling interest that flowed from a racially diverse student body.[36] Since each applicant is judged individually on his or her merits, race remains only one among many factors that enter into the admissions decision.

The Politics of Affirmative Action

A comprehensive review of nationwide surveys conducted over the past twenty years reveals an unsurprising truth: blacks favor affirmative action programs, and whites do not. Women and men do not differ on this issue. The gulf between the races was wider in the 1970s than it is today, but the moderation results from shifts among blacks, not whites. Perhaps the most important finding is that "whites' views have remained essentially unchanged over twenty-five years."[37]

How do we account for the persistence of equal outcomes policies? A majority of Americans have consistently rejected explicit race or gender preferences for the awarding of contracts, employment decisions, and college admissions, regardless of the groups such preferences benefit. Nevertheless, preference policies have survived and thrived under both Democrats and Republicans. The list of protected groups has expanded beyond African Americans to include Hispanic Americans, Native Americans, Asian Pacific Americans, Subcontinental Asian Americans, and women. Politicians have a powerful motive—votes—to expand the number of protected groups and the benefits such policies provide.

The conflict between freedom and equality will continue as other individuals and groups press their demands through litigation and legislation.

The choice the country makes will depend on whether and to what extent Americans are prepared to change their minds on these thorny issues.

Summary

Americans want equality, but they disagree on the extent to which government should guarantee it. At the heart of this conflict is the distinction between equal opportunities and equal outcomes.

Congress enacted the Civil War amendments—the Thirteenth, Fourteenth, and Fifteenth amendments—to provide full civil rights to black Americans. In the late nineteenth century, the Supreme Court interpreted the amendments very narrowly, declaring that they did not restrain individuals from denying civil rights to blacks and did not apply to powers that were reserved for the states. The Court's rulings had the effect of denying the vote to most blacks and of institutionalizing racism, making racial segregation a fact of daily life.

Through a series of court cases spanning two decades, the Court slowly dismantled segregation in the schools. The battle for desegregation culminated in the *Brown* cases in 1954 and 1955, in which a now-supportive Supreme Court declared segregated schools to be inherently unequal and therefore unconstitutional. The Court also ordered the desegregation of all schools and upheld the use of busing to do so.

Gains in other civil rights areas came more slowly. The motivating force was the civil rights movement, led by Martin Luther King Jr. until his assassination in 1968. King believed strongly in civil disobedience and nonviolence, strategies that helped secure for blacks equality in voting rights, public accommodations, higher education, housing, and employment opportunity.

Civil rights activism and the civil rights movement worked to the benefit of all minority groups; in fact, they benefited all Americans. Native Americans obtained some redress for past injustices. Hispanic Americans came to recognize the importance of group action to achieve economic and political equality. Disabled Americans won civil rights protections enjoyed by African Americans and others. And civil rights legislation removed most of the protectionism that was, in effect, legalized discrimination against women in education and employment.

Despite legislative advances in the area of women's rights, the states did not ratify the equal rights amendment. Still, the struggle for ratification produced several positive results, heightening awareness of women's roles in society and mobilizing their political power. And legislation and judicial rulings implemented much of the amendment's provisions in practice. The Supreme Court now judges sex-based classification with "skeptical scrutiny," meaning that distinctions based on sex are almost as suspect as distinctions based on race.

Government and business instituted affirmative action programs to counteract the results of past discrimination. These provide preferential treatment for women, minorities, and the disabled in a number of areas that affect individuals' economic opportunity and

well-being. In effect, such programs discriminate to remedy earlier discrimination. When programs make race the determining factor in awarding contracts, offering employment, or granting admission to educational institutions, the courts will be skeptical of their validity. Racial preference policies once again pass constitutional muster, provided they are narrowly tailored and serve a compelling interest.

We can guarantee equal outcomes only if we restrict the free competition that is an integral part of equal opportunity. Many Americans object to policies that restrict individual freedom, such as quotas and set-asides that arbitrarily change the outcome of the race. The challenge of pluralist democracy is to balance the need for freedom with demands for equality.

KEY CASES

Plessy v. *Ferguson*
Brown v. *Board of Education*
Brown v. *Board of Education II*
United States v. *Virginia*
Regents of the University of California v. *Bakke*
Gratz v. *Bollinger*
Grutter v. *Bollinger*

CL **Resources:** Videos, Simulations, News, Timelines, Primary Sources

- Government Purposes and Public Policies
- Fragmentation and Coordination
- Economic Policy and the Budget

This icon will direct
you to resources and
activities on the website:
www.cengage.com/polisci/janda/
chall_dem_brief/7e

CL

THE ECONOMIC SKY WAS FALLING in foreign markets. On Monday, January 21, 2008, European stocks fell 7 percent, the largest drop since the September 11 attack on the United States in 2001.[1] The crash was worse in Asia and the Pacific Rim, where markets fell even lower. In Japan, one investor said, "America is the culprit. If the U.S. problems didn't exist, Japan's stock market wouldn't be down this much."[2] He was reflecting on the global bank losses from the U.S. subprime mortgage crisis.

On Tuesday, Ben Bernanke, chair of the Federal Reserve Board, announced a 0.75 percent cut in interest rates—the largest ever for a single day—to stimulate lending and improve the economy.[3] A week later, the Fed cut rates another 0.5 percent. Economists viewed these unprecedented, rapid rate cuts as superficial bandages for an economy deeply troubled by a record decline in housing values. On February 13, Congress passed a bipartisan bill to give $168 billion in tax rebates to people with low to middle incomes. Officials hoped that these rebate checks would boost the economy. Few were confident that these actions would be successful.

In the fall, a rapid series of events revealed just how deep the economic crisis was. On September 7, the federal government took con-trol of mortgage giants Fannie Mae and Freddie Mac. A week later Wall Street investment bank Lehman Brothers declared bankruptcy. On September 16 the government stepped in with an $85 billion loan to prevent the world's largest insurance company, AIG, from collapsing, lest it drag other financial giants with it. AIG had guaranteed mortgage-related securities for financial institutions and had incurred enormous losses. Bernanke and Secretary of the Treasury Henry Paulson went to Congress with a sobering message of potential economic calamity, and after two weeks of frenzied debate, Congress enacted a $700 billion bailout plan for the banking industry.[4] In mid-October, the Treasury undertook the partial purchase of nine of the largest banks in the United States.[5] The stock market dropped steadily, with the Dow losing over a quarter of its value between the beginning of 2008 and Election Day in November. A week after the election, the AIG bailout cost reached $150 billion.

How much control of the domestic economy can government really exercise? More concretely, how is the national budget formulated, and what role do taxes, spending, and deficits play? From another perspective, how do issues such as these arise, and what happens to them once they catch the public's attention?

Previous chapters have focused on individual institutions of government. Here we focus on government more broadly and ask how policymaking takes place across institutions. We first identify different types of public policies and then analyze the stages in the policymaking process. We examine how policy is made when many competing interest groups are trying to influence the outcome and how relationships between those groups, and between such groups and different parts of government, structure the policymaking process. Finally, we take a closer look at budgeting and policies relating to the economy.

 # Government Purposes and Public Policies

In Chapter 1, we noted that nearly all citizens are willing to accept limitations on their personal freedom in return for various benefits of government. We defined the major purposes of government as maintaining order, providing public benefits, and promoting equality. Different governments place different values on each broad purpose, and those differences are reflected in their public policies. A **public policy** is a general plan of action adopted by a government to solve a social problem, counter a threat, or pursue an objective.

Whatever their form and effectiveness, all policies have this in common: they are the means by which government pursues certain goals in specific situations. People disagree about public policies because they disagree about one or more of the following elements: the goals that government should have, the means it should use to achieve goals, and the perception of the situation at hand.

When people in and outside government disagree on goals, that disagreement is often rooted in a basic difference in values. As emphasized throughout this book, such value conflict is often manifested as disputes pitting freedom versus order or freedom versus equality. The roots of the values we hold can run deep, beginning with childhood socialization as the values of parents are transmitted to their children. Disputes involving values are in many ways the hardest to bridge since they reflect a basic worldview and go to the core of one's sense of right and wrong.

The problem of illegal drugs illustrates how different core values lead us to prefer different public policies. Everyone is in agreement that government should address the problems created by drugs. Yet there are sharply contrasting views of what should be done. Recall from Chapter 1 that libertarians put individual freedom above all else and want to limit government as much as possible. Many libertarians argue that drugs should be decriminalized; if people want to take drugs, they should be free to do so, just as they are free to drink alcohol if they want. If drugs were decriminalized, they could be sold openly, the prices would fall dramatically, and the crime associated with illegal drugs would largely evaporate. Conservatives' value system places considerable emphasis on order. In their mind, a decent, safe, and civilized society does not allow people to debase themselves through drug abuse. Pointing to the broad costs to society brought on through alcoholism, such as drunk driving accidents, conservatives argue that government should punish those who violate the law rather than decriminalize the behavior. Liberals place greater emphasis on treatment as a policy option. They regard drug addiction as a medical or emotional problem and believe that government should offer the services that addicts can

public policy A general plan of action adopted by the government to solve a social problem, counter a threat, or pursue an objective.

use to stop their self-destructive behavior. Liberals value equality, and their view on this issue is that government should be expansive so that it can help people in need. Many drug offenders are impoverished because of their spending on drugs and cannot pay for private treatment.

Types of Policies

Although values underlie choices, analysis of public policy does not usually focus explicitly on core beliefs. Political scientists often try to categorize public policy choices by their objectives. That is, in the broad scheme of things, what are policymakers trying to do by choosing a particular policy direction? One common purpose is to allocate resources so that some segment of society can receive a service or benefit. We can call these **distributive policies**. Consider, for example, budgetary earmarks for colleges and universities. In 2007 Congress appropriated $2.3 billion in projects designated for specific schools. Included was a $1.9 million grant to the City College of New York to help create the new Charles Rangel Center for Public Service, named for Representative Charles Rangel, who not coincidentally sponsored the earmark. Three Iowa legislators placed a $196,000 earmark into the budget for research on reducing swine and poultry odors.[6] Some projects seem vital, while others are derided as "pork barrel."

Distributional policies are not all projects or new buildings. Some are social programs designed to help a disadvantaged group in society. What distributional policies have in common is that all of us pay through our taxes to support those who receive the benefit, presumably because that benefit works toward the common good, such as enhanced security, a better-trained work force, or a cleaner environment. In contrast, **redistributional policies** are explicitly designed to take resources from one sector of society and transfer them to another (reflecting the core value of greater equality). In a rather unusual redistributional proposal in Seattle, Washington, in 2003, proponents of early childhood education programs succeeded in getting an initiative on a citywide ballot that would have added a 10 cent tax on every cup of espresso sold in the city. The new revenues brought in by this tax were to fund early childhood programs and, as such, the plan was to redistribute revenues from espresso drinkers to families with small children. The voters rejected the initiative, and no such redistribution took place.[7]

Another basic policy approach is **regulation**. In Chapter 10, we noted that regulations are the rules that guide the operation of government programs. When regulations apply to business markets, they are an attempt to structure the operations of that market in a particular way. Government intersperses itself as a referee, setting rules as to what kinds of companies can participate in what kinds of market activities. Trucking is a case in point. The United States used to restrict the entrance of Mexican trucks into this country, barring them from traveling more than 20 miles into the United States. Thus, they would have to unload their cargo at a transfer

distributive policies
Government policies designed to confer a benefit on a particular institution or group.

redistributional policies
Policies that take government resources, such as tax funds, from one sector of society and transfer them to another.

regulation Rules that guide the operation of government programs and business markets.

station, where it would be placed on an American carrier that would take the merchandise to its destination. The United States said it forbade Mexican trucks from traveling on their own to wherever their cargo was headed because they were not always safe and they polluted more than American trucks did. An international trade panel determined, however, that these regulatory rules violated the North American Free Trade Agreement. In response, Congress passed a new law providing for inspection stations at border crossings to ensure that the Mexican trucks were safe and that their drivers met the same licensing standards as American drivers. In the case of the Mexican trucks, the restrictive regulations were largely the product of lobbying by American trucking firms and the Teamsters union, which wanted to preserve business for themselves.[8]

This framework of distributional, redistributional, and regulatory policies is rather general, and there are surely policy approaches that do not fit neatly into one of these categories.[9] Nevertheless, this framework is a useful prism to examine public policymaking. Understanding the broad purposes of public policy allows a better evaluation of the tools necessary to attain these objectives.

A Policymaking Model

Not only do political scientists distinguish among the different types of policies, they also distinguish among different stages of the policymaking process and try to identify patterns in the way people attempt to influence decisions and in the way decisions are reached. We can separate the policymaking process into four stages: agenda setting, policy formulation, implementation, and policy evaluation.[10] Figure 14.1 shows the four stages in sequence. As the figure indicates, policymaking is a circular process: the end of one phase is the beginning of another.

Agenda setting is the stage at which problems are defined as political issues. Many problems confront Americans in their daily lives, but government is not actively working to solve them all. For example, the problem of poverty among the elderly did not suddenly arise during the 1930s, but that is when inadequate income for the elderly was defined as a political problem. When the government begins to consider acting on an issue it has previously ignored, we say that the issue has become part of the political agenda.

Why does an existing social problem become redefined as a political problem? There is no single reason; many factors can stimulate new thinking about a problem. Sometimes highly visible events or developments push issues onto the agenda. Issues may also reach the agenda through the efforts of scholars and activists to get more people to pay attention to a condition about which the general public seems unaware. The likelihood that a certain problem will move onto the agenda is also affected by who controls the government and by broad ideological shifts. Agenda building also may involve redefining old issues so that people look at them in different ways.[11]

agenda setting The stage of the policymaking process during which problems get defined as political issues.

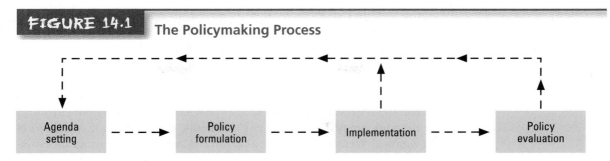

FIGURE 14.1 The Policymaking Process

This model, one of many possible ways to depict the policymaking process, shows four stages. Feedback on program operations and on performance from the last two stages stimulates new cycles of the process.

Policy formulation is the stage of the policymaking process in which formal policy proposals are developed and officials decide whether to adopt them. The most obvious kind of policy formulation is the proposal of a measure by the president or the development of legislation by Congress. Administrative agencies also formulate policy through the regulatory process. Courts too formulate policy when their decisions establish new interpretations of the law.

Policies are not self-executing; **implementation** is the stage at which they are carried out. When agencies in Washington issue regulations, some government bodies must put those policies into effect. In the case of the Americans with Disabilities Act, for example, the owners of office buildings probably would not have repositioned their water fountains simply because Washington had published new regulations. Administrative bodies at the regional, state, or local level had to inform them of the rules, give them a timetable for compliance, communicate the penalties for noncompliance, answer questions, and report to Washington on how well the regulations were working.

As pointed out in Chapter 10, one of the biggest problems at the implementation stage of policymaking is coordination. After officials in Washington enact a law and write the new regulations, people outside Washington typically are designated to implement the policy. The agents may be local officials, state administrators, or federal bureaucrats headquartered in regional offices around the country. Although implementation may sound highly technical, it is very much a political process calling for a great deal of bargaining and negotiation among different groups of people in and out of government.

Policy evaluation is the analysis of how well a policy is working. Evaluation tends to draw heavily on approaches used by academics, including cost-effectiveness analysis and statistical methods designed to provide quantitative measurements of program outcomes. Technical studies can be

policy formulation The stage of the policymaking process during which formal proposals are developed and adopted.

implementation The process of putting specific policies into operation.

policy evaluation Analysis of a public policy so as to determine how well it is working.

quite influential in decisions about whether to continue, expand, alter, reduce, or eliminate programs.

Evaluation is part of the policymaking process because it helps to identify problems and issues arising from current policy. In other words, evaluation studies provide **feedback** about program performance. (The dotted line in Figure 14.1 represents a feedback loop. Problems that emerge during the implementation stage also provide feedback to policymakers.) By drawing attention to emerging problems, policy evaluation influences the political agenda. Thus, we come full circle. Frequently, program evaluations reveal shortcomings in a program. The ambitious No Child Left Behind Act, passed by Congress in 2001, mandated improvements in schools' performance. Schools whose students do not score high enough on standardized tests can lose funding after receiving a warning. As soon as the first round of testing was completed under the new requirements, individual schools with significant percentages of students falling below the required performance thresholds were easily identified. Yet an evaluation providing feedback that a program is failing does not mean that the problem will be solved. After the first round of testing, some states, including Colorado and Michigan, reduced the performance standard for their students rather than risk eventually losing their funding under No Child Left Behind.[12] The states' changes solved the immediate political problem, but they did not address the underlying learning issues. The end of the policy process—evaluating whether the policy is being implemented as it was envisioned when it was formulated—marks the beginning of a new cycle of public policymaking.

Fragmentation and Coordination

The policymaking process encompasses many different stages and includes many different participants at each stage. Here we examine some forces that pull the government in different directions and make problem solving less coherent than it might otherwise be. In the next section, we look at some structural elements of American government that work to coordinate competing and sometimes conflicting approaches to the same problems.

Multiplicity and Fragmentation

A single policy problem may be attacked in different and sometimes competing ways by government for many reasons. At the heart of this **fragmentation** of policymaking is the fundamental nature of government in America. The separation of powers divides authority among the branches of the national government, and federalism divides authority among national, state, and local levels of government. These multiple centers of power are, of course, a primary component of pluralist democracy. Additionally, within any issue area, a number—often a very large number—of interest groups try to

feedback Information received by policymakers about the effectiveness of public policy.

fragmentation In policymaking, the phenomenon of attacking a single problem in different and sometimes competing ways.

influence policy decisions. Representatives from these organizations interact with one another and with government officials on a recurring basis. The ongoing interaction produces both conflict and cooperation.

Fragmentation is often the result of many different agencies being created at different times to address different problems. Over time, however, as those problems evolve and mutate, they can become more closely related even as the different agencies do little or nothing to try to coordinate their efforts. Many of the intelligence and operational failures associated with the September 11 terrorist attacks can be traced in part to the lack of coordination among various security-related agencies. In the area of border and transportation security, for example, responsibility was split among the Immigration and Naturalization Service, the Customs Service, the Coast Guard, the Federal Protective Services, and other agencies.

The first post-9/11 attempt to overcome this fragmentation was the Office of Homeland Security within the White House. However, it was a conspicuous failure as the relevant agencies spread throughout the government were tenacious in resisting encroachments on their autonomy and authority from the new White House unit.[13]

So powerful was the resistance (and so vast was the job to be done) that the Bush administration and Congress created a new cabinet department incorporating twenty-two existing agencies of the government. Thus, the solution was to break up the existing government agencies and rearrange their offices and duties into new administrative structures.[14] Even so, the new Department of Homeland Security went only part of the way in overcoming fragmentation in this area. To coordinate the efforts of the sixteen-member intelligence community, Congress passed a separate law in 2004 to create a new director of national intelligence.[15]

Congress is characterized by the same diffusion of authority. At the time the Department of Homeland Security was created, sixty-one House and Senate committees and subcommittees possessed some degree of jurisdiction over the agencies that were incorporated into the new organization.[16]

The Pursuit of Coordination

How does the government overcome fragmentation so that it can make its public policies more coherent? One common response to the problem of coordination is the formation of interagency task forces within the executive branch. Their common goal is to develop a broad policy response that all relevant agencies will endorse. Such task forces include representatives of all agencies claiming responsibility for a particular issue. They attempt to forge good policy as well as goodwill among competing agencies.

As illustrated with the case of homeland security, reorganization of disparate parts of government working in related areas is a fundamental approach to enhancing coordination. Despite the obstacles that administrators trying to protect their turf put up, reorganization across agencies is possible. The involvement and commitment of the president is often critical, as his status and willingness to expend political capital can put reorganizations on the agenda and push them forward.

The Office of Management and Budget (OMB) also fosters coordination within the executive branch. OMB can do much more than review budgets and look for ways to improve management practices. Since the Reagan administration, presidents have used this office to clear regulations before they were proposed publicly by the administrative agencies. OMB's regulatory review role centralizes control of the executive branch.

In a decentralized, federal system of government with large numbers of interest groups, fragmentation is inevitable. Beyond the structural factors is the natural tendency of people and organizations to defend their base of power. Government officials understand, however, that mechanisms of coordination are necessary so that fragmentation does not overwhelm policymaking. Mechanisms such as interagency task forces, reorganizations, and White House review can bring some coherence to policymaking.

Government by Policy Area

Policy formulation takes place across different institutions. Participants from these institutions do not patiently wait their turn as policymaking proceeds from one institution to the next. Rather, they try to influence policy at whatever stage they can. Suppose that Congress is considering amendments to the Clean Air Act. Because Congress does not function in a vacuum, the other parts of government that will be affected by the legislation participate in the process too. The Environmental Protection Agency (EPA) has an interest in the outcome because it will have to administer the law. The White House is concerned about any legislation that affects such vital sectors of the economy as the steel and coal industries. As a result, officials from both the EPA and the White House work with members of Congress and the appropriate committee staffs to try to ensure that their interests are protected. At the same time, lobbyists representing corporations, trade associations, and environmental groups do their best to influence Congress, agency officials, and White House aides. Trade associations might hire public relations firms to sway public opinion toward their industry's point of view. Experts from think tanks and universities might be asked to testify at hearings or to serve in an informal advisory capacity in regard to the technical, economic, and social effects of the proposed amendments.

The various individuals and organizations that work in a particular policy area form a loosely knit community. The boundaries and membership of an **issue network** are hardly precise, but participants share expertise in a policy domain and interact frequently.[17] In general terms, such networks include members of Congress, committee staffers, agency officials, lawyers, lobbyists, consultants, scholars, and public relations specialists. This makes for a large number of participants. One study identified over twelve hundred interest groups that had some contact with government officials in Washington in relation to health care over a five-year period.[18] Not all of

issue network A shared-knowledge group consisting of representatives of various interests involved in some particular aspect of public policy.

the participants in an issue network have a working relationship with all the others. Indeed, some may be chronic antagonists. Others tend to be allies.

The common denominator in a network is not the same political outlook; it is policy expertise. One must have the necessary expertise to enter the community of activists and politicians that influence policymaking in an issue area. Consider Medicare, for example. The program is crucial to the health of the elderly, and with millions of baby boomers rapidly approaching retirement age, it needs to be restructured to make sure there will be enough money available to care for them all. But to enter the political debate on this issue requires specialized knowledge. What is the difference between a "defined benefit" and a "defined contribution" or between a "provider-sponsored organization" and a "health maintenance organization"? Without getting into "portability" or "capitated" arrangements, is it better to have "medical savings accounts" or "fee-for-service" plans?[19]

The members of an issue network speak the same language. They can participate in the negotiation and compromise of policymaking because they can offer concrete, detailed solutions to the problems at hand. They understand the substance of policy, the way Washington works, and one another's viewpoints.

In a number of ways, issue networks promote pluralist democracy. They are open systems, populated by a wide range of interest groups. Decision making is not centralized in the hands of a few key players; policies are formulated in a participatory fashion. But there is still no guarantee that all relevant interests are represented, and those with the greatest financial resources have an advantage. Nevertheless, issue networks provide access to government for a diverse set of competing interests and thus further the pluralist ideal.[20]

Those who prefer majoritarian democracy, however, see issue networks as an obstacle to achieving their vision of how government should operate. The technical complexity of contemporary issues makes it especially difficult for the public at large to exert control over policy outcomes. However, although issue networks promote pluralism, keep in mind that majoritarian influences on policymaking are still significant. The broad contours of public opinion can be a dominant force on highly visible issues. Elections, too, send messages to policymakers about the most widely discussed campaign issues. What issue networks have done, however, is facilitate pluralist politics in policy areas in which majoritarian influences are weak.

 ## Economic Policy and the Budget

While the Washington policy community includes thousands of actors scattered throughout many issue networks, their issues share one thing in common. Whether large or small, there are economic and budgetary consequences to the acceptance of their policy proposals. Policymakers must consider not only the direct costs of a new antipollution measure or health program, but also the broader impact that starting such programs might have on the nation's economy. Tinkering with the economy is not a task to be undertaken lightly. Economists often disagree about the budgetary impact of various programs and whether they would help or hurt broader efforts to control the ups and downs of the nation's economy.

Economic Theory

Government efforts to control the economy rely on theories about how the economy responds to government taxing and spending policies and its control of the money supply. How policymakers tax and spend, or loosen and tighten interest rates, depends on their beliefs about how the economy functions and the proper role of government in the economy.

Keynesian theory, developed by John Maynard Keynes, a British economist, holds that government can stabilize the economy through a combination of fiscal and monetary policies.[21] **Fiscal policies,** which are enacted by the president and Congress, involve changes in government spending and taxing. When demand for goods and services is too low, according to Keynes, government should either spend more itself—hiring people and thus giving them money—or cut taxes, giving people more of their own money to spend. When demand is too great, the government should either spend less or raise taxes, giving people less money to spend. **Monetary policies,** which are largely determined by the Federal Reserve Board, involve changes in the money supply and operate less directly on the economy. Increasing the amount of money in circulation increases demand and thus increases **inflation,** price increases that decrease the value of currency. Decreasing the money supply decreases aggregate demand and inflationary pressures.

Governments frequently use the Keynesian technique of **deficit financing**— spending in excess of tax revenues—to combat an economic slump. The objective of deficit financing is to inject extra money into the economy to stimulate aggregate demand.

In 1946, the year Keynes died, Congress passed an employment act establishing "the continuing responsibility of the national government to . . . promote maximum employment, production and purchasing power." It also created the **Council of Economic Advisers (CEA)** within the Executive Office of the President to advise the president on maintaining a stable economy.

Monetary policies in the United States are under the control of the **Federal Reserve System,** which acts as the country's central bank. At the top of the system is the board of governors, seven members who are appointed by the president for staggered terms of fourteen years. The president designates one member of the board to be its chairperson, serving a four-year term that extends beyond the president's term of office.

Keynesian theory An economic theory stating that the government can stabilize the economy—that is, can smooth business cycles—by controlling the level of aggregate demand, and that the level of aggregate demand can be controlled by means of fiscal and monetary policies.

fiscal policies Economic policies that involve government spending and taxing.

monetary policies Economic policies that involve control of, and changes in, the supply of money.

inflation An economic condition characterized by price increases linked to a decrease in the value of the currency.

deficit financing The Keynesian technique of spending beyond government income to combat an economic slump. Its purpose is to inject extra money into the economy to stimulate aggregate demand.

Council of Economic Advisers (CEA) A group that works within the executive branch to provide advice on maintaining a stable economy.

Federal Reserve System The system of banks that acts as the central bank of the United States and controls major monetary policies.

Budgeting for Public Policy

To most people—college students included—the national budget is B-O-R-I-N-G. To national politicians, it is an exciting script for high drama. The numbers, categories, and percentages that numb normal minds cause politicians' nostrils to flare and their hearts to pound. The budget is a battlefield on which politicians wage war over the programs they support.

Today, the president prepares the budget, and Congress approves it. This was not always the case. Before 1921, Congress prepared the budget under its constitutional authority to raise taxes and appropriate funds. The budget was formed piecemeal by enacting a series of laws that originated in the many committees involved in the highly decentralized process of raising revenue, authorizing expenditures, and appropriating funds.

Congressional budgeting (such as it was) worked well enough for a nation of farmers but not for an industrialized nation with a growing population and an increasingly active government. Soon after World War I, Congress realized that the budget-making process needed to be centralized. With the Budget and Accounting Act of 1921, it thrust the responsibility for preparing the budget onto the president. The act established the Bureau of the Budget to prepare the president's budget for submission to Congress each January. Congress retained its constitutional authority to raise and spend funds, but now it would begin its work with the president's budget as its starting point. And all executive agencies' budget requests had to be funneled for review through the Bureau of the Budget (which became the Office of Management and Budget in 1970); requests that were consistent with the president's overall economic and legislative program were incorporated into the president's budget.

The Nature of the Budget

The national budget is complex, but its basic elements are not beyond understanding. We begin with some definitions. The *Budget of the United States Government* is the annual financial plan that the president is required to submit to Congress at the start of each year. It applies to the next **fiscal year (FY)**, the interval the government uses for accounting purposes. Currently, the fiscal year runs from October 1 to September 30. The budget is named for the year in which it *ends*, so the FY 2009 budget applies to the twelve months from October 1, 2008, to September 30, 2009.

Broadly, the budget defines **budget authority** (how much government agencies are authorized to spend on current and future programs); **budget outlays**, or expenditures (how much agencies are expected to spend this year); and **receipts** (how much is expected in taxes and other revenues). Figure 14.2 shows the relative size of eighteen categories of budget outlays for FY 2009. President Bush's FY 2009 budget proposal contained *authority* for expenditures of $3,026 billion, but it called for outlays of $3,107 billion. His budget also anticipated receipts of $2,700 billion, leaving an

fiscal year (FY) The twelve-month period from October 1 to September 30 used by the government for accounting purposes. A fiscal year budget is named for the year in which it ends.

budget authority The amounts that government agencies are authorized to spend for current and future programs.

budget outlays The amounts that government agencies are expected to spend in the fiscal year.

receipts For a government, the amount expected or obtained in taxes and other revenues.

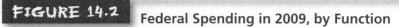

Federal Spending in 2009, by Function

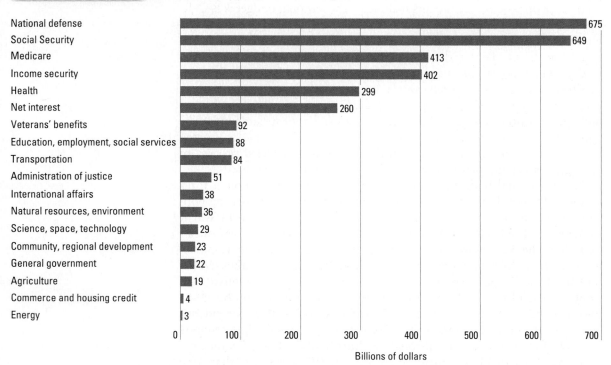

Billions of dollars

Federal budget authorities and outlays are organized into about twenty categories, some of which are mainly for bookkeeping purposes. This graph shows expected outlays for each of eighteen substantive functions for the year 2009 in President Bush's FY 2009 budget. The final budget differed somewhat from this distribution because Congress amended some of the president's spending proposals. The graph makes clear the huge differences among spending categories. Military spending accounts for the largest share of the budget (22 percent) and is the largest amount in inflation-adjusted dollars since World War II. About 35 percent of government outlays are for Social Security and income security—that is, payments to individuals. Health costs (including Medicare) account for almost 25 percent more, more than national defense, and net interest consumes about 8 percent. This leaves relatively little for transportation, agriculture, justice, science, and energy—matters often regarded as important centers of government activity—which fall under the heading of "discretionary spending." The budget data in this figure do not include $700 billion authorized by Congress to assist the financial services / banking industries and free up credit markets.

Source: Executive Office of the President, *Budget of the United States Government, Analytical Perspectives Fiscal Year 2009* (Washington, D.C.: U.S. Government Printing Office, 2008), Table 27-1.

estimated *deficit* of $407 billion—the difference between receipts and out-lays in a single fiscal year.[22] A deficit is different from the **national debt**, which represents the accumulated sum of borrowing (mainly to finance past an-nual deficits) that remains to be paid. The total national debt on Election Day 2008 was a staggering $10.6 *trillion*, with estimates of adding an an-nual half trillion dollar deficit to the debt in subsequent years.[23]

Bush's FY 2009 budget, with appendixes, was thousands of pages long and weighed several pounds. (The president's budget document contains more than numbers. It also explains individual spending programs in terms of national needs and agency objectives, and it analyzes proposed taxes and other receipts.) Each year, reporters, lobbyists, and political analysts anxiously await the publication of the president's budget, eager to learn his plans for government spending in the coming year.

Preparing the President's Budget

The budget that the president submits to Congress each winter is the end product of a process that begins the previous spring under the supervision of the **Office of Management and Budget (OMB)**. OMB is located within the Ex-ecutive Office of the President and is headed by a director appointed by the president with the approval of the Senate. The OMB, with a staff of more than five hundred, is the most powerful domestic agency in the bureau-cracy, and its director, who attends meetings of the president's cabinet, is one of the most powerful figures in government.

The OMB initiates the budget process each spring by meeting with the president to discuss the economic situation and his budgetary priorities. It then sends broad budgeting guidelines to every government agency and re-quests their initial projection of how much money they will need for the next fiscal year. The OMB assembles this information and makes recom-mendations to the president, who then develops more precise guidelines describing how much each is likely to get. By summer, the agencies are asked to prepare budgets based on the new guidelines. By fall, they submit their formal budgets to the OMB, where budget analysts scrutinize agency requests, considering both their costs and their consistency with the presi-dent's legislative program. A lot of politicking goes on at this stage as agency heads try to circumvent the OMB by pleading for their pet projects with presidential advisers and perhaps even with the president himself.

Political negotiations over the budget may extend into the early win-ter, often until it goes to the printer. The voluminous document looks very much like a finished product, but the figures it contains are not final. In giving the president the responsibility for preparing the budget in 1921, Congress simply provided itself with a starting point for its own work.

Passing the Congressional Budget

The president's budget must be approved by Congress. Its process for do-ing so is a creaky conglomeration of traditional procedures overlaid with

DO IT!
Paw over the budget yourself at www.gpoaccess.gov/usbudget.

national debt The accumulated sum of past government borrowing that remains to be paid.

Office of Management and Budget (OMB) The budgeting arm of the Executive Office; prepares the president's budget.

structural reforms from the 1970s, external constraints from the 1980s, and changes introduced by the 1990 Budget Enforcement Act. The cumbersome process has had difficulty producing a budget according to Congress's own timetable.

The Traditional Procedure: The Committee Structure. Traditionally, the tasks of budget making were divided among a number of committees, a process that has been retained. Three types of committees are involved in budgeting:

- **Tax committees** are responsible for raising the revenues to run the government. The Ways and Means Committee in the House and the Finance Committee in the Senate consider all proposals for taxes, tariffs, and other receipts contained in the president's budget.

- **Authorization committees** (such as the House Armed Services Committee and the Senate Banking, Housing, and Urban Affairs Committee) have jurisdiction over particular legislative subjects. The House has about twenty committees that can authorize spending and the Senate about fifteen. Each pores over the portions of the budget that pertain to its area of responsibility. However, in recent years, power has shifted from the authorization committees to the appropriations committees.

- **Appropriations committees** decide which of the programs approved by the authorization committees will actually be funded (that is, given money to spend). For example, the House Armed Services Committee might propose building a new line of tanks for the army, and it might succeed in getting this proposal enacted into law. But the tanks will never be built unless the appropriations committees appropriate funds for that purpose. Thirteen distinct appropriations bills are supposed to be enacted each year to fund the nation's spending.

Two serious problems are inherent in a budgeting process that involves three distinct kinds of congressional committees. First, the two-step spending process (first authorization, then appropriation) is complex; it offers wonderful opportunities for interest groups to get into the budgeting act in the spirit of pluralist democracy. Second, because one group of legislators in each house plans for revenues and many other groups plan for spending, no one is responsible for the budget as a whole.

Three Decades of Budgetary Reforms. Congress surrendered considerable authority in 1921 when it gave the president the responsibility of preparing the budget. During the next fifty years, attempts by Congress to regain control of the budgeting process failed because of jurisdictional squabbles between the revenue and appropriations committees.

In the 1970s, Congress added a new committee structure to combat the pluralist politics inherent in the old procedures and to make budget

tax committees The two committees of Congress responsible for raising the revenue with which to run the government.

authorization committees Committees of Congress that can authorize spending in their particular areas of responsibility.

appropriations committees Committees of Congress that decide which of the programs passed by the authorization committees will actually be funded.

choices in a more majoritarian manner, by roll-call votes in both chambers. The Budget and Impoundment Control Act of 1974 fashioned a typically political solution to the problems of wounded egos and competing jurisdictions that had frustrated previous attempts to change the budget-making process. All the tax and appropriations committees (and chairpersons) were retained, but new House and Senate budget committees were superimposed over the old committee structure. The **budget committees** supervise a comprehensive budget review process, aided by the Congressional Budget Office. The **Congressional Budget Office (CBO)**, with a staff of more than two hundred, has acquired a budgetary expertise equal to that of the president's OMB, so it can prepare credible alternative budgets for Congress.

The 1974 reforms also set up a timetable for the congressional budgeting process. By April 15, both houses were to vote on a budget resolution, proposed by the budget committees, stating overall revenue and spending levels for twenty-one different "budget functions," such as national defense, agriculture, and health. Between May 15 and June 30, the appropriations committees were to draft thirteen appropriations bills for government spending. The levels of spending set by majority vote in the budget resolution were to constrain pressures by special interests for increased spending. This process worked reasonably well for the first few years, but it broke down when President Reagan submitted annual budgets heavy with military spending and huge deficits. The Democratic Congress refused to propose a tax increase to reduce the deficit without the president's cooperation, and Congress encountered increasing difficulty in enacting its budget resolutions according to its own timetable.

In the 1980s, Congress tried to force itself to balance the budget by setting targets. Republican senators Phil Gramm of Texas and Warren Rudman of New Hampshire tried in 1985 to force a balanced budget by gradually eliminating the deficit. Known simply as **Gramm-Rudman,** this act mandated that the budget deficit be lowered to a specified level each year until the budget was balanced by FY 1991. If Congress did not meet the deficit level in any year, the act would trigger across-the-board budget cuts. Unable to make the deficit meet the law in 1986 or 1987, Congress and the president simply changed the law to match the deficit. Gramm-Rudman showed that Congress lacked the will to force itself to balance the budget by an orderly plan of deficit reduction.

In the 1990s, Congress introduced some belt-tightening reforms and passed important tax increases that led to a balanced budget. Threatened by another huge deficit for FY 1991, Congress and President George H. W. Bush agreed on a new package of reforms and deficit targets in the **Budget Enforcement Act (BEA)** of 1990. Instead of defining annual deficit targets, the BEA defined two types of spending: **mandatory spending** and **discretionary spending.** Spending is mandatory for **entitlement** programs (such as Social Security and veterans' pensions) that provide benefits to individuals legally entitled to them and cannot be reduced without changing the law. Discretionary spending entails expenditures authorized by annual appropriations,

budget committees One committee in each house of Congress that supervises a comprehensive budget review process.

Congressional Budget Office (CBO) The budgeting arm of Congress, which prepares alternative budgets to those prepared by the president's OMB.

Gramm-Rudman Popular name for an act passed by Congress in 1985 that, in its original form, sought to lower the national deficit to a specified level each year, culminating in a balanced budget in FY 1991. New reforms and deficit targets were agreed on in 1990.

Budget Enforcement Act (BEA) A 1990 law that distinguished between mandatory and discretionary spending.

mandatory spending In the Budget Enforcement Act of 1990, expenditures required by previous commitments.

discretionary spending In the Budget Enforcement Act of 1990, authorized expenditures from annual appropriations.

entitlement A benefit to which every eligible person has a legal right and that the government cannot deny without changing the law.

such as for the military. The law also established **pay-as-you-go** restrictions on mandatory spending: any proposed expansion of an entitlement program must be offset by cuts to another program or by a tax increase. Similarly, any tax cut must be offset by a tax increase somewhere else or by spending cuts.[24] The law also imposed limits, or "caps," on discretionary spending.

To get the Democratic Congress to pass the BEA, President George H. W. Bush accepted some modest tax increases—despite having vowed at the 1988 Republican National Convention: "Read my lips: no new taxes." Consequently, he faced a rebellion from members of his own party in Congress, who bitterly opposed the tax increase. Indeed, the tax hike may have cost him reelection in 1992. Nevertheless, the 1990 law did limit discretionary spending and slowed unfinanced entitlements and tax cuts. The 1993 Deficit Reduction Act under President Bill Clinton made even more progress in reducing the deficit by cutting spending cuts and raising taxes. By 1997, the deficit declined to $22 billion.[25]

The 1990 and 1993 budget agreements, both of which encountered strong opposition in Congress, helped pave the way for the historic **Balanced Budget Act (BBA)** that President Clinton and Congress negotiated in 1997. Empowered by strong tax revenues during a long period of economic growth, the BBA accomplished what most observers thought was beyond political possibility. It not only led to the balanced budget it promised but actually produced a budget surplus ahead of schedule—the first surplus since 1969.

INTERACTIVE 14.1

AP | *Balancing a Budget*

The End of Budgetary Reform, 2000–Present. In the early 2000s, President Bush and Republicans in Congress advocated using the budget surplus for large across-the-board tax cuts to return money to taxpayers (and to maintain spending discipline in the federal government).[26] Although the caps on discretionary spending and pay-as-you-go requirements, established by the 1990 Budget Enforcement Act, helped balance the budget entering 2000, many members of Congress in both parties resented its restrictions on their freedom to make fiscal decisions. Accordingly, Congress allowed the caps on discretionary spending and the pay-as-you-go requirements to expire at the end of 2002.[27] Since 2002, the government has run budget deficits, not surpluses. When Democrats regained control of Congress in 2007, they reinstated pay-as-you-go rules, but they had little effect in controlling the deficit.

Taxing and Spending Decisions

Ultimately, the budget is a policy document in which programs are funded in an effort to achieve policy objectives and address national problems. Decisions on how to raise and spend government funds are inherently political, because members of the public, governmental leaders, and the political parties all hold diverse and competing perspectives on what policies

pay-as-you-go In the Budget Enforcement Act of 1990, the requirement that any tax cut or expansion of an entitlement program must be offset by a tax increase or other savings.

Balanced Budget Act (BBA) A 1997 law that promised to balance the budget by 2002.

should be adopted. Many of these policy decisions are shaped by circumstances outside the government's immediate control.

Tax Policies.   Tax policy is designed to provide a continuous flow of income. A major text on government finance says that tax policy is sometimes changed to accomplish one or more of several objectives:

- To adjust overall revenue to meet budget outlays

- To make the tax burden more equitable for taxpayers

- To help control the economy by raising taxes (thus decreasing demand) or lowering taxes (thus increasing demand)[28]

In 1986 Congress passed one of the most sweeping tax reform laws in history. The new policy reclaimed a great deal of revenue by eliminating many deductions for corporations and wealthy citizens. By eliminating many tax brackets, the new tax policy approached the idea of a flat tax—one that requires everyone to pay at the same rate. A flat tax has the appeal of simplicity, but it violates the principle of **progressive taxation,** under which the rich pay proportionately higher taxes than the poor. Governments can rely on progressive taxation to redistribute wealth and thus promote economic equality.

After the 1986 tax reform, there were only two tax rates: 15 and 28 percent. In 1990 George H. W. Bush was forced to violate his pledge of "no new taxes" by creating a third tax rate, 31 percent. Clinton created a fourth level, 40 percent in 1993, moving toward a more progressive tax structure.

Soon after his election, George W. Bush got Congress to pass a complex $1.35 trillion tax cut. The 2001 law, amended in 2003, created six tax brackets: 10, 15, 25, 28, 33, and 35 percent. Intended to stimulate the economy, the tax cuts also reduced the government's tax revenue needed to match spending. Changes in the economy can also have a strong impact on tax revenues. The government taxes income from the sale of real estate and stocks (capital gains tax). When the value of the stock market declines, there is less of this capital gains income to tax. When government revenues from this source decline, the budget deficit grows.[29]

Spending Policies.   The FY 2009 budget projects spending over $3,000,000,000,000—that's three *trillion* dollars (or three thousand billions, if you prefer). Where does the money go? To understand current expenditures, it is a good idea to examine national expenditures over time, as shown in Figure 14.3. The effect of World War II is clear: spending for national defense rose sharply after 1940, peaked at about 90 percent of the budget in 1945, and fell to about 30 percent in peacetime. The percentage allocated to defense rose again in the early 1950s, reflecting rearmament during the Cold War with the Soviet Union. Thereafter, the share of the budget devoted to defense decreased steadily (except for the bump during

INTERACTIVE 14.2

 Taxes

progressive taxation A system of taxation whereby the rich pay proportionately higher taxes than the poor; used by governments to redistribute wealth and thus promote equality.

FIGURE 14.3   National Government Outlays Over Time

This chart plots the percentage of the annual budget devoted to four major expense categories over time. It shows that significant changes have occurred in national spending since 1940. During World War II, defense spending consumed more than 80 percent of the national budget. Defense again accounted for most national expenditures during the Cold War of the 1950s. Since then, the military's share of expenditures has declined, while payments to individuals (mostly in the form of Social Security benefits) have increased dramatically. Also, as the graph shows, the proportion of the budget paid in interest on the national debt has increased substantially since the 1970s.

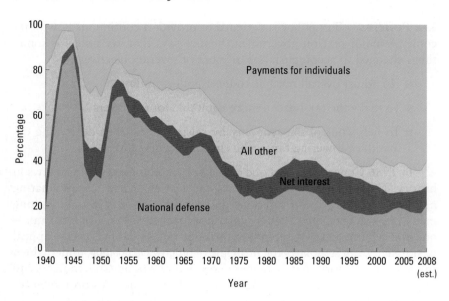

Source: Executive Office of the President, *Budget of the United States Government, Fiscal Year 2009: Historical Tables* (Washington, D.C.: U.S. Government Printing Office, 2008), Table 6-1.

the Vietnam War in the late 1960s). This trend was reversed by the Carter administration in the 1970s and shot up during the Reagan presidency. Defense spending significantly decreased under George H. W. Bush and continued to fall under Clinton. Following the September 11 terrorist attacks, however, defense spending rose sharply. President George W. Bush's proposed FY 2009 budget estimated outlays for national defense more than double the national defense budget for FY 2001. Even taking inflation into account, this represented a 59.5 percent increase in constant dollars.[30] The Iraq war alone cost an estimated $600 billion over the first five years.[31]

Government payments to individuals (Social Security checks) consistently consumed less of the budget than national defense until 1971. Since then, payments to individuals have accounted for the largest portion of the national budget, and they have been increasing. Net interest payments also increased substantially during the years of budget deficits. Pressure from payments for national defense, individuals, and interest on the national debt has squeezed all other government outlays.

National spending has increased from about 15 percent of gross domestic product (GDP) soon after World War II to over 20 percent, for

Compared with What?

Tax Burdens in Thirty Countries

All nations tax their citizens, but some nations impose a heavier tax burden than do others. This graph compares tax burdens in 2004 in thirty countries as a percentage of gross domestic product (GDP), which is the market value of goods produced inside the country by workers, businesses, and government. The percentages encompass national, state, and local taxes and Social Security contributions. By this measure, the U.S. government extracts less in taxes from its citizens than do the governments of almost every other democratic nation.

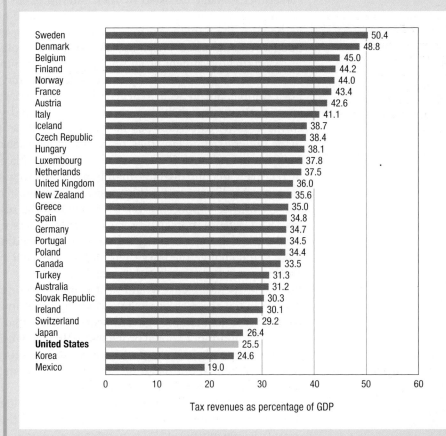

Tax revenues as percentage of GDP

Source: "Public Finance > Taxation, 2004," *OECD in Figures: Statistics on the Member Countries, 2007 Edition* (Paris: Organization for Economic Cooperation and Development, 2007), pp. 58–59.

many years at the price of a growing national deficit. There are two major explanations for this steady increase in government spending. One is bureaucratic, the other political.

The bureaucratic explanation for spending increases involves **incremental budgeting.** When compiling their funding requests for the coming year, bureaucrats traditionally ask for the amount they received in the current year, plus some increment to fund new projects. Because Congress already approved the agency's budget for the current year, it pays little attention to the agency's current size (the largest part of its budget) and focuses instead on the extra money (the increment) requested for the next year. As a result, few agencies are ever cut back, and spending continually goes up.

Incremental budgeting produces a sort of bureaucratic momentum that continually pushes up spending. Once an agency is established, it attracts a clientele that defends its existence and supports the agency's requests for extra funds to do more year after year. Because budgeting is a two-step process, agencies that get cut back in the authorizing committees sometimes manage (assisted by their interest group clientele) to get funds restored in the appropriations committees—and if not in the House, then perhaps in the Senate. So incremental budgeting and the congressional budget-making process itself are ideally suited to pluralist politics.

Certain government programs are effectively immune to budget reductions, because they have been enacted into law and enshrined in politics. For example, Social Security legislation guarantees certain benefits to program participants when they retire. Medicare and veterans' benefits also entitle citizens to certain payments. Because these payments have to be made under existing law, they represent **uncontrollable outlays.** In Bush's FY 2009 budget, almost 60 percent of all budget outlays were uncontrollable or relatively uncontrollable—mainly payments to individuals under Social Security, Medicare, and public assistance; interest on the national debt; and farm price supports. Over 60 percent of the rest went for "security" (national defense, homeland security), leaving less than 18 percent of the total outlays in "nonsecurity" discretionary spending.[32] To be sure, Congress could change the laws to abolish entitlement payments. But politics argues against large-scale reductions.

What spending cuts would be acceptable to or even popular with the public? In the abstract, voters favor cutting government spending, but they tend to favor maintaining "government programs that help needy people and deal with important national problems."[33] In fact, when a national poll asked whether respondents thought federal spending should be "increased, decreased, or kept about the same" for eleven different purposes—highways, welfare, public schools, crime, child care, border security, terrorism, aid to the poor, Social Security, science and technology, and foreign aid—respondents favored increasing or keeping about the same level of spending for *every* purpose!"[34] A perplexed Congress, trying to reduce the budget deficit, faces a public that favors funding programs at even higher levels than those favored by most lawmakers.[35] Moreover, spending for the

incremental budgeting
A method of budget making that involves adding new funds (an increment) onto the amount previously budgeted (in last year's budget).

uncontrollable outlay A payment that government must make by law.

most expensive of these programs—Social Security and Medicare—is uncontrollable.

Social Security.   The largest entitlement program is **Social Security**, a social insurance program that provides economic assistance to people faced with unemployment, disability, or old age; it is financed by taxes on employers and employees. Initially, Social Security benefits were distributed only to the aged, the unemployed, and surviving spouses—most of whom were widows—with dependent children. Today, Social Security also provides medical care for the elderly and income support for the disabled.

The Social Security taxes collected today pay the benefits of today's retirees, with surpluses held over, in theory at least, to help finance the retirement of future generations. Thus, Social Security is not a form of savings; it is a pay-as-you-go tax system. Today's workers support today's elderly.

When the program began, it had many contributors and few beneficiaries. The program could thus provide relatively large benefits with low taxes. In 1937, for example, the tax rate was 1 percent, and the Social Security taxes of nine workers supported each beneficiary. As the program matured and more people retired or became disabled, the ratio of workers to recipients decreased.

In 2008, the Social Security system paid old age, survivor, and disability benefits of a little over $600 billion to 50 million people and collected tax revenue from 164 million, a ratio of roughly 3.3 workers for every beneficiary. In October 2007, the first baby boomer, Kathleen Casey-Kirschling, signed up for Social Security benefits. The problem is that there are 80 million other baby boomers in line behind her.[36] As the bulk of the baby boom generation retires between 2010 and 2030, the number of retirees will grow at a much faster rate than the number of workers. By 2030, the ratio will decline to two workers for every beneficiary.

To minimize the impact of the aging population and the impending retirement of the large baby boomer generation, the government has been collecting substantially more taxes each year than it needs to pay out in current benefits. The surplus has been put into a trust fund account. By 2017, benefit payments will exceed receipts, and the Social Security Administration will need to tap into the trust fund to help cover monthly payments.[37] That will create a new challenge. The money in the trust fund has been invested in government securities. In other words, the Social Security funds for the future have been borrowed by the Treasury Department (and spent) to finance part of the government's general debt.

Politicians will face an inevitable dilemma: whether to lower benefits and generate the ire of retirees or to raise taxes and generate the ire of taxpayers. As a group, older Americans exercise enormous political power. People at or near retirement age now make up almost 30 percent of the potential electorate, and voter turnout among older Americans is reported to be about twice that of younger people.[38]

Social Security Social insurance that provides economic assistance to persons faced with unemployment, disability, or old age; it is financed by taxes on employers and employees.

That's the Trust Fund?
President George W. Bush visited the Bureau of the Public Debt (BPD) to highlight the problems facing the Social Security program. Notice the white filing cabinet next to him? That holds the actual Social Security Trust Fund, made up of special Treasury Department securities (government IOUs) such as that held here by the director of the BPD. As baby boomers retire, the Social Security Administration will need to cash these IOUs in, and the Treasury Department will have to find money to repay the money it borrowed. *(© Luke Frazza/AFP/Getty Images)*

Medicare. On July 30, 1965, President Lyndon Johnson signed a bill that provided several health benefits to the elderly and the poor. The **Social Security Act** was amended to provide **Medicare,** health care for all people aged sixty-five or older. Fearful of the power of the American Medical Association (AMA), which then opposed any form of government-provided medical care, the Democrats confined their efforts to a compulsory hospitalization insurance plan for the elderly (this is known today as Part A of Medicare). In addition, the bill contained a version of an alternative Republican plan that called for voluntary government-subsidized insurance to cover physicians' fees (this is known today as Part B of Medicare). A third program, added a year later, is called Medicaid; it provides medical aid to the poor through federally assisted state health programs. **Medicaid** is a need-based comprehensive medical and hospitalization program; those who are very poor qualify. Finally, in 2003, the Congress passed the Medicare Prescription Drug, Improvement, and Modernization Act to provide beneficiaries with prescription drug coverage. Revised estimates for the new program indicate that it will be much more costly than first expected.

Medicare costs continue to increase at rates in excess of the cost of living. In 1985 the government adopted a new payment system under which hospitals are paid a fixed fee based on the patient's diagnosis. If the patient's stay costs more than the fee schedule allows, the hospital pays the difference. But if the hospital treats a patient for less than the fixed fee, the hospital reaps a profit. This cost containment system provides an incentive

Social Security Act The law that provided for Social Security and is the basis of modern American social welfare.

Medicare A health insurance program for all persons older than sixty-five, as well as for some younger individuals with disabilities.

Medicaid A need-based comprehensive medical and hospitalization program.

for hospitals to discharge patients sooner, perhaps in some cases before they are completely well.

Summary

Government tries to solve problems through a variety of approaches. Some public policies prohibit, some protect, some promote, and some provide. The approach chosen can significantly affect the policymaking process.

Although there is much variation in the policymaking process, we can conceive of it as consisting of four stages. The first stage is agenda setting, the process by which problems become defined as political issues worthy of government attention. Once people in government feel that they should be doing something about a problem, an attempt at policy formulation follows. All three branches of the national government formulate policy. Once policies have been formulated and ratified, administrative units of government must implement them. Finally, once policies are being carried out, they need to be evaluated. Implementation and program evaluation influence agenda building, because program shortcomings become evident during these stages. Thus, the process is really circular, with the end often marking the beginning of a new round of policymaking.

Policymaking in many areas can be viewed as an ongoing process of interaction within issue networks composed of actors inside and outside government. Each network offers a way to communicate and exchange information and ideas about a particular policy area. In a network, lobbying coalitions form easily and dissolve rapidly as new issues arise. Issue networks

place a high premium on expertise as public policy problems grow ever more complex.

Congress alone prepared the budget until 1921, when it thrust the responsibility onto the president. Later, Congress restructured the process under the House and Senate budget committees. The new process worked well until it confronted the huge budget deficits of the 1980s. Because so much of the budget involves military spending and uncontrollable payments to individuals, balancing the budget by reducing what remains—mainly spending for nonentitlement domestic programs—was regarded as impossible. Unwilling to accept responsibility for passing a tax increase, Congress passed the Gramm-Rudman deficit-reduction law in 1985. The deficit problem proved so intractable, however, that Congress had to amend the law in 1987 to extend the deadline to 1993—and the budget still was not balanced. When the Republicans gained control of Congress in 1995, they abandoned the informal policy of incremental budgeting and drastically cut spending on discretionary programs.

President George H. W. Bush promised "no new taxes" when he was campaigning for office in 1988, but he had to acknowledge the need for revenue increases to cut the deficit and was forced to accept the Budget Enforcement Act of 1990, which raised the income tax. This act modified the budgeting procedure and made it easier to meet the Gramm-Rudman targets. In 1993, President Clinton narrowly won approval of a fourth income tax bracket, at

40 percent. Responding to increased revenue and a hold on spending, the deficit declined. Aided by a growth economy, Clinton engineered taxing and spending changes in 1997 that produced a budget surplus in FY 1998—the first surplus since 1969. The budget surplus disappeared in FY 2002, after President George W. Bush and the Congress cut taxes and increased spending to combat terrorism.

Often disagreements about public policy are disagreements about values. Some of the oldest and most costly domestic policies, such as Social Security and Medicare, pose choices between freedom and equality. Gradually, programs to aid the elderly and the poor have been transformed into entitlements. These government programs have reduced poverty among some groups, especially the elderly. However, there are significant concerns about the long-term economic viability of these programs as the American public ages.

CL **Resources:** Videos, Simulations, News, Timelines, Primary Sources

Appendix

The Declaration of Independence, July 4, 1776
The Constitution of the United States of America

THE DECLARATION OF INDEPENDENCE, JULY 4, 1776

The unanimous Declaration of the thirteen United States of America

When in the course of human events, it becomes necessary for one people to dissolve the political bands which have connected them with another, and to assume, among the powers of the earth the separate and equal station to which the Laws of Nature and of Nature's God entitle them, a decent respect to the opinions of mankind requires that they should declare the causes which impel them to the separation.

We hold these truths to be self-evident, that all men are created equal, that they are endowed by their Creator with certain unalienable rights, that among these are life, liberty, and the pursuit of happiness. That to secure these rights, governments are instituted among men, deriving their just powers from the consent of the governed. That whenever any form of government becomes destructive of these ends, it is the right of the people to alter or to abolish it, and to institute new government, laying its foundation on such principles, and organizing its power in such form, as to them shall seem most likely to effect their safety and happiness. Prudence, indeed, will dictate that governments long established should not be changed for light and transient causes; and accordingly all experience hath shown, that mankind are more disposed to suffer, while evils are sufferable, than to right themselves by abolishing the forms to which they are accustomed. But when a long train of abuses and usurpations, pursuing invariably the same object evinces a design to reduce them under absolute despotism, it is their right, it is their duty, to throw off such government, and to provide new guards for their future security. Such has been the patient sufferance of these Colonies; and such is now the necessity which constrains them to alter their former systems of government. The history of the present King of Great Britain is a history of repeated injuries and usurpations, all having in direct object the establishment of an absolute tyranny over these States. To prove this, let facts be submitted to a candid world.

He has refused his assent to laws, the most wholesome and necessary for the public good.

He has forbidden his governors to pass laws of immediate and pressing importance, unless suspended in their operation till his assent should be obtained; and, when so suspended, he has utterly neglected to attend to them.

He has refused to pass other laws for the accommodation of large districts of people, unless those people would relinquish the right of representation in the legislature, a right inestimable to them, and formidable to tyrants only.

He has called together legislative bodies at places unusual, uncomfortable, and distant from the depository of their public records, for the sole purpose of fatiguing them into compliance with his measures.

He has dissolved representative houses repeatedly, for opposing, with manly firmness, his invasions on the rights of the people.

He has refused for a long time, after such dissolutions, to cause others to be elected; whereby the legislative powers, incapable of annihilation, have returned to the people at large for their exercise; the State remaining, in the meantime exposed to all the dangers of invasions from without and convulsions within.

He has endeavored to prevent the population of these States; for that purpose obstructing the laws for naturalization of foreigners; refusing to pass others to encourage their migration hither, and raising the conditions of new appropriations of lands.

He has obstructed the administration of justice, by refusing his assent to laws for establishing judiciary powers.

He has made judges dependent on his will alone, for the tenure of their offices, and the amount and payment of their salaries.

He has erected a multitude of new offices, and sent hither swarms of officers to harass our people, and eat out their substance.

He has kept among us, in times of peace, standing armies, without the consent of our legislatures.

He has affected to render the military independent of and superior to the civil power.

He has combined with others to subject us to a jurisdiction foreign to our constitution, and unacknowledged by our laws; giving his assent to their acts of pretended legislation:

For quartering large bodies of armed troops among us;

For protecting them, by a mock trial, from punishment for any murders which they should commit on the inhabitants of these states;

For cutting off our trade with all parts of the world;

For imposing taxes on us without our consent;

For depriving us, in many cases, of the benefits of trial by jury;

For transporting us beyond seas, to be tried for pretended offenses;

For abolishing the free system of English laws in a neighboring province, establishing therein an arbitrary government, and enlarging its boundaries, so as to render it at once an example and fit instrument for introducing the same absolute rule into these Colonies;

For taking away our Charters, abolishing our most valuable laws, and altering fundamentally the forms of our governments;

For suspending our own Legislatures, and declaring themselves invested with power to legislate for us in all cases whatsoever.

He has abdicated government here, by declaring us out of his protection and waging war against us.

He has plundered our seas, ravaged our coasts, burned our towns, and destroyed the lives of our people.

He is at this time transporting large armies of foreign mercenaries to complete the works of death, desolation, and tyranny, already begun with circumstances of cruelty and perfidy scarcely paralleled in the most barbarous ages, and totally unworthy the head of a civilized nation.

He has constrained our fellow-citizens taken captive on the high seas to bear arms against their country, to become the executioners of their friends and brethren, or to fall themselves by their hands.

He has excited domestic insurrection among us, and has endeavored to bring on the inhabitants of our frontiers the merciless Indian savages, whose known rule of warfare is an undistinguished destruction of all ages, sexes, and conditions.

In every stage of these oppressions we have petitioned for redress in the most humble terms: our repeated petitions have been answered only by repeated injury. A prince whose character is thus marked by every act which may define a tyrant, is unfit to be the ruler of a free people.

Nor have we been wanting in our attentions to our British brethren. We have warned them, from time to time, of attempts by their Legislature to extend an unwarrantable jurisdiction over us. We have reminded them of the circumstances of our emigration and settlement here. We have appealed to their native justice and magnanimity, and we have conjured them by the ties of our common kindred to disavow these usurpations, which would inevitably interrupt our connections and correspondence. They too have been deaf to the voice of justice and of consanguinity. We must, therefore, acquiesce in the necessity, which denounces our separation, and hold them, as we hold the rest of mankind, enemies in war, in peace friends.

We, therefore, the Representatives of the United States of America, in General Congress assembled, appealing to the Supreme Judge of the world for the rectitude of our intentions, do, in the name, and by the authority of the good people of these Colonies, solemnly publish and declare, That these United Colonies are, and of right ought to be, FREE AND INDEPENDENT STATES; that they are absolved from all allegiance to the British Crown, and that all political connection between them and the State of Great Britain is, and ought to be, totally dissolved; and that, as Free and Independent States they have full power to levy war, conclude peace, contract alliances, establish commerce, and do all other acts and things which independent States may of right do. And for the support of this declaration, with a firm reliance on the protection of Divine Providence, we mutually pledge to each other our lives, our fortunes and our sacred honor.

JOHN HANCOCK
and fifty-five others

THE CONSTITUTION OF THE UNITED STATES OF AMERICA*

[Preamble: outlines goals and effect]

We the people of the United States, in order to form a more perfect Union, establish Justice, insure domestic Tranquility, provide for the common defence, promote the general Welfare, and secure the Blessings of Liberty to ourselves and our Posterity, do ordain and establish this Constitution for the United States of America.

ARTICLE I
[The legislative branch]

[Powers vested]

SECTION 1   All legislative Powers herein granted shall be vested in a Congress of the United States, which shall consist of a Senate and a House of Representatives.

---

*Passages no longer in effect are printed in italic type.

[House of Representatives: selection, term, qualifications, apportionment of seats, census requirement, exclusive power to impeach]

SECTION 2   The House of Representatives shall be composed of Members chosen every second Year by the people of the several States, and the Electors in each State shall have the Qualifications requisite for Electors of the most numerous Branch of the State Legislature.

No person shall be a Representative who shall not have attained to the Age of twenty five Years, and been seven Years a Citizen of the United States, and who shall not, when elected, be an Inhabitant of that State in which he shall be chosen.

Representatives and direct Taxes shall be apportioned among the several States which may be included within this Union, according to their respective numbers, *which shall be determined by adding to the whole Number of free Persons, including those bound to Service for a Term of Years and excluding Indians not taxed, three-fifths of all other Persons.* The actual Enumeration shall be made within three Years after the first Meeting of the Congress of the United States, and within every subsequent Term of ten Years, in such Manner as they shall by Law direct. The number of Representatives shall not exceed one for every thirty Thousand, but each State shall have at Least one Representative; *and until such enumeration shall be made, the State of New Hampshire shall be entitled to choose three, Massachusetts eight, Rhode Island and Providence Plantations one, Connecticut five, New York six, New Jersey four, Pennsylvania eight, Delaware one, Maryland six, Virginia ten, North Carolina five, South Carolina five, and Georgia three.*

When vacancies happen in the Representation from any State, the Executive Authority thereof shall issue Writs of Election to fill such Vacancies.

The House of Representatives shall chuse their Speaker and other Officers; and shall have the sole Power of Impeachment.

[Senate: selection, term, qualifications, exclusive power to try impeachments]

SECTION 3   The Senate of the United States shall be composed of two Senators from each State, *chosen by the Legislature thereof,* for six years; and each Senator shall have one Vote.

Immediately after they shall be assembled in Consequence of the first Election, they shall be divided as equally as may be into three Classes. The Seats of the Senators of the first Class shall be vacated at the Expiration of the second Year, of the second Class at the expiration of the fourth Year, and of the third Class at the expiration of the sixth Year, so that one-third may be chosen every second Year; *and if Vacancies happen by Resignation or otherwise, during the Recess of the Legislature of any State, the Executive thereof may make temporary Appointments until the next meeting of the legislature, which shall then fill such Vacancies.*

No person shall be a Senator who shall not have attained to the Age of thirty Years, and been nine Years a Citizen of the United States, and who shall not, when elected, be an Inhabitant of that State for which he shall be chosen.

The Vice-President of the United States shall be President of the Senate, but shall have no Vote, unless they be equally divided.

The Senate shall choose their other officers, and also a President pro tempore, in the absence of the Vice-President, or when he shall exercise the Office of President of the United States.

The Senate shall have the sole Power to try all impeachments. When sitting for that purpose, they shall be on Oath or Affirmation. When the President of the

United States is tried, the Chief Justice shall preside: and no Person shall be convicted without the Concurrence of two-thirds of the members Present.

Judgment in Cases of Impeachment shall not extend further than to removal from the Office, and disqualification to hold and enjoy any Office of honor, Trust or Profit under the United States: but the Party convicted shall nevertheless be liable and subject to Indictment, Trial, Judgment and Punishment, according to Law.

[Elections]

SECTION 4   The Times, Places and Manner of holding Elections for Senators and Representatives shall be prescribed in each State by the Legislature thereof; but the Congress may at any time by Law make or alter such regulations, except as to the Places of chusing Senators.

The Congress shall assemble at least once in every Year, and such meeting *shall be on the first Monday in December, unless they shall by Law appoint a different Day.*

[Powers and duties of the two chambers: rules of procedure, power over members]

SECTION 5   Each House shall be the Judge of the Elections, Returns and Qualifications of its own Members, and a Majority of each shall constitute a Quorum to do Business; but a smaller Number may adjourn from day to day, and may be authorized to compel the Attendance of absent Members, in such Manner, and under such Penalties as each House may provide.

Each House may determine the Rules of its proceedings, punish its Members for disorderly behaviour, and with the Concurrence of two thirds, expel a Member.

Each House shall keep a Journal of its Proceedings, and from time to time publish the same, excepting such Parts as may in their Judgment require Secrecy; and the Yeas and Nays of the Members of either House on any question shall, at the Desire of one fifth of those Present, be entered on the Journal.

Neither House, during the Session of Congress, shall, without the Consent of the other, adjourn for more than three days, nor to any other Place than that in which the two Houses shall be sitting.

[Compensation, privilege from arrest, privilege of speech, disabilities of members]

SECTION 6   The Senators and Representatives shall receive a Compensation for their services, to be ascertained by Law, and paid out of the Treasury of the United States. They shall in all Cases, except Treason, Felony and Breach of the Peace, be privileged from Arrest during their Attendance at the Session of their respective Houses, and in going to and returning from the same; and for any Speech or Debate in either House, they shall not be questioned in any other Place.

No Senator or Representative shall, during the Time for which he was elected, be appointed to any civil office under the Authority of the United States, which shall have been created, or the Emoluments whereof shall have been increased, during such time; and no Person holding any Office under the United States, shall be a Member of either House during his Continuance in Office.

[Legislative process: revenue bills, approval or veto power of president]

SECTION 7   All bills for raising Revenue shall originate in the House of Representatives; but the Senate may propose or concur with Amendments as on other Bills.

Every Bill which shall have passed the House of Representatives and the Senate, shall, before it become a Law, be presented to the President of the United States; if he approve he shall sign it, but if not he shall return it with Objections to that House in which it originated, who shall enter the Objections at large on their journal, and proceed to reconsider it. If after such Reconsideration two thirds of that House shall agree to pass the Bill, it shall be sent, together with the Objections, to the other House, by which it shall likewise be reconsidered, and, if approved by two thirds of that house, it shall become a Law. But in all such Cases the Votes of both houses shall be determined by yeas and Nays, and the Names of the Persons voting for and against the Bill shall be entered on the journal of each House respectively. If any Bill shall not be returned by the President within ten Days (Sundays excepted) after it shall have been presented to him, the Same shall be a Law, in like Manner as if he had signed it, unless the Congress by their Adjournment prevent its Return, in which Case it shall not be a Law.

Every Order, Resolution, or Vote to which the Concurrence of the Senate and House of Representatives may be necessary (except on a question of Adjournment) shall be presented to the President of the United States; and before the Same shall take Effect, shall be approved by him, or being disapproved by him, shall be repassed by two thirds of the Senate and House of Representatives, according to the Rules and Limitations prescribed in the Case of a Bill.

[Powers of Congress enumerated]

SECTION 8   The Congress shall have Power

To lay and collect Taxes, Duties, Imposts, and Excises, to pay the Debts and provide for the common Defence and general Welfare of the United States; but all Duties, Imposts and Excises shall be uniform throughout the United States;

To borrow Money on the credit of the United States;

To regulate Commerce with foreign Nations, and among the several States, and with the Indian tribes;

To establish an uniform Rule of Naturalization, and uniform Laws on the subject of Bankruptcies throughout the United States;

To coin Money, regulate the Value thereof, and of foreign Coin, and fix the Standard of Weights and Measures;

To provide for the Punishment of counterfeiting the Securities and current Coin of the United States;

To establish Post Offices and post Roads;

To promote the Progress of Science and useful Arts by securing for limited Times to Authors and Inventors the exclusive Right to their respective Writings and Discoveries;

To constitute Tribunals inferior to the supreme Court;

To define and punish Piracies and Felonies committed on the high Seas, and offenses against the Law of Nations;

To declare War, grant Letters of Marque and Reprisal, and make Rules concerning Captures on Land and Water;

To raise and support Armies, but no Appropriation of Money to that Use shall be for a longer Term than two Years;

To provide and maintain a Navy;

To make rules for the Government and Regulation of the land and naval Forces;

To provide for calling forth the Militia to execute the Laws of the Union, suppress Insurrections, and repel Invasions;

To provide for organizing, arming, and disciplining the Militia, and for governing such Part of them as may be employed in the Service of the United States, reserving to the States respectively the Appointment of the Officers, and the Authority of training the Militia according to the discipline prescribed by Congress;

To exercise exclusive Legislation in all Cases whatsoever, over such District (not exceeding ten Miles square) as may, by cession of particular States, and the Acceptance of Congress, become the Seat of Government of the United States, and to exercise like Authority over all places purchased by the Consent of the Legislature of the State in which the Same shall be, for Erection of Forts, Magazines, Arsenals, dock-Yards, and other needful Buildings;—And

[Elastic clause]

To make all Laws which shall be necessary and proper for carrying into Execution the foregoing Powers, and all other powers vested by this Constitution in the Government of the United States, or in any Department or Officer thereof.

[Powers denied Congress]

SECTION 9 *The Migration or Importation of such persons as any of the States now existing shall think proper to admit, shall not be prohibited by the Congress prior to the Year 1808; but a Tax or duty may be imposed on such Importation, not exceeding $10 for each Person.*

The Privilege of the Writ of Habeas Corpus shall not be suspended, unless when in Cases of Rebellion or Invasion the public Safety may require it.

No Bill of Attainder or ex post facto Law shall be passed.

No Capitation, or other direct, Tax shall be laid, unless in Proportion to the Census or Enumeration herein before directed to be taken.

No Tax or Duty shall be laid on Articles exported from any State.

No Preference shall be given by any Regulation of Commerce or Revenue to the Ports of one State over those of another; nor shall Vessels bound to, or from, one State, be obliged to enter, clear, or pay Duties in another.

No Money shall be drawn from the Treasury, but in Consequence of Appropriations made by Law; and a regular Statement and Account of the receipts and Expenditures of all public Money shall be published from time to time.

No Title of Nobility shall be granted by the United States: And no Person holding any Office or Profit or trust under them, shall, without the Consent of the Congress, accept of any present, Emolument, Office, or Title, of any kind whatever, from any King, Prince, or foreign State.

[Powers denied the states]

SECTION 10 No State shall enter into any Treaty, Alliance, or Confederation; grant Letters of Marque and Reprisal; coin Money; emit Bills of Credit; make any Thing but gold and silver Coin a Tender in Payment of Debts; pass any Bill of Attainder, ex post facto law, or Law impairing the obligation of Contracts, or grant any Title of Nobility.

No State shall, without the Consent of Congress, lay any Imposts or Duties on Imports or Exports, except what may be absolutely necessary for executing its inspection Laws: and the net Produce of all duties and imposts, laid by any State on Imports or Exports, shall be for the Use of the Treasury of the United States; and all such Laws shall be subject to the Revision and Controul of the Congress.

No State shall, without the consent of Congress, lay any Duty of Tonnage, keep Troops or Ships of War in time of Peace, enter into any Agreement or Compact with another State, or with a foreign Power, or engage in War, unless actually invaded, or in such imminent Danger as will not admit of delay.

ARTICLE II
[The executive branch]

[The president: power vested, term, electoral college, qualifications, presidential succession, compensation, oath of office]

SECTION 1   The executive Power shall be vested in a President of the United States of America. He shall hold his office during the Term of four Years, and, together with the Vice President, chosen for the same Term, be elected as follows:

Each State shall appoint, in such Manner as the Legislature thereof may direct, a Number of Electors, equal to the whole Number of Senators and Representatives to which the State may be entitled in the Congress; but no Senator or Representative, or Person holding an Office of Trust or Profit under the United States, shall be appointed an Elector.

The Electors shall meet in their respective States, and vote by Ballot for two Persons, of whom one at least shall not be an inhabitant of the same State with themselves. And they shall make a List of all the Persons voted for, and of the Number of Votes for each: which List they shall sign and certify, and transmit sealed to the Seat of Government of the United States, directed to the President of the Senate. The President of the Senate shall, in the presence of the Senate and House of Representatives, open all the Certificates, and the Votes shall then be counted. The Person having the greatest Number of Votes shall be the President, if such Number be a Majority of the whole number of Electors appointed; and if there be more than one who have such Majority, and have an equal Number of Votes, then the House of Representatives shall immediately chuse by Ballot one of them for President; and if no Person have a Majority, then from the five highest on the List said House shall in like Manner chuse the President. But in chusing the President the Votes shall be taken by States, the Representation from each State having one Vote; a quorum for this purpose shall consist of a Member or Members from two thirds of the States, and a Majority of all the States shall be necessary to a Choice. In every Case, after the Choice of the President, the person having the greatest Number of Votes of the Electors shall be the Vice President. But if there should remain two or more who have equal Votes, the Senate shall chuse from them by Ballot the Vice President.

The Congress may determine the Time of chusing the Electors and the Day on which they shall give their Votes; which Day shall be the same throughout the United States.

No person except a natural born Citizen, or a Citizen of the United States at the time of the Adoption of this Constitution, shall be eligible to the Office of President; neither shall any Person be eligible to that Office who shall not have attained to the age of thirty-five Years, and been fourteen Years a Resident within the United States.

In cases of the Removal of the President from Office or of his Death, Resignation, or Inability to discharge the Powers and Duties of the said Office, the same shall devolve on the Vice President, and the Congress may by law provide for the case of Removal, Death, Resignation, or inability, both of the President and

Vice President, declaring what Officer shall then act as President, and such Officer shall act accordingly, until the Disability be removed, or a President shall be elected.

The President shall, at stated Times, receive for his Services, a Compensation, which shall neither be increased nor diminished during the Period for which he shall have been elected, and he shall not receive within that Period any other emolument from the United States, or any of them.

Before he enter on the Execution of his Office, he shall take the following Oath or Affirmation:—"I do solemnly swear (or affirm) that I will faithfully execute the Office of the President of the United States, and will to the best of my Ability preserve, protect and defend the Constitution of the United States."

[Powers and duties: as commander in chief, over advisers, to pardon, to make treaties and appoint officers]

SECTION 2   The President shall be Commander in Chief of the Army and Navy of the United States, and of the Militia of the several States, when called into the actual service of the United States; he may require the Opinion, in writing, of the principal Officer in each of the executive Departments, upon any Subject relating to the Duties of their respective Offices, and he shall have Power to grant Reprieves and Pardons for Offences against the United States, except in Cases of Impeachment.

He shall have Power, by and with the Advice and Consent of the Senate, to make Treaties, provided two-thirds of the Senators present concur; and he shall nominate, and by and with the Advice and Consent of the Senate, shall appoint Ambassadors, other public Ministers and Consuls, Judges of the supreme Court, and all other Officers of the United States, whose Appointments are not herein otherwise provided for, and which shall be established by Law: but Congress may by Law vest the Appointment of such inferior Officers, as they think proper, in the President alone, in the courts of Law, or in the Heads of Departments.

The President shall have Power to fill up all Vacancies that may happen during the Recess of the Senate, by granting Commissions which shall expire at the end of their next Session.

[Legislative, diplomatic, and law-enforcement duties]

SECTION 3   He shall from time to time give to the Congress Information of the State of the Union, and recommend to their Consideration such Measures as he shall judge necessary and expedient; he may, on extraordinary Occasions, convene both Houses, or either of them, and in Case of Disagreement between them, with Respect to the Time of Adjournment, he may adjourn them to such Time as he shall think proper; he shall receive Ambassadors and other public Ministers; he shall take Care that the Laws be faithfully executed, and shall Commission all the Officers of the United States.

[Impeachment]

SECTION 4   The President, Vice President and all civil Officers of the United States shall be removed from Office on Impeachment for, and on Conviction of, Treason, Bribery, or other high Crimes and Misdemeanors.

ARTICLE III
[The judicial branch]

[Power vested; Supreme Court; lower courts; judges]

SECTION 1   The judicial Power of the United States shall be vested in one supreme Court, and in such inferior Courts as the Congress may from time to time ordain and establish. The Judges, both of the supreme and inferior Courts, shall hold their Offices during good Behaviour, and shall, at stated Times, receive for their Services a Compensation which shall not be diminished during their Continuance in Office.

[Jurisdiction; trial by jury]

SECTION 2   The judicial Power shall extend to all Cases, in Law and Equity, arising under this Constitution, the Laws of the United States, and Treaties made, or which shall be made, under their Authority;—to all Cases affecting Ambassadors, other public Ministers and Consuls;—to all Cases of admiralty and maritime Jurisdiction;—to Controversies to which the United States shall be a Party;—to controversies between two or more States;—*between a State and Citizens of another State;*—between Citizens of different States—between Citizens of the same State claiming Lands under grants of different States, and between a State, or the Citizens thereof, and foreign States, Citizens or Subjects.

In all cases affecting Ambassadors, other public Ministers and Consuls, and those in which a State shall be Party, the supreme Court shall have original Jurisdiction. In all the other Cases before mentioned, the supreme Court shall have appellate Jurisdiction, both as to Law and Fact, with such Exceptions, and under such Regulations, as the Congress shall make.

The Trial of all Crimes, except in cases of Impeachment, shall be by Jury; and such Trial shall be held in the State where said Crimes shall have been committed; but when not committed within any State, the Trial shall be at such Place or Places as the Congress may by Law have directed.

[Treason: definition, punishment]

SECTION 3   Treason against the United States shall consist only in levying War against them, or in adhering to their Enemies, giving them Aid and Comfort. No Person shall be convicted of Treason unless on the Testimony of two Witnesses to the same overt Act, or on confession in open Court.

The Congress shall have power to declare the Punishment of Treason, but no Attainder of Treason shall work Corruption of Blood, or Forfeiture except during the Life of the Person attainted.

ARTICLE IV
[States' relations]

[Full faith and credit]

SECTION 1   Full Faith and Credit shall be given in each State to the public Acts, Records, and judicial Proceedings of every other State. And the Congress may by general laws prescribe the Manner in which such Acts, Records, and Proceedings shall be proved, and the Effect thereof.

[Interstate comity, rendition]

SECTION 2   The Citizens of each State shall be entitled to all Privileges and Immunities of Citizens in the several States.

A Person charged in any State with Treason, Felony, or other Crime, who shall flee from Justice, and be found in another State, shall on Demand of the executive Authority of the State from which he fled, be delivered up, to be removed to the State having Jurisdiction of the Crime.

No person held to Service or Labor in one State, under the Laws thereof, escaping into another, shall, in consequence of any Law or Regulation therein, be discharged from such Service or Labor, but shall be delivered up on Claim of the Party to whom such Service or Labor may be due.

[New states]

SECTION 3   New States may be admitted by the Congress into this Union; but no new State shall be formed or erected within the Jurisdiction of any other State; nor any State be formed by the Junction of two or more States, or parts of States, without the Consent of the Legislatures of the States concerned as well as of the Congress.

The Congress shall have Power to dispose of and make all needful Rules and Regulations respecting the Territory or other Property belonging to the United States; and nothing in this Constitution shall be so construed as to Prejudice any Claims of the United States, or of any particular State.

[Obligations of the United States to the states]

SECTION 4   The United States shall guarantee to every State in this Union a Republican Form of Government, and shall protect each of them against Invasion; and on Application of the Legislature, or of the Executive (when the Legislature cannot be convened), against domestic Violence.

ARTICLE V
[Mode of amendment]

The Congress, whenever two-thirds of both Houses shall deem it necessary, shall propose Amendments to this Constitution, or, on the Application of the Legislatures of two-thirds of the several States, shall call a Convention for proposing Amendments, which, in either Case, shall be valid to all Intents and Purposes, as part of this Constitution, when ratified by the legislatures of three-fourths of the several States, or by Conventions in three-fourths thereof, as the one or the other Mode of Ratification may be proposed by the Congress; Provided *that no Amendment which may be made prior to the Year One thousand eight hundred and eight shall in any Manner affect the first and fourth clauses in the Ninth Section of the first Article;* and that no State, without its Consent, shall be deprived of its equal suffrage in the Senate.

ARTICLE VI
[Prior debts, supremacy of Constitution, oaths of office]

All Debts contracted and Engagements entered into, before the Adoption of this Constitution, shall be as valid against the United States under this Constitution, as under the Confederation.

This Constitution, and the Laws of the United States which shall be made in Pursuance thereof; and all Treaties made, or which shall be made, under the Authority of the United States, shall be the supreme Law of the Land; and the judges in every State shall be bound thereby, anything in the Constitution or Laws of any State to the Contrary notwithstanding.

The Senators and Representatives before mentioned, and the Members of the several State Legislatures, and all executive and judicial Officers, both of the United States and of the several States, shall be bound by Oath or Affirmation to support this Constitution; but no religious test shall ever be required as a Qualification to any Office or public Trust under the United States.

ARTICLE VII
[Ratification]

The ratification of the Conventions of nine States shall be sufficient for the Establishment of this Constitution between the States so ratifying the Same.

Done in Convention by the Unanimous Consent of the States present, the seventeenth day of September in the Year of our Lord one thousand seven hundred and eighty-seven and of the Independence of the United States of America the twelfth. In WITNESS whereof We have hereunto subscribed our Names.

GEORGE WASHINGTON
and thirty-seven others

Amendments to the Constitution

[The first ten amendments—the Bill of Rights—were adopted in 1791.]

AMENDMENT I
[Freedom of religion, speech, press, assembly]

Congress shall make no law respecting an establishment of religion, or prohibiting the free exercise thereof; or abridging the freedom of speech, or of the press; or the right of the people peaceably to assemble, and to petition the Government for a redress of grievances.

AMENDMENT II
[Right to bear arms]

A well-regulated militia being necessary to the security of a free State, the right of the people to keep and bear arms shall not be infringed.

AMENDMENT III
[Quartering of soldiers]

No Soldier shall, in time of peace, be quartered in any house without the consent of the Owner, nor in time of war, but in a manner to be prescribed by law.

AMENDMENT IV
[Searches and seizures]

The right of the people to be secure in their persons, houses, papers, and effects, against unreasonable searches and seizures, shall not be violated, and no Warrants shall issue but upon probable cause, supported by Oath or affirmation, and particularly describing the place to be searched, and the persons or things to be seized.

AMENDMENT V
[Rights of persons: grand juries, double jeopardy, self-incrimination, due process, eminent domain]

No person shall be held to answer for a capital, or otherwise infamous crime, unless on a presentment or indictment of a Grand Jury, except in cases arising in the land or naval forces, or in the Militia, when in actual service in time of War or public danger; nor shall any person be subject for the same offense to be twice put in jeopardy of life or limb; nor shall be compelled in any criminal case to be a witness against himself, nor be deprived of life, liberty, or property, without due process of law; nor shall private property be taken for public use without just compensation.

AMENDMENT VI
[Rights of accused in criminal prosecutions]

In all criminal prosecutions, the accused shall enjoy the right to a speedy and public trial, by an impartial jury of the State and district wherein the crime shall have been committed, which district shall have been previously ascertained by law, and to be informed of the nature and cause of the accusation; to be confronted with the witnesses against him; to have compulsory process for obtaining Witnesses in his favor, and to have the assistance of counsel for his defence.

AMENDMENT VII
[Civil trials]

In Suits at common law, where the value in controversy shall exceed twenty dollars, the right of trial by jury shall be preserved, and no fact tried by a jury shall be otherwise reexamined in any Court of the United States, than according to the rules of the common law.

AMENDMENT VIII
[Punishment for crime]

Excessive bail shall not be required, nor excessive fines imposed, nor cruel and unusual punishments inflicted.

AMENDMENT IX
[Rights retained by the people]

The enumeration in the Constitution, of certain rights, shall not be construed to deny or disparage others retained by the people.

AMENDMENT X
[Rights reserved to the states]

The powers not delegated to the United States by the Constitution, nor prohibited by it to the States, are reserved to the States respectively, or to the people.

AMENDMENT XI
[Suits against the states; adopted 1798]

The Judicial power of the United States shall not be construed to extend to any suit in law or equity, commenced or prosecuted against one of the United States by Citizens of another state, or by Citizens or Subjects of any Foreign State.

AMENDMENT XII
[Election of the president; adopted 1804]

The electors shall meet in their respective States, and vote by ballot for President and Vice-President, one of whom, at least, shall not be an inhabitant of the same state with themselves; they shall name in their ballots the person voted for as President, and in distinct ballots the person voted for as Vice-President, and they shall make distinct lists of all persons voted for as President, and of all persons voted for as Vice-President, and of the number of votes for each, which lists they shall sign and certify, and transmit sealed to the seat of government of the United States, directed to the President of the Senate;—the President of the Senate shall, in the presence of the Senate and House of Representatives, open all the certificates and the votes shall then be counted;—the person having the greatest number of votes for President shall be the President, if such number be a majority of the whole number of electors appointed; and if no person have such majority, then from the persons having the highest numbers not exceeding three on the list of those voted for as President, the House of Representatives shall choose immediately, by ballot, the President. But in choosing the President, the votes shall be taken by States, the representation from each State having one vote; a quorum for this purpose shall consist of a member or members from two-thirds of the States, and a majority of all the States shall be necessary to a choice. And if the House of Representatives shall not choose a President whenever the right of choice shall devolve upon them, before *the fourth day of March* next following, then the Vice-President shall act as President, as in the case of the death or other constitutional disability of the President.—The person having the greatest number of votes as Vice-President shall be the Vice-President, if such number be a majority of the whole number of electors appointed; and if no person have a majority, then from the two highest numbers on the list the Senate shall choose the Vice-President; a quorum for the purpose shall consist of two-thirds of the whole number of Senators, and a majority of the whole number shall be necessary to a choice. But no person constitutionally ineligible to the office of President shall be eligible to that of Vice-President of the United States.

AMENDMENT XIII
[Abolition of slavery; adopted 1865]

SECTION 1   Neither slavery nor involuntary servitude, except as a punishment for crime whereof the party shall have been duly convicted, shall exist within the United States, or any place subject to their jurisdiction.

SECTION 2   Congress shall have power to enforce this article by appropriate legislation.

AMENDMENT XIV
[Adopted 1868]

[Citizenship rights; privileges and immunities; due process; equal protection]

SECTION 1   All persons born or naturalized in the United States, and subject to the jurisdiction thereof, are citizens of the United States and of the State wherein they reside. No State shall make or enforce any law which shall abridge the privileges or immunities of citizens of the United States; nor shall any State deprive any person of life, liberty, or property, without due process of law; nor deny to any person within its jurisdiction the equal protection of the laws.

[Apportionment of representation]

SECTION 2   Representatives shall be apportioned among the several States according to their respective numbers, counting the whole number of persons in each State, excluding Indians not taxed. But when the right to vote at any election for the choice of Electors for President and Vice-President of the United States, Representatives in Congress, the Executive and Judicial officers of a State, or the members of the Legislature thereof, is denied to any of the male inhabitants of such State, being twenty-one years of age and citizens of the United States, or in any way abridged, except for participation in rebellion, or other crime, the basis of representation therein shall be reduced in the proportion which the number of such male citizens shall bear to the whole number of male citizens twenty-one years of age in such State.

[Disqualification of Confederate officials]

SECTION 3   No person shall be a Senator or Representative in Congress, or Elector of President and Vice-President, or hold any office, civil or military, under the United States, or under any State, who, having previously taken an oath, as a member of Congress, or as an officer of the United States, or as a member of any State legislature, or as an executive or judicial officer of any State, to support the Constitution of the United States, shall have engaged in insurrection or rebellion against the same, or given aid or comfort to the enemies thereof. Congress may, by a vote of two-thirds of each house, remove such disability.

[Public debts]

SECTION 4   The validity of the public debt of the United States, authorized by law, including debts incurred for payment of pensions and bounties for services in suppressing insurrection or rebellion, shall not be questioned. But neither the United States nor any State shall assume or pay any debt or obligation incurred in aid of insurrection or rebellion against the United States, or any claim for the loss of emancipation of any slave; but all such debts, obligations, and claims shall be held illegal and void.

[Enforcement]

SECTION 5 The Congress shall have power to enforce, by appropriate legislation, the provisions of this article.

AMENDMENT XV
[Extension of right to vote; adopted 1870]

SECTION 1 The right of citizens of the United States to vote shall not be denied or abridged by the United States or by any State on account of race, color, or previous condition of servitude.

SECTION 2 The Congress shall have power to enforce this article by appropriate legislation.

AMENDMENT XVI
[Income tax; adopted 1913]

The Congress shall have power to lay and collect taxes on incomes, from whatever source derived, without apportionment among the several States, and without regard to any census or enumeration.

AMENDMENT XVII
[Popular election of senators; adopted 1913]

SECTION 1 The Senate of the United States shall be composed of two Senators from each State, elected by the people thereof, for six years; and each Senator shall have one vote. The electors in each State shall have the qualifications requisite for electors of the most numerous branch of the State legislatures.

SECTION 2 When vacancies happen in the representation of any State in the Senate, the executive authority of such State shall issue writs of election to fill such vacancies: Provided, that the Legislature of any State may empower the executive thereof to make temporary appointments until the people fill the vacancies by election as the Legislature may direct.

SECTION 3 This amendment shall not be so construed as to affect the election or term of any Senator chosen before it becomes valid as part of the Constitution.

AMENDMENT XVIII
[Prohibition of intoxicating liquors; adopted 1919, repealed 1933]

SECTION 1 After one year from the ratification of this article the manufacture, sale or transportation of intoxicating liquors within, the importation thereof into, or the exportation thereof from the United States and all territory subject to the jurisdiction thereof, for beverage purposes, is hereby prohibited.

SECTION 2 The Congress and the several States shall have concurrent power to enforce this article by appropriate legislation.

SECTION 3   This article shall be inoperative unless it shall have been ratified as an amendment to the Constitution by the legislatures of the several States, as provided by the Constitution, within seven years from the date of the submission thereof to the States by the Congress.

AMENDMENT XIX
[Right of women to vote; adopted 1920]

SECTION 1   The right of citizens of the United States to vote shall not be denied or abridged by the United States or by any State on account of sex.

SECTION 2   The Congress shall have power to enforce this article by appropriate legislation.

AMENDMENT XX
[Commencement of terms of office; adopted 1933]

SECTION 1   The terms of the President and Vice-President shall end at noon on the 20th day of January, and the terms of Senators and Representatives at noon on the 3d day of January, of the years in which such terms would have ended if this article had not been ratified; and the terms of their successors shall then begin.

SECTION 2   The Congress shall assemble at least once in every year, and such meetings shall begin at noon on the 3d day of January, unless they shall by law appoint a different day.

[Extension of presidential succession]

SECTION 3   If, at the time fixed for the beginning of the term of the President, the President-elect shall have died, the Vice-President-elect shall become President. If a President shall not have been chosen before the time fixed for the beginning of his term, or if the President-elect shall have failed to qualify, then the Vice-President-elect shall act as President until a President shall have qualified; and the Congress may by law provide for the case wherein neither a President-elect nor a Vice-President-elect shall have qualified, declaring who shall then act as President, or the manner in which one who is to act shall be selected, and such persons shall act accordingly until a President or Vice-President shall have qualified.

SECTION 4   The Congress may by law provide for the case of the death of any of the persons from whom the House of Representatives may choose a President whenever the right of choice shall have devolved upon them, and for the case of the death of any of the persons from whom the Senate may choose a Vice-President whenever the right of choice shall have devolved upon them.

SECTION 5   Sections 1 and 2 shall take effect on the 15th day of October following the ratification of this article.

SECTION 6   This article shall be inoperative unless it shall have been ratified as an amendment to the Constitution by the Legislatures of three-fourths of the several States within seven years from the date of its submission.

AMENDMENT XXI
[Repeal of Eighteenth Amendment; adopted 1933]

SECTION 1   The eighteenth article of amendment to the Constitution of the United States is hereby repealed.

SECTION 2   The transportation or importation into any State, Territory, or Possession of the United States for delivery or use therein of intoxicating liquors, in violation of the laws thereof, is hereby prohibited.

SECTION 3   This article shall be inoperative unless it shall have been ratified as an amendment to the Constitution by conventions in the several States, as provided in the Constitution, within seven years from the date of submission thereof to the States by the Congress.

AMENDMENT XXII
[Limit on presidential tenure; adopted 1951]

SECTION 1   No person shall be elected to the office of President more than twice, and no person who has held the office of President, or acted as President, for more than two years of a term to which some other person was elected President shall be elected to the office of President more than once. But this article shall not apply to any person holding the office of President when this article was proposed by the Congress, and shall not prevent any person who may be holding the office of President, or acting as President, during the term within which this article becomes operative from holding the office of President or acting as President during the remainder of such term.

SECTION 2   This article shall be inoperative unless it shall have been ratified as an amendment to the Constitution by the legislatures of three-fourths of the several States within seven years from the date of its submission to the States by the Congress.

AMENDMENT XXIII
[Presidential electors for the District of Columbia; adopted 1961]

SECTION 1   The District constituting the seat of Government of the United States shall appoint in such manner as the Congress may direct:
   A number of electors of President and Vice President equal to the whole number of Senators and Representatives in Congress to which the District would be entitled if it were a State, but in no event more than the least populous State; they shall be in addition to those appointed by the States, but they shall be considered for the purposes of the election of President and Vice President, to be electors appointed by a State; and they shall meet in the District and perform such duties as provided by the twelfth article of amendment.

SECTION 2   The Congress shall have the power to enforce this article by appropriate legislation.

AMENDMENT XXIV
[Poll tax outlawed in national elections; adopted 1964]

SECTION 1   The right of citizens of the United States to vote in any primary or other election for President or Vice President, for electors for President or Vice President, or for Senator or Representative in Congress, shall not be denied or abridged by the United States or any State by reason of failure to pay any poll tax or other tax.

SECTION 2   The Congress shall have the power to enforce this article by appropriate legislation.

AMENDMENT XXV
[Presidential succession; adopted 1967]

SECTION 1   In case of the removal of the President from office or of his death or resignation, the Vice President shall become President.

[Vice-presidential vacancy]

SECTION 2   Whenever there is a vacancy in the office of the Vice President, the President shall nominate a Vice President who shall take office upon confirmation by a majority vote of both Houses of Congress.

SECTION 3   Whenever the President transmits to the President pro tempore of the Senate and the Speaker of the House of Representatives his written declaration that he is unable to discharge the powers and duties of his office, and until he transmits to them a written declaration to the contrary, such powers and duties shall be discharged by the Vice President as Acting President.

[Presidential disability]

SECTION 4   Whenever the Vice President and a majority of either the principal officers of the executive departments or of such other body as Congress may by law provide, transmit to the President pro tempore of the Senate and the Speaker of the House of Representatives their written declaration that the President is unable to discharge the powers and duties of his office, the Vice President shall immediately assume the powers and duties of the office as Acting President.

Thereafter, when the President transmits to the President pro tempore of the Senate and the Speaker of the House of Representatives his written declaration that no inability exists, he shall resume the powers and duties of his office unless the Vice President and a majority of either the principal officers of the executive department(s) or of such other body as Congress may by law provide, transmit within four days to the President pro tempore of the Senate and the Speaker of the House of Representatives their written declaration that the President is unable to discharge the powers and duties of his office. Thereupon Congress shall decide the issue, assembling within forty-eight hours for that purpose if not in session. If the Congress, within twenty-one days after receipt of the latter written declaration, or, if Congress is not in session, within twenty-one days after Congress is required to assemble, determines by two-thirds vote of both Houses that the President is unable to discharge the powers and duties of his office, the Vice President shall continue to discharge the same as Acting President; otherwise, the President shall resume the powers and duties of his office.

AMENDMENT XXVI
[Right of eighteen-year-olds to vote; adopted 1971]

SECTION 1   The right of citizens of the United States, who are eighteen years of age or older, to vote shall not be denied or abridged by the United States or by any State on account of age.

SECTION 2   The Congress shall have power to enforce this article by appropriate legislation.

AMENDMENT XXVII
[Congressional pay raises; adopted 1992]

No law, varying the compensation for the services of the Senators and Representatives shall take effect, until an election of Representatives shall have intervened.

References

Chapter 1 / Dilemmas of Democracy / pages 1–31

1. The information about the Roger Rodriguez case discussed below comes from Carrick Mollenkamp and Ian McDonald, "Behind Subprime Woes, a Cascade of Bad Debts," *Wall Street Journal,* 17 October 2007, p. 1.

2. Mark Landler, "U.S. Credit Crisis Adds to Gloom of Arctic Norway's Long Night," *New York Times,* 2 December 2007, pp. 1 and 11.

3. Organization for Economic Co-Operation and Development, "Highlights of Recent Trends in Financial Markets, November 2007" (Paris: OECD, 21 November 2007), p. 17.

4. Greg Ip and Joellen Perry, "Central Banks Launch Effort to Free Up Credit," *Wall Street Journal,* 13 December 2007, pp. A1 and A20.

5. Mark Andreas Kayser, "How Domestic Is Domestic Politics? Globalization and Elections," *Annual Review of Political Science* 10 (2007): 341–362.

6. David Easton, *The Political System* (New York: Knopf, 1953), p. 65.

7. Thomas Biersteker and Cynthia Weber (eds.), *State Sovereignty as Social Construct* (Cambridge: Cambridge University Press, 1996), p. 12. For a definition of sovereignty at the national level, see Bernard Crick, "Sovereignty," in *International Encyclopedia of the Social Sciences,* Vol. 15 (New York: Macmillan and the Free Press, 1968), p. 77. In the same encyclopedia, David Apter, "Government," Vol. 6, links sovereignty to "a national autonomous community," p. 215.

8. Nick Timiraos, "Arctic Thaw Defrosts a Sea Treaty," *Wall Street Journal,* 3 November 2007, p. 11.

9. Jess Bravin, "U.S. to Pull Out of World Court on War Crimes," *Wall Street Journal,* 6 May 2002, p. A4.

10. Charles M. Madigan and Colin McMahon, "A Slow, Painful Quest for Justice," *Chicago Tribune,* 7 September 1999, pp. 1, 8.

11. Tom Hundley, "Europe Seeks to Convert U.S. on Death Penalty," *Chicago Tribune,* 26 June 2000, p. 1; Salim Muwakkil, "The Capital of Capital Punishment," *Chicago Tribune,* 12 July 1999, p. 18.

12. 1977 Constitution of the Union of Soviet Socialist Republics, Article 11, in *Constitutions of Countries of the World,* ed. A. P. Blaustein and G. H. Flanz (Dobbs Ferry, N.Y.: Oceana, 1971).

13. Edward Cody, "Chinese Lawmakers Approve Measure to Protect Private Property Rights, *Washington Post,* 17 March 2007, p. A10.

14. Karl Marx and Friedrich Engels, *Critique of the Gotha Programme* (New York: International Publishers, 1938), p. 10. Originally written in 1875 but published in 1891.

15. See the argument in Amy Gutman, *Liberal Equality* (Cambridge: Cambridge University Press, 1980), pp. 9–10.

16. See John H. Schaar, "Equality of Opportunity and Beyond," in *Equality,* NOMOS IX, ed. J. Roland Pennock and John W. Chapman (New York: Atherton Press, 1967), pp. 228–249.

17. Gallup Poll, released 9 January 2003.

18. See generally Milton Friedman, *Capitalism and Freedom* (Chicago: University of Chicago Press, 1962).

19. Joseph Kahn, "Anarchism, the Creed That Won't Stay Dead," *New York Times,* 5 August 2000, p. A15.

20. The communitarian category was labeled "Populist" in early editions of this book. We have relabeled it for two reasons. First, we believe that *communitarian* is more descriptive of the category. Second, we recognize that the term *populist* has been used increasingly to refer to the political styles of candidates such as Pat Buchanan and Ralph Nader. In this sense, a populist appeals to mass resentment against those in power. Given the debate over what *populist* really means, we have decided to use *communitarian,* a less familiar term with fewer connotations. For a discussion of definitions in print, see Michael Kazin, *The Populist Persuasion: An American History* (New York: Basic Books, 1995).

21. The communitarian movement was founded by a group of ethicists and social scientists who met in Washington, D.C., in 1990 at the invitation of sociologist Amitai Etzioni and political theorist William Galston to discuss the declining state of morality and values in the United States. Etzioni became the leading spokesperson for the movement. See his *Rights and the Common Good: The Communitarian Perspective* (New York: St. Martin's Press, 1995), pp. iii–iv. The communitarian political movement should be distinguished from communitarian thought in political philosophy, which is associated with theorists such as Alasdair MacIntyre, Michael Sandel, and Charles Taylor, who wrote in the late 1970s and early 1980s. In essence, communitarian theorists criticized liberalism, which stressed freedom and individualism, as excessively individualistic. Their fundamental critique was that liberalism slights the values of community life. See Allen E. Buchanan, "Assessing the Communitarian Critique of Liberalism," *Ethics* 99 (July 1989): 852–882, and Patrick Neal and David Paris, "Liberalism and the Communitarian Critique: A Guide for the Perplexed," *Canadian Journal of Political Science* 23 (September 1990): 419–439. Communitarian philosophers attacked liberalism over the inviolability of civil liberties. In our framework, such issues involve the tradeoff between freedom and order. Communitarian and liberal theorists differ less concerning the tradeoff between freedom and equality. See William R. Lund, "Communitarian Politics and the Problem of Equality," *Political Research Quarterly* 46 (September 1993): 577–600. But see also Susan Hekman, "The Embodiment of the Subject: Feminism and the Communitarian Critique of Liberalism," *Journal of Politics* 54 (November 1992): 1098–1119.

22. Etzioni, *Rights and the Common Good,* p. iv, and Etzioni, "Communitarian Solutions/What Communitarians

Think," *Journal of State Government* 65 (January–March): 9–11. For a critical review of the communitarian program, see Jeremiah Creedon, "Communitarian Manifesto," *Utne Reader* (July–August 1992): 38–40.

23. Etzioni, "Communitarian Solutions/What Communitarians Think," p. 10. See also Lester Thurow, "Communitarian vs. Individualistic Capitalism," in Etzioni, *Rights and the Common Good*, pp. 277–282. Note, however, that government's role in dealing with issues of social and economic inequality is far less developed in communitarian writings than is its role in dealing with issues of order. In the same volume, an article by David Osborne, "Beyond Left and Right: A New Political Paradigm" (pp. 283–290), downplays the role of government in guaranteeing entitlements.

24. Etzioni, *Rights and the Common Good*, p. 17.

25. David M. Herszenhorn, "Farm Subsidies Seem Immune to an Overhaul," *New York Times*, 26 July 2007, p. A1; Stephen J. Hedges, "Farm Bill Subsidies Remain," from Chicagotribune.com; and "Green Acres," *Wall Street Journal*, 16 December 2007, from WSJ.com.

26. Kenneth Janda, "What's in a Name? Party Labels Across the World," in *The CONTA Conference: Proceedings of the Conference of Conceptual and Terminological Analysis of the Social Sciences*, ed. F. W. Riggs (Frankfurt: Indeks Verlage, 1982), pp. 46–62.

27. See James A. Stimson, Michael B. MacKuen, and Robert S. Erikson, "Dynamic Representation," *American Political Science Review* 89 (September 1995): 543–565.

28. See C. B. Macpherson, *The Real World of Democracy* (New York: Oxford University Press, 1975), pp. 58–59.

29. Thomas E. Cronin, *Direct Democracy* (Cambridge, Mass.: Harvard University Press, 1989), p. 47.

30. Jack Citrin, "Who's the Boss? Direct Democracy and Popular Control of Government," in *Broken Contract?* ed. Stephen C. Craig (Boulder, Colo.: Westview, 1996), p. 271.

31. Lawrence K. Grossman, *The Electronic Republic* (New York: Viking, 1995).

32. American National Election Study, 2004. Conducted by the Center for Political Studies of the Institute for Social Research, University of Michigan. On the implications of voters being poorly informed, see Bryan Caplan, *The Myth of the Rational Voter* (Princeton, N.J.: Princeton University Press, 2007).

33. Benjamin I. Page and Robert Y. Shapiro, *The Rational Public* (Chicago: University of Chicago Press, 1992), p. 387.

34. See Robert A. Dahl, *Dilemmas of Pluralist Democracy* (New Haven, Conn.: Yale University Press, 1982), p. 5.

35. Jeffrey M. Berry, *The New Liberalism* (Washington, D.C.: The Brookings Institution, 1999).

36. Robert D. Putnam, *Bowling Alone* (New York: Simon & Schuster, 2000).

37. The classic statement on elite theory is C. Wright Mills, *The Power Elite* (New York: Oxford University Press, 1956).

38. See Robert A. Dahl, *Who Governs?* (New Haven, Conn.: Yale University Press, 1961). See also Clarence N. Stone, *Regime Politics* (Lawrence: University of Kansas Press, 1989); and John P. Heinz, Edward O. Laumann, Robert
L. Nelson, and Robert H. Salisbury, *The Hollow Core* (Cambridge, Mass.: Harvard University Press, 1993).

39. Peter Bachrach and Morton S. Baratz, "Two Faces of Power," *American Political Science Review* 56 (December 1962): 947–952; and John Gaventa, *Power and Powerlessness* (Urbana: University of Illinois Press, 1980).

40. See, for example, Dan Clawson, Alan Neustadtl, and Denise Scott, *Money Talks* (New York: Basic Books, 1992).

41. Kay Lehman Schlozman and John T. Tierney, *Organized Interests and American Politics* (New York: Harper & Row, 1986).

42. Arend Lijphart, *Democracies* (New Haven, Conn.: Yale University Press, 1984).

43. *Africa Demos* 3 (May 1996): 1, 27; Michael Bratton and Nicholas van de Walle, "Popular Protest and Political Reform in Africa," *Comparative Politics* 24 (July 1992): 419–442.

44. See Thomas L. Friedman, *Longitudes and Attitudes: The World After September 11* (New York: Farrar, Straus & Giroux, 2002).

45. E. E. Schattschneider, *The Semi-Sovereign People* (New York: Holt, Rinehart, & Winston, 1960), p. 35.

Chapter 2 / The Constitution / pages 32–62

1. Introductory speech by President V. Giscard d'Estaing to the Convention on the Future of Europe, 28 February 2002, available at http://european-convention.eu.int/docs/speeches/1.

2. Letter from George Washington to James Madison, 31 March 1787, available at http://gwpapers.virginia.edu/constitution/1787/madison3.html.

3. Center for Political Studies, Institute for Social Research, *American National Election Study, 2000* (Ann Arbor: University of Michigan, 2001).

4. Hungary was the first country to ratify the Reform Treaty, with only 5 out of 386 members of parliament opposed the ratification. See EurActiv.com, available at www.euractiv.com/en/future-eu/hungary-country-ratify-new-eu-treaty/article-169183 (accessed 30 March 2008). Kevin Sullivan, "Ireland Shoots Down Plan for a More Unified E.U.," *Washington Post*, 14 June 2008, p. A8.

5. Samuel Eliot Morison, *Oxford History of the American People* (New York: Oxford University Press, 1965), p. 172.

6. John Plamentz, *Man and Society*, rev. ed., ed. M. E. Plamentz and Robert Wokler, Vol. 1: *From the Middle Ages to Locke* (New York: Longman, 1992), pp. 216–218.

7. Extrapolated from U.S. Department of Defense, *Selected Manpower Statistics, FY 1982* (Washington, D.C.: U.S. Government Printing Office, 1983), Table 2-30, p. 130; and U.S. Bureau of the Census, *1985 Statistical Abstract of the United States* (Washington, D.C.: U.S. Government Printing Office, 1985), Tables 1 and 2, p. 6.

8. Joseph T. Keenan, *The Constitution of the United States* (Homewood, Ill.: Dow-Jones-Irwin, 1975).

9. David P. Szatmary, *Shays' Rebellion: The Making of an Agrarian Insurrection* (Amherst: University of Massachusetts Press, 1980), pp. 82–102.

10. Robert H. Jackson, *The Struggle for Judicial Supremacy* (New York: Knopf, 1941), p. 8.
11. Forrest McDonald, *Novus Ordo Seclorum: The Intellectual Origins of the Constitution* (Lawrence: University Press of Kansas, 1985), pp. 205–209.
12. Donald S. Lutz, "The Preamble to the Constitution of the United States," *This Constitution* 1 (September 1983): 23–30.
13. Richard E. Neustadt, *Presidential Power: The Politics of Leadership* (New York: Wiley, 1960), p. 33.
14. Robert A. Goldwin, Letter to the Editor, *Wall Street Journal*, 30 August 1993, p. A11.
15. Herbert J. Storing (ed.), *The Complete Anti-Federalist*, 7 vols. (Chicago: University of Chicago Press, 1981).
16. Alexis de Tocqueville, *Democracy in America, 1835–1839*, ed. J. P. Mayer and Max Lerner (New York: Harper & Row, 1966), p. 102.
17. Jerold L. Waltman, *Political Origins of the U.S. Income Tax* (Jackson: University Press of Mississippi, 1985), p. 10.

Chapter 3 / Federalism / pages 63–87

1. Dan Baum, "When Katrina Hit, Where Were the Police?" *New Yorker*, 9 January 2006, available at www.newyorker.com/fact/content/articles/060109fa_fact.
2. Evan Thomas, "How Bush Blew It," *Newsweek*, 19 September 2005, available at www.newsweek.com/id/104464.
3. As part of a major government restructuring that took place after September 11, FEMA lost its independent status and became a subdepartment under the Department of Homeland Security. September 11 profoundly changed the list of priorities in the United States, as terrorism replaced natural disasters as a clear and present danger. Unfortunately, these situations require different measures. What is good for fighting terrorism may be inadequate for handling natural catastrophes.
4. Testimony from affected people, from "The Storm," *Frontline-PBS*, 22 November 2005, available at www.pbs.org/wgbh/pages/frontline/storm/view.
5. William H. Stewart, *Concepts of Federalism* (Lanham, Md.: University Press of America, 1984).
6. Edward Corwin, "The Passing of Dual Federalism," *University of Virginia Law Review* 36 (1950): 4.
7. See Daniel J. Elazar, *The American Partnership* (Chicago: University of Chicago Press, 1962); Morton Grodzins, *The American System* (Chicago: Rand McNally, 1966).
8. James T. Patterson, *The New Deal and the States: Federalism in Transition* (Princeton, N.J.: Princeton University Press, 1969).
9. For more information on the USA-PATRIOT Act, see http://thomas.loc.gov/cgibin/bdquery/z?d107:h.r.03162:. For the Department of Homeland Security, see www.dhs.gov/dhspublic/.
10. *McCulloch* v. *Maryland*, 4 Wheat. 316 (1819).
11. *Gibbons* v. *Ogden*, 22 U.S. 1 (1824).
12. *Dred Scott* v. *Sanford*, 19 How. 393, 426 (1857).
13. *United States* v. *Lopez*, 514 U.S. 549 (1995).
14. *Printz* v. *United States*, 521 U.S. 98 (1997).
15. *United States* v. *Morrison*, 120 S. Ct. 1740 (2000).
16. *Lawrence and Garner* v. *Texas*, 539 U.S. 558 (2003).

This decision overturned *Bowers* v. *Hardwick*, 478 U.S. 186 (1986).
17. Brandy Anderson, "Congress Passes National .08 BAC Law," *DRIVEN* (Fall 2000), available at www.madd.org/news/1,1056,1253,00.html.
18. Terry Sanford, *Storm Over the States* (New York: McGraw-Hill, 1967).
19. Quoted in Cynthia J. Bowling and Deil S. Wright, "Public Administration in the Fifty States: A Half-Century Administrative Revolution," *State and Local Government Review* 30 (Winter 1998): 52.
20. David M. Hedge, *Governance and the Changing American States* (Boulder, Colo.: Westview Press, 1998).
21. Bureau of Labor Statistics, U.S. Department of Labor, *Career Guide to Industries, 2008–09 Edition*, State and Local Government, Excluding Education and Hospitals, available at www.bls.gov/oco/cg/cgs042.htm, accessed 15 March 2008.
22. Paul Manna, "Federalism, Agenda Setting, and the Development of Federal Education Policy, 1965–2001" (Ph.D. diss., University of Wisconsin, 2003).
23. Ronald Reagan, "Statement on Signing Executive Order Establishing the Presidential Advisory Committee on Federalism," 1981 Pub. Papers 341, 8 April 1981.
24. Joseph F. Zimmerman, *Contemporary American Federalism: The Growth of National Power* (New York: Praeger, 1992), Chap. 4.
25. Internet Tax Nondiscrimination Act of 2004.
26. Joseph Zimmerman, "Congressional Preemption During the George W. Bush Administration," *Publius* 37, 3 (2007): 432–452.
27. Ibid., 436.
28. Ibid., 432.
29. John Kincaid, "From Cooperative to Coercive Federalism," *Annals of the American Academy of Political and Social Science* 509, (May 1990): 139–152.
30. "Unfunded Federal Mandates," *Congressional Digest* (March 1995): 68.
31. Paul Posner, "The Politics of Coercive Federalism," *Publius* 37, 3 (2007): 390–412.
32. National Conference of State Legislatures, *NCSL News*, "States Legislatures Face Unsettled Conditions in 2008," 14 December 2007. Available at www.ncsl.org/programs/press/2007/pr121007.htm, accessed 26 January 2008.
33. National Conference of State Legislatures, *NCSL News*, "State Lawmakers Intercept Shipment of Federal Unfunded Mandates and Cost-Shifts," 5 August 2007, available at www.ncsl.org/programs/press/2007/pr070805.htm, accessed 28 January 2008.
34. CNN, "Texas House Paralyzed by Democratic Walkout," 19 May 2002, available at www.cnn.com/2003/ALLPOLITICS/05/13/texas.legislature; R. Jeffrey Smith, "DeLay, FAA Roles in Texas Redistricting Flap Detailed," *Washington Post*, 12 July 2003, p. A3; Karen Masterson, "Transportation Investigator Says Agency Erred in Seeking Democrats," *Houston Chronicle*, 16 July 2003, p. A6.
35. U.S. Bureau of the Census, *Statistical Abstract of the United States: 2008* (Washington, D.C.: U.S. Government Printing Office, 2008), Table 414, p. 263.
36. *U.S. Term Limits* v. *Thornton*, 514 U.S. 779 (1995).

Chapter 4 / Public Opinion, Political Socialization, and the Media / pages 88–120

1. Julia Preston, "New U.N. Chief Invites Controversy by Declining to Oppose Hussein Execution," *New York Times*, 3 January 2007.
2. "Death Penalty Statistics 2006," *Amnesty International*, 27 April 2007, available at www.amnesty.org.
3. But 91 percent of all executions in 1996 took place in China, Iran, Iraq, Sudan, Pakistan, and the United States. "Death Penalty Statistics 2006."
4. Gallup Poll conducted 4–7 October 2007, reported by Frank Newport, "Sixty-nine Percent of Americans Support Death Penalty," 12 October 2007, available at www.gallup.com. For opinion from 1957 to 2007, see Robert Ruby, "Capital Punishment's Constant Constituency: An American Majority," Pew Forum on Religion and Public Life, 27 June 2007, available at http://pewforum.org/docs/index.php?DocID=231.
5. Warren Weaver Jr., "Death Penalty a 300-Year Issue in America," *New York Times*, 3 July 1976.
6. *Furman* v. *Georgia*, 408 U.S. 238 (1972).
7. *Gregg* v. *Georgia*, 248 U.S. 153 (1976).
8. U.S. Department of Justice, Bureau of Justice Statistics, "Number of Persons Executed in the U.S. 1930–2006," available at www.ojp.usdoj.gov/bjs/glance/tables/exetab.htm.
9. Seventy percent of whites favor the death penalty, while 56 percent of African Americans oppose it. Lydia Saad, "Racial Disagreement Over Death Penalty Has Varied Historically," Gallup News Service, 30 July 2007, available at www.gallup.com. For a discussion of the effects of the disenfranchisement of felons see Jeff Manza and Christopher Uggen, *Locked Out: Felon Disenfranchisement and American Democracy* (New York: Oxford University Press, 2006).
10. Frank Newport, "Sixty-nine Percent of Americans Support Death Penalty," 12 October 2007, available at www.gallup.com.
11. Death Penalty Information website, "Facts About the Death Penalty, March 1, 2008," available at www.deathpenaltyinfo.org/FactSheet.pdf.
12. Adam Liptak, "At 60% of Total, Texas Is Bucking Execution Trend," *New York Times*, 26 December 2007, p. A1.
13. Jess Bravin and Gary Fields, "Top Cases Reflect Political Fray," *Wall Street Journal*, 7 January 2008, p. A4, and Kavan Peterson, Stateline.org, "Lethal Injection on Trial," 17 January 2007, *Pew Research Center*, available at http://pewresearch.org/obdeck/?ObDeckID=122. Tim Craig, "Va. Executions Are Put on Hold," *Washington Post*, 2 April 2008, p. B01. *Baze et al.* v. *Rees*, 553 U.S. ___(2008). *Kennedy* v. *Louisiana*, 554 U.S. ___(2008).
14. David Masci, "An Impassioned Debate: An Overview of the Death Penalty in America," Pew Forum on Religion and Public Life, 19 December 2007, available at http://pewforum.org/docs/?DocID=270.
15. U.S. Department of Justice, Bureau of Justice Statistics, "Advance Count of Execution: January 1, 2007–December 31, 2007," available at www.ojp.usdoj.gov/bjs/pub/html/cp/2006/tables/cp06sta.htm.
16. See Roberta S. Sigel (ed.), *Political Learning in Adulthood: A Sourcebook of Theory and Research* (Chicago: University of Chicago Press, 1989).
17. Pew Center for the People and the Press, "Public's News Habits Little Changed by September 11," 9 June 2002, available at http://people-press.org//reports/display.php3?ReportID=156.
18. Other scholars have analyzed opinion on abortion using six questions from the General Social Survey (GSS). See R. Michael Alvarez and John Brehm, "American Ambivalence Toward Abortion Policy," *American Journal of Political Science* 39 (1995): 1055–1082; Elizabeth Adell Cook, Ted G. Jelen, and Clyde Wilcox, *Between Two Absolutes: Public Opinion and the Politics of Abortion* (Boulder, Colo.: Westview Press, 1992).
19. Although some people view the politics of abortion as single-issue politics, the issue has broader political significance. In their book on the subject, Cook, Jelen, and Wilcox say, "Although embryonic life is one important value in the abortion debate, it is not the only value at stake." They contend that the politics is tied to alternative sexual relationships and traditional roles of women in the home, which are "social order" issues. See *Between Two Absolutes*, pp. 8–9.
20. Russell J. Dalton, *The Good Citizen* (Washington, D.C.: Congressional Quarterly Press, 2008), Chap. 5.
21. Ibid., p. 50.
22. The increasing wealth in industrialized societies may or may not be replacing class conflict with conflict over values. See the exchange between Ronald Inglehart and Scott C. Flanagan, "Value Change in Industrial Societies," *American Political Science Review* 81 (December 1987): 1289–1319.
23. Nathan Glazer, "The Structure of Ethnicity," *Public Opinion* 7 (October–November 1984): 4.
24. D'Vera Cohn, "Hispanics Declared Largest Minority," *Washington Post*, 19 June 2003, p. A1.
25. U.S. Census Bureau, "Race and Hispanic Origin in 2005," Population Profile of the United States: Dynamic Version, available online at www.census.gov/population/pop-profile/dynamic/RACEHO.pdf. U.S. Bureau of the Census, Hispanics in the United States, Slide 11, "Current Population Trends in the Hispanic Population." Internet Presentation available at www.census.gov/population/www/socdemo/hispanic/files/Internet_Hispanic_in_US_2006.pdf.
26. Michael Dawson, *Black Visions: The Roots of Contemporary African American Political Ideologies* (Chicago: University of Chicago Press, 2001) and *Behind the Mule* (Princeton, N.J.: Princeton University Press, 1994); John Garcia, *Latino Politics in America* (Lanham, Md.: Rowman and Littlefield, 2003); Peite Lien, *The Making of Asian America Through Political Participation* (Philadelphia: Temple University Press, 2001); Wendy Tam, "Asians—A Monolithic Voting Bloc?" *Political Behavior* 17 (1995): 223–249; Katherine Tate, *Black Faces in the Mirror: African Americans and Their Representatives in the U.S. Congress* (Princeton, N.J.: Princeton University Press, 2003). See U.S. Census Bureau, "Population Profile of the United States: Dynamic Version" for up-to-date population statistics, available at

www.census.gov/population/www/pop-profile/profiledynamic.html.

27. Glazer, "Structure of Ethnicity," p. 5.

28. U.S. Religious Landscape Survey: Religious Beliefs and Practices, Diverse and Politically Relevant (Washington, D.C.: Pew Forum on Religion and Public Life, 2008), p. 8, available at religions.pewforum.org/pdf/report2-religious-landscape-study-full.pdf.

29. See David C. Leege and Lyman A. Kellstedt (eds.), *Rediscovering the Religious Factor in American Politics* (Armonk, N.Y.: Sharpe, 1993), for a comprehensive examination of religion in political life that goes far beyond the analysis here. However, some scholars have argued that Americans are not as polarized as the news media would have us think. See Morris P. Fiorina, *Culture Wars? The Myth of a Polarized America* (White Plains, N.Y.: Longman, 2004).

30. Jeffrey M. Jones, "Understanding Americans' Support for the Death Penalty," Gallup News Service, 3 June 2003.

31. Center for American Women and Politics, Eagleton Institute of Politics, "Gender Gap Persists in the 2004 Election," press release, 5 November 2004, available at www.cawp.rutgers.edu/Facts/Elections/GG2004facts.pdf.

32. John Robinson, "The Ups and Downs and Ins and Outs of Ideology," *Public Opinion* 7 (February–March 1984): 12.

33. For a more positive interpretation of ideological attitudes within the public, see William G. Jacoby, "The Structure of Ideological Thinking in the American Electorate" (paper presented at the Annual Meeting of the American Political Science Association, Washington, D.C., September 1993). Jacoby applies a new method to survey data for the 1984 and 1988 elections and concludes "that there is a systematic, cumulative structure underlying liberal-conservative thinking in the American public" (p. 1).

34. When asked to describe the parties and candidates in the 1956 election, only about 12 percent of respondents volunteered responses that contained ideological terms (such as *liberal, conservative,* and *capitalism*). Most respondents (42 percent) evaluated the parties and candidates in terms of "benefits to groups" (farmers, workers, or businesspeople, for example). Others (24 percent) spoke more generally about "the nature of the times" (for example, inflation, unemployment, and the threat of war). Finally, a good portion of the sample (22 percent) gave answers that contained no classifiable issue content. See Angus Campbell, Philip E. Converse, Warren E. Miller, and Donald E. Stokes, *The American Voter* (New York: Wiley, 1960), Chap. 10.

35. Marjorie Connelly, "A 'Conservative' Is (Fill in the Blank)," *New York Times,* 3 November 1996, sec. 4, p. 5.

36. Ibid.

37. A relationship between liberalism and political tolerance was found by John L. Sullivan et al., "The Sources of Political Tolerance: A Multivariate Analysis," *American Political Science Review* 75 (March 1981): 102. See also Robinson, "Ups and Downs," pp. 13–15.

38. Herbert Asher, *Presidential Elections and American Politics* (Homewood, Ill.: Dorsey, 1980), pp. 14–20.

Asher also constructs a two-dimensional framework, distinguishing between "traditional New Deal" issues and "new lifestyle" issues.

39. John E. Jackson, "The Systematic Beliefs of the Mass Public: Estimating Policy Preferences with Survey Data," *Journal of Politics* 45 (November 1983): 840–865.

40. Milton Rokeach also proposed a two-dimensional model of political ideology grounded in the terminal values of freedom and equality. See *The Nature of Human Values* (New York: Free Press, 1973), especially Chap. 6. Rokeach found that positive and negative references to the two values permeate the writings of socialists, communists, fascists, and conservatives and clearly differentiate the four bodies of writing from one another (pp. 173–174). However, Rokeach built his two-dimensional model around only the values of freedom and equality; he did not deal with the question of freedom versus order.

41. In our framework, opposition to abortion is classified as a communitarian position. However, the communitarian movement led by Amitai Etzioni adopted no position on abortion. Personal communication from Vanessa Hoffman by e-mail, in reply to my query of 5 February 1996.

42. Two researchers who compared the public's knowledge on various topics in 1989 with its knowledge of the same topics in the 1940s and 1950s found similar levels of knowledge across the years. They point out, however, "that knowledge has been stable during a period of rapid changes in education, communication, and the public role of women seems paradoxical." They suspect, but cannot demonstrate, that the expected increase in knowledge did not materialize because of a decline in the public's interest in politics over time. See Michael X. Delli Carpini and Scott Keeter, "Stability and Change in the U.S. Public's Knowledge of Politics," *Public Opinion Quarterly* 55 (Winter 1991): 607.

43. Michael X. Delli Carpini and Scott Keeter, *What Americans Know About Politics and Why It Matters* (New Haven, Conn.: Yale University Press, 1996).

44. Ibid., p. 269.

45. There is evidence that the educational system and parental practices hamper the ability of women to develop their political knowledge. See Linda L. M. Bennett and Stephen Earl Bennett, "Enduring Gender Differences in Political Interests," *American Politics Quarterly* 17 (January 1989): 105–122.

46. "Public Knowledge of Current Affairs Little Changed by News and Information Revolution: What Americans Know 1989–2007," Pew Research Center for the People and the Press, 15 April 2007, available at http://people-press.org/reports/display.php3?ReportID=319.

47. W. Russell Neuman, *The Paradox of Mass Politics: Knowledge and Opinion in the American Electorate* (Cambridge, Mass.: Harvard University Press, 1986), p. 81.

48. Stephan Lewandowsky, Werner Stritzke, Klaus Oberauer, and Michael Morales, "Memory for Fact, Fiction, and Misinformation: The Iraq War 2003," *Psychological Science* 16 (March 2005): 190–195.

49. A significant literature exists on the limitations of self-interest in explaining political life. See Jane J. Mans-

bridge (ed.), *Beyond Self-Interest* (Chicago: University of Chicago Press, 1990).

50. Aaron Wildavsky, "Choosing Preferences by Constructing Institutions: A Cultural Theory of Preference Formation," *American Political Science Review* 81 (March 1987): 3–21.

51. Henry Brady and Paul Sniderman, "Attitude Attribution: A Group Basis for Political Reasoning," *American Political Science Review* 79 (1985): 1061–1078; Samuel Popkin, *The Reasoning Voter*, 2nd ed. (Chicago: University of Chicago Press, 1994); Paul M. Sniderman, Richard A. Brody, and Philip E. Tetlock, *Reasoning and Choice* (Cambridge: Cambridge University Press, 1991). Psychologists have tended to emphasize the distorting effects of heuristics. See Daniel Kahneman, Paul Slovic, and Amos Tversky (eds.), *Judgment Under Uncertainty: Heuristics and Biases* (Cambridge: Cambridge University Press, 1982), and Richard Nisbett and Lee Ross, *Human Inference: Strategies and Shortcomings of Social Judgment* (Englewood Cliffs, N.J.: Prentice-Hall, 1980).

52. Political psychologists refer to beliefs that guide information processing as opinion "schemas." See Pamela Johnston Conover and Stanley Feldman, "How People Organize the Political World: A Schematic Model," *American Journal of Political Science* 28 (February 1984): 95–127; Milton Lodge and Kathleen M. McGraw, *Political Judgment: Structure and Process* (Ann Arbor: University of Michigan Press, 1995). For an excellent review of schema structures in contemporary psychology, especially as they relate to political science, see Reid Hastie, "A Primer of Information-Processing Theory for the Political Scientist," in *Political Cognition,* ed. Richard R. Lau and David O. Sears (Hillsdale, N.J.: Erlbaum, 1986), pp. 11–39.

53. Pew Center for the People and the Press, "Religion and Politics: Contention and Consensus," 24 July 2003, available at http://people-press.org/reports/display .php3?ReportID=189.

54. J. Kuklinski and N. L. Hurley, "On Hearing and Interpreting Political Messages," *Journal of Politics* 56 (1994): 729–751.

55. On framing, see William Jacoby, "Issue Framing and Public Opinion on Government Spending," *American Journal of Political Science* 44 (October 2000): 750–767; James N. Druckman, "The Implications of Framing Effects for Citizen Competence," *Political Behavior* 23 (September 2001): 225–253. On political spin, see Lawrence Jacobs and Robert Y. Shapiro, *Politicians Don't Pander* (Chicago: University of Chicago Press, 2000).

56. Benjamin I. Page, Robert Y. Shapiro, and Glenn R. Dempsey, "What Moves Public Opinion?" *American Political Science Review* 81 (March 1987): 23–43.

57. Michael Margolis and Gary A. Mauser, *Manipulating Public Opinion: Essays on Public Opinion as a Dependent Variable* (Pacific Grove, Calif.: Brooks/Cole, 1989).

58. John December, Neil Randall, and Wes Tatters, *Discover the World Wide Web with Your Sportster* (Indianapolis, Ind.: Sams.net Publishing, 1995), pp. 11–12.

59. Marsha Walton, CNN, "Web Reaches New Milestone: 100 Million Sites," 1 November 2006, available at www .cnn.com/2006/TECH/internet/11/01/ 100millionwebsites/index.html.

60. "Demographics of Internet Users," Pew Internet and American Life 2007 survey, available at www .pewinternet.org.

61. "Internet News Audience Highly Critical of News Organizations," Pew Research Center for the People and the Press, 9 August 2007, available at http://people-press.org.

62. Katherine Q. Seelye, Jacques Steinberg, and David F. Gallagher, "Bloggers as News Media Trophy Hunters," *New York Times,* 14 February 2005, p. C1; Bill Carter, "Post-Mortem of a Broadcast Disaster," *New York Times,* 11 January 2005, p. C1.

63. Doris A. Graber, *Mass Media and American Politics,* 6th ed. (Washington, D.C.: Congressional Quarterly Press, 2002), pp. 107–109. See also W. Lance Bennett, *News: The Politics of Illusion,* 3rd ed. (White Plains, N.Y.: Longman, 1996), Chap. 2.

64. Joe Flint, "Viacom to Split, Create 2 Companies," *Wall Street Journal,* 15 June 2005, p. B5.

65. Frank Ahrens, "At *Wall Street Journal,* Change of Accents," *Washington Post,* 5 March 2008, p. D01.

66. Paige Albiniak, "Court Scraps Reply Rules," *Broadcasting and Cable,* 16 October 2000, pp. 6–7. Stephen Labaton, "In Test F.C.C. Lifts Requirements on Broadcasting Political Replies," *New York Times,* 5 October 2000, pp. A1, A27.

67. Martha Joynt Kumar, "The President and the News Media," in *The President, the Public, and the Parties,* 2nd ed. (Washington, D.C.: Congressional Quarterly Press, 1997), p. 119.

68. Bennett, *News: The Politics of Illusion,* p. 26.

69. Stephen J. Farnsworth and S. Robert Lichter, *The Nightly News Nightmare: Network Television's Coverage of U.S. Presidential Elections, 1988–2000* (Lanham, Md.: Rowman & Littlefield, 2003), p. 51.

70. "Summary of Findings: Modest Interest in 2008 Campaign News," Pew Research Center for the People and the Press, 23 October 2007, available at http:// people-press.org.

71. "Television: Primary Media Sources for News," TVB, Nielsen Media Research Survey 2006, Media Information Center, available at www.mediainfocenter.org/ television/content/leading_news.asap.

72. "Online Papers Modestly Boost Newspaper Readership," Pew Research Center for the People and the Press, 30 July 2006, available at http://people-press.org.

73. Ibid.

74. "Top Online News Sites (Nielsen ratings)," January–December 2006, the State of the News Media 2007, available at www.stateofthemedia.org.

75. Pew Research Center, "Public Knowledge of Current Affairs Little Changed by News and Information Revolutions: What Americans Know: 1989–2007," *Survey Report,* 15 April 2007, available at http://people-press. org/reports/pdf/319.pdf.

76. William P. Eveland Jr. and Dietram A. Scheufele, "Connecting News Media Use with Gaps in Knowledge and Participation," *Political Communication* 17 (July–September, 2000): 215–237.

77. W. Russell Neuman, Marion R. Just, and Ann N. Crigler, *Common Knowledge: News and the Construction of Political Meaning* (Chicago: University of Chicago Press, 1992), p. 10. One seasoned journalist argues that technology has set back the quality of news coverage. Now a television crew can fly to the scene of a crisis and immediately televise information without knowing much about the local politics or culture, which was not true of foreign correspondents in the past. See David R. Gergen, "Diplomacy in a Television Age: The Dangers of Teledemocracy," in *The Media and Foreign Policy,* ed. Simon Serfaty (New York: St. Martin's Press, 1990), p. 51.

78. Doris A. Graber, *Processing the News: How People Tame the Information Tide,* 2nd ed. (New York: Longman, 1988), pp. 166–169.

79. Neuman, Just, and Crigler, *Common Knowledge,* p. 113.

80. Laurence Parisot, "Attitudes About the Media: A Five-Country Comparison," *Public Opinion* 10 (January–February 1988): 60.

81. The statistical difficulties in determining media effects owing to measurement error are discussed in Larry M. Bartels, "Messages Received: The Political Impact of Media Exposure" (paper prepared for delivery at the annual meeting of the American Political Science Association, Washington, D.C., September 1993). According to Bartels, "More direct and convincing demonstrations of significant opinion changes due to media exposure will require data collections spanning considerably longer periods of time" (p. 27).

82. "Clinton Gets a Bounce: Most People Who Watched Give His State of Union Speech High Marks," 27 January 1998, CNN/Time All-Politics website, available at www.allpolitics.com. The Nielsen estimates of total number of viewers was 53.1 million, reported in "Clinton's Troubles Built TV Ratings," *New York Times,* 29 January 1998, p. A19.

83. Doris Graber, *Media Power in Politics* (Washington, D.C.: Congressional Quarterly Press, 2007), pp. 278–279.

84. Daniel J. Wakin, "Report Calls Networks' Election Night Coverage a Disaster," *New York Times,* 3 February 2001, p. A8.

85. Shanto Iyengar and Donald R. Kinder, *News That Matters: Television and American Opinion* (Chicago: University of Chicago Press, 1987), p. 33.

86. Ibid., p. 60.

87. W. Russell Neuman, "The Threshold of Public Attention," *Public Opinion Quarterly* 54 (Summer 1990): 159–176.

88. Robert Entman, *Democracy Without Citizens: Media and the Decay of American Politics* (New York: Oxford University Press, 1989), p. 86.

89. A panel study of ten- to seventeen-year-olds during the 1988 presidential campaign found that the campaign helped these young people crystallize their party identifications and their attitudes toward the candidates but had little effect on their political ideology and views on central campaign issues. See David O. Sears, Nicholas A. Valentino, and Rick Kosterman, "Domain Specificity in the Effects of Political Events on Pre-Adult Socialization" (paper prepared for delivery at the annual meeting of the American Political Science Association, Washington, D.C., September 1993).

90. John J. O'Connor, "Soothing Bromides? Not on TV," *New York Times,* 28 October 1990, Arts and Leisure section, pp. 1, 35.

91. James Fallows, *Breaking the News: How the Media Undermine American Democracy* (New York: Pantheon Books, 1996).

92. See Bernard Goldberg, *Bias: A CBS Insider Exposes How the Media Distort the News* (Washington, D.C.: Regnery Publishing, 2002); and Ann Coulter, *Slander: Liberal Lies About the American Right* (New York: Crown, 2002).

93. See Eric Alterman, *What Liberal Media? The Truth About Bias and the News* (New York: Basic Books, 2003); and Al Franken, *Lies (and the Lying Liars Who Tell Them): A Fair and Balanced Look at the Right* (New York: Penguin, 2003).

94. Pew Research Center of the People and the Press, "Bottom Line Pressures Now Hurting Coverage, Say Journalists," press release, 23 May 2004, available at http://people-press.org/reports/.

95. Stephen J. Farnsworth and S. Robert Lichter, "The Nightly News Nightmare Revisited: Network Television's Coverage of the 2004 Presidential Election" (paper prepared for presentation at the annual meeting of the American Political Science Association, Washington, D.C., 2005), p. 31.

96. *The People, the Press, and Their Leaders* (Washington, D.C.: Times-Mirror Center for the People and the Press, 1995).

97. "Bird in the Hand for Bush," *Editor and Publisher,* 6 November 2000, pp. 24–27.

98. Greg Mitchell, "Daily Endorsement Tally: Kerry Wins Without Recount," *Editor and Publisher,* 5 November 2004, available at www.editorandpublisher.com/eandp/search/article_display.jsp?vnu_content_id=1000707329.

99. Greg Mitchell, "Endorsement Analysis: Breaking Down the Chains," *Editor and Publisher,* 27 October 2004, available at www.editorandpublisher.com/eandp/search/article_display.jsp?vnu_content_id=1000691964.

100. Maura Clancey and Michael J. Robinson, "General Election Coverage: Part I," *Public Opinion* 7 (December–January 1985): 54. Some journalists take their watchdog role seriously. See Pew Research Center, "Striking the Balance, Audience Interests, Business Pressures and Journalists' Values," 30 March 1999, available at http://people-press.org/reports/display.php3?ReportID=67.

101. Todd Shields, "Media Accentuates the Negative," *Editor and Publisher,* 27 November 2000, p. 12.

102. W. Lance Bennett and William Serrin, "The Watchdog Role," in Geneva Overholser and Kathleen Hall Jamieson, *Institutions of American Democracy: The Press* (Oxford: Oxford University Press, 2005), pp. 169–188.

103. For a critique of the press on these grounds, see W. Lance Bennett et al., *When the Press Fails* (Chicago: University of Chicago Press, 2007).

104. William Schneider and I. A. Lewis, "Views on the News," *Public Opinion* 8 (August/September 1985): 11. For similar findings from a 1994 study, see Times-Mirror Center for the People and the Press, "Mixed Message About Press Freedom on Both Sides of the Atlantic," press release, 16 March 1994, p. 65. See also Thomas E. Patterson and Wolfgang Donsbach, "News Decisions: Journalists as Partisan Actors," *Political Communication* 13, 4 (October–December 1996): 455–468.

105. Pew Research Center for the People and the Press, News Interest Final Topline, 1–5 February 2006, available at http://people-press.org/reports/display .php3?ReportID=270.

Chapter 5 / Participation and Voting / pages 121–147

1. Choe Sang-Hun, "Myanmar Magic: Tell a Joke, and You Disappear," *New York Times,* 29 October 2007, p. A4.

2. Choe Sang-Hun, "Myanmar's Monks and Junta: Fragile Coexistence Is Shattered," *New York Times,* 24 October 2007, p. A10.

3. For an overview, see the Associated Press, "Myanmar Monks' Protests Again," 21 September 2007, available at www.msnbc.msn.com, and Seth Mydans, "Monks' Protest Is Challenging Burmese Junta," *New York Times,* 24 September 2007, p. A1.

4. The Associated Press, "U.S. Tightens Sanctions on Myanmar," 5 February 2008, available at www.msnbc .msn.com.

5. Lester W. Milbrath and M. L. Goel, *Political Participation* (Chicago: Rand McNally, 1977), p. 2.

6. U.S. Department of State, "Patterns of Global Terrorism 2001" (Washington, D.C.: U.S. Department of State, May 2002), p. 17. The definition is contained in Title 22 of the U.S. Code, Section 2656f(d). On the problem of defining terrorism, see Walter Laqueur, *No End to War: Terrorism in the 21st Century* (New York: Continuum International, 2003), esp. the appendix.

7. Lou Nichel and Dan Herbeck, *American Terrorist: Timothy McVeigh and the Oklahoma City Bombing* (New York: HarperCollins, 2001), pp. 350–354.

8. William E. Schmidt, "Selma Marchers Mark 1965 Clash," *New York Times,* 4 March 1985.

9. See Sidney Verba and Norman H. Nie, *Participation in America: Political Democracy and Social Equality* (New York: Harper & Row, 1972), p. 3.

10. Russell J. Dalton, *Citizen Politics,* 2nd ed. (Chatham, N.J.: Chatham House, 1996).

11. International Social Survey Programme (ISSP) 2004: Citizenship Survey, available at zacat.gesis.org.

12. Stephen C. Craig and Michael A. Magiotto, "Political Discontent and Political Action," *Journal of Politics* 43 (May 1981): 514–522. But see Mitchell A. Seligson, "Trust Efficacy and Modes of Political Participation: A Study of Costa Rican Peasants," *British Journal of Political Science* 10 (January 1980): 75–98, for a review of studies that came to different conclusions.

13. Philip H. Pollock III, "Organizations as Agents of Mobi-lization: How Does Group Activity Affect Political Participation?" *American Journal of Political Science* 26 (August 1982): 485–503. Also see Jan E. Leighley, "Social Interaction and Contextual Influence on Political Participation," *American Politics Quarterly* 18 (October 1990): 459–475.

14. Arthur H. Miller et al., "Group Consciousness and Political Participation," *American Journal of Political Science* 25 (August 1981): 495. See also Susan J. Carroll, "Gender Politics and the Socializing Impact of the Women's Movement," in *Political Learning in Adulthood: A Sourcebook of Theory and Research,* ed. Roberta S. Sigel (Chicago: University of Chicago Press, 1989), p. 307.

15. International Social Survey Programme (ISSP) 2004: Citizenship Survey, available at www.zacat.gesis.org.

16. See James L. Gibson, "The Policy Consequences of Political Intolerance: Political Repression During the Vietnam War Era," *Journal of Politics* 51 (February 1989): 13–35. Gibson found that individual state legislatures reacted quite differently in response to antiwar demonstrations on college campuses, but the laws passed to discourage dissent were not related directly to public opinion within the state.

17. See Verba and Nie, *Participation in America,* p. 69. See also John Clayton Thomas, "Citizen-Initiated Contacts with Government Agencies: A Test of Three Theories," *American Journal of Political Science* 26 (August 1982): 504–522; Elaine B. Sharp, "Citizen-Initiated Contacting of Government Officials and Socioeconomic Status: Determining the Relationship and Accounting for It," *American Political Science Review* 76 (March 1982): 109–115.

18. Elaine B. Sharp, "Citizen Demand Making in the Urban Context," *American Journal of Political Science* 28 (November 1984): 654–670, esp. pp. 654, 665.

19. Verba and Nie, *Participation in America,* p. 67; Sharp, "Citizen Demand Making," p. 660.

20. See Joel B. Grossman et al., "Dimensions of Institutional Participation: Who Uses the Courts and How?" *Journal of Politics* 44 (February 1982): 86–114; Frances Kahn Zemans, "Legal Mobilization: The Neglected Role of the Law in the Political System," *American Political Science Review* 77 (September 1983): 690–703.

21. *Brown* v. *Board of Education,* 347 U.S. 483 (1954).

22. Jan-Erik Lane and Svante Ersson, *Democracy: A Comparative Approach* (New York: Routledge, 2003), p. 238; International Institute for Democracy and Educational Assistance, "Voter Turnout," online database available at www.idea.int/vt/index.cfm.

23. Max Kaase and Alan Marsh, "Political Action: A Theoretical Perspective," in *Political Action: Mass Participation in Five Western Democracies,* ed. Samuel H. Barnes and Max Kaase (Beverly Hills, Calif.: Sage, 1979), p. 168.

24. *Smith* v. *Allwright,* 321 U.S. 649 (1944).

25. *Harper* v. *Virginia State Board of Elections,* 383 U.S. 663 (1966).

26. Everett Carll Ladd, *The American Polity* (New York: Norton, 1985), p. 392.

27. Ivor Crewe, "Electoral Participation," in *Democracy at the Polls: A Comparative Study of Competitive National*

Elections, ed. David Butler, Howard R. Penniman, and Austin Ranney (Washington, D.C.: American Enterprise Institute, 1981), pp. 219–223.

28. Faiza Saleh Ambah, "For Women in Kuwait, a Landmark Election," *Washington Post,* 29 June 2006, p. A20.

29. Initiative and Referendum Institute, "Election Results 2008: A First Look at Results," *Ballot Watch* (November 2008), available at www.iandrinstitute.org/ballotwatch.htm.

30. David B. Magleby, *Direct Legislation: Voting on Ballot Propositions in the United States* (Baltimore: Johns Hopkins University Press, 1984), p. 59. See also Ernest Tollerson, "In 90's Ritual, Hired Hands Carry Democracy's Petitions," *New York Times,* 9 July 1996, p. 1.

31. David S. Broder, "A Snake in the Grass Roots," *Washington Post,* 26 March 2000, pp. B1–B2.

32. Data on individual states may be found at www.census.gov/census2000/states.

33. Crewe, "Electoral Participation," p. 232. A rich literature has grown to explain turnout across nations. See Pippa Norris, *Democratic Phoenix: Reinventing Political Activism* (Cambridge: Cambridge University Press, 2002), Chap. 3; Mark N. Franklin, "The Dynamics of Electoral Participation," in *Comparing Democracies 2: New Challenges in the Study of Elections and Voting,* ed. Lawrence LeDuc, Richard G. Niemi, and Pippa Norris (London: Sage, 2002), pp. 148–168.

34. Verba and Nie, *Participation in America,* p. 13.

35. Russell J. Dalton, *Citizen Policies,* 3rd ed. (New York: Seven Bridges, 2002), pp. 67–68. For the argument that greater economic inequality leads to greater political inequality, see Frederick Solt, "Economic Inequality and Democratic Political Engagement," *American Journal of Political Science* 52, 1 (January 2008): 48–60.

36. Russell J. Dalton, *The Good Citizen: How a Younger Generation Is Reshaping American Politics* (Washington, D.C.: Congressional Quarterly Press, 2008).

37. Cliff Zukin et al., *A New Engagement?* (New York: Oxford University Press, 2006), pp. 188–191.

38. For a concise summary of the effect of age on voting turnout, see William H. Flanigan and Nancy H. Zingale, *Political Behavior of the American Electorate,* 11th ed. (Washington, D.C.: Congressional Quarterly Press, 2005).

39. Richard Murray and Arnold Vedlitz, "Race, Socioeconomic Status, and Voting Participation in Large Southern Cities," *Journal of Politics* 39 (November 1977): 1064–1072; Verba and Nie, *Participation in America,* p. 157. See also Bobo and Gilliam, "Race, Sociopolitical Participation, and Black Empowerment," *American Political Science Review* 84, 2 (June 1990): 377–393. Their study of 1987 national survey data with a black oversample found that African Americans participated more than whites of comparable socioeconomic status in cities in which the mayor's office was held by an African American.

40. William H. Flanigan and Nancy H. Zingale, *Political Behavior of the American Electorate,* 8th ed. (Washington, D.C.: Congressional Quarterly Press, 1994), pp. 41–43.

41. Ronald B. Rapoport, "The Sex Gap in Political Persuad-ing: Where the 'Structuring Principle' Works," *American Journal of Political Science* 25 (February 1981): 32–48.

42. Bruce C. Straits, "The Social Context of Voter Turnout," *Public Opinion Quarterly* 54 (Spring 1990): 64–73.

43. See Sidney Verba, Kay Lehman Scholzman, and Henry E. Brady, *Voice and Equality: Civic Voluntarism in American Politics* (Cambridge, Mass.: Harvard University Press, 1995), p. 433.

44. Stephen D. Shaffer, "A Multivariate Explanation of Decreasing Turnout in Presidential Elections, 1960–1976," *American Journal of Political Science* 25 (February 1981): 68–95; Paul R. Abramson and John H. Aldrich, "The Decline of Electoral Participation in America," *American Political Science Review* 76 (September 1981): 603–620. However, one scholar argues that this research suffers because it looks at voters and nonvoters only in a single election. When the focus shifts to people who vote only sometimes, the models do not fit so well. See M. Margaret Conway and John E. Hughes, "Political Mobilization and Patterns of Voter Turnout" (paper prepared for delivery at the annual meeting of the American Political Science Association, Washington, D.C., September 1993).

45. Apparently Richard A. Brody was the first scholar to pose this problem as a puzzle. See his "The Puzzle of Political Participation in America," in *The New American Political System,* ed. Anthony King (Washington, D.C.: American Enterprise Institute, 1978), pp. 287–324. Since then, a sizable literature has attempted to explain the decline in voter turnout in the United States. Some authors have claimed to account for the decline with just a few variables, but their work has been criticized for being too simplistic. See Carol A. Cassel and Robert C. Luskin, "Simple Explanations of Turnout Decline," *American Political Science Review* 82 (December 1988): 1321–1330. They contend that most of the post-1960 decline is still unexplained. If it is any comfort, voter turnout in Western European elections has seen a somewhat milder decline. See International Institute for Democracy and Electoral Assistance, *Voter Turnout in Western Europe* (Stockholm, Sweden: IDEA, 2004).

46. Abramson and Aldrich, "Decline of Electoral Participation," p. 519; Shaffer, "Multivariate Explanation," pp. 78, 90.

47. See Eric Pultzer, "Becoming a Habitual Voter: Inertia, Resources, and Growth in Young Adulthood," *American Political Science Review* (March 2002): 41–56; Alan S. Gerber, Donald P. Green, and Ron Shachar, "Voting May Be Habit-Forming: Evidence from a Randomized Field Experiment," *American Journal of Political Science* (July 2003): 540–550; and David Dreyer Lassen, "The Effect of Information on Voter Turnout: Evidence from a Natural Experiment," *American Journal of Political Science* 49 (January 2005): 103–11. For the argument that turnout may be genetic, see "The Genetics of Politics," *Scientific American* (November 2007): 18–21.

48. The negative effect of registration laws on voter turnout is argued in Frances Fox Piven and Richard Cloward, "Government Statistics and Conflicting Explanations of Nonvoting," *PS: Political Science and Politics* 22 (September 1989): 580–588. Their analysis was hotly

contested in Stephen Earl Bennett, "The Uses and Abuses of Registration and Turnout Data: An Analysis of Piven and Cloward's Studies of Nonvoting in America," *PS: Political Science and Politics* 23 (June 1990): 166–171. Bennett showed that turnout declined 10 to 13 percent after 1960, despite efforts to remove or lower legal hurdles to registration. For their reply, see Frances Fox Piven and Richard Cloward, "A Reply to Bennett," *PS: Political Science and Politics* 23 (June 1990): 172–173. You can see that reasonable people can disagree on this matter.

49. Nonprofit Voter Engagement Network, "America Goes to the Polls: A Report on Voter Turnout in the 2006 Election," available at www.nonprofitvote.org.

50. Ruth Goldway, "The Election Is in the Mail," *New York Times*, 6 December 2006; Randal C. Archibold, "Mail-In Voters Become the Latest Prize," *New York Times*, 14 January 2008.

51. David Glass, Peverill Squire, and Raymond Wolfinger, "Voter Turnout: An International Comparison," *Public Opinion* 6 (December–January 1984): 52. Wolfinger says that because of the strong effect of registration on turnout, most rational choice analyses of voting would be better suited to analyzing turnout of only registered voters. See Raymond E. Wolfinger, "The Rational Citizen Faces Election Day," *Public Affairs Report* 6 (November 1992): 12.

52. Data from a League of Women Voters Study published on the NBC News website at www.decision96.msn.com/vote/motor.htm and dated 16 May 1996.

53. Federal Election Commission, "NVRA Report Submitted to Congress: Almost 148 Million Registered to Vote in States Covered by Act," press release, 1 July 2003, www.fec.gov/press/20030701nvrareport.html.

54. Federal Election Commission, *The Impact of the National Voter Registration Act of 1993 on the Administration of Elections for Federal Office 1997–1998* (Washington, D.C.: Federal Election Commission, 1999), available at www.fec.gov/pages/9798NVRAexec.htm.

55. Recent research finds that "party contact is clearly a statistically and substantively important factor in predicting and explaining political behavior." See Peter W. Wielhouwer and Brad Lockerbie, "Party Contacting and Political Participation, 1952–1990" (paper prepared for delivery at the annual meeting of the American Political Science Association, Chicago, 1992), p. 14. Of course, parties strategically target the groups that they want to vote in elections. See Peter W. Wielhouwer, "Strategic Canvassing by Political Parties, 1952–1990," *American Review of Politics* 16 (Fall 1995): 213–238.

56. Nonprofit Voter Engagement Network, "America Goes to the Polls: A Report on Voter Turnout in the 2006 Election," available at www.nonprofitvote.org.

57. See Charles Krauthammer, "In Praise of Low Voter Turnout," *Time*, 21 May 1990, p. 88. Krauthammer says, "Low voter turnout means that people see politics as quite marginal to their lives, as neither salvation nor ruin. . . . Low voter turnout is a leading indicator of contentment." A major study in 1996 that compared one thousand likely nonvoters with twenty-three hundred likely voters found that 24 percent of the nonvoters said they "hardly ever" followed public affairs versus

5 percent of likely voters. See Dwight Morris, "No-Show '96: Americans Who Don't Vote," summary report to the Medill News Service and WTTW Television, Northwestern University School of Journalism, 1996.

58. Crewe, "Electoral Participation," p. 262.

59. Barnes and Kaase, *Political Action,* p. 532.

60. *1971 Congressional Quarterly Almanac* (Washington, D.C.: Congressional Quarterly Press, 1972), p. 475.

61. Benjamin Ginsberg, *The Consequences of Consent: Elections, Citizen Control, and Popular Acquiescence* (Reading, Mass.: Addison-Wesley, 1982), pp. 13–14.

62. Ibid., pp. 6–7.

63. Some people have argued that the decline in voter turnout during the 1980s served to increase the class bias in the electorate because people of lower socioeconomic status stayed home. But others have concluded that "class bias has not increased since 1964." Jan E. Leighley and Jonathan Nagler, "Socioeconomic Class Bias in Turnout, 1964–1988: The Voters Remain the Same," *American Political Science Review* 86 (September 1992): 734. Nevertheless, Rosenstone and Hansen say, "The economic inequalities in political participation that prevail in the United States today are as large as the racial disparities in political participation that prevailed in the 1950s. America's leaders today face few incentives to attend to the needs of the disadvantaged." Steven J. Rosenstone and John Mark Hansen, *Mobilization, Participation, and Democracy in America* (New York: Macmillan, 1993), p. 248.

Chapter 6 / Political Parties, Campaigns, and Elections / pages 148–186

1. CNN, "Election Center 2008: Results." Internet vote tally available at www.cnn.com/ELECTION/2008/results/president/allcandidates. Accessed 9 November 2008.

2. Adopted in convention at Denver, Colorado, in May 2008 and available at www.lp.org/platform.

3. Counts of Libertarian Party congressional candidates in 2004 were compiled from election data in Clerk of the House of Representatives, *Statistics of the Presidential and Congressional Election of November 2, 2004* (Washington, D.C., 2005); and *Federal Elections 2004*.

4. The Ultimate Third Party Encyclopedia at www.thirdpartywatch.com/encyclopedia/index.php?title=Libertarian_Party.

5. Statistics of the Presidential and Congressional Election of November 2, 2004, pp. 65–67.

6. Center for Political Studies of the Institute for Social Research, *American National Election Study 2004* (Ann Arbor: University of Michigan, 2005).

7. David W. Moore, "Perot Supporters: For the Man, Not a Third Party," *Gallup Organization Newsletter Archive*, 17 August 1995, available at www.gallup.com/newsletter/aug95.

8. See Jerome M. Clubb, William H. Flanigan, and Nancy H. Zingale, *Partisan Realignment: Voters, Parties, and Government in American History* (Beverly Hills, Calif.: Sage, 1980), p. 163.

9. See Gerald M. Pomper, "Classification of Presidential Elections," *Journal of Politics* 29 (August 1967): 535–566.

10. Seth C. McKeen, "Rural Voters and the Polarization of American Presidential Elections," *PS: Political Science and Politics* 41 (January 2008): 101–108.

11. Jeffrey M. Stonecash, *Political Parties Matter: Realignment and the Return of Partisan Voting* (Boulder, Colo.: Lynne Rienner, 2006), pp. 129–130.

12. The discussion that follows draws heavily on Austin Ranney and Willmoore Kendall, *Democracy and the American Party System* (New York: Harcourt, Brace, 1956), Chaps. 18 and 19.

13. See Steven J. Rosenstone, Roy L. Behr, and Edward H. Lazarus, *Third Parties in America: Citizen Response to Major Party Failure* (Princeton, N.J.: Princeton University Press, 1984), pp. 5–6.

14. Ibid., p. 8.

15. Samuel Issacharoff, Pamela S. Karlan, and Richard H. Pildes, *The Law of Democracy*, rev. 2nd ed. (New York: Foundation Press, 2002), pp. 417–436.

16. See James Gimpel, *National Elections and the Autonomy of American State Party Systems* (Pittsburgh, Pa.: University of Pittsburgh Press, 1996).

17. Measuring the concept of party identification has had its problems. See R. Michael Alvarez, "The Puzzle of Party Identification," *American Politics Quarterly* 18 (October 1990): 476–491; and Donald Philip Green and Bradley Palmquist, "Of Artifacts and Partisan Instability," *American Journal of Political Science* 34 (August 1990): 872–902.

18. Rhodes Cook, "GOP Shows Dramatic Growth, Especially in the South," *Congressional Quarterly Weekly Report*, 13 January 1996, pp. 97–100.

19. Two scholars on voting behavior describe partisanship as "the feeling of sympathy for and loyalty to a political party that an individual acquires—sometimes during childhood—and holds through life, often with increasing intensity." See William H. Flanigan and Nancy H. Zingale, *Political Behavior of the American Electorate*, 10th ed. (Washington, D.C.: Congressional Quarterly Press, 2002), p. 60.

20. "The GOP's Spending Spree," *Wall Street Journal*, 25 November 2003, p. A18.

21. See, for example, Gerald M. Pomper, *Elections in America* (New York: Dodd, Mead, 1968); Benjamin Ginsberg, "Election and Public Policy," *American Political Science Review* 70 (March 1976): 41–50; and Jeff Fishel, *Presidents and Promises* (Washington, D.C.: Congressional Quarterly Press, 1985).

22. The platforms are available at www.gop.com/2008Platform and www.democrats.org/a/party/platform.html.

23. Ian Budge et al., *Mapping Policy Preferences: Estimates for Parties, Electors, and Governments 1945–1998,* (Oxford: Oxford University Press, 2001), p. 49.

24. See Ralph M. Goldman, *The National Party Chairmen and Committees: Factionalism at the Top* (Armonk, N.Y.: Sharpe, 1990). The subtitle is revealing.

25. Cornelius P. Cotter and Bernard C. Hennessy, *Political Without Power: The National Party Committees* (New York: Atherton Press, 1964).

26. William Crotty and John S. Jackson III, *Presidential Primaries and Nominations* (Washington, D.C.: Congressional Quarterly Press, 1985), p. 33.

27. Phillip A. Klinkner, "Party Culture and Party Behavior," in Daniel M. Shea and John C. Green, (eds.), *The State of the Parties* (Lanham, Md.: Rowman and Littlefield, 1994), pp. 275–287; and Philip A. Klinkner, *The Losing Parties: Out-Party National Committees, 1956–1993* (New Haven, Conn.: Yale University Press, 1994).

28. Jeff Zeleny, "His Meteoric Days Behind Him, A Less Fiery Dean Leads Party," *New York Times,* 21 October 2007, pp. 1 and 16; and Naftali Bendavid, "The House That Rahm Built," *Chicago Tribune,* Special Report, 12 November 2007.

29. John Frendreis, Alan R. Gitelson, Gregory Flemming, and Anne Layzell, "Local Political Parties and Legislative Races in 1992," in Shea and Green, *The State of the Parties,* p. 139.

30. Robert Biersack, "Hard Facts and Soft Money: State Party Finance in the 1992 Federal Elections," in Shea and Green, *The State of the Parties,* p. 114.

31. Martin P. Wattenberg, *The Decline of American Political Parties, 1952–1994* (Cambridge, Mass.: Harvard University Press, 1996).

32. Taylor Dark III, "The Rise of the Global Party? American Party Organizations Abroad," *Party Politics* 9 (March 2003): 241–255.

33. Barbara Sinclair, "The Congressional Party: Evolving Organizational, Agenda-Setting, and Policy Roles," in L. Sandy Maisel (ed.), *The Parties Respond: Changes in American Parties and Campaigns,* 3rd ed. (Boulder, Colo.: Westview Press, 1998), p. 227.

34. The model is articulated most clearly in a report by the American Political Science Association, "Toward a More Responsible Two-Party System," *American Political Science Review* 44 (September 1950): pt. II. See also Gerald M. Pomper, "Toward a More Responsible Party System? What, Again?" *Journal of Politics* 33 (November 1971): 916–940. See also the seven essays in the symposium, "Divided Government and the Politics of Constitutional Reform," *PS: Political Science and Politics* 24 (December 1991): 634–657.

35. This is essentially the framework for studying campaigns set forth in Barbara G. Salmore and Stephen A. Salmore, *Candidates, Parties, and Campaigns: Electoral Politics in America,* 2nd ed. (Washington, D.C.: Congressional Quarterly Press, 1989).

36. Adam Nagourney, "Internet Injects Sweeping Change into U.S. Politics," *New York Times,* 2 April 2006, pp. 1 and 17.

37. Martin P. Wattenberg, *The Rise of Candidate-Centered Politics: Presidential Elections of the 1980s* (Cambridge, Mass.: Harvard University Press, 1991).

38. Michael Gallagher, "Conclusion," in *Candidate Selection in Comparative Perspective: The Secret Garden of Politics,* ed. Michael Gallagher and Michael Marsh (London: Sage, 1988), p. 238.

39. *The Book of the States, 2003* (Lexington, Ky.: Council of State Governments, 2003), pp. 295–296. See also Federal Election Commission, "2004 Presidential and

Congressional Primary Dates," available at www.fec.gov/pubrec/fe2004/2004pdates.pdf.

40. Talar Aslanian et al., "Recapturing Voter Intent: The Nonpartisan Primary in California" (capstone seminar report, Pepperdine University, April 2003), appendix C, available at http://publicpolicy.pepperdine.edu/academics/mpp/capstone/primary.pdf.

41. Harold W. Stanley and Richard G. Niemi, *Vital Statistics on American Politics, 1788–2008* (Washington, D.C.: Congressional Quarterly Press, 2008). According to state-by-state delegate totals in "The Green Papers" website, about 15 percent of the delegates to each party's 2008 presidential nominating convention were selected through the caucus/convention system.

42. William G. Mayer and Andrew E. Busch, *The Front-Loading Problem in Presidential Nominations* (Washington, D.C.: The Brookings Institution, 2004).

43. See Rhodes Cook, *The Presidential Nominating Process: A Place for Us?* (Lanham, Md.: Rowman & Littlefield, 2004), Chap. 5. Nations that have copied the American model have experienced mixed results. See James A. McCann, "The Emerging International Trend Toward Open Presidential Primaries," in William G. Mayer, *The Making of the Presidential Candidates 2004* (Lanham, Md.: Rowman & Littlefield, 2004), pp. 265–293.

44. Gary R. Orren and Nelson W. Polsby (eds.), *Media and Momentum: The New Hampshire Primary and Nomination Politics* (Chatham, N.J.: Chatham House, 1987), p. 23.

45. Dan Balz, "Fla., Mich. Delegates Each Get Half a Vote," *Washington Post,* 1 June 2008, p. A1.

46. See James R. Beniger, "Winning the Presidential Nomination: National Polls and State Primary Elections, 1936–1972," *Public Opinion Quarterly* 40 (Spring 1976): 22–38.

47. See Alexis Simendinger, James A. Barnes, and Carl M. Cannon, "Pondering a Popular Vote," *National Journal,* 18 November 2000, pp. 3650–3656.

48. Harold W. Stanley and Richard G. Niemi, *Vital Statistics on American Politics,* 2nd ed. (Washington, D.C.: Congressional Quarterly Press, 1990), p. 132; and the 1992 and 1996 National Election Study, Center for Political Studies, University of Michigan.

49. Carl Hulse and David M. Herszenhorn, "G.O.P. Exodus in House Bodes Ill for Fall Success," *New York Times,* 31 January 2008, p. A16.

50. Salmore and Salmore, *Candidates, Parties, and Campaigns.*

51. Quoted in E. J. Dionne Jr., "On the Trail of Corporation Donations," *New York Times,* 6 October 1980.

52. Salmore and Salmore, *Candidates, Parties, and Campaigns,* p. 11. See also David Himes, "Strategy and Tactics for Campaign Fund-Raising," in *Campaigns and Elections: American Style,* ed. James A. Thurber and Candice J. Nelson (Boulder, Colo.: Westview Press, 1995), pp. 62–77.

53. "Corzine Spent $20 per Vote on Election Day," *USA Today,* 8 November 2000, available at www.usatoday.com/news/vote2000/nj/main01.htm.

54. New York City Campaign Finance Board, "The Impact of High-Spending Non-Participants on the Campaign Finance Program" (2006), report available at www.nyccfb.info/PDF/publications/highspending_white_paper.pdf.

55. For tactical reasons in Congress, the bill that actually passed was the Shays-Meehan bill, sponsored by representatives Christopher Shays (R-Conn.) and Martin Meehan (D-Mass.), but it became known as McCain-Feingold for the early work done by both senators.

56. Robert Barnes, "5–4 Supreme Court Weakens Curbs on Pre-Election TV Ads," *Washington Post,* 26 June 2007, p. A1. See *Federal Election Commission* v. *Wisconsin Right to Life, Inc.,* 511 U.S. ___ (2007).

57. *Davis* v. *Federal Election Commission,* 554 U.S. ___ (2008).

58. Federal Election Commission, "2004 Presidential Campaign Financial Activity Summarized," news release, 3 February 2005.

59. James A. Barnes, "Matching Funds, R.I.P.," *National Journal Magazine,* 26 April 2008, available at www.nationaljournal.com/njmagazine/pi_20080426_9817.php.

60. Steve Weissman and Ruth Hassan, "BCRA and the 527 Groups," in *The Election After Reform,* ed. Michael J. Malbin (Lanham, Md.: Rowman and Littlefield, 2006).

61. Salmore and Salmore, *Candidates, Parties, and Campaigns,* p. 11.

62. David Moon, "What You Use Depends on What You Have: Information Effects on the Determinants of Electoral Choice," *American Politics Quarterly* 18 (January 1990): 3–24.

63. See the "Marketplace" section in monthly issues of the magazine *Campaigns and Elections,* which contains scores of names, addresses, and telephone numbers of people who supply "political products and services"—from "campaign schools" to "voter files and mailing lists."

64. Bruce I. Newman, "A Predictive Model of Voter Behavior," in Bruce I. Newman (ed.), *Handbook of Political Marketing* (Thousand Oaks, Calif.: Sage, 1999), pp. 259–282. For studies on campaign consultants at work, see James A. Thurber and Candice J. Nelson (eds.), *Campaign Warriors: The Role of Political Consultants in Elections* (Washington, D.C.: Brookings Institution, 2000).

65. See Darrell M. West, *Air Wars: Television Advertising in Election Campaigns, 1952–2004,* 4th ed. (Washington, D.C.: Congressional Quarterly Press, 2005).

66. Lee Rainie, Michael Cornfield, and John Horrigan, "The Internet and Campaign 2004," report released by the Pew Internet and American Life Project, 6 March 2005, p. i, available at www.pewinternet.org/pdfs/PIP_2004_Campaign.pdf.

67. Leslie Wayne and Jeff Zeleny, "Enlisting New Donors, Obama Reaped $32 Million in January," *New York Times,* 1 February 2008, pp. A1 and A14.

68. Katharine Q. Seelye and Leslie Wayne, "The Web Finds Its Man, and Takes Him for a Ride," *New York Times,* 11 November 2007, p. 22.

69. Pew Research Center for the People and the Press, "Internet's Broader Role in Campaign 2008," News Release, 11 January 2008.

70. Emily Steel, "Why Web Campaign Spending Trails TV," *Wall Street Journal,* 14 December 2008, p. B4.

71. Pamela Johnston Conover and Stanley Feldman, "Candidate Perception in an Ambiguous World: Campaigns, Cues, and Inference Processes," *American Journal of Political Science* 33 (November 1989): 912–940.

72. Kevin Merida, "Racist Incidents Give Some Campaigners Pause," *Washington Post,* 13 May 2008, p. A01.

73. Michael M. Gant and Norman R. Luttbeg, *American Electoral Behavior* (Itasca, Ill.: Peacock, 1991), pp. 63–64. For recent research indicating a growth in issue voting, see Martin Gilens, Jynn Vavreck, and Martin Cohen, "The Mass Media and the Public's Assessments of Presidential Candidates, 1952–2000," *Journal of Politics* 69 (November 2007): 1160–1175.

74. Craig Goodman and Gregg R. Murray, "Do You See What I See? Perceptions of Party Differences and Voting Behavior," *American Politics Research* 35 (November 2007): 905–931.

75. Conover and Feldman, "Candidate Perception," p. 938.

76. Party identification has been assumed to be relatively resistant to short-term campaign effects, but see Dee Allsop and Herbert F. Weisberg, "Measuring Change in Party Identification in an Election Campaign," *American Journal of Political Science* 32 (November 1988): 996–1017. They conclude that partisanship is more volatile than we have thought.

Chapter 7 / Interest Groups / pages 187–208

1. John M. Broder, "Crossing a Threshold on Energy Legislation," *New York Times,* 5 December 2007; Daniel Whitten, "Light Bulbs, Gas Changing as U.S. Energy Bill Passes, Bloomberg.wire service, 18 December 2007; and Steven Mufson, "House Sends President an Energy Bill to Sign," *Washington Post,* 19 December 2007, p. A1.

2. Alexis de Tocqueville, *Democracy in America, 1835–1839,* reprint, ed. Richard D. Heffner (New York: Mentor Books, 1956), p. 79.

3. *The Federalist Papers* (New York: Mentor Books, 1961), p. 79.

4. Ibid., p. 78.

5. See Robert A. Dahl, *A Preface to Democratic Theory* (Chicago: University of Chicago Press, 1956), pp. 4–33.

6. Alan Rosenthal, *The Third House* (Washington, D.C.: Congressional Quarterly Press, 1993), p. 7.

7. This discussion follows from Jeffrey M. Berry, *The Interest Group Society* (New York: Longman, 1997), pp. 6–8.

8. John Mark Hansen, *Gaining Access* (Chicago: University of Chicago Press, 1991), pp. 11–17.

9. David B. Truman, *The Governmental Process* (New York: Knopf, 1951).

10. Herbert Gans, *The Urban Villagers* (New York: Free Press, 1962).

11. Robert H. Salisbury, "An Exchange Theory of Interest Groups," *Midwest Journal of Political Science* 13 (February 1969): 1–32.

12. See Mancur Olson Jr., *The Logic of Collective Action* (New York: Schocken, 1968).

13. Lori A. Brainard and Patricia D. Siplon, "Cyberspace Challenges to Mainstream Nonprofit Health Organizations," *Administration and Society* 34 (May 2002): 141–175.

14. See ibid.

15. See, for example, Edward O. Laumann and David Knoke, *The Organizational State* (Madison: University of Wisconsin Press, 1987), p. 3, cited in Robert H. Salisbury, "The Paradox of Interest Groups in Washington—More Groups, Less Clout," in *The New American Political System,* 2nd ed., ed. Anthony King (Washington, D.C.: American Enterprise Institute, 1990), p. 226.

16. William M. Welch, "Tauzin Switches Sides from Drug Industry Overseer to Lobbyist," *USA Today,* 15 December 2004.

17. Federal Election Commission, "PAC Contributions 2005–2006 Through December 31, 2006," available at www.fec.gov/press/press2007/20071009pac/contrib2006.pdf; Federal Election Commission, "FEC Records Slight Increase in the Number of PACs." 17 January 2008 News Release, available at www.fec.gov/press/press2008/20080117paccount.shtml.

18. PAC expenditure data are available online from the Federal Election Commission through its "Summary Report Search" at www.fec.gov/finance/disclosure/srssea.shtml.

19. Michael Forsythe and Kristin Jensen, "Democratic Lobbyists Relish Return to Washington's Power Elite," Bloomberg.wire service, 10 November 2006.

20. Federal Election Commission, "PAC Contributions 2005–2006 Through December 31, 2006," available at www.fec.gov/press/press2007/20071009pac/contrib2006.pdf.

21. Ibid.

22. Stephen Ansolabehere, John de Figueredo, and James N. Snyder Jr., "Why Is There So Little Money in U.S. Politics?" *Journal of Economic Perspectives* 17 (Winter 2003): 161–181; Mark Smith, *American Business and Political Power* (Chicago: University of Chicago Press, 2000): 115–141.

23. Marie Hojnacki and David Kimball, "The Contribution and Lobbying Strategies of PAC Sponsors in Committee" (paper delivered at the annual meeting of the American Political Science Association, Boston, September 1998); John R. Wright, "Contributions, Lobbying, and Committee Voting in the U.S. House of Representatives," *American Political Science Review* 84 (June 1990): 417–438; and Richard L. Hall and Frank W. Wayman, "Buying Time: Money Interests and the Mobilization of Bias in Congressional Committees," *American Political Science Review* 84 (September 1990): 797–820.

24. Center for Responsive Politics, "Top Contributors to 527 Committees, 2004 Election Cycle," online database available at www.opensecrets.org/527s/527contribs.asp?cycle =2004.

25. Kay Lehman Schlozman and John T. Tierney, *Organized Interests and American Democracy* (New York: Harper & Row, 1986), p. 150.

26. Berry, *The Interest Group Society,* p. 166.

27. Frank R. Baumgartner, Jeffrey M. Berry, Marie

Hojnacki, David C. Kimball, and Beth L. Leech, *Advocacy and Policy Change* (forthcoming).

28. Eric Pianin, "For Environmentalists, Victories in the Courts," *Washington Post*, 27 January 2003, p. A3.

29. Clay Risen, "Store Lobby," *New Republic*, 25 July 2005, pp. 10–11.

30. Marc K. Landy and Mary Hague, "Private Interests and Superfund," *Public Interest* 108 (Summer 1992): 97–115.

31. Dara Z. Strolovitch, *Affirmative Advocacy* (Chicago: University of Chicago Press, 2007), p. 181.

32. Kay Lehman Schlozman, Traci Burch, and Samuel Lampert, "Still an Upper-Class Accent?" (paper delivered at the annual meeting of the American Political Science Association, Chicago, Ill., September 2004), pp. 16, 25.

33. Jeffrey M. Berry, *The New Liberalism* (Washington, D.C.: The Brookings Institution, 1999), pp. 120–130.

34. Schlozman and Tierney, *Organized Interests*, pp. 58–87.

35. Jonathan Rauch, *Demosclerosis* (New York: Times Books, 1994), p. 91. The latter figure is interpolated from Rauch and Michael T. Heaney, "Coalitions and Interest Group Influence over Health Care Policy" (paper delivered at the annual meeting of the American Political Science Association, Philadelphia, August 2003), p. 16.

36. Baumgartner et al., *Advocacy and Policy Change*.

37. Federal Election Commission, attachment for "PAC Financial Activity 2005–2006," available at www.fec.gov/press/press2007/20071009pac/summary2006.pdf.

38. Brody Mullins, "Interest Groups Gain in Election Case Quest," *Wall Street Journal*, 19 December 2007, p. A1.

39. *Federal Election Commission* v. *Wisconsin Right to Life, Inc.*, 511 U.S. ___ (2007).

40. Jeff Zeleny and Carl Hulse, "Congress Votes to Tighten Rules on Lobbyist Ties," *New York Times*, 3 August 2007, p. A1.

Chapter 8 / Congress / pages 209–236

1. Carl Hulse, "Congress Passes War Funds Bill, Ending Impasse," *New York Times*, 25 May 2007.

2. Clinton Rossiter, *1787: The Grand Convention* (New York: Mentor, 1968), p. 158.

3. James M. Lindsay and Randall B. Ripley, "How Congress Influences Foreign and Defense Policy," in *Congress Resurgent*, ed. Randall B. Ripley and James M. Lindsay (Ann Arbor: University of Michigan Press, 1993), pp. 25–28.

4. Gregory L. Giroux, "Voter Discontent Fuels Democrats' Day," *CQ Weekly*, 13 November 2006, p. 2983.

5. Norman J. Ornstein, Thomas E. Mann, and Michael J. Malbin, *Vital Statistics on Congress, 2001–2002* (Washington, D.C.: AEI Press, 2002), pp. 75–76.

6. Ibid.

7. Thomas E. Mann, "Polarizing the House of Representatives: How Much Does Gerrymandering Matter?" in *Red and Blue Nation*, ed. Pietro S. Nivola and David W. Brady (Washington, D.C.: The Brookings Institution and Hoover Institution, 2006), pp. 263–283.

8. Timothy E. Cook, *Making Laws and Making News*

(Washington, D.C.: The Brookings Institution, 1989), p. 83.

9. Dennis Conrad, "House Spends Big on Home Mailings," *Boston Globe*, 28 December 2007, p. A2.

10. Katharine Q. Seeyle, "Congress Online: Much Sizzle, Little Steak," *New York Times*, 24 June 2003, p. A16.

11. Federal Election Commission, "Congressional Campaigns Spend $966 Million Through Mid October," press release, 2 November 2006. Calculated from supplemental table, "Financial Activity of General Election Congressional Candidates—1994–2006," available at www.fec.gov/press2006/20061102can/hselong12g2006.pdf.

12. Jonathan S. Krasno, *Challengers, Competition, and Reelection* (New Haven, Conn.: Yale University Press, 1994).

13. Paul S. Herrnson, *Congressional Elections*, 5th ed. (Washington, D.C.: Congressional Quarterly Press, 2008), pp. 65–66.

14. Lois Romano, "Hill Demographic Goes Slightly More Female," *Washington Post*, 9 November 2006, p. A39.

15. Hanna Fenichel Ptikin, *The Concept of Representation* (Berkeley: University of California Press, 1967), pp. 60–91; Jane Mansbridge, "Should Blacks Represent Blacks and Women Represent Women? A Contingent 'Yes,'" *Journal of Politics* 61 (1999): 628–657.

16. Carol M. Swain, *Black Faces, Black Interests* (Cambridge, Mass.: Harvard University Press, 1993), p. 197.

17. See the Census Bureau website at www.census.gov/population/www/pop-profile/profiledynamic.html.

18. *Shaw* v. *Reno*, 509 U.S. 630 (1993).

19. *Bush* v. *Vera*, 116 S. Ct. 1941 (1996).

20. *Easley* v. *Cromartie*, 532 U.S. 234 (2001).

21. See David Lublin, *The Paradox of Representation* (Princeton, N.J.: Princeton University Press, 1997). Kenneth W. Shotts, "Does Racial Redistricting Cause Conservative Policy Outcomes?" *Journal of Politics* 65 (2003): 216–226, presents an alternative view.

22. Walter J. Oleszek, *Congressional Procedures and the Policy Process* (Washington, D.C.: Congressional Quarterly Press, 1996), p. 91.

23. See Frank R. Baumgartner, Jeffrey M. Berry, Marie Hojnacki, David C. Kimball, and Beth L. Leech, *Advocacy and Policy Change* (forthcoming).

24. Adriel Bettelheim, "Reluctant Congress Drafted into Bioengineering Battle," *CQ Weekly*, 22 April 2000, pp. 938–944.

25. Woodrow Wilson, *Congressional Government* (Boston: Houghton Mifflin, 1885), p. 79.

26. Karen Foerstal, "Gingrich Flexes His Power in Picking Panel Chiefs," *Congressional Quarterly Weekly Report*, 7 January 1995, p. 3326.

27. Jonathan Weisman and Peter Slevin, "Hastings, Harman Rejected for Chairmanship," *Washington Post*, 29 November 2006, p. A1.

28. Joel D. Aberbach, *Keeping a Watchful Eye* (Washington, D.C.: The Brookings Institution, 1990), pp. 162–183.

29. John D. Huber and Charles R. Shipan, *Deliberate Discretion?* (Cambridge: Cambridge University Press, 2002.)

30. Gary W. Cox and Mathew D. McCubbins, *Legislative Leviathan* (Berkeley: University of California Press,

1993); and Keith Krehbiel, *Information and Legislative Organization* (Ann Arbor: University of Michigan Press, 1992).

31. Jonathan Franzen, "The Listener," *New Yorker,* 6 October 2003, p. 85.

32. David M. Herszenhorn, "Fuel Bill Shows House Speaker's Muscle," *New York Times,* 2 December 2007, p. 22.

33. Charles O. Jones, *The United States Congress* (Homewood, Ill.: Dorsey Press, 1982), p. 322.

34. Eric M. Uslaner, "Is the Senate More Civil Than the House?" in *Esteemed Colleagues,* ed. Burdett A. Loomis (Washington, D.C.: The Brookings Institution Press, 2000), pp. 32–55.

35. Cox and McCubbins, *Legislative Leviathan;* D. Roderick Kiewiet and Mathew D. McCubbins, *The Logic of Delegation* (Chicago: University of Chicago Press, 1991); and Krehbiel, *Information and Legislative Organization.*

36. Dan Carney, "As Hostilities Rage on the Hill, Partisan-Vote Rate Soars," *Congressional Quarterly Weekly Report,* 27 January 1996, pp. 199–201; and Martin P. Wattenberg, *The Decline of American Political Parties, 1994* (Cambridge, Mass.: Harvard University Press, 1996), Chap. 11.

37. See Mark A. Peterson, *Legislating Together* (Cambridge, Mass.: Harvard University Press, 1990).

38. James Sterling Young, *The Washington Community* (New York: Harcourt, Brace, 1964).

39. Barry C. Burden, *The Personal Roots of Representation* (Princeton, N.J.: Princeton University Press, 2007).

40. Richard F. Fenno Jr., *Home Style* (Boston: Little, Brown, 1978), p. 32.

41. Louis I. Bredvold and Ralph G. Ross (eds.), *The Philosophy of Edmund Burke* (Ann Arbor: University of Michigan Press, 1960), p. 148.

42. For an alternative and more highly differentiated set of representation models, see Jane Mansbridge, "Rethinking Representation," *American Political Science Review* 97 (November 2003): 515–528.

43. Warren E. Miller and Donald E. Stokes, "Constituency Influence in Congress," *American Political Science Review* 57 (March 1963): 45–57. On minority legislators, see James B. Johnson and Philip E. Secret, "Focus and Style: Representational Roles of Congressional Black and Hispanic Caucus Members," *Journal of Black Studies* 26 (January 1996): 245–273.

44. John R. Wilke, "How Lawmaker Rebuilt Hometown on Earmarks," *Wall Street Journal,* 30 October 2007, p. A1; and Robert Pear, "One Lawmaker's Waste Is Another's Namesake," *New York Times,* 13 November 2007, p. A23.

45. Cheryl Gay Stolberg, "Ease a Little Guilt, Provide Some Jobs: It's Pork on the Hill," *New York Times,* 20 December 2003, p. A1.

46. Robert Weissberg, "Collective vs. Dyadic Representation in Congress," *American Political Science Review* 72 (June 1978): 535–547.

47. E. Scott Adler, *Why Congressional Reforms Fail* (Chicago: University of Chicago Press, 2002); Eric Schickler, *Disjointed Pluralism* (Princeton, N.J.: Princeton University Press, 2001).

Chapter 9 / The Presidency / pages 237–263

1. Janet Elder, "Poll Shows Americans Divided Over Election, Indicating That Bush Must Build Public Support," *New York Times,* 18 December 2000, p. A21. For an account of the political and legal issues surrounding the 2000 presidential election, see Howard Gillman, *The Votes That Counted* (Chicago: University of Chicago Press, 2001); and Cass Sunstein and Richard Epstein (eds.), *The Vote: Bush, Gore, and the Supreme Court* (Chicago: University of Chicago Press, 2001).

2. Sheryl Gay Stolberg, "In Global Battle on AIDS, Bush Creates Legacy," *New York Times,* 5 January 2008.

3. See Jeffrey M. Jones, "Bush Finishes 19th Quarter in Office on Low Note: Quarterly Average Only in 18th Percentile," Gallup Poll, 21 October 2005, and "Independents, Moderate Republicans Lead Decline in Bush Ratings," Gallup Poll, 8 November 2005, available at poll.gallup.com.

4. Department of Defense, "Military Casualty Information," July 2008. Available online at siadapp.dmdc.osd .mil/personnel/CASUALTY/castop.htm. A regularly updated summary count for Afghanistan and Iraq is available online at www.defenselink.mil/news/casualty .pdf.

5. Christopher Dickey, "The Constitution in Peril," *Newsweek,* 8 October 2007, pp. 60–66; Jameel Jaffer and Amrit Singh, *Administration of Torture* (New York: Columbia University Press, 2007); James Pfiffner, "Constraining Executive Power: George W. Bush and the Constitution," *Presidential Studies Quarterly* 38, no. 1 (March 2008): 123–143; and Charlie Savage, *Takeover: The Return of the Imperial Presidency and the Subversion of American Democracy* (Boston: Back Bay Books, 2008).

6. Ed Henry, "With One Year to Go, Bush's Legacy Is a Mixed Bag," 24 December 2007, available at www.cnn .com; David Nather, "New Handshake, Same Grip," *Congressional Quarterly Weekly Report,* 17 December 2007, p. 3702 and "Last Year for the History Books," *Congressional Quarterly Weekly Report,* 21 January 2008, p. 196; Sheryl Gay Stolberg, "Bush, Facing Woes in '08, Focuses on War and Taxes," *New York Times,* 29 January 2008, p. A1. For more on Bush's legacy, see Colin Campbell, Bert Rockman, and Andrew Rudalevige, *The George W. Bush Legacy* (Washington, D.C.: Congressional Quarterly Press, 2007); and Lou Cannon and Carl M. Cannon, *Reagan's Disciple: George W. Bush's Troubled Quest for a Presidential Legacy* (New York: Public Affairs, 2008).

7. Sheryl Gay Stolberg, "Echo of First Bush: Good Economy Turns Sour," *New York Times,* 28 January 2008, p. A1; Jon Cohen and Dan Balz, "U.S. Outlook Is Worst Since '92, Poll Finds," *Washington Post,* 13 May 2008, p. A01.

8. See Louis Fisher, *Presidential War Power* (Lawrence: University Press of Kansas, 1995).

9. Lyn Ragsdale, *Vital Statistics on the Presidency: Washington to Clinton* (Washington, D.C.: Congressional Quarterly Press, 1996), p. 396.

10. Charles Cameron, *Veto Bargaining: Presidents and the Politics of Negative Power* (Cambridge: Cambridge University Press, 2000).

11. Jeffrey Tulis, *The Rhetorical Presidency* (Princeton, N.J.: Princeton University Press, 1987).

12. Cecil V. Crabb Jr. and Pat M. Holt, *Invitation to Struggle: Congress, the President and Foreign Policy,* 2nd ed. (Washington, D.C.: Congressional Quarterly Press, 1984); Arthur Schlesinger Jr., *The Imperial Presidency* (Boston: Houghton Mifflin, 1989).

13. Text of Joint Resolution to Authorize Use of Military Force Against Iraq, *Congressional Quarterly Weekly Report,* 12 October 2002, p. 2697.

14. *Hamdan v. Rumsfeld,* 548 U.S. 557 (2006).

15. Wilfred E. Binkley, *President and Congress,* 3rd ed. (New York: Vintage, 1962), p. 155.

16. William G. Howell, *Power Without Persuasion: The Politics of Direct Presidential Action* (Princeton, N.J.: Princeton University Press, 2003); Kenneth R. Mayer, *With the Stroke of a Pen: Executive Orders and Presidential Power* (Princeton, N.J.: Princeton University Press, 2001).

17. 2007 budget figures, *Statistical Abstract of the United States,* available at www.census.gov/compendia/statab/cats/federal_govt_finances_employment.html.

18. Richard Tanner Johnson, *Managing the White House* (New York: Harper and Row, 1974); John P. Burke, *The Institutional Presidency* (Baltimore, Md.: Johns Hopkins University Press, 1992).

19. Irving Janus, *Victims of Groupthink: A Psychological Study of Foreign Policy Decisions and Fiascoes* (Boston: Houghton Mifflin, 1972); Andrew Rudalevige, "The Structure of Leadership: Presidents, Hierarchies, and Information Flow," *Presidential Studies Quarterly* 35 (June 2005): 333–360.

20. John Cochran, "GOP Turns to Cheney to Get the Job Done," *Congressional Quarterly Weekly Report,* 31 May 2003, pp. 1306–1308.

21. Edward Weisband and Thomas M. Franck, *Resignation in Protest* (New York: Penguin, 1975), p. 139, quoted in Thomas E. Cronin, *The State of the Presidency,* 2nd ed. (Boston: Little, Brown, 1980), p. 253.

22. See Richard W. Waterman, "Combining Political Resources: The Internalization of the President's Appointment Power," in *The Presidency Reconsidered,* ed. Richard W. Waterman (Itasca, Ill.: Peacock, 1993), pp. 172–210.

23. Doris Kearns, *Lyndon Johnson and the American Dream* (New York: Signet, 1977), p. 363.

24. See Merrill McLoughlin (ed.), *The Impeachment and Trial of President Clinton: The Official Transcripts, from the House Judiciary Committee Hearings to the Senate Trial* (New York: Random House, 1999); Richard Posner, *An Affair of State* (Cambridge, Mass.: Harvard University Press, 1999); Jeffrey Toobin, *A Vast Conspiracy* (New York: Touchstone, 1999).

25. James David Barber, *Presidential Character,* 4th ed. (Englewood Cliffs, N.J.: Prentice Hall, 1992); Fred I. Greenstein, *The Presidential Difference: Leadership Style from FDR to Clinton* (Princeton, N.J.: Princeton University Press, 2000); Stanley Renshon, *High Hopes: The Clinton Presidency and the Politics of Ambition* (New York: Routledge, 1998).

26. Donald Kinder, "Presidential Character Revisited," in *Political Cognition,* ed. Richard Lau and David O. Sears (Hillsdale, N.J.: Erlbaum, 1986), pp. 233–255; W. E. Miller and J. M. Shanks, *The New American Voter* (Cambridge, Mass.: Harvard University Press, 1996).

27. Richard E. Neustadt, *Presidential Power,* rev. ed. (New York: Wiley, 1980), p. 10.

28. Ibid., p. 9.

29. George C. Edwards III, *At the Margins* (New Haven, Conn.: Yale University Press, 1989). See also Jon R. Bond and Richard Fleisher, *The President in the Legislative Arena* (Chicago: University of Chicago Press, 1990).

30. See Edwards, *At the Margins,* pp. 101–125.

31. Samuel Kernell, *Going Public: New Strategies of Presidential Leadership,* 3rd ed. (Washington, D.C.: Congressional Quarterly Press, 1997), p. 2.

32. Richard A. Brody, *Assessing the President* (Stanford, Calif.: Stanford University Press, 1991), pp. 27–44; Gary C. Jacobson, "The Bush Presidency and the American Electorate," in *The George W. Bush Presidency,* ed. Fred I. Greenstein (Baltimore, Md.: Johns Hopkins University Press, 2003), pp. 197–227.

33. Paul Brace and Barbara Hinckley, *Follow the Leader* (New York: Basic Books, 1992); Richard Brody, "President Bush and the Public," in *The George W. Bush Presidency,* ed. Greenstein, pp. 228–244; George C. Edwards III and Tami Swenson, "Who Rallies? The Anatomy of a Rally Event," *Journal of Politics* 59 (February 1997): 200–212.

34. Richard C. Eichenberg and Richard J. Stoll, *The Political Fortunes of War: Iraq and the Domestic Standing of President George W. Bush* (London: The Foreign Policy Centre, 2004), p. 8.

35. Jeffrey M. Jones, "Bush Approval Showing Only Slight Decline Six Months After Record High," *Gallup News Service,* 21 March 2002, p. 1.

36. Jeffrey E. Cohen, *Presidential Responsiveness and Public Policy-Making* (Ann Arbor: University of Michigan Press, 1999); Lawrence C. Jacobs and Robert Y. Shapiro, *Politicians Don't Pander* (Chicago: University of Chicago Press, 2000).

37. David McCullough, *Truman* (New York: Simon & Schuster, 1992), p. 914.

38. Bond and Fleisher, *The President in the Legislative Arena;* Mark Peterson, *Legislating Together* (Cambridge, Mass.: Harvard University Press, 1990).

39. Clea Benson, "Presidential Support: The Power of No," *Congressional Quarterly Weekly Report,* 14 January 2008, p. 137.

40. "Two Cheers for United Government," *American Enterprise* 4 (January–February 1993): 107–108.

41. Morris Fiorina, *Divided Government,* 2nd ed. (Needham Heights, Mass.: Allyn & Bacon, 1996), p. 153.

42. See generally Charles O. Jones, *The Presidency in a Separated System* (Washington, D.C.: The Brookings Institution, 1994).

43. David R. Mayhew, *Divided We Govern* (New Haven, Conn.: Yale University Press, 1991); and David R. Mayhew, "The Return to Unified Government Under Clinton:

How Much of a Difference in Lawmaking," in *The New American Politics*, ed. Bryan D. Jones (Boulder, Colo.: Westview Press, 1995), pp. 111–121.

44. See Jon Bond and Richard Fleisher (eds.), *Polarized Politics: Congress and the President in a Partisan Era* (Washington, D.C.: CQ Press, 2000); Sean Kelley, "Divided We Govern: A Reassessment," *Polity* 25 (Spring 1993): 475–484.

45. See Sarah H. Binder, "The Dynamics of Legislative Gridlock, 1947–96," *American Political Science Review* 93 (September 1999): 519–534.

46. See Charles O. Jones, *The Presidency in a Separated System*, 2nd ed. (Washington, D.C.: The Brookings Institution, 2005).

47. "Prepared Text of Carter's Farewell Address," *New York Times*, 15 January 1981, p. B10.

48. Stephen Skowronek, *The Politics Presidents Make*, 2nd ed. (Cambridge, Mass.: Harvard University Press, 1997).

49. Stephen Skowronek, "Presidential Leadership in Political Time," in *The Presidency in the Political System*, 6th ed., ed. Michael Nelson (Washington, D.C.: Congressional Quarterly Press, 2000), p. 164; Stephen Skowronek, "The Setting: Change and Continuity in the Politics of Leadership," in *The Elections of 2000*, ed. Michael Nelson (Washington, D.C.: Congressional Quarterly Press, 2001), pp. 1–25.

50. *Public Papers of the President, Lyndon B. Johnson, 1965* (Washington, D.C.: Government Printing Office, 1966), 1:72.

51. Kevin Phillips, *The Politics of Rich and Poor* (New York: Random House, 1990), p. 88.

52. John W. Kingdon, *Agendas, Alternatives, and Public Policies* (Boston: Little, Brown, 1984), p. 25.

53. Richard E. Neustadt, "Presidency and Legislation: The Growth of Central Clearance," *American Political Science Review* 48 (September 1954): 641–671.

54. Seth King, "Reagan, in Bid for Budget Votes, Reported to Yield on Sugar Prices," *New York Times*, 27 June 1981, p. A1.

55. Jeffrey M. Berry and Kent E. Portney, "Centralizing Regulatory Control and Interest Group Access: The Quayle Council on Competitiveness," in *Interest Group Politics*, 4th ed., ed. Allan J. Cigler and Burdett A. Loomis (Washington, D.C.: Congressional Quarterly Press, 1994), pp. 319–347.

56. The extent to which popularity affects presidential influence in Congress is difficult to determine with any precision. For an overview of this issue, see Jon R. Bond, Richard Fleisher, and Glen S. Katz, "An Overview of the Empirical Findings on Presidential-Congressional Relations," in *Rivals for Power*, ed. James A. Thurber (Washington, D.C.: Congressional Quarterly Press, 1996), pp. 103–139.

57. For an inside account of the Bush administration's response to September 11, see Bob Woodward, *Bush at War* (New York: Simon & Schuster, 2002). For an account of the decision to go to war with Iraq, see Bob Woodward, *Plan of Attack* (New York: Simon & Schuster, 2004).

58. For more on Iraq and foreign policy in the George W. Bush administration, see Jacob Weisberg, *The Bush Tragedy* (New York: Random House, 2008).

59. Gallup polls find that respondents in countries in the Middle East and North Africa are more likely to approve of the national leadership of Japan, China, France, and Germany, than the leadership of the United States and Great Britain. See Cynthia English, "In Mideast, North Africa, Views of Powerful Nations Differ," 13 November 2007, available at www.gallup.com.

60. Alexander George, "The Case for Multiple Advocacy in Foreign Policy," *American Political Science Review* (September 1972): 751–782.

61. John P. Burke and Fred I. Greenstein, *How Presidents Test Reality* (New York: Russell Sage Foundation, 1989); Richard E. Neustadt and Ernest R. May, *Thinking in Time* (New York: Free Press, 1986).

Chapter 10 / The Bureaucracy / pages 264–282

1. The National Commission on Terrorist Attacks Upon the United States (also known as the 9-11 Commission) was an independent, bipartisan commission created by congressional legislation and President George W. Bush in late 2002. Their 2004 final report stated that they found no links between Iraq and Al Qaeda. For the full report, see www.9-11commission.gov.

2. United States Department of Defense, Office of the Inspector General, "Review of the Pre-Iraqi War Activities of the Office of the Under Secretary of Defense for Policy," 9 February 2007, available at www.dodig.osd .mil/fo/Foia/pre-iraqi.htm.

3. This account draws on Rajiv Chandrasekaran, *Imperial Life in the Emerald City* (New York: Vintage Books, 2006); Jeffrey Goldberg, "A Little Learning," *New Yorker*, 9 May 2005; Walter Pincus and R. Jeffrey Smith, "Official's Key Report on Iraq is Faulted," *Washington Post*, 9 February 2007; Thomas Ricks, *Fiasco* (New York: Penguin Press, 2006); and Bob Woodward, *State of Denial* (New York: Simon and Schuster, 2006).

4. James Q. Wilson, *Bureaucracy* (New York: Basic Books, 1989), p. 25.

5. Bruce D. Porter, "Parkinson's Law Revisited: War and the Growth of American Government," *Public Interest* 60 (Summer 1980): 50.

6. See generally Ballard C. Campbell, *The Growth of American Government* (Bloomington: Indiana University Press, 1995).

7. See generally Marc Allen Eisner, *Regulatory Politics in Transition*, 2nd ed. (Baltimore: Johns Hopkins University Press, 2000).

8. See Anne Schneider and Helen Ingram, "Social Construction of Target Populations: Implications for Politics and Policy," *American Political Science Review* 87 (June 1993): 334–347.

9. Theda Skocpol, *Protecting Soldiers and Mothers: The Political Origins of Social Policy in the United States* (Cambridge, Mass.: Harvard University Press, 1992).

10. Paul C. Light, *The True Size of Government* (Washington, D.C.: The Brookings Institution, 1999).

11. U.S. Department of Defense, "Civilian Employment Statistics, May 2008," released 1 July 2008, available at siadapp.dmdc.osd.mil/personnel/CIVILIAN/fy2008/ may2008/may2008.pdf; and U.S. Department of

Defense, "Armed Forces Strength Figures for June 30, 2008," available at siadapp.dmdc.osd.mil/personnel/MILITARY/ms0.pdf, accessed 22 July 2008.

12. John T. Tierney, "Government Corporations and Managing the Public's Business," *Political Science Quarterly* 99 (Spring 1984): 73–92.

13. U.S. Census Bureau, *Statistical Abstract of the United States, 2004–2005,* Table 485, available at www.census.gov/prod/2004pubs/04statab/fedgov.pdf.

14. Presidential Appointee Initiative, *Staffing a New Administration: A Guide to Personnel Appointments in a Presidential Transition* (Washington, D.C.: The Brookings Institution, 2000), available at www.appointee.brookings.edu/resourcecenter/journalismguide.pdf.

15. Though formally located within the executive branch, the bureaucracy is "caught in the middle" between the Congress and the president. See Barry Weingast, "Caught in the Middle: The President, Congress, and the Political-Bureaucratic System," in *The Executive Branch,* ed. J. Aberbach and M. Peterson (New York: Oxford University Press, 2005), pp. 312–343.

16. Theodore J. Lowi Jr., *The End of Liberalism,* 2nd ed. (New York: Norton, 1979).

17. Doris A. Graber, *Mass Media and American Politics,* 3rd ed. (Washington, D.C.: Congressional Quarterly Press, 1989), p. 51.

18. Lauren Etter, "Is Someone Listening to Your Phone Calls?" *Wall Street Journal,* 7 January 2006, p. A5; James Risen and Eric Lichtblau, "Bush Lets U.S. Spy on Callers Without Courts," *New York Times,* 16 December 2005, p. A1.

19. Tom A. Peter, "Warrantless Wiretaps Expanded," *Christian Science Monitor,* 7 August 2007; and Lawrence Wright, "The Spymaster," *New Yorker,* 21 January 2008, pp. 42–59.

20. Jeffrey M. Berry, *Feeding Hungry People* (New Brunswick, N.J.: Rutgers University Press, 1984).

21. Cornelius M. Kerwin, *Rulemaking: How Government Agencies Write Law and Make Policy,* 3d ed. (Washington, D.C.: Congressional Quarterly Press, 2003).

22. Stuart Shapiro, "The Role of Procedural Controls in OSHA's Ergonomics Rulemaking," *Public Administration Review* 67 (July/August 2007): 688–701.

23. Stephen Labaton, "Trucking Rules Are Eased, a Debate on Safety Intensifies," *New York Times,* 3 December 2006, p. 1.

24. Charles E. Lindblom, "The Science of Muddling Through," *Public Administration Review* 19 (Spring 1959): 79–88.

25. See Michael T. Hayes, *Incrementalism and Public Policy* (White Plains, N.Y.: Longman, 1992).

26. Frank R. Baumgartner, Jeffrey M. Berry, Marie Hojnacki, David C. Kimball, and Beth L. Leech, *Advocacy and Policy Change* (Chicago: University of Chicago Press, forthcoming); and Bryan D. Jones and Frank R. Baumgartner, *The Politics of Attention* (Chicago: University of Chicago Press, 2005).

27. "Bureaucratic culture" is a particularly slippery concept but can be conceived of as the interplay of artifacts, values, and underlying assumptions. See Irene Lurie and Norma Riccucci, "Changing the 'Culture' of Welfare Offices," *Administration and Society* 34 (January 2003): 653–677.

28. Thomas W. Church and Robert T. Nakamura, *Cleaning Up the Mess* (Washington, D.C.: The Brookings Institution, 1993).

29. Ronald Daniels (ed.), *On Risk and Disaster: Lessons from Hurricane Katrina* (Philadelphia: University of Pennsylvania Press, 2006); Saundra Schneider, "Administrative Breakdowns in Governmental Response to Hurricane Katrina," *Public Administration Review* 65 (September–October 2005): 515–516.

30. Spencer Hsu and Amy Goldstein, "Administration Faulted on Katrina," *Washington Post,* 2 February 2006, p. A5.

31. See generally Terry M. Moe, "The Politics of Bureaucratic Structure," in *Can the Government Govern?* ed. John E. Chubb and Paul E. Peterson (Washington, D.C.: The Brookings Institution, 1989), pp. 267–329.

32. Daniel J. Fiorino, *The New Environmental Regulation* (Cambridge, Mass.: MIT Press, 2006). Del Quentin Wilber and Marc Kaufman, "Judges Toss EPA Rule to Reduce Smog, Soot," *Washington Post,* 12 July 2008, p. A01.

33. Archon Fung, Mary Graham, and David Weil, *Full Disclosure* (New York: Cambridge University Press, 2007).

34. See generally E. S. Savas, *Privatization and Public-Private Partnerships* (New York: Chatham House, 2000).

35. Steven Rathgeb Smith, "Social Services," in *The State of Nonprofit America,* ed. Lester M. Salamon (Washington, D.C.: The Brookings Institution and Aspen Institute, 2002), p. 165.

36. Beryl A. Radin, *Beyond Machiavelli: Policy Analysis Comes of Age* (Washington, D.C.: Georgetown University Press, 2000), pp. 168–169.

37. David G. Frederickson and H. George Frederickson, *Measuring the Performance of the Hollow State* (Washington, D.C.: Georgetown University Press, 2006), pp. 56–57.

38. See Carolyn J. Heinrich, "Outcomes-Based Performance in the Public Sector," *Public Administration Review* 62 (November–December 2002): 712–725; David Hirschmann, "Thermometers or Sauna? Performance Measurement and Democratic Assistance in the United States Agency for International Development (USAID)," *Public Administration* 80 (2002): 235–255.

39. See Amahai Glazer and Lawrence S. Rothenberg, *Why Government Succeeds and Why It Fails* (Cambridge, Mass.: Harvard University Press, 2001).

Chapter 11 / The Courts / pages 283–308

1. Philip Elman (interviewed by Norman Silber), *The Solicitor General's Office, Justice Frankfurter, and Civil Rights Litigation, 1946–1960: An Oral History,* 100 Harv. L. Rev. 817 at 840 (1987).

2. David O'Brien, *Storm Center,* 2nd ed. (New York: Norton, 1990), p. 324.

3. Bernard Schwartz, *The Unpublished Opinions of the Warren Court* (New York: Oxford University Press, 1985), p. 446.

4. Ibid., pp. 445–448.

5. Felix Frankfurter and James M. Landis, *The Business of the Supreme Court* (New York: Macmillan, 1928), pp. 5–14; and Julius Goebel Jr., *Antecedents and Beginnings to 1801*, Vol. 1 of *The History of the Supreme Court of the United States* (New York: Macmillan, 1971).

6. Maeva Marcus (ed.), *The Justices on Circuit, 1795–1800*, Vol. 3 of *The Documentary History of the Supreme Court of the United States, 1789–1800* (New York: Columbia University Press, 1990).

7. Robert G. McCloskey, *The United States Supreme Court* (Chicago: University of Chicago Press, 1960), p. 31.

8. *Marbury v. Madison,* 1 Cranch 137 at 177, 178 (1803).

9. Interestingly, the term *judicial review* dates only to 1910. It was apparently unknown to Marshall and his contemporaries. Robert Lowry Clinton, *Marbury v. Madison and Judicial Review* (Lawrence: University Press of Kansas, 1989), p. 7.

10. Lee Epstein et al., *The Supreme Court Compendium,* 4th ed. (Washington, D.C.: Congressional Quarterly Press, 2007), Table 2-15.

11. *Ware v. Hylton,* 3 Dallas 199 (1796).

12. *Martin v. Hunter's Lessee,* 1 Wheat. 304 (1816).

13. Epstein et al., *The Supreme Court Compendium,* Table 2-16.

14. Garry Wills, *Explaining America: The Federalist* (Garden City, N.Y.: Doubleday, 1981), pp. 127–136.

15. *State Justice Institute News* 4 (Spring 1993): 1.

16. Charles Alan Wright, *Handbook on the Law of Federal Courts,* 3rd ed. (St. Paul, Minn.: West, 1976), p. 7.

17. James C. Duff, *Judicial Business of the United States Courts,* 2007 Annual Report of the Director, Administrative Office of the U.S. Courts. Table 11, "Status of Article III Judgeship Positions," p. 42. Available at www.uscourts.gov/judbus2007/contents.html.

18. James C. Duff, *Judicial Business of the United States Courts,* 2007 Annual Report of the Director, Administrative Office of the U.S. Courts. "Caseload Highlights," p. 14. Available at www.uscourts.gov/judbus2007/contents.html.

19. James C. Duff, *Judicial Business of the United States Courts,* 2007 Annual Report of the Director, Administrative Office of the U.S. Courts. Table 13, "U.S. Magistrate Judge Positions Authorized by the Judicial Conference," p. 44. Available at www.uscourts.gov/judbus2007/contents.html.

20. James C. Duff, *Judicial Business of the United States Courts,* 2007 Annual Report of the Director, Administrative Office of the U.S. Courts. Table 11, "Status of Article III Judgeship Positions," p. 42, and Table 1, "U.S. Courts of Appeals: Appeals Filed, Terminated, and Pending," p. 19. Available at www.uscourts.gov/judbus2007/contents.html.

21. Linda Greenhouse, "Precedent for Lower Courts: Tyrant or Teacher?" *New York Times,* 29 January 1988, p. B7.

22. *Texas v. Johnson,* 491 U.S. 397 (1989); *United States v. Eichman,* 496 U.S. 310 (1990).

23. *Regents of the University of California v. Bakke,* 438 U.S. 265 (1978).

24. *Grutter v. Bollinger,* 539 U.S. 244 (2003); *Gratz v. Bollinger,* 539 U.S. 306 (2003).

25. *Parents Involved in Community Schools v. Seattle School Dist. No. 1,* 551 U.S.___ (2007).

26. "Reading Petitions Is for Clerks Only at High Court Now," *Wall Street Journal,* 11 October 1990, p. B7. Robert Barnes, "Justices Continue Trend of Hearing Fewer Cases," *Washington Post,* 7 January 2007, p. A4.

27. Jeffrey Rosen, "Supreme Court Inc: How the Nation's Highest Court Has Come to Side with Business," *New York Times Magazine,* 16 March 2008, pp. 38 et seq.

28. H. W. Perry Jr., *Deciding to Decide: Agenda Setting in the United States Supreme Court* (Cambridge, Mass.: Harvard University Press, 1991); Gregory A. Caldiera and John R. Wright, "The Discuss List: Agenda Building in the Supreme Court," *Law and Society Review* 24, no. 3 (1990): 807.

29. Doris M. Provine, *Case Selection in the United States Supreme Court* (Chicago: University of Chicago Press, 1980), pp. 74–102.

30. Perry, *Deciding to Decide,* p. 286.

31. "Rising Fixed Opinions," *New York Times,* 22 February 1988, p. 14. See also Linda Greenhouse, "At the Bar," *New York Times,* 28 July 1989, p. 21.

32. Jeffrey A. Segal and Harold J. Spaeth, *The Supreme Court and the Attitudinal Model* (Cambridge: Cambridge University Press, 1993).

33. Thomas G. Walker, Lee Epstein, and William J. Dixon, "On the Mysterious Demise of Consensual Norms in the United States Supreme Court," *Journal of Politics* 50 (1988): 361–389.

34. See, for example, Walter F. Murphy, *Elements of Judicial Strategy* (Chicago: University of Chicago Press, 1964); and Bob Woodward and Scott Armstrong, *The Brethren* (New York: Simon & Schuster, 1979).

35. Greenhouse, "At the Bar," p. 21.

36. James Sample, Lauren Jones, and Rachel Weiss, *The New Politics of Judicial Elections 2006* (Washington, D.C.: Justice at Stake, 2007), p. vi–vii. Available at www.justiceatstake.org.

37. Stephen L. Wasby, *The Supreme Court in the Federal Judicial System,* 3rd ed. (Chicago: Nelson-Hall, 1988), pp. 107–110.

38. Jeffrey Toobin, *The Nine: Inside the Secret World of the Supreme Court* (New York: Doubleday, 2007), p. 269.

39. Federal Judicial Center, "Judges of the United States Courts," available at http://air.fjc.gov/history/judges_frm.html.

40. Ronald Stidham, Robert A. Carp, and Donald R. Songer, "The Voting Behavior of Judges Appointed by President Clinton" (paper presented at the annual meeting of the Southwestern Political Science Association, Houston, Texas, March 1996). See also Susan B. Haire, Martha Anne Humphries, and Donald R. Songer, "The Voting Behavior of Clinton's Courts of Appeals Appointees," *Judicature* 84 (March–April 2001): 274–281.

41. Robert A. Carp, Ronald Stidham, and Kenneth L. Manning, "The Voting Behavior of George W. Bush's Judges: How Sharp a Turn to the Right?" in *Principles and Practice of American Politics: Classic and Contemporary Readings,* 3rd ed., ed. Samuel Kernell and Steven S.

Smith (Washington, D.C.: Congressional Quarterly Press, 2006).

42. Information from the U.S. Senate, "Supreme Court Nominations, Present–1789," available at www.senate.gov/pagelayout/reference/nominations/Nominations.htm.
43. *Brown v. Board of Education II*, 349 U.S. 294 (1955).
44. Alexander M. Bickel, *The Least Dangerous Branch* (Indianapolis: Bobbs-Merrill, 1962); and Robert A. Dahl, "Decision-Making in a Democracy: The Supreme Court as a National Policy-Maker," *Journal of Public Law* 6 (1962): 279.
45. William Mishler and Reginal S. Sheehan, "The Supreme Court as a Countermajoritarian Institution? The Impact of Public Opinion on Supreme Court Decisions," *American Political Science Review* 87 (1993): 87–101.
46. Thomas R. Marshall, *Public Opinion and the Supreme Court* (Boston: Unwin Hyman, 1989).
47. *Kelo v. City of New London*, 545 U.S. 469 (2005).
48. Jeffrey M. Jones, "Nearly 6 in 10 Approve of Supreme Court," *Social Issues & Policy*, Gallup Poll News Service (17 June 2003).
49. Ibid., pp. 192–193; Gerald N. Rosenberg, *The Hollow Hope: Can Courts Bring About Social Change?* (Chicago: University of Chicago Press, 1991).
50. William J. Brennan Jr., "State Supreme Court Judge Versus United States Supreme Court Justice: A Change in Function and Perspective," *University of Florida Law Review* 19 (1966): 225.

Chapter 12 / Order and Civil Liberties / pages 310–337

1. Learned Hand, *The Bill of Rights* (Boston: Atheneum, 1958), p. 1.
2. Leonard W. Levy, *The Establishment Clause: Religion and the First Amendment* (New York: Macmillan, 1986); Leo Pfeffer, *Church, State, and Freedom* (Boston: Beacon Press, 1953); and Leonard W. Levy, "The Original Meaning of the Establishment Clause of the First Amendment," in *Religion and the State*, ed. James E. Wood Jr. (Waco, Tex.: Baylor University Press, 1985), pp. 43–83.
3. *Reynolds v. United States*, 98 U.S. 145 (1879).
4. *Everson v. Board of Education*, 330 U.S. 1 (1947).
5. *Board of Education v. Allen*, 392 U.S. 236 (1968).
6. *Lemon v. Kurtzman*, 403 U.S. 602 (1971).
7. *Agostini v. Felton*, 96 U.S. 552 (1997).
8. *Zelman, Superintendent of Public Instruction of Ohio, et al. v. Simmons-Harris et al.*, 536 U.S. 639 (2002).
9. *Engle v. Vitale*, 370 U.S. 421 (1962); *Wallace v. Jaffree*, 472 U.S. 38 (1985).
10. *Lee v. Weisman*, 505 U.S. 577 (1992).
11. *Santa Fe Independent School District v. Doe*, 530 U.S. 290 (2000).
12. *Good News Club v. Milford Central School*, 533 U.S. 98 (2001).
13. Michael W. McConnell, "The Origins and Historical Understanding of the Free Exercise of Religion," *Harvard Law Review* 103 (1990): 1409.
14. Herbert v. *Verner*, 374 U.S. 398 (1963).

15. *Employment Division v. Smith*, 494 U.S. 872 (1990).
16. *Boerne v. Flores*, 95 U.S. 2074 (1997).
17. *Gonzales v. O Centro Espírita Beneficente União do Vegetal*, 546 U.S. 418 (2006).
18. Laurence Tribe, *Treatise on American Constitutional Law*, 2nd ed. (St. Paul, Minn.: West, 1988), p. 566.
19. Zechariah Chafee, *Free Speech in the United States* (Cambridge, Mass.: Harvard University Press, 1941).
20. Leonard W. Levy, *The Emergence of a Free Press* (New York: Oxford University Press, 1985).
21. *Schenck v. United States*, 249 U.S. 47 (1919).
22. *Gitlow v. New York*, 268 U.S. 652 (1925).
23. *Dennis v. United States*, 341 U.S. 494 (1951).
24. *Brandenburg v. Ohio*, 395 U.S. 444 (1969).
25. *Tinker v. Des Moines Independent County School District*, 393 U.S. 503 at 508 (1969).
26. *DePinto and LaRocco v. Bayonne Board of Education*, 514 F.Supp.2d 663 (2007).
27. *Morse v. Frederick*, 551 U.S. ____ (2007); Charles Lane, "Court Backs School on Speech Curbs," *Washington Post*, 26 June 2007, p. A6.
28. *Miller v. California*, 413 U.S. 15 (1973).
29. *ACLU v. Reno* (1996 U.S. Dist. LEXIS) (12 June 1996).
30. *Reno v. ACLU*, 96 U.S. 511 (1997).
31. *Ashcroft v. ACLU*, 524 U.S. 656 (2004). *ACLU v. Gonzales*, 22 March 2007, Eastern District of Pennsylvania, Final Order in Civil Action No. 98-5591.
32. *United States v. Williams*, 553 U.S. ____ (2008).
33. *New York Times v. Sullivan*, 376 U.S. 254 (1964).
34. *Near v. Minnesota*, 283 U.S. 697 (1931).
35. For a detailed account of *Near*, see Fred W. Friendly, *Minnesota Rag* (New York: Random House, 1981).
36. *New York Times v. United States*, 403 U.S. 713 (1971).
37. *Branzburg v. Hayes*, 408 U.S. 665 (1972).
38. *Zurcher v. Stanford Daily*, 436 U.S. 547 (1978).
39. *Hazelwood School District v. Kuhlmeier*, 484 U.S. 260 (1988).
40. *United States v. Cruikshank*, 92 U.S. 542 (1876); *Constitution of the United States of America: Annotated and Interpreted* (Washington, D.C.: U.S. Government Printing Office, 1973), p. 1031.
41. *DeJonge v. Oregon*, 299 U.S. 353 (1937).
42. *United States v. Miller*, 307 U.S. 174 (1939).
43. *District of Columbia v. Heller*, 554 U.S. ____ (2008).
44. *Barron v. Baltimore*, 32 U.S. (7 Pet.) 243 (1833).
45. *Chicago, Burlington & Quincy R.R. v. Chicago*, 166 U.S. 226 (1897).
46. *Gitlow v. New York*, 268 U.S. 666 (1925).
47. *Palko v. Connecticut*, 302 U.S. 319 (1937).
48. *Duncan v. Louisiana*, 391 U.S. 145 (1968).
49. *McNabb v. United States*, 318 U.S. 332 (1943).
50. *Baldwin v. New York*, 399 U.S. 66 (1970).
51. Anthony Lewis, *Gideon's Trumpet* (New York: Random House, 1964).
52. *Gideon v. Wainwright*, 372 U.S. 335 (1963).
53. *Miranda v. Arizona*, 384 U.S. 436 (1966).
54. *Dickerson v. United States*, 530 U.S. 428 (2000).
55. *Missouri v. Seibert*, 542 U.S. 600 (2004).
56. *Wolf v. Colorado*, 338 U.S. 25 (1949).
57. *Mapp v. Ohio*, 367 U.S. 643 (1961).
58. *United States v. Leon*, 468 U.S. 897 (1984).

59. Liane Hansen, "Voices in the News This Week," *NPR Weekend Edition,* 28 October 2001 (NEXIS transcript).
60. Dan Eggen, "Tough Anti-Terror Campaign Pledged: Ashcroft Tells Mayors He Will Use New Law to Fullest Extent," *Washington Post,* 26 October 2001, p. A1.
61. *Rasul* v. *Bush,* 542 U.S. 466 (2004).
62. *Hamdi* v. *Rumsfeld,* 542 U.S. 507 (2004). Charles Lane, "Justices Back Detainee Access to U.S. Courts," *Washington Post,* 29 June 2004, p. A1.
63. *Hamdan* v. *Rumsfeld,* 548 U.S. 557 (2006).
64. Michael A. Fletcher, "Bush Signs Terrorism Measure," *Washington Post,* 18 October 2006, p. A4.
65. *Boumediene* v. *Bush,* 553 U.S. ____ (2008)
66. Article I, Sec. 9.
67. Paul Brest, *Processes of Constitutional Decision-Making* (Boston: Little, Brown, 1975), p. 708.
68. *Griswold* v. *Connecticut,* 381 U.S. 479 (1965).
69. *Roe* v. *Wade,* 410 U.S. 113 (1973).
70. See John Hart Ely, "The Wages of Crying Wolf: A Comment on *Roe* v. *Wade,*" *Yale Law Journal* 82 (1973): 920.
71. *Webster* v. *Reproductive Health Services,* 492 U.S. 490 (1989).
72. *Steinberg* v. *Carhart,* 530 U.S. 914 (2000); *Gonzales* v. *Carhart,* 550 U.S. ____ (2007).
73. *Bowers* v. *Hardwick,* 478 U.S. 186 (1986).
74. *Lawrence and Garner* v. *Texas,* 539 U.S. 558 (2003).
75. Ibid.
76. Glenn Kessler, "California Voters Narrowly Approve Same-Sex Marriage Ban," *Washington Post,* 6 November 2008, p. A44.

Chapter 13 / Equality and Civil Rights / pages 338–359

1. Nina Bernstein, "100 Years in the Back Door, Out the Front," *New York Times,* 21 May 2006, sec. 4, p. 4, quoted in Aristide Zolberg, *A Nation By Design: Immigration Policy in the Fashioning of America* (New York: Russell Sage Foundation, 2006).
2. Sam Howe Verhovek, "In Poll, Americans Reject Means But Not Ends of Racial Diversity," *New York Times,* 14 December 1997, sec. 1, p. 1; Jack Citrin, "Affirmative Action in the People's Court," *Public Interest* 122 (1996): 40–41; Charlotte Steeh and Maria Krysan, "Affirmative Action and the Public, 1970–1995," *Public Opinion Quarterly* 60 (1996): 128–158; Gallup Poll, 25–28 October 2000: "Would you vote . . . for or against a law which would allow your state to give preferences in job hiring and school admission on the basis of race?" For, 13 percent; against, 85 percent; and no opinion, 2 percent.
3. *The Slaughterhouse Cases,* 83 U.S. 36 (1873).
4. *Civil Rights Cases,* 109 U.S. 3 (1883).
5. Mary Beth Norton et al., *A People and a Nation: A History of the United States,* 3rd ed. (Boston: Houghton Mifflin, 1990), p. 490.
6. *Plessy* v. *Ferguson,* 163 U.S. 537 (1896).
7. Ibid., p. 562 (Harlan, J., dissenting).
8. *Cummings* v. *County Board of Education,* 175 U.S. 528 (1899).
9. *Brown* v. *Board of Education,* 347 U.S. 483 (1954).
10. Ibid., pp. 483, 495.
11. Ibid., pp. 483, 494.
12. *Brown* v. *Board of Education II,* 349 U.S. 294 (1955).
13. Jack W. Peltason, *Fifty-Eight Lonely Men,* rev. ed. (Urbana: University of Illinois Press, 1971).
14. *Alexander* v. *Holmes County Board of Education,* 396 U.S. 19 (1969).
15. *Milliken* v. *Bradley,* 418 U.S. 717 (1974).
16. Norton et al., *People and a Nation,* p. 943.
17. But see Abigail M. Thernstrom, *Whose Vote Counts? Affirmative Action and Minority Voting Rights* (Cambridge, Mass.: Harvard University Press, 1987).
18. *Richmond* v. *J. A. Croson Co.,* 488 U.S. 469 (1989).
19. *Martin* v. *Wilks,* 490 U.S. 755 (1989); *Wards Cove Packing Co.* v. *Atonio,* 490 U.S. 642 (1989); *Patterson* v. *McLean Credit Union,* 491 U.S. 164 (1989); *Price Waterhouse* v. *Hopkins,* 490 U.S. 228 (1989); *Lorance* v. *AT&T Technologies,* 490 U.S. 900 (1989); and *EEOC* v. *Arabian American Oil Co.,* 499 U.S. 244 (1991).
20. *Saint Francis College* v. *Al-Khazraji,* 481 U.S. 604 (1987).
21. Dee Brown, *Bury My Heart at Wounded Knee: An Indian History of the American West* (New York: Holt, Rinehart & Winston, 1971).
22. U.S. Bureau of the Census, *Hispanics in the United States,* Slide 11, "Current Population Trends in the Hispanic Population." Internet presentation available at www.census.gov/population/www/socdemo/hispanic/files/Internet_Hispanic_in_US_2006.pdf. Midred L. Amer, "Membership in the 110th Congress: A Profile," Congressional Research Service, report for Congress RS22555, 15 December 2006, pp. 5–6. These statistics do not include nonvoting delegates from American territories or the resident commissioner of Puerto Rico.
23. The U.S. Equal Employment Opportunities Commission, "Americans with Disabilities Act of 1990 (ADA) FY 1997–FY 2007," available at www.eeoc.gov/stats/ada-charges.html.
24. *Reed* v. *Reed,* 404 U.S. 71 (1971).
25. *Frontiero* v. *Richardson,* 411 U.S. 677 (1973).
26. *Craig* v. *Boren,* 429 U.S. 190 (1976).
27. *J.E.B.* v. *Alabama exrel. T.B.,* 511 U.S. 127 (1994).
28. *United States* v. *Virginia,* slip op. 94–1941 & 94–2107 (decided 26 June 1996).
29. Melvin I. Urofsky, *A March of Liberty* (New York: Knopf, 1988), p. 902.
30. *Harris* v. *Forklift Systems,* 510 U.S. 17 (1993).
31. *Facts on File* 206B2 (4 June 1965).
32. As quoted in Melvin I. Urofsky, *A Conflict of Rights: The Supreme Court and Affirmative Action* (New York: Scribner's, 1991), p. 29.
33. *Regents of the University of California* v. *Bakke,* 438 U.S. 265 (1978).
34. *Adarand Constructors, Inc.* v. *Peña,* 518 U.S. (1995).
35. *Gratz* v. *Bollinger,* 539 U.S. 244 (2003).
36. *Grutter* v. *Bollinger,* 539 U.S. 306 (2003).
37. Stephen Earl Bennett et al., *Americans' Opinions About Affirmative Action* (Cincinnati: University of Cincinnati, Institute for Policy Research, 1995), p. 4; Lawrence Bobo, "Race and Beliefs About Affirmative Action," in

Racialized Politics: The Debate About Racism in America, ed. David O. Sears, Jim Sidanius, and Lawrence Bobo (Chicago: University of Chicago Press, 2000).

Chapter 14 / Policymaking and the Budget / pages 360–384

1. Ian Campbell et al., "European Shares Take a Punch as Pessimism Gains Upper Hand," *Wall Street Journal Europe,* 22 January 2008, available at http://online.wsj.com/article/SB120096919555205505.html.
2. James T. Areddy, "Small Investors Are in Hot Seat as Stocks Recoil," *Wall Street Journal Europe,* 22 January 2008, available at http://online.wsj.com/article/SB120102173724506961.html.
3. Edmund L. Andrews, "Fed, in Surprise, Sets Big Rate Cut to Ease Markets," *New York Times,* 23 January 2008, p. A1.
4. Lori Montgomery and Paul Kane, "Bush Enacts Historic Financial Rescue," *Washington Post,* 4 October 2008, p. A01.
5. David Cho, Neil Irwin and Peter Whoriskey, "U.S. Forces Nine Major Banks to Accept Partial Nationalization," *Washington Post,* 14 October 2008, p. A01.
6. Alan Finder, "Study Finds Record Education Earmarks," *New York Times,* 24 March 2008, p. A15.
7. "Espresso Tax Is Defeated," *New York Times,* 18 September 2003, p. A17.
8. Steven Greenhouse, "Mexican Trucks Gain Approval to Haul Cargo Throughout U.S.," *New York Times,* 28 November 2002, p. A1.
9. This typology is adapted from Theodore Lowi's classic article, "American Business, Public Policy Case Studies, and Political Theory," *World Politics* 16 (July 1964): 677–715.
10. The policymaking process can be depicted in many ways. Another approach, a bit more elaborate than this, is described in James E. Anderson, *Public Policymaking,* 2nd ed. (Boston: Houghton Mifflin, 1994), p. 37.
11. See Christopher J. Bosso, "The Contextual Bases of Problem Definition," in *The Politics of Problem Definition,* ed. David A. Rochefort and Roger W. Cobb (Lawrence: University Press of Kansas, 1994), pp. 182–203.
12. Sam Dillon, "States Are Relaxing Education Standards to Avoid Sanctions from Federal Law," *New York Times,* 22 May 2003, p. A25.
13. Elizabeth Becker, "Big Visions for Security Post Shrink amid Political Drama," *New York Times,* 3 May 2002, p. A1.
14. Mary Dalrymple, "Homeland Security Department Another Victory for Administration," *CQ Weekly,* 16 November 2002, pp. 3002–3007.
15. Walter Pincus, "Intelligence Bill Clears Congress," *Washington Post,* 9 December 2004, p. A04.
16. Derek Willis, "Turf Battles Could Lie Ahead in Fight to Oversee Homeland Department," *CQ Weekly,* 16 November 2002, p. 3006.
17. Jeffrey M. Berry, *The Interest Group Society,* 3rd ed. (New York: Longman, 1997), p. 187.
18. Michael T. Heaney, "Coalitions and Interest Group Influence Over Health Care Policy" (paper delivered at the annual meeting of the American Political Science Association, Philadelphia, August 2003), p. 16.
19. Steve Langdon, "On Medicare, Negotiators Split Over Policy, Not Just Figures," *Congressional Quarterly Weekly Report,* 22 February 1997, pp. 488–490.
20. Jeffrey M. Berry, "Subgovernments, Issue Networks, and Political Conflict," in *Remaking American Politics,* ed. Richard A. Harris and Sidney M. Milkis (Boulder, Colo.: Westview Press, 1989), pp. 239–260.
21. Paul Peretz, "The Politics of Fiscal and Monetary Policy," in *The Politics of American Economic Policy Making,* 2nd ed., ed. Paul Peretz (Armonk, N.Y.: M. E. Sharp, 1996), pp. 101–113.
22. Executive Office of the President, *Budget of the United States Government, Fiscal Year 2007* (Washington, D.C.: U.S. Government Printing Office, 2006), Table 26-1, p. 381.
23. Jonathan Weisman, "Record $482 Billion '09 Deficit Forecast," *Washington Post,* 29 July 2008, p. A04. The Bureau of the Public Debt publishes historical data and a revised total debt figure daily at www.treasurydirect.gov/NP/BPDLogin?application=np.
24. For a concise discussion of the 1990 budget reforms, see James A. Thurber, "Congressional-Presidential Battles to Balance the Budget," in James A. Thurber (ed.), *Rivals for Power: Presidential-Congressional Relations* (Washington, D.C.: Congressional Quarterly Press, 1996), pp. 196–202.
25. For a brief account of presidential attempts, from Carter to Clinton, to deal with budget deficits, see Alexis Simendinger, David Baumann, Carl M. Cannon, and John Maggs, "Sky High," *National Journal,* 7 February 2004, pp. 370–373.
26. Ibid., p. 377; Concord Coalition, "Budget Process Reform: An Important Tool for Fiscal Discipline, But Not a Magic Bullet," *Issue Brief,* 5 February 2004.
27. Concord Coalition, "Budget Process Reform," p. 3.
28. Richard A. Musgrave and Peggy B. Musgrave, *Public Finance in Theory and Practice,* 2nd ed. (New York: McGraw-Hill, 1976), p. 42.
29. Office of Management and Budget, *Fiscal Year 2003 Budget of the United States Government, Mid-Session Review,* 15 July 2002, pp. 4–5, available at www.gpoaccess.gov/usbudget/fy03/pdf/msr.pdf.
30. Executive Office of the President, "Table 8.7: Outlays for Discretionary Programs: 1962–2009" and "Table 8.8: Outlays for Discretionary Programs in Constant (FY2000) Dollars: 1962–2009," in *Budget of the United States Government, Fiscal Year 2009, Historical Tables* (Washington, D.C.: Government Printing Office, 2007), pp. 154–155, 160–161.
31. David M. Herszenhorn, "Estimates of Iraq War Cost Were Not Close to Ballpark," *New York Times,* 19 March 2008, p. A9.
32. Executive Office of the President, "Table S-8: Budget Summary by Category" in *Budget of the United States Government, Fiscal Year 2009, Summary Tables* (Washington, D.C.: Government Printing Office, 2008), p. 162.
33. Times-Mirror Center for the People and the Press, "Voter

Anxiety Dividing GOP: Energized Democrats Backing Clinton," press release, 14 November 1995, p. 88.

34. These questions were asked in the 2004 American National Election Survey conducted by the Survey Research Center at the University of Michigan.

35. Fay Lomax Cook et al., *Convergent Perspectives on Social Welfare Policy: The Views from the General Public, Members of Congress, and AFDC Recipients* (Evanston, Ill.: Center for Urban Affairs and Policy Research, Northwestern University, 1988), Table 4-1.

36. Social Security Administration, "Nation's First Baby Boomer Files for Social Security Retirement Benefits—Online!" News release, 15 October 2007, available at www.ssa.gov/pressoffice/pr/babyboomerfiles-pr.pdf.

37. *Annual Report of the Board of Trustees of the Federal Old-Age and Survivors Insurance and Disability Insurance Trust Funds, 2008*, p. 18; available at www.ssa.gov/OACT/TR/TR08/tr08.pdf.

38. U.S. Bureau of the Census, U.S. Department of Commerce, *Statistical Abstract of the United States, 1995* (Washington, D.C.: U.S. Government Printing Office, 1995), p. 289.

Acknowledgments

Text Credits

p. 105: From Pew Global Attitudes Project, "Global Unease with Major World Powers," June 27, 2007, http://pewglobal.org/reports/display.php?ReportID=256. Reprinted by permission of Pew Global Attitudes Project.

p. 229: "United We Stand Opposed," *CQ Weekly,* 14 January 2008, p. 144.

p. 303: *Wall Street Journal (Eastern Edition)* by n/a. Copyright 2007 by Dow Jones & Company, Inc. Reproduced with permission of Dow Jones & Company, Inc. in the format Textbook via Copyright Clearance Center.

Chapter-Opening Photo Credits

p. 1: © Jeff Greenberg/The Image Works.

p. 32: © Terry Why/Index Stock Imagery.

p. 63: © Wesley Bocx/The Image Works.

p. 88: © Salah Malkawi/Getty Images.

p. 121: AFP/Getty Images.

p. 148: Photo by Chuck Timm/Libertarian Party of LaPorte County, Indiana.

p. 187: © Catherine Karnow/Corbis.

p. 209: © Karen Bleier/AFP/Getty Images.

p. 237: Ethan Miller/Getty Images.

p. 264: SpencerPlatt/Getty Images.

p. 283: © Robert Schafer/Stock Connection.

p. 310: © Michael Greenlar/The Image Works.

p. 338: © Danny Moloshok/AP Photo.

p. 360: Roberto Schmidt/AFP/Getty Images.

Index